GONE WILD

BOOK TWO OF THE ALASKA OFF GRID SURVIVAL SERIES

MILES MARTIN

ALASKADREAMS
PUBLISHING

Gone Wild
By Miles Martin

Book Two of The Alaska Off Grid Survival Series
©2021 Miles Martin
Artwork, Photos, Original Poetry ©2021 by Miles Martin - All rights reserved

Published by:
Alaska Dreams Publishing
www.alaskadp.com
1st ADP Edition August 2021
PRINT PAPERBACK ISBN: 978-1-956303-01-8
PRINT HARDCOVER ISBN: 978-1-956303-00-1
This book was previously published by Miles of Alaska

Visit www.milesofalaska.com to find a bio of Miles, additional photos, stories, how-to videos, handmade artwork, and raw materials for sale.

Denali view from the river near my homestead.

One of my sled dogs named 'Distance.'

CONTENTS

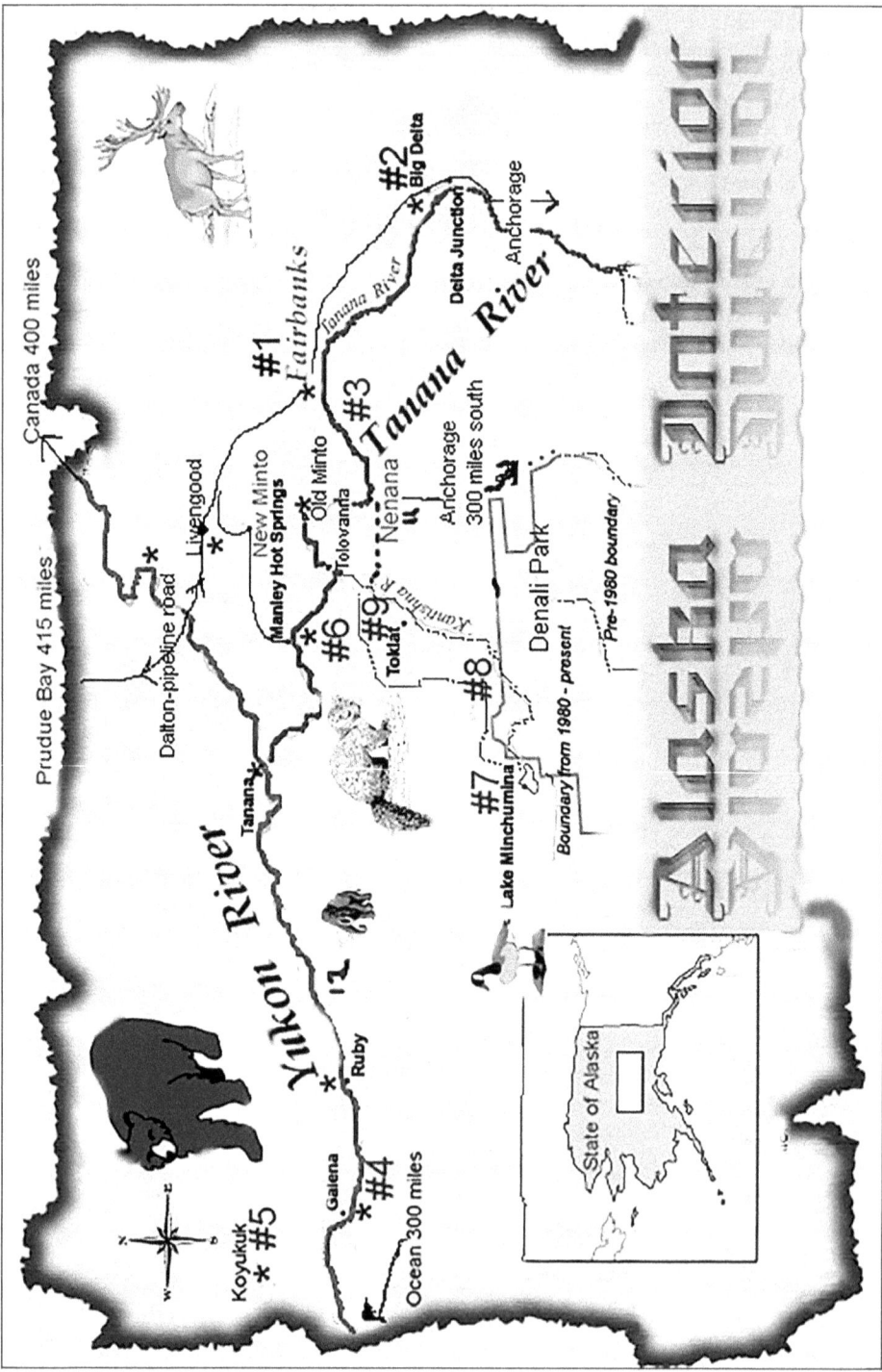

MAP NOTES

When you step into this map, you have left civilization. This area is so different from the civilized world that it is almost like coming to another planet. In an area that covers 400,000 square miles (Alaska's Interior,) the largest community is Fairbanks. Fairbanks has a population of about 40,000. There are more communities on this map with under 100 people than over 100 people. There are more bears than people. Disobeying Man's laws can get you in prison. Disobeying Natures Laws can get you killed. The two sets of laws do not always agree.

I have given numbers to the places various things happened that will be referred to throughout the book. You can come back to the map to see where that is.

#1- I arrive in Fairbanks knowing of no other place.

#2 I get flown into the wilderness to a fish camp on the Yukon.

#3 I walk out to the Dalton highway- just being built and end up not far from Livengood.

#4 I decide to build a houseboat and meet a builder in Big Delta.

#5 I take off with the houseboat and end up in Fairbanks, the hub of the interior of Alaska. Book one, Going Wild ends here.

#6 Old Minto was an abandoned native village, a landmark as I travel.

#7 Manley Hot Springs. A river community I spend a lot of time at.

#8 Tanana is the first community I run into when I get to the Yukon River. An important gas stop.

#9 Ruby. Near where my boat almost sinks in a storm.

#10 Galena. The furthest downstream I travel, spend a winter, learn a lot.

#11 The Koyukuk Country. The land I dream of and inquire about going to.

#12 Lake Minchumina. Exact center of the state, and largest lake. I backtrack to here, and live a while.

#13 Kantishna River Homestead site.

#14 Hansen Lake area, where I live and trap before homesteading. Note the dotted trail between 13 and 14, which is the trapline I begin to cut connecting the two areas.

INTRODUCTION

This is book two in an ongoing series. It is best to have read book one, 'Going Wild' before this book. Much of the purpose of the series is to show change, growth in my thinking, and how I got from 'there' to 'here.' Many issues I follow take more than one book to explain. This edition, in 2021, is a major change, having been heavily re-edited as I have turned sixty-nine years old. The original was written when I was twenty. I was so sure then it was perfect! The older I get, the less I know. After over thirty years of writing, and eight books out, I learned a little more about writing, so feel a need to go back and fix glaring errors. Issues with to and too, coarse and course, and using past and present tense. I also tone down personal legal issues no one wants to hear, stuff like that. Same stories, easier to read.

At eighteen years, I wanted to write a fast pace mountain man first person true present time story. I later feel I cannot pull this off as I hoped, because I am not as successful at being a hero as I was sure I would be. I did not die, which I was convinced would happen if I failed. I was surprised when so many people enjoyed my first book. Many readers think it is funny! Being funny is far from what I wanted. I see my writing more as a story of being human, going for dreams, facing the good, the bad and the ugly. It's about 'life,' those who choose to live, rather than give up, and accept the rat race. My story is the road taken, the other side of the fence, marching to a different drummer, a square peg dealing with round holes.

I'd like it to be like Hemingway, Mark Twain, with some aspects of 'Alive,' 'Donner Pass,' 'In Cold Blood,' or James Bond, Star Trek, Indiana Jones, Tarzan, Jim Bridger, Daniel Boone, the Wizard of Oz. What do all these characters have in common? Dreams, ambitions, hope, adventure. This is all about heroes. Who we look up to, and why. I wonder what works, what does not. There are various ways to solve life problems. My story reads like I'm stuck in the 1880s, but what if it is the cutting edge of a brave new future world? What is reality? What is fiction? The truth about life in the wild, that resonates to the frequencies of all mankind. The vibrations all living things share. We all have the desire to survive, to eat, to have shelter, to avoid pain. I offer something for those who can hold their breath and dive deep. But also excite those who can only play and dog paddle on the surface. Something for those who look for balls, but also those with misty eyes. Along this ambitious path, I may or may not get far, never see the end of the road. Here is the journey through my eyes. It's a biography. It's a historical novel. It's a science fiction, horror, mountain man story. This is at once Tarzan and Daniel Boone, but at the same time, Star Wars and going through the star gate.

Some stories are out of chronological order, names and events changed to protect various things. Obviously I wouldn't want to get sued, needlessly hurt anyone, go to jail for anything illegal. Much of what I say is my opinion. Obviously, it is just a story, nothing that is supposed to hold up in court (smile). As I say in book one, my accuracy is in feelings and how it is, not numbers, names, dates. This is me talking, with no one in between you and I. The advantage is real and raw. The disadvantage is rough around the edges.

Chris McCandless did the same thing. His story became famous through Jon Krakauer's 'Into the Wild.' Similar title, similar upbringing, problems, same events. I lived, he died.

I can tell it in first person, and answer why. But the answer may take many books. Mostly, I do not quit or give up, under conditions that should be overwhelming. I'm crawling in the snow at fifty below zero, five days without food.

I had to be rescued, making international headlines. Several times I almost died. I could have, should have died, but didn't, which is what matters. I'm not exactly sky rocketing into stardom. Many people are saying the 'dumb' part might be right. But we just won't talk to those people, right? *Those in the peanut gallery, not in the ring with the bull!* My grandfather, father, and I, and later in life my son, have the same name. Dad got three Ph.D. degrees and became Dean of a college. I have shamed the family name with this nonsense dream. I am so far, proving the family correct. I have serious mental problems, one step away from needing a shrink, being on welfare, ward of the state. I stubbornly refuse to go down for the count. I am driven to prove the entire world wrong about me.

Surely, there is something on the other side of the fence, besides the mud and crap I observe in the sheep pen called civilization. *But wait! I left the green grass, climbed the fence, and found the mud! Ha! The joke is on me.* However, I am discovering positive things I never considered, or dreamed of. The reality might even be better than the dream! Instead of 'learning my lesson' and never going back to that God awful life in the wilds, I plan to make it my life. There is a sense of freedom, strength, being in control of my life. I tan leather, make my own clothes, make my own soap, provide my own fuel to keep warm, fetch my food from the land. I am king of all I can see from horizon to horizon. I kill a few bears in self-defense, get lost, fall through the ice, have all the expected adventures of a greenhorn.

The tusk is over 8 feet long when I finaly get it loose

CHAPTER ONE

POLICE TROUBLE, FAIR TIME, HOUSEBOAT FROM FAIRBANKS TO TANANA, BEAR ON BOAT, WOODCUTTERS, BUSHY CHARLIE, MAMMOTH GRAVEYARD, HOUSEBOAT SINKS

"How can we catch these fish swimming around the houseboat? We lost the pole when it got swept off the roof by a sweeper branch?" Hmm. My conscience and I have learned to be friends since we have spent a lot of time alone together. The alternative would be to go schizoid. I have a few feet of loose line lying on the floor. I hunt around in the toolbox and find a rusty hook. Hmm. "Nothing for bait; no flies or spoons." I answer my conscience with "Hmmm." I tie a piece of bright plastic trail flagging to the hook with a simple knot that sort of looks like the wings of a big bug. The four feet of line with hook is jiggled over the side of the boat on the surface of the water. The clear water shows me the fish. They stop, get nervous, and almost swim away. I move slower. The fish come in closer. I pretend I'm a struggling bug, and "how would a bug yell for help?" I pretend I'm a bug yelling for his life. As I think "help!" I'm the bug, thrashing a little, catching my breath as I suck in water. "I can't get my wings loose off the water!" I jiggle only one wing in the water, like I got one free, but I'm getting weaker. I watch the fish and see them thinking.

"It's a big bug all right, but it's dying, come on, let's move in on it, it's getting weaker, and if we let it get away, some bigger fish downstream will have our meal!"

"Help!" I wiggle more weakly, as I lay on the deck, hand and line over the water, only a few feet from the fish. One big fat one gets brave and moves in. This is fifty pound test line, and the grayling isn't even a pound, so I do not need to play with

him. Unceremoniously I heft him into the boat. I wait until the other stupid fish forget what they saw, so I can do this again.

The wood stove in the houseboat is happily purring like a cat, which likes fish sizzling in a frying pan, covered with flour and pepper. I hungrily yawn, as I sit and read a book by kerosene light, smelling dinner.

"What would a meal like this cost if I had to buy it huh? Huh? Why you couldn't get Grayling this fresh for under $50!" I feel sorry for people who can't eat this good. I even feel guilty for being so happy. "What right do we have to escape going off the cliff with the rest of the Lemming?" I smile, as I look out the window facing the Chena River at the Fairbanks, Alaska city lights. A beaver on the river slaps its tail. "He smells the boat and smoke, and tells the world there is something strange out here, to be careful till he checks it out." I know where the beaver will be now, bravely swimming to the boat to check it out. "I give him exactly two minutes to get to the window, what do you think?" I weigh in my mind all the factors. I go over in my mind anything that would affect the time. There is a good probability he has seen a boat before. Though not connecting a boat directly to smoke, he has smelled smoke before. There is no sound coming from the boat, no person in sight. I judge the age of the beaver by the loudness of the slap on the water. I think about the sound of the dive, after a slap. He came back up right away. He is not very afraid, but even so, he's old enough to be wise.

"I say five minutes." We wait to see who is right, me or I. I keep a thumb in the book to keep my place, as we stare out the window waiting for the beaver. *"Two minutes, like I said."* I'm puzzled. I'd a sworn it would be five. Oh well. I thoughtfully think on this, as I eat my fish, pretending I am the beaver. With enough concentration, I 'become the beaver.' My head turns, and my eyes are just above the water, as I slowly move my feet, smelling the boat ahead.

The beaver tail slaps again. I frown. I know the different tail slap sounds, and this means there is great danger coming. This is not about the boat, "something is going on." The beaver already made his report about the boat. This is about something new. *"If this were the wilderness I'd know a bear is coming, and I'd be ready, and shoot it if it came on the boat."* But this is town, and there wouldn't be a bear, so I'm confused about what to do. *"It must be a person sneaking around."* Who would be here in the dark? I have to ask myself what I would, could do, if it is a thief. Would it be better to let him rob me, rather than risk going to jail for hurting someone? What does society say these days about our right to defend our property? The rights are being lost so fast I am unsure what we can do anymore, besides let people rob us and then calling 911. Because of this, I am terrified as I hear feet, a pause, and someone on my boat deck.

"Hey, anyone in here!" Pause.

"Hold on!" I go to the door and open it, but my gun's handy, 'in case.'

There's a cop standing here. He looks at my long hair . . . and scowls. He looks around in the boat, takes in the smell of fish I just ate. I'd guess it's not legal to catch a fish without a pole. Not legal to catch a fish with a rusty big hook. Illegal to use ribbon as bait. Illegal to eat fish the same day you caught it. Illegal to have long hair at the same time you catch a fish. . . but the evidence is gone now, so not a thing he can do. *"Gosh, how awful! He doesn't get to cart me off to jail."* He scowls again.

"Got a report of funny stuff going on here. What are you doing? You can't stay here like this! Where do you live! Let's see some ID." He's ready for trouble, wants trouble, ready to reach for his club so he can beat up another long hair. He is not trying to solve a problem, be helpful by protecting the innocent. I gulp. *"Here we go again! Assume the position!"* Of course, the cop can't hear my conscience. Only I can. I reply out loud,

"I just got this boat; it's my first trip with it. I have engine trouble and my friend is getting parts," I say with as much apology as I can muster. This appeases him.

"Well..., you can't stay here; in the morning you better be gone!" Past experience tells me there is no use reminding him of my 'legal rights.' I cannot say, "Where's your warrant to be on my boat? Am I under arrest? Then get off my boat!" That's a good way to end up dead. Or he'd laugh a reply like, "So tell it to the judge!" As he carted me off, and this, only if he's in an especially good mood. The judge of course would have his hands full as he tried to find test cases involving questions about the legal right of a person to park a houseboat on the river and live on it for a while, eating fish he catches there. There is no use pointing out the law saying anything within 100 ft of the river is public land with an easement. It is legal to camp; stop and stay, in emergencies.

There is no reason the cop couldn't get his answers by politely asking, "Hey how are you? Is everything ok here? I saw your boat and wondered if you needed help! What are you doing here anyhow? A place to park? Hey, I know a great place." I wonder what's wrong with that approach. I sigh again. At least the cop is gone and I'm safe again.

'Where then can we park? No one will want us around.' "Maybe we can make it to Alaskaland." I tell my conscience. If I walk in the water with the rope, I can drag the boat a mile in the shallow water. Maybe we will be safe there. We have friends, members of society who could vouch for us. *Alaskaland is a gold rush theme park for tourists along the river. We hang out there sometimes and get along because we look like one of those old time characters tourists like to take pictures of and hear stories from.*

I'm not far from the power plant. In 1977 this is a residential area with run down houses. There is a row of tall tangled willows between the river and grass lawns. The river is not being utilized much. There are no docks, no tied up boats, just jumbles of rocks and a place to dump garbage off the bank. This is not an image of people who appreciate or respect the river. The waterfront is almost a slum area. I had passed Alaskaland without stopping when I came up the Chena trying to get to 'downtown,' because I have to get last minute supplies. It takes two fifteen-hour days of backbreaking work, dragging my houseboat through the shallows and freezing water with a rope over my shoulder to get it to Alaskaland, where I might be safe. If I slip and fall in a hole in this cold water I will probably die. The terror of the thought of being found floating face down in the river (or worse, much worse, going to jail) after being found by the police, drives me on.

Alaskaland is like 'home.' The tourist season is winding down. It's mid-August. Nights get cold now, and the first freeze is around the corner. It is already freezing in the mountains, where this water comes from. The 'windy-bag-goes,' usually parked in the parking lot out front are in smaller numbers. In mid-summer, I see them packed like sardines, full of people coming all the way to Alaska, so they can set the TV up on the asphalt, get out the lawn chair, and fill out postcards about their 'Alaska experience,' to send home to children and grandchildren. Now, it's too cold for them, so they head south, taking their 'made in Korea' totem poles bought at a hand crafted Alaskaland shop with them. Willows along the riverbank are bright red and yellow. Kingfisher birds sit on dead tree stumps and give an agitated chatter as I approach, showing red throats and white fronts as they glide to the next dead tree. Now and then one grabs a small fish near the surface of the water, takes it to his perch and glares at me. These birds are more a part of my reality than the tourists.

"Some of them are all right, Miles." Bill and Nora are friends who own the Diamond Willow wood shop, chuckling at my description of tourists.

I tell them, "I know. I meet some of these tourists. People who truly want to know about 'us,' and are excited about another way to live and think."

Nora points out, "Some even stay and become Alaskans like we did! It's one thing we like about you, Miles, you talk to everyone, and try to give them insight into what Alaska is about. Many people come to us after talking to you and tell us how you are the highlight of their trip, even the highlight of their whole life. So don't get discouraged by those who do not understand. You can't please everyone, Miles. Try to dwell on the good things going on."

The sun is out, and fall is one of the nicest times in Alaska, with clear sky and wonderful colors. It is hard to stay 'negative.' I am soon, once again, laughing, making jokes, and talking to everyone about everything, blade of grass in my mouth, bearskin hat blocking the sun, long hair pulled back like Wild Bill Hickok. A tourist stops me, asking,

"Can we take your picture? Are you related to Pedro?"

I have to think fast, 'Pedro?' But before my unconscious thought becomes real words they go on, "The one in the Alaskaland flier here, who discovered gold and founded Fairbanks! You look like him!" I only smile and wink mischievously with that mysterious, 'maybe I'm related to him' look. They take my picture, and slip me $5. "No, no we insist! It will be the highlight of our photo album! It is so refreshing to see such historical people on our trip." I could be one of the sheep so easily, and stay out of trouble, being cute, conning tourists out of their money. *They happily go along with it too. Does anyone want the truth?* Another tourist is standing in front of me. This is, I don't know, 'disgusting'– considering the image of myself I have as a Mountain Man. This is 'humiliating,' I think the word is.

"Huh? Oh yes, sorry one more mug here? And what is your name? Are you having a good time here in our wonderful Alaska?"

The tourist replies, "Oh yes! Everyone here treats us so nice! We are having such a good time! We go see Mount McKinley tomorrow! We are so excited! Have you seen the mountain before?"

I smile, appropriately wise, and get my famous 'faraway look,' as I reply, "But it is best in the winter, with the northern lights over it, while sleeping by a campfire. There is the warmth of the fire, the flicker of its flames through the webbing of my snowshoes stuck in the snow in front of me. The wolves howl, and far, far away Mount McKinley stands out, white, cold, against those red northern lights." They all look starry eyed and sigh, as I think, 'It is so easy to lead people where you wish, with words.'

The tourists eat it up and hastily invite me to dinner. "We'd be honored if you would join us at the salmon feed for dinner...."

The daughter coos, "Could you take us out sometime to see wolves? We'd pay you!" The cute daughter is leaning toward me so I get a whiff of her female odors, perfume, hair and . . .

Everyone agrees eagerly, and the tourist father adds, "I bet the wolves are so majestic to see, and I read how they mate for life, and are so social and wonderful! I bet you respect them a lot! Have you ever seen them play?" Everyone waits for me to speak.

I almost tell them a nice story.... about wolves at play. But a very vivid image of screams, blood everywhere; a scene from one of my first wolf encounters fills my head. I do not let it show. Nor do I ask if they ever saw the movie 'Deliverance.'

I smile, saying, "Well... not everything about wolves is wonderful you know. I respect them all right, but they are not people, and do not have human feelings. They are animals, and they kill." I leave it at that. The tourists get nervous and quiet; this is leading into forbidden territory.

One hastily adds, "Yes of course, but only for food right? They only take the weak and old, helping nature stay in a healthy balance!" They all look at each other for confirmation, and I know this is as far as they will listen, so I only smile at their wisdom, and say nothing. We promise to write each other, stay in touch. I thank them for a good dinner. They had a good time with me. I wish they could leave it at that, accept that. Why do we have to be friends? Like so many other people I meet, they would lynch me if they knew the truth. There is no way I will get a letter from these people. In a week I will have no address. I drop off the face of the civilized earth. For now I am sad and bitter about this, thinking of the girl so inviting. After sucking on the blade of grass, I take it out of my mouth, realizing I could have the real thing if I'd give up my dream. I stare at the succulent end of the weed and sadly sigh.

"It's fair time again Miles, you going to be there? Got any new art?"

I do not recognize this guy, but obviously he knows me, so I reply, "Yea, I got some new art. I'll have it at the fair if I run into you. You bet I'll be there!" The guilt returns. This person looks up to me, yet I do not have a clue who he is. I hadn't really planned on going to the fair, and if the houseboat engine had been ok; I would be in the wilderness by now, but as long as I'm still in town, may as well go! As this guy reminds me, it might be a chance for me to make some needed money. My guess is, I will need engine parts, and will have other money outflow issues. *No place to spend money in the wilds though.*

I'm at the BLM office-where I had worked all summer with the fire fighters. I hear a faint holler from way back in the office, "Is that Miles out front there? Didn't we lay him off? What's he doing still hanging around, the secretaries have work to do, Christ!" I hear another one of the honchos in the back laughing.

This secretary had bought a lot of art from me, and says, "Sorry Miles, going to have to get back to work." The other people are the same way. I shrug my shoulders and head for the door. No one hollers at me to have a good trip, or good luck, or see you later, next season, or anything. *"Yeah well, who needs any of them anyway."*

WAITING to hear from Will is depressing. He had traveled with me in the new houseboat, and showed me he has a lot of knowledge about how engines run. The trip from Delta to Fairbanks had been a real test, as this is not normally a stretch of river people boat. It's very braided and shallow. We had passed a canoe that was stuck and being hand lined. Will has promised to get word to Steamer whom I built the boat with. There is that wonder about my engine, if it is easy to fix, if I'll have the money, time, and more, *"will this motor hold up for the use I need it for? Or will it be too delicate!"* People had asked me why the heck I got a Chrysler. Since neither I, nor anyone I talk to has heard that Chrysler even makes outboards. I have little faith in the engines. Steamer had promised me Mercury engines, but he couldn't get the dealership, so told me these would be every bit as good....., *yeah right, gosh will I ever be glad when I don't have to depend on anyone anymore!*

I have my mail coming to the downtown post office general delivery, since I have no address. *"I do have a home now though, my houseboat!"* There is a pile of mail today. I sit in the fall sun on the steps of the post office, off to the side reading.

"Hey, move along! You can't stay here!" A policeman has come up on me while I was reading. I open my mouth to protest...

"I'm only....."

"I don't care what you are only doing, move along or go to jail, you're loitering!" I wonder; depressingly, what kind of a society I live in, and how I will be glad to leave it! *Thank you kind officer for pointing out how worthless I am!* A note from Steamer.

Hey Miles,

Hi. Pretty busy around here, glad you made it to Fairbanks. As I said; I knew you could do it! I looked at the engine lower unit, and think it cannot be covered under warranty. It looks like you hit something and broke the main gear. You need a whole new lower unit. I can get one for you for $600. You need to call or let me know if you want me to order one or not.

Take care----**Steamer**

I'm at the bank. "Yes, I have a savings account here already. I'd like to have a checking account so I can pay bills when I'm in the villages, and can't get to the bank to withdraw cash from my savings. I've never had a checking account before. Maybe you could tell me how it works?"

"Sure, no problem. You fill it out as it shows on each line, with the amount, and sign it, when you use it in a store you put the store's name on this line, and they will ask for ID, you show that. It's pretty simple." I doubt it, but decide I better have an account, and quit carrying all this cash around. Will told me it would be easy. It seems a good idea to pay Steamer by check, instead of sending cash in the mail, or a series of money orders. So I get the instructions on how it works, but I really wanted someone with me who I trusted, and could explain it better.

I head for the store to try using checks, and see how it works. I've seen it done before, but want to learn firsthand. I watch the lady in front of me, as she writes out her check, just as the bank guy has described to me. She shows ID, and 'that's that.' With confidence and an artificial, elaborate unconcerned air, blade of grass working in my mouth, bear hat pulled down low, I put my groceries down on the counter.

The Cashier asks, "Cash or check"

I reply – just like the lady in front of me did, "Oh that will be check." I look at the amount; write it down carefully on the correct line (I have to study it for a moment to see which line the amount goes on, I've never done this before).

I get told, "I need two ID's please."

"No problem. I have three." So I get them out, and she studies the ID's carefully, and calls the manager over, *"Oh,…. Oh"* goes my conscience. But I do not let my concern show. I pretend to read the instructions on the Jell-O box, like I haven't a care in the world. The manager comes over, and I look up.

He takes one glance at my ID, another glance at me, scowls, and hollers at the top of his voice, "Hell No!" Throws it down, and stomps off. *"Holy Crap,"* Goes my conscience. Everyone in the store heard him, and is now staring at me. I haven't the cash to pay. I have to leave all my groceries in the cart, and in humiliation, walk out, to the whispers of everyone around me, treated like a criminal.

I explain my experience to my buddy Will. His arms are as big around as my body. He lays them on the table.

"So Miles, tell me again what you did?"

I'm trying to figure out what went wrong at the store. I swear it is because I have long hair or something. I understand how lame that sounds. I tell Will in exasperation, "I told you a hundred times! I did just like the woman in front of me! Yes! I showed my ID, even three separate ID's!" Will can't figure it out either. He has me repeat it all over.

"I walk up, I put my groceries down. Yes, I write the amount on the right line. Yes, I put the right amount down. No, I didn't try to write a check for more and want change." Will sighs, puzzled, trying to figure out along with me, what went wrong. I'm still embarrassed.

"Will, what good did school do us? What a waste of time. We didn't learn a darn thing about real life!"

Will ignores my outburst as he asks, "You had the amount in your account to cover the check, and they didn't call in?"

I reply, "I already told you, No!" I think about it again. As I say: "She never used the phone, I would have seen her. The guy looks at my ID and doesn't like it maybe." Will picks up the 'ID' part.

"Ok Miles, show me the ID you showed him. Is it expired?" "I already said, "No!" But I get out my wallet and show him my ID's.

"My library card," I throw that down. "My trappers license!" I put that down. "My residency card!" I put that down. I scowl at Will.

Will puts his hands over his face, starts shaking his head back and forth, and then bursts out laughing.

"Will, what's so damn funny!"

"Miles! They need photo ID!"

"Well now how the hell am I supposed to know that, Will? No one ever told me that! Oh yes, everyone said it would be so easy! But did anyone want to go with me? Show me? Oh no, everything will be just fine! Isn't that what you told me?"

Will can't stop laughing. "You should write a book, Miles! I can't believe this!"

With folded arms I reply, "Go to hell." I don't like being made fun of. Will sees I'm really upset, so backs off.

"Miles, you can survive in the wilderness where few others could, so if you have problems in town when no one else does, maybe God just put you together different. Don't worry about it."

I respond, "Yeah well, I'm scared shitless of banks, phones and women. Don't think I ever want to be alone with any of them." I sigh.

Will is about to laugh again, but sees how serious and scared I am. "Hey Miles, anytime you want to go do the check thing, just let me know, I'll be glad to go with you."

"Thanks, but you're a little bit late. That's not what you said a week ago when I asked," My conscience says in my head so Will can't hear.

FAIR TIME AGAIN, all right! "Hey, Miles, so what you got to show me?"

I get out the cigar box I carry with my latest art in it. Here is a bear claw, and a belt buckle of ivory, with a silver polar bear and a brass sun on it. I get out some jade pieces with flowers. Mostly I do flowers and birds in metalwork hand- cut scenes.

"Cool buckle! How much?" I turn it over to look at the price I put on it. "It's $75, but I can do a deal on it for you, how about $65?" He gets out the cash and pays me.

While he had been buying, someone I don't know, out of curiosity, is looking over my shoulder asking, "You do this work? How lovely, how much is that copper flower with the shell center, the one on jade?"

I turn it over, "$45."

They do not ask for a discount. Since I don't know them, they pay the full tourist price, and seem happy to do so. *"The piece only took us an hour to make, man, this is all right! Sure beats working for a living!"* My conscience is good at trying to make me feel good. I just made over $100 in an hour. What I'm worth just went through the roof. I hitch my pants up and stroll down the fair isles like a millionaire. *"A hundred dollars an hour. Imagine that!"*

Every morning I arrive at the fair early, and pretend I'm carrying something in for the fair. Empty box in hand I am waved through as I say: "Delivery!" The gate people recognize me by now, heck; they recognize me years later after seeing me one time! I guess it's hard to forget a short guy in bearskin hat, leather shirt, knife at my side, blade of grass in his mouth, walking fast, with a big smile all the time.

"Wild Miles!" I stop and spin on my heels. My cigar box comes out again, another sale. I'm on my way to the dry fruit guy, if I can ever get that far without selling out. The dry fruit guy is not in the best of moods this year.

"I don't know Miles—" I almost have a relieved look because he doesn't want any art. Conscience,"*I'm not sure my cigar box full of goods is going to last through this fair.*" Someone comes up beside us, asks about my work, and almost buys a $100 piece. I'm about to leave. I don't care if this fruit guy gets anything or not! He expected me to dicker and push it on him. I'm surprised when the dry fruit guy asks me back, and does our usual $200 trade. He gives me an envious look at my carefree attitude about business and money. I stroll off, as if I own the world.

The craft market guy, I think his name is Crafty, is ahead. I store my dry fruit there with the owner, whom I trade with and am getting to know. I drop off more handmade pottery, ivory, and other raw material from other crafters set up at the fair selling, so I have materials to work with. As every year, I do more wholesale work and trades with vendors than I do retail business. All the regular vendors know me now, and are happy to see me. Well a few scowl and do not like me selling, not even paying to get in, much less not having a vendor booth, but I don't notice. I rarely walk more than ten feet before someone hollers my name out. It takes me all day to make one trip around the fair.

While gnawing on a butter dripping corn cob, not caring where it drips, as if I'd never eaten before, I ask one of the vendors on a lunch break how it's going. He seems to be a little glum. Conscience: *How can you be glum at a fair, good grief!*" He can't hear my conscience talking. He tells me his money problems and his 'happiness level' seems low. I interrupt him: "Do you really want to be doing this?!"

He says."Heck no!"

"So why are you here?" He looks puzzled. He never thought of it before. I ask, "What would you like to be doing?"

There is no hesitation before he replies-as if I might think his dream stupid."I've always loved airplanes!"

I look around with my hands up in a, 'So where is this airplane' gesture.

He laughs, "You don't understand! I got house payments, bills, responsibilities—"

I interrupt, "Oh no! It is you who don't understand! Your first obligation is to yourself. If you are miserable, you can't help anyone! You think you're going to sell stuff at a fair with that hang dog look?"

He interrupts, "Yeah but—"

And I go on, "I bet if you sold everything you owned you could buy an airplane."

He thinks about it, and says thoughtfully, "Yea, you're right, but then what! I'd be broke, no place to live."

I shake my head sorrowfully telling him, "You got the wrong attitude. You got high blood pressure, ulcers, can't sleep, and not eating right. How can anyone in your life who sees all that, say they 'care.' Or let me put it in another way. Let's say you were a car and people depended on you for transportation. But no one changed your oil, or greased you, or rotated your tires. How long could you provide reliable transportation? Put another way—you could use a lube job with loving hands—get the bugs washed off your windshield. You need an overhaul and could be good for another 200,000 miles instead of another ten. No place to live? Well as it is, you will not be alive at all in a year or two. This much misery will kill you. You live in the plane if you have to! You go to the small airlines and ask if you can wash planes, ask if you can sweep floors, you'll do anything in return for flying lessons, trade for food. You tell 'em all that you live for is flying. Tell 'em all you own in the whole world is your plane, and some day you're going to fly it, for a living. Show em your plane. Maybe you can rent it out. Maybe they'd let you live in the shop, or put a tent up in the yard."

His reply is, "Yeah but my parents, my girlfriend—"

I go on, " How much can they love you, watching you slowly die. Huh?"

Again, he interrupts, "But if they ask what I did with the house, my job, my car, my—"

Understanding his line of thought I interrupt, "You tell 'em you traded it all for something worth ten times as much, your life! Of course it wouldn't be easy, you may even fail! But you'll fail reaching for what you want! And, who knows, you might end up flying instead of being stuck at the fair!" I talk with a big smile, and wink, as I walk away, leaving him perplexed… but with fire in his eyes.

Future Flash:

Ten years down the road a guy comes up to me at the fair. Some happy healthy guy I never saw before. He seems to know me. This is common. His hand is out to shake mine. I smile back and put my hand out.

"I'm glad to see you again, and wondered if I ever would. I wanted to thank you for saving my life." How does one respond to that, not having a clue what the person is talking about, or who this is? He goes on, as I listen for clues in the conversation that might indicate who he is, and how we know each other.

"I got that airplane after thinking over what you said. My parents disowned me, my girlfriend left me, and I had a hard couple of years at first." *So this is the guy I vaguely recall chatting with so long ago who had looked so miserable at the fair!* He does not look the same. Now he is thinner, with color to his skin, a smile on his face, and the confidence of someone who owns the world. He found a new woman who understands his love of flying, has a child, and is a commercial bush pilot. He makes twice the money he ever could have with his old life. Everything he had to give up as a sacrifice, he got back again ten-fold.

"Miles, it is all because of you, thank you!" Well of course, it is all because of him. All I did was point out what he already knew. It is nice however, to have helped. It has me thinking how we never know what affect some small thing we do or say might have on someone.

Future flash ends and I have other things on my mind.

It's been several weeks now. The engine lower unit is not here yet. *'So much for fast reliable service I'm gonna get'* my conscience quietly reminds me. I'm leaning over the boat, watching the fish, trying to figure out which one is going to go for the lure. *'The fattest biggest one!'* I reply to myself: "No, I think it will be that smaller more aggressive one off to the side, taking in the whole situation." The lure jiggles from the end of my new pole. The big fat one goes for it. "Hmmm," the boat gently rocks and bumps the dock. The wood stove smoke blows downriver. Rush hour traffic is at a walking pace on the road above me. A few people honk. I smile and wave. Conscience, *'They wish they could be fishing, those rich people in their suits and ties, coming home from their rat race jobs.'* We own the world, because we envy no one. Steamer problems, the police, boat hold ups, it is all only 'stuff' to wave aside. If it was easy, everyone would do it, and then the river and wilderness would be crowded! We are lucky it is so hard, and so few people will do it! So we have it to ourselves! I'm sure glad!

Little do I know that the paddlewheel tour boat that goes by here every day has been taking note of me. The loudspeaker goes on. The tourists are told, "Here on your right, is a trapper outfitting himself for the winter. You can see his supplies all around, and it looks like he is ready for winter!" There are Ooo's and Ahh's with pictures taken, unknown to me, as I poach fish, and scratch my armpits, without a care in the world.

THE TOURIST PADDLEWHEEL boat toots its horn. I wake up slowly; tilt my bearskin hat back so I can see. I squint in the sun, lazily wave hello, and go back to sleep. *'Now that we are awake, should we put another stick of wood in the stove?'* My buddy in my head is trying to be helpful, but I reply (maybe just to show whose boss), "I think not, I like the sun too much, let's just lay here." I go back to sleep. I have picked berries in the woods, am eating fish and greens I pick along the shore. When I'm in the mood, I work on my art. There is a place in the house on the boat to do my artwork. There is little I 'must' do, so long as I keep my life simple. I review what I have done, or need to do yet.

I recall that I should be in deep water once I leave Fairbanks for the next thousand miles, so I am not so concerned about the two feet the boat is drawing now.

Coming down from the village of Delta, the boat needed only four inches! But the boat had no supplies on board and was new-dry and now 'wet.' I have 300 gallons of gas on board in fifty five gallon drums I scrounged at the dump. I have enough food to last all winter. Everything is with me. I don't really have to work again for another year, unless I wish. I hope to trap of course, but I'm not under any stress to do well, catch a lot, or make any money at it. I have enough art materials to work all winter creating, and only need simple hand tools to do my work. The tools still fit in a shoe box. I can fit a thousand dollars' worth of art in my cigar box. Alaska House will do a show for me next spring, where all the art I make all winter will probably sell. *So? What worries have I got?*

Will and I found a covered pit hidden in the woods. We store some things in there so no one will find and steal them. Someone finds and steals everything. Will is really bummed out, and me too, for a while, but all in all I'm doing all right. I can live without the things; it's all luxuries anyway. It's amazing how little is really 'necessary!' I have already learned how little it takes to be happy. Conscience, *'Just about all my unhappiness has to do with 'people.' Just get me away from people, and I'll be fine!'*

"WILL, the engine lower unit is here in Alaska now, but more money is owed before I can pick it up."

"Ok, Miles, this is how we can do it. You got a check from BLM, and you need to pay Steamer, who wants cash. So I can pay Steamer, and you write me a check, and put your BLM check in the bank later today, to cover this check you write me now. It's pretty simple. People do it all the time." How town people live, seems so complicated to me but, "Whatever."

At the bank, "I'm headed out to the wilderness on my houseboat. I don't expect to see anyone for many months. I'm just depositing my last check in my account. I'm pretty excited to be leaving." I'm talking to the teller.

She shakes her head and doesn't understand how anyone could want to do that, asking, "Aren't you afraid? What if you get sick?"

I wink at her saying, "Then I'll die." She thinks I'm crazy and suicidal. I think she is, I mean how can one knowingly be among the lemmings headed for the cliff and say they are not suicidal?

On the street I'm whistling, grass stem bouncing along in my mouth, hunting knife swinging at my side, weaving my way through the lemmings. The lights are on in my eyes, as everyone else looks like zombies. A police siren comes closer. I turn to look at what is going on; *"Must be a wreck somewhere."*

The crowd stops as the police pull up, and a cop with a club gets out, runs up to me. "Up against the wall, spread your legs! Now!" I open my mouth to ask what is going on. "I said now!" A club is slammed into my side; I'm forced against the wall. My nose hits the wall and starts bleeding. The cop gets my wallet out and looks in it. I assume, to see who I am. He hands it back to me. "Ok, you can go."

He simply walks away. "What do you mean, I can go!? What kind of crap is this? No apology? Was I mistaken for someone else? You almost break my nose and I can go?" The sheep are confused and bleating.

They look at me; they look at the police leaving, and do not know what to do, till someone tells them, "Ok break it up, move along."

Nobody asks any questions. I wipe the blood from my nose. No one asks me if I am ok. Some even look like they are sorry I was not carted off. "Is this how people live? Business as usual? Hope you are not the Jew singled out next?" I have no idea what is going on. *There I was, minding my own business, happy, not bothering anyone, and 'Bam.'* As usual I get all wound up, ever more convinced I need to get out of here.

In the morning, I am glad to have a fire going on the houseboat in the chill of the fall and the first freeze. There is no one around to send me off. Nora, from the Alaskaland Willow Shop, has hinted that I am to meet a woman who loves me. She is supposed to simply show up. I wait a while for her, then end up sighing that it will not be this year, or at least this place. *Nora's dream must have been wrong.* With another sigh, I warm up the engines. The new lower unit is working well. I have full power now. This is the first test of the new unit on the engines. This is one advantage of having twin engines. Each one can be lifted easily. Installing the new lower unit took only a crescent wrench and screwdriver.

Alaskaland has long since shut down. A few ducks in the water are the only noise I hear. With wood smoke wafting off in the dawn, I idle down the Chena River, and out to the Tanana. The next stop should be the Village of Nenana in seventy miles.

There is no sun out on this gray day. I do not touch bottom, and feel good that the water is deeper, calmer, than the trip had been down from Delta. As I travel, there is the thought of what Don has told me. There is a bet on, for how many days I will last in the wilderness. I can picture Don, redneck that he is, thoughtfully putting tobacco chew in his mouth. Don and the honchos at BLM think it will be a short time, and I will come back with my tail between my legs, or die. Don never did say which side he bet on, or let on how many people, or who might think I'll make it. I'm a lot less concerned than I was when I first went out. I only snort briefly, that they know so little about me. *'They only see me laughing, and never being serious, being such a klutz in town about the phone, my not driving, bank accounts and such. …'* I'm sure Don wants me to do well though. During the seasonal work with firefighters, my boss and I had gotten to know each other. Don, in winter, is the fur buyer I sell to.

My eyes go to my new 270 rifle. I decided I needed a new rifle besides the fifty caliber black powder, and the twenty-two. The 270 is purchased at the pawnshop. I think it will work well. I haven't gotten the reloading press yet, but this is on my list to get, if I see another big wad of money come in. I have a hand loader though, and have molds to cast my own lead for the 357 pistol and the 270 rifle. I have worked out light loads for the 270, and practiced some with this. I almost lost my job with the forest firefighters for reloading ammunition in my room. My thoughts drift into neutral.

The boat is handling slow and sluggish, compared to how it handled empty. I cannot get on step with this set of engines, so now I know I will go upstream very slowly, with the engines wound out burning ten gallons of fuel an hour. This trip is downstream, so I'm not very concerned, but already I see this power set up is not right, and Steamer has steered me wrong; *Just to sell me engines he is the dealer of.* Rather than get angry, I feel sorry for him. I know he will never have anything in life. Few people trust him. Without trust, there is nothing. My conscience is full of piss and vinegar today, piping up loudly and firmly, *'I will overcome this set back.'* I smile, "Steamer was pretty slick all right." On the bright side, I think the boat is well built and will serve me well. *'After all, here we are going downriver, with a year's supplies.'* Sometimes my conscience says, "I," and sometimes "We," and I notice the difference.

Evening finds me at a slough that looks like a good place to get off the river for the night. I shoot a duck for dinner as I pull in. I realize the Howling Dog, where I dance, is not very far from here, maybe even within walking distance. I see lights up on the hill. I remember where the road comes down near the river.

In the morning I see I cannot turn the boat around in this narrow slough I pulled into the evening before. I try to back up, but there is little backing power with the riffle runners-which is a new- fangled thing we put on the engine propeller that helps it run shallower. The boat has drifted over a log. The engines will not run over the log. The obstruction is across the whole slough, and well attached to the bottom. I decide it would be better to just follow this slough forward to the main river, rather than try to back up over the log. I assume this slough will connect to the main river around the next bend. I cannot find this place on the map. If this were a 'creek,' and not a slough connecting back to the river, the water would be clear, or be a different color.

The slough goes on and on, forks, divides, and gets shallower. I have to line the boat by hand, slogging through the freezing water, dragging the boat over the sand. I spend a great deal of time back in this slough, and decide I will be more careful about pulling into these types of places. *'I had trouble before in a spot like this coming out of Delta.'* The land is very pretty back here though. The white birch trees have sun-yellow fall leaves. The trees bend with graceful curves out over the water, whose surface reflects the colors back. Sometimes I boat under these arches, and it is like a yellow brick road to Oz. The sun dapples the water, ducks fly up; fish disturb the water ahead of me. I do not mind the time spent back here. *What is my hurry? If it takes a day, a week, a month, what does it matter? When winter comes, I will stop, and make that spot my home for eight months.* I do not even have to know where I am. I certainly hope I get far enough away to get into some good trapping country though, but wherever I end up, there will be fur around.

I spend almost a full day just getting out of this unknown slough. There are no other boats, even this close to Fairbanks. I am baffled that so few people think of going out on the river, but choose to stay in the city. There is a fish camp here and there to let me know I'm not really in the wilderness yet, but they are deserted camps, with empty smokehouses. There are more moose tracks than people tracks.

THE THIRD DAY I come to Nenana early in the day. I see the railroad bridge first. There are a lot of barges here, and I do not feel comfortable trying to dock with all these big boats at the docking area. This looks like a busy place. I know a few people here, but not well. I am unsure how to find them. I have no reason to stop, so do not. I still have not run into a single boat on the river.

I whisper to my conscience, "Where are all the trappers? The bush folks heading out for winter like me." I still have never met another serious trapper. I know they exist because Don is a fur buyer, who tells me about other trappers. I guess I expected more people to have the love of life in the wilderness. I had heard Alaska is full of those who love the wild! I'd think the rivers would be bank to bank full of people who love the outdoors. *Surely so many tell me how much they love the wilderness, but is it all talk?* They have jobs, the reality of life comes to play I think. They really want the clothes washer and TV more. They want the light when they flip the switch. They want the hot water to come out when they turn a knob. They want the car, the furniture, and of course, it takes the job to pay the bills, and no time to go out in the wilderness, except on the two weeks, once a year vacation. They can't afford the boat. When it comes down to a choice between the boat and the car, or the new TV, the boat dream gets set aside. I am glad for this, that the wilderness and river are left free and open. *'There are the talkers and then doers.'* My conscience reminds me of our outlook on life. When I say I love the wilderness, it has a different meaning than when the tourist says so. *'I put my money where my mouth is.'* I sigh, as I think of the river, and my mind drifts along with the gurgling of the water. Music to my ears.

The river spreads out past Nenana. The hills disappear. The flats open up into willow country. The fall smells of drying sedge grass in the swamps is familiar to me. I think the Indian village of Old Minto should be coming up any time. The map tells me it should be about thirty-five miles down from Nenana. I'm anxious to view an Indian village, which I have never done.

Two days go by. I know for sure I have gone over thirty-five miles! *How could I have missed Minto?* I see fish camps every few miles. Some are just an old tent frame beside a small tin shed. Others have a small cabin and several sheds. I'm still not seeing any boats. None of these camps have anyone in them. I thought I would see Indians out checking fish wheels, or nets. This looks like a neglected, poor area to me. *Minto may have been a collection of these smokehouses that I went by.* I've read so much about Indians, how proud they are, and what a wonderful life they live. *Surely they must be rich, and prosperous!* Where are the dog teams? Where are the well tended gardens, moose hanging from poles, next to fish put up for winter? Where is the hustle and bustle of an active people wearing eagle feather bonnets? Where are the giggling, pretty native women in smoke tan hide dresses tending cook fires? I am not ignorant on such matters, for I have read books, seen documentaries, admired paintings of this lifestyle, the lifestyle of the subsistence Indian. *'Everything human looks 100 years old and deserted. Oh well!'* I do not dwell on it. The beauty is good to see, and if I see no proud Indians, what's it to me?

I am more concerned with the fact that I do not know where I am, to the nearest 100 miles. I wish to know what kind of time I am making, what kind of gas mileage I'm getting. I do have some half-formed plans. I'd like to get to the Koyukuk before winter, since I have looked at the maps and dreamed so much. But another year's wait? *'It doesn't really matter, because we live on 'bush time' now, not 'city time'!'*

There is no more tying up in shallow or narrow creeks. I learn to trust the main river. In the morning I wake up to sounds I do not understand. The boat is rocking. My main concern, and thought, is that the current is too strong here, it is not safe. *'Maybe a big tree has hung up on the boat.'* The bed is set up across the front door. A section gets set aside in the daytime, holding the rolled up foam pad out of the way. This same board is set in place to complete the bed frame at night. I actually sleep against the door.

I listen intently with a frown, distinguishing the various sounds. There is the gurgle of the river, call of a jay, chatter of a squirrel. Something isn't right in the world outside, but I'm unsure in the morning fog of wakefulness, just what isn't right. A scratching sound on the front of the boat has me thinking. *'Is this the branches of the birch I'm parked under, scrapping the front of the boat, as it sways in the current?"* I look out the window and see the current isn't moving the boat. *'Maybe a grouse is on the front of the boat, scratching for the gravel it needs, as they do early in the morning.'* Yes, that is what it must be. I wonder if there is a way to get this grouse for breakfast. The scraping sound again. The sound of little grouse claws on the boat deck.

I push on the door to open it enough to see the grouse. *'If it flies to a tree as it should, I will see which tree, and be able to go out and get my breakfast.'* The door slams back in my face. This astonishes me! *"What the heck?"* I slowly push on the door again. It slams back in my face again! As my astonishment turns to questions, the boat rocks back and forth, and black hairs come through the crack of the door.

I know it is a bear. He is scratching his back on the doorknob, just a foot away on the other side. The boat rocks gently back and forth. The hairs go up and down the door through the crack. There is a pause. I think the bear must have turned around. I think if I move, I am so close the bear will hear me, and know someone is in here.

There is a sniffing at the crack. Then claws come through the crack as if the bear has smelled something, and wants in. I understand a bear's strength enough to know that it wouldn't take much to pull the door off, and I'd be right here on the other side, an appetizer in a box. There is another pause, as the bear must be debating if he wishes to pull the door off or not.

I keep the 357 pistol on a nail by the door within easy reach from the bed, for just such an event. My hand slowly works its way toward the gun, hoping not to make even the slightest sound. After what seems an hour, I manage to get hold of the gun, as the bear keeps rubbing his back on the knob, and his claws on the door. I have no idea what the bear has on his mind. *'When we don't know what is on a bear's mind, we kill him.'* I am unwilling to take a chance that the bear will not, in one swipe, tear the door off, and if he does this, I could not stop him and it is not predictable what he might do if suddenly confronted with the unexpected. Neither can I let him know I am in here, or he may intentionally rip the door off. With conscience choice, I pull the hammer back, muffled by my pillow. I do not want to blow my eardrums out in this confined space, or blow my door up shooting through it, or not know where I'm hitting the bear. *'I should never shoot anything without being absolutely sure what it is anyway.'* But in this case, I've seen the claws come through the cracks of the door.

I slowly push on the door so I can get it open enough to stick the gun out. *'I will make too much noise, and it will take too long, to work my way out the back door and up over the roof.'* As I open the door, the door slams back in my face. The bear has his back to me, and the door pushes him toward the edge of the bow. There is little room for him on the bow, so he slams the door shut, not knowing I push on the other side.

After several attempts, which are almost humorous, of shoving the door open and the bear slamming it shut, I am able to get the pistol out the front door. I feel fur, and do not want the bear to see, or realize, and maybe attack my hand. As soon as I feel fur, I pull the trigger. All hell breaks loose. The blast is almost in the cabin, so slams my eardrums "Blam!" I yank the pistol back inside, cover my ears and rock back and forth. I hear the scream of the bear over the ringing in my ears. The way the boat rocks and feels lighter, I know the bear dove off the front of the boat.

I open the door, knowing if he is only wounded, I might get another shot as he tries to get up the steep river bank. The door flies open, and the bear is lying on the bank in front of the boat, dead. The bear is not huge, but big enough. I have to take the time to get dressed. I'm now fully awake. I get the fire stoked up, knife sharpened, and spend this day skinning the bear, and cutting up the meat.

I work the hide on a lovely fall day, under the yellow birch leaves and blue sky. *'The dead animal in front of me seems as natural as the rest of the scene.'* I know the reason my conscience says this. There is concern that somehow there is something evil—wrong-about killing, and surely God will strike us down or cause bad karma over this. I'm so programmed by civilization's views.

The smell of the cooking heart works its way out of the boat. *'We will eat well for a while!'* I am unsure though, how the meat will keep. Past experience gives me some insight into the probable length of time before there is serious spoilage. *'I bet there is spoilage before we can eat it all up, so we better be eating bear for breakfast, lunch, supper, and stuffing ourselves.'*

There is a lot of blood to clean up off the front of the boat, and even on the door knob. The bullet had hit him in the side, mostly a liver shot, but tore up a lot of the insides. *'Anyone who thinks this 357 gun is not enough, needs to see this.'* I give a lot of thought to where the bullet hit, what it did, angle it went, rate of expansion, and the fragmentation. I study exactly where the best place is to hit a bear and what happens. This is part of what I need to know to survive here. *'Do we want to load a lighter bullet that will move faster? Or should we load heavier, have it move slower, but have more energy?'* Too much of what I read turns out to be hog wash. I will remember this damage with the heavier bullet. *'We used the lighter, faster bullet last time and it worked better at longer distances. So we will reload, and keep a heavy bullet first, for up close emergency, then a hot light load, for the longer shot, where we have time to advance the cylinder twice.'* This is stuff I'm not going to read in any book. There's been all kinds of advice discussed at jobs I've had, given by people who read a lot, but not much firsthand knowledge. I read about loading wad cutters backwards, loading hot and heavy, hot and light, hollow points, steel points, soft lead, hard copper, and any number of other combinations.

The bear, and what stops him, ends up being a common topic of discussion. My conscience reminds me of our view on this, *'Because we humans are afraid. The real answer is to understand the bear better, and be able to make reasonable assumptions about what he is likely to do, and not do, and try our best to leave him alone when possible, but till then, we can't take chances.'* Maybe we never will understand the bear enough to leave him alone, but with understanding comes less fear, and with less fear comes less aggression. This is really more meat then I want right now, and has been a lot of work. *'But I killed him, so I will eat him. Do you notice how, in our new lifestyle, we do not choose how much, or what kind of food goes in our basket?'* Yes, I surely do notice.

There is salt on board to take care of the hide, but I use it all up. Salt is added to the list of things to replace when I next get to a store, which may be a while. The hide is draped on the roof to dry in the air and sun as I continue down the river, wondering where I am, and if I've passed Manley Hot Springs, or maybe not even come to Minto yet. I'm going through about thirty gallons of fuel a day, so decide to slow down, and just let the current take me, using the engine for steering only.

'Where the heck is Manley Hot Springs, good grief, where are these towns?' I see from the map that this place is off the main river. I am looking for places the size of Fairbanks. I've never seen a real village. My first year up here I was in Fairbanks and the wilderness, but no village. To a city dweller, 'Fairbanks,' with 40,000 people, is a small quaint place, and 'out in the toolies.' Anyplace that has big letters on the map, and is the only name listed for fifty miles, has got to be fairly big. The concept of 'twenty people,' warranting a name on a map is funny, unregistered on the mind. Even though I lived extremely remote, I consider it 'another planet' in my mind, not even related to 'this world.' I've seen single families bigger than these villages are. Conscience, *'Could any of these collections of outhouse looking buildings actually be villages? These buildings back where I come from would be called shacks, woodsheds, outhouses, and be apologized for.'* The concept that someone might live in one is not discussable. There would be a hush in the room, and red faces, to even ask. The fact I built and lived in one is also not really discussable.

Thinking of the map I have memorized, I remember I had seen that there is 'Minto,' off the river a long way, and 'Old Minto,' on the river, but maybe deserted. *'How can a village that says it depends on the land, distance itself from the river? The river is life!'* Surely there should be a major dock at these places. Well, for sure I should recognize the Yukon River when I get to it. *'Man may come and go, but the Yukon is forever.'* I finish the thought out loud, "It cannot go away, or fool me about its location! I've seen the Yukon, and know I will recognize it. The water will change color, for one thing."

This day, it is raining heavily. *'Winter wants to be here. The weather is at war.'* It is true that most storms come between season changes, and major weather fronts come ahead of a big storm, so if it has been nice and warm and a storm comes, chances are, after the storm, the weather will get cold. I am not conscience of thinking this, but I 'sense' it. This is very different from looking in the paper to know the weather.

The geese are nervous, and I pick up on it. Up on the roof I am out in the cold rain. I remember Steamer saying how crazy this is, when I have a house on the boat from which I could be running the boat, warm and comfortable, and that is why I have a house on the boat! But I am not unhappy with my choice. I like steering the boat from the roof, out in the weather. I actually like being out in the rain! I am reminded of Hemingway's, 'Old Man and the Sea' tying himself to the mast in a storm. I love the smell of the wet. The sounds of the rain and wind. I do not mind the cold and wet, as long as I can get out of it at night.

"All our heroes were out in the weather! The Mountain Men, the sailor, all of them in the stories show the pirate swinging his sword in the rain and lightning. Clint Eastwood comes in out of the rain and storm in his poncho, laughing. The great cattle drives, the Indians, all of them live outdoors, and laugh in the rain." That's only part of it. I truly love the outdoors. I take a deep breath, and smile at the smell of wet poplar trees. The way the sheets of rain dimple the surface of the river in waves, soothes my troubled mind.

'Shhh, do you hear that?' I stop and hold my breath to listen. *'A chain saw.'* This is the first human sound I have heard in weeks. The sound of a tree falling comes to me through the fog. *'Someone else is out here.'* Mountain men of yesteryear would have thought, *'Check to see the powder is dry,'* while reaching to the black powder rifle, wondering ..... *'Is this a friend or foe?'* The sounds get louder, and I hear two people talking. Through the rain's misty gloom, a log raft is made out against the far cut bank, so I head over to see who this is. *'Maybe they can tell us where Manly is, Minto, the Yukon (whichever one we are closest to).'*

Sheets of rain fall at intervals of a few minutes apart. It takes me ten minutes to cross the river. Two Athabascan Indians from Tanana stand in the rain, waiting for me to dock. I'm not sure where to land, since there is a steep cut bank where they are. My cumbersome houseboat approaches the log raft. The boat is very heavy and I'm not using much power, so the current takes over more than I realize. I touch the raft with a 'thump.' The houseboat doesn't even stop, but slowly climbs up on the raft's corner, stops, slowly slides off and back into the water. I don't quite understand yet that one must always approach a landing heading upstream into the current, even if you are going downstream. It may look silly to swing out and make a big loop, and come upstream to dock, but this is how it's done because there is more control, allowing the current to slow you down, instead of speed you up. My engines however are too weak to confidently come back upstream with any control.

"Hi, I'm Wild Miles. How far am I from the Yukon? Have I passed Manley yet?" The two Indians just stare at me. My bear skin hat is no longer 'tanned leather,' but more like wet skin, draping over my smiling face like my own hair. The blade of grass in my mouth droops in the rain. I stand before them proudly, expecting a compliment on my boat. *'They are so quiet because this has got to be the coolest thing they ever saw!'*

One of them clears his throat. "I'm Scott Summers from Tanana." His hand comes out and I shake it.

There is awkwardness as the other says, "You fu*&^ed up our raft." I look at the raft with concern. I didn't think I hit it very hard. It is tied with rope, and a dowel

33

peg through a hole in each corner. The peg in this corner is broken, and the raft wants to come apart.

"I'm not used to my new boat I guess; sorry, let me help you fix it."

We spend half an hour fixing the raft, and I help them cut trees down. "This raft is our firewood for the winter. We'll float it down to Tanana and leave it on the beach till winter, then haul it up to the cabin with the dogs."

My conscience replies, so the Natives can't hear me, *'Dogs will haul all these logs?'* I have trouble believing horses could do it! These logs are a couple hundred pounds each! I keep my mouth shut. I wouldn't want these Indians thinking I'm an idiot.

Scott says, "Well.... um; Wild Miles is it? We are headed for Tanana now, why not stick with us, and we'll show you where the Yukon is. Squaw Crossing is just ahead, and it's pretty tricky to get through. You have to know the channel."

My conscience replies: "Gosh these Indians are friendly, but I guess it's because I'm like one of them now, you know, a bush person. They haven't said anything about it, but they must really like my boat, just too shy to say anything, but that's ok. They are just a little jealous, so I won't say anything to make it worse. I'm not going to hurt their feelings by letting them think I'm better than them or have a cooler boat or anything." I'm just staring at them saying nothing till we get to work shoving the raft off into the current and heading off for the Yukon River.

They go slower than I was going, but I stick with them in case they need help. The Indians have a small skiff they tie to the raft, that they use to steer it. The raft is about thirty by thirty feet, and is all dry firewood. A barge comes toward us in Squaw Crossing. This is not good, but the barge sees us, toots it's horn, and wants us to get out of the way I think, but there is no way to control the raft, and we can only stay in the main channel. The barge slows down. The front swings around, as they choose another channel that takes the barge behind an island, so I do not get a good look at it.

The waves of the barge are huge, even though ten minutes has gone by and the barge is a quarter mile away when it turned. I see the Athabascan's have to turn the raft into the waves, which works the raft and makes it creak dangerously. One end of the raft lets loose, (couldn't possibly be the part I smashed up), and a single log drifts off.

"I'll get it!" I yell, knowing they are tied to the raft and must stay with it. *'They are lucky we came along to help. We'll show them how skilled, and what good workers we are!'* I go fetch the log, but the Indians are out of sight now. They have told me where to find them in Tanana.

There is an old graveyard I see first, up on a hill, with old Russian crosses and fences. It looks well kept, and looks nice in the fall-colored hillside. The village is around the bend a little. I see the river water color change as I come around an island. I would have known where I was without help, but it is nice to have confirmation from someone. The log raft is tied ashore where the Indians said it would be. I drop the towed log off at the raft, and re-lash it in place with pieces of rope trailing from the raft.

"Where do I get gas?" is my first question when I spot someone.

"Oh you can't get gas today, not for three more days."

'What do you mean we can't get gas! What's going on?' I ask my conscience to pipe down so I can think. Gas is only sold four days a week in Tanana. *'How absurd,'* my civilized mind thinks. *'This is more like what I expected Minto to look like, or Manley, so probably that collection of outhouses was a village!'* I do not reply, but guess this must be so. In front of me is a mile stretch of a hundred boats of all sizes and shapes. I see dog teams on the gravel beach, all tied up by fish racks. Almost all the dog yards look alike, with a fifty-five gallon rusty drum cut up to be a cooker for dog food, set over a rock fire pit. The dogs are all on chains about seven feet long, just out of reach of each other. They each have a number ten can in their area as the water and food dish. The fish racks look alike, and are made of drift wood frameworks six feet off the ground, supported on upright logs, with lots of cross poles. Some racks have a lot of split fish hanging, similar to what I hung at Piper's camp. This reminds me that Piper is the only one who thinks I can make it, and wants to help and gave me a job at his fish camp. He taught me how to use the boat, catch the salmon in his nets, and dry the salmon as, 'Squaw Candy' in thin strips. I notice that instead of 'strips,' these salmon are just cut in half. They dry partly spoiled, but good enough for the dogs. I had heard the term before, and now know what 'split fish' means.

I see a lot of log cabins up on shore, with wood smoke curling up in the wet air. A few frame 'white man' buildings are up too, mostly the business places. Everyone seems to speak English. I figured they would, but had hoped to see maybe a village where a lot of people spoke the native language. I agree with the few Indians I've talked to in the past, like the firefighters, who said that white man can't go anywhere without cramming his ways down everyone's throat. About the time he conquers a race, he tells them how wonderful the old ways were, puts it in his art, and makes it romantic, 'the majestic Indian.' I can't blame the Indian for laughing, being puzzled, and even hostile. *'But don't take it out on me! I'm on your side!'* I feel puzzled by white man's behavior myself. I was born and raised white, so I can only imagine how odd we must seem to the Native. Because of this, I'm willing to over-look a certain amount of crap from the Indians.

"Hi, Harry!" This is one of the Indian firefighters I worked with this past summer.

He is glad to see me saying, "So you really did it huh?!" He's looking at my houseboat.

I proudly reply, "Yeah and I got all my winter supplies with me, so I can go out and trap all winter!"

My Athabascan friend nods in the affirmative but replies, "You're in Indian country now, and you're a White man, so you be careful! Don't be a know-it-all tourist." He warns me fondly, then asks me, "Hey Wild Miles, you want to come to the beer party? Frank just made a beer run to Nenana."

I don't understand why they would have to go all the way to Nenana to get beer, but I keep my mouth shut. "We don't want to be a know-it-all tourist, or asking too many questions. Maybe this is a dry village. We've heard of this... a place where the people vote not to drink, and it can't be bought, but the drinkers must ignore this, it looks like? Whatever. We better just go along with the program. We better go to this party, would be an insult not to go, and maybe we can mingle with the locals, and learn something, try and make some friends, at least get along."

I agree with my other half so say out loud, "Sure, sounds like fun!" He puts his arm around my shoulder like we are best buddies, *'I think he's drunk!'* My other half agrees. Arm in arm, we march off through the village. I have little time to take it in, as he talks and expects me to hold a conversation, but out of the corner of my eyes I see there are no streets! Well there are sort of, but its' all dirt! After we leave the one main dirt mud hole of a road full of ponds you could loose a tractor in, we get off on footpaths through the grass, that serve as the means to get from one home to another. The homes look to me to be cracker boxes, with wood doors falling off rusty hinges. Flattened gas cans are roof shingles. Broken snow machines, wrecked cars, dog shit, toys, and a mixture of 'stuff' lays in most yards. People step outside the front door to piss on the path as we walk by, and holler out greetings to everyone.

There are a few nice homes, but we do not go near them, and I assume there is a better section of the village, just as there is with the white people. We stop in front of a twenty x twenty one room log cabin. Harry waves me in ahead of him, where he introduces me to seven to eight, half drunk and passed out Indians. I'm the only white person here.

One of them grabs my hair saying, "You brought us a Pilgrim? Should we scalp him?" Everyone laughs at this guy's remark.

Harry speaks up for me, "He's all right. We worked together this summer. He just boated down from Fairbanks."

Someone in the corner burps, "Hey, you want a beer?" I, of course, better take the beer or I'm in trouble, even though I don't drink. This is not the time to get prissy. The pipe with the pot in it gets passed around ritually with great reverence. I politely take it, hold it a little bit, and pass it on to someone else, saying the sacred words, 'Hey man – good stuff,' while bobbing my head like a duck. I never let on I didn't smoke the peace pipe. I nurse the one beer all evening, pretending to enjoy it. I think it tastes like hot green pee.

Someone comes over with a guitar and plays some native traditional songs. "I left my heart in Texas—"

A few of the drunks stand up to dance, grab a couple of women I hadn't seen come in. I wouldn't dare grab one of their women, maybe start a fight. I enjoy just watching, and learning. I spot a barrel stove that heats the room, and a kerosene light on a bare wood table. My conscience, *'It looks like they live a great deal like we have lived ourselves in the wilderness, that first cabin we built before the houseboat.'*

"Yeah but we got off on nature and not drugs." Conscience, *'And starvation we got off on that too, don't forget!'* No I wasn't forgetting that. We'd had a rough time, but not as rough as life in town, but yes we'd had to be rescued. The 'whup whup' of Chinook military rescue helicopter blades in the -50° blowing snow is fried in my memory.

It would be impolite to leave early. I do not know my way back, and I would be afraid of the hostility here without my body guard, Harry, who is now passed out against a log wall. I don't blame these people for their feelings about whites, heck, I feel ashamed to be one! I'd be glad to be an Indian and live on the trapline in the old way! You bet! Surely I am in the wrong part of town, just like the white city has places you don't want to be! Surely there is an 'uptown' I have not seen, where the proud Indian lives wearing bear claws, and feathers with clear eyes looking wise.

My new friends look like 'pick up sticks' in a child game, all 'crisscrossed' on the floor, next to pools of vomit. I sneak out the door in the darkness and rain. Can I find my way back to the houseboat? I know where the river is, and just cut a straight line for it, as hostile dogs bark at me. I wonder if I will be spotted and scalped. I don't think I would like village life. Anyhow, I remember Canada. I'm not going to get conned by a village again.

Conscience, 'Yes Canada. Remember Canada? Didn't we get deported or something?'

"Don't start that crap again, 'remember' my ass, of course I remember! Lost everything we owned, the house, the boat, the photography equipment. You and your bright ideas, 'Go live in Canada, young man!'"

The next day I talk Scott into selling me some of his personal stash of gas, so I can get out of here. I have time to stop at the Tanana store, and this seems like a nice place. The 'fresh' things are not quite 'fresh,' and high priced, but there are nice frozen things, chips, soda, canned goods, books, and the things I'd expect to see maybe in a mom and pop type general store in the south. (As seen in the movies). I see enough here to know that if I stayed around and wanted to trap, there would be some hostility. There are Indians who would run my line, steal my traps, fur, and play games with me, and probably no one else would care enough to put a stop to it. If I put a stop to it myself, I'd get run out. I think I could make a few good friends here, but they'd be in a minority. I know right off I would get along with the store people. I also sense whose side they'd be on if trouble came along. Over a few years of hard times I might get accepted by the general population. Conscience, *'I'm glad we have a houseboat so we can move on, and not get stuck anyplace!'*

'Hey, what in the heck is going on down the beach over there?' I look down the beach and see a sailboat being launched into the river. A crowd is gathered around some event on the beach. Someone is using roller logs and a chute to send an ocean looking sailboat into the water by methods I've seen on TV from 3rd world countries. Out of curiosity I amble over, and mingle with the crowd. This boat is built by, 'The Nine Mile Flash,' who saw the design in a popular mechanics magazine, and decided to build it. He ordered the materials that came on the barge, (which took a year) and spent another two years building it. He's never seen a sailboat, never done carpentry work, and has no other help or advice than the drawing in a magazine. I gather all this information from the crowd. He did a wonderful job anyone would be proud of. He's got to be gifted to do this with no help.

"Nine Mile Flash?" I ask.

Now I'm told, "Oh, he had his house burn down and had to run nine miles to town." The guy talking to me puts out his hand, "Bush Charley," and I shake his hand. He is a Mountain Man or hippie looking guy in leathers, with beer bottle caps crimped on all the fringes of his jacket. I find out he can start a fire with flint and steel, traps, and is kind of the local 'White Mountain Man,' accepted by the Indians. This whole scene, and the people, could as well come from a story in the lower forty-eight states from 200 years ago. I have to remind myself: *'This is not a movie set.'* Bush Charley tells me that the Nine Mile Flash is starting off today on a trip to Siberia, using this sailboat, and this is his send-off day. The connection of Alaska to Russia is brought home in this story. There were the Russian grave designs, Russian church, and this guy is going to sail over.

Bush Charlie gets my attention, "Wild Miles, I heard of you from the firefighters. I hear you're one of us, so I can tell you about the bone yard." He explains this as a place where people find mammoth tusks. The local name is not located on any maps, and few people know about it, certainly not tourists. (Or scientists, who I find out, are excluded, and am curious, 'why.') He tells me it is a long way, and off the river a bit, but I could find it.

Bush Charlie goes on, "You don't know about Mammoths? They lived here over 10,000 years ago, up to 80,000 years ago, and are the big wooly elephants that roamed the earth. There were other animals too, bison, camel, tigers, all sorts of cave man type ice age stuff. If you're an artist, you should stop and get some material!" He only tells me because I'm 'one of us.' So this is nice, much better then, 'one of them.'

There is a roar from the crowd as the sailboat splashes into the water, and settles in the element where it belongs. "Doesn't want to roll over anyway!" I'm talking to Bushy Charley. We talk about what it would be like to go to Siberia.

Bushy tells me of his own dream, "I'm headed for the headwaters of the Amazon next year myself. I know the Yukon, now I want to try the Amazon."

I reply, "The river itself sounds ok, Bushy, but I wouldn't like all the disease and heat, but it'd be a challenge all right!"

I'M anxious to get my show on the road, so start the engines, and houseboat warmed up in the rain. I head on down the river with 300 gallons of gas, and all my winter supplies. Conscience: *'We gotta find this bone yard place.'* I can't get there in a day though, so camp out on the river. There are grizzly tracks on the sand. I keep the guns handy. The bear meat on board has me worried. Grizzlies eat black bears, and these smells would make great bait. The hide is not drying well, and has been moved into the cabin with me, since I'm reluctant to let it go to waste. I have to put up with the strong bear smell. My conscience reminds me of the Mountain Man—Indian code we live by, "You kill it, you deal with it."

I find the ice age boneyard. After walking in a long way, the bone yard is recognized by the odor described to me, of old things rotting. The mud cliffs slide into the creek. The water acts as a sluice box, leaving behind bones and tusks. The soil has been frozen for 10,000 years, and as the creek cuts into the frozen soil, it thaws for the first time. There are jungle leaves floating in the water. Tropical ferns are growing, and an 'ice fog' hangs in the deep cut. There are bones lying right in the open. I pick them up, but I do not know what they are. One is a rib bone five feet long, another is a leg bone as big as I am. It is not possible to be here and not get covered in mud. Everything is 'mud.' There is a constant plop, pop, with a rumble and 'SSSSSSS,' every few minutes as a slide fills the bottom somewhere up ahead, or behind. Hopefully it doesn't bury me.

The soil is jet black, oil rich, and filled with old things. A frozen pond, trapped in the mud slide, tips and falls into the cut within sight. This looks like it came from a many ton tea cup. I walk up to it and see pure ice eight feet thick. This prehistoric pond has shells on its bottom. I look to see if there are any prehistoric fish trapped in the ice, but see none. I do see sticks that have been cut by 700 pound beaver, leaving inch wide teeth marks.

I find only a small piece of mammoth ivory, but big enough to make into a belt buckle. *'This is a place it would be good to come back to.'* Wolverine, bears, every kind of predator comes around here to feed off the bones as they become exposed. Some of the bones still have flesh on them. *'There is a prehistoric steppe bison in the Fairbanks University museum called 'Blue Babe,' that was found around here.'* "The bison is intact and even the eyelashes are there. It had been killed by a cave cat of some kind, and the claw marks are still visible on the haunches." I have little time this trip to look the area over good. The weather is cold, and wet. I wish to get going further down the river, maybe get to my destination up the Koyukuk. I'm reluctant to dip water from near here when it is time to eat. Because, as my conscience puts it to us… *'This may be water from that prehistoric ice cube? What if it has prehistoric germs? What if I come down with mastodon itch, or the mammoth crud -- Saber Tooth heebie jeebies that there is no cure for?'* My body gives an involuntary shudder.

There are fish in the next stream I come to, so I have salmon for dinner, but also eat some of the bear meat just because I must. It has green spots. I have to cut maggots out of it. An antique hand blown blue bottle is found the following day while getting water to drink, in a slough that has some bootleg history. I can tell by the names of nearby islands and creeks 'hooch slough,' 'Whiskey Run', etc. The bottle goes on a shelf in the boat. At night I tie up on the main river because I see no big creeks or quiet sloughs to tie up in, and I have had bad experience getting back out of the small shallow creeks.

During the night the wind picks up, so I sleep fitfully as the boat rocks in protest. In the dark there is little I can do. There is a flashlight, but no flood light. I recall there are rocks just downstream from me and if I turn myself loose, I fear I may be dashed on the rocks! The waves get to four feet, as the boat is pushed broadside into the shore. Each wave picks up the boat and slams it on the gravel bar; over and over, "Slam! Grind, Bam." Hour after hour. I keep thinking, "I have seen the worse," yet I am wrong. There is worse yet to come. I wonder now if the rope will break, and if I will get swept downriver in the dark, or if the boat will get smashed into pieces with this hammering. The hollow hull magnifies the sounds, but surely this cannot be good for the boat! Even if I 'only' spring a leak, it would be a major problem, with all my food aboard that can't get wet!

Water is coming into the boat. Waves are washing over the side because I am now broadside to the waves, but maybe the boat is falling apart. The emergency hand pump is found and put to use. *'Thank God we remembered to consider we might need one of these in just such an emergency!'* The pump lasts only a few minutes before it quits, and needs looking after. It is only plugged up. After fixing, it lasts another minute before it wears out, will not work, and upon being worked on again, breaks. Conscience, *'Look at this, cheap plastic parts inside, what a piece of crap! Look at the price we paid! It should be illegal to sell stuff like this, and con people into believing their life can depend on this product!'* Yes, I've about had it with advertising. Ever since I came to Alaska, I've felt ripped off by products advertised to do what I'm doing with it, that turns out to be an outright lie. Conscience, *'Look at the picture on the box! Get a load of this! Airplanes crash, boats are sinking, and everyone is saving the day with this product.'*

After looking around I find a gas pump, used to transfer gas from barrels. This works as a bilge pump. A bucket to dip with will not work, because there is the 'subfloor' four inches above the bilge's, with no hole in it big enough to accept a bucket. Conscience, *'If we have to, before the boat fills with water and sinks, we should use the crowbar to make the needed hole in this sub floor!'*

The waves wash the boat further ashore, making it lean more and more. Now there is three feet of water in the bilges on one side, and no water on the other side. With this distribution of water I can now use the bucket. The supplies on the floor on this side are now wet; full of silt and gas. The leaning boat is unbalanced, so the shelves dump their goods onto the floor. Books, maps, the lamp, my diary, everything is now sloshing around in the water in the dark.

I have an idea. I tear the shelves out of the walls. These boards are taken outside and used as props against the hull of the boat, so the waves can't shake the boat, or cause it to lean with each blow. I have not been able to rest for more than half an hour at a time up till now. With these new prop boards, the waves stop cresting over the gunwale, so I gain on the water inside by bailing. The 100 gallons in the bilges is thrown out one bucket at a time. About the time I think I am done bailing, the storm increases, and water starts coming in again. I stay awake two straight days bailing. Ketchup, syrup, gas, and assorted other things mix and spread into every crevice in the boat. The smells are overwhelming. The gas fumes bother me the most, and are the most dangerous. There is no place outside the boat where I will be safe though, so I remain with the boat, bailing while breathing in the fumes. *'To leave the boat would mean to loose it.'* my conscience says; but I am unsure if I agree, yet am unwilling to argue. I cannot get the stove started of course, everything is wet and would not burn, but there are the gas fumes. In a quieter lull, I try to get some sleep. I'm soaking wet, cold and tired. I do not know how many of my supplies are being ruined, maybe my whole boat, and who knows how much gas I'm losing. Any spark, even static electricity, would light up the night with 300 gallons of gas.

Living on houseboat as I build Kantishna R. cabin

Me finding a mammoth tusk

CHAPTER TWO

BOAT RESCUE, RUBY, KIDS, CANADA PAST FLASH,
GALENA, BEAR, BULLET RELOADS, FREEZE
HOUSEBOAT IN FOR WINTER, SWANS, TRAPPING
SEASON, OTTER, LETTERS, CROSS YUKON ICE,
INDIAN VIEWS, DAD AND TRIP OUTSIDE, SELL
FURS, BAD CHECK

I n the morning I'm still alive. The gas fumes leave me groggy, sick, and throwing up, but I am unwilling to abandon my boat. I have to be ready to do whatever it takes to save it, like the emergency bailing. My conscience reminds me, *'Abandon our boat and go where? The storm is raging. The rain is sleet, and the night is Raven black.* After three solid days of storm, the wind has died down enough to where there are no more waves hammering the boat. I can go out now and check the hull, and take stock of damages. I need to see what can be done.

The repetitious pounding on the gravel has not broken up the hull. I don't think it even leaks! There are a few scrapes, and even places that should be patched, but nothing serious, and no structural damage. The extra money I spent building the boat from marine grade plywood, clear lumber, and bronze screws, is what helped save the boat I'm convinced. I'm missing maybe twenty gallons of gas, which is a lot less than my imagination allowed. The main damage is to my winter supplies. The clean-up job to make the boat livable is horrendous. Honey and other food is soaking into the wood now. Fifty pound bags of rice have gotten wet, swollen, broken, and scattered everywhere. A mischievous God has been let loose. I had put a lot of perishables up high, considering there could be water down low. Yet it had been the up high things that spilled off the shelves, and are the most damaged.

Some things like rice had just been too heavy to put up high in an already top-heavy boat. Flour is ok, spices, matches; quite a lot is ok actually. This just looks so terrible it is hard to believe anything survives.

'How do we get Sable off the sandbar though?' I use the feminine name of my boat, as all boats need a name, so called her 'Sable,' because Sable is a fur that trappers value, is a land animal, but related to mink and otter from the water. Sable is from Russia, or the Russian name for Alaskan Marten, an exotic far off romantic sounding place of adventure. Right now I need to think of this set of events as an adventure, not a disaster! The waves left me high and dry on the sandbar, and not sitting level. The first thing I do is get the handy jack out and level the boat on logs. *'Will we have to unload the heavy things to get us back to the water?'* I have one empty barrel. This barrel is set outside the boat. I transfer one barrel of fuel from the boat into the empty one on shore with a siphon hose. Now I have an empty one in the boat, which I put out on shore and transfer another full one into. I have six barrels to go through. As I work, my conscience sets this up like a high school algebra problem; *'We have six barrels of gas, one pump, and want it all out of the boat intact, and it's too heavy to lift...'* This will take forever, but I think has to be done before I can even consider jerking the boat around. This gas transfer relieves the boat of 2,000 pounds. I read somewhere to figure about seven pounds a gallon for gas.

The boat is only five feet from the water, but there is no way to move it without help from tools. I can jack the boat up, and push it off the jack onto roller logs, then keep jacking and pushing off, gaining a foot each time maybe. This could be done in about a day. I have a fire going on shore to dry out clothes and keep warm. There is a coating of frost on the sand this morning. This is to be expected, since it is now into September. My damp clothes cause me to shiver, until I get into the heavy work.

I do not hear the engine until an Indian in a big powerful boat pulls up.

"Need any help?" I'm not sure what he can do that wouldn't require him hanging around here all day, which I wouldn't ask of anyone.

He pulls ashore, looks over my situation, and says, "I think my boat could pull you into the water, if you set some roller logs up." I'm dubious, from my limited experience with boat engines, but I've always been under powered. My conscience reminds me, *'When they say 'horsepower' I think 'one horsepower,' like the work one horse can do. I go 'wow!' I think five horses should be able to move a house, rip this boat apart. I do not understand how a total of fifty horses shouldn't be able to move an entire village in one yank.'* That's a lot of horses strung in front of me. I'd think fifty dogs could do a lot. So it's just more bullshit we hear. I could hold one motor horse back with a single finger!

So anyhow I answer the guy, "We can give it a try, you got a strong rope, or should I try to find one. My gear is pretty scattered now."

"I have rope, here!" He tosses me one end of a 100 foot rope. The stern of my boat is facing the water, not the bow, so I tie around my two engines; the only thing back here to tie to. He nods that he understands as I wave for him to 'go for it.' He's sitting in his boat with it in idle, keeping his bow into the current. Eighty horses are in harness.

The rope tightens as the horses rumble. He doesn't want to try yanking on it unless this straight pull will not work. No use yanking my transom out, or the engines off my boat. The houseboat groans, so I know we are getting close, and wave him to slap the horses. All eighty horses bend heads, wave tails, shake manes, and with a roar, water flies. The rope stretches enough to squeeze all the water out of it, and make it vibrate. The houseboat slowly moves, then slides on the skid poles. With a few thumps and bumps the houseboat splashes into the water.

This saves me a couple of days work, and only took us fifteen minutes. He tells me he's one of the Mark's family from Huslia. Giving the family name seems the bush custom. It is assumed if you are from Alaska you will recognize the family name, and thus have a clue what sort this person is, from the blood line.

Arnold Marks throws a wave, saying he wants to go on his way, not stop to visit saying, "I have friends caught in this storm, and a lot of people got in trouble." I feel a little better that this was not all my fault because I did something wrong. A lot of boats in the next village of Ruby were sunk, and a lot of people got into trouble. One fisherman lost his life in this storm. These are all seasoned river people, so think there was not much else I could have done. I'm actually one of the lucky ones.

Conscience, '*Next time though, I think we could tie off the bow to keep the boat from swinging crossways, or even tie us 'bow out' so the waves wash harmlessly over the bow, and not over the stern into the boat itself. Because there is little glass up front, it would be safer in storms like this.*' I'm glad then, that I didn't build a luxury boat with lots of glass, which would have impressed the town people more, but not been as practical.

Now I have to transfer all the gas on shore back to the boat, and do this in the reverse order that I used getting it out. This takes half a day. Meanwhile there is plenty to do, fixing the shelf I ripped out, sorting goods that can be saved and dried, from goods that have to be tossed out. The front and back door are left open to air and dry things, but mostly to get the gas fumes out so I can get a fire going in the stove. There is plenty of room on the beach to spread out on the gravel to dry and sort things as my conscience mumbles under our breath, '*and no cop telling me to move on! No one ripping it off as fast as I set it ashore!*' I feel sorry, once again, for people who will never know what it is like to live without locks, contracts, or the threat of a club every time they get the idea to try something different.

I'M TOTALLY EXHAUSTED, but in a happy way. The fire is crackling in the stove. My gear is dry. I still have lots of food. What I lost is fairly inexpensive stuff that can be replaced for a hundred dollars. *"Probably I can get these things in one of the villages"* The bear hide will not dry now. After the damp rain, Then a river soaking, I have to give up on saving it. The hair is starting to slip. I have to toss it out, and feel bad. The meat is green, and full of boat gas and silt. The meat makes me sick, but I feel very strongly about eating what I kill, and will not part with it till I absolutely cannot keep it down. Lots of cooking, and strong spices helps keep the meat eatable. *'Soaking in vinegar seems to help preserve it longer too! Also we now know why curry is a preferred spice in hot India! It sure masks the taste of rotten meat better than anything else we know!'*

The engines do not start. Common sense tells me it has to be related to what has gone on. I was raised where, if something breaks, you call someone who can fix it. I have had only a little experience with a snow machine engine. I also had Piper's small outboard, but only long enough to know how to change a spark plug. *'We know it takes three things to make the engine run, right? Spark, gas-air, and mechanics. So we isolate which category the problem lies in.'* My conscience helps me get started. My buddy Will had steered me in the right direction. I doubt it's a compression related mechanical problem, since the engine ran well last time, nothing should have happened to it since, and two engines are involved. Spark is easy to check. I pull the plugs, ground them and see if there is spark. I have spark, so I can assume it is a fuel problem. This is most likely, because this would affect both engines.

I disconnect the lines and use the hand squeeze bulb to pump gas out the end of the hose into a can. There is a little water in it. I keep squeezing till I get pure fuel. I then take the sediment bowls off the engine carburetors and dump the water out. *'We need to get a water separator for this system; how come it's not standard? Huh?'* I do not bother explaining the obvious; "Because boat owners do not put their boats engines underwater as a rule. Most boat owners are weekend warriors." My conscience already knows that. I put the carburetor back together and the engines start.

I arrive in Ruby in the dark. I decide to stop for the night so I can see what Ruby is like in the daylight. It is nice to have a level, warm bed, and wood stove heat. In the morning I forget where I am and am momentarily puzzled when I hear whispers outside the boat. *'Sounds like kids.'* I yawn and wonder if I should get up and have breakfast first, or yell at these kids to go away. Maybe I could ask them if they know what day it is.

☹

Instead I just shove the door open from the bed. The startled children scatter.

"Hi kids! What's going on?" They shyly come back to talk to me and ask questions about my boat and my lifestyle.

47

Athabascan kid, "Way you from, Mista?"

I think about this as he stares in my boat in astonishment and I reply to this, "I'm from another planet."

Another Athabascan kid, "No way man! You from Mars or something? How come you're not green? What planet you from then?"

All five kids laugh and I laugh too saying, "I come from Earth, what planet is this?"

They all giggle. "This is Earth!" one says.

I look puzzled, grab a map and look at it. Scratch my head. "This couldn't be Earth, because it is so different from the Earth I come from." I pause before going on. "How many people you got in your village here?"

Another one says, "About 300 people."

I look impressed, "That's a lot of people huh?" They all agree. Most of the villages are smaller, much smaller. The biggest place any of these children have seen is Fairbanks, and even that is like 'unreal.' With this in mind I tell them, "Well, how about a place where 300 people fit in just one building?" They think this is hilariously impossible.

They all start talking and asking questions at once. "Can we see the inside yer boat?"

I laugh. "Ok, but let me get up and get dressed first ok. I'll shut the door, but I'll be right back. There are even more children gathered when I open the door again. I am suddenly Oz—the great and powerful. Word has gone around that there is someone from another planet visiting them. They all want to come aboard to visit. I show them how the boat is set up to live on, and this is my home.

They are full of questions that show a lot of insight. "Is your planet contaminated, and is that why you left?" They have been watching Star Trek. I do not know how to answer.

Someone else asks, "You aren't going to contaminate our planet too, are you?" They think I come from a very sad planet where you can't even look up and see the sun. No wonder I left. The children are laughing and throwing rocks into the river. I tell them about the big storm and how it was.

They know about storms and one twelve-year-old asks, "Did ya check your carbs for water?" I had told him about the engines not starting. These Indian kids wouldn't last five minutes in New York, but they are not stupid, and know how to take care of themselves on their planet.

I say, "Many things on your planet are new to me, and it will take me a while to understand how everything works."

They all nod in understanding. One kid is up on the roof at the console, pretending to run the boat. I hear other little feet up there, so decide I better step out where I can keep an eye out and make sure no one falls into the river.

As the dozen or so children scamper around the boat I daydream about what it would be like to have a wife and a houseful of children and wonder why I am on the lonely path I am on. My conscience speaks to me, *'This life is rewarding in its own way but everything has a price.'* Sigh. My mind drifts into a—

Flash-past: Canada 1972. There is a young boy about fourteen who comes around to visit me regularly. I'm not so many years older than him. His parents drink. It is winter. His home is often empty and freezing cold when he gets home from school. The house depends on wood heat. The parents do not keep enough firewood around, and are too preoccupied with other matters to keep the fire going. This kid is too young to know how to go get wood, split it, and tend the fire. The family may not even have a chain saw that runs. So instead he goes out and wanders on the streets, stopping in any warm place he can find. Sometimes he hangs out at the store, but they run him out. Sometimes he stops at the library, but he gets too noisy and disruptive. He is labeled a 'problem child.' Sometimes he steals, starts fights, and throws rocks at dogs. Sometimes he wanders over to my place and we talk. Sometimes we talk about getting into trouble and how fun it is. Sometimes we talk about the price trouble costs. Sometimes we talk about other things to do that are fun, that keep us out of trouble, like going out in the woods snaring rabbits.

One day he says to me, "My teacher said today, if we don't pay attention in school we will end up like you! What does that mean?" He's puzzled because he admires me. No one is really interested in this kid, and I know that he gets bored. He's too young to think of as a friend, but I think of this town as my home, and this kid, as part of my community, and as such, is part of my responsibility. I couldn't put my feelings into words, maybe because no one has ever suggested this line of thinking to me, about helping others for no reason. I'm just over being a kid myself. I am hanging around the library, have gotten a few of the neighborhood children to start hanging out there and staying out of trouble by reading and talking. I try to make it a warm, friendly place where they are welcome, slipping a little learning in without them knowing it, by making it 'fun.'

This kid needs more than just this though, and I know it, but I also know it is up to his parents, not me. Still, if he wasn't at my place, he'd be out on the street throwing rocks at windows. For some reason he looks up to me, listens to me, and I do not have any problem at all with him. He minds very well, and is amazingly bright. I find it a shame that he will probably end up in jail with the way his life is going. Maybe just a little bit of my time can change that. I have my own life to live, and know I can't save the world, or raise someone else's child, but it's hard to tell him to go away and quit bothering me like everyone else does. He reminds me of myself when I was his age. My parents took care of me though, materially anyhow, but like this kid, it was common for no one to be home, or if they were home, not noticing if I was or not.

This kid and I go out hunting rabbits a couple of times, for fun and for food. He comes from a very poor family where there is often no food in the house. I also do not have extra food to be feeding the local hungry children, since I cannot legally work in Canada yet, and have to live on the money I saved till my papers come through, and I cannot sell my paintings.

One day there is a big ruckus over this kid's visit. I don't even remember his name. He's just a local kid. But the parents tell him to stay away from me. He's crying, angry. He does something or other. Next thing is; I hear how he got sent to reform school and good riddance, and not needing his kind around. No, not exactly a tragedy. Just a fact of life. There is talk going around how he used to come visit me and we went out in the woods together, with speculations on why a guy takes a kid into the woods. No one wants their children to come near me. I'm probably a child molester. Just another fact of life to ponder. **My past flash ends**

One of the Ruby village children is asking, "Hey Mister, how long are you going to stay around here anyway? Can we come and visit again?"

I smile and explain that I'll be on my way, and don't know how to tell them that it isn't such a good idea to talk to strangers. Not that this is what I myself believe, but I parrot what society teaches, knowing this is what the parents of these children will believe.

My conscience knows the brainwash ritual, but comments to me: *'Everyone is your enemy until proven different, because one in 10,000 just might be a bad person. What a concept!'* Yeah well, it's none of my concern. Should have just told these little brats to stay away from my boat. Now look, they are happy, and want to come back. I take time to talk to 'em and obviously, I have to be up to no good. Obviously, I'm about to molest them. Why else would a human being enjoy children or want to answer their questions? 'Nice' is not going to get rewarded. Now I feel guilty for being nice to them. Societies' middle name is 'Guilt.' No, not for everyone, just those who take the different fork in the road, march to another sheet of music then the rest of society.

An adult up on the bank yells at the children, "What are you kids doing? Get away from that boat! Get up here!"

The adult scowls at me from a distance and calls to the children, who do not wish to go. I say, "You all better leave. They might think I'm a monster from the other planet and it wouldn't be safe for me if the adults got scared and angry. It might not be safe for me if they think I am trying to eat little children."

The children wisely nod in agreement, as more adults come with stern faces.

"Bye" they shyly say as they run off. I have to chuckle. Ruby seems like a nice enough place, kind of up against a hill, not like the Minto flats country. I have the impression it's about the size of Tanana, but I'm not really paying attention. There's nothing I want to get here. I think I can wait till the next village, Galena, which is bigger, and is more of a hub for this part of the world, or so I've been told by the village forest fire fighters I met in the past while working for BLM. The barge runs in and out of Galena, so fuel prices should be better. My conscience thinks: *'Maybe this is smaller than Tanana. These villages are so spread out.'* I reply "hmm."

"Emit Peters, where's his place at?" This is the only person I know here. He's one of the Indians I met and respected from the firefighting job. I'm directed to his log cabin up the path. A dog chews on a moose leg bone out front. Trash burns in a fifty five gallon drum. About 100 sled dogs are chained up beside a log cabin with an outhouse. Emit and I chat a little while. He just won the Iditarod, the new sled dog race getting started. It's not so well known yet. Emit tells me the race is promising, and we talk about it, and the strategy he used to win it.

Emit explains, "It's over a thousand miles long through the wilderness, and takes about twelve days to run." He shows me his dog team, as he rambles on about the race. "You have to teach the dogs to drink water every day, and not eat snow. Snow takes calories to melt, more calories than the good the water produced gives! " Emit tells me about sled dogs. The dogs are all barking like crazy with happiness to see us, and jump all over me as we laugh about it. They all look healthy and well cared for.

Emit brings up the subject of my art. "I like your artwork, Miles. Could you do my dog on a necklace, my dog, Lucky, that was the leader in the race?" I tell him I can do it, and can send it from Galena. Emit looks down the hill at my boat and comments, "You rode out the storm all right I see!"

I reply, "Yea, hear it was a nasty one around here." We discuss the weather for a while, and I tell him I want to be on my way, headed for the Koyukuk.

He clucks his tongue, "Not sure you want to go there, Miles, Indians running the white people out. They shot a plane down a week ago."

I can't believe the war is that out front, that anyone could shoot a plane down and not get nuked, not have a big FBI investigation going on to get to the bottom of it, which would happen if I shot a plane down. He tells me boats are being sunk, a teacher run out, houses burned. Nothing in the paper about it though.

Emit thinks I'm funny, thinking all the news worth knowing is in the paper, and explains, "This is bush news, Miles; nobody in town cares what happens out here."

Again, I don't believe it. My conscience explains to me, *'I'll get more news from Galena, it's closer, and I know people there. There is a firefighting station there. Galena is the largest village on the Yukon I think. Prices will be better there for re-outfitting too.'* Galena is another sixty miles.

Future Flash:
Twenty years from now. One of the Ruby 'kids' is now an adult, remembers and

confides in me. "Wild Miles, I was one of the children you talked to in Ruby. You spoke of your planet you are from. Ever since, I wished to understand more about this. Because of meeting you, I was not like others, and tried to understand views and perspective when visitors come from far away, and not judge or try to harm them. I wished to get along with whites. I am now head of a big multimillion dollar Indian corporation, encouraging Natives to get along with your people, who are from another planet. I believe your people mean well because of meeting you as a child. I am again reminded how some small event in our lives can have big consequences in the future.

Past Flash ends

Two miles out of Galena I run out of gas. My conscience is angry, *'How'd this happen?'* My conscience figured it was my responsibility, not his. I have to explain: "I think there was more water in the gas when I measured it out than I thought. Maybe lost more than I figured in the storm, burned more than I thought I would with the engines, but I thought I had 300 gallons from Tanana!" My conscience shares some of the blame, using 'we' when replying: *'If we had watched closer, we could have drifted more in the middle section, and not had to drift into the village. This isn't going to look good. Who would ever have guessed 300 gallons wouldn't get us to hell and back.'* I do not have to be reminded that the more I try to prove I am a sourdough, the more I prove I am not. There's some village fisherman out as I drift along, and I wave and want to know if they have any extra gas to sell. I'd only need a gallon. They ignore me. Figure I'm just an ignorant tourist. "Let him float!" This puts my conscience in a bad mood saying: *'I hope they never need help!'*

Luckily no one is out and about as I pole and paddle my way out of the current and into the village. This would not be a cool entry to see. There is an 'old village' and a 'new' village, just like Minto. The 'new,' is the white man's doing, just like Minto. I land in the old village. The one connected spiritually to the water, and has boats, dogs, fish racks, and log cabins with wood smoke. The new village is frame places burning oil, and away from the water.

There are benches along the top of the river bank that I wonder about. I ask a stranger what the benches are for! A polite reply:

"People sit and visit, watch the river, watch the fish wheels turn." I wonder how anyone could be so bored as to find entertainment in watching a wheel turn! Good grief!

It doesn't take me long to run into BLM people I know. There is a military base here, so a lot of white influence. It wouldn't be so easy here to make a white person disappear without a ripple. I bring the subject up right away:

"What's up in Huslia and the Koyukuk country? White people being run out and it being unsafe and all that!" I can't believe the reply:

"It's true enough. No way in hell I'd go up with a brand new boat. Indians would sniper you out. It's only a handful of radicals, but no one in the village will turn them in, or do anything about it."

I reply: "Come on, that's got to be paranoid talk! You're telling me there's a place in this United States where I can't go because there's a war against American citizens? I mean, if it's true, and the Indian wants to go to war, why not treat it like Vietnam? How can they be at war with the U.S. and get away with it! Shooting planes down! That's crazy!"

My friend shrugs his shoulders as he informs me: "Wouldn't be politically correct to move the troops in to win, just like Vietnam." I'm dumbfounded and will not believe him, but politely hear: "Too many voters in the lower states think the Indians shit doesn't stink- and feel guilty for running them off their land and want to make up for it and understand why they are upset and protesting. It is not their plane getting shot down or their kids getting sniped." I think this guy is nuts but it does seem odd. Either it is all not true, and no boats are sunk, or planes shot down or schools burned, or if true, why is there no news of it? And why isn't it being stopped? Very strange. I'm looked at like I am nuts and stupid, so I drop the subject. I hold up my winter plans till I hear more about these killings and burnings. It's got to be exaggerated out of proportion! Meanwhile I have supplies to get, and gas to buy. While getting gas I run into one of the BLM honchos, out wrapping up the fire season here.

He greets me. "Hey Miles, what are you doing here! Did the main office send you?"

I know nothing about what is going on at the main office so say: "No, I'm just passing through. I need some supplies."

"Well, we could use you here if you want about two weeks of work. The buildings need wrapping up here for winter, and you have experience and are in the system as an employee." It's true. This is part of the work I did in Fairbanks, drained water pipes, put boards over windows, shut down all systems.

I think it over. I need more money now to replace gas and supplies after that storm set me back. This new information about Huslia running whites off needs to be checked out. Who knows when I might have work again, or the chance to make any money? This would be a good reason to be here while I check things out. It goes over a lot better to say, 'Yea, working for the BLM firefighters!' Than, 'Just a bum hanging around.' So I say: "Sounds good to me!" The paperwork is done up to re-open my work status, and I'm back on the payroll.

On the job I work with a guy I knew a little in Fairbanks, who remembers me. The local native, Larry, tells me there is a place across the river, "Go up this slough, where you can park your houseboat, and trap if you want." I hadn't been thinking of stopping here for the winter till now. My conscience gives the advice: *'But it would be nice to have a place to stay and also trap. An advantage is to have the backing of someone local who gives the ok, and so not be in trouble like if I went into country where I don't know anyone, and try and trap, especially up in hostile Indian country.'* Winter is not so far away. October is around the corner, and the ice will run anytime early in October.

I tell Larry: "I'll go check it out! I wanted to get further downriver and get to the Koyukuk, but may not get there this year; we'll see how it goes."

Larry nods and says: "There might be less trouble next year, and you might be able to go up there then, Miles. You know, a lot of the Huslia Indians come down this way. If you were around here, you would meet them, and get to know them, and maybe be accepted better later, rather than coming in as a stranger." I nod that this is good advice and mention meeting someone from Huslia already, who seemed nice:

"I met Arnold Marks. He said he is from Huslia, and he helped me get my boat back in the water after that big storm a couple of weeks ago. He seemed nice enough." Larry opens his mouth to say something, but thinks better of it. I see his hesitation and know what it means, so speak his thoughts: "Yea, I know how it is. As long as I remain an outsider, it's ok, but when I say I want to move in, and trap, everything changes. It's the same where I come from. People are friendly, till you want a job, or look for a house in the area. All of a sudden the questions come about who you are. You need to have references. Your race and religion suddenly matter. I understand."

Larry is relieved that I know how it is. He doesn't want me in trouble and may not want to take me on as a friend and stand up for me if I am going to do something stupid and embarrass him or put him on the spot. Larry shrugs his shoulders saying: "Yeah Miles, it's like that, what else can you expect? The white man isn't exactly the Indian's friend you know. It's fine when you bring your money and all that, but it's a whole different thing to want to live among us! Just hang in there and be patient." I like Larry for being honest. He seems smart, sober, hard working with a lot going for him.

The slough across the Yukon from Galena winds around like a long creek. The place Larry speaks of is called Jack Slough. A white man once lived here and made hooch. His grave is still here with an iron fence around it. There are nice birch trees, rosehips, with dry grass on the high bank. The area is protected from the wind and has tall spruce trees not far back from the water. No one is back here, and I see a lot of animal sign. No one claims it as a trapping area. Larry says he has as much claim as anyone, so can transfer his rights to the area to me. Very little in the wilds is done with paperwork. Deals are handshakes. In the wilds your word is all you have.

The houseboat can come out of the water here, and it would be safe. I do not wish to be on the main river. I already know the main river is too open, busy, and windy. There are not many other creeks or rivers near Galena where I could move to, or explore as an alternative. I'd have to go fifty miles to find another place like this. My conscience helps me decide, *'It is good to hang around at least a little and get to know the local people, and be accepted first, then figure out where a better place might be. Maybe some opportunity will present itself later. If we go off in the wilderness and see no one all winter, locals will get suspicious, just like what happened before. There is no such thing as being left alone.'*

I've traveled 800 miles since Delta, and am well into Indian country, away from the big city. My life is pointing in this direction for now. I shrug my shoulders with a smile, and head back across the river. A few days later I set up permanent camp with a tent, and start drying my supplies better. The boat needs to be completely emptied of its ton of supplies, and thoroughly cleaned before winter. During the two weeks of working for BLM I keep a low profile in Galena. I've seen enough trouble, and just feel shy or something. I watch. I listen. I don't want to make any waves, cause any problems, stand out in any negative way. I do not go to the bar. I don't hang out anywhere at night where there might be trouble or confrontations. The military here brings confrontations and hostility between the White and Indian. It is kept under wraps, but I see the tension. There are fights at the hobo bar, which is a pretty famous place from what I hear. There are bullet holes in the walls from 'incidents' over the years; that are bragged about, and famous fights go down in history. I stay in the old village, where the Indians and trappers will be. A few people start to recognize me and greet me.

Winter will be here soon. Once I pull the houseboat out of the water and I'm across the river, I will not be able to cross anymore till the river freezes, most likely a month or more.

One day on the job I holler at someone I recognize: "Oh, Hi Don! You here to wrap things up, too?"

"Well, well, if it isn't the Wild Miles! You're not dead."

I laugh. We spend a day working together. He was flown in for the last day to make sure everything is shut down and signed off. Water is drained from all the pipes in the buildings. We disconnect pipes, wrap insulation here and there, pull water pumps, inventory fire extinguishers, linen, and furniture, lock up store rooms and all these kind of things we are used to doing.

Don sadly says when he leaves, "Guess I'll have to report you made it huh?"

I know this is his form of humor, and I'm pleased he will be able to tell everyone 'Wild Miles made it.' To let him know my situation, I inform him. "I'll be staying across the river in my houseboat about five miles away. I'll have fur to sell this winter, so you'll be seeing me." Don is still the only fur buyer I have sold to in the past. I remember bets were made on the job, where he was my boss, on how many 'days' I'd survive. I think he was the only one betting on me, and saying to the rest how I might be made of the stuff it takes to survive in the wilderness. Few believe him. It was Don who liked the part about how I wanted this houseboat to be a steam paddle boat, reminding me by pretending to pull the cord on the steam whistle going 'Toot, toot!" as he walked by. We'd both laugh. The guy I built the boat under had said he knew how to put steam in, but in the end he wouldn't, and it looked harder to install than I was ready for, however, the boat is still set up to fit the steam engine in if I decide later. This is usually a laughable subject, especially when I take my thoughts to the next level and suggest the price of fuel might go up. Few can imagine the fuel price getting much over a dollar a gallon, without a revolution.

I cross the river for the last time with the houseboat, and plan to set it up for the winter. I have a come along hand winch to pull the boat out. Roller poles are cut to slide it up on. A lot of tools want to rust, so have to be cleaned and oiled or they will be ruined. I stop to do this. Most of the canned goods were on the floor during the storm and submerged in water and gas. Most cans have no labels. This means I will not know what I am eating till I open the can. It might be a meal like beans, or vegetables, or it might be a dessert, like peaches. I'm just glad I have any food at all. If I open a can and it is not exactly what I want, I can save it for a couple of days, and try opening another can for a better choice.

The first day I'm in hopes of a main meal like meatballs, but get pears. I try again, and get peaches; "Hmm." So rather than try again and have all these open cans of food around, I decide to be content with a main meal of peaches and pears. I empty gas and silt off the top of thirty pounds of honey. I hadn't realized the lid was not waterproof. Conscience: *'I'm sure not going to throw away all this honey! Only the top few inches will taste like gas.'* Rice is spread out on a blanket to dry in the fall sun. Birds come to eat it and poop in it.

Conscience: *'It's going to get cooked anyway. We've eaten worse.'* I smile, recalling what got eaten in the past *'and we never even got sick!'* I chuckle because I had been taught it would kill you if you ate something from the refrigerator that was over a week old. Conscience: *'Yes we eat ten times that old or 100 times that old! Ha!'*

There is plenty to do to get ready for winter I see. The boat is now totally empty for cleaning. Buckets of water are heated on the wood stove. All surfaces are scrubbed. I have been putting it off, but finally my conscience says, *'It is time to pull the boat out.'* It takes a few days of hard work. The winch is fastened to a big spruce tree and fifty feet of cable stretched to the boat. I work the winch handle to put tension on the cable, then go pry on the boat till it slides a few inches, then take up the slack back at the come along handle again. The one ton winch will not move the empty boat and I do not understand, but there is a lot of friction between the river silt and the bottom of the boat. I do not really work hard, just long, slow and patiently. The weather is wonderful, with freezing crisp mornings, hot dry sun, with warmth in the afternoon. In the middle of a several hour stretch of working the winch, my conscience goes *'shhhhh- I think I heard something!'* I didn't hear anything, but stop and listen close, and wonder what was heard that my conscience would interrupt the work. Conscience: *'The clucking of grouse. Should we go get it?'* I always like fresh food. The mixed up canned goods and rice is ok, but fresh grouse sure sounds good! I shoot two grouse and cook them on the wood stove as I level the boat.

A willow hoop structure goes up over the back of the boat and extends the boat another ten feet to act as a shelter for things I can store out of the boat to give me more living space. I make pole shelves, and then cover the whole thing in plastic. It will all get burned in the spring, so I do not do a fancy job. The engines are left on the boat. They do not seem to be in the way, and this means no messing with the steering cables and console on the roof. Every day I spend an hour cutting and gathering winter firewood. I prefer to use the handsaw. I gather rosehips and dry them on the stove top in a frying pan for winter tea and vitamin C. A small fish net is used to get pike and whitefish out of the slough. I cut them like salmon strips to dry for winter. I had learned how to do this my first winter out working Piper's fish camp. The flies are gone, so the fish will not spoil as easily as they would in the summer. A few mushrooms are gathered for adding to stews. Berry season is over, but a few high bush cranberries have dried on the bush and can be gathered.

I keep my eyes open for moose, since it is time to get one for winter. I think anyway, one would keep now because of the freezing each night, and lack of flies. I do not think of what I do as 'work' but just fun things to do. It is good to be away from people, and I am glad for this time of year, when no one can cross the river, and I cannot cross, and so I am safe. The river is running ice now. There is ice on the slough. It is a world filled with Nature, and God, but not man. Most evenings are spent sipping tea by the wood stove on the houseboat, reading books, keeping up with my diary notes, writing poetry, and doing my art.

Poem
Winter Coming—Galena Oct. 77
The cracking of the ice
falling to water level,
its sighs and pings, and screams,
are like the moose walk, wolf howl,
the loon, rabbit scream, bird call.
The coming winter sounds
flood the memory with the past,
a repeat of the questions,
enough wood? This a good spot?
Am I ready? And, 'for what?'
The time between 'summer'
(when people are boat traveling),

and the frozen 'winter',
(the time for snow machining),
is a time of no communication.
For a woodsman it means,
there will be no one around
for at least a few more weeks,
and he's alone with the sound
of the forming ice and winds.

From outside the boat in the evening, the kerosene light shines out the window and looks very inviting. The outline of the house on a boat, surrounded by the plastic shelter, woodpile, clothes drying, and other evidence of a long time camp has a very special look to it; something out of time, out of context, incongruous here. Yet the intrusion is very human looking and nostalgic. My conscience and I are on the same wavelength, *I wonder how many times in my past, my ancestors came back after a days hunt, seeing camp off in the distance; the warmth of the home light, and a fire waiting. Surely after thousands of years, something of this scene would be impregnated in a permanent memory bank, common to all human beings? Why is it that a camp fire is so hypnotic? Why is it that bending down to get a drink at a creek is so familiar? What can the past fifty – hundred years of civilization mean, compared to the million years before that?'*

Such things I think about. I stare into a camp fire, listening to the wood pop, seeing sparks mingle with the smoke around a rabbit cooking on a stick. I am camped out on a hunting trip.

When I come back, after being gone a day, I see my camp has been raided by a bear. My still drying rice has been scattered. The clothes on the line torn down; ripped apart. Canned goods have been bitten into. The houseboat itself has not been invaded, but could have been. The damage could have been like a total loss of all my winter supplies, and a disaster. Such a raid by a bear could cost me my life. I am lucky the damage is so little. Never the less I have to sigh, at all the work I'd gone through to save the rice, now all for nothing. Conscience: *'The bear will be back; just keep an eye out. We can have bear meat for winter to make up for his damage.'*

The guns are kept handy and loaded. The black powder fifty caliber named 'Holy Shit' is by the front door, 270 Winchester by the back door, and the 357 magnum pistol on its nail by the bed. I do not answer my conscience for I already know: "Probably we will need the rifle here." The 357 has three light loads, and three heavy loads. The three light loads are for grouse, heavy loads are for bear. I keep the three bear loads so they are the first loads to come up when I pull the hammer back.

While reading a book by the kerosene light at the window I see the bear starting to cross the log that is the bridge over the open water from one side of the slough to the other. He's headed this way, and doesn't know I'm here. There is little time to think. Once he crosses the log he will be in thick brush. Once he hears me coming he will make a dash for this brush. He has to be caught out in the open on the log. I almost grab the black powder, but change my mind because it has only one shot, and sometimes it does not fire. In my haste, I grab up the pistol, which I have used to shoot bears before, and know works.

I'm at the creek before the bear sees me running toward him. There is no room for the bear to turn around fast on the narrow log, so he wants to hurry across, and beat me to the shore. He will want to run off in the alder and willow trees. I knew this is what he would want to do. I am faster. I stand here and block his way. The hammer comes back, sights line up in an instant, and I fire, just to the left of the head, and into the neck, heart-lung area. The gun only goes 'pop!'

I know right away what has happened. Conscience: "I do not have the three heavy loads lined up, but a light grouse load because we just shot a grouse and have not had time to rearrange the loads." Without being flustered, I pull the hammer back and fire again, as the bear increases speed toward me. I will not budge from this spot. The second shot is also a light load, and the bear does not even flinch. The loads are so light; the bullets are not going through the hide. There is only one way for the bear to go, over me. I'm blocking his way to safety. I calmly pull the hammer back again, knowing somewhere in this pistol are the heavy loads. I'm aware I better find them fast. I fire again. "Pop!" Conscience: *Well, the next load for sure will be a heavy one.'* The bear is coming like a cannon ball. Only one jump away when I pull the trigger for the 4th time. "Bam!" The heavy bear load goes off, driving a copper jacketed 158 grain semi wad cutter from a zero speed to over 2,000 feet a second, in a thousandth of a second, and within seven inches of barrel length. I hear the explosion as my hand loaded mercury fulminate primer torches off fourteen grains of red dot powder, taking it from fifty degrees, to a temperature with lots of zeros after it in units of time measured in thousandths of a second. The copper missile scrambles out the guns mouth trying to stay ahead of the explosion, cutting a path through the sound barrier, stabilizing, and rotating, in peaceful silence ahead of the shock wave. The single moment burned into the brain begins with an explosion, and ends the same instant with the slap of the bullet hitting, mixed with the sound of breaking bones, flesh being mangled; the scream of a soul passing to the next world. A lot to take in during the blink of an eye.

The bear drops like a downed plane, with a sliding -- 'crash and burn' aspect, of flying parts. Arms and legs windmill into the slide, as dirt and trees are ripped up along the flight path. I do not even take a step back, or change my expression as the slide stops at my feet. I slowly put a foot out and touch the bear, politely saying: "Don't be messing with my things no more, ok?" In truth a very concentrated effort at stabilizing fear. Not of the bear, as much as the loss of my supplies if I fail.

Conscience: *'See? It's not that hard to teach a bear to mind! Stay! Lay down! Roll over!'* I think this is funny, so I smile. Conscience: *'Well, this isn't the moose I was in hopes of getting, and all in all I don't like bear meat that much, it's to rich and fatty, but, meat is meat, and I'll eat it, and have meat for a long time.'*

I'm skinning the bear, looking for where I hit him with each shot, as I always do. My conscience records the data for further reference in our survival: *'Hmm, the light loads just barely went under the skin and didn't mushroom.'* I reply: "They were all hits anyway, so my accuracy in a hurry and under pressure is good." I get to the part with all the meat damage, where the heavy load hit. I feel as clinical as a doctor doing an autopsy. *'Small entry hole through the skin in the neck, second vertebrae smashed, changing the trajectory of the projectile downward, breaking through the collar bone, causing projectile to split into two pieces, resulting in bullet disintegration.'* As my conscience rambles on I wonder if I should try a more solid bullet next time, as a comparison. "Hmmmm." My conscience is still reciting away, *'One lung penetrated, one main artery cut, one chamber of the heart penetrated; yup and here's the empty copper jacket.'* I take it away from my conscience and roll it around between my fingers thoughtfully. My conscience is looking over my shoulder still recording data, *'Fair mushrooming, and copper peeled back to three times the diameter with two thirds of the mass missing. Concave bullet base from excessive powder charge, probably affecting accuracy drastically.'* I know this concave base in the copper was caused at the instant of the powder ignition. And my thoughts go on. Maybe I can try a slightly slower burning powder to get the weight moving slower, increasing accuracy, yet keeping velocity. Such a load cannot be bought in the store, and is worked out for my personal gun and situation.

This is the only way I can stand there and face the bear without fear. I must have answers. I must know what is going on; what is going to happen, and why. I know I have worked out a pistol load when making my own bullets that is off the charts in the books. My bullet load has the powder behind it of the forty- four magnum, and is borderline 'ready to blow the gun up.' I see my accuracy is all gone to hell, but to quote my conscience: *'But this is one screaming Tasmanian Devil when it hits!'* I smile as I thoughtfully toss the bullet up and catch it in my hand, then put it in my pocket. I save it for; I don't know why. My conscience is still rambling, *'Maybe thirteen and a half grains of powder? Let's try a different brand powder? Maybe we can get the pressures down after the initial primer ignition. We need a little less start up pressure and a little longer burning time.'* It will be a long time yet before I move on in reloading to changing the primer, or the various projectiles offered to reloaders. Thousands of shots, thousands of holes in paper, and years of watching the tapes recorded in my mind over and over accumulate in a final hot load. But for now, I already have something you can't just go and buy off the shelf. I've already thrown away the book, and learned to skip the part that follows the word 'recommended,' 'safe' and 'talk to your dealer.'

Conscience: *'We need to get a pressure cooker and canning jars so we can put up game we get like this, and not worry about spoilage.'* I put this on the 'if we ever get any money to do this' list. Maybe this hide and meat will keep though, since the weather is so cool.

Because my diary is mostly ruined now by the water, the damp air in the boat, the bear tearing pages up as they dry outside, I spend evenings reconstructing old work, recopying wet pages I can still read before throwing them away. I'm working from a still fresh memory, and putting the diary into a 'story' form. A dry blank spiral notebook is found, and I start the first page of 'the red book.' At the top of the first page, but in different color ink, so I don't know when it is put there, I make a copyright symbol, and write:

Diary: ©"1977" I'd always known a bit more than the average person about the wilderness, it's just that up till now it was just 'read about theory.' All the theory fell into place well enough once I got out here. I could have learned more from people out here in the bush.

Several times I'd been offered partnerships on a trapline, and outdoor jobs among experienced people. I'd have maybe learned faster, and easier, but it's just not my way. I'm willing to listen to someone, but not believe them just because they say it is so. Too many times I found out different, or that it's not the only or best way. I've heard for example that if you can get a bear in his den he will not bother you; you can go in after him. He won't fight in the den. I'll be darned if I'm crawling in a hole after a bear! Ha Ha! I've heard it from maybe half a dozen people.

Oh well, at any rate, I do not believe much of what I hear. Had a new way to get a fire going this year, with gasoline.

Diary ends

The red book rambles on for about six pages, dwelling on how I get the fire going with gas, and how exciting it is, then jumps to watching the ice go out, Steamer and I building the boat, then back to my first boat. The cabin building doesn't even get mentioned, (?) and a bear only gets one sentence. (?)

By the time the first snow comes I'm well settled in, pleased that I did not have the pressure of having to build a cabin! I'm not even sure I could be here at all if the idea was to build a cabin! Larry says it is ok to be here because he knows it is just a houseboat, and I'll be moving on. Not having to be pressured about building has meant I spent the time gathering food for winter, and enjoying the fall more.

Now that there is snow and winter near, there will be no more bears. They will be hibernating now, so I am able to keep more things outdoors under the shelter, and in my tent. The extra room in the boat is appreciated. One of the first things I do is to set up a work area to do my art. I'm really excited about this. For the first time I have a place to work, and no one can say I can't. Or shouldn't! On my mind because I had gotten into trouble while doing art in my idle time sitting at a desk waiting for firefighters to return from a fire when I was the guy issuing rooms and linen at BLM.

Diary: Early Nov. 1977 When the creek and swamp freezes I can get out better, so set out to scout areas to trap, and since there is no snow yet it is easy to slide along the smooth ice and make good time using a pair of cross-country skis as 'ice-skates.' I zoom right along. A vast amount of country now opens to me with the freeze, and I wander miles and miles back through the swamps. There are endless lakes, creeks, beaver damns, and colorful clumps of frozen goose grass, moss, birch trees, mountains off in the distance, and tracks in the frost on the ice. Skid marks are identified as a place where a lynx slid, catching a rabbit in a tight cornered chase. There is a place a fox got a late duck, and everywhere, sign of animal activity. **Diary ends**

In my diary is the thrill through my descriptions of the land, of being back in the wilderness again. I so often write of the animals, and the beauty, but rarely about people. There is page after page of descriptions with no dates. Conscience: *'Yes it is well and good to enjoy the beauty but just like in town, while you enjoy the beauty you best remember to keep your hand on your wallet and remember the phone number of your lawyer and accountant - the weapons of survival in civilization. Same rules here - just different weapons.'* My next entry reads:

Diary: Come upon a pair of trumpeter swans in a small, unfrozen section of a creek. This is my first up close encounter with these huge white majestic birds. I have read they weigh 30 pounds, and have an eight foot wing spread. They see me coming and sit alert, with heads straight up, giving a nervous short trumpet blast. They stretch five feet above the water. These swans are nervous, and go to take off, but I soon see they are unused to the newly formed ice around them. They hit the ice before they get airborne, slip and slide, getting into a tangle with each other. They indignantly beat on each other, the one blaming the other for the disaster. There is now a problem about getting airborne as they crash into the tundra tussocks.

This is a memory that will stay with me, seeing the frozen grass throwing off frost as the swans hit it, with the sound of trumpeting, wings beating the air, and the huge birds finally getting airborne, against the backdrop of the mountains. **Diary ends**

Past flash: I always loved art, and always loved doing flowers and birds. Being an artist was a sissy thing to do though. Being physically short, and cute, didn't help any. Plus always moving and being the new kid around who has to prove himself. I got in trouble for drawing naked women, but at least the other kids didn't think I was a sissy, or a faggot. My parents must have thought I had a problem about courage, self-image, masculinity and such things, and thought it would be solved by 'sports' maybe 'make a man out of me.' My father had been a wrestler, top judo guy. I had been told to join the wrestling team. I quit. A fellow student on the wrestling team 'cross faced' me – deliberately tried to break my nose and thought it was funny. I decided I couldn't do this to someone, didn't want to learn how. Why would I want to hurt a fellow student who I liked? He wanted me to fight back, try to hurt him in return. Most people sadly thought I wasn't capable.

I chose going to tap dancing school for a while, and really liked it. As a child I'm thinking. "What is the message society puts out? Who and what is rewarded? Is there money available in schools to keep an art class? Do dancers get funding — scholarships?? No! It is football, violent sports that the money goes to. Who gets remembered? Who are our heroes? Can any of us remember the names of famous tap dancers? Famous guys who specialize in painting flowers? No! We remember the big guys who can knock down the most people, draw the most blood! I'm shocked and disgusted when people have the nerve to tell me they think society is civilized, and has changed in the past 10,000 years. People who can, and who enjoy, breaking noses get scholarships. Nice comes in last. Nice is an embarrassment. This was a conscience thought when I was thirteen years old. **Past flash ends**

I sigh at the flood of past events in my life. As I sit in the houseboat reworking my notes and diary entries, I think about 'things' I must confront. Things I'm not really prepared for.

Trapping season begins! There is still little snow on the creek, so I'm traveling along through the country easily on skis. I'm out on the creek setting traps for mink and fox today. Constantly my conscience speaks to me as a friend and advisor. Across a bend in the creek I see something big and dark move. I freeze, with my rifle in my hand. I still hope to see a moose, but this is too small to be a moose or bear. The grass rustles and parts. Hop slide. Pause. Hop slide, Pause. *It is an otter coming toward me that hasn't seen me yet.* I freeze in place, rifle at the ready, as the unsuspecting otter comes around the corner.

Thirty feet away the otter senses something isn't right. Conscience: *'Maybe he smells us?'* I'm right out in the open, in plain sight, but I haven't moved, so am not registered visually yet. It doesn't take much of a move to line the sights up on the otter. I have the 270 with me, and a hot moose load in the chamber, with no time to expel it and jack a light load in. I shoot before I'm really ready because the otter is about to bolt. "Blam!" The 150 grain bullet takes off. On the flip side of that instant, the otter turns and runs. I don't know if he's been hit or not. The sights on the gun are set at 200 yards, so this thirty foot shot is hard to judge, since the sight pattern will not be the same up close.

There is blood on the ice. *"I have a hit!"* I take off after the otter. I would have been much happier with an instant kill, but if not, I will learn something here. There are fresh tracks, only a little snow, and no open water for the otter to dive into. He's caught above ground. I'm curious what he will do. I see he has not stopped to rest, or gone into shock yet from the bullet strike. Will he try to cover the most ground, thinking he will outrun me? Will he turn to fight? Will he try to hide? It all has to do with understanding the world I live in. To catch an animal I have to understand it!

The blood trail disappears. At first the otter stays to the creek, remembering when it was water, and the best place to escape. Later the otter realizes this is not safe anymore, so cuts out across country, conscience: *'maybe in search of open water?'* The tracks lead to an old abandoned beaver house I've never seen before, so I've been lead into new country I will wish to explore later. There is a panic at the beaver house when he can't find a way in. A little way ahead is a hole in the bank above the ice, and the otter went in here.

When I look around I see there are no tracks indicating he has come out anywhere. Conscience: *'So he's still in here!'* I wish to keep after him because he is wounded and might die needlessly without me even getting his fur. If he was not wounded I would have given up here. Conscience: *'How can we get him out?'* I decide to smoke him out. I start a handful of wet green grass on fire, and stuff it in the hole. I look around to see if I see smoke coming out any other place to indicate there is another entrance to keep an eye on. I get bored after a while, and think he has found a way to get fresh air, like a very long network of tunnels.

I tell my conscience. "You keep an eye out to the left; I'll watch the right, he must be ready to bolt someplace by now!" Conscience: *'But the otter can hold his breath for a long time, don't forget that!'* Hmm. But I do not know how long an otter can stay under water, or hold his breath. In twenty minutes I hear a very distinct sound of 'throwing up' way back in the hole. "Blaw, Blaw!" I smile. Conscience: *'He has the dry heaves, and is inhaling smoke.'* I know he will have to come out now. I have a snare ready with a loop in it. There are more very human sounding throwing up gasps, followed by a disturbance in the smoke around the hole. I know he is moving to the entrance. I move the burning grass out of the way.

The head comes out, and the eyes are closed. He is gagging, and can't see or smell a thing. I have to laugh a little. I gently put the snare around his neck. He doesn't even know I'm here. I give a gentle tug to make sure the snare will stay on and fit snug, before giving a sharp pull. I do not want the hide damaged.

I see now that the bullet had only hit the tail, and he would have survived. If I had known this I might have let him go. To gain such knowledge, like if an animal will survive or not, or how injured he is, takes a great deal of learning and experience that I do not now have, but one day hope to.

"This otter is very big, and stretches out 'six feet." I show my conscience, who nods in agreement, but can tell that my conscience thinks closer to five ft. I decide to keep it myself, tan it, and make something out of it, to remember this otter by. He is heavier then I wish to carry, maybe fifty pounds, (My conscience says twenty-five). I drag him on the ice, stopping to make a predator set in my trail, in case some critter follows the blood trail on the ice. Conscience: *'Here comes the mighty Jeremiah Johnson, back from the trapline, leaving a scent trail, in hopes some big animal will follow to the cabin.'* And adds, *'Hey, you remember that part in the movie where the mentor says 'You take care of this one, I'll go get another,' when the bear comes into the cabin, and the mentor dives out the back?'* I reply; "Uh huh" Conscience: *'Well if some big critter follows this blood trail to the houseboat. I'm going out the back and you take care of it ok?'* I stop in the trail, shocked, saying, "You mean to tell me you wouldn't kill and skin it while I went out the back to find another one?"

When I skin the otter I see the teeth are worn, so this one is very old. There are many scars on the hide from fights he has won. I have to make a stretcher board for this guy and hope this time I will get it right, and will receive no comments about using muskrat boards! The fur buyer, Don, had suggested politely that maybe I had used a muskrat stretcher board to stretch my Marten furs. Humph! I have no idea why a book would suggest a hoop type branch stretcher, or why wire stretchers are even sold. To use one of them wire ones is to deduct at least $10 off every fur they are used on. They make the hide look very ugly, a proper wood one with a rounded back, makes the fur stand up natural like. You have to make them yourself; there are no perfect stretchers on the market. *Just another example for me to file away, under 'bullcrap' sold in stores as 'just what you need.'*

Days and weeks go by. I get very involved in my days of trapping and exploring, skinning and hunting, making things for the houseboat, and making art pieces. I do not feel lonely. I have no wasted or bored time on my hands. I go out with the black powder rifle sometimes and practice with it. I write a few letters. This has become my social life as time has gone by. Since I cannot mail the letters till I go to the village, I keep letters on going and send them as a 'package' whenever I get in to the village. Sometimes the letters are months old by the time they get mailed. There is one woman I write regularly. I have had a crush on her since we were both fourteen. I went into the Navy at sixteen years old. Dad thought it would be a good idea. I still miss my—

Dearest Maggie: Nov.—do not know the day

Good morning! I have been working on this letter now for a month and it is 300 pages long now. I wonder how long it will take you to read and what you will think!

As I glance over the past entries I see my moods going up and down. I'm in a pretty good mood today for sure - new snow and nice sunrise. I am excited to go out and check my traps. I know this is something you wouldn't know much about. I think of you in college now, studying to be? Well no, you do not know yet what you are studying for - mostly looking for a good guy to settle down with! As you say, your frog you will kiss and turn into a prince! Ha! I know you worry about me, but I am fine. Yes it is true; my first year here in the Alaska wilderness went great. It was my second year out alone I almost died! That bothers me some too - concerns me. Indians stole my food - tried to kill me. Here in Galena relations between the whites and Athabascan's is pretty good, but the area I told you about that I looked at on the map up the Koyukuk River has a village named Huslia and it is said the Indians there are killing white people – running them off. Supposedly they shot a plane down just a month ago. It is hard to believe however that a plane could get shot down and nothing gets done about it, so this must be an untrue rumor. Still it goes to show how remote it is here, and the sort of situation I could find myself in. Most locals laugh that I would attempt to take a new boat up to that country, saying, "The Huslia Indians will sink it for sure!" So I am hesitant now to see my plans through and do not know what to do. I am holed up here in Galena now for winter. I arrived here late in the season anyhow, probably couldn't have made it to the Koyukuk. I am in hopes of meeting people from that area. I'm told Galena is a hub for Natives from far off, so my chances of meeting them here is pretty good. Maybe something will work out, some plan will show itself. I must keep an open mind. Meanwhile I will enjoy what life has to offer. Anyhow, enough for today. Talk to ya tomorrow! **Sunshine, Miles**

A letter has to be mailed I'm reluctant to send off but must. It shows a little of the frustration and feelings about phones, forms, deadlines, and such. I try to collect unemployment from the BLM job that ended. I feel like I get a run around and finally give up in disgust.

Dear Unemployment,

Don't understand what's going on, help, help, hello? Hello? I spent two hours trying the phone and running up my long distance calls to where I have to miss a meal now to pay for it, and didn't get anywhere, just recordings. The toll free number doesn't work, for reasons I do not understand.

I do not know if I have a problem or not, only that I didn't get a check, and I seem to have a form here I may have not filled out and sent in, but maybe I did, because I often get duplicate forms from you that confuse me, so I never know if I sent it in already or not. I mark it on the calendar, but maybe I sent it, and forgot to mark it.

So I may or may not need to open another claim. If I do, it looks like I need forms I do not have, that need to be sent to me, which complicates things even more. Hmm.

But maybe I'm lucky and, but no, I didn't get a check. Sigh. So what's the deal now? I hold my breath and wait for forms? Sigh. Yes, I know, I'm really bad with dates and times and forms, and no, I do not understand all this 'pin numbers, and punch it all in' stuff on the phone. I'd have to write it all out anyway just to get it right on the phone, and 'IT' (the computer voice) doesn't answer questions. It doesn't even ask how the weather is, or say; "Have a nice day." People don't answer phones anymore?

Anyway, I filled these forms out, but I'm sure you will laugh, "Yea! Right! Dream on! You screwed up! Go back to square one! Do not pass go! Do not collect $200!"

So 'um', ok, tell me what 'square one is again?'

I'm puzzled. You know, some folks think I'm really bright, some say even 'genius.' I sure wonder how 'stupid' people manage all these forms. Hmm.

Have a nice Day Miles

The letter is mailed in one of my hand painted envelopes. Otter tracks going nowhere up a creek to nothing. Blades of grass along the ice, far distant nondescript hill far, far away, that the otter will never reach.

One day I see a rabbit hopping along. It stops just behind a big tree. I'm out hunting with the black powder rifle. I know if I move, the rabbit will run. It is listening for me to move. I can see his shadow, but not him. I look at the tree and try to guess where his head would be on the other side of the tree. I aim for that spot on the tree. The smoke pole is torched off. After the six foot of flame and gagging cloud of smoke clears, I go over to the tree and see the headless rabbit on the other side. There is a hole in the tree out the back side of it that a basketball would set in "Holy shit!" It seems every time I fire this rifle that's all that can be said.

Sometime after this, on a day when I do not have anything on my mind, the creek ice overflows with water three feet deep. Something has happened out on the main river, and I assume it can only be that it has frozen, and backed the water up the slough. It is time to take a walk out to the main river and see. I'm not especially anxious to get across, and in fact am nervous, and not happy that now there is a way for people to come over. Conscience: *'My life is fine, till people come into it.'* But I'm curious too, and do not really wish to avoid the opportunity. Just that, if I never saw another human being in the rest of my lifetime, I'd be perfectly content. The world without people makes for good dreams. *Perhaps the world would heal someday, air might clean up, water be pure again, some other creature could take our place and be king of the forest for a while.*

With a black powder rifle, fox hat on my head, I head out to walk the five miles to the river. Ice all the way across. A long pole is under my arm as I walk, in case I fall through. My conscience reminds me we read once: *'The pole will stop me from going all the way under, and gives me something to climb out on. It is also my 'thumper' pole, to test ice ahead of me as I go.'*

The day is a warm, gray, -5 degrees. I 'tappity' tap the ice with my pole and weave a zig-zag path across the river that is half a mile wide here. A cold breeze flaps the fringes on my leather jacket, and waves the tail of the fox on my hat off to the side. While I'm stopped and warming my fingers under my arm pits, I see something red flit between two ice hummocks not far away, and my head turns to catch what I saw; a fox is high - tailing it across the ice in front of me. He saw the fox hat flapping in the wind, and had been startled to find out this cute fox is on the head of a trapper. The fox is the only thing I see that is not gray.

Two Indians silently wait for me on the Galena side of the river. When I approach out of the gray they tell me I am the first one across the river, and I must be crazy, it just froze a few hours ago. I was careful, so I have no concern for this. They ask, "So what were you dynamiting over there?" I'm momentarily puzzled, till I realize they have heard my black powder rifle. I explain by pointing to the rifle. They have never seen such a rifle before and are mystified by it.

This whole scene suddenly hits me as a perfect scene in a movie. The all white frozen river. The mad trapper crossing it with the thumper pole, weaving his way, a fox dashes out front. The trapper is 'out of time' and we think this is a movie about the 1800's. There are the Indians to confirm this belief, but the viewer is puzzled that they do not understand the rifle. Maybe the film is the 1700's not the 1800's. A wild man in leathers, but the viewer is puzzled by the more modern Indian dress. A snow machine zooms across the background. No one looks up. Now the viewer has no idea what time period this movie is about. All of a sudden we know this is not an ordinary movie, and we want to know what is going on. Why are the Indians dressed like white men? Why is the white man dressed like an Indian? Is this a comedy? A parody? The Athabascan's do not know why I am smiling and act like they know why, because I have gone mad. I bid good bye to the Indians. The movie skit ends.

"Gotta check my mail"

There are other people carrying rifles in the village. A snow machine pulling a sled full of dead fox zooms by on the snow covered road. A child screams for a ride, jumps on the runners of the sled. No one pays attention. Dead moose hang in yards around town, and the scene looks like I would expect an Indian village to look like. Conscience: *And this isn't even a movie, it's real, and I'm part of it, not a play or act, but 'real life!'* I get my mail and head back towards my houseboat.

"Did you get your moose yet?" I'm startled by an old time Indian addressing me with such a question. I pause, unsure how to answer. Conscience: *How does this old man know I've been looking for a moose? It's not legal to get a moose this time of year; is he setting me up, working for Fish and Game?* I walk closer to the Indian to strike up a conversation before I decide what I will tell him. He's maybe in his 80's, and he is out in front of his log cabin splitting firewood. He looks at me closer.

"You're not my grandson!" Conscience: *'No shit old timer!'* but of course only I can hear my conscience. I am not sure I know how to talk yet, for I have not spoken much over the past two months. In the silence before I speak I realize I could sort of pass for an Indian, in that the Indians are shorter than white people, and I tan easily. I now have dark skin. Conscience: *'He must have so many grandchildren he can't keep track of them.'* It would be fun to screw with him and play a joke, indignantly claim to be his grandchild and how he should remember me! For some reason I like this old man right away. He's all smiles, out here splitting wood in the cold, with no complaint. I reply finally, "No I didn't get a moose yet, but I'm looking."

He only nods. His eyes go to my black powder rifle. "Haven't seen one of these in a while, what you doing with one of these? It was almost the 1800's when I had mine; a long time ago." He goes back in time as he sits on the stump he has been splitting wood on, waves me to sit on the edge of the firewood pile. Conscience: *'As if I have nothing better to do then sit and listen to the ramblings of an old man, oh well, guess I'm really not that busy, may as well indulge the stupid old codger,'* Edgar is still talking: "See that bridge over there? Over by the airport?"

I have no idea why he brought this up, of course I see it. I'm not half blind like he is. I reply, "Yea, there's a bridge, another road, a culvert."

He nods his head in confirmation and explains, "When I first came here, none of this was here. I was the first one to cross that creek. I remember I laid a log down right there where the bridge is, so I could get across. I was tracking a moose." He looks around at the village and adds, "None of this was here. It was all wilderness." Conscience: *'Gosh! I guess this old guy has seen it all, imagine what those days were like!'* He nods at the memory adding; "Used to cut firewood for the steamboat. We used a hand axe back then. Got paid fifty cents a cord. That was big money for an Indian back in those days. I was rich and well respected." He stands up and looks upriver. There's a pause. "You can't see the spot now. The steamboat used to pull up right over there. Yup, we had rifles just like yours back in them days."

I have to ask, "And did you like the six foot of flame, and the smell of rotten eggs?"

He pauses and smiles at some memory he does not speak of and says, "It was cool!" I have to laugh out loud. He's trying to use the language younger people use these days, so I will understand that nothing ever changes. He goes on after the pause, "I called my stick – that - throws - smoke, 'sheekum,' after my first sled dog. My father gave me this dog when I was seven years old. Have you given a name to yours?"

I have never told anyone about this, because no one these days gives names to guns, and it would seem odd to do so, but I tell him shyly: "I call her 'Holy Shit'." The old man looks puzzled. This does not seem like the name of a gun. I say, "If I aimed at that window over there, and torched her off, I bet the ball would put a hole through everyone's house in Galena."

He looks at the row of houses all lined up along the river bank, before saying; "Holy Shit."

I nod. I know this old man has got his wood to cut and I'm holding him up. He has to work slowly, being so old and all. I offer: "Hey, I may as well help you split wood while we talk."

He smiles his reply: "My children, grandchildren, don't come by much to bring me moose or cut wood. The old way is gone." He smiles, unflustered by this thought. I reflect on this:

"Yes, the young Indians are in a hurry to be like white people, and the young white people are in a hurry to be like Indians." He moves his head with a 'yes, it is so' nod. I split wood while we talk. "What do you think of the Koyukuk country? I'd like to go live there I think." Conscience: *This old man might know a lot about the area and people.'*

"The Indians there will scalp you for sure white man."

I snap back: "Maybe it will be me who does the scalping!" He only nods at my outburst, and looks again at my smoke - pole. I thought he might make some rude comment about the wolf pup thinking it has fangs.

"But you will not do it carrying this." Touching my rifle as he says: "The Indian has modern magnum repeating rifle, with power scope!" We talk about guns, ballistics, reloading time, trajectory, killing power of various calibers, and the old days, when the Indian and Eskimo were at war, killing each other.

"They used to come down the Koyukuk River, steal our children, and kill us. I remember that." The old man stares upriver lost in thought. He can still see them coming. *In the days when wars were fought with stone clubs, flint knives, a very few black powder rifles, bows and arrows.* I picture Eskimos sneaking into camp on snowshoes. The Indians still hate the Eskimos, don't trust them. The upper Koyukuk is the border line between Eskimo and Indian country. "You go up there, you kill lots of them." He nods. "I think I'm right, you are my grandson."

I know he speaks with seriousness, but I make a joke of it: "Ok Grandpa!" But after this he always calls me 'grandson' and I call him 'grandpa,' and I am now part of his family. "It is done!" *Just as it would have been in the old days.* I help him get firewood and moose meat in his old age, and in return, he gives me the protection of his position as an elder on the village council, and we just seem to bond. I hang out in the old village, and stay with the Indians mostly. *I'm always looking for substitute parents, a mentor, someone to look up to and hang around.*

Hey Will—How's it hanging?

Long time no hear from- you keeping your powder dry? Remember how we looked at maps and we both thought the Koyukuk country looked mighty fine on the map? Turns out the Indians there are killing off the white folk. Sounds like 150 years ago in the Wild West, huh? Remember reading about the mountain men and how it was - with the Spanish claiming the remote area and the Mexicans saying to the U.S. it was their land - like around Texas? The Indians claimed it and any of 'em could mess a trapper over and if the trapper did any retaliating it was war? That's the bitch of it. I don't mind the Indians wanting to kill people - I mind that it isn't both ways. So what are you up to? Got work? Getting ready to head out someplace like I did? **Later, Miles**

A letter arrives having to do with unemployment and BLM work questions.

Dear Sir

You stated on the form provided that you are a subsistence person. You did not answer the question as to what day you intend to go subsistence hunting for a moose. You did not answer how much money you intend to make trapping so we may consider your wages and unemployment claim. Bla bla bla.

Unemployment office

I toss it in the waste basket. I'm pissed. Both I and my employer paid into unemployment and I can't collect it. No subsistence person can say what day they will hunt, and no trapper can say how much fur they will catch, and what it will be worth. *You may as well ask what day the sun will shine. What day will you win the lottery, how big will the gold nugget be you hope to find and what will it be worth. Any answer I give would be a lie, and I am not anxious to lie to the government. I'm not interested in committing a crime in order to collect unemployment.*

An Indian about my age named John sits with me at the cafe, and I tell him with enthusiasm how much I like the old village compared to the new, and how the Indian way seems like a good way. He laughs. I ask why?

"You ever hear the joke about the Lone Ranger, and Tonto?" I have never heard about such a joke. I have never heard an Indian joke before, so am very interested in the Indian humor.

"No, tell me this joke!"

He explains it in long drawn out descriptions, summed up: "The Lone Ranger and Tonto were out with dog teams in the Minto flats." I have to smile, Conscience: *'This is a new twist to the ole Lone Ranger story.'* The Athabascan goes on: "They have been traveling together many days, and are tired, hungry. Up ahead across the flats the Lone Ranger spots hostile Indians coming in a big group. He stops his dog team. Tonto pulls up behind, sets his snow hook, and walks up to talk to the Lone Ranger." I try to picture the white man and Indian out on the Minto flats in winter. "The Lone Ranger asks nervously, 'What we do now Tonto?' Tonto looks out across

71

the flats at the Indians coming, turns to the Lone Ranger and says, "What do you mean 'We' White man?"

There is a message in this for me, but pretend I do not get it. I laugh along with my friend. But am reminded of my outlook expressed to Will, about anyone meaning me harm. We both have a thing about being 'victims.' We both believe it would be a nice place to live, and nice way to live, to be able to protect ourselves, defend ourselves when our lives are threatened. Neither of us has found such a place among people. These feelings go all the way back to childhood. *When you cannot trust your parents, who can you trust?*

I find out Edgar Noller, the old time Indian, my adopted Grandpa, is the last one alive who was on the original serum run that the Iditarod dog sled race is based on, where dog teams ran in relays to haul diphtheria serum from Nenana to Nome to save people from the outbreak, back before the days of airplanes. I hear all about these days. I hear from the old time Indians who remember the days before white people, and can remember when they saw the first white man. The days when the Russians owned Alaska, and what that was like. The days of the big fur trade, and Hudson Bay outposts. The days of steamboats, and serious trouble between white and Indian, and the killings. The days of the influx of prospectors looking for the yellow metal. I hear funny stories about the white man, from the Indians perspective, that give me insight into my own people. I try to answer questions truthfully.

I ask: "If I go to the Koyukuk country, and the people there try to sink my boat – run me off - kill me – how should I handle that?"

The Athabascan elder replies; "The white man is the invader of the land- moving in like a pack of wolves cleaning the land of all that is good - giving the Indian nothing in return. This is not good."

I agree and explain: "Yes," but I pause. "We have the same enemy, it is civilization, government, waste, lying , stealing. I am on your side if there is a war." But I am a white man with white man knowledge and your people do not understand that white man is powerful and devious. Our numbers are so great you have no hope to win a war in an outright battle. You have not been outside Alaska to see. I am not a modern white man. I am like the old time Mountain Man who wishes to be left in peace to live in the old way, the Indian way, at one with the land. I do not want to move in on someone's land. The world is getting crowded. It looks like there is room enough for one more trapper, someone who can be an ally when you have trouble with the white people. I have trouble with Natives who mean me harm, especially the ones who are trying to live like white people with white man jobs, white man clothes, white man guns, but do not accept the price of white man's shit that goes with all the nice things. The Indian cannot expect to have the white man's gifts, and at the same time give the white man the finger, and tell him to go home. I will respect the Indian who wishes to live in the old ways and be left alone, and the Indian who will judge me for my actions, and not my race. "Just as I will not hate anyone for being an Indian, only for wishing me harm!"

The reply I get is, "Yes this is all right, but not all Indians feel the same way. We cannot control our young people who have been taught another way and will not listen to wisdom of elders. We are torn between wanting to help our young people, and not wanting problems with the white people."

I nod: "We have said enough for now. We have both spoken from our hearts. Let us talk later. I do not want trouble. I have had a dream all my life to be a trapper. I will not back down from this dream as a coward because of unfair threats. I wish to be fair and just. I will have to learn more and try to understand this situation. It is not easy to understand another culture, but I will try."

Sometime before Christmas there is a letter from my father, who speaks of me visiting. I know it has been a few years, maybe four - five since I have seen him, and it had only been for a few days. Things here in Galena are going well enough. I could get away for a couple of weeks and it wouldn't matter so much.

> **Dear Dad**, it's good to hear from you, and yes, I know it's been a long time since I've seen you and this might be a good time to take a trip 'outside' as we Alaskans call the lower forty-eight states. I can only visit a couple of weeks at the most, but I'll look into flights, times, prices and let you know when to expect me.
> **Sunshine, Miles**

I don't want my father to pay for this trip, even though he offers. I have to sell fur to get the money for the ticket. I will keep some fur for the Seattle fur exchange though. I hear I might get a better price at the auction there. Seattle is a very long the way, so I can do a layover there. A gal here in Galena has been buying some of my artwork. She took some with her on a trip outside this winter, and tells me she sold enough to pay for her trip. I have been working hard, and building up a jewelry inventory. I hope on that stop in Seattle I can also sell my artwork. If this gal did all right, then I can do better I think, since I can tell about it, having made it. Conscience: *'Maybe like her, I could pay for the trip from the profit of selling the art on the trip!'* I have the fur money though, if this is what it will take to do it.

> **Dearest Maggie,**
> It looks like I might make a trip outside. Dad wants to see me. I know you think my art will do well, but you are my friend so say nice things. I might lack some confidence...Well it is hard you know, when all your life you have been told art is not important. Told no money can be made at it, and it is an unworthy occupation, just a hobby to entertain yourself so you do not get bored with your free time. Sometimes I feel like a train with a full head of steam, but the emergency brake is on.

Well I think I am getting along with most of the local Indians, an interesting people. Some of them are very smart, even though they have not been to formal school. They are wise in the ways of the world. Some could hold their own anyplace in any group of people anywhere in the world. I wonder sometimes if greatness transcends all races and is a human trait not a racial one. Certainly I am proud to know some of these people. But no, this race does not have all the answers and no one is 'good' just because they are Indian. Like every group, there are some bad ones too! I wish you could be sharing some of this experience with me. It would be nice to get your perspective on the situation here.

Sunshine, Miles

I have two coffee cans full of change I've accumulated over the years. I have a habit of emptying my pocket each day when in town, or when I come home from a town trip, and the change goes in this can. I have enough to buy a return trip ticket to Fairbanks. There are only two other people today going to Fairbanks. We wait for our flight in someone's house. Tea is served, and we are asked to watch the children as the mother cleans house. We are told to make ourselves at home, and one of the other strangers goes over and changes the channel on the TV, opens the refrigerator and gets a glass of milk. We all sit and watch the tube, as we wait for our flight.

When the plane arrives, the pilot asks us to unload cargo from his plane. Hmm. We all go out in the blowing snow and unload the plane, then load the plane up with mail headed for Fairbanks. The plane is a six-passenger type, well dinged up from years of bush use.

"Time to leave!" The pilot hollers out, and asks me to sit next to him. I have to speak up:

"Yea, well, I haven't paid yet, who do I see about that?" I haven't seen anyone that looks in charge here, and wonder vaguely if I should have paid the mother in the house.

"Oh, you pay when you get to Fairbanks," the pilot says with no apparent misgivings. I am used to paying for meals after eating, but never flying first, and paying later!

My 357 pistol bangs against the side of the plane as I climb in next to the pilot. No one suggests I leave it behind, or take it off, or asks if it is loaded. A gun is part of a way of life here and is as common as belt buckles, and worn with as little concern or threat. Once in the air, the ground below looks familiar to me! I tell the pilot I think this is my trapline below.

He replies: "Oh yea? On the other side of this hill here? Let's turn around and go look at it!" He turns the plane around, and none of the other passengers wonders, or asks what is going on, so I assume the pilots here are used to flying wherever they like. The aerial view of my trapline is appreciated. The passengers, pilot and I talk 'trapping' the rest of the way to Fairbanks. By the time we arrive, we all know the price wolves are fetching—how to skin an otter the right way—and why Cynthia has been crying the past two weeks.

When we get to town the pilot says, "You pay in there," turns, goes away, without knowing if I went in and paid or not. The loose arrangement is mentioned to the gal behind the desk inside the tin shed.

I ask: "Don't some people just walk away without paying?" She smiles at me politely-saying, as if to a child needing education, "Some try, but everyone who flies here from Galena are local there, and so must return. We are the only airline. If they ever want to go home, they better pay!" There is a thoughtful pause before she adds: "Sometimes people do not pay for weeks or months, till a pay check they wait for comes in, or they sell furs. People who have a reputation for not paying are known, and we do not extend the courtesy. We assume people will be honest until proven otherwise." Conscience: 'How different from where I came from, and how refreshing. 'Innocent until proven guilty'! What a concept! Where have we heard such odd talk before?' It is ...'interesting' to be hearing it from an Indian. Conscience: 'What a twist in history. Getting lessons on my form of government from a Native American who couldn't participate in the constitution, could not vote, had no rights, was not a citizen - yet under-stands it better than my government.' I pay with my cans of pennies, and she is used to this too. This way of life suits me, and though I'm not quite 'at ease,' I at least relax a little. I know Fairbanks now, and this is familiar to me. We are in the same section of the airport that I came to when I met Piper Wright, in fact think his building is just a few doors down, but I can't tell in the dark. There is about three hours of daylight this time of year. I remember it seems so long ago now - how it was Piper who flew me out to the wilderness and let me cut salmon for him. *He flew all my supplies out for me my first year- and gave me my first trapline!*

The passengers and I are five miles away from downtown. "Miles, you need a ride into town? I got my car here, come on, give you a lift." It is nice to have a stranger be so friendly, and I accept the ride. "Oh, Miles, maybe you should put your gun in your back pack while we are in town?" I forgot all about it, I'm so used to wearing it. Conscience: 'I guess I've always liked guns, and it is really nice to live in a place where they are common and accepted and non-threatening. It is so easy to get into the habit of carrying one, talking about them, and I have to remember that every place is not so accepting.'

Fairbanks has changed even in the past few years since I first saw it. The pipeline days have made the change I think, and like other Alaskans, I'm not happy about 'outsiders' cramming their ideas down our throat. One change is that, when I first got here, it was common to see guns at people's sides. Now I think it is not so common. I put my pistol in the pack.

Rather than stay at the Salvation Army, as I had been doing my first two years, I

75

decide to get a room. For the first time in my life I stay in a paid for room. When it is time to go to bed I cannot find a thermostat to turn down. I find it stifling hot in here. I'm used to being more out in the cold. I end up opening the bathroom window, and sleeping on the floor there. Conscience: *'For my $50 a night, what a waste!'* In the morning I take my furs to see Don, in a cab. This is so much different for me than past memories of bringing furs to town.

"Your furs are looking good, Miles. You're learning how to handle fur. Galena doing all right by you?"

I reply to this inquiry from Don; "I'm doing fine." We don't really have a lot to talk about, though I like Don a lot, and hope he thinks of me as 'one of us' now, a trapper, a wilderness person. If not, at least well on my way to being proper material for such. If I talk too much he will know how green I still am, so I keep my mouth shut. I get over a thousand dollars for just part of my furs.

"Don, how is the Seattle Fur Exchange? I might give that a try with some of my furs."

"You might do ok and might not. Furs are sold there in lots of 200. Dealers like myself try to match furs to get the 200 matched, and we can get a better deal. If you offer only a few, and they are not matched you do not get as good a price. On the other hand it is the last sale at the auction that sets the trend for the next month or so for prices dealers like myself will pay you. If you get lucky there is an unexpected demand, then your furs might sell high. It's a gamble." He pauses and decides to tell me how to get more money for my fur. "You could make your own stretchers Miles. Make them rounded on the back so the fur stands up. Wash the fur too, using shampoo. Your tails are split better than last year, and look ok, but you might get a few dollars more with that extra effort." Don pays me the going average for fur, and I feel good about this. I'm still not handling my furs as well as I'd like, and he tries to give me some more pointers, but I'm not paying enough attention. Conscience: *'But at least I get the 'average' price.'* My first two seasons I got less than the average and even felt flat out ripped off. Don likes my otter story, and I tell him about the marten I'm getting, and what I'm learning about them. He doesn't say much about a lot of it, and gives the impression he doesn't agree, but appreciates my enthusiasm for the fur business. I've loosened up a little. I breathe in the smell of furs. My eyes play over the hundreds of marten, fox, wolf, in piles in the 'fur room,' extension of his home.

"I'm headed outside Don."

Don nods sagely: "Yea, I know how it is, the relatives pull at us. They never really do accept that this is our home now. Well, it's a crazy place out there, you be careful!" We both agree: "It's safer in the wilderness for sure!" We both laugh in agreement.

"See you later Don, I better go get my tickets."

Don thoughtfully gets his can of tobacco chew out, and with a show of much ceremony puts a plug under his lip, then hands the can to me as a joke, knowing I don't chew, saying: "You should try it; make a man out of you!" I wave a laughing good bye.

"Will! What a surprise, good to see you! Seems like I run into you when I come to town."

Will replies: "I'm not sure what to say, Miles. That check you wrote me bounced. I had just started a new job, and needed the money to fix my truck so I could go to work. I couldn't fix the truck, missed to many days of work, lost the job. I thought maybe you ripped me off."

Conscience: *'How did this happen? I put my last pay check in the account to cover the check to Will, just as Will told me is the way it works.'* I answer Will out loud: "I don't understand, Will! I had the money in the account. I put the last paycheck in the bank, and then took off for the wilderness. What could have gone wrong? I haven't been to the bank yet. I assume my account will be just as I left it. I haven't used the account since I put the money in it. I'm really sorry, Will."

I hand Will the cash I owe him, which does not seem like very much money now, $300. Big deal. Conscience: *'But it cost my friend his job, and he thinks I set him up.'* I take Will out to lunch and explain I don't understand banks and checking accounts. I'm not sure if he believes this or not, but we sort of part as friends, I hope. He remembers how it was helping me get the account.

The bank is on the way to where I'm going. Conscience: *'I better see if I can find out what the heck is going on.'* After standing in a long line I explain to the teller, who gets my records up on the computer. Computers are new and I think: *The Beast. - Do we run it, or does it run us! This newfangled contraption that's smarter than the human.* I say nothing before the teller speaks:"There's no record of $300 ever going into this account, sir." I remember back to that check, and recall saying to that teller how I'm going into the wilderness and would be out of touch for a while. I think she did not give me a receipt, and didn't put the money in my account. After so many months have gone by, I cannot remember which teller it is, and I know I have no proof of anything. No records. The checking account has caused me nothing but grief and humiliation. The few times I need money, I end up going to the bank and standing in line to cash my own checks I write to myself. Without ID, what good is this account?

"I'd like to close this account please." I'm now a cash only person. I can keep track of my money better than anyone else can. *No one cares about my money as much as I do, so who is the most qualified to keep track of it?*

I get out two letters I have not read yet:

Dear Miles

Nice to hear from you! You sound like you are getting along all right. It is always interesting to hear from you. You are very special. I am glad to hear you are trying to get along with the Indians there. I know you are a very kind person and shouldn't have any trouble as they will see you for who you are! As for me I got a new car again and same old problems with Dave. I need to get away from him but can't seem to do it. School is good. I am getting good grades. My mother and father say hi. My sister Mimi says hi too! We all miss you! Stay warm up there!

Love Maggie

Hey Miles—Will here,

You haven't been scalped yet huh? Well if you have to, you scalp them first, ya hear? No work, you know how winters are. A time to hole up and collect unemployment - wait till spring. I got a deal on some traps and a tent at a garage sale in the fall. I have to keep it at my dad's. I hope to save up enough to get out maybe next year! Sometimes I have some welding work to do for someone but other than that pretty slow! Watch your top knot!

Will

I already saw Will, so he must have wrote this a long time ago. No mention of the missing $300. I don't stay in Fairbanks long. When I'm at the airport I see people ahead of me going through some newfangled gate of some kind. Conscience: *'It must be a metal detector of some sort.'* The last time I had flown was maybe four years ago? Things have changed so much? The first thing that crosses my mind is the book '1984.' I got this situation figured out by watching though. I got it figured out because it was all in the science fiction books. Conscience: *'You put all metal things in a tray, and hand them around. You walk through, and as long as you do not have any metal left on you, it lets you through. It must have to do with stuff I see in the news, about terrorists, bombs, skyjacking and stuff like this happening in 3rd world countries.'* Nothing has ever happened over here, but the fear is spreading like fire, and so that explains all this. I find it funny how easily people become afraid, and how little it takes to make the sheep nervous, and start bleating. I smile to myself and wonder how Americans survive in the world, but the metal detector? *Piece of cake! No problem!*

As I walk the line I notice how many people know each other here. I must know a quarter of these people by sight, though no names come to mind. Everyone is in a good mood because it's close to Christmas. Most people, like me, are going outside to see relatives, and aren't looking forward to the trip, though we all want to see our folks. Everyone is nervous about how crazy thing are outside, and we exchange horror stories. When it's my turn at the metal detector the security lady asks me about the furs over my shoulder.

She says, "My brother traps too!" I tell her I want to hand carry them, and hope to sell them on my five hour stop in Seattle. I put all my metal in the tray. I take off my knife so I can go through the detector. She suggests I put the hunting knife in my carryon bag. I don't understand why it would be a big deal one way or the other, but smile and comply. Everything is friendly, and I just don't understand how things have changed since I last flew. I've worn a hunting knife since I was ten years old, and even wore one to school for years. No one suggested anything other than, 'it's a bit odd,' but no one was especially concerned or afraid, but times are changing. My conscience pipes up: *'A man with a knife is master of a thousand tasks.'* The phrase has a nice ring to it. It is the single symbol that stands for everything I believe in, about being an outdoor person, and wanting to be a self-sufficient Mountain Man. Other people in line besides me also have to put hunting knives into carryon bags, out of sight.

When we all board the plane, everyone sits where they wish. It never occurred to me that seats might be assigned, but there is a rumor going around that further on in the trip there will be assigned seats! Conscience: *'What an absurd concept! What if I don't like the person sitting next to me! What if I have to sit next to a nun, or a redneck, someone in a suit and tie! Someone I have nothing in common with! No one is going to make me sit next to some dip shit! Why should I when there is probably someone a few seats up, who wears a knife and Mountain Man hat and with who I could talk about the good life. More to the point - what's it to them where I sit?'* I spot the uniform of the Mountain Man and with pride. I stop him with the passwords: "Stringing steal?"

The passenger looks pleased to have another trapper on board, and replies: "No just wire - but have a seat." If he's stringing wire I know he is after only wolves, maybe a few lynx. A starting point for a long involved conversation. The passengers change seats a lot during the flight. Some seek out quiet areas so they can sleep, others want to be near the rest room or whatever, maybe near a window, or a woman they can try to hit on. Women with babies all sit together.

The stewardesses stop, sit and chat with the passengers a while. Before taking off I think about the big jets I see. Only a few years ago I would see at least a few prop planes on the runway. *Now it is all jets!* My art work comes out and I start to polish it. Like any good salesman, I have an eye out for a customer. I tilt the polished art in the light so it catches the eye of the stewardess going by.

She asks, "Do you make this lovely art?" With appropriate modesty, I shyly tell her I do. Her thrilled reply: "I'll be back to look at it once I have a break!" When she comes back, she sits next to me. Her hypnotic perfume tickles my hormones, *Being a trapper I understand the use of lure.* A set of classic legs dangle like a rabbit in front of a lynx.

I tell her how I live on a houseboat in the wilderness. "This art is done by kerosene light with hand tools, No electricity."

The bunny replies, "You're very talented. This is passionate work. I love those earrings, would you give me a deal on them?" I remind her how no one does work anything like this, and it is very one of a kind. Just when she's primed to hear how I can't come down on my prices, I give her a deal.

😊 :)

She picks out a pair of mammoth ivory earrings with brass hand cut flowers, silver stem, copper leaves, pays for them and gives me her phone number saying: "I pass through Galena a lot and sometimes have time off. Your life on a houseboat sounds so peaceful. I'd love to get out of the rat race for a while." There is a significant pause as she slowly unfolds her long legs in front of me. I can only gulp. *Now who is the helpless 'rabbit,' and who is the 'mischievous wolf'?*

Visiting Karen

Salmon drying at fish camp along Kantishna River

CHAPTER THREE

SELL MORE FURS, PIKES MARKET, METAL DETECTOR, CHICAGO AIRPORT BULLETS, THE HE, SHE, DAD VISIT, SISTER, BACK TO ALASKA, EAGLE CLAW ORDER, MARTEN, OVERNIGHT CAMP, SLED DOG TRIP, WOLVERINE

"Good luck selling your furs, hope you get a good price! I wish I could afford them. They are so gorgeous!" As I get the furs down from the overhead, the stewardess says her good byes. Other passengers wish me good luck selling here. There is a five hour wait before my connection through Chicago, and on to New York. I hail a cab. No one suggests I need a permit to export fur, sell fur, or carry fur. This simply would never occur to an Alaskan. There is however a hint of the question on some minds. Conscience: *'Permit? Where do you think this is- Russia???'*

"Seattle Fur Exchange?" The cab driver asks.

"Yea," is all I reply. The driver is used to taking Alaskans and their fur to the fur clearing house. This is the biggest fur place in the west. Montreal would be the next biggest place to sell. At the fur exchange I get paid about the same as I would get in Alaska. I'm unclear why. It is explained, similar to what the fur dealer told me.

"We sell in lots of 200 furs. The furs are graded, bundled, and big buyers bid on the whole bundle. These furs of yours will have to be graded and put in separate bundles with others of the same color and class."

Conscience: *'So the secret to getting twice the money would be to organize trapping friends, and put together a bundle of 200 matched furs, which is what the fur dealer does.'* I reply to my conscience: "It is better to just let the fur buyer do this for his share, it's probably worth it. The only way to make more money is to get lucky, or have reason to believe the price of fur has gone up since the fur buyer last got word." The Fur Exchange pays with a check, which causes me to frown. Don pays cash. Even after the explanation, it does not make sense to me that I'm closer to the source, cut out the fur buyer, but do not make more money. Something is fishy here, but I cannot figure it out. Wearing my fox hat, tail flying, I head for 'Pikes Market,' where I was told this Galena gal sold all my art and paid for her trip. I carry my bag of art. The art is packed in moss I collected. I have no boxes or chains, since I have no source to get these things in Galena, and have no catalog or brochure yet.

At Pike's I spot a vendor who might be interested, and ask: "I see you got belts for sale, how's it doing?"

A jolly good humored guy replies from behind a six foot table with his wears set up on the street:"Oh Hi! You looking for a belt?"

I nod 'no' as I answer: "What I'm thinking is that I make belt buckles, and you make belts, and maybe we need to combine our work."

He's interested and says: "Let's see what you do." I get out my box and sort out six buckles from the string ties and necklaces. Two are on mammoth ivory, one is on Dall sheep horn, the rest are moose antler. The themes vary, but are all metal animals of copper, silver, brass, and bronze.

I explain to the vendor as I sort them: "They are all hand drawn, hand cut, with hand tools, one of a kind." He looks closer and seems impressed. I see he does not have a good selection of buckles. I explain the deal: "The prices marked are retail. You could get them all at wholesale, for half what's marked, but you'd have to get them all. Sell three and the other half are paid for, and all profit." He thinks about it. I see his mind working. I'm not sure if he needs more persuasion but add: "You'll never see buckles like this again; I'm the only one doing this work."

"Ok, I think I can sell them before Christmas, and you do good work, prices are right. I'll take them." He counts out $295 cash.

I give him my new business card, saying: "If you need more, this is how to get hold of me!" Pike's is a bustling place with lots going on. Nothing but street vendors as far as the eye can see. I've never been around anything like it. Conscience: *'There must be 100 people set up to sell!'* I've never seen so many vendors in one spot! *Amazing!* I sell about half of all I've made, in two hours. I want to hang on to a few pieces to use as Christmas presents when I get to Dad's. A bunch of relatives are supposed to be getting together, my sister, Dad's wife's sister and brother, and her son. *I don't know Dad's wife well…*

Past-flash: She came into the family just before I went in the Navy. It was awkward. I hadn't known my step mother and dad were unhappy and divorcing till the day before Mom left. *I call my step mother, Mom.* This new woman, who is closer to my age than Dad's, moved in the next day. I'm fourteen, about the time I meet Maggie.

I think this new woman in Dad's life is the one who decided it would be good for her and Dad to be alone, and send the kids away. My sister goes to our real mother. *It's complicated, our real mother was gone when I was seven but this 'Mom' I refer to is a step Mom who was like a real Mom to me who Dad is divorcing for a second step Mom.* Well if you 'get it,' that's more than I do. I'm sent off to the Navy. It had been a sudden decision. I had no time to say bye to my girlfriend, Debbie or to Maggie. This was considered a minor detail by the family. The relationships I had, will lose, or how we children feel, means nothing. What matters is that it is time to serve my country, give my parents freedom, and become a man. I pretty much always went along with the program, trying to please everyone. This is the last decision my father ever makes for me. **My past flash ends**

I have no real feelings for my Dad's new wife, do not know her, and wonder how this visit will go, and what there will be to talk about. I don't understand why they ask me to come see them. They have their life, and I have mine, and our lives do not overlap anyplace. But I want them to be happy, and, well, whatever. Seeing family is not exactly something you can get out of. It's costing me half a year's wages to visit.

The metal detector is in front of me now. I had been day dreaming in line. I understand how it works, so am not concerned. My carryon bag is x-rayed. Conscience: *'I don't remember the bags being x-rayed in Fairbanks?'* Oh well. This lady wants to know what is in the bag, and I tell her, "Jewelry, mostly metal."

She sees my knife in the bag and says: "Can you put this in your check in luggage—might not be appropriate in your carry on."

I reply: "I don't have access to it till Chicago, it's already checked in. I didn't know. I had no problems in Alaska about it. I'm used to carrying it everywhere I go."

She is not so concerned and lets me leave it in the bag, but tells me, "Next time!" I decide I will save a lot of hassle, and just put it in my check in luggage in Chicago if I can. I'm nervous and uncomfortable without the knife at my side. It is like my arm, my sense of 'who I am.' I cannot explain the feeling, but will be glad when I can put it back on again. I guess a city slicker would feel the same, if going somewhere new and strange, and not having a tie to wear, told to keep it far away because you might strangle someone with it. Or being asked to remove the cross you wear around your neck- credit card or car keys. These are all are symbols of what we believe in and stand for. My thoughts are interrupted by the security gal's: "You make this art? It's so lovely!"

"Yeah, it's hand done without electricity, one of a kind" I say shyly.

She's busy looking at my art and holding up the line. No one seems especially concerned or in a hurry. She asks: "Do you have any wolves? The guy running the camera collects wolves!" *Camera?* I'm looking around. I know nothing about hidden cameras. This is some scene from some horrible future where big brother watches everything we do from hiding. I thought it was illegal to film someone without their consent. Conscience: *'Or it used to be! When did things change?'* I missed out on a lot of things while I spent those years in the wilderness, and overseas in the service. I don't really have time to follow through with my thought of: *How can people live like this, being spied on!* The security gal is holding my wolf pieces up to the camera so the guy monitoring the spy camera can see my art. This was certainly non-threatening, so I do not think much on it. The security gal beams at me: "Hey the guy upstairs says his shift is over in a few minutes, you going to be around by the boarding gate?" I tell her I can hang around off to the side for a little while. My plane doesn't leave for an hour yet. I realize however, that this guy with the camera and this security gal must have some secret way to talk to each other. I never heard anything exchanged between the two.

A lady I hadn't seen behind me has been looking over my shoulder at the art work the security gal has set out. "Can I buy that?"

What am I going to do? Say no! I don't even have to make the sale. Another person buys something as I step off to the side to wait for the camera monitor guy. I'm stuffing money in my pocket and handing out art hand over fist it seems like. I got bills hanging out of my pocket, as the camera guy thanks me for waiting, and walks off with a wolf bolo tie for $150. I'm not keeping track of what I'm selling, and can only 'guess,' I've made $800 or so in the past few hours; a good months wages for most hard working people. The plane ticket cost me $250 - so I'm doing good.

On the plane I'm not assigned a seat, but I'm asked 'smoking or non-smoking' *Huh?* This is new to me. I missed out on something else I see. I remember when us nonsmokers were tolerant of people who smoked. It was their life, and I wouldn't presume to impose my opinion on them! Conscience: *'Second hand smoke? How silly! I breathe second hand exhaust from cars, should I complain, and put a stop to driving? If someone has a cold, they will give it to me and affect my health, should we put restrictions on people who have a cold? Make them sit somewhere else? No! It's one of the prices we pay for being social animals, we pay the price for other people's problems, to a certain extent, in return for the social advantage of having others around, but, "anyway" – whatever- sure is curious though.'* So the smokers are segregated out these days, I'll be darn, just one more restriction and imposition on me. Now I can choose from only half the plane, of places I'd like to sit. But I only smile and shake my head at the wonders of the world.

People here are 'somewhat friendly,' but not as friendly as Alaska. The stewardess will not sit next to anyone, or give out her private phone number to a stranger, and no one actually hollers across the plane at a friend at the other end. The person next to you might talk, once the plane is up, and the conversation is 'stiffly polite.' I have a memory of living like this a long time ago in a past life. A life I'm about to visit.

The Chicago airport floors me. I have never in my life seen so many people in one place. Chicago at Christmas. I vow to never again complain at how crowded Fairbanks is getting! Everyone here is moving fast, angry, reminding me of a stirred up hornet nest, where one wrong move and they will all turn and sting. Just looking for trouble. I pick up on the fear in everyone and it scares me, confuses me. No one is smiling, or talking to strangers, or helping anyone out. There are lines every-where. If I want a drink of water, there is a line! *How absurd!* How can people live this way! I never stand in line. My time is worth too much to waste it in a line. When I'm in the post office, if there's more than four to five people, I consider it 'crowded.' I'm in line though, forced to be, and not liking it one bit. I have to get a seat assign-ment. Can you believe it? I cannot choose who I sit next to? I practically want my money back! I'm picking up on the tension around me, and feeding off it.

"How are your feet?" A perfect stranger is asking me this absurd question.

Conscience: *'I wonder if he's been smoking loco weed, dropped some acid and sees snakes at my feet.'* I frown, puzzled, look down at my feet, and reply: "Just fine, how are yours?"

He quickly adds: "I mean your feet are in casts, I just wondered if you burned them."

Casts? I look down at my feet again. It dawns on me—so I explain: "These are bunny boots, not casts. We wear them in Alaska to keep warm." Conscience: *'I suppose they do look like casts if you've never seen them before. They are big and bulky, all white, smooth, weigh five pounds each.'*

"Bunny boots?" He asks, and starts to smile. I nod in agreement, he heard me right. He bursts out laughing as loud as he can, right there in the airport, wheezing, "Bunny boots! Ha! Bunny boots, Ha!" He thinks it's the funniest thing he ever heard.

Conscience:*' Everyone in Alaska wears them. I even go out dancing in them at the Howling Dog sometimes."* I never really thought how 'odd' this must look here. Yes, in Galena, 'bunny boots' are considered my formal dress. I've only left there a day ago. This is quite a change for me. My conscience reminds me: *'Not like the change I went through coming in off the Yukon to Fairbanks after my first year in the wilderness though! Ha!'*

But I feel it, a tension, approaching sensory overload. The desire to cover my eyes and ears, drop to the ground and go catatonic. The edge of a nervous break-down. But not to panic: *we've been here before and survived worse, we'll manage.* This feeling gets heightened when I know I'm not fitting in, and I'm being scrutinized. This is the fear of the pack, as it's on the verge of turning on me, the object of a lynch mob. The way an injured wolf feels when the pack starts to circle. The way an albino raven would feel. A black person, who inadvertently walks into a Ku Klux Klan meeting, or the white business man who takes a wrong turn somewhere and ends up in Harlem, at night. The nervous smile, the sweat, wanting to gracefully get out of this alive. *I don't belong here. I'm not welcome here.*

In the restroom I nervously put my knife in my check in luggage that will not be x-rayed. I see well enough now, looking in people's faces what would happen if they saw a knife. I'd never see the light of day. I wonder if one of the spy cameras is in the restroom. Nothing would surprise me. A lady comes in the restroom; *Gosh Golly!* And I think I must be in the wrong restroom. Conscience: *'All I need now! Here I am in a lady's room, carrying a knife!'* No one else has come in to let me know which restroom I'm in. "Should I go back out and check the symbol again?" I ask my conscience. *But wait a minute, do women's restrooms have urinals?* I've never been in a lady's room so I wouldn't know. If I find out what women are trying to do in the restroom, trying to be 'equal,' I promise myself to only smile and nod.

The 'lady' walks up to the nearest urinal, and lifts her dress. *Jesus Christ, I can't believe this, what's happened since I've been gone, this is spooky! It's a man!* I'm not going to say a thing. I smile and nod, like I see a man in high heels, and nylons every day. *Those don't look like false tits either, oh my God, this is worse than 1984, maybe it's a robot, more likely 'grafting and splicing' has come a long way since I last heard.... wonder if this 'he/she' looks like Frankenstein under the clothes, with a lot of scars...."* But I give my "Have a nice day!" smile, as 'it' passes by. *I'm going to be open minded, and not scream.* I hightail it out of there. Surely this is not earth. My reaction would be the same if I discovered a green Martian impersonating a human.

I'm across the hall at a newsstand and overhear the guy running it saying, "Yea! I'm sure it's a guy!"

I put in my two cents worth. "Yea, it's a guy, I was there." We all speculate at where things are going, and at least I'm not the only one wondering.

The newsstand guy says: "I'm gonna ask from now on, 'Are you really a woman?', before I play touchy feely."

"For sure!" We all agree.

One guy in the group says: "Yeah and you don't have to like your body no more, you can order a new one! Yup! If you're fat, they got this new vacuum cleaner thing that sucks all the fat out. They can cut and splice about anything."

Another guy adds: "Yeah? Well I'd like a part off a horse!"

We all go, 'Hmm' speculatively.

"There's a bank now full of organ parts you can donate to, withdraw from and all that. There's a drawer I guess, and the surgeon picks out what you need, you know, eyeballs, livers and all this" We all nod we have heard such a thing, more, seen the proof of it. Conscience: *'But I thought it was all like, in the experimental stages!*

But here I am, meeting one in a Chicago airport, and there's no nurse, no oxygen tank in a cart, it gives new meaning to the expression 'Are you for real!' and 'Who are you anyway!'

The damn metal detector thing again. I've been through this a bunch of times now and it's getting beyond 'fun and interesting.' I know the routine. I set my metal in the tray. My compass, my bullets, my change, and my pen knife. Conscience: *'There isn't much metal artwork left now, but I bet these stern face robots wouldn't stop to buy something! Christmas, and look at them, looks like they are going to a funeral! How can people live like this?'* I reply: "Oh, brave new world that has such things in it."

"Pardon me?" The security lady heard me.

With a smile I reply, "Just a private thought, a line from a book I read—said by someone who saw the future."

The security lady seems to be delaying me, but I don't notice; there's a security guy running down the hall, and there's a lot of commotion. I'm as interested as anyone else in 'who the terrorist is.' The commotion and buzzing of the bees gets closer and closer as we all wonder who it will be, and then there is a rush at me. Conscience: *'What have I done now? Was there a camera in the restroom, and the sheep are nervous about the knife I hid? Did that 'he/she' say something against me, the look on your face? Arrested for discrimination?'* Have I offended someone? Conscience reply to all this: *'I bet it was the bunny boot guy who thought we were weird - bet he reported us to the Gestapo.'* These are the things going through my mind, as I'm taken away in handcuffs. I'm scared of course. I'm a stranger in a strange land. I know no one. *Canada all over again.* I do not need reminding how I got deported and lost my home and everything I owned for making $200 trying to keep a library open. I feel like a caged animal, and here comes the stick. I'll be lucky if I make it back to Alaska with only a broken nose. Here I am being drug along through the crowd in handcuffs, in my bunny boots, fox hat, and long hair. Conscience: *Maybe all that's illegal, maybe that's what it's all about? And people ask me how I can live such a dangerous life in the wilds! Ha! I thought I would at least live long enough to make it to the folks for Christmas! Little did I know…?'*

I'm taken to a small room. There is one chair. I'm pushed down in it. A bare bulb burns above me. There are two guys. The first thing I hear is: "Ok, where's the gun!" I'm puzzled. I thought I had all the possibilities covered. Am I going to get framed for something I didn't even do, like almost happened at the fair over the stolen jackets? I'm still looking puzzled. "We'll ask you one more time! Where's the gun!"

My puzzled reply: "What gun?"

They ignore me; act like they didn't hear me. Whisper to each other. The other guy who hasn't spoken comes up to me and is real nice. "Why not just explain about the gun, and it'll be ok. You made a mistake, things happen. Tell us what happened and we'll see what we can do for you." Conscience: *'Said the SS to the Jew!'* Then it hits me, *Good guy, bad guy, bare bulb, one chair, empty room, God, it's just like the movies!*

GONE WILD

"Ok one more time, tell us about the gun and the bullets!" They are trying to wear me down. The word 'bullets' clicks.

"Bullets! Yes, is this what it's all about? I left the gun back home of course! I just forgot to take the bullets out of my pocket. I live in the Alaska wilderness, and every day I check my pockets for matches, compass and bullets. It's just a habit. Bullets are no use without a gun, they are harmless. Is it illegal to have bullets?"

"Ok, where's the gun!"

Conscience: *'They haven't heard a word I said. I might as well recite the Koran to them.'* Finally they give up though. Apparently I am correct; there is nothing illegal about having bullets. They have to let me go. Conscience: *'What a freaked out paranoid society I've come to, imagine all this fear over 'bullets,' you'd think I had an atom bomb with me!'* I'm still able to make the connections for my New York flight. I let them keep the bullets. *My own reloads. I should make them pay for them. What they did is stealing.*

While I sit around by the gate, ready for my flight to New York from here, a lady comes up to me asking: "Why are you wearing fur?" She is very angry, and I have no idea what to make of her. I glance around at the other people, to see if someone is running to a phone to tell security there is a nut case loose here. No one makes a move, in fact everyone else is 'minding their own business,' some are even scowling. My conscience is taking all this in thinking: *'It's a lynch mob!'* She gets in my face again. I'm trying to ignore her, turn away, and pretend she isn't there. Conscience: *'Obviously demented, I hope she's not dangerous.'* She's ranting away like a lunatic: "You should be taken out and shot! Don't you have any feelings! You think you can just go out and wear fur, then smile about it!"

"I killed it myself!" I say with a grin, proudly. Conscience: *'Oh indeed lady, I not only wear fur, I kill it, so digest that one.'* She goes ballistic. I think it's funny. *Poor lady.* Might as well entertain myself by pressing her buttons - yawn.

Pretty soon though she irritates me, getting in my face and yelling on and on and saying crazy things about…. "The poor animals, aren't you ashamed! They have a right to live too!" and stuff I can't remember, mixed with threats.

I finally sigh: "Lady, could you go sit somewhere else please? I'd like some peace and quiet. Can't you keep your personal opinion to yourself? It's been fun talking to you, but it's not fun anymore." I'd be happy to enter a friendly, educational discussion on the subject, but she's not here to debate, or listen, or learn, or teach. She's here to punish. She's a terrorist. A person full of anger and hate. I feel like getting caught up in it - teach her the facts of life like 'Those who stick fingers in faces loose finger.' My conscience reminds me: *'A few years ago this would have never been happening, there would have been sirens by now, and this irritating person would have been carted away in a strait jacket. I don't wish her any harm, I just want her to go away, this is embarrassing, everyone is starring at us.'* But strangely, I get the funny feeling it is me, not her, who is at fault here. *What'd I do?* Again I'm puzzled, and a little afraid. I know I would never in a million years get in someone's face, embarrass, threaten -- yell at anyone because I didn't agree with them. *Where would society be if we all got in each other's business about everything?* There is very little I see that I agree with, but feel everyone has a right to an opinion, and a way of life of their choice. We are social animals; we need to learn to get along with each other. No wonder civilized people aren't allowed to carry sharp objects - they'd kill each other off-probably good riddance too.

On this leg of the trip we are assigned specific seats. *How can people live like this? This is insane!!*At the New York airport I'm terrified. I thought Chicago was crowded. Ha! I didn't know this many people were on the planet! Fairbanks is 'crowded,' but at least if there is a 'big crowd' of say 100 people, I'd recognize at least a few faces. This, before me, is a faceless mass of humanity. I have to move where the crowd goes. There is no stopping, or I get swept along. God help anyone who drops anything here, or decides they need to go to the restroom. Where I live, when I gotta pee, I just stop and whip it out. The concept of using the restroom only one or two times a day, and at specific times and places seems 'nuttso,' but I have a vague memory far away in my mind of a past life, living like this. It makes me shiver. *Thank God I found another way!* I honestly believe I'd be dead now if I hadn't found the wilderness. I couldn't live like this.

I have to get from this airport to another New York Airport, all the way across the city. I know there is a way to do it. I try to ask someone, and everyone I speak to treats me like a non-person. I'm not there; they turn away and go blank. Conscience: *'Holy shit! What kind of place is this? How do people live like this?'* I reply: "When in Rome, imitate the Romans." I remember this about 'survival' in strange places. I try to imitate everyone else, scowl, and never make eye contact. Waddle like a duck with a hernia when there is a gap ahead of me.

Finally I'm at the curb, and know this is somehow connected to going to the other airport, 'Kennedy'? There is a sign and an arrow every now and then. *A person could fall down, die here, and it would be about the time the carcass started to stink full of maggots a week later before anyone would bother to look down. And these people tell me 'bears' are scary? As long as I live, I will never come through here again. This is 100 times scarier than bears!*

A cab pulls up, screeches to a halt, driver jumps out, "Anyone for Kennedy?" I leap forward, assuming this swarming mass will jump me to the gun. No one else steps forward, or acknowledges that there is a cab here, and the driver just asked us a question. *How rude these people are!* But in the back of my mind, *Oh, oh, something isn't right here. I got to act like the Romans, and none of the Romans are taking the cab, something is fishy here!* But I have no idea what. *Isn't this a cab? Would it be stolen? How would these people know? What do all these people know in common, that I wouldn't know? Is this guy going to roll me?* I'm in deep trouble again, for the hundredth time. The cab driver is asking for another rider: "Hey come on, I need at least one more rider, you there, want to go?" Everyone ignores him. He can't find another rider. He asks if I want to be the only passenger. *This is my way out!*

I politely say, "No thank you." He cusses and drives off. Some kind of bus comes by, and there is a scramble. I get the second bus. I get to the other airport, and the last connection to Plattsburgh, New York, where my father now lives. I've never been here. We lived in Syracuse when I last knew him.

He was 'only' a professor then. He has a few degrees. I don't know how many, or in what subjects. He never told me, or I never asked. Or he told me once, and I forgot. Now he's Dean of a college, and that's pretty slick, and I'm proud of him for accomplishing what he wanted. That's real dedication. He was born in the slums of New York City, and now look! College at sixteen and never looked back! Got to hand it to him. He taught me how to be alone and I thank him. I'm puzzled however that he wants to see me. Why? *He's sorry he taught me how to be alone?* I'm puzzled. I'm embarrassed. What am I supposed to do about it? I am what I am - a product of how I was raised. I'm happy and glad. Why can't he be? Parents are very strange.

The flight to Plattsburgh is a short hop and I'm there before I realize it. It's just a short cab ride from the airport. The home is a spread out mansion looking place on Lake Champlain. There are no neighbors I see, and lots of trees. A feeling of quiet and peace, which is surprising to find so close to the city. There's a manicured lawn, a sailboat at a private dock, a couple of cars, a thing I heard is called a gazebo, sort of an out building just for relaxing in.

I nervously ring the bell. Dad's wife answers. She is glad to see me at first, but then asks me why I'm dressed like this. "You better go out and get some descent clothes before you come in this house!" I'm flabbergasted. I went out and got brand new jeans just for this trip, and a new plaid shirt. Cost me a week's wages. I'm used to shopping at thrift stores and dumpsters. I open my mouth to comment, but "why bother." I'm just about to smile and say, "Bye," turn around and go back to Alaska, and never come back again, when I hear my father's voice in the background.

"Hey, is that Miles here?" He steps out from behind the door and gives me a big hug and pulls me in. Having to go buy a suit and tie before I'm allowed in the house is forgotten. She will just have to suffer the embarrassment and indignity.

"Did you have a good trip? How's life going anyway? Gosh it's good to see you, been a long time!"

No use telling him about the trip, ha, ha. "Yea, good trip, everything's great!" There's a Persian rug on the floor, a new stereo in a walnut case. The picture window overlooking the lake is spotless, and I see the gazebo there that I'd heard about. I'm lead down the hall, and around a few corners to my own room with its own bath. Conscience: *'The bathroom is bigger than my houseboat.'* My father wants to be proud of me; tries to be proud of me, but doesn't quite know what to make of me. I sympathize with his dilemma. He wants to love me, but I'm a stranger. His wife suggested that while I visit, I wear a suit and tie my father has. We are the same size. It would be less embarrassing for my father. I know he wishes to introduce me around the university. Certainly I can't be going around in bunny boots and fox hat!

I reply: "Sure, no problem. I guess I can dress up and feel like a clown for my father." I was sorry I said that, Conscience: *'But no one seems to consider accepting me for me, thinks about who I am, my feelings in all this. It's all to please everyone else.'* It's Christmas, and I've got to get along. I wear the suit and tie. I sort of remember which is the desert fork, which is the water glass, and which is for wine. I vaguely recall which side of the plate the napkin ring goes on. I try not to put my elbows on the table, cut only two pieces of meat delicately at a time. Stick my pinkie out when I pick up the tea cup, and say ... just the right things in just the right way. But what is there to say? Conscience: *'Why, back home I'd pick up that whole roast between my two paws, slam it to my face, grab it with my teeth, shake my head, and swallow what came off!'*

"Miles, tell us about Alaska? What is the university there like?"

I have to pause. The only part of the university I've seen is the museum. I have pictures and stories of Indians, fish racks of salmon, log cabins, dog teams.... but no one here is interested in my stories or pictures, so the conversation becomes 'polite awkwardness.' They think I'm stupid as I go "ummm."

My step brother, who I don't know well, has been to Alaska. He went to Anchorage. The Alaskans I know consider 'Anchorage' a suburb of Seattle, and not Alaska, insultingly calling it calling it 'Los Anchorage.' Its climate is not like the rest of the state, and does not see the cold or dark. It is much like city life anyplace. It has more in common with the lower states than it does with the rest of Alaska. Yet Anchorage contains half the state's population, gets half the federal funding, half the voters, half the control, and regulates the rest of us. Interior Alaskans have no good feelings for Anchorage. Seeing only Anchorage and thinking this means knowing Alaska, and being proud to have been there, is not saying much. It's naive. Anchorage knows little about, and has had no experience with, issues of subsistence, hunting, native villages, wilderness issues of all kinds.

My step-brother was there looking for work for a few days; one of those pipe-line jobs. Alaskans I know feel the pipeline is for and about 'outsiders,' and is not a good subject, just a way for people to come up, make the big money, and go back to where ever they came from to spend it. My step-brother is saying proudly he was trying to do just that. While there, he bought some slides at a gift shop. My father gets a screen out. The lights are dimmed, and we 'ooh' and 'ahh' over the slide show. I smile and make no comment. I'm aware my father is trying to show interest in Alaska and thus bonding us. Anchorage is all he can comprehend, and even this is on the edge of incredibility. "Miles?" My father takes me aside: "Would you mind not wearing that knife? Everyone worries it might cut the furniture when you sit down." That's ridiculous, it's in a sheath and cannot cut anything. I'm pretty sure what happened was, 'she' went to him and said, "You know we can't have that in the house! It scares me! It isn't right! That big knife! I know he's your son, but this is just too much! I won't have it." And he said, "Now, now dear, calm down, I'll have a talk with him." I'm not trying to scare anyone, or even impress anyone. I'm just a terrified kid, clinging to things familiar to me. She's some kind of shrink for a living. Child psychologist or something. I have heard it before, the psychological reasons, the symbolism. I can guess what she'd say 'hanging on to my knife, symbolizes. It's sharp and pointy and represents the penis. I sigh. I cannot say it is just a tool, opens boxes, and is a symbol of my ability to perform many tasks, is something familiar and important to me. *Oh well, no use saying anything like that.* Where is the kindness, sympathy, forgiveness, and understanding? But I know it will be 'immature' of me to try and insist on carrying my knife. I know that if my father came to visit me, and he wanted to wear his suit and tie in the wilderness, I would find it a bit odd, and so would my friends, but we would understand, and no one would make him take his tie off.

I'd proudly say, "This is my father, Dean of a college," and dare anyone to make anything of it. If my friends whispered, "Educated idiot then, huh." I'd stand up for him, "Well he's the best educated idiot of them all!" Hell yes!

When in Rome, do as the Romans do. So I remember my promise to make a game of imitating those around me. Survival depends on it. I happily try to walk the walk, talk the talk. Some of Dad's friends actually nod approval. Too bad I can't hang around, and find a place in some big company and work my way up, be the head of a bank or something. There are hints that maybe there would be a place for me. I smile politely and nod and say, "I'll think it over."

My sister wants to see me alone. "Do you remember when we were five?"

My mind does not spin back to a place I do not want to be. If I went there, I might not come back. I haven't seen my sister in a long time. She used to laugh, and have pretty white blonde, long hair. Her hair is short, dark, just 'different.' Her speech is slow and labored, like she has trouble forming the words. I can guess why. I ask, "Want to go on a canoe ride?"

She brightens: "But it's snowy out!"

I laugh: "Hey, in Alaska, this would be like summer weather. She lives in Maine so I'd think it would be the same for her. I go out in my boat when it's much colder than this, as long as there is open water!" We go out for a while on the peaceful lake.

She confides: "I wish we lived closer to each other, Miles. I miss having you around!" What can I say? What can I say to anyone? As far as they are concerned, I selfishly deserted everyone, ran away, to do some foolish dangerous thing. I'm sick, and everyone is polite about it. She says: "Let's paddle all the way across the lake and never come back, Miles!"

"I think we shouldn't try to go across the lake, Eileen. It's too far in a canoe." I wonder briefly, if she knows that.

Hanging around in this 'Turkey' costume, I feel my blood pressure going right through the roof, with all this pretending for the sake of everyone else. Dad's wife tells me how nice I look, and how much I please my father dressed like this. Now I know it's all my fault. If only I were someone else. Conscience: *'What? No one here wants to hear how we finally learned how to catch mice!'* I chuckle to myself. Conscience: *'It's actually kind of fun, pretending to be someone else.'* The waiter in the restaurant calls me "sir." People hold doors open. Not because of who I am, how I think, but because of how I dress.

We all go to a French place to eat, where meals are $100 each, and it's pretty cool to look around. Ten waiters stand there, and if you drop a napkin, they all rush to pick it up at once. My sister orders 'hamburgers.' She was always like that. Our real mother is like that. Me, I might be like that – but maybe not. I wave my hand in dismissal, so 'hoity toity,' like everyone else. I find it 'fun' to pick the right French dish, and think about what the proper combinations might be; if the lemon, or the cucumber, would be 'proper' for the African snails. And I guess if a person has the money, 'why not!' I'm young, I don't understand it all. I only see there's a fly in the soup, and no one else sees it. Money makes the world go round, everyone knows that but me.

The main problem I have is the sorts of things a person has to do, and put up with, to get that kind of money. I look around at what my father has, and its 'nice,' but it cost. It cost him --me, my sister, two wives, who knows how many friends, who knows what bullshit he had to promise along the way, what dreams he had to let go of. I saw a little of it growing up, and 'the top' is not always such a wonderful place to be. But I'm a lot like him – not that he'd admit it - so what can I say?

"Hey, thanks Dad, a real Russian Cossack hat?" I look at the label and it's written in Russian. He was over there, and the hat has the real Russian label in it. It is pretty nice. I wear it with my suit and tie and fresh washed skin. The dried fresh rosehips, to be used for tea, that I hand out as Christmas presents gets a polite response that I notice. No one cares that I picked them myself - and they have a lot of vitamin C.

The daughter of one of my father's friends, about my age and very pretty in her white dress and jewels, says to me; "I can tell you are an Alaskan trapper!" I'm puzzled, till she adds, "Because of your fur hat!" I nod politely with a 'you are very clever!' smile. She wants to hear some wilderness stories, but I can't think of any. I see her father beaming his approval. Conscience: *'I have the proper blood line, and connections.'* I get the impression he's having 'problems' with her, and it's about time she left the nest, and he is hopeful he can pawn her off on me. She's tired of his bullshit, and wants freedom, adventure, and my life sounds ever so exciting, and rebellious. But with me, she'd be jumping from the frying pan, into the fire. My conscience is hopeful or doesn't care saying: *'She'd be amazingly fun for about a week; I think she would be one of the 'wrap her legs around and scream' types. Don't you think?'* She knows that's what I think, and she's saying "yes," with her eyes, and it would be so easy to ... But I let the moment pass; give a vague response, about leaving soon. The pull is there, but I do not really want to get involved in something with no possible way of working out and misleading her for a short time of fun. That little fun could be very costly.

My father doesn't know why I don't want to stay longer. I fit right in, get along and impress everyone, Dad: "It could be like old times!"

I stutter: "Well Dad..." I have to pause. I don't want to hurt my father's feelings, but at the same time, I don't want him to think there's even a chance I might come back, or live like this. I'm staring at the rug. Conscience: *'The wear marks are still on the Persian rug, from the path I wore on it in the other house. Pace from one window, stare out, pace to another window, stare out, pace to another, back to the first, and stare out. I did this for hours, days, and years. No one noticed. A wild animal in a cage. Now that I'm loose, there's no way in hell I'd come back. I'd rather be dead.'*

Dad interrupts before I can make up a story - saying: "I need to go to the store, why don't you come with me?" On the highway the truck has engine trouble. Dad says: "It's gas, water and dirt in the tank." We pull over to fiddle with it. He says the gas cap was off for a while and dirt got in. The hood of the truck is up. I see a cop car in the distance coming toward us.

My first words are, "Oh shit! Now we are in real trouble, hurry up!" My father is puzzled. I'm sure, thinks I'm paranoid. The cop pulls over. I expect him to tell us to go against the car, spread our legs, don't move, while he gets ID and calls the numbers in on the radio. I'm ready to 'assume the position.' The cop smiles, and asks us if we are ok. I can't believe this. My father calmly tells him its water in the gas.

The cop goes back to his car, gets out a bottle of gas heet, that stuff that mixed gas with water so the water burns, and puts it in the gas tank for us, saying: "Let me follow you a ways, to make sure you will be ok, Sir." My father thanks him, as if it is no big deal, as if this is how cops treat people all the time, and is to be expected. This is sort of how I remember things from a long time ago, but it means times have not changed after all, so what is going on? *This is weird!* I can only assume then, the problem is mine, that it is me, who deserves to be treated like shit. I'm, of coarse, puzzled 'why,' and hope I can figure it out so I can survive. It seems to me there is a whole class of people who are not 'glad' to see the police, and they aren't just the criminals. Hmmm.

On the way home Dad tells me he had one of his two fuel tanks contaminated somehow, maybe a lost gas cap, and it's full of water and dirt, but it runs for a while, and then messes up the engine. The people at the shop told him he needs a whole new tank and it's going to cost a cool zillion dollars.

I only chuckle. I explain how it can be fixed for about $20. The solution is simple, "Doesn't require any brainstorming and is the kind of problem I solve ten times a day every day." I repeat: "You cut the fuel line and put in this gas filter that has a water separator. The filter will take water and dirt out. There is a valve at the bottom to drain the water out that it catches. It holds a cup or so. Eventually you'll have all the dirt and water out of the tank." I laugh. That's always the answer here "get a new one." Dad thinks I'm just the smartest guy, to think of that. I have no idea why he latches on that one thing, and thinks it's really something. Perhaps of all the things I've done, it's the only thing he can relate to, and understand. But it's nice that he's proud of me for something. It would be like me being proud of Dad because he can make change at the restaurant, that being as close as I could come to understanding what a PhD degree is.

Back at the house I ask Dad if I can use the phone. His wife starts a burst of laughter, immediately stifled, because I'm using the wrong spoon for the dessert. Conscience: *'Sometimes I remember, but it's almost like I have a mental block. Anyhow, I may not do that well in her world, but I can last longer then she would in mine! I'd give her about ten seconds, before it would be 'freak out time.' Probably she'd be dead in an hour.'* I smile, she's embarrassed she let it out, how stupid I am; everyone is supposed to be polite about that, how I have a mental disability, and not let it show. But if she visited me, I wouldn't laugh. I'd know she understands her world, and I know mine, and people can't be expected to be knowledgeable about everything, or good in every environment. I'd take care of her in my world, not expect her to understand. Maybe she would understand who the savages in the world are.

After dinner I'm appalled by how much gets thrown in the trash, but don't say anything. Conscience: *'A whole village in a third world country could live off what is thrown out in this house.'*

"No, Miles, don't save that salad, it will be wilted by tomorrow, just toss it out." I eat some of it before tossing it, but there is only so much I can eat. It bothers me very much to throw out good food. I almost starved to death last year. I know too many friends who would almost die for these throw away leftovers. She is still talking to me: "That cheese is drying out in the refrigerator, toss that out too, Miles." She looks at me in distaste that I would eat out of the main salad bowl, and not go get a bowl, and sit at the table. Her expression tells me she thinks I am an uncivilized pig, and if it were not for my father we certainly wouldn't know each other.

After the next meal I hear, "Oh, Miles will eat it, just give it to Miles!" Now I'm the family garbage disposal, for whatever people put on their plate but couldn't eat, 'Just give it to Miles.' I hear her from the other room: "Miles, you need to measure the water when you make the juice, did you do that? Otherwise no one will drink it and we'll have to throw it out!" Once again I goofed. I have this 'thing' about measuring or following directions. I think now, I know where it comes from. I smile. I'm considered incompetent to make a pitcher of juice, and need supervision. She stands over me, patiently shows me how it's done, talking very slowly so I understand. I thank her politely. At first I wanted to have two pitchers of juice, one pitcher, the way I like it, another pitcher, measured exactly, "but this sounds absurd." So I make the juice by measuring, swearing no one will ever make me measure juice again, as my unconscious daydreams while I stir.

"We don't wear furs, Miles, it's a personal preference. We don't believe in hurting living things." Dad's wife is explaining, telling me how she collects aluminum cans and recycles them sometimes, because she believes in 'preserving the environment.' Doing her part to save the planet. I pick up on all these new catchy phrases. I nod my head at how noble this is of her. There will of course be no conversation about trapping in her house. I'm sincere when I tell her it is good to keep conservation on one's mind. Each of us in this world does what we think is right in the best way we know how. I leave the room to go see what Dad is up to.

In the living room my father plays his Haines flute. The concert tape leaves out one instrument so he can play along. He calls it 'music minus one.' He practices for the band he plays with, a Beethoven piece. The metronome clicks, my father's foot taps, as he waits for his part to come in on. His face is filled with peace. I remember this from the past. His escape. Far, far away from his insane wife, and idiot son. My father and I are a lot alike? *After all, didn't he have a goal too? A goal no one could stop? Not his parents, not his wife or children, and didn't he move from one planet to another, and never look back? Didn't he overcome us all, to be the great person he is? Can I do any less?* "Rewards and prices to pay." I smile and ask how his music is going. He nods and doesn't want to be interrupted. I stutter in a soft polite voice as I back away.

ON THE WAY home to Alaska, I do not have my bunny boots on, do not wear my knife, do not have bullets in my pocket, and am too afraid to wear a fur hat. I am not happy, cocky, carefree or lucky. I pass myself off as one of the lemming. But as I get closer to home the rules loosen up, and so do the people. In Seattle, I have my fur hat back on, my trusty knife at my side, and toes wiggling in bunny boots. Someone asks me if I'm from Alaska.

"How can you tell?" The guy laughs at my joke. He's in bunny boots too. We both exchange horror stories of the crazy lemming march over the cliff. We are both glad we will soon be safe back 'home.' We both enjoy, once again, being able to sit anywhere on the plane, flirt with the stewardess, slap other passengers we know on the back, and basically act like 'one of us,' an Alaskan. A banner across the isle of the plane headed for Alaska reads, "Welcome back." Every passenger lets out a cheer, and we all get a free drink. I accept a coke with my usual line: "When I look down the barrel, I want to see one bear and one set of sights!" I wink at the guy next to me. We all vow never to return to the madness of 'outside' again. This seems to be the universal feeling on the plane. Only a few people are puzzled, those who are making their first trip. But certainly no one was 'afraid', or made to feel unwelcome. Strangers were not made fun of, but welcomed, and wished good luck.

The pilot interrupts the flight with an announcement. There is a beautiful river and mountain below. He tells us what mountain and river. The jet is tipped one way then other so we all can see. The whole package is so unlike a 'lower 48' flight. On the flight from Anchorage to Fairbanks, there are only a few passengers. The stewardess sits next to me and looks at my art. I tell her about the other stewardess and this one knows her. We talk about how so many people cross paths here in Alaska, know people or have friends in common.

When we land, all the passengers laugh. None of us are used to the -30° air because we've been gone. We all choke on it, and laugh again. "Isn't it great!?" We all wish each other well, as if we had shared in some great adventure of danger that bonded us together. Anyone with a car offers a ride to any of us that needed one, and insisted we not take a cab. The guy I get a ride with stops for coffee and we hang around a little while. I get compliments on my hat. I tell my bunny boot story and it gets a lot of laughs. Everyone in the coffee house is wearing bunny boots.

BACK IN GALENA none of my Indian friends believe you have to pay for a flight before you even take it. "What if you don't like it?"

I answer them with, "Well you just better like it, you haven't got a choice!"

They reply. "Well they can kiss my ass then!"

This makes me smile. I can just picture that. One old timer has never been as far away as Fairbanks in his life. He's in his 70's. He sends someone else with a grocery list when he needs supplies.

"Why don't you just go in and get supplies yourself?" I ask him.

He gives a shocked reply, "I can't do that; I don't know anyone to stay with!"

I step out into the snow-covered street, followed by a few of the natives. Looking up and down the street, nothing stirs. There is wood smoke drifting lazily up and trailing across the river. A chainsaw 'revs' up, far in the distance. We are all dressed in furs, bunny boots, or fur mukluks on our feet. We take a short cut across an empty lot where a well-used path leads across Huntington's yard. The old man waves out the window when we walk by. We wave back.

"In the city, you could not just cut across an empty lot, or walk across someone's property because it is a shortcut. You have to stay on the sidewalk where everyone else walks." My Native friends think this is funny; that I'm making up a story to entertain them, and think I have a great imagination. They do not know that when I try and describe Galena and this life to the city people, the city people think I am making up a story and think I have a great imagination. Even though these village people watch TV, so should know what I am talking about! This is like the city people who watch Nova or a National Geographic specials, and should know about other cultures, but seem not to. It's like enjoying a cartoon. No one thinks rabbits are like Bugs Bunny, even though there it is in the TV.

Back at the houseboat across the river I am anxious to get my traps back out. I see lots of new tracks on the old trail, still visible since I left. No one else has been on it, and no one has visited the boat while I was gone. I hadn't had to lock it. Snow covers the boat so it can hardly be seen now. It looks like a snow mound with a window in it. I have shoveled snow against the walls to help insulate against cold.

The temperature is -50° zero, and I have to get a fire going. I had left newspaper, kindling, and split wood by the stove, knowing I'd have to get a fire going as soon as I got here. The small boat does not take so long to warm up. The frosted window clears up and I can see out. A letter is written to Maggie, telling her about my trip outside.

Dearest Maggie,

It has been a while since I saw life outside Alaska. I still remember the 60s. Things have changed quite a bit. People in general seem angrier, or maybe I'm just older, and my perception of what I see has changed? So many women talk about how rough their life is. What a rotten thing it is to be a women in this day and age, discrimination, no rights, blah, blah. I see all the anger and hurt in them. I am puzzled. I look at the role of a woman and do not understand what is so bad about it. You are a city gal and do not seem crazy or angry – so explain it to me. No it was not a great visit.

I go on for twenty pages in my usual way...

The situation with my family is reviewed. It is not a bad family or anything. No one is evil. All are respected members of society with jobs, friends, and loved ones. It is me without all that, so this suggests the problem is me, I just can't figure out what is wrong with me.

But you seem different, I've always been able to tell you what is on my mind, open and honestly. Saw the relatives, had my time in the big city under the bright lights. It's all right I guess, just glad I don't have to live like that. I understand that some do, and like it, and that's how it is. You seem to do ok, all in all. I'm just different.

Anyhow, I'm rambling again! Hope you are well! Haven't heard from you in a while.

Sunshine, Miles

It takes me a while to begin to get my strength back after my visit outside Alaska.

In the morning I wake up groggily to the boat rocking, and a scraping sound. I have no idea what could cause this. *An earthquake?* No. *Just a dream?* No, *I'm awake?* Uh huh. The movement stops, so I forget about it, but decide to get up, now that I'm awake. There is a crescent moon against black night. There are only a few hours of light each day. My mind is on getting out with some traps, but I think about doing some art since it is still dark. I sold all I had with me on the trip, yet I come home with little of the money. It cost so much to live in town, with the round trip ticket, and staying in Fairbanks, eating there and what not. My father earns in a week what I earn in a year.

It is cheap to live here in the houseboat, no rent, no electric, small heat cost for cutting wood. No bills, so money goes a long way. Yet the art has to be sold where there are people, and it cost a lot to be there. What a dilemma. I'm thinking of this as I step out the door to get a pot of snow to melt for water. When I look to the wall of snow against the boat, I see why the boat had been rocking. A moose had been sleeping in the snow up against the boat. Maybe there had been some heat escaping through the wall that the moose was attracted to. When he got up, he rubbed his back on the boat, rocking it. I see some hairs in the wood. The snow has not even frozen yet where he was bedded down. I still haven't got my winter meat yet and here it had been within arm's reach all night. There is still bear meat left, but not very much, and I'm stretching it to make it last.

'*A grouse! I hear a grouse!*' My conscience is hollering at me. The door is opened and I look around, knowing the bird will be at the very top of a tree, sitting as still as he can, stretched out to look like the top of the tree. Knowing the habits of grouse, it will likely be a tree within fifty feet, the usual distance grouse here fly away when startled. *There he is!* I spot him a ways off in the spruce thicket. I knew it would be a spruce tree; *that's why they call him a Spruce Chicken!* Off through the deep snow I go, taking the fifty caliber with me. When I think I'm close enough, I get the bead on him. "Va---rooommm." The usual six foot of flame; the usual gagging smoke and "Holy Shit!"

I took the head off the grouse. The last grouse had been center punched. There hadn't been a speck left bigger than a period at the end of a sentence. As I walk over to get the grouse out of the snow, a moose is spotted. He had been sleeping when I shot, jumped up when I fired, and is now looking around, wondering what in the heck 'that' was. There is no way I could reload in time to shoot him. I can only watch as he wanders off. Conscience: '*Now I know why repeating rifles were invented, and people gave these black powder guns up! Will must be right, this is outdated.*' I had built this gun from a kit and Will had laughed about how outdated it was, how it couldn't be depended on. I really need meat bad, and it is hard to watch this winter's worth of meat walk away, and such an easy shot, so close to home. I can only sigh.

Compared to the past though, I'm living like a king! I have fresh potatoes, eggs sometimes, cheese, and all sorts of things I did without in the past. The propane light is such an improvement over the 'gee whiz-light' that it is really appreciated. I feel very lucky! (And rich!) The whiz light had been an empty cheese whiz jar. I had put a hole in the lid, used diesel fuel and a string. This had been my winter light through the dark and cold. The trap line is extended each trip out and I am doing pretty well. There are some marten around, and otter, mink, fox, wolf, wolverine, and lynx. It is exciting to see the tracks, and know the thrill of thinking like them, then being right.

Conscience: *'Someone's been out here with a snow machine.'* I look down at the fresh tracks. This is the first time anyone's been up the slough here on a machine. I know the GI's on the base get out and fool around sometimes. This doesn't look like a local Indian. After following the tracks, I see whoever it was has been checking my traps! A couple of the bigger traps are missing! I've heard of this happening, but have never seen it. I wonder what I'm to do. Bushwhack the culprit? I sigh. I get advice from the local cop in Galena, asking, "What should I do? I can't be losing my traps and furs. I make little enough money at this as it is, to have someone else collecting from my work."

The cop has heard of trouble like this before. He says, "What I'd do?" He confides after a pause, "Make a wolverine set." He pauses before going on to see if I 'get it' but I'm puzzled, wondering what wolverines have to do with this problem. It's a people problem. He goes on. "Use a 330 Conibear, one of them new style humane traps. I'd cut the locks off, and chain it good to a tree. Then I'd set it in my footprints leading to one of my sets." I immediately get the point. I know about these new type traps we trappers are being forced to use, replacing what was good enough for the past 100 years. They are supposed to be humane because they kill instantly. Problem is, they'll break your arm or leg and grab you, like way up by the knee. Without the locks it would be impossible to get the trap open again once set off, without the setting tool. Setting a Conibear as described would catch the thief permanently.

In shock I ask: "But wouldn't that be like... murder? I mean how can you suggest it?"

The cop shrugs his shoulders with: "I'm just telling you what I'd do. The only thing that works. You of course can't say you set it up like this to catch a thief. You have to have the 'oh my goodness how could such a tragic thing have happened' attitude."

If I followed the cop's suggestion, I'd only have to catch one, and the problem would be stopped around here for many years. To hell with depending on the system. The system is way back in Fairbanks. They don't have money to come way out here. Even in Fairbanks a person would be lucky if the police helped, even if I had the money, interest, would the police have the time to cross the street, unless it was 'politically correct'! I wish, I hope, but that's not what I'm seeing. It is not 'honesty, protection, justice for all.' I'm far from pleased. I had hoped the local cop would say something like, "Glad you told me - I'll ask around and tell you what I hear, maybe we can salvage a bad situation here, have a talk with someone, get your traps back." I'm wondering just what the cop is getting paid for? What if I get the wrong person? Why should it be in my hands? Conscience: *'Oh well, - in a tough country got to live like the Romans when in Rome. People around here think you are an easy mark or soft and it's the end. Have to let it be known you don't put up with crap from people. That's the code of the wild…'*

I cut the locks off of a 330 Conibear trap, and chain it to a tree as one of my 'wolverine' sets. It may not actually 'kill' someone, *maybe they'd only lose their foot.* I'm curious how long it would take to get out, and all the various ways a person might think of to try. But at least I no longer feel a helpless victim. Someone is going to be laughing over messing with me, and I'm going to 'wipe that smile off someone's face.' Not that I'm going to enjoy it, or want it to be this way. I will sigh at the way Karma works. "What goes around comes around," I remind my conscience. I wonder if the thief will be willing to cut his leg off at the knee with his rusty Swiss army knife in order to survive. We'll see.

One day I run into a guy out setting a fish net under the ice. I'm curious about this. He's setting in an eddy out in the river.

"John Stam." He introduces himself with outstretched hand. I watch how this is done. He puts in a series of holes a few feet apart, then feeds a rope through the holes with a stick. The rope is tied to the net so the net can be pulled through. After helping him set the net in the bitter wind, he tells me he fishes for his dog team. He explains: "I trap with the dogs; maybe I'll race that Iditarod."

I ask, "How many do you have?"

"I don't really know. Over twenty, I have pups coming and going, always trading and buying." He tells me all of the dog's names and history, as if they were children. I can't believe it, so much to remember, knowing the parents, bloodline to listen to him talk about going back four generations of twenty dogs. John goes on, "You should come out with me some time, see how you like mushing! Thanks for helping me with the net!" I have crossed the river with John while we were talking. It is about time to get to the post office anyway, so I head on up. The post office lady says her husband runs the sporting goods store, and I should go see him about selling art work there.

"It is up in the new village." I haven't been up to the new village much, but follow her directions. Gordy Cruger introduces himself, and I like him right off. He picks out a few belt buckles on consignment.

"The GI's are my big customers," he tells me. They want guns and outdoor gear, Alaska related things, also gifts for loved ones they left back where they come from.

His shop is run out of his home, and has all kinds of things on shelves and on the wall. He doesn't run regular hours. People just call up and say they'd like to come up. He tells them if it's a good time to come shop or not. If he says it is a nice day and he is going out to hunt, the customers say, "Ok, maybe tomorrow?" He doesn't make a lot of money at this, but is retired military himself, I think, so has some other money coming in.

Gordy introduced me to a jet pilot who likes my work. Pilot, "Hey I like your work. Could you do some work on an eagle claw? I just got one from a good friend. Eagles are my totem animal you know. I fly like the eagle, and have the power of the eagle!" I'm not so sure about that, but he hands me the claw before I can comment, and I tell him I can put a cap on it, do some inlay work.

I tell him, "I'll leave it here at the sporting goods store when I come back across the river."

"Wow! You live across the river in a houseboat? I heard about you from the other jet pilots!"

I'm tired of telling stories today, and say I got things to do. I try to end the conversation: "I'll see you when I come in again maybe!" This hot shot pilot thinks he's made of the right stuff, and has what it takes. He thinks he's the Eagle. Well, whatever. I leave saying: "Hey guys, I got to go, catch you later!"

"Nice meeting you, Miles!"

Before I leave the new site, I meet Ed and Dawn, who are an older retired couple and like to stay active. Dawn tells me: "I used to manage a gift shop, maybe I can use my connections to help you sell?" She likes my work and buys a few things outright. They are into 'religion,' and hang out a lot with the local pastor. "Why not come over for dinner when you can?" I'm still not sure how much I want to be involved with people, so I'm pretty noncommittal. *Canada and all that.* I don't need to be getting close to people and getting stabbed in the back.

I go back across the river and don't come back for a month. There is wood to cut, books to read, furs to catch, and I never seem to run out of things to do, and never get bored, or lonely. Conscience: *'Just sometimes, but I've been more lonely around people than when isolated in the wilderness.'* There is only one month left in the trapping season and I want to hit it hard, since it will be a while before I can trap again. The skis are working all right, but I think I will just use snowshoes in the future. The skis do not make a good enough trail to find again on my way home in the dark. I had discovered this early on, but kept using the skis anyway, out of habit. The animals do not like the ski trail as much as the snowshoe trails either. Hmmm.

Another marten? The number one trap on the pole set got a marten. There he is, hanging frozen. Another had been by, and I could have got it too, if I had checked the trap earlier. The dwarf birch trees snag at my skis; so I avoid this section. The spruce thickets seem the best place to travel. Conscience: *'Let the animal come to me, why go out in bum country to find them?'* This doesn't always work, but it is also not the best idea to bust through hard going country for a long ways and wear myself out. I have a new twenty two rifle with me this trip and get a couple of willow grouse. I traded some art for a rifle with Gordy. The black powder is just too heavy to carry, and gives me only the one shot. There is a beaver house I want to set a trap at this trip. It is a long way out so I will not be back till late. The beaver house is twenty feet tall and as big as a house. A fire is built. I cook one of the grouse over the open fire. There are some dry rosehips that I pick and make tea from.

A hole in the ice is made for an otter set. Noticing the cattails, I take a stick and get at the mud in the bottom of the lake, and dig up some cattail roots. They are cooked inside the grouse, mostly for the moisture. The cattail roots this time of year are shriveled up and not as tasty as they would be in the spring, but it's a meal I take from the land. Spruce bows are cut to lie down on. I take a nap after eating. The ski trip home will take four hours, so I rest up with an hour nap. When I wake, it is like starting a new day. I am refreshed and not tired at all. Many days are like this, where nothing truly eventful happens, just a series of days and weeks that run together into a pleasant memory. Some days go in the diary.

Diary: February 20, 1978.

Another long ski to beaver house number three. Got an otter from the hole I made to get cattail roots for dinner last trip. Eating a lot of grouse and rabbits, but no moose. Too late to get one, spring will be here before I could eat it all up, but sure miss the meat. Weather has been nice.

The dogs are screaming frantically. I'm in John's dog yard and we are going on his trapline today. All the screaming hurts my ears. There is jumping, lunging, pulling, barking, as all twenty dogs hope they are among the eight that get run today. They seem hard to control. I do not see how John gets the harness on such a pile of squirming fur. I learn the front one is called 'The Leader,' and is supposed to know more than the rest, and know commands to turn. There is a name for other positions, but it's all too much to remember with all the noise and confusion. I cannot make sense out of the tangle of lines and harnesses either, though I gather that there is a common line all the dogs are hooked to. They run in tandem on either side of the main line.

John built the sled himself, which is a nice wood basket sled about six feet long. The two runners are two inches wide. The bed of the sled is about six inches above the runners. John's ready saying: "Climb in, Miles, the dogs are ready to go!" I climb in and sit with the wood box of traps and bait between my knees. A rope connects the sled to a tree by a quick release snap. John pulls it loose as I'm still trying to figure out how to sit. I grab the side rails as we take off like a rocket after lighting the fuse. We bounce airborne over the first few bumps and I feel like I'm riding a bronco out of the chute. The two command words to turn are 'gee' and 'haw,' but I do not know which is which and wonder why 'mushers' don't just teach dogs English.

After the dogs settle down, we are traveling about ten miles an hour. John's voice interrupt's the other sounds: "The dogs can keep this pace up for ten straight hours if they are trained for it. This is the kind of speed it takes to win the Iditarod, for ten straight days." I know from earlier talks it takes five gallons of feed a day to take care of eight dogs. They can each consume one whole salmon a day. "One dog can haul a 500 pound load of firewood by himself from the wood lot to the cabin, a half a mile." I listen to John tell me about what it's like working with dogs.

I add what I know. "I know Emit, who won the first race. I made a necklace with his lead dog done in metalwork. I sent it before Christmas from Galena."

John knows Emit, even got a dog from him. "Miles, could you make me a necklace, too?"

I have another special order to fill. The sun is just coming up on the mountains as the dogs scramble up the river bank on the other side. I know no machine of any kind could climb such a steep bank. Conscience: 'It's nice all right, but it's a lot of work, and a person needs a place to keep them, and be settled to have them, as well as have more money than I do now, so I may as well forget about having dogs.'

"Pole set ahead!" John warns me we are about to stop. He doesn't have to say anything to the dogs. There is a marten in the trap. The dogs know to stop without being told. All the dogs drop at once and start chewing ice out from between their paws as John gets the marten and resets the trap. I take note on how John does his pole set. Conscience: 'It looks a lot like mine, but he uses a thicker tree, and staples the trap, where I wire the trap, but it works the same.' This is the first time I have met another trapper and seen how it's really done, besides drawings in books. It took three years to meet another trapper!

The dogs know that when John gets on the runners it is time to go, but he says, "Hike!" All the dogs pull in unison. I'm impressed by the quiet travel, and the musher being able to look around as the dogs stay on the trail. John says, "The next one is a wolf set. I used a moose head with its rack on it for bait." John had got his winter moose early on, before the bull shed his rack. When we get to this set, John frowns. I do not know why, till he says: "I know I put it right here!" I see no set. The wind has blown here.

Conscience: *'I figured out like John has, it is good to make wolf sets in windy country where the tracks will blow out so the wolf does not know you were ever here.'* I look around for a moose head in the trees nearby, maybe he just forgot which tree it was next to.

John mumbles, "I know I put it here next to this tree, Miles. I think I caught something." Now I'm alert and excited. *It has to be a wolf!* John has told me the moose head weighs over 200 pounds with the rack on it. The spread of the rack would be close to five feet. Surely it would be hard to hide, and hard to move, so it has to be nearby.

I spot an anomaly in the environment, so holler: "Hey John, over here, looks like a broken tree!"

Up the trail a bit is a broken spruce tree. We are in a thicket of dwarf spruce that grow on the permafrost. They can be 200 years old and only three feet tall. One of them is broken. When we inspect the area, there is another broken one, then we can make out a direction. As we get into the trees ahead, we see more and more are broken treetops, till it looks like a bulldozer came through and mowed the trees down. There are maybe a hundred broken trees ahead of us in a row, about the width of a moose rack. It reminds me of the Tasmanian Devil cartoons, with devastation everywhere, made by a tornado animal. The arctic sun glares upon us. Stunted odd shaped dark trees stick up as teeth in the jaws of a dragon. All around is white. Nothing human is seen in any direction. No plane overhead, or road, or building, or power lines. Just God's work.

"Maybe a grizzly, Miles, I'm glad I have my rifle with me!"

We look at a set of tracks and know it cannot be a grizzly. I give my opinion: "Maybe wolf, but I don't think so." We are both puzzled. Up ahead we see the dead frozen animal that did this, and say at the same time; "Wolverine!" This thirty pound animal had run off with a 200 pound moose rack. Each time it tangled with a tree, he chewed it down. John and I exchange 'wolverine' stories. We both agree they are amazing:

"Miles, when they make up their mind to do something, it gets done! They never give up!" I agree. We talk about wolverines the rest of the trip. More miles are covered than I could snowshoe in a day, and we cover the ground so easily, talking, as the dogs do the work.

"This is all right John!" I don't know enough to help unhook the dogs from harness, but he tells me where each dog goes when he hands them to me to take to the dog yard. Each dog has a house with straw in it. Each dog dives in and looks around like he never saw it before, checks it out, and comes back out again. Hmm. They seem very happy, obviously love their work. There is much about this dog trip to ponder. I had been raised being told of the vast difference between us humans and animals. How we humans have nothing at all in common with animals that were put on this earth as food for us by God and have no soul. Animals do not think, or have feelings, and cannot reason or have human – like thoughts. It is mostly about stimulus response with animals, and is studied as a science, as one studies rocks. Discussing animals and spirituality in the same conversation is sacrilegious. Animals can be 'pets,' as one waters plants. But there is no discussion on a working relationship of trust. Animals depend on man; man does not depend on animals! I'm not seeing anything here with Johns dogs that can be 'proven' by science, but on the other hand, I know what 'happy' is when I see it on any animals face.

John and I get into a conversation about 'happy,' and what it means, revolving around our lifestyle. Then on to companionship and women. "Miles, I heard you put an advertisement out in 'Mother Earth News' and got some replies. How many, and what are these women like, I'm curious and might try it myself."

"It's not a yes or no question, John. Nothing has really worked out, even though I have had maybe hundreds of letters over the years. Yes, some of the women seem nice and sincere, but not all are. Here is a letter I got not long ago just so you can see what some of the women are like. I'll just show you parts of it."

This is an eight page letter hand written on yellow lined notepad paper. Dated Tuesday Jan 25.

Dear Miles,

Hi Sweetie, it's me again. You said you'd spoil me if you wrote too often. And maybe I'm spoiling you by writing so much but I want to spoil you! Also you wanted me to write more often and so I'm trying to.

Actually it was a boring day today. I didn't have work and I won't have to until Thursday. My girlfriend Dinah and her husband both work, and their kids, Scott and John were both in school, so I was on my own all day. I mostly just lay around with thoughts of you, read your letters and look at your pictures. Could you send more pictures!!

Maybe I ought to tell you a little bit more about my life here. As I told you, I live with my girlfriend and her husband Milt. I have lived with them three years. You asked me if I'd miss my relatives and friends. Not so much my relatives, but I would miss Dinah and the kids. She is like a sister to me. We are very close! But she is behind me 100% in this and thinks you and I will get along perfectly. She would never advise me to do something that she didn't think I could do or wouldn't like doing.

I've been going through my drawers and cleaning out stuff in anticipation of coming to Alaska. I figured I might as well get rid of some of the junk I've accumulated now, and not wait until the last minute.

My girlfriend Dinah said that just before I get ready to leave she'd give me a going away shower, and have everyone get me personal items like heavy sweaters, long johns, flannel nightgowns and stuff like that. I thought that was nice of her to suggest, because it's not fair that you should have to outfit me completely when I get there. I like to give people I care about things. You asked about material things meaning a lot. They don't mean all that much to me. I'd rather give things. It gives me a greater pleasure. I guess it wouldn't mean much for me to give up the material things here. I think I'd much rather be in the wilderness with you in a cabin we built snuggled together **in a sleeping bag!!**

The first two pages end, and June signs off before continuing another day. In this break John comments as he flips the pages.

"Dang, Miles. She sounds serious! Where is she? This sounds like love. I hear wedding bells!"

"Well John, she is quite the dreamer with a vivid image of our life together. You know the cute cabin with white picket fence we build together. Time spent snuggled up together."

"This doesn't sound too bad to me, Miles!"

"I look forward to meeting her all right, and she is a pretty gal, a good one to dream about. I do notice she talks about, and sees the good side from a 'females' viewpoint, but does not ask much about the rest, or indicate she comprehends the price for all this good stuff. There is that part where she is in a snow storm where she lives, lasting a few days and she is freaked out, talking about cabin fever. She is afraid and cannot imagine what it would be like to be outdoors at such a time."

"I didn't see that part, Miles, but hey she never lived this life, she's bound to be nervous. Snuggle up to her and keep her safe! Tell her what she needs to hear!" I let John know I can take care of a woman all right, while hunting for that part of the letter he didn't see.

Wed Jan 26th

We are in the middle of a blizzard! Visibility is zero, and they have declared Western Michigan under a state of emergency! The drifts are about 6 ft! I hear Alaska is having 50 degree weather. I guess you're luckier than me right now. I tried to picture myself out in the wilderness in this and it's a really scary feeling!

There is a pause and interruption as I try to find another place in the letter as John has not got time to read eight pages. I can't find it but John focuses on another part.

I feel so restless. I keep hoping for a letter from you, but the mail man didn't make it through today. I'm wondering if you have my letter yet and I'm worried about your answer, yet anxious too! I hope you don't think that I come on too strong? I just want to be with you in person, as soon as I can get there. I keep worrying that you won't wait for me; that you'll decide on the girl on the lake with the child? I hope you give me a chance first!

John interrupts, "So who is the girl on the lake?"

"It's complicated, or maybe simple. Letters arrive, some new – some from women I thought went away that come back again with a new letter, and most make assumptions of some kind. Out of the blue one might say, 'I decided to come up after all!' Other times, women think there is more going on between us than there is. It is unrealistic to keep everyone updated on what others are saying, doing, feeling, and how it is with me. There is this thought I have that the right woman will simply work out and at some point I'll know it. This woman here, June, has only written twice before. I made no commitment, just asking questions, telling her about myself, and asking her about herself. On the one hand it would be nice to meet in person all right. But on the other hand I do not want to make a serious mistake I cannot easily undo. More than one woman got me all involved before, sending me a picture of what they look like and then I find out they weigh 300 pounds, or are bald, or have one eye, stuff like that. One gal sent me a picture of her daughter instead of herself. I'd probably rather someone comes up on vacation for a visit and we see how it is between us. Not have a going away party, sell everything, and come up here to be with me as an only option."

"Wow! So what does this one look like, I forgot about that! Looks are not everything, but dang, they kind of need to be in the top 50% right?"

"Well, John, I do agree you can tell a lot by how they look to ya, and part of the bonding and attraction is going to be looks, it's a factor all right. A foxy playboy pin up is not required, and I do not want to be real picky, but yes, in the top 50% would be nice. Ha! Actually I told you already this one is in the top 10%."

"Oh, here's a part. Miles, it says here:

"I have to say you look healthy! I don't know, your complexion is so tan and you have color in your cheeks. Your cabin sure looks like a bachelor pad! I can identify some of the objects like your sleeping bag, stove, mirror, etc.... but the rest of the stuff, well???"

So what's this about a cabin?"

"I think she is looking at the houseboat and not understanding it is a boat."

"Do you think she would like a houseboat?"

"That's part of it; she says she hates the water and can't swim."

"That's a hard thing Miles, when we are river rats huh?"

"Yes, and she seems interesting, and maybe it will work out. Who knows? Do I want to give it a try? There are other women as well, who also sound interesting. Do I, at this point, choose and drop everyone else? This is what would be fair to the woman. The problem is, when I did this in the past, the woman, more than once, did not show up, got cold feet. There are other women who wrote just like this one. Can I then go back to all the rest saying, "False alarm, she never showed, now where were we?" I get an indignant line about, "How dare you," and "You made your choice, now live with it!" I pause and think, and see this is not quit how John sees it, so I finish,

"She's good looking and she's hot for me. Even if it only lasts a few days, it will be a few days without sleep." Followed by a crafty wink.

"Wow! Miles, you are so lucky. Dang. Sounds like a good idea! I think I'll put an ad out!"

Hansen Lake bear gets engine, so have to switch out engines.

CHAPTER FOUR

IN THE NEWS, BOATING SEASON, VILLAGE
ROUTINE, A MOOSE, GALLERY ART SHOW, STOLEN
RIFLE, STICK DANCE, LOST ENGINE, NEW TYPE
ENGINE, HARVEST GARDEN, LEAVE GALENA TO
NEW DESTINATION

"Wild Miles!" I turn around to see who hails me. It's one of the GI hot shot jet pilots who asks:"Did you hear the news about Nate?" I can't recall which pilot is 'Nate.' As usual, I smile and assume something will click at some point in the conversation, and I'll access the brain file called 'Nate.' "He crashed his jet three days after he got that Eagle claw necklace from you! He was wearing it! Flew his plane right into the ground in a white out. Thought he knew where he was and wouldn't follow instruments! The jet was upside down when it hit, somewhere on the Yukon." I'd had a funny feeling about his project, and hadn't really wanted to do it, but I'd needed the money. I don't believe so much in 'totem animals,' the native belief in special animal powers given to people. It didn't seem healthy to me to go around believing you are an eagle.

I answer: "Huh, well, I'm sorry to hear that. He was a friend of yours?"

"We all know each other pretty good around here on the base."

I sigh: "I hope the eagle claw gets buried with him."

The pilot has to think about that a little before answering. "No one else would wear it now, it's bad luck."

I nod: "Uh huh, well, take care, sorry again about your friend." I think about this guy on my walk across the river, and getting involved in people and their totem animals. Hmm.

I recognize this as a major event, and the beginning of an important concept in my 'animal parts' business that may take many years to gel, but begins here with a hot shot pilot crashing, wearing my work. No I'm not 'responsible' but even so, I want to be careful who I do work for and what it is I'm being part of, and why. I begin to be referred to as a 'Shaman' by many customers, especially Natives. Defined by the Eskimo as, 'One who lives in two worlds, and belongs in neither.' More times than I can count in my life I get told how some 'animal part' I transferred to someone was 'blessed,' gave them courage, changed their life in some important way. That's good for business, and I feel good to be told I am responsible for something positive. But if I am a Shaman or not, is up to others to decide.

ONCE AGAIN I think how happy I am being on 'bush time,' sleeping when I'm tired, eating when I'm hungry, going outdoors when the weather is nice. I'm reading a book when I hear footsteps outside, followed by:

"Hello! Anyone home?" There is female twittering. I open the houseboat back door and two lovely women greet me on cross country skis. I'm puzzled what they are doing here. One steps forward saying:

"We want to interview you for the local paper, is this a good time?" I nod:

"Sure, come on in, warm up, have some tea."

They furiously take notes as I ramble on about past experiences, present lifestyle, and future dreams. When I am done they look at my artwork. Both say "Oh, you do this? It's so different!" They end up each buying a necklace. One laughs:

"You should put up a sign on the river, a blinking neon one, with an arrow coming up the slough!" The other says, "When you come into town, you should see us, stop by to see me and visit for a while." They both giggle. Conscience: *"Hmm, eligible women, and I even sold some art. But a lot of talk going on these past many months not amounting to anything but flirting! But I know, am sure, we could be getting some if we really wanted. Yet no woman so far seems like real potential for something long term or serious."*

When I make my usual 'every two week' run to town, I'm wondering what the article on me is like. A lot of strangers say "Hi" to me, stop, and want to chat. The weather had got cold again. I am able to cross the river, even though I thought when I saw John last, it would be my last trip across the ice. When I check my mail and see the paper, I understand why suddenly folks are greeting me. There is my picture on the front page. An article was done, describing my life and goals. My artwork is mentioned. Hmmmm, I read it over.

Galena Snowshoe Messenger—April 15 1978

113

There's a real old fashioned Mountain Man in our midst folks, who lives alone just like the old time mountain men of the west, trapping and hunting with a black powder rifle. For his bullets, he melts down lead from old batteries, and pours and casts the bullets himself for about two cents each. Miles Martin lives alone on his river boat on the bank of a slough a few miles out of Galena. He came down last summer from Delta Junction in his boat to work for BLM, which he plans to do again this summer. He's got six months' worth of beans, flour and rice stored in his boat. Sourdough bread and rabbits are the mainstay of his diet.

Out of polished sheep's horn, agate, and fossil ivory, Miles makes medallions, earrings and necklaces with animals of Alaska inlaid in intricate metal designs. Some of his jewelry is on sale at Gordy's, Galena Commercial, and stores in Fairbanks. When his pants from the Salvation Army get to dirty, Miles throws them out. He claims this is cheaper than buying new clothes and washing them. Miles remembers when he moored his houseboat right on the Chena River in the middle of downtown Fairbanks. He got a lot of stares from people driving by the bank on their way to work as he was standing out on the deck of his boat brushing his teeth and cooking his breakfast.

Living near Galena, Miles says, is like living in the suburbs. "I see someone go by at least once a week!" When he lived in the Rampart area several years ago (see article in Alaska Magazine July of 77) he saw no people for eight full months. This year he has had about six visitors to his winter retreat. He's happy to say that his experience here has been a good one; in the Rampart area he had to hike out after his fish and meat were stolen out of his cache. His most faithful visitors this year have been a cow and calf moose who occasionally bed down against the boat.

So when you see a genuine Mountain Man on one of his rare trips to the Post Office, a man wearing homemade leather clothing and a squirrel skin cap, give him an old fashioned handshake! **There aren't many like Miles Martin left!**

I put the paper down and smile. Hmmm. Conscience: "Not quite what I'd write about myself, or quite how I see myself, but certainly this would never have been written several years ago." My private thoughts are interrupted with:

"Hi Miles, how's it going," a stranger saying hi. Conscience: "I don't seem to be the butt of all the jokes anymore. People aren't making fun of how I dress, how I think, what my plans are." Such are my thoughts as I absentmindedly open a letter.

Dear Wild Miles:

Sorry I didn't get to your letter sooner. That is a lovely watercolor on the envelope! Did you do it? What kind of feather was that you taped to the letter? It looked like some kind of duck. Anyway I put it on my mirror. I will not be able to come see you! I know you were expecting me and I thought it would work out, but other things came up. I got my job transferred so will not be coming through Galena. I will be thinking of you and your wonderful life! You are an inspiration to me, and give me hope that there are good people in the world! I hope you find someone. Oh- do you always address your envelopes upside down? What is the significance of that? Take care! **Your Stewardess Friend**

I chuckle at the letter. Conscience: "She notices we always address our envelopes upside down—ha! Will you tell her why? That the world spins the other direction for us- what's up to others is down for us? And why do all of us do things the way they have always been done- why not try it another direction?" I do not bother to reply as we have had this conversation many times. It is time to think about 'boating' more seriously, and what I want to do, where I want to go. I still have no real answers about the Koyukuk country. I hear good things about the land, and the trapping. The maps show a lot of river miles, with lots of room. There is still no one I met from there who could put in a good word, except the guy who helped me pull my boat off the sandbar during the storm. Certainly then, there must be some good people there, but I do not know how to get hold of this guy and I do not really know him, and don't feel like imposing.

I'm concerned about my boat power in the twin outboards. I know I cannot go upstream very well, and I burn way to much fuel running two engines. I think it was poor advice to set it up this way. But my chances of affording steam, for now, seem slim. I'm more remote, and for sure there is no knowledge here, and getting all the parts, the right parts would be tough. The maps are well worn by now, after a year's worth of opening, closing, folding, and dreaming. I can no longer read the map at the seams, but I have the maps memorized anyway. I lean toward trying the Koyukuk.

After making this decision I think about how I am going to make money to get supplies for the following winter. Conscience: *"It takes all summer to get ready for winter. Can I make enough money doing my art? Trapping?"* When I review the past year I know that without the BLM money I couldn't have made it. But I hadn't devoted all my time to my art either. I had to eat bum food all winter. There had been the moldy wet rice, the maggoty bear meat and gas tainted honey. I couldn't afford to replace it. Society's teachings die hard, as I realize the concept of 'a regular job' is very ingrained in all of us. 'The paycheck.' Everything else is 'just a hobby.' I do not know what kind of work would be up the Koyukuk, maybe they are 'Indian hire only' jobs. I think out loud: "Can I can fly to Fairbanks and sell the art at the art shows for Alaska House!?" This could be my plan.

Many hours have been spent reading, or doing my art, and looking up to admire the view out the houseboat window of virgin snow, spruce branches dipping and rising in the wind. There have been chickadees, ravens, and constant change of scenery. Sunsets and sunrises are filled with orange and reds. The yellow orb of the sun at high noon-barely above the trees gives a purple haze light. Now we gain seven minutes a day of light. Half an hour a week becomes noticeable. Now there is warmth to the spring sun.

My thinking is interrupted by the sound of geese. They land on the sandbar, now exposed through the snow. With the twenty-two in hand, I jump out the door and sneak through the woods. I haven't had meat like this in a couple of months. I never did really like the bear meat, and only ate it because I killed the bear. All the bears I have eaten have been full of worms. Tapeworm of some kind, but also worms I can see in the meat itself. I really look forward to something fresh that tastes good.[1] Nothing is better tasting than geese that have been eating Iowa corn—yum. The same geese in fall are skinny, tasting like seaweed. I've been eating a lot of frozen potatoes lately. They got black. They taste mushy. Eating is not fun. Grouse are good, but taste like the spruce needles they eat; not that I complain, but when there's a choice? Why not enjoy food? I'm also sure fresh food is healthier then my old food.

"Honk Honk." There is a pause. I know one of them has seen something that doesn't look right and is telling the rest to keep quiet and listen. I haven't been spotted yet, but they know I'm around. It's curious how, after a few years of listening carefully, I know by the sounds what is going on and what is going to happen. As I lay there waiting for these geese to un-nervous themselves, I get bit by the first mosquito of the year. *"I'll be darn,"* I think with a smile. *The first green shoots are yellow green on the tan sandbar.*

This is what the geese are feeding on. Behind them, the snow on the river shimmers heat waves like the Sahara. I wiggle on my belly through the still frozen snow in the shade of some red alders. The geese are even more nervous now, knowing I am here, but think I am far enough away to be of no danger. None has screamed "Oh No! Fly for your lives!" Just the quiet nervous sounds. I study them for a while as they feed on the horsetail on the edge of the slough. It takes half an hour for them to calm down. I inch closer, much like the lynx, fox, wolves do, trying to accomplish the same thing.

'Pop.' One of the geese falls over without a sound. The geese hush up and look around with long outstretched necks. Conscience: *"I thought they would have flown by now! Maybe they haven't been shot at in a while."* 'Pop,' and another one is hit, but this one flaps his wings against the wet sand a few times before falling over. All the rest take off in a wave. Maybe twenty-four geese circle overhead to memorize what I look like.

The first goose of the season is cooked in the woodstove. I take the time to pluck it, which I only do with the first goose of each season because it takes so long. I stuff this one with last year's blueberries mixed with rice, new shoots, sage, and pepper. The meal is remembered the whole rest of the year. This is a yearly ritual. Eating 'The first goose' is almost a sacred ceremony, in thanks for earth's bounty.

Poem
Upon the water's edge at dusk is such a peaceful sight
To hear the loon at sunset
Makes me think of the quiet
As the sun flattens
And changes colors
Shimmering on the surface
I sit on a rock and just look.
A duck flies
Into the weeds
And disappears

A 'squib' load is worked out for the 270 rifle. I want to be able to shoot small game with it, but have the powerful loads for the moose and bear handy, like I do with the pistol. A squib load is a load using lead, not copper, and the projectile travels at under a grand, so close to subsonic, meaning 'quiet.' A normal 270 bullet travels three times faster, at three grand. A lot of paper is filled with little holes. A lot of data collecting followed by 'hmmm.' My conscience and I have a lot of conversations.... *"Let's try the gas check, looks like the base of the lead is deforming."* That is tried, but the powder charge has to be increased too much to drive it down the barrel. *Hmmm.* That idea is scratched. I find some old beer bottles, and practice shooting through the opening, and blowing the backs out, without touching the sides at 200 feet. I can do a dozen in a row now. At the same distance I can put a bullet through the opening of a beer can without touching the top at 100ft, and hit the can at 300 yards (my conscience says more like 200 yards). This is 'good enough.' I still practice though, just because it is 'fun.'

More ducks, cranes, swans, robins, and geese come each day till there is a non-stop sound of bird life twenty-four hours a day. At first it is hard to get used to, hard to sleep, but then I get used to it, just as I had on the Yukon in past years.

Once the snow melts I can work on the bottom of the boat. There are places that need fiberglass repairing. One piece hangs down from the bottom. I wonder if this caused increased fuel consumption, and contributes to running out of gas getting here. This would relive me of the issue of being all my fault for not carrying enough gas. The engines are looked over. New oil is put in the lower units, fresh gas in the tank, a new fuel filter installed, controls greased. All these things like grease, and lock washers, had been on a list and acquired over the winter. I take my time, and work on the boat an hour a day, then go out hunting, or doing my art work. I use up all my art supplies, so metalwork comes to a grinding halt. I am able to continue art using items from the garbage pile—bones, claws, antler, teeth and such. The boat is ready to run. There is not much to do now until the ice goes out, and I can cross the river by boat.

I have learned when hunting, that it is better to let the game come to me, instead of me doing a lot of walking and making noise. I find a patch of dry grass on the slough bank, and just sit and read for a while. Nothing stirs. The birds would let me know if anything is moving around me. I set the book aside and take a nap in the heat of the spring sun.

I awake with a start, but know enough, even in my sleep, not to make a sudden move or noise. Something is different, but I do not know what that is yet. I wait for brain cells to come up to speed. My unsleeping conscience has alerted me. Then I hear it, steps coming toward me on the path. The squirrels chatter to let the world know. I do not move, but keep an eye out. The walking comes closer and louder, but I do not know for sure what it is.

A small moose walks out in the grass, passes only twenty feet by me, and stands in the water on the ice of the slough. I hadn't planned on shooting a moose, since it is a lot of meat. I had made up my mind a month ago on that. But this is a small moose, and such a perfect shot, in a good location. Conscience: *"Sometimes in this lifestyle it is not us that decides how life will be, but life, that tells us what we shall eat, and when!"* I know I have the squib load in the chamber, and if I try to eject it, the moose will hear me and be gone before I can get a good shot off. I think the squib load will work at this close range, but I'm not sure.

I'm already laying in a perfect position for the shot, do not even have to move. I had expected any animal I shot at to be near the slough. I ease the safety off. From only forty feet away, I take careful aim at where I've studied the heart is from this position, from doing many an autopsy. *"Right behind the elbow and up six inches."* There is a small 'pop,' not even as loud as a twenty-two. A twenty -two bullet is .22 inches in diameter and the 270 is .270 inches, so not a huge difference in diameter! The moose slowly turns to see what made the noise. I do not move. I know from past experience the moose is fatally hit, because he didn't feel or hear the hit. He bends over to get a drink of water and looks puzzled. He wonders why his vision is failing, but before that thought gets far, he falls over dead. I'm glad he didn't feel anything.

The houseboat is just around the corner. The moose is on the slick ice. It is easy to move the moose on the ice after gutting and skinning. The meat floats in the foot deep freezing cold water, and is cleaned and cooled within minutes of death. The ice is very clean and slick, so the meat is transported with a rope, and is slithered to the boat. Quarters are hung from a tree by the boat. There are no flies out yet. The night temperatures hover at freezing. The day temperatures in the sun might be sixty, but in the shade under fifty, so this is perfect meat hanging conditions. This had been considered when deciding if I should take this moose. Sometimes such a situation is a gift from the Gods—and it is easy for me to understand primitive people who believe in such things. I mean, I had hunted all winter and never seen a moose. I could plan a perfect shot all my life and never would it turn out as expected- no matter how much effort –thinking, planning, money, got spent. Here I was, sleeping without a care in the world and the perfect situation is given to me. How is this possible? What would the odds be if one tried to plan it out? *"What day do you plan to get your subsistence hunt?"* This hunt shows what a silly question that is.

I do not know what to do with the meat in the long term though, because the weather is warmer each day, flies will be out within days. The ice will go out and I'll be leaving here soon. *"Let's make jerky!"* I put string between trees and cut thin slices of moose to hang up. Some of the meat is partially frozen so shaves paper thin, other parts are soft and bloody and are hard to keep an inch thick. It all gets hung up, except the 50 pounds of heart, liver, and kidney, which is my breakfast lunch and dinner. The thin pieces dry in a day, and still look red. This taste good. This is so much different than the jerky I had made in the past. *Surely there is an art to making jerky, and it is not as simple to do as we read about in 'how to' books!* Some of the thicker pieces have trouble drying. Flies start coming around. The sun burns the hanging meat. The first rain gets it wet again. Most of it dries 'ok,' but some is not drying out. The fly eggs are hatching before the jerky dries. I'm picking maggots out of the last pieces as they dry. I save this anyway, because you just never know when hungry times might come along, and no use wondering why I threw out food! There is only twenty pounds of really top quality jerky you'd be proud to serve your mother. This equals about fifty pounds of fresh meat. There is some OK jerky, and then some jerky most dogs would turn down. I'm just so excited that I'm eating real Mountain Man food, I do not care how it comes out, so long as my tummy holds it down!

I come across the bullet I fired, The bullet lodged in one of the chambers of the heart, *'dead center.'* The bullet is still in perfect shape, without a scratch on it. Conscience: *"I can re-load it; put it in front of another charge of powder. Wouldn't it be cool to wait, and kill another moose with it! Tell the story, on how I killed two moose with one bullet!"*

😊 :)

"Yeah yeah sure right!" I roll my eyes up- "You and your hair brained ideas." But I stop chewing long enough to smile.

The water rises fast when the Yukon finally breaks up. I'm used to this, but it is always amazing to me. It is like water in a bathtub. The houseboat is safe in the trees, but I want the water to rise enough to set it afloat. That would save me a lot of work. But the water drops without setting the boat free, and there is a lot of mud left behind. I set the jack under the boat to get the weight off the barrels it sets on. The jack sinks in mud. I have to go find a piece of plywood to set the jack on. The jack almost slips off the plywood and I save it just in time, or the boat would have fallen to the ground!

Once the boat is setting in the mud it will not budge. *"I should have lowered it on poles!"* I reply to my conscience: "Hey you are supposed to be awake and looking out for me- what's going on?" The suction of the mud holds the houseboat in place. I have to wade the slough with a rope and winch to get the right purchase to pull the boat in the water from a tree across the slough. The first effort pulls the tree up by the roots. I have to wade back over in the ice filled water. My feet go numb. My boots fill with water. There is the 'ft ft' sound each time I take a step. *"This better work now."* I crank on the winch, but the boat will not budge. I have to pry on it, then the boat slides a few inches forward. I have to crank up tension with the winch again. It is a very slow process, of walking the cold water, coming back to the boat, going back to the tree, then back to the boat. Three hard days later I'm still at it. This is not fun or romantic; it's just bitching hard backbreaking, cold, muddy, work! I'm anxious to get out on the river, and frustrated at the 'many days' delay! I heard a boat, so now feel like summer has started without me!

With one last heave-ho, the houseboat slides into its element. There is the tinkle of ice bumping the sides, and gentle rocking. I feel like an olive in an icy Martini. The houseboat no longer looks new, but a dozen years old. The deck and sides are covered in mud. Smoke stains from the chimney and chipping paint from a winter cold outside, hot inside, gives a patchwork quilt look to it. The hull has been scraped, banged, pushed on, pulled with a winch, and loaded like a barge. I smile though because it's 'mine.' My conscience reminds me: *"A houseboat that maybe only the father of it could love. Certainly it hasn't helped me pick up any women. Sigh. You ain't exactly spiffy."* My houseboat just bobs in the water in front of me. The happily grinning olive in the mixed drink, making me drunk with affection.

The engines both start on the first crank. *"Way to go!"* The Gods smile on me. The purr of the engines sounds like the hoofs of all those horses on a dirt road, waiting to open up. I have to smile at all the memories that sound brings. All the hours I've spent hearing it, as I try to read a map, wondering where I am, all those hills, swamps, and lakes I passed. Conscience: *"Ready to do her again? The Koyukuk? Warpath Indians be damned? I'll be a target up on the roof as I am steering."* I sigh. Hate to get picked off by a sniper. Country where white man hasn't got any say so, and isn't welcome, and a place still part of the United States that no civilized person even knows exists. It is rather intriguing.

I ease the houseboat out to the main river. The water level is still above flood stage, and running with trees and icebergs. The current stirring up the mud banks gives the river turbulence, and the color of chocolate malt being mixed in a blender.

I have to go very slow through the churning foam and weave between forty ft drift logs. I end up a mile downstream of Galena by the time I get across the Yukon. In the slack water against the bank, I work my way back upstream. The fish rack where John Stam keeps his dogs and gear seems like a good enough place to pull in.

"You're the first boat in the water Miles, what you doing out there in that crap?"

"I heard a boat the other day John!" "Yea, probably someone on the water at the edge of the ice before it broke up!"

As John looks out across the river I crossed, he is shaking his head mumbling about 'insanity.' I tell him it's time for me to mosey on over to the post office. Someone from a log cabin with a blanket for a door hollers.

"I thought you were spending breakup across the river Miles." I holler back to a face in a window:

"I did. The river just broke." An answer from the window:

"Of course it just broke! It is customary to wait at least a week before going out on it. It's very unpredictable after it breaks." I laugh:

"Guess I just broke tradition huh?" Conscience: "I'm a river man, and how can I explain how it is? Wanting to see it in all its moods. ..... but I sort of am concerned about my mail too, and BLM." I wonder if there will be an early job here opening the buildings for the season. I probably have to send in an application, and there will be a deadline date for this. I'd guess it would be 'soon.' But there is no word from BLM. I wonder if politics has come into play here, seeing how I don't get along with the honchos. Hmm. The people here who know me are glad to see me. I yell, "Hey Grandpa, I got my winter moose!" I give my grandpa some meat and he chuckles, doesn't say anything about a winter moose in spring. I see Edgar, the Huntington's, and others. New art goes to the two stores, Dawns and Gordy's. The Dall Sheep piece I did sells for $200 to the first person I show it to. I know that in Fairbanks I could have got twice that much. In Seattle, twice that again. But the civilized world is far away. Life is less costly here, with no rent, electric or phone, so I settle for what I can get. Some of the GIs know my work now and look me up. They like my stories too, but they are such suckers, and so green about Alaska. Kids from Nebraska, never been out of state till now, sent to Alaska, never been off the base.

The jets fly over us constantly, looking like real high tech stuff. Rumor has it this is a place for the best training and testing of military secret stuff, nice and 'out of the way.' Some 'weird stuff' sometimes gets seen, with stealth planes, whisper helicopters, and top secret honchos in fancy cars with tinted windows. No one knows who they are, why they are here, and it is not wise to ask many questions. There's a line on the runway that reads, "If you cross this line you may be shot." That makes itself pretty clear. These are not 'wilderness lovers,' this is the forefront of civilization, and a prime target in a war. Not especially the place I want to be. The guys are all right, fighter pilots and such; real smart about jets and war, but amazingly ignorant about winter, Alaska, basic survival, and more important, 'killing,' 'death' and 'courage.' Never seen blood before, scared shitless of bears, and other related subjects. I find this amazing. The top trained killers in the country, squeamish about blood. Most seem to have never killed nothing 'one-on-one.' Can drop a bomb on a village and kill every living thing though. The whole 'war' subject is touchy.

They like my art. I sell it to them. But most military buyers haven't got a clue about where they are, or what they are involved in. "A real brainwash job. I remember it was the same when I was in." I try to smile about it… so as not to work myself into a dither over something that I can't do anything about.

I get into a routine of spending the early hours of the morning, like 4:00 am doing my artwork. When everyone else gets up I make my rounds. There is a coke to sip at the cafe, check my mail, go see Grandpa, on up to Gordy's, visit Dawn, check with the GI's, over to the cafe for lunch, where I meet with people I made appointments with. Then do my deals there while I eat. Everyone laughingly calls the cafe 'my office.' I bring in about $50 a day. I work maybe two hours a day. My conscience reminds me: *"Well, I don't work at all really. I make my money having fun."* But $50 a day keeps me even, ahead a little, $100 a day is what it takes to get ready for next winter. I need gas and supplies to head out. I want to leave like, 'soon.' I spend evenings reading, then go to bed early. The time on my boat is my 'private time' that most everyone respects, and I get few visitors here. I 'make the rounds' and people know where I will be at any given time, or they meet me at 'the office,' so know where to leave money or messages. I drop art off at various places, give people a cut for letting me use them as a drop. This way I don't need a place of business. *"Purdy slick Wild Miles."*

😄 :)

I'm expecting word to come from BLM on my usual summer job. I almost feel guilty for getting paid having fun. *"What do you do for a living?"* I answer myself: "I get paid doing what I love!" next question: *"What do you do for entertainment?"* Reply: "I work!" It isn't the usual way of thinking. I'm almost relived when I get word I'm not rehired at BLM. I do not look forward to having a boss. This does mean though, that it might be longer before I can 'move on' toward Koyukuk country. *"But surely by winter."*

Every few days I move the boat to somewhere else, just so the view out the window changes. There are always ducks out the window, fish off the bow. I eat well. I have a trade going at the cafe, and can eat all summer in trade for my art. I get reloading supplies from Gordy in trade. I have a deal going at the store and trade for gas for the boat. It's a nice life, all in all. Not how I'd like to live 'forever,' to boring, but in a lazy way, it's peaceful.

"Hey John, how's life treating you?" John answers up: "Pretty good Miles, what's happening?" I mention a previously discussed subject, "Well you know that knife I made, that you were looking at? I'd like to do the trade you mentioned before, for your wood boat. I know it's old, but it should work just to get back and forth across the river when I want to keep the houseboat up the slough." John answers: "Sure Miles sounds good. I'm never going to use that boat anyway, and that's a nice knife!"

I set one of the twin outboards from the houseboat on this old style wood long narrow twenty-four ft boat. The lines of it are very beautiful, with a nice pointed upswept bow. I do not transfer any controls from the houseboat, only the one engine, and I use it with the tiller. So now I keep the houseboat at different places up and down the slough. I cross back and forth every day in my new 'runabout.' *"We're coming up in the world now, a two boat family."*

I finally decide I need to go to Fairbanks. I can get some fresh food for summer, and check with BLM on work and sell my art, even do a show. I had been told at Alaska House I could just show up in early summer and they would plan a show within a few days, advertise it and make it happen. It's nice for me as I do not like running the cash register. Someone else making change while I talk and hand over art works well.

The flight to town goes as expected. I sell all my inventory of art in three days. I get needed supplies. BLM had no answer for me, but I have a contact to keep in touch with who will keep me posted about job openings to apply for.

BACK IN GALENA.

Every morning I pass the benches on the riverbank I'd seen when I first got here and had asked about. People sit here, and it is always full. Sometimes I have to meet people here to close trade deals. I have to wait today as someone is late showing up. I ask curiously: "So how many fish in the box?" I see everyone is watching the fish wheel turn. I get an answer. "Over 200 in four hours." Someone else says.

"Yesterday there were 800 before it got checked, and that's about the max it can hold!" Hmmm I'm more curious and ask:

"How many females and males?" I know enough by now to know the males run first, ahead of the females, so the ratio tells how far into the run we are.

"Not even 50/50 yet." So I know the run hasn't peaked yet. A boat is way off in the distance. Someone makes a comment:

"Looks like Bob's right on time, making his run of illegal eggs. Must have a good load, boat sits low. Must be what, 1,000 pounds?" Another Native: "Naw, more like 800, no way it's a thousand" I give my opinion:

"Closer to a thousand, if that's a fifty horse merc." A snort of a reply: "She-it, you can't run no merc and haul that, he needs Johnson, I've told him that!" Someone else joins in:

"You heard of them new Yamaha's? I hear George has one and swears he gets twelve mile to a gallon with a load!" the guy who snorted replies:

"He's full of… fish scales, no two cycle does that! He wishes!" First guy:

"Hey, have you heard who his girlfriend is sleeping with?" I don't hear the reply but hear the answer:

"Sally? No shit? I thought it was Paul she had it in for!" back and forth: "Naw, seen 'em together myself." Someone passing by overhears and mumbles :

"I'll be darn"

"Game warden isn't coming till tomorrow noon, spread the word." I chime in: "You mean you guys know when the game warden is coming?" the snorter:

"God Miles, you need to be on the bench more often and keep up on things or you'll get in trouble!" *Hmmmm.*

And I cannot believe, that this conversation goes on from six am 'till midnight, non-stop seven days a week. What scares me? What scares me is, I find myself actually sitting here, thinking it's a great life. We talk about how many fish today compared to yesterday, last year, other years, other wheels, future catches, catches by various fisherman. We then compare boats and loads, and who can run the boat best, compared to last year, next year, and this person's son, and wife. This leads to who they all sleep with, will sleep with, might sleep with, and, well, it's easy to see how the conversation can go on and never end! All very fascinating stuff! I add:

"I still say closer to 1,000 pounds! Look at how it's on step. Any less weight and it would climb out better, any more weight, and it wouldn't get up at all. Unless he doesn't load the boat right!" all say at once:

"Hey, he knows how to load a boat!" I add,

"Unless he wants to fool us?"

"No, he cares about how much gas he burns."

"Hey look, here comes his pick-up plane, it's ole Henry flying again, he must be out of jail!"

"Hasn't got his pilots permit." "What a bunch a crap, he flies better than…."

"Hey did you hear how he landed crossways on the runway in Fairbanks? Like freaked those guys out! He figured he had enough room, why bother to land and do all that taxi stuff. He headed right where he wanted. He only needs 100 feet. Book says 300, but you know how the books are." We all agree. We know how the books are. We talk about how stupid White people are, and how forked their tongues are.

I start showing up on the bench, like a regular. *"This is better than TV!"* I learn more about the Indians, the land, and the river. I learn what they want, what they dream about. There are no secrets here. Who and what you are comes out. There is no place to hide here. These people know when you get up, go to bed, who you look at. They know what your income is, ('reported' and otherwise). Nothing escapes these people. We think pretty much alike. We do not understand the government, Fish and Game, civilization. I shrug my shoulders.

"Hey Wild Miles, You want a plot in the community garden?" I curiously ask,

"What's that all about?" Someone I don't know tells me,

"If you want a garden you can have as much room as you want. We have a community plot, and a rotor-tiller. The university gives us experimental seeds. We tell them how they work out, and in return we get the seeds for free. You can grow as much as you want, just let us know how much to plow up!" I reply:

"I'm not sure I will be around here long enough to harvest a garden! But I can get a garden started, and someone else can harvest it I guess. But it would be nice to grow my own food and not have to buy it." I think to myself: *"Maybe I could plant, and come back to harvest. Anyhow, worth giving this a shot, see where it goes."*

With the usual blade of grass bouncing from my mouth, I walk the dirt path through Galena making my rounds. As time passes I get more restless. At the cafe I regularly jump up and head out. The waitress asks,

"Places to go, things to do Miles," I look puzzled- asking:

"Have I said that before?" Waitress:

"Only about a hundred times! Ha ha!" I sheepishly:

"Yeah well...." Conscience: "I can't think of where it is I need to go, but it's somewhere, hmmm."

I grin, "Gotta go see a man about a horse!" and I'm off to who knows where. Conscience: "Is this life is getting to boring, or am I just horny? Maybe a woman would settle me down."

While hanging out in the café one day I write a poem. It's not a true story but it could be.

Poem
The Talk of The Cafe
He couldn't deny,
that it wasn't true,
because they say,
that it was them two.

And at the cafe',
well him and Mary,
was the talk of the day.
So if you ask me,
well I guess that Sue,
she just couldn't see.

But then we all knew,
beforehand anyway,
what she would do to her guy.

I was the one you know,
who heard her yell that day,
"That's good enough for you!"
Then she began to cry,
when she shot those two,
right there in the cafe'

"Oh what did I do!"
She started to say,
as she shot herself too.

Well they buried them three,
All'n the same awful day,
which is all they could do.
Sue Hated Mary,
and he hated Sue,
but they all died that day.

Between you and me?
Their boy's the same way,
and tis what they all say,
over there at the cafe

"Wild Miles weren't you in Ruby last summer? Ran into someone who met you there." I reply:

"I was only there briefly. I was in Tanana first." A conversation is started with someone I don't know, and don't ask who this is, but they ask me,

"Tanana huh? Did you meet the nine Mile Flash? Heard he only got as far as Ruby, his sailboat caught on fire, some woodstove problem. I hear it's still on the beach, and he's there working."

"Yes I'd heard of the nine Mile Flash, met him with Bush Charlie."

"I'll be darn. I kind of hoped he'd make it to the ocean. He spent a lot of time working on the boat, seemed like he had a lot of stick to it energy. Sorry to hear about him. Think he'll rebuild it and go on?" A shrug,

"Who knows?" I end the conversation,

"Well, see ya around!" Conscience: "Now what in the heck is that guys name anyway--I should know it.... Oh well."

I write to Maggie my longtime friend from New York.

Dear Maggie,

I know you will not understand all these 'name places' but it does help me think to write it down! If I don't go to the Koyukuk country, another idea would be, to follow the Yukon to the mouth and the ocean, then around the coast, and up the Kuskokwim River. There are no roads at all to the Kusko country. This river looks about a thousand miles long. There are only small villages on the whole river, and no white villages. I don't know much about this country though, but there are no rumors about hostility. I imagine going on's in this country is pretty unlikely to ever reach white man news. I do not believe there are any roads through here—not even winter roads.

I ramble on to someone I will never see again who I once loved.

Sunshine, Miles

Once again I go over the names circled on my well-worn maps. I have heard about all these places. There is the Koyukuk, Innoko, Porcupine, Black, Chandler, Charley, Kobuk, Sheenjek, Nowitna, Kantishna, and many others. I could get to any of them from here if I wished. I'm on the river community bench talking to the elders. Old Edgar is in his 90's. He frowns as a boat comes around the corner. Immediately everyone guesses who it is, how many fish they haul. Edgar tells me:

"I remember the days before these motor boats. The days of pole boats. We used to use dogs to line the boats along the beach. It used to take three days to get to fish camp. If it takes an hour now, people complain!" He spots a log coming.

"Got to run, going to fetch that log for firewood!" He dashes off to his boat, hobbling like all get out in his enthusiasm to have this great log. I go with him just for something to do. We lash the log to his boat and he slowly drags it to shore. It will take a while because he only has a small motor.

We talk about the Kantishna River again. He's telling me of memories from thirty years ago.

"It's 300 miles long, all twisty and shallow, but don't be fooled! I used to get the barge through. There were no trappers or homesteads or no one for 300 miles. I'd get to Lake Minchumina. This is the largest lake in the interior; eight miles across, in the exact center of the state, only fifty miles from Mt. McKinley. They have a maintained runway there to get mail in. About twenty people live there." He goes on to tell me about the muddy flats again. I've had him tell the story a few times.

"Hundreds of lakes, more than you can count, with no one there. I would see moose, bear, swans, fish like you wouldn't believe. This area must be fifty X twenty miles of nothing but lakes connected to each other." I try to picture what this must be like, as we tow the forty foot log toward the shore. "There are spruce trees along the banks, and places with a lot of white birch hanging over the water too. Every bend has a beaver house. Some houses are as big as our Galena houses, with many generations of untouched beaver in them." This sounds like a tale from 200 years ago, and the kind of talk heard by the fur traders, stories read in old books and journals, repeated with a sigh of 'those must have been the days huh?' Yet here I am, and they are not 'stories of long ago.' It is possible nothing here in the Kantishna country has changed. No one I have talked to knows.

There are other places with more sketchy information, country with even more room than this, like the Kuskokwim country. I'd guess there are not ten white people there in a thousand miles of country. Edgar and I tie off his log on the beach. Everyone will know it is his, and leave it alone. "Edgar, I heard the White people are coming to your home to put in water and a toilet!" He snarls:

"Yea! Now I will have to pay all this money to get water, and I can't use the outhouse. I told them I don't want this, but there is no choice, they come in my home without permission and put it in." Even as we speak, times are changing. I keep notes in my journal that no one listens to. They think this life will be forever, this life they talk about and live. I know we are part of 'the ending times.' I know about civilization. What civilization does not understand, it destroys. If someone is doing something other people cannot do, it is discrimination, jealousy, and it is stopped. I don't bother upsetting Edgar about this. He says:

"Thanks Miles" I wave.

"See you on the bench I guess." As I walk the path back to the river front, seagulls swirl in the clear blue sky. Spruce trees jut up at all angles along the river front as far as the eye can see. I take a deep breath of the fresh air.

I've got my houseboat in the water in a new place up the slough. I make the daily trip across the river, at a different time than usual. I already know everyone on the bench is watching, and speculating on my change in routine. I can hear them now:

"Ole Wild Miles is getting restless I think."

"Could be, could be. My guess is he isn't going to stay around for another winter. Wonder what his past is that he always has to keep moving on? Notice how he never talks about it?"

"Yeah well if he starts sleeping with that waitress, she'll keep him here, settle him down!"

"You think he's getting any?"

"If he was, he wouldn't be so restless now, would he?" A village knows more about you than you know about yourself. All the things you don't want to think about, that's what gets talked about all over the village the most. Conscience: *"The only thing I have to remember is; they mean well. It's just the village way, it is not considered rude. It is part of survival in a small place."* It doesn't bother me like it does some people. I'm not someone who cares to keep secrets. I'm someone who, if given half a chance, is open and honest. With me it is more about 'trust.' It is not what you know about me I care about. It is what you do with that information. Use it to help me or use it to hurt me.

When I get to my houseboat with the runabout, there is a change. The back door is open. I have had a visitor. Someone has run off with my 270 rifle. "Some God *&%#!! GI Thieving mother&*%$!" I look around to see what else might be missing. I see nothing else stolen. I've about had it with those hot shot jet pilots. *I'm sure it must be one of them.* They have little respect for Alaska, another way of living, other cultures. Whoever it was, probably is the one who took my traps earlier. As long as it didn't become a continuing problem that is ok, but it's depressing to think of some pilot who makes 100 grand a year, coming around on a snow machine that cost more than all the money I've made in my life, taking some traps and $100 of fur, that might represent several weeks of wages to me, as a trapper. What is an appropriate response here? A gun set? Maybe I should get advice from the cop again.

Dear Dad: Hello! So how did you like the jerky I sent? I haven't heard if you got it. I haven't heard from you since I saw you over Christmas. I hope life is treating you good these days. I am fine. As I write this letter, a duck lands on the water in front of the window I look out. I have been selling and trading my artwork, and though I'm not getting rich at it, I enjoy it. I have a garden going in the community garden plot. Cold weather root crops grow best in Alaska. Beets, turnips, carrots, all grow good...

I write about what I've been doing the past month or so since I last wrote...

Hope all's going well with you! **Sunshine, Miles**

"So Grandpa, you know about the lower Yukon? What would I be getting into if I went that way? What about the ocean, would my houseboat handle it for a few days along the coast?" Grandpa studies me thoughtfully before answering:

"Long way to go to chase a dream." This is not the answer I'm looking for. I don't need a lecture on wisdom. I say:

"I know Grandpa, but this isn't where I belong. I like Galena ok, but I'd like a smaller river. There is too much open space here. Too much waves and wind on the river. There is too much traffic on this big river, with barges and fisherman, and everyone knowing my business even if I cross the river. I do not like the military so close. The jets coming in low over me on the trapline ruins the peace of the whole day. I cannot think good thoughts when a fighter jet comes in just over the treetops, breaking the sound barrier." Grandpa shrugs his shoulders in understanding. I go on:

"I'm still young. I can settle down later. This is the time in life to see places, decide what I want to do, where I want to be. Once a person makes a decision, they have to live with it. Then it becomes very hard to ever pull up roots and check out alternatives." Grandpa:

"Well, you could get to the mouth, but the ocean is not a good place for your top heavy flat bottom boat. Maybe you could get it on a barge though. There is always a way if it is what you decide to do." I sigh:

"Well, there is still trouble up the Koyukuk, and it looks like it will get worse before it gets better." I hear in Galena that part of the problem in the remote native villages is the White people who bring in alcohol, illegal to sell, and create drinking problems the village is trying to get away from.[2]

I spend time talking to the old timers and Indians, about places I might go that would suit what I'm looking for. Nothing sounds quite right. I continue to make my rounds, and bring in money. I really don't have a handle on 'profit,' since I have no concept of 'business' yet. I do not know how to measure 'trades.' I trade for things I do not need, then re-trade what I traded for, and trade at a loss! I enjoy it, but in terms of 'making a living' where does it leave me? Often I have to go track people down more than one time to collect my money, which occupies my time. Sometimes people do not pay at all! What can I really do about it? Mostly I write it off, but I do not want to face this, that this is a 'loss.' All I focus on is the days I sold $100 of art, and am excited about it. The bottom line though, is that after time goes by, have I got money saved up? No! I eat, I live. I keep even. I pay for gas to cross the river every day, keep up with 'parts' for the travel, spark plugs, oil, filters, props I ding up. I still do not know what it cost to run a boat, which I later average out to be about $10 an hour for every hour it's run. Boating is an amazingly high cost of transportation. I'd guess it's costing me a good $15 a day just to run the boat back and forth across the river. I forget my 'material cost and shipping' for the art things I make. Even business people who study such matters often have trouble knowing for sure what their profit margin is. I have had no training in such matters, and do not know how to do bookwork. I'm an artist, not a business man. *I cant afford an accountant! Geez!*

I'm trying to get ahead enough to buy a big wad of gas and food for winter, like I have done in the past. I can't go into 'winter' with no supplies! There will be little art business going on once winter comes. This is information I'm only vaguely conscience of and do not want to face, or it would discourage me too much. This may well be why I'm so nervous and restless. I'm still 'happy' but not entirely at peace. A person can't live forever on vacation. At some point a person has to get serious about the bills, and basic needs.

I'm doing my artwork in the early morning as usual. It's 4:00 am and the sun is up; coming through the window as the boat lazily drifts at its mooring. This early morning low sun through the window is great light for me to get my delicate sawing done by. There is a loud 'twang.' The boat vibrates. With puzzled frown I stop my work. Again 'twang,' and another vibration through the boat. A third time this happens. "Something is going on with my bow rope," is all I can think. I open the front door to look. "Maybe the wind has drifted me, and spun the boat around a log or something." A cow moose with twin calves, calmly looks up at me with no fear. They had all three tripped over my bow rope while crossing the slough here. The three moose stand there making eye contact with me and are only curious. The sun is behind them in a still low sunrise. The reflection of the moose in the water, all the green willow leaves hanging over the water, and the backdrop of the tan sandbar in the distance is postcard material. I am able to get a picture with my camera from this twenty foot distance. The cow bends her head and nudges the calves out of the water. I talk to them, wish them well. They stand on shore and shiver a moment, before walking up to the willows to feed. As I work on my art, I hear them feeding around my boat.

"Hello!" I hear voices outside the houseboat, and wonder who is visiting. It is two of the Indians I visit sometimes in the old village. I greet them and invite them in.

"Sit down, I'm just finishing up my art piece for the day, then I'll head across to the village. What's going on?" I'm munching on some of the last of the jerky I made. The best is already gone, and now I'm into the maggoty stuff. They ask,

"Have you got any coffee? Aren't you going to offer us anything to eat. That's polite when you have guests you know." I am reluctant to offer the jerky I'm eating because it is so bad. The 'once froze' potatoes thawed, turned black and mushy and fermented. I'm still eating them. I really haven't got anything better to offer, so I'm embarrassed. I explain:

"This is all I have, old jerky. It didn't come out very good. Flies got to it. I had to wipe the eggs off, but some dried on the outside and I didn't get it off."

They both grin. "Oh, that's fine. You should have seen how ours came out! The eggs hatched, and we have dried maggots to eat with the jerky!" we all laugh. They think my meat is just fine.

Conscience: "Are they just being polite? Maybe then, I'm not the only one having trouble making jerky and maybe even Indians get flies in the meat. They seem to honestly like the meat, it's hard to say." They seem hungry, and ask for more, so it can't be too bad to eat. They wave good bye, and I get back to my routine on the boat.

The very next day.... "Hello!" I frown: *"Another visitor?"* I guess I like to cross the river and see people on my own terms, but I like my space, and my houseboat is sort of my place to be left alone. I open the door.

"Oh Hi John John!" A lot of the Indians have the same last and first name. When the White people gave them names not so long ago, this came about somehow.

There is 'Sam Sam' 'Piper Piper' and here is 'John John' coming to visit. He ducks his head and comes aboard the houseboat saying,

"Here's your gun, thanks!" I'm flabbergasted. I glance at my gun and it is muddy, rusted, banged up, like it's been in the bottom of a boat for a month. I kept it well oiled, cleaned it after every shooting, and put it in a gun case, except when actually hunting. I absolutely do not know what to say. He sees my expression and frowns:

"What's wrong with you? I thought we were friends!" I angrily reply:

"I thought we were friends too John John! How come you stole my rifle?"

Now he is angry saying: "You White people are all alike, never understand Indian! I thought you were different! But you're not!"

Normally I do all I can to smooth things over, try to get along, overlook small slights and problems. This is my rifle, that my life depends on. I cannot afford to replace it. I have learned about this gun, know how it shoots. A man's gun is like a sacred thing. Like the old mountain men of the past, you could steal his horse, his traps, his cabin, but never, never screw with his gun! So I blow up. "You come into my home without asking me, you walk off with my only rifle I need to survive with, you don't leave a note, you don't ask me, you keep it for a month, then have the gall to return it to me all messed up, and want to know why I'm upset? You're lucky I don't break it over your head! Why did you steal it! Why didn't you just ask to borrow it?"

"Because I thought we were friends, but we are not I see! Indian way is that what is mine is yours! There is nothing I have that you cannot take if you need it! What's yours is mine! If I need to use something of yours, I can. This is Indian way!" He glowers at me and throws me my rifle, adding, "You keep your gun! For you White man, it is 'things' you own. You don't want people to touch what is yours! Your land, your home, your gun! Make big pile, call it yours, mad at rest of world!" He stomps out the door, and that is the last I ever see of him.[3] I write to Maggie…

Dearest Maggie: Hello! How you doing? You never commented on the jerky I sent. I think it's pretty cool to make jerky. I read about it all those years! Now I finally get to actually make some. A very exciting time for me, and want to share it with others, but all I get is silence. My dad never answered, you never answered, my mail order women never answered. I only got one comment, "What did you send me Miles, a dried dead mouse? Ha Ha, what utensil do you eat this with? A hammer? Ha Ha." So I assume it either got moldy in the mail, or it isn't something anyone understands or something. (Not quite Slim Jim's' huh?) It is a big thing for me, but part of a new life I can't seem to share with my past. Oh well. Just try to understand, I didn't mean any harm, and you don't have to eat it. I was just over excited about this Mountain Man food.

😄 :)

Speaking of the mail order gal. I talked about her before. June is her name, and yes I know 'here we go again.' She got mad at me for who knows what. She changed her mind and is not coming up to see me. All that love was so much dust in the wind, so much ink on paper. In some ways I've about had it with love. I suspect at least part of the problem is me though, because logic tells me it is not likely the entire world has gone mad, but me. Me who has issues. Me there is something wrong with. If I were a woman, would I want me? Probably I'm a handful to say the least. So I'm not entirely optimistic about me learning all about love. There are others now, always it is others – something just around the corner. The next one will be the right one. But never this one. Never mind.

I still do not know where I'm going from here, and I need to save up more money to move on. I'm happy enough here for now, I just know this is not the place I will settle down. There are a lot of good people here…

and I go on to tell her about things happening in my life. The good people I meet, Grandpa, and selling art. I explain my feelings about 'John John…

He honestly believes what he tells me, and I wonder if it was just a cultural misunderstanding. I am unsure I can accept this way of thinking, though I hear it sometimes, even among the Whites. It is basically a communist thought, that there is no private ownership. Those goods belong to the community, and get shared. Those who need it, use it. It doesn't matter who paid for it. When I think about it, I can understand how it works well in certain cultures. Like where everyone has about equal things. You go borrow someone's bow and arrows; next time, he borrows yours. If you get a moose, you share, next time it might be him who gets a moose, and that too gets shared. It 'sounds good' in theory.

This Indian lives in a broken down cabin and doesn't own any more than a tin can to cook coffee in. He can't even afford bullets for this gun. He has nothing at all I would wish to borrow. He has no concept of how to take care of White man's equipment. 'Guns' are like 'magic.' The Indians I know are mostly poor shots, do not know how to clean a gun, do not understand 'reloading' ballistics, nor wish to know all the details. They want to pick it up, point it, and have it, by magic, bring game to them. This Indian has no comprehension that he has ruined my rifle that might cost me several months' wages to replace.

I think I cannot overcome this 'White man' concept, that if I pay for it, it is mine. If you want one, get a job; buy your own, go screw your own gun up! Nor do I like the concept that my home is open for anyone to come into when I'm gone. I am reluctant to think like an 'Indian,' "Come into my home! Make tea; help yourself to whatever I have." I believe too much in a 'private life' and will not give this up. I believe too much in 'the way to get ahead is to work for things.' I believe too much in private ownership, free enterprise, and the old American way. I understand better why the White people's way, and Indian way will never come together. I understand a little, about the Lone Ranger and Tonto. To the White man, Tonto mostly says "Ugh" and "Kemosabe." There is no place for insight, wisdom, or real equality. We do not expect Tonto to ever desert his 'good buddy' the Lone Ranger. But in reality, what is so great about the relationship, from the Indians standpoint?

This becomes one of my long winded letters to Maggie that ends up over 300 pages long, rambling about all sorts of things... "bla bla."…

Love—Miles

I HEAD BACK to the houseboat I call 'home' across the river at the end of another day in Galena. The wind is picking up. The trip home is a little rough. Back home I get involved in some special order art pieces for GI's. The next day is very windy, so I do not even bother crossing the river. I am actually glad to be home for a few days to get into my art and relax. The storm rages out my window. while the woodstove keeps me cozy warm at 70 degrees. The boat gently rocks as I watch Raven clouds fly overhead with wings of rain flapping down. My conscience friend: *"A nice day to sit, read, sip tea, and contemplate the evils of the rat race in the city."*

The rain does not give up for three days, but on the fourth, seems to slow up. I decide I wish to get out and cross the river. I have art to deliver, and maybe I will look at these engines of Harvey's. Harvey has inboard engines he wants to sell cheap that might work on my houseboat. He had them in a barge. The slough is out of the main wind, so the slough looks navigable. I get the engine on the John boat going all right and am dressed for the weather. It is good to feel the wind and rain in my face. I love the smell of wet trees, and the sounds of the storm.

The Yukon is looking rough as I approach from the mouth of the slough. If I could have seen it out my window I would have waited, but now that I'm dressed, and have run the slough, am primed for crossing, I think I will 'have at it.' The twenty-five horse engine is running good. I like how this boat handles. I have to ease the bow into the waves and wind. There are whitecaps of foam on four ft. swells. I go slow and easy, nose to the right angle. It takes a while to work my way across the river. There is drift to dodge, but I have done this a lot of times. I'm only doing three miles an hour. The water blows in my face as I crest each wave, but no water is getting in the boat. The boat feels safe and stable. I see John now at his boat, bailing water out of it during this slack in the storm.

I come over another ordinary wave, and see a big log crossways to me that I will run over. I throttle back, put the engine in neutral, so when I slide over the log, and the prop hits, there will be no power on the prop. The boat slides over the log with only a slight thump. The log hooks on the engine, and as the boat slides down the crest of the wave, the log grabs the engine and lifts it straight up. I do not have it securely bolted to the transom, only clamped. The engine goes straight up, off the transom, and into the river. The hose runs out, followed by the fuel tank. Before I can register in my mind what has happened, the running engine disappears under water.

Before I have time to even think, *"Oh Oh!"* the bow swings with the wind and wants to go crossways to the waves. If I let this happen, the boat will capsize, and I will likely drown. I grab the emergency paddle and am able to keep the bow to the wind, but an unable to gain any forward motion toward shore. I simply drift downstream away from Galena. There is too much wind to expect to be heard yelling at John, but he has heard my engine quit, and while I work the paddle and pay attention to what I'm doing, John gets his boat going and heads out after me.

He is able to get along side. I hand him my bow rope to tie to his stern. I get a tow back to his camp on the beach. A concerned John:

"Looks like you lost your new motor Miles, what happened!" I explain about the log. He tells me everyone bolts the engine through the transom. I didn't know that, or had 'heard,' but it didn't seem at the time like good advice. It is hard to believe anything could lift the heavy engine that is 'clamped.' I have to say:

"Well John, guess I'll be looking at Harvey's engines huh? I never did like these twin 25's on the houseboat anyway." John offers to try and drag for the engine later after the storm, but in thirty feet of water I doubt dragging will work, and the engine will be full of silt. We cannot even mark the spot where it went down.

"Yup, time to see Harvey John" Harvey greets me from his log cabin,

"Hey Miles, heard you lost your engine. Too bad. Yeah I got the inboard—outboards I told you about. It will require work getting one in your boat. You only need one. They are eighty horse Volvo Penta's. Same four cylinder as is in the car, only with marine bearings and water cooled exhaust manifolds." He shows me the engines and they are not very massive looking. He explains how the engine goes in the boat.

"This is four cycle Miles, you will see more power for your horses! The engine is in your boat and hooks through the transom to the out drive. Harvey looks around at his junk pile under the shed eaves. Here are the gears, and this is the propeller that goes in the water." I know I need healthier horses for sure. I say:

"So ok Harvey, what's the bottom line here, how much is it gonna set me back?" I still remember the wonderful kayak deal I just couldn't turn down when I first came to Alaska. I got conned into something I didn't need. Harvey explains:

"Well Miles they are 1960 engines. One runs, and one is for spare parts. I used them in a barge I prospected with, and they have about a million miles on them. Both have been overhauled twice. You can have them both for $200. I'll throw in a box of props, and spare parts, oil filters, spark plugs, special tools it needs." It's pretty hard to find fault with a deal like this, considering I can't hardly get one prop for that price. I ask:

"How can I get these to my houseboat? They weigh 300 pounds each." He happily says:

"Just get some people together to haul one on a pole!"

I snort, "Yeah right!"

Harvey laughs. "Sure, just get a case of beer and invite a bunch of guys to come around." I answer like he's crazy: "They'd drink the beer, say the job can be done easier when everyone is sober in the morning and all disappear." I'm someone who depends on myself, and no one else.

Four guys from the base I sold art to who like my stories, show up and we use a pole and get one engine at time into the John boat. It only takes an hour. I give them a case of beer and "thanks!" I'm surprised it works. This is probably the first time in my life I ever asked anyone to help me. The houseboat has been set up to be ready for the engines. I have a hole in the transom and bolt holes drilled to hold it. I pull the John boat under a tripod I set up in the shallow water. I hook the come along winch that is hanging from the peak of the tripod, to the engine I think is most likely to run. The engine is winched out of the johnboat carefully. I crank it up as high as I can, then move the houseboat under it. A few adjustments have to be made so it fits perfect in the holes, which are all above the waterline, as long as the weight of the engine is not in the boat, and the bow is loaded heavy with the full gas barrels to keep the stern high.

I have no electricity, so holes are drilled with hand drill, and keyhole saw. There is no book on this engine. I have little knowledge of how an engine runs, but decide I can figure it out if I just look at the engine and think about it. All I have for tools are a crescent wrench, screwdriver, and hammer. I have two engine blocks, a box of parts, and more duplicate engine parts. I know a little about how an outboard runs, as well as a chainsaw. I have confidence I can figure it out.

A coil comes off one, a rocker arm off the other, valve cover out of the box. I still do not know which engine block will work best, so switch back and forth as I come to a stumbling block with one. I find a stripped stud, and have to try the other block, then something cracked, and go back and try and thread the hole on the first block, then move on with it. Wires hang everywhere. I have to figure out what goes to the coil, starter, switch, heater, or just an idiot light. I have no way to know what the color code is. I do not even know what would be standard, or even what color is normally positive or negative. Sometimes the length of the wire is a hint. I hold it out at the length that would seem reasonable, and see, at that length, what it could even possibly hook to. Conscience: *"Well, it can't be the points, it won't reach."* Hmmm *"Oh! Here we go; I bet it's the oil light!"*

I take a break every few days to go across the river in the John boat with the remaining twenty-five horse powering it. There is a bolt, or a pack of washers, or a roll of electrical tape to buy, and it takes a special trip, and holds up the project till I get it. This is very inefficient.

I check on the garden. The seeds are up, growing, and doing well. My plot is twenty feet long and ten feet wide, but could have been forty X forty if I'd wanted. Usually seeds get planted June first in the interior of Alaska, after the last frost. Harvest is expected to be by September first, before the first freeze. The first freeze can come in the middle of August, but many things can survive a light freeze, or can be covered beforehand if we know it is coming. This is a three month growing season, so it's pretty intense, with the twenty-four hours of light, and not many cloudy days. Under these conditions, every single day makes a difference, and the garden needs all the help it can get. I put rotten fish water John gives me over the plot to help fertilize it.

"You going to get a commercial fish permit Miles? They are $10, I have the forms." I laugh at John.

"Yeah right! Just what I need, another form, another permit. How many game wardens you ever see? I never met one, wouldn't know what one looks like. No one I know uses a permit. Who you going to show it to? You're far away from anyone who cares about permits!" John admits I'm right, and he's about the only one who bothers to pay his $10.

"It doesn't matter so much now Miles, but maybe down the road it will." "Yeah well, down the road is down the road John, maybe I'll pay my $10 then, if I have to."[4]

There's good money in fishing all right. All I'd need would be the $10 permit, the John boat, my twenty-five horse engine, and a net. Salmon sells pretty high, and the caviar eggs even higher. A guy could build a fish wheel for $100 and catch 6-700 salmon a day. I haven't followed the details, but assume someone here is a processor and does the buying. There's even more money in the bootleg eggs, but I don't understand how that works. Maybe fishing during the closed season? I do not know about such things. Fishing for a living doesn't interest me. I don't like the smell of fish slime, nor working around other people, depending on the one local buyer who sets the price as he pleases, and a government that regulates things. If I wanted to live right in the village it might work, but it is not an occupation for someone who wants to be 100 miles from his nearest neighbor, and hates regulations. When I worked the fish camp for Piper my first year in Alaska, someone with a plane had stopped by sometimes to ask about eggs and I had sold some- rather than throw them away. Waste is a crime. Now I do not understand why fish eggs are illegal to sell. It doesn't make sense that subsistence fisherman are supposed to throw fish eggs back in the river with the guts. What I'm told for a reason, is that many people would catch the fish, who do not need them, just to strip eggs out to sell. Subsistence people could, in theory, make a big business out of stripping eggs and tossing fish back in the river. The law ensures only commercial fisherman who are designated, controlled, and who are in business can make money at fishing.

"You coming to the stick dance Miles?" I answer,

"Yea, guess so, that waitress gal wants to dance with me, and it might be fun to see what goes on here." There are two or three women sort of interested in me actually. No one I think I could be serious about. If I was willing to call this 'home' though, I could have a girlfriend here. But I'll be moving on. If one of the gals seemed like a good 'life partner,' I'd have interest in bringing her along if she'd have me, but think none of the gals interested, are that interested. This is more of a 'let's have fun' interest.

"Your boat engine running yet Wild Miles?" I answer,

"No, but pretty soon I think." Most of the time I do not know the name of the person addressing me. I wave as I head over to the river bank where the grease pole climbing contest starts. There's a $100 bill on top of the pole. Several people try before me. I give it a shot, but there's no getting a grip on that greased pole. Someone manages to do it though, but there must be a trick to it! We all laugh at the efforts.

"Tea making contest, find a partner, grab a boat!" Everyone laughs, and chooses a partner. A giggling Indian gal grabs my elbow, asking me:

"You have boat?" We have to cross the Yukon, get kindling to build a fire, come back to this shore, get a fire going on the beach, put a kettle of river water on the fire and make a pot of tea. Whoever can serve a cup of tea first wins. It is partly a test in 'working together.' One has to keep the fire going hot, while the other runs for water, and one has to set the wood on while the other tends to the tea. Those who argue waste time. There is skill in crossing the river, in choosing the right wood for the fire. It is a contest that any couple could be part of, and it's all in fun. Some elder couples enjoy it, some teenage lovers enjoy it.

My partner and I lose our chance to win in the boat trip over. My boat is not a fast one. We do all right on all the rest. I speak up:

"Everything connected to the tea, you deal with, everything connected to the fire, I'll deal with; does this sound good?" She nods yes, this sounds good. We hear a lot of screaming. The wood scatters when someone trips going to the boat. Those on the opposite shore scream at the top of their voice. Motors start again, back to the Galena side to start the fire. We are about fifth to get ashore, not so bad, out of about twenty couples. I use a knife to shave some dry wood to get the fire started hot and fast, while she runs to the water with the kettle. I overhear screams of,

"That wood is wet, quick, get another piece in the fire!" Somewhere else, "Blow harder, it's going out!"

"Too much water in the kettle, it's going to spill in the fire!"

I look up to see my partner bumping into another gal who is also getting water. My partner bursts out laughing, which wastes a little time, but really, who cares? It is not 'who wins,' but 'who has the most fun'! I have to join the fun and yell at her,

"What kind of woman is this? Do you have to stop and gossip while doing your chores?" Everyone finds this hilarious and laughs. She yells at me,

"If you weren't so busy watching the women bend over at the water, maybe you would have a hot fire waiting for me by now!" Everyone laughs even harder.

"But if I didn't watch you bend over getting water, you would be mad at me, and I would be worried where you might pour your first cup of boiling tea!" This brings more laughs.

The couple who wins are elders who know how to work together. One couple took all this quite seriously and the two are yelling at each other at the top of their voice.

"Because you're drunk you no good blankity blank!" We all laugh.

"I bet you put water in my boat gas" We all think this is hilarious. The one's who won collect a rifle that someone else put up as a prize. It is a used rifle, but this is the custom it seems, gifts are offered and exchanged. There is much talk about the winners. I yell,

"I'm glad I lost, it was more fun!" This becomes the joke of the day everyone repeats.

My tea making partner is only thirteen years old. As we sit around after the contest, her father looks at me and winks. The relatives try to line me up with her. There is a dance later, and it is hinted it is appropriate for me to take her, and what follows is also hinted at.

I hadn't understood what I'd said 'yes' to, when I'd entered the 'tea making contest,' and had assumed it was all in fun and just a simple tea contest. But in fact it seems to be an elaborate social event with a lot of levels to it. I see it is a time when the villages get together up and down the river. It is an old, old custom.

The purpose as I see it, is to make good feelings to ease tensions between villages that do not see each other much. This is a chance to share customs, gifts, food, and to exchange women between cultures. There are contests. Some are fun, some more serious, to show off your village; show off your personal ability as a hunter, fisherman, provider. This is a chance to check each other out, and see who might be interested in whom as a mate. This is a chance for women to watch the men run the boat, while the women get checked out, to see who might listen, who has a temper, who moves with grace.

It is out in the open in the public in front of the village elders who approve or do not approve of what they see going on. This way there is no sneaking around. The Indians flirt right here in front of everyone. It is a time to say yes or no, if you approve or not, or if you are jealous or have a problem about this, it is a time to make a challenge or enter a contest to win this person back. It may also be a time to give someone away, show the community that you are no longer a couple, and someone else may wish to step in. So, though it is 'fun,' it is also a very important social time. Wives and husbands get chosen here. Yet an elder Athabascan tells me this event is mostly about honoring loved ones who have passed away in a tradi-tional 'potlatch' ceremony given a year or so after a loved one passes away. Clearly there are different reasons to be here.

I watch everything now in a new light, and am amazed at what a great way this is to do things. These people are not so primitive. There is not so much crime or problems as I see in White society. I think back to my entry into the world of the opposite sex. Absolutely no guidance whatsoever. I had to sneak girls into my home before the parents got home from work, and we had to hide everything and do a lot of pretending nothing was going on.

My whole generation was about making out in the back seat of a car on some back road, trying not to get caught. Making 'sex' something forbidden, evil, to be avoided, and full of fear of getting someone pregnant, getting a disease you have no information on, but vaguely hear, 'makes it shrivel up and fall off.' My first girl-friend's mother told her she could get pregnant from a toilet seat. I remember debating with her if this could happen. She was afraid to use a toilet in a public place. There was no way in hell she'd find sex 'enjoyable fun, rewarding.' What did we learn about the roll we were to play later in life? Were there fun games designed to teach us? Did any adult look at us and wink and smile? Adults frowned, and tried to keep us apart! It was only the 'bad' children who disobeyed, and met secretly, to do forbidden things. What did this teach my generation? Now? There is a whole generation of dysfunctional families, and no wonder!

This thirteen year old has been shyly following me around since spring, and now she's holding my hand and squeezing it seductively. Conscience: *"What have I gotten myself into here? Am I going to insult her family now if I don't take her? Break some taboo if I turn her down? Hurt her feelings in front of her people?"* Is this like I read about in all the Mountain Man books from 200 years ago, of when the trapper comes to the Indian village, and the elders select a young virgin out of respect, and expect him to marry her and all this? Oh my, what a mess, and bet these early trappers in the books felt the same way sometimes?

She is breathtakingly beautiful, I must admit. But realistically, she is more like a child than an adult, and it is hard to think of her as cooking and taking care of busi-ness, giving any advice. She would be someone I'd have to take care of, but not like an equal partner.

Conscience: "In civilization, the very act of me holding her hand like this and being next to her flirting, would get me life without parole! This behavior would be considered socially deviant, 'disgusting'." It is not 'the law' that stops me from this, it is simply 'reality!' Not wanting to hurt her feelings, or get involved in something that can't work out. But it is a good thing maybe to have the chance, at thirteen, to test your sexual abilities under supervision. To practice, learn, talk openly. I wish very much I had been raised like this, that my generation had been raised like this. We had to rebel finally, fight the establishment, and shock everyone.

This little girl senses my trepidation, seems to sense my confusion. She does not make a big deal of it, or feel embarrassed, hurt, insulted. She kisses my hand, says "Thank you!" Jumps up, and runs off with one of her girlfriends, giggling over to the river bank, throwing sticks in the water. The elders cluck their tongues and smile, remembering what it was like to be young.

"So Miles, how come you didn't go for it? You could have had a good time!" someone who knows me that I don't know has addressed me and I reply:

"Ya well, I'm leaving, places to go, things to do. She's a bit young." Stranger:

"A bit ripe too Miles." I don't want to hear about it-saying,

"Well, someone else can have a taste then, not me. I just don't want to be that way."

I wander off to be by myself for a while.

"Hey Wild Miles! What you doing over here alone on the river bank looking so glum!? I thought you were having a good time? Come on, the dance is starting!" I laugh:

"Go on by yourself, I just want to be alone for a while, I'll catch up to you later."

After being alone and staring at the river I decide to go to the dance. The different villages downriver put on a dance for the others in turn. There are dancers from the village of Kaltag, and think Holy Cross has dancers. I have never seen dancing like this in my life, or even heard of such dancing in my life, and it puts the Twist, the Frug, and all the White man dances to shame. The one I record and remember the most is a dance called "Goose coming in for landing." The arms are outstretched, and the dancer is looking around for a place to land, back-winging, feet out, hitting the water, settling down in the water, then looking well pleased. Anyone who knows geese will understand all the gestures.

I'd gone to opera before when young, and watched all the twirling and graceful moves. I remember most though; trying to understand the Latin program, hearing all the high pitched yodeling, which I suppose is 'all right' for the stuffy British types. I mean, I'm sure it takes talent, but it had no meaning to me. This dance here is full of things I understand, about hunting, animals, and things connected to the land. One old Eskimo woman did a dance called "Starting the Snow Machine." She goes through the motions of yanking on the cord, checking the plugs. .... all done in dance-to drums. The darn thing still will not start, so she kicks it, and then it starts. She is content and beams, she calls her grandson over to watch, and ride with her. This is so wonderful because we have all in Galena seen the grandmothers trying to get these things going on a cold day, and calling the grandson over to help, or watch. She throws a leg up to straddle it, goes bumpity bump down the trail, looking around for rabbits. She stops to shoot one, throws it on the machine and takes off again. It is all done to traditional drum music. I watch men hunt caribou in dance, and it is just as if I am there. I can see the caribou, the hunter, the chase. There is the kill, the feast, all in a dance. As far as I'm concerned, there is no better dancing anywhere in the world. This brings the people together in a special way because we all see what we have in common, and share the same things we think are funny, or graceful. It makes us all human, with similar problems. It is time to dance. There are dances where we can all join in. I make up a dance.

"I call this, 'Kicking the Bear!' I show, to the beat of the drum, how it was. Everyone can see what happened and follows. It is easy to do this to the beat of the drum, because I am there, and it becomes intense, and real, around the flickering haunting flames of a snapping fire.

"You make good Indian!" Everyone nods. No one thinks my story is bullshit. I take them there, and they can see. Everyone here knows a lot about bears. There are no words, no talking when dancing, but when done sometimes we say something, and I end mine like the caribou hunters did, with "It is so!" Which I understand to mean, "I have brought it to life for you to see, and so there can be no doubt now, that this happened, and you see it as I saw it, behold!" "Dancing is magic."

We are all outdoors around a big bonfire. People sit on logs. There are stumps with buckets of cooling stew sitting on them for people to help themselves from. There is no 'program,' and no entry fee. Everyone chips in and helps cook, helps take care of babies, helps organize. I see moose stew, fresh geese, salmon, and steaming things hanging from wire over the fire, maybe beaver meat. There is no eating utensil, no plate or fork. We stab our hunting knife in the pot and a hunk of whatever comes up. We walk off with it dripping from our paws. No one needs a permit to handle food. No one thinks of a health inspector, or thinks about getting sick. But I know this day will come, and we are in the ending times, so I record it. This is not the sort of thing tourists get to see. Most of us smell like fish, are wearing muddy boots, jeans, knives at our side. I am recording the ending days dutifully in my diary.

I'M AT MY HOUSEBOAT.

The engine controls have to be moved up to the console on the roof. It is an effort to scramble up on the roof, jump back down to the bilges, every time I want to trace a wire out. I get the gauges up here, and the key switch. The intake for water is fitted. After a month of hard work I think there is not much more to do. I squirt some gas down the carb throat, squeeze the primer bulb, and jump up on the roof to turn the key, just to see if it will even turn over. Conscience: *"That's a lot of wires, I doubt I have them all hooked up right, but when I turn it on, I can see where the shorts are."* I turn the key.

There is no 'click' of the key. There is no 'click' of the starter engaging, as I expected. There is only an instant "Vrooooom," and an engine running full throttle without a muffler. "Jesus Christ!" Me and I are both startled, and look for the kill switch, then realize I have disconnected it, thinking it might have a short in it. I have to jump down into the bilge's, and run to the screaming engine. I am so scared I start pulling wires, before this blows itself up. I have to pull an amazing number of wires to strangle it. When it is finally quiet, my heart is still pounding. It is instant, total, all-consuming love at first sound. Tears of joy are in my eyes.

"You really want to haul ass don't you!" I smile at my lover. "I thought you might have trouble starting, not trouble stopping!" I smile again. Damn you're beautiful. I hug my engine.

I hook up all the wires again, make sure the kill switch is working, (the key didn't shut the engine off). I hook the throttle cable up, so I can control the gas supply. I hook up the shifter. I know this engine inside out. I've had every nut and bolt on it, off and on a dozen times. I've put new rings in, honed it, lapped the valves, everything, with the most primitive tools, no book, and nothing but common sense. I'm sure things need proper torque, valves need adjusting, timing perfected, parts micro metered, but it runs, doesn't like to stop, and that's good enough for me.

I turn the key again and it starts quiet, sits and just growls like a lion purring. I call her "Cat," but this reminds me too, of a bulldozer cat when it idles....Wumba-wumba-wumba. There is no thump, no clunk, no tic. None of the sounds I dreaded hearing were present. Conscience: *"Till death do you part, I now pronounce you, man and engine!"* That's God in the background, also quite pleased with my efforts. Conscience: *"God after all, gets quite bored up there in the sky, crossing each morning hauling the sun, looking down on mankind to see what is new. Where has Miles been? I wouldn't want God to be bored. I will make sure God is entertained."*

I put the engine in gear. The prop slowly turns, in rpms I can see. *"Lots of low end power!"* The mud swirls off the bottom and the stern raises, and I see spirit here my twin outboards could never show me. The houseboat is not as light as it was when it was built. The wood has soaked up some water. A lot of new shelving has gone in, and all my normal gear I travel with adds to the weight. I now draw at least six inches, instead of four. With the prop, I bet I draw two feet. Wuba-wuba-, I shift gears, thugga thugga thugga, reverse, sssssssss. I shut her down. Oil pressure seems fine. I want to get a temperature gauge, but water temp discharge feels like I think it should, not too hot. The steering cable is reinforced with hose clamps (the new ones didn't work). The lower unit doesn't line up perfect and has to be bailing wired on, because of housing parts missing. A lot of parts are just amazingly worn out.

I take it on a test run upstream. Conscience: *"Ten miles an hour, three gallons an hour at maximum throttle."* I get to much vibration at full throttle, and can only run about half. Cruising is about two gallons an hour. Conscience: *"The outboards went through about eight gallons an hour."*

"HEY MILES! How come your garden's getting harvested, you expecting a frost?" Looking up from my garden plot I see Dawn coming toward me and reply,

"Oh hi Dawn! I got my engine going and I'm about ready to head out. I know I've been talking about it all summer, but I'm about ready and I'm doing it."

"I didn't think you'd really go Miles. We'll miss you. I thought you were happy here?"

"Sure Dawn, but you know, places to go, things to see. I might check out the Kantishna country Edgar talked about, or I may decide to go downstream and up into Koyukuk country, I haven't decided yet. I only know I expect to cover a lot of ground, see a lot of country, have a lot of adventures, and learn a lot of things."

Dawn shakes her head, waves a good bye—obviously not understanding. I smile as I watch her walk the grassy path between the Indian shacks in the old village, pulling her shawl over her shoulders against the wind.

Conscience: "One of God's sheep, who shall inherit the Earth, after it is well used up and trampled. Someone who is not cause' over her life, but blows in the wind and is only 'affected'....." I have to smile and admire her though. It must be tough being a sheep. I smile again realizing she would say to me how she feels sorry for me- that being outside the flock must be so hard and lonely. As I feel sorry for her being in the herd so restricted. I see no insult worse than being called a sheep. She probably sees being the wolf as the worse fate she could imagine, destined for hell. Hell does not scare me, heaven does. I smile at this comparison between us. Even so, 'friends.' I recognize in her a decent person, and for her I am someone she would wish to be responsible for bringing into the flock. It would win her a lot of points with God. Yet God has put a sword in my hand. She'd say it was the devil, not God. Interesting how all of us find facts that support who we are.

I go over my supplies once again. Most supplies I traded my art for. I've got 300 pounds of flour, 100 pounds of beans, fifty pounds of dry fruit, oh yes, can't forget rice! I got 200 pounds of whole grain rice. I remembered honey, instead of sugar. I have a box of spices. There is not much room for the garden produce. If I waited another few weeks I could double my harvest weight, but I can't wait for everything to be perfect. The time comes when things get set aside and you 'go for it.' There is

300 gallons of gas in the barrels. I have enough food to be gone a year out of touch, and enough gas to go 1,500 miles.

I know everyone on the bench is watching me pull out, talking, speculating on how much weight I carry, my boating ability, who I might or might not have slept with, or wanted to or could have. I know they will hold their breath and watch to see if I go up, or downstream. They talk and speculate on where I will be when winter comes, and if I will be back or die out there. There will be guesses on my true nature, if I'm really a trapper, and just where my bullshit begins and ends. But my guess would be that someone points out the magazine story on me, where I'm called a Mountain Man. Someone will point out how I sold my furs, my art, lived, and made enough in the subsistence lifestyle without working for wages, to outfit myself for the winter. Heads will nod in confirmation, even if some others still speculate. The proof shall be in the pudding. Conscience: *"Will I or will I not come back? To be or not to be- that is the question!"*

I'm not just a green horn 'going wild' anymore. I have arrived. I have become what I set out to be when I was five years old, a trapper, a subsistence person, living with the land, selling crafts from the land. Wild and free. I have things to learn yet, but I've been at it a few years now. I'm Gone Wild." I chuckle to myself as I come out of the mouth of the slough to the main river. The cat sounding engine purrs contentedly. There is the sound of the water on the hull, 'shhhshhhhshhhhh.' The sun is out. The sky is blue. Smoke from my woodstove swirls in the light breeze, following behind me like fairy dust. *"Where shall we go? Upstream or down?"* I take in a deep breath, and smile the reply without words to my conscience: *"We will go anywhere we wish!"*

CHAPTER FIVE

THE BARGE, FINDING MAMMOTH IVORY, ENGINE QUITS, VILLAGE OF TANANA

Future flash:

I write this in January of 2003 on a -40° day, and have to pause. The old diaries and writings I am working with come to a drastic change. After I left Galena in the houseboat in such a mad rush toward my destiny, I started a new diary notebook. But more than that, this is where I had ended the manuscript destined to be one book. All the work I had redone ten times with a pencil, then manual typewriter with a ribbon, till it was almost memorized has come to its end.

I am now staring in a box of letters calendars, diaries, that have not been looked at since they were written in longhand in 1978. In the box I find a spare typewriter ribbon for the manual typewriter all the work was to be rewritten on. I find moss in the bottom of the box. Moss that was in the box from the first cabin I built. A cabin I had to walk away from so long ago when my food was stolen, that I walked out and had to be rescued from.

A bear had broken in, but never got into the box, yet left moss behind. There are dry dead mice. There are once wet diaries from the houseboat boat sinking. I realize this box, all these papers, have survived two forest fires, been hauled to four homesteads, and have traveled thousands of miles by boat, and dog sled over these past years. A lot of memories here. Since I am now working from original material the style may change. I have fifty pounds of extremely detailed information from this time period, down to conversations, weather, land descriptions. This spot in the work might be somewhat of a turning point in the flow of things. **Future flash ends**

When leaving Galena's Jack Slough in the houseboat I do not know for sure where I will go. I have heard of a lot of good places, but there are two main places that most interest me. One is upstream a long way. One is downstream a long way. I am not wishy washy or indecisive here. Much depends on what the well-used engine will do when I hit the main river fully loaded, and if I can make any time at all upstream or am 'stuck,' going downriver. In much of my thinking I have adopted an Indian way of thinking and viewing life. This Indian way seems more workable in the environment I find myself in, compared to the white man's. The native ways are very strange to the white man, until the white man tries to walk in the Indian's moccasins. He then discovers the Indian way works. This is the concept of letting the land, the situation, speak to me. Show me what 'wishes to be,' rather than forcing some notion on nature. I have maybe a month of travel time before I ought to be where I need to be. In a month the weather will get stormy, cold, and the river water level will drop. In about a month the moose will be in rut and easy to get. In a month the first snow can arrive, and before that it would be nice to pick a few berries, mushrooms, and herbs for tea that help me make it through the winter. There is no substitute for fresh vitamins, especially when my diet tends to be less than perfectly preserved foods.

Also if there is a problem with the new place, like I can't get ready in time for the freeze up, I can have an emergency 'out,' and get back to civilization.

Diary: On that note I left Galena - the first of August 1978 - bound for Lake Minchumina at the headwaters of the Kantishna River 600 miles away.

As I'm pulling out into the Yukon River off the slough I am thinking to myself; *The engine sounds strong. I think we can make it upstream - where we couldn't before with those twin twenty-five horse outboards. I don't know about you, but I had enough for a while of Indians trying to kill me. That walk out and rescue a few years ago was close. As interesting as that Koyukuk River sounds downstream of here, I think we should try upstream on the Kantishna. Sounds just as nice, that 300 miles of river with no one on it and that village of twenty people on Lake Minchumina that was there thirty years ago, and still should be there.* Such are my thoughts. I answer myself: "Ya, well I hate to give up a plan of the Koyuk country, be a quitter, but in truth, new information has come to us since the plan was thought of. I mean we worked a whole year to be here and get this far on a dream trip to the Koyukuk. It cost us a lot of time and money to get here. But no, it is not worth getting scalped over, or even worse, me defending myself, scalping someone, and ending up getting tortured for it or put in prison. We are seeking peace in life anyway. Why go where we are not welcome? It irks me that some low life's are messing with my dream, but being adaptable is part of survival—right?

So while me, myself, and I are rambling, the houseboat is already going back upstream.

Diary: This time I am going upstream. I'd never put in any time that direction, and it will be new to me. The water reads different. Like taking a book and reading from back to front. Right off I see an advantage in it. I can hold even with the current while I study the river situation, or creep along testing the water depth and not having to commit to that direction. Going downstream is not so easy, because even holding back in reverse I can't overcome the current and am committed even if I make a mistake. This isn't any light riverboat. I'm drawing three ft of water with two tons on board. This is more like a barge. I have the riverboat I had traded a knife for with John which is tied up alongside, filled with supplies. Coming down stream last year in a new boat I was only drawing six inches, (didn't have all these supplies with me for weight). My speed going up is much slower than coming down. I'm doing four to five miles an hour against a six mile an hour current. I can make maybe twenty to thirty miles in a ten hour day.

Sometimes I get only ten miles in ten hours. I have to learn how to work the river eddies and find the slack water. In reading water, it is not like reading the signs on the street! Reading water means paying attention to the drift going by, the foam going by, the color of the water, the size of the whirlpools, the shape of the islands, and much more. It all has to be figured out as I go along. Making a mistake can mean spending hours in the frigid water with a pry pole, getting off a sandbar.

For those who wouldn't understand the situation, it is like figuring out how to drive a car as you go, and going 'whoops,' when you drift into oncoming traffic, suggesting to yourself this isn't the thing to do again. "Whoops! Need to stay out of the ditch!" and "Gosh! That light must have something to do with the flow of traffic. I wonder if the changing colors mean anything." Few people know why I am still alive. It isn't people's respect I get. People on the river are **making the sign of the cross.**

I'm convinced I have a natural instinct about this river reading.[1] Conscience: *'Because we are still alive – or is it because we have a high Jesus factor?'* I answer myself: "Well sure - both I guess, but don't you notice the few times we are around other river people we see the change in the water surface that others do not see?" We feel the change in the boat hitting a new depth of water and others go, 'Huh?' When we mention it? I'm sure all we need is practice. I'm so convinced I'd bet my life on it! The houseboat is a little different in construction now than it had been. I had to adapt it for the new engine. This eighty horse Volvo Penta sounds like a cat dozer without a good muffler, blowing blue smoke. *Well, heck it has well over 500,000 miles on it.* I have baling wire holding things on. The steering and throttle cable are patched, and wind around and up to the roof top where I sit on a bar stool to steer.

So we can be up high and see the water better in the distance! This makes perfect sense to me. I am puzzled that almost everyone just shakes their head in wonder.

Many or most people I see are civilized. Many of their views would not work for me in my lifestyle. Most river travelers wish to go fast, compare her speed to the fastest, not the slowest they can go! Traveling only ten miles in a day would not be acceptable! I compare the speed to the old days of lining with dogs! In this way I feel lucky, and blessed, rather than ashamed and disappointed. I am thus out of communication with the rest of the world. Necessary for my survival. A price, choice I make to be where I am, have what I have. I live my lifestyle with pride.

The Yukon is a mile wide here in some places. The water is the color of coffee with cream in it. A gurgle is the constant sound, as whirlpools splash. The silt in the river hisses against the hull. The river seems to always be in the flats, but in the distance I can always see mountains. Dark spruce trees at the skyline look like jagged teeth. Usually there are birds present, ravens, seagulls an eagle or a kingfisher. The scene looks very much like all the pictures in the mountain-man books, Lewis and Clark sketches, and famous paintings from our nation's past. Huck Finn, Mark Twain stuff; in the background of the paddle boats. The air is always pure. I can take a deep breath, hold it with a smile, and not want to gag it back out like when in the city.

There is no traffic to speak of. Days can go by and I never see anyone. Maybe once a week a barge goes either up or down stream. Maybe every twenty miles there's a fish camp with a tent and sled dogs out front, with one or two people living here fishing. This will not be their permanent home, but only a place to come get fish every year. The words, 'Fish camp,' are almost sacred. Barges sometimes stop and drop major supplies off at these camps. Ramps are run to shore from the deck and a forklift takes wood pallets loaded with supplies off. Gear is stacked on the beach. Usually it is gas. The barge Taku Chief is pulling out of a fish camp ahead.

I think: *Let's wait a minute - we can follow the barge – maybe learn more about reading water!* So we slow up and wait for the barge to get out in the current and head upstream, with my houseboat following. Taku is traveling about the same speed as I am, so it is not hard to stay in her wake.

Diary: I'd been following Taku Chief all day - which saved eyestrain trying to figure out where to go. Up ahead she took the left side of an island in a left turn. On my own I wouldn't have chosen that side of the island. Almost always the outside turn carries the most water. This must be shorter, and there must be enough water because the barge knows what it is doing - so I follow. I hang back as I see the barge slow - turn this way - then that - then go broadside to me. I am not far behind - trying to memorize the moves as this must be how to get through. I realize the barge is stuck. There is not enough room for me to turn around and go back the other way. I get stuck too. With its bigger engines the Taku back flushes the silt out from under herself – and gets through. I spend hours working the engine, then finally shut the engine off - and jump in the water. I spent half a day doing back breaking work to get free. I should have been reading my own water, not depending on someone else to do it for me. Just goes to show no one else is doing it any better.

I am not always sure where I am, but doing better than I had coming downstream. Conscience: *'Isn't the bone yard up ahead here someplace soon? We should recognize it by the cliff—and the smell!'* So we were both keeping our eye out for this place we want to stop. My conscience reminds me: *'If we find some ivory, we can do some art work on it and sell it, and it will be cool to say we found it ourselves!'* I have not been to Fairbanks or a store where I might get art supplies in over a year, so the only hope I have for material is to find it. There are no signs, for of course there are no signs marking anything on the river, not even the villages. To quote the villagers: "If you don't know where you are, you shouldn't be here." I'm thinking about this as I keep my eyes on the land going by. *'Of course I know where we are – don't you?'* "Of course, just seeing if you know! But just in case - for verification only - get the map out - not that we need it or anything ..." We already determined we had gone by Ruby in the dark and not known it, or gone on the other side of an island and missed it or something. No big deal. I had no reason to stop there... except Emit still owes me for the dog pendant I made and mailed him. For sure I do not want to miss the mammoth graveyard.

The area is recognized by the strength of the current. Trees that were floating are getting sucked under water in whirlpools. Entire thirty ft. trees disappear under the murky water without a sound. *'That's what happens to us if we screw up you know!'* I didn't need a reminder. But to get to the good part of the graveyard requires getting in the most dangerous areas.

From half a mile away I see a cliff on a bluff give way. This is like a skyscraper falling, peeling off the face of a cliff. The nose of the houseboat has to be turned into the waves from a quarter mile away. To have been there when it fell would have been to die. Five minutes later we are right at that spot where the cliff fell, looking for mammoth tusks. Another section of cliff falls, but not on top of me, maybe 100 ft upriver. The wake is big, but I hold the bow rope as I stand on the beach. The boat rocks violently a while, and I retie it, then get back to looking.

The waves of this last avalanche expose some mammoth rib bones. My conscience is trying to tell me the facts of life: *'I figure this - there are two ways to get what you want in life. One is to work really long and hard, standing in line with the sheep. The other way is to take great risk ...'* "Uh huh, yeah, well if you would stop talking and do more looking we might find a tusk." A tusk is worth about a year's wages. *'You remember that tusk the GI in Galena found?'* I remember it well. How could I forget? It was twelve ft. long. When the tip and the base were on the ground, I could walk under it without bending over. It weighed 300 pounds. Such tusks are found right here.

This is a curious place, 40,000 years ago something happened here; in the days of the ice age. All sorts of animal parts, bones, sometimes flesh, comes out of the ice here. Grizzly tracks show that he comes here to feed on such meat.

I feel a rumble, and the cliff here changes. Dust along a fault line sifts along a growing crack. Judging the length, direction of the crack, and where the corresponding weak spot is on the other side, *'Time to get out of this spot—lets' get a move on!'* My conscience is right behind me. The boat is shoved out, engine started quickly, and under full power we head away. A few seconds later the cliff gives way, and slams right where the houseboat had been. There's no time to go back and look to see if anything interesting got exposed. Fall weather is in the air.

I have miles to cover yet. [2]

I'm nervous about the lack of speed we are making. Wondering if we will get to the Kantishna before winter. The engine is acting up. As we travel, we review that little adventure at the bone yard. Conscience: *'Ya, we could have died back there. Do you think we were just foolish—you know another idiot born every day - as so many believe.'* 'I and me' pass the hundreds of hours we sit together up here on the bar stool on a houseboat roof listening to the drone of a sick engine discussing death, the weather, the meaning of life.

> **Diary:** The engine is old and acting up. It doesn't want to start on cold days. The starter brushes are going. I have to drain the oil in a pan, take the oil strainer off to get the starter off. I take the starter apart, clean the brushes, shove some cardboard spacers in, then put it all back together. I'm good for maybe three to four cranks. I then have to do this all over again. The carburetor is acting up as well.

If I can't get the engine going and it quits for good I can only travel back downstream and end up in Galena where I started almost a month ago. But worse, if the engine quits as it sometimes tries to in the middle of a bad current corner with logs and other dangers, I will be in serious trouble.

I find myself in a swift corner, trying to handle the turn without the power to overcome the current, which tries to swing the bow into the sweepers. Before the bow gets into those treetops that are over the water I give the engine full power. The engine quits. As the houseboat drifts backwards, the lower unit and propeller hits bottom. The current takes the bow and swings it around. No paddle or pole can overcome this current now that I am going sideways. The boat spins so fast, that the pivot point in the back corner squats down and below the water line. In a flash we take on fifty gallons of water. The boat continues to swing around until it is pointed downstream. Once the boat streamlines downstream, it starts moving and the lower unit is washed off the bottom. We are drifting downstream safely out of the sweepers. Only blind luck saved the situation. If the bow had been interrupted in its swing around by a sweeper, or if the lower unit had not washed off , the boat would have gone under in an instant. I have no doubt. All I can do us gulp, with my eyes bugged open.

The engine is fixed, this time an air leak in the fuel line, later water in the gas. Progress is made upriver with various engine problems, mixed with rewards, like fresh duck meals, and good scenery. Days go by.

Fall colors are showing. Mountains far off, show up red and yellow against a robin egg blue sky. Trumpeter swans and geese are coming to the river from the nesting ground swamps. With deep tan face I smile. My favorite fish is burbot. I catch some on overnight lines that I set out. These get cooked on the morning fire that takes the night chill out of the air. Burbot reminds me of catfish. They look the same and can get as big, but usually four to five pounds is normal. Most mornings while breakfast is cooking, I do some art work or read a book. Most evenings I spend getting another fire going in the wood stove and cooking dinner as I clean fish or game, tinker with the engine, transfer gas, or sit around reading by kerosene light looking out the window at the constantly changing view.

When I get to the village of Tanana I decide I have to get to Fairbanks for engine parts. It isn't what I want to do. I do not look forward to it, but Tanana is my last chance. There is an air strip here, with regular flights on the mail plane. I have made a list of all the parts I need, and maybe get advice from Will, who knows engines. I also have done enough art that it would be worth going to the gallery or new shops and sell my latest creations for winter money. This trip will cut into my already low funds, but not if I can get some 'end of the tourist season' art sales in. *It is hard to count on anything, or have a plan, for it constantly changes!* After finding out the price to fly, plans change again. I don't have enough money. I hope I can make it to Manley Hot Springs, another eighty miles maybe. There is a road to Fairbanks from there. Maybe I can hitch a ride, or it will be cheaper to fly from Manley than from Tanana.

In Tanana I run into some BLM forest firefighters I know. I can't exactly brag, since I'm limping in and need help, parts, which of course only confirms to them that it is only a matter of 'days,' and I will either die or give up, so these people can collect on their bets. I do not have a lot to say, but know word will get back to Don, and the bosses at the main office. My heart is broken. More than anything in the world I wanted to look good, come in proudly, prove I'm everything I say I am, a trapper, a river man. A few of the secretaries will be concerned and want to be my mother. Most of the guys will tell a joke ending with; 'Wild Miles,' and a laugh. I would see them in hell before I asked for help, or had word get out I couldn't take care of myself. If I make it, then it is because, it is, because um… *'We are Oz! The great and powerful!'* "Exactly!" *'Don't pay attention to that man behind the curtain!'* Their view and my view are at different ends of the rainbow. Their view is on the rainy side. My view is on the side that has the pot of gold. To me, engine troubles are just one more exciting part of a fascinating adventure. The sort of things legends and movies are made of. There is no doubt whatever in my mind I will overcome every and all obstacles. *Nothing worth having is free. Nothing hard is acquired with ease. If it was easy; everyone would do it! The river would be crowded! I rejoice it is hard! This leaves the true believers - lots of room! A culling, weeding out process!*

I have to hang around Tanana for a few more days getting the engine in good enough shape to go on. I figure if I need anything I don't have, it would be good to be here where there is a hardware store, a dump where I might find a part from which I can make something I need. There is not a part I can't make if I have to, rings, head gaskets, rewinding starters. This, of course, gives even more cause for laughs. Me, with my baling wire, chewing gum and crescent wrench, overhauling an engine, upside down with my feet in the air. Not everyone finds it hilarious, but enough people that I figure I don't need their shit. Screw 'em. *The joke will be on them in the long haul when they meet God, even before that! It will be them stuck in the rat race living their meaningless lives on a treadmill. Who will remember them in thirty years?* Humph. I answer myself; "One of the hardest spots is up ahead yet, Squaw Crossing; the mouth of the Tanana river." Windy as hell this time of year, only a foot of water in most places. We will have to find that three ft. deep channel that winds through the flats. We will also face the wind. Me, myself and my woman (the boat), are a team working together, a threesome.

Once through Squaw Crossing we will be on a smaller river, less current, less dangerous, maybe shallower, hard to say. This is the time of year when the weather is freezing in the hills. The source of the water, and the water level, can drop a foot in a day and never come back up. This is not likely for another two to three weeks but 'possible." We are both silent and nervous. A little short shit with broken rusty sword turns to face the dragon - and yells "Charge!" As the world laughs.

In late fall there can be ice to dodge coming in the main river from the creeks.

Meat Cache

CHAPTER SIX

SQUAW CROSSING, MANLEY HOT SPRINGS, WOMAN QUALITY TIME, BEAR, LIFE THREATENED BY A CRAZY PERSON

S quaw crossing is no big deal. There is no way to know this ahead of time. The wind is calm, day is clear and crisp. *I'm reading from the log of the Starship Enterprise.* Fall colors reflect in the calm mirror of the crossing. Geese are getting nervous and wanting to go south soon. There is plenty of food along the river to eat as I travel. Fresh goose and duck stuffed with rice and mushrooms is standard fare. The smell of birch wood from the wood stove reminds me of the dinner cooking inside. Every now and then I have to climb down off the roof to go inside and poke at the cooking goose to see if it is done yet.

I have been traveling like this for a month. At ten hours or more a day. It has become a way of life. The flats defining Squaw Crossing extend as far as the eye can see, like a big lake. Looking behind me, there is a trail of my wood smoke wrapping around upturned driftwood tree roots hung up on sandbars. There is no current to show where the channel is. I have to send my unconscious out in front of me to tell me the depth. Sandbars are exposed above the water. The dried out sandbars are exposed to the wind. The clouds of silt look like my wood smoke. *Galaxies as seen through the windshield of the space ship.* There is nothing but water, silt, trees, and blue sky. Just as it has been for a hundred thousand years. My hurt, anger, and frustration with society goes away when I am alone in the wilderness. Only here, do I know peace.

Early in the morning while garden potatoes are frying, I work on a piece of jewelry at the bench set up by the window. The sounds are good sounds. Swans are trumpeting, and sand hill cranes are crooning. The splash of a beaver on the water, the gurgle of the current are familiar background sounds. I have a wild Dall sheep horn I acquired in a trade in Galena and have been working on the same art display all summer. This will be a major art piece with a story told in thirty-five separate scenes. I expect to have hundreds of hours into it before it is done. I am unsure how the story will unfold, but the horn must be polished and some background metals prepared. *What this piece wishes to be will reveal itself all in good time.* Against this back-drop there seems to be no hurry.

Manley Hot Springs is not really looked forward to. I am not even sure where this Kantishna River is I am headed for. As much as I dislike it, I really must stop and get directions, word on trapping grounds, and I need engine parts. I'd asked mail to get forwarded to Manley when I was in Tanana so any mail sent should be waiting for me there. I'll need gas maybe.

'Must be this slough here on the left.' My conscience has been keeping an eye out while I had my eye on the maps. I had missed Manley on the way downstream. It is not on the main river, but up a hot clear slough. The map shows me that the slough mouth should be up against a bluff called 'Bean Ridge,' and this should be a land-mark to spot. The slough is deep and slow moving. According to the map, the village should be about six miles up this slough. I find Bean Ridge and head up the slough.

There are some log cabins with wood smoke coming from each chimney like a big fish camp, or like an Indian village in the movies. There are a few boats tied up here and there, a float plane, some fishnets set out. The bridge across the slough shows me where the middle of town is. The postmaster, Mike, tells me about 80 people pick up their mail here, but there are no post boxes. Everyone gets mail general delivery. The roadhouse is not far off. I go there without much conversation. I can use a burger and fries washed down with an ice cold coke, while I think about what to do. Maybe someone will know where the Kantishna River is, and I can get some information. I have a map, but I want to know if I can find a place to trap, and anything else relevant to living there, like if this village of Lake Minchumina is hostile or not. Will I be killed if I go there?

The Manley Roadhouse is a historical place where dog sled mail carriers used to stop, as well as trappers and miners. Stepping inside is like stepping into someone's home. There is a wood stove crackling away, an inviting sofa in front of it. Log walls are lined with bookshelves loaded with paperbacks. It looks like people just borrow or drop off used books. Leaded glass windows have antiques on the sills. I spot gold rush items, furs, and mammoth bones. A few people are hanging out here. One of them I sort of remember from Tanana, on my first stop there on the way down to Galena, a year, maybe it is two years now. I am not good with time, but Chris remembers me, and reminds me I got gas from him when the gas pump was closed.

It must be so, but I don't remember. Beside him is a Native gal from Tanana about my age, real pretty, who looks at me invitingly. I'm always interested in a gal who might be the one God has put in my path. I miss Nancy a lot, the gal I met dancing at the Howling Dog in Fairbanks a few years back. I don't want to let on to this native gal I'm overly interested. These matters have to be handled delicately after all. Even the stupid grouse knows he has to bow and fluff up. I wait for Chris to introduce us so I can say "Yeah I just arrived by houseboat…" so she can be appropriately impressed. Swoon would be nice—kind of melt in my arm or something. I'd settle for, 'raised eyebrows of interest' right now. Damsel in distress, dragon slayer, you know, maybe somehow it fits together or something.

Chris introduces us and it is 'time'… Here we go.

"Ya hi! I just arrived by houseboat…"

She doesn't swoon. She says: "You mean that dumb looking boat everyone is talking about where you have to look over the roof to see?"

Well of course this can't possibly be the one God has put on this earth for me to please! But I don't let on. I'm used to this. I happily smile: "Uh huh! That's me!" I play the role of the village idiot, which seems a better choice than getting defensive. That pretty much ends the conversation. I order my burger, sip my coke, wondering what's going to happen next. The roadhouse owner is also the store clerk, and his wife is the postmaster. Looking out the window I can see the runway, and the log cabin store is there someplace. I can't see it, but Mike tells me there is a gas pump next to the store. Sounds like there is someone with a fuel truck who will come down and pump fuel into a boat if you call him. I nod. Mike wants to know what I am doing here, and where I am headed.

I begin: "Well I heard a lot about the Kantishna River when I was in Galena, but no one I have talked to really knows much about it. You know that river?"

Mike replies, "Sure I have heard of it. Never been on it. This operation keeps me pretty busy here. I know a few people from here trap up there, and a lot of people from here go up there moose hunting." So I finally have a chance to get some updated information about this place after two years of hearing and asking. This is an exciting time for me, but I don't want to let on. People might think I was a pup, green around the gills. Probably I don't have to say or do much to prove I am an idiot, but what the heck.

Mike's wife over at the store/post office is wearing a piece of my jewelry! I say, "Yes I'm the one who made that, wondering where you got it." We get to talking. Others come join in and I meet some nice enough folks here who want to help. Some of the news though is not so good to hear.

"Yeah as far as I know the whole river is being trapped from the mouth all the way up by different trappers" and "Not a good year to try to go up it. Those who tried are coming back saying it is a low water year and too shallow up there a ways, and this is with regular shallow draft river boats! If you draw three ft., I doubt you could make it!" Conscience: *'We better find out more then, before we take off. Wouldn't be good to get part way up and get stuck and have to spend a winter, and not even be able to trap or be someplace where there would be trouble over it.'* I don't say much out loud to people, just listen and gather data. I still need to get to Fairbanks for parts no matter what I do. This is the first of September and I hear, "Well you have to be settled in wherever you are spending a winter by Sept 15th, after that you'll be froze in!" The old timer saying this looks like he has been around, so should know what he is talking about. This does not give me much time. Every single day counts right now. Glad enough now I didn't spend an extra day at the bone yard, even though at the time it looked like there was plenty of days of freedom. I'm also glad I didn't wait around Galena to harvest a better garden.

No one is interested in seeing my cool houseboat. So I sit alone in the boat as if I were in the wilderness. Wood stove going, kerosene lantern aglow, reading mail I picked up. There are letters still coming in from my magazine ad looking for a woman. Some new ones, and some I have written to for a while now. It is hard to know if any of them would work out or not. I had to write John in Galena that June never showed up. I'm glad enough I did not have my heart on the line from all those devoted words she wrote. *Yet my very caution might have run her off!* So how much is my own fault? I write John,

Hey John!

How's life with you? Staying out of trouble? I've got to keep this short, been pretty busy. Oh, yeah, you asked me to tell you about how things work out with June and how it goes. It turned out ok. But you know how it is, something a person should keep to themselves. You'll just have to have your own experiences. I'll write again, and you can write me general delivery here in Manley Hot Springs.

Later, Wild Miles

"Hey, some incoming mail, smells like it's from a woman!"

Dear Miles—There's no other way to put it. You said a letter is just words on paper. But, I can tell you have been sincere and truthful. I want the man to be the boss for I don't quite know where to begin or what to say! Three letters and so many beautiful pictures! I'm just stunned. I figured there were a lot of girls writing to you. You're a rare breed (and a good one!). I never believed I had a chance! Well as you've probably read from the other letter, I am working to get it together to come to Alaska. I just can't explain how you make me feel when I read your letters. I guess deep down inside I'm an emotional person. One minute I'm smiling as I read one of your adventures. Then I feel real important when you tell me about your boat and plans, and then I'm actually crying (I never cry!) when you write about your feelings!

I have never read anything with so much emotion as your letters! I love it. You make me feel really good! Right now I'm sitting in my room looking at you in the picture of you on the houseboat. This may sound terribly forward, but I'm going to say it anyway... you are so cuddly looking I'd just like to hold you forever! Please don't think I'm being silly... and I'm exactly as you said! Everything in your letter was me to a T- incredible. I don't mean to brag but I'm exactly what you want. I guess that's pretty blunt, but sure... I don't want money or clothes or fine home. I want a good relationship. Please don't give up on me. I'm trying to get it together to come to Alaska! Isn't it exciting to want to see someone you have never seen-but feel you know so well? It's driving me crazy!

Your cabin was just as I imagined. Your knife case was so pretty. The pelts were incredible. I can't believe it—we are so much alike. I love the piece of moose antler you sent. I will try my hand at scrimshaw on it and send it back. The pictures and poems were super- as usual! I think I got the message from the poems. Did you say you wrote for Alaska Magazine? I read it all the time! I wanted to ask how you decided to put an ad in Mother Earth News! What kind of responses did you get?

By the way you never did say what you thought of my pictures! It's important to hear what you have to say. I feel that you like me because I'm me because I didn't send pictures at first and you were very sincere before you even saw me- so let me know ok? I wish I could fly up there right now! I can't wait. Do you think you can wait?

This letter is very scrambled because there is so much to say at once! Seven pages have gone by so fast! Believe me I understand exactly where you are.

She encloses a poem she wrote for me. I inspired her to write this poem?

Poem
I dreamed about a prince one time
A handsome noble man
Who came upon my window sill
And took me by the hand.
"Step forth ye lovely lady
and I shall lead the way,
to a better life in wonderland
now dare ye say 'Nay'?"

I stepped across the window sill
And jumped upon his horse
Then a whirlwind gently lifted us

And set us on our course.

Through valley streams and mountains high
We traveled and we lived.
We worked and played and laughed and kissed
And gave all we had to give.
Now I grew to dearly love the prince
A magical mystical man
And we are living happily
In 'forever and ever' land.

'Wow she sounds about perfect for us huh? All except for a few minor details. Huh? What choo think?' I answer my conscience by strumming my finger on the table top. I have to get up and go look out the window- step out on the deck. An owl is disturbed and hoots. A fox runs off through the grass. The Northern lights are out. I stare at them thinking. The boat gently rocks as I step back to the warmth and glow of the wood stove inside. I sit in my chair by the bed that doubles as my table in the daytime and write a letter—but not to this gal—to Maggie.

Dearest Maggie,

So she sounds perfect for me right? I have mentioned her before I think. She answered my ad a while back but never sent a picture. I was of course curious what she looked like. She assured me looks would never be a problem, and so I set that thought aside. We wrote back and forth. I'm 'interested' for sure! Who wouldn't be—words like that!

But I get a picture and she weighs 300 pounds. She is not the age she told me she was, and she has serious permanent health problems from an accident, problems that would not allow her to live in the wilderness. Now, I might have overcome all that under some conditions, but I have trouble trusting her—like I had been deceived. The trouble is though, I think she is sincere in her perception of herself and her situation. She truly believes what she says, and she never lied to me or deceived me—in her eyes. But I said in my ad I was looking for a small woman-in the physical description.

I said I lived in the wilderness and would not likely leave. How we see ourselves needs to relate to how others see us maybe. She feels healthy and believes she is, and by some standards 'is' and she is very beautiful—to someone- to many even. But I'll put it like this—if a woman had an ad out that went "Looking for big man." If I replied at all I'd say "Well we have many things in common but up front you need to know I'm a short guy. That matters to some—not to others, so if it matters, may as well say so and we can move along! If it is not a big deal—Hi! I'm Miles."

For sure I want someone to have a picture right off. I thought if I got to know this woman, maybe the things between us would not matter—but here she is being as she is. I wish I was better at speaking up about stuff I don't like—in that it is pretty easy to be open and honest about the good stuff! It is dealing with things we know will hurt someone that puts communication to the test. My Oh My, Whatever am I going to do! What a mess. Ten years older than me, 300 pounds, can't live in the wilderness and in love with me. Is that a pickle or what? Meanwhile back at the ranch—how the heck are you anyhow?

Sunshine Miles

Maggie does not write to me often, and it is never a long letter, but she is a good listener. She has never been mad at me. I tell her a lot of crap. She accepts all I say in stride without judgment. She rarely even gives advice- just "I'm sure you'll figure it out!" She's the best friend a person could ever hope for. I had thought I might get a letter from my father, mother, or sister. I haven't heard from any of them in a few months now. I had written them all before I left Galena. *Well whatever. I have other things on my mind.*

I'M TRYING to find out if I can get a ride to Fairbanks, and what it costs to fly, when the plane leaves etc. This village is different from the others I have seen. There are a lot of white people here. Since a road comes to it and ends, people can drive here. People here are more civilization savvy than more remote places. The standard of living seems higher.

Being on the road, there is some tourism and work for people. It looks like some of these nice homes are vacation homes for rich people in town. I see retired elders who have money here. For sure there are trappers, miners, and homesteaders. A public laundry is nice to see, catering to the visitors off the river. The hot springs is the big attraction. I see the hot water runs into the building as a hot creek, without pipes. Tropical vegetation grows along the hot creek, I'm told, year round! So far, no answer to the trip to town. Hmmm. I sit at the table outside the post office and write, waiting for the village to wake up, so I can ask about Fairbanks. Blade of grass in my mouth...

Dear Susie,

It has been a while since I heard from you. I didn't know how things were going. I met someone else. Well more like someone I already knew worked out! What a bummer about the timing and your feelings and all. I was interested but didn't hear from you. I thought maybe my last letter was too much or something. You seem so nice and beautiful I'm sure 'the right guy' will come into your life! It will be like magic and you will be glad you waited I hope! Certainly you deserve…(etc etc) **Sunshine, Miles**

Conscience: *'You lied to me you fat old bitch! I think you need to write that.'* I answer my conscience: "Now, now, that's enough of that! It does no harm to be nice, and if I'm full of shit? What is the harm huh?" I seal the letter and drop it in the box outside the post office. It seems such a bummer that misdirected affection can be worse than none at all. It is six in the morning and no one seems to be up. I've been up as usual since five a.m. The blade of grass I'm chewing on gets shifted.

I seek out a new blade to suck on while I contemplate this 'Susie' situation. It would be nice to figure out – in general, what is going on with my nonexistent love life. See if we see a pattern, a way to… *'So what is wrong with this picture? You know, the lovely letter from Susie, and our reply.'* "Maybe there is nothing wrong with the letter or her, it is us…" *'Could be, but consider this, her letter sounds pretty off in La la land! - I mean it is nice and all, but still La la land.'* "And the point would be?" *'Well it might be hard to live up to all this. Haven't met and thinks we are perfect. Anyone with their head on straight would know we are complicated, not easy to know, or love, and have serious problems. Our lifestyle alone should require a lot of questions and concerns, that someone should at least be saying they can't make any promise but might give it a try.'* "All well and true, but how come we get so many letters just like this one? It stands to reason – the problem originates in us someplace, if this happens so often. Logic tells us it is not the human race that is messed up, but us!" *'Ok, well maybe we come across to the rest of the world as off in la la land ourselves, a make believe type world, not connected to reality.'* There might be some truth to this. I may not mind a partner able to dream. It's just that we need to be in the same dream? No, more like the dream needs to be workable. I have a dream, and I am living it. Not perfectly, but I am taking care of myself. *Do we face the truth of what and who we are?* I get my unconscious drift, like being fat and thinking you are not, like believing you are a centerfold model, while being a tub of lard… *'Hey here comes the postmaster!'*

The postmistress and I chat on the topic of the trip to Fairbanks. It sounds like people go back and forth on the mail plane which flies at least three days a week. Ticket is $25, so no big deal. I have my list, money, and late that day fly to Fairbanks-about a half hour flight.

ON THE STREET.

"Hey, Will fancy meeting you here. I just got here and was going to try and call!" Will is glad to see me saying: "Yeah, it is weird how whenever you come to town

GONE WILD

you seem to run into me right off on the street!" We wonder what the odds of that are, just randomly having that happen, and both think again how weird it is!

"I need parts for the engine, Will. You'd like it, old car Volvo engine set up for marine use." Will helps me get all the parts. He asks me about the black powder rifle he likes so much now. We both find it funny, how he had insulted it through the whole time I was building it. Now I give up on it and it is Will who is an avid Black Powder Man! I explain how I might have had a nice winter moose if I had a gun that fired more than one shot. I took up the 270 rifle. Just using the black powder now for fun because it is cheap, and because if there were ever hard times, black powder can be made to work.

"Yeah, Miles, if you have to. you can even make your own powder from stuff in the land and make your own lead balls!"

The way civilization is going we seriously consider these are ending times. I remind Will: "My rabbit cycle theory of civilization!"

I get some last minute supplies. Will and I hit a few garage sales- and catch the last day of the state fair. I do not have time to really enjoy it. I'm nervous about the future and all.

Will tells me, "Hey buddy you are out there doing it, when most of us are just talking. I really admire that!"

I thank Will for the confidence in me. I have to remember there are some all right people in my life. Thinking of this I ask Will, "Hey, you ever hear anything about the Koyukuk area and Huslia? Remember we talked about planes getting shot down there? I still wonder what would have happened if I had chosen to go there and live. I wonder if the rumors were even correct or if more went on since I last heard!"

"I guess you know as much as me, but did hear from a moose hunter who went that direction a year or so ago. He said his gas was stolen, and he was run off. He said the only school teacher has been burned out and run off at gunpoint. The hunter told me he heard they did not want any white teachers there. Who knows, Miles, if it is true or not but I also heard from a fire fighter who went out on a forest fire in the area. This was first hand. He told me the fire crew was runoff at gunpoint. The reason was the locals felt the fire fighters were protecting white man hunting camps and homes more than the native land and homes. He confessed they go save the most valuable first, whoever owns them, and many native homes look like empty outhouses, and the white homes are often $100,000 homes completely outfitted with valuables."

"Hard to know, Will, what that was all about. I live the life myself, and some-times even an outhouse looking place is the best someone has, and their life depends on it, while a $100,000 place is just a vacation place the owner can live without. How do you place a value on something? Is it just in dollars. Value to civi-lization is cutting trees down and making a clearing, building a bridge, an air strip, a ranch, a farm. That's what proving up on a homestead means, a list of accepted improvements, all involving replacing nature with something better. So I sort of see the native's point of view. Just that dang ,Will, I can't help that I'm white! I'm the wrong color! I do not want to be punished for my color, Will! I asked because we were talking about good and bad folks. I remembered that one guy from Huslia, Arnold, who helped me out in that storm by Ruby and pulled my houseboat off the sandbar. I was a stranger to him and he helped out with no thought of being paid, just being a nice human being. So not everyone there will shoot you for being white. Still amazes me, Will, how that stuff can go on and the outside world does not care or do anything. I bet if you and I boated up there and started killing Indians there'd be hell to pay, huh?"

"You got that right, while it's open season with a bounty on us white folk! Indians taking scalps and all that. Anyone takes shots at me, tries to sink my boat it's war. I'm not afraid of that. I'm scared what would happen if I defended myself!"

"Better have more than black powder, Will!" He's got a new 375 H & H he says'll knock an Indian on his ass at half a mile. Wipe out the whole village from across the river." But no, it is better just never to go there. Let them live in the stone age as they wish. I'm all for that, just wish I could join them.

"Marry yourself one, Miles!"

"Yeah? I've seen some nice ones actually, even some good catches by any standards, but none that would have me! Ha!" We change the subject and look at my list of needs again. Some things got ruined when the water got in the boat. I have to buy these items all over again. I laugh, "Seems like you either got money or you got time, but never both! Those who can afford all the right things and can afford all the supplies don't want or need them, or never have time to get out to use what they bought, or have the knowledge of how to use the tools. Those with all the time seem to not have the money to make it happen! Those living the life are going around with broke down stuff that doesn't work." We have talked about this before, but I bring it up again as here we are in that situation. Will wants to live like me but is trying to save money and get good supplies first. Meanwhile the years pass. I have a lot on my mind- wondering if I can make it to the Kantishna before winter. This situation is a little like Galena last winter. I do not want to spend another winter in a village unless I have to. I miss the wilderness. The village is better than living in town at least, but still. Part of me wonders if I could fit into society. Life gets lonesome alone out there. There is at least a little pull to mingle, to see if I might meet my soul mate, or fit in someplace or? Some sort of restlessness or something I can't explain, that I'm fighting with.

Will doesn't like to dance, so he just drops me off at the Howling Dog and we part. I hope to run into people I know. Tomorrow is my trip back to Manley with engine parts, so may as well get some social life in. Might be the last of it I see till next spring. I spot a gal I know.

"Hey, Becky, how are you! Where's Bob?" I know her from Hippie Hill back in Delta where the houseboat was built.

She hesitates and says, "Not with Bob anymore, Miles, we parted after we both got Pipeline jobs. He got into the money and drugs, too much for my taste." I thought I heard how she and Bob had a $200,000 home with a swimming pool and sports car and all the trimmings. In fact most of those I stood in line with to get pipeline jobs ended up becoming rich. I would have been one of them if I hadn't had my dream to follow. So she's rich now. So are the former street people I thought I was so much better than. Those with no ambition, blank stares, no brains. Many were thieves. Nothing going for them. Now they are rich, respected members of society… and here I am. It's hard to swallow. It doesn't seem fair. *I guess we are not supposed to judge huh?* I have my dream, my adventures, but somehow- it's not like I thought it would be.

Becky seems to be with someone else, *darn*. She is a good bush woman. We had been out in the woods off and on together. She seemed to like me, so, if I had been around? Who knows? We talk about the old days on Quartz Lake and life in Delta. I tell her about my latest adventures with the houseboat. She was around when it was being built. She says, "Well Manley Hot Springs, huh? I was thinking of going there actually, hmm, sounds like a nice place. Maybe take a dip in the springs and enjoy getting out of town! Even though it's a five hour drive, if you pay for gas I can take you there with all your stuff if you like? I'd like to see the houseboat too! I never did see it in the water after all that time you spent in the shop building it!"

So this will work out good. I have a way to get my things to Manley. I ask if she has seen Nancy, who I had met here and am still fond of. Nancy met the drummer of one of the Howling Dog bands, but maybe they broke up, but no, she got married, is happy. I can't seem to accept that, or have it sink in. All these 'situations' seem to slip through my fingers. So many opportunities it looks like on the surface, yet none work out, and I'm left wondering if I set it up that way, or if my conscience works behind my back and doesn't tell me. Who knows if we share everything or not!

This is all forgotten as Becky and I get into the music and dance our hearts out. I tend to be a marathon dancer. My own opinion is that my mind shoots me full of drugs when I hear music, and it is a high of some kind. I will dance, and cannot be stopped till the drug wears off. So I become the music and scream like I'm at a rock concert, dancing till I drop. Since I'm in good shape, that takes a long time –like five hours of nonstop dancing. After dancing all night I crash on the floor at Becky's place. We plan our Manley trip for tomorrow.

The road from Fairbanks to Manley is unpaved - two lanes of twisty mudded potholes for five hours. The scenery is spectacular at least. Rolling hills of yellow and orange interspersed with views of valleys and gold rush camps. Several times we see moose feeding alongside the road. Blueberries are still out, and turn some hills blue. There is a fog hanging in the hills adding magic to the sun dappling through it.

"I have heard it is sort of a private springs, but the owner lets people use the bathhouse and collects some money. If I hear right, you pay, and that reserves the springs for an hour and it is all yours!" We knock on Chuck Dart's door and get the key, pay him the three dollars. He gives us a towel, and tells us to have a good time. The path to the log bathhouse is a windy dirt one that goes by wild flowers, tall grass, tropical ferns, and fall colored yellow birch trees. I hadn't thought ahead about using the bathhouse, and how to handle this procedure and all. *We get it alone huh?* We go in the small cabin and see the cement pool. Steam invitingly rises off water that is like hot bath water, right out of the ground. The hot stream gurgles in one end of the pool and out the other side. A cold stream also comes in. The temperature can be changed by using rocks provided, to limit one stream or the other. There is no changing room. We get down to our underwear and climb in the soothing water. All we can do is groan and sigh at how good it feels.

She laughs: "This is the life huh! I envy you being by here and able to jump in any time you like." She walks in the hot water over to me. The water is up to our chins. She takes the blade of grass out of my mouth and sets it on the ledge. She gets right up against me and puts her mouth over mine. We float in the hot water for a long time against each other. After a while she sighs: "My Oh My! This isn't a good idea, but the water is so soothing and you are so hot and I am so horny and well…" The words trail off as she runs her tongue deep down my throat. We eventually part —and end things there, for a while. She has a boyfriend, a job, a life to go back to. She looks at me longingly as she says all that though. I'm not saying much, but not letting go. For all the talk and flirting and opportunities, I haven't been this close to anyone in what, five years? Since Nancy, when I first came up here. She was the university student who didn't want me to leave for the wilderness, and promised to take care of me, support me if I stayed. She didn't wait for me though, and was married by the time I came back to town in spring.

I am fascinated by how a person knows by instinct what to do next. I feel her body temperature change even in the hot tub. We circle in on the rhythm of her breathing. I'm pretty sensitive to my environment all in all. She is about my height, short, even for a woman, with long dark hair almost to her waist. She might weigh 120 pounds. All distributed perfectly. She is olive skinned, dark eyes, hard to know her race or origin, maybe Spanish, maybe Jewish. Not that it matters. She says, "But don't look at my feet! I have ugly big feet!" Where she got such a notion I have no idea!

We are both giggling, and I giggle as seriously as I can: "Don't worry I won't stare at your feet." My eyes are closed, mouth over her breast. We see there are candle stubs along the edge of the water. It looks like lovers pay for the bath at night, light candles, and make love in the shallow hot water.

"Miles, it is getting too late for me to drive back to Fairbanks today? Maybe I can spend the night on the houseboat?"

"Sure, might be fun for you! It's nice being out on the water and hearing the night sounds out the window, as the boat rocks you to sleep." No one else but Will, and some kids in Galena, maybe those gals who skied out to buy art, and maybe John, but no one else has been on the boat in all these years. One person a year. When I had built it I was so sure it would be so great for picking up chicks. I thought I might need a stick to keep them off. Life however is not always as we dream it to be. "We have to take this small run about boat up the slough to where I have the houseboat parked." We pack all my things in the small boat. I have all the engine parts and extra goods that go to the houseboat. The fall colors are out, and the slough is clear and calm. Mosquitoes are gone now because we have had our first night freeze. The mile trip in the small boat is made with no talking, but I see Becky has her head back smelling the woods, eyes closed, smile on her face.

She opens her eyes with a start. Something has occurred to her: "Miles, isn't it moose season? I want a moose! What if we shoot a moose?"

I laugh at a woman being so enthusiastic about hunting, "Sure if we get a moose you can pack part of it in the truck and take it to Fairbanks if you have a freezer. But we are more likely to get a bear!" I had seen a lot of bear sign around. Becky shivers and tells me she is afraid of bears!

It is getting dark. We have had a long day, so we get ready for bed. I want her to have the bed by the door up high. I will sleep on the floor. We had made love in the bathhouse, then in the small boat, and now on the houseboat. I think she said "God!" a few times and I may have said "Dear!" a time or two or more – whose counting? I suppose it is like the dancing. I either want none, or all.

The morning is cold, with mist hugging the water, giving a surrealistic look to the fall colors along the edge. I step out the back door to pee in the water. I'm in my underwear yawning, scratching my chin and eyes, as I lazily see how far I can piss, vaguely wondering if any fish are screaming and gagging below. While looking across the sort of pond we are on, I see a bear is sitting there, just watching me through the sedge grass. I calmly step inside and shake sleeping Becky. When she is awake I ask her to hand me the rifle.

"There above the door the bed is against." I can't reach it, so she has to hand it to me. When she looks at me puzzled I simply say, "Bear" I had said it so casually it didn't register on her half asleep mind.

She nods "uh huh" and hands me the rifle, then goes back asleep. In my underwear I open the squeaky back door and peer out to see the bear is still staring at the boat; an intrusion is on his turf he doesn't understand. Conscience: *'Hi my name is Wild Miles, I'm the new King of the forest here. Would you like to be my dinner? Could you please turn you head just a trifle more to the left so I can put a lead ball in your brain pan? Thank you!'* As if the bear heard me, he turns his head and offers me a clear shot at the brain pan. The fifty caliber 'Holy Shit' does her usual thing. Like a stick of dynamite going off. Six ft. of flame. A cloud of blue smoke I can't see through, and the boat rocks with a mighty Whump! From over by the bed I hear the scream . "Jesus F —uk!" She is out of bed now. It wouldn't be polite to laugh, but… She has fallen out of bed and is on the floor, hair dragging in the wood chips.

"You should see the expression on your face. I wish I had a camera!" When her heart starts to beat again she starts laughing. After she is dressed I show her how to skin a bear. She's pretty excited. All this has been quite an adventure for her. We cook a fresh bear steak. I give her the hide and some meat, get her off on the road for an early start to Fairbanks.

"Miles this is the most exciting two days I have ever had in my life. I will remember this as long as I live." I can only nod dumbly and wave good-bye mumbling about thanks for the ride. She doesn't mind having an adventure as a change of pace, but this is not how she wants to live.

I tell myself how anxious I am to get these new parts on my engine. As I work on the engine I am glad I have this bear meat. Possibly the weather is cold enough now this meat will keep till next May. Becky has a boyfriend, a life, and plans. Loving her means setting her free. My life is an exciting vacation. Who wants to really live like this forever? Not her.

My conscience tells me what I already figured: *'Looks like it is too late to go to the Kantishna for winter. The engine is still untested. River water is dropping fast. We still do not know where we can trap on that river and …'* I don't want to hear any more and just say: "Yeah, yeah I know!" We'll make the best of it. The owner of the hot springs has a son named Johnny who is a miner. On the side, he is the local distributor for snow machines. I might need a snow machine. If I was to be on the Kantishna River, of course a machine would be no use without gas and parts. But in Manley, the temperature is now below freezing and winter is in the air.

Dearest Maggie:

I'm pretty bummed out I will not make it to the Kantishna and the wilderness this year, just too late in the season and too many factors not going my way. I mentioned Becky I think? I know, maybe I should have tried to keep her around. Is it because I still miss Nancy? Yet I know she is married now and no use thinking of her! I'm thinking of getting a snow machine. (?) Yeah. Well I could use it to trap and maybe it will pay for itself. Certainly I should find out if they are useful or not. I had one in

Delta where the houseboat was built and liked it, but there was no trapline available around there. Back to Becky—well I go to the post office and am asked "So where's your girlfriend?" There is talk about our time at the hot springs. Not much is a secret in a village it looks like, so I am the subject of gossip now. Anyhow talk to ya later!
Sunshine, Miles

The boat engine runs good I think, so at least there will be no unknowns when it is time to make the long trip up the Kantishna. The water starts dropping. I decide on a place to park for winter. In the past there had been trouble winching the boat out of the water for winter. Now I made up my mind it is much better to pull in the shallows someplace, jam logs under the boat, and just let the water drop out from under it. There is a pond at the end of a dead end slough—called 'Hagan Slough' on an old map I have. I could have parked in the hot water of the springs, but this is right in the village, and I am uncertain what will happen at -50°. I bet there is a lot of ice fog! This pond is about three miles from the village. I feel more comfortable being away a little bit.

One day I hear a splash next to the houseboat. My conscience thinks, 'Hey a moose!' I grab 'Holy Shit' resting by the back door. When I ease the door open there is a moose swimming the pond without a care in the world. I already have bear meat, but this bear will not be nearly enough to last the winter. I had let Becky have a lot of it. A fresh cap is put on the nipple and when I pull the hammer back, the bull turns and looks at me. It's an easy shot-only 100 ft. I squeeze the trigger after sighting in on the head. The hammer falls on the cap and all there is, is "click." The cap has not gone off - must be damp. I quickly set aside 'Holy Shit,' and grab my 270 rifle with its reloaded ammunition in it. Now the shot is not easy. The moose has swum the pond, climbed out the other side and is trotting off into the brush, having got nervous with all the sounds I made. I make a quick shot through the brush and hit the moose. The brush deflected the bullet or my aim was not perfect but a moose is a big target. Even though I missed the heart shot, the hit was vital and kills the moose.

While skinning the moose, another bull shows up, hangs around, and would have been easy to shoot as well. I let it be, and only hoped it would not charge or make trouble. The bulls are in rut now, angry and unpredictable. This seems a good omen to me to have got a bear and then a moose and seen yet another moose. I will not have to worry about food all winter now.

Conscience 'Half the time that black powder fails us—maybe we shouldn't be depending on it so much!' I reply to myself, "Yes, it is fun and cheap to shoot but we wouldn't have got this moose if we didn't have the 270 as back up!" I depend on the black powder less and less.

There is a party at the roadhouse. Chuck from the hot springs explains: "Every year there is a big celebration when the tourist season ends. The road gets closed, or at least the state will not maintain it once winter arrives, so there will be no plowing. We are all socked in for winter. Most Manley people stockpile supplies. There is a co-op for those who want to share large orders of bulk food." The entire population of fifty winter residents show up for the big party. The celebration will be talked about the rest of the winter. This seems like a tight knit community that is refreshing to see. We laugh and dance to local fiddle music in the Roadhouse. I meet more of the village members as well as the town characters.

I'm still wondering about Manley and what kind of community it is. I'm chatting with someone at the post office, the local gathering place, explaining how I am getting a snow machine and expect to go up and down the slough in winter. Out of the blue, someone behind me, who I wasn't even speaking to says, "Well you're not going by my place and I own the land right down to the slough! The first time you go by I'll just shoot over your head…"

I turn to see it is not even a guy, but a woman. I, of course, have to wonder what kind of place this is, and how many people here I want to get to know. She had spoken loudly with great anger and insanity. No one who heard her said anything like, "Hey that's enough of that kind of talk!" and apologized to me, made me feel welcome. I vaguely wonder whether I should shoot her first, rather than get sniped off my snow machine and blindsided. The reality is there are people, who would kill you just for giggles. If no one is going to lock this woman up, and it's everyone for themselves, then maybe this is the sort of place where if your mouth gets too big for your britches you tend to disappear. One thing I want to do is survive. There are things I wish to accomplish. Being a victim of a drive by is not what I want to be known for. I have no intention of trembling in my boots and not using the public slough, due to the words of a crazy person. I have courage, understand the wonderful world of firearms, and understand no one will look out for me. There are no police around. If there are dead bodies to pick up, it's not going to be mine if I can help it. Let them pile up. I will be the last one standing.

Not long after this I am in the roadhouse, minding my own business, sipping a coke at the bar, the only place to socialize in the village. Mike is bartending and comes over, real friendly. I smile. Mike shows me an ad he clipped out of the paper. "Miles, I thought you could use these!" Everyone in the bar is watching. I take a look, and it is an ad for elevator shoes. Mike is at least a foot taller than I am and weighs twice as much. What is there to say? I assume I'm different, do not fit in, and am not welcome here. Partly I think because I'm sipping a coke instead of a beer. Partly because I travel with a nick name like 'Wild Miles,' but I am short, and do not appear to be very tough, or not tough by the standards of these men here. Getting angry is not going to help much, nor is feeling hurt. I play dumb like I don't get it.

"No thanks, I'm happy with my height, but thanks for your concern, Mike." He gets angry as I get up. He's toe to toe looking down on me, to show me the difference in our height.

"Shorty, I could pick you up with one hand and toss you thorough the window!" Everyone else laughs.

I reply, "Uh huh, you are three times stronger than me, and probably could." He smiles and I add "But I'm three times faster than you are, and if you made a move on me, before you could blink, I'd have your throat slit. So what's your point?" I stand there waiting for him to make his move. Go for it. We no longer live in the Stone Age. The mean bully is not always the last one standing.[1]

Later someone shows me bullet holes in the roadhouse wall, and proudly tells me this is the result of settling a dispute. I assume from all this, that people around here must be dropping like flies. Shootings and killing is a way of life. We'll remain armed and watch our back. I'm up to it, but feel sorry for the young, old, and weak. I wish the world was a more peaceful place.

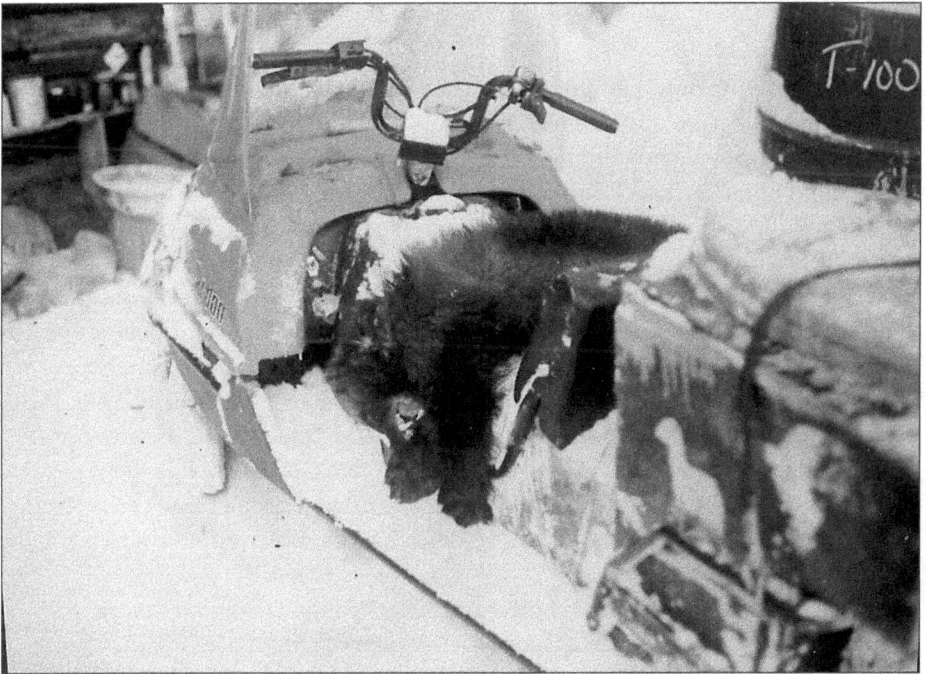

Wolverine

CHAPTER SEVEN

WINTER WALK TO MANLEY, NEW SNOW MACHINE, OTHER TRAPPERS, TRAPPING

Ice forms on the dead end pond I'm at so I can no longer take the run about boat in to the village, and there is not enough ice to walk on. This is that happy time called 'freeze up,' when we hunker down and no one travels till winter sets in for good. The fall colors had been gorgeous this year. The birch trees are still bright yellow, and the low willows along the slough have more reds. The whole mountain top is filled with colors. The mountain comes right down to the slough with a rock face cliff. The slough is six ft. deep and 100 ft across, twisting around through a series of hairpin turns for six miles. There are no roads to see, and only a few fish camps. No houses exist till the village is reached. Nothing but beaver houses the size of human houses. The water color is not like the main river, which is filled with silt. This water is slow, dark, reflecting the sky and colors more. In one picture I took, it is hard to tell which is the sky and mountains, and which is the reflection. Turning it one way or the other, it looks the same till you spot a beaver stick floating in what must be the water, since it is unlikely a beaver stick would be floating in the sky. Ha!

When the ice starts to form it only adds to the beauty. This is the time of year the sky can be expected to be blue as long as a full month. Often there is not a breeze. In some places I was raised, this is called an Indian summer. Alaskans just call it 'freeze up.' Otter play on the ice and leave skid marks in the frost on the ice. There are fish in the slough. Some residents set nets out to catch them. Mostly it is tourists who go out with fish poles to catch them for sport. There are not many places in the whole interior of Alaska that match Manley Hot Springs for beauty. The view from the houseboat window takes my breath away. The richest millionaire can't get a better view out their window. I can only smile, yawn, and greet each day as a blessing. One of the best views on the planet and no rent, no fee. Can life get much better?

I spend the time setting up a shelter outside the boat to move things into so there is more room to live on the boat. This is like the winter in Galena, with just a simple pole frame, draping a twenty foot tarp over it. Some shelving is made of poles to hold boxes and crates. I have a new propane light, with several twenty pound propane bottles to set out. I have bags of clothes, and anything else I think can stay frozen all winter. I have been eating the garden vegetables I had harvested and carried with me from Galena. That free community garden had been nice, but it was a shame to have harvested it way too early with everything still so small. All in the hopes I could make it to the Kantishna before winter. I only have twenty-thirty pounds left. I spend some time blanching, slicing, and drying some of these vegetables. I decide not to bother with potatoes as they should keep ok, but I dry carrots and beets. Probably I will have it all eaten before any of it would go bad, but maybe I just want to see how this drying thing works, so I know. Reading about it is one thing, but doing it quite another! I'm finding this to be true of about everything! All those Mountain Man books I read when young make life sound free and easy- but try to live the life!!

The moose hide is saved. I am determined to not waste anything this year. In the past I had so much go bad it made me sick. My first moose was half wasted by maggots and the first bear... *so this will be different!* I make a stretching rack to lash the moose hide in so I can scrape it- just like I have read about, and seen in pictures. I will tan it later on. I have already experimented with all the ways to tan when I had been at the fish camp working for Piper. There was the ashes, the bark water, the battery acid ,the moose brain, smoke, tide soap, and of course the piss soak fiasco. I could practically write a book on the 101 ways to tan skins. All give a different type of leather, depending on what is needed.

Grouse hunting is fun this time of year, and as usual there are plenty! Feathers and guts are saved to be used later for trapping bait. A few fish are caught in a small net, and they are hung to dry as I was taught by Piper. The salmon run is over, at least the Kings. There are a few chums and silvers. I get more pike than anything else. Cranberries are picked, as well as Labrador leaves, and rose hips for tea. The days turn into weeks. I am happy, healthy, and wish it could go on forever. Well maybe not, because I look forward to snow and trapping! I do not look forward to seeing people, or I do, but what am I going to do about this woman who wants to shoot me off my snow machine? In civilization one might go cry to the police. This is supposed to stop killings. People get locked up before they kill someone, in theory. I'm not sure how it works in actuality but suspect folks get locked up after the deed, not before. No one else seems to care what this woman said. It is clearly 'my problem,' not the community's. It is only the community's problem when there are dead bodies to sort out.

Anyhow there is plenty of time to sit and contemplate the ways of the world out alone in the wilderness. Especially when it gets dark so early now, and here I am in a one room six by seven ft. space. There is not much room for projects. I set up my space to do my art work with more room, now that so much can be stored outside. The single propane light is not great. I read a lot, but one can only read so many books. I average a book every two days but I only brought twenty books. That's all the weight I could afford. It cost a dollar a pound to get things out here. I sit in the dark and think a lot.

"Hey we can walk into the village!" I tell my conscience one cold morning. The temperature has dropped to -20.° The slough ice looks good enough to walk on. There are open places from the warm spring's water, but think there is enough ice along the edges. I look forward to picking up my new snow machine! The walk is a little tricky, and a little dangerous, *"But so is life!"* I fall through the ice, but nothing serious, just the usual.

AT THE POST OFFICE:

"Hi, Mike—got mail for me?"

Mike is not especially glad to see me and says, "Yes, but you are lucky. I only have to hold it for fifteen days you know." He explains again how there are no boxes here. How all mail is general delivery, and Federal postal laws state that general delivery only has to be held for fifteen days, after that it can get sent back as undeliverable. I wonder what trappers—homesteaders around here do. Mike tells me what a favor he is doing for me, holding my mail like this, and not to let it happen again.

He is surprised I am still alive. He thinks I am going to cost the tax payers a lot of money carting me out in a body bag. I thank him for his opinion. I hope if I do die, I will not be a burden on society, and will not be found. I tell him if I disappear, not to have any search parties. He doesn't like the grin on my face. I think by his expression he is afraid to die, and is angry that I am not. I can tell by his behavior he is not happy, works hard, has a hard life, and is resentful my life is so easy, and I don't have to work. I get to go fishing, do my art, live how I like, and he can't. He's convinced his tax dollars are supporting me, as with most bums.

Mike stands there swelled up—big strong looking guy, an ex-cop-being a typical bully. He's the postmaster. I need my mail. I don't need to be pissing him off. Behind my laugh I think someday someone is going to clean his clock. That's what usually happens to bullies. I smile.

"My snow machine is here? All right!" The local dealer, John shows it to me. It is a ski doo citation. Similar to the Elan, same engine. This has got to be the coolest thing I ever saw, except for maybe my boat.

Johnny adds, "But I don't know where you are going to trap around here. Me and my brother have everything north of the river. Joe has quite an area south of the river." I reply, "Well I'm not out to take anything away for anyone else. I'll go out and look around and get back to you with any questions after I see what's going on. We can look over maps. I'll go talk to Joe so he knows who is out running around the country."

We both know trappers have no legal rights. Trappers are considered using public lands that belong to all of us. Trails we cut are public trails. We can register traplines, but that means what? Register with who? Register with a Trapper's Association, sort of like the Boy Scouts. It is not legal to steal fur from another's trap or steal traps, but legally a trapper can set his own trap on your pole or cubby set. Most trappers know none of us can make any money like that. 90% of the trappers honor the bush code. We live by a set of laws not in writing anyplace, not enforceable except by the laws of the gun. I want Johnny to know I want to do the right thing here. I'm still trying to get a handle on just what the bush laws are. Sounds though like there are only two to three trappers in an area the size of some states. Surely there is room 'someplace.' No one seems to be coming down the slough itself, and going downriver. Downriver is where I had just come from with the houseboat. I know there are no more roads, and no villages till the Yukon River. Looking over the maps – it looks like a lot of country.

Joe lives across the Tanana River from the village. I run my snow machine down the slough to see him. The river is not frozen yet. I see smoke across the river. Joe has been out running his dog team in the new snow. He is able to mush to within yelling distance and hollers. "What month is this? Is trapping season open yet?!" I have to laugh. *Someone else besides me forgets what month it is.* He is freezing in like me, out of the village, and cannot come in till the main river freezes. He lives alone. I assume faces the same things I do, so I feel a kinship toward him. "Did you get a moose?"

I holler back I got my winter moose. I could have shot one for him too if I knew or trusted him. It is not legal to kill a winter moose the way all of us do. The legal season is at a time meat will not keep without a refrigerator requiring electricity. So the legal season is set for city sport hunters. Joe is running out of food, especially for his dog team. I think a minute, and holler a reply: "Hey Joe, I still have some bear meat if you can use it!" The meat is not frozen, and was not in the best shape. I have been eating it, but this moose is so much better that I'm kind of leaving the bear alone. Though I cut a lot of fat off the bear to fry stuff up in through the winter.

Joe replies: "I can haul a boat to the edge of the ice with the dogs and come across to your side!" The boat he has is small, but will work just to get across this narrow channel of open water. This of course is highly unsafe, and not recommended. If the shelf ice broke and either of us went in the river we would die, that simple.

I go back to the houseboat with the snow machine and drag the bear carcass on the snow with a rope behind the snow machine. Joe gets the meat, which he will mostly feed to his sled dogs. It is not the time to bring up the trapline issue. I can talk to him later after I look around and know more about the country. I can then have knowledge outside what rival trappers are telling me.

While waiting for the main river to freeze, which is the wilderness highway, I make art pieces and snow machine into Manley every few days. The Roadhouse is closed, so there is no public place to eat or stay in winter. I am seeing some of the Manley residents I met at the Roadhouse closing party. They invite each other to their houses for dinner. I get included. I enjoy some nice home cooked meals.

One gal is in the process of buying the store, and is sort of new here herself. She invites me and a few of the other bachelors over for dinner regularly. We become sort of friends. We talk a lot. I help her get firewood and do guy stuff for her. She is against selling liquor in the store to the Indians. Locals think she will go under. Booze is where the money is that subsidizes everything else. She thinks everyone will be glad to get good food instead of booze. We shall see.

I meet a local pilot and his family. He is very religious, I think Seventh Day Adventist. He likes to talk about the Lord and His plans for mankind. I enjoy a good discussion. He has a big family with lots of children. He lives in a house he is still building. They do not have a lot of money, but seem to get by and are all close and good people. I teach art to his children, and help Maul, the pilot, out by loading his plane and bringing firewood into the house. He pays me by having me over to dinner often. Maul supplements his income by flying supplies for the bush folk with his private plane. Homesteaders and trappers who need things come to Maul. Flying weather is marginal still, with open water and ice not thick yet. He wants his plane on skies now. I helped him take the floats off. I meet a few really nice people living here. Some become lifelong friends.

No. The nut who threatened to shoot me is just that, a local nut everyone tolerates. Apparently she means no harm, just gets a French fry short of a happy meal every now and then. I wish I had the ability to know when someone is harmless. If I told someone I was going to shoot them, you could take that to the bank. I never lived in a world where people make idle threats. My father and everyone I was raised around said what they meant, and meant what they said. But anyhow it is nice to know, 'probably' I'm not going to have to kill anyone in self-defense.

"Hey, Joe good to see you, river must have frozen huh?" Joe shows up at my houseboat with his dog team. He ties them up to a tree near the boat. The seven dogs lay right down without a sound, still in harness. Joe is tall and thin, He has long stringy blondish hair. He is wearing dirty jeans, wore out military surplus bunny boots, an old army coat, with gray wool cap. I invite him in. There is barely room in my houseboat for two people to fit. Two people couldn't pass each other in here, and two chairs wouldn't fit in here. Joe looks around and nods. No one else wants to visit me here.

"There enough room in here?"

"Enough room for what? I spend more time outdoors than indoors. All I need is room to sit, eat, read, do my art, and have a place to sleep. Anything else is kind of wasted space." After talk of the weather and such I say, "I'd like to trap Joe, just this winter till I get to the Kantishna River. I don't want to put in a trail in the trees and do any cutting. I was thinking of going downriver maybe, depending on where you go and what you claim."

"Miles, I don't own the cabin across the river I live in. The cabin belongs to a Native called Navaho. He is getting old and doesn't get around much anymore. He is in Tanana and used to come up here with dogs all the way from there. It all used to be his trapline, but no more. He lets me use his cabin. I guess it is ok if you trap downriver, and up some of the sloughs. I trap everything south of the river pretty much. Up the zits to almost Wien Lake about 200 miles, then across to the hills before the Kantishna drainage. Maybe 100 miles wide." I don't have to get the maps out. I know all the places he is speaking of by heart, and can picture it in my mind.

"Can you boat up the zits in summer?" I wonder if he can supply a line camp from the river.

"Just at break up." Joe goes on telling me where the other trappers are. No one has a map. It is just all a verbal understanding. Joe explains, "Steve is out of Moose Heart lake. He goes in by ski plane. He claims everything in a circle around there maybe 100 miles, good country there, lots of rolling hills with marten. Hard to cut through country though. You'll meet Art. He traps by plane up in the Brooks Range, but not around here. There are some Cosna River people who do not get into Manley much, but they are way up at the headwaters, maybe 100 miles from here. So you can have that hundred miles from here to there. It's not much room, but you're kind of last in line here."[1]

I run into Maul, the Seventh Day Adventist friend I now know is called 'The Flying Peddler,' who invites me over for dinner. Maul tells me, "I believe in supplying the bush people with good things like fruit and good fresh food. No booze and no junk food. I deliver propane when most pilots won't because it's a hazard. I know people need and depend on propane." Sounds like a good thing he is doing. He likes to trade. Only half his business is in cash. He trades for furs, fish, and services. It all fits in with his religious views. "There wasn't a big place in the bible for money people." Maul tells me the ways of the Lord. I find out he likes to tell one story over and over. I look at this tall skinny nervous energy guy as he tells it… "Yes, Miles, I was alone in the world and wanted a wife, so I took it to the Lord and prayed. As I was praying in an empty church, a woman comes in, looking lost, looking for some other church. We introduce ourselves, talk, and that was that. The Lord brought her to me. She is the one. I don't know what I would have done without her. That was over ten years ago" His beautiful wife smiles and nods as all the kids giggle, for they have all heard the story many times. I envy him that it was so simple and straight forward. Making a mistake about such matters is pretty awful. They don't have much money, so we eat a lot of salmon, which everyone catches. There is so much of it that all the dogs in town get fed salmon till it runs out everyone's ears. In this village you can have all the salmon you want for free, just by asking. Maul's house is not finished, so is cold. The entire family hunkers down under all their blankets at night. None seem to complain. The big plan is to finish the house then sell it for a great profit and move into something else.

The village is small enough most everyone walks, runs sled dogs, or snow machine. The roads are not plowed. We do not see cars or trucks much. There is no TV station. The community is lucky to have a phone line that works sometimes. There is no form of government of any kind. No taxes, no cop, no fire department, no garbage pickup, no street lights, no signs. If the community needs something they call a town meeting and discuss it. Pretty cut off from the outside world. A lot of people here work the tourist trade or mine seasonally, and do not choose to work all winter, or supplement their main job in summer with some side thing in winter like trapping, sled dog racing, or some craft of some kind. One guy builds dog sleds by hand to sell to racers in Fairbanks. Some people are retired. No one seems very stressed out about anything. Certainly no one is in a hurry. A visit might last an hour or all day. The post office is also sort of a store with a few items, and sells gas so snow machines can pull right up to the pump as cars do in summer.

There are places all over town to tie up sled dogs. Several students and the school teacher arrive each day by sled dog, and tie them up in the schoolyard. The school is one-room, two teachers, and all grades. Most residents do not have electricity, unless they run their own generator. One guy who sells fuel sells power I think, so a few people have power of some sort, but I see a lot of kerosene lanterns, and wood stove or propane cooking stoves. I find out about all this from dinner talks and observing.

Maul asks, "Miles, will we see you on movie night? I hear it's a good movie this week!"

I had heard of this in Manley, so reply, "Sure!" Movies are shown at the community center, a log cabin with barrel wood stove. This happens every two weeks for the community. A projector is got out, and we all sit in school chairs to watch old black and white movies. I join the pottery club. This is at the school which has a kiln.

We all donate what we can to help pay for the power and clay and such. Being an artist, I really look forward to this.

On pottery day I get asked, "Miles, since you are an artist, are you interested in teaching art at the school? There is a program with funding to pay you if you are interested."

"Well I'm not a certified teacher. Isn't that a problem?" Everyone laughs. They see it as, I know about art. The kids want to know about art. Put the two of us together, what's the problem? My thinking as well. I don't have to have the money. I can use it, but I'm ok, not desperate. I can get by until real work comes along. In this case I have furs accumulating I can sell. Not enough to pay for the snow machine yet, but I think I will have that much before the season ends. One thing I am finding out is, I am not alone. Many people end up in the Alaska wilderness because of some trauma in their life. Some reason they maxed out in some way on stress, on life in the fast lane. Some got taken to the cleaners in some way or other, with a story to tell about it. As a result, some of us just want peace, want simple things. Or say they do, but may not know how to get there from here. Others take that feeling and feel angry, want to hurt someone to get even for having been hurt themselves. So I do not answer right away on this offer. I am not interested in getting involved in this community, care about it and all that. I am headed for the Kantishna River. This is just a stopping place along the way! *Humph!*

The hot springs is open all winter. Most residents have no running water in their homes so rely on going to the bathhouse to get clean. The water runs out of a hose along the road for anyone to stop and use. Many of us fill jugs from it to take home for water. After a hot bath I go to 'pottery night.' About ten people show up regularly. We talk, and get to know each other. *Almost like being friends, given enough time.* The subject of teaching comes up again. There is another artist in the community who does stained glass who I am getting to know. I brought up the offer made to me, and asked if he wanted to be part of the deal. If there was a problem with the deal, at least I wouldn't be the only one getting the shaft. I agreed to work with Steve. We teach every other day. It is just a two week class, but it's a thousand dollars. Really good money for two weeks of work. *This would almost pay for the snow machine.*

I'm a little nervous. I've never taught before, and do not consider myself a very social person. I'm surprised I'm not considered too weird to be around people's children. Again, like in Canada, the kid I had befriended is on my mind.

There are twenty-five students in the Manley school, covering all grades. It will be a challenge to teach all levels from first grade to twelfth. With the younger crowd, and especially those who have no attention span or interest in art, there is an extra challenge. The plan is to occupy them with finger painting and basics that the regular teacher could cover, while I plan to teach block printing Christmas cards with the rest, and if time, in the second week get into ivory scrimshaw. This is two weeks of full time nothing but art work. The first half of the day is to be spent on the basics of drawing, coming up with a design for the card. Every year I cut a linoleum block, get out my roller and ink, cut my own paper and print my own Christmas cards. I have been doing this since I was a child. This saves money, but is also a gift that is from 'me,' something with a personal connection.

> **Diary:** I've been getting letters from Linda, a gal I've never met, and who was supposed to come here after her trip to England. The last letter casually mentioned she is back from England. No reference to her coming to Alaska. I reply and ask if she still plans to come—she says, "Don't push me!" She calls me 'Her Trapper.' I considered going to visit her, since I am not on the Kantishna. I have this extra money from the teaching job, and will have furs to sell. She gets cool and distant, not excited to have me visit. I call her on the phone. She tells me she has been seeing this other guy and can't kick him out of the house. A guy she had told me it was all over with a year ago. Whatever. I think I am just entertainment for her. A fantasy about someone far away that the reality would not suit. **This happens a lot.**

I am pretty touched by the community that wants me to teach its kids. All my 'problems' in society, my parents, relatives, civilized people, seem to be saying about me is, "Christ, Miles, get real and what do you expect! Dress like a freak, long hair, dirty, wear a knife; you're getting what you deserve!" Living on the outside of society, I shouldn't be expected to be accepted by society! But I feel… Well… I don't like everyone or accept everyone. So what. I don't get involved, or help them, or be part of whatever they are doing, but I also do not interfere. People are innocent unless they show me otherwise. Say, do, be, and dress anyway you want! Just do not mess with anyone else's rights. Don't insult me, threaten me, and we will get along just fine. I expect to be treated the same way. I don't ask for acceptance by everyone. But I do ask not to be messed with if I have done nothing wrong. I expect polite tolerance.

"Miles, what do you do for a living?" Someone, one of the parents is asking me.

I tell them with a straight face, "I kill cute fuzzy defenseless creatures and sell their skin."

There is a pause followed by, "Right on! What have you killed so far?"

"Well let's see… about ten fox, maybe twenty marten, a lynx."

A nod of the head followed by, "How's the price of marten this season? I hear it's gone up!"

I nod yes, saying, "Market looks strong so far. No word back from the auctions, but hear the buyers are paying a $60 average. I'm holding out, thinking the price will get better yet, based on how the season ended last year."

Another nod of the head followed by, "Yes but trappers saw last year's prices end high and are all geared up this year, so there could be more supplied than demanded?"

This is possible, but I give my opinion, "My guess is the trappers will be out in greater numbers, but the marten cycle is on a downslide, especially felt around the larger towns like Fairbanks. In the remote villages, trappers do not keep up as much on the news, so are less likely to know what is happening in the big picture. Some will understand, but I'm betting most will not, and will make no extra effort. We'll see!" It is nice to talk to someone about furs, who understands the market, and has something to add to the conversation. I change the subject. "I have to do something besides trap. I do art work, and sell it mostly in Fairbanks, wholesale to the shops there."

"Christmas must be a good time to sell then! Are you going in to town to sell for Christmas?"

I explain I am reluctant to spend the money to go in, but might have to. Maul overhears the conversation and says, "Miles, I am headed in by plane, going empty to bring back a load. I can give you a ride in, but you would have to catch the mail plane back!" This would work out great.

"Thanks Maul!" My art teaching class is over now. Everyone is happy. We designed Christmas cards. Printed them so all the kids have cards to send out. We had time to do some scrimshaw. Most kids were able to make a necklace for parents. There are some pretty artistically talented children in Manley.

FLYING with Maul is only a little bit like flying with Piper, who had flown me into the wilderness my first year. Piper had been a cautious flier, 'by the book.' The line goes, 'There are a lot of old pilots, there are a lot of bold pilots, but there are not a lot of old bold pilots.' Maul is a bold pilot, word has it. Many will not fly with him. He takes on all the jobs no one else will take; the heaviest loads, going to the shortest runways, in the worst weather. I do not understand planes much, but Maul is obviously proud of his plane as he explains: "This used to be a 180 maul—but I had it converted to a 185. Every instrument is duplicated in case one fails." The seats have been taken out. Piper told me his plane could haul about 500 pounds. Maul tells me this is rated for 800, but winks at me saying, "Which means it can handle twice that." He explains what really matters is how the plane feels and behaves—not the stated numbers. "Many things affect the payload, from the type of oil used, to the air temperature, the pitch of the prop, how the load is distributed, more things than the book can ever mention." I had noticed how Maul paid a lot of attention to the sound of the engine. He revved the engine and rocked the plane up on its nose and back down, watching all the gauges. When he was ready, and feels right, there is no hesitation to him. Peddle to the metal, thrust back in the seat, straight up into the air, and an immediate bank at 90 degrees. Lord help anyone with a queasy tummy. My understanding is, he has been flying like this for a few years and has not had an accident or serious close calls. Maul has a high Jesus factor. I'm not afraid to fly with him, and enjoy it.

"HELLO KAREN, Charley! How are things going at the Alaska House this season?" I'm in Fairbanks at my favorite gallery.

They are happy to see me, and get a look at my latest art, saying, "You get better every time we see your work Miles, amazing!" I have art packed in empty soup cans with moss. We both laugh at that. $500 art pieces, and can't afford boxes to put them in.

Karen is looking at a dog team scene I did in metals on mammoth ivory and exclaims, "Gee, Miles, this metal scene must have several hundred pieces in it! How do you keep it all sorted!" I shrug my shoulders. This piece is of Joe, when he came to visit the houseboat. I have copper traps in the sled with brass tarp. I have dog dishes, chains, each harness on all seven dogs, as well as collars on all the dogs. Karen laughs, "Look at the expression on the dogs, priceless!" They look tired. One is looking for a good place to lie down, but doesn't want to disturb the dog next to him. Another looks like it just wants to eat, another is looking towards the human leader for instructions. Spruce trees bend under the weight of new snow. All is told in metal work. I have less expensive items of simple scenes like a flying duck, a single flower on a slice of moose antler, a piece of jade, a tooth from a fox and bone from a wolf.

Charley is a state senator. Sometimes we chat politics. "I do not agree with you, Miles. Once I am elected, a politician decides what he likes. The process allows the public to vote if they want him or not. After that the politician has access to information the public does not, and votes as he sees fit, with no regard for how the public feels! Well I care, but I need not share my thoughts with the public, or vote how the public wishes, because the public does not have all the information I have."

"Charley, I feel the politician represents the people, even after he is elected, and needs to listen to how the majority of the people feel." We rarely talk specifics. I do not want to use our friendship to alter things, even though I have strong feelings about specific topics. It is enough we are becoming friends, and I am known through my art. We do not always agree, but respect each other. *What better way to communicate through the back door? What better way to make a statement about a lifestyle than to show its beauty through art? Isn't it so–a picture is worth a thousand words?*

Some items are bought outright so I have some upfront money to work with. Most of it is left on consignment. I'm told by Karen, "Let me get the books out, Miles. I think we owe you some money from consignment things that sold since you were last in!"

I get cash. I am not sure for what items. I am not keeping records. I make stuff. I get paid, it is enough. I'm not interested in the details. I laugh. "It takes as long to keep track of it as it does to make it!"

"I recall a lot of requests for belt buckles with animals on them, if you want to keep that in mind when looking for ideas!" They are good about letting me do whatever I wish, and being happy with it.

I do say, "If you get stuck with anything you can't sell, I'll trade it for something new." They have one item that needs repair which I pick up saying, "No charge. I'll get it back to you when it is fixed." Karen asks me if I have time to do a show, even though advertising on short notice would be tough. I have people collecting my art who want to know when I bring new things in. We work out a date a few days from now. It's the off season, but locals may come.

ON THE STREET I holler out, "Hey, how you doing, looks like it happens again! First day in town and I run into you!"

Will is dumbfounded once again saying, "This is the first time I have been in town in over a month!" Will is pretty busy. We have lunch together. He has to get things done, then takes off. I have time to tell him all the engine parts for the boat were the right ones, and there should be no problem. He wants to know if I am still using the black powder rifle.

Over time I'm getting kind of fond of my buddy, Will. One smart cookie when it comes to engines. More than that, he is kind, generous, level headed, honest, all the things that really matter in a friend. He and I share a passion for the wilderness. I still hope he makes it out there. I ask, "Saved enough money yet, Will?" He is trying to save enough to outfit himself to go out.

He shakes his head sadly, "Miles, work is tight. You wouldn't believe how it is here in town!" He tells me how it is and I am all the more glad I 'escaped' to the wilderness. He lives from hand to mouth, working hard, barely keeping even with life. He's such a talented guy too, can fix anything. I feel for him.

Will asks, "Miles, can I borrow twenty bucks?" I give a look with my eyebrows that he answers with, "Need a raffle ticket on a $70,000 jet boat. I'm going to win."

Now, I don't agree a broke guy should be borrowing money to buy a darn raffle ticket. But on the other hand Will is my friend and it is not my place to lecture, for after all, it is just an opinion. An opinion obviously he doesn't hold. He's a big boy.

As long as he pays it back, I put no restrictions on what he wants it for. I smile back, "Sure, Will, long as you're good for it. I'm sure you know my opinion, but hey, hope you win it!"

Will adds, "Oh yeah, I need another ten bucks for the hitch. My truck hasn't got a hitch."

I look at him a moment thinking how incredible this is. Guy can't buy lunch, and he wants a trailer hitch for a boat he is sure he is going to win on a raffle? Is he nuts? I sigh—smile- shrug my shoulders. "Sure, Will, here you go, but no more. I don't want you to end up in a bind over borrowing money." We are cruising down third Avenue and I slap Will saying, "Hey, Will, what's going on there with that lady on the street?" She is walking along crying, and trying to get someone's attention, but no one is stopping or caring. Will hasn't said anything, just watching. So I speak up. "Will we got to stop and help this woman, find out what's wrong, and see if we can do something for her!"

Finally Will speaks up, "Miles, it's none of our business. We need to keep going."

In shock I say, "Will, we can't be like that! When people need help you got to help them!" I roll the window down and holler to the lady, "What's wrong?! Can we help!?"

She sniffles as she points. I follow her finger and see there's a guy running up ahead with a purse. She sniffles again. "That man took my purse."

"Well, get in, we'll have it back for you!"

Will glowers at me as she gets in, but I give him a, 'shut up,' look and he drives after this guy with the purse. The guy goes into a local hotel on the corner, so I have Will slam the breaks on as I jump out and follow into the hotel. As I get next to the guy to confront him, I over hear him saying to the clerk behind the desk: "Call the police!"

This puzzles me momentarily, as it seems odd for a thief to ask for the police, but I do not have time to think about it. The purse is on the counter loose. Another clerk says to me, "Here, quick, take it out the back!"

My only concern is getting the purse back to the rightful owner. So without thinking, I grab the purse and turn to run with it. The thief turns and grabs me, throws me against the wall. He lifts me off my feet as he says to me, "First I'm going to rip your arms off. Then I'm going to. . ."

Just then Will comes through the door. Will takes it all in and says, "I was just leaving," and turns to go back out. He doesn't want to get involved, never did. It's my mess, and I can deal with it. But the thief thinks Will is scared, and sees I am not. The thief lets go of me and goes to grab Will. When he lets go of me, I grab the purse and make a dash out the back door. The back door is alarmed, so there is a scream of a siren, as I run down the street with a purse in my hand. This does not look good. I make it around to the front where I know Will has the truck, and the lady whose purse this is. Will has made it to the truck with the thief hot on his heels. Tires squeal as Will gets the heck out of there. I jump in as he goes by me and we leave the thief screaming profanities in the empty alley.

I finally look around as the adrenaline rush leaves, and notice the gal has different color hair now. This is all quite strange. She has a wig in her purse. Will stops, and I hand the lady her purse as she gets out, and I say, "Lady you better take this and get out of here, who knows if that thief has a car, good luck to ya!" and with that Will takes off. Will and I get out of the neighborhood. I am quite pleased, and look over to Will, thinking he would be like me, and we'd be slapping each other on the great deed we had done today. But Will is staring out the window shaking his head sadly. I ask, "Will, what is wrong with you. Don't you feel good we helped that nice lady?"

Will takes a while replying as is his way. "Miles, did you hear what that guy was saying?"

I give a puzzled, "Yeah… well it was all pretty strange if you ask me."

Will tells me what we were part of, as he figures it. This gal is a hooker. This hotel is working with her. She took this guy, customer upstairs. While he is undressed, she grabs his wallet, throws it in her purse and runs. He doesn't catch up to her till she is down the street. He grabs the purse with his wallet in it, and marches over to the hotel to report this.

Now that Will mentions it I do recollect. "Will, that clerk put her finger down on the receiver while she was dialing the police so the call wouldn't go through while he wasn't looking. I wondered why she would do that!" I pause and think and say, "So Will you are telling me we just helped a hooker rip off her John?" Will only sighs. I feel bad, should have listened to Will, minded our own business. Will is more street wise than I am. After a while I add, "I'll never understand town, Will."

THE ALASKA HOUSE Art Show is good for me. Maybe 100 people show up. Not like in a big city, but they all want to buy, and I sell almost everything I have for full price. I have to give 20% to the gallery, but I still leave with almost $3,000. Not bad for a few hours of show time.[2] This is good for my ego. I sign autographs, tell bear stories, and give a story for almost all the pieces I sell. I get so many compliments on my art, I laugh to Karen, "I need a tape player so when I am alone doing this art I can turn it on for motivation." hearing, "Oh Miles this is so good!" And such things. We both laugh.

I only want to spend a short time in town. It cost too much to stay here. I have a reservation on the mail plane, and head back to Manley. I have traps out that I do not want to leave set for more than a few days without checking. I had agreed to let Maul use my snow machine, since he hasn't got one.

On the way to the houseboat I notice the snow machine isn't running as it should. I stop and lift the cowling. Maul has used string to tie up the carburetor. It really needs a bolt, which would require something from Fairbanks. The string is getting sucked into the carb so I cut the loose ends of the string. Not long afterwards, the engine seizes up. It looks like a piece of string got sucked in and blocked something inside… no it tangled in the cooling fan belt and locked it up. I think it is Maul's fault. I know he hasn't got any money to speak of. Anyhow he doesn't think it had anything to do with the string on the carb. The problem is solved if I simply don't let other people use equipment I depend on. Fixing the engine cost me $300 and a week of down time.

Pups playing, 'learning the ropes!'

CHAPTER EIGHT

SELBY LAKE BROOKS RANGE, FIRST SLED DOGS, READY TO TRAVEL AGAIN

C hristmas came and went and didn't even get mentioned in my diary. I have never liked Christmas much. Christmas is for those who have loved ones, close friends. I did meet a couple about this time though, Dem, the school teacher, and her husband, Van who traps in the Brooks Range by plane.

Van: "Yes I have heard of the Kantishna River and even the lake at the headwaters. I have a ham radio license and talk to someone from the lake. I gather there are eighteen people there, a post office, no store. Don't know much else."

I scratch my beard thoughtfully before replying, "Well I'm not ready for you to mention me to this guy or ask questions. I think it would be better to show up and see what is going on first. I know a lot of remote places get inquiries from would be visitors wanting information, people who never show up. I'd get better answers maybe if I was there!" I'm glad to know at least the rumors I heard a year ago seem to be true. There is a big lake with a small community. "I would think it would be very beautiful there since it is a huge lake and only fifty miles from Denali Mountain."

Van nods,"I flew by it once, but it was raining, with no view, so can't tell you much. Those muddy flats on the map extend a long way, and are nothing but hundreds of unnamed lakes. My guess is there would be a lot of fish and ducks and such there." This sounds like a place to settle to me. Van has something else on his mind."Miles, I wasn't able to come out off the trapline for Christmas. I want to make it up to my wife. I have my dog team out there on Selby Lake in the Brooks Range so I cannot come out for more than a couple of days at a time. Would you look after the dog team if I flew you out, so I can come in for two weeks?"

"Sure Van, sounds like it would be fun, and give me a chance to see another part of the Alaska wilderness, maybe find out about sled dogs!" I have to pull my traps and get ready to go. My art tools fit in a shoebox, and are all hand tools, so I am able to do my art anyplace. I think it is pretty slick that I can fly into the Alaska Brooks Range and get dropped off for two weeks in the mountains at a remote cabin, and it is not a vacation that cost me. Conscience: *'It is a job and I'm making money! With jobs like this, who needs vacations? It is like being retired. It is like getting paid for having fun!'*

The flight with Van is spectacular. The Brooks Range is a different climate and different country than the interior flats. This mountain range is the Northern boundary of the interior and separates the arctic from the interior. The separation includes a separation between Indian and Eskimo, separates lifestyles, and animal life. This is Dall Sheep country. Grizzly Bear country. There is lots of wind, snow, and northern lights. The plane struggles to gain altitude to get over the top of the mountains. Van tilts the wings in the two-seater plane so I can look down on the lakes and mountains below. I'm actually spending more hours in a private plane than in a car.

"Miles, one in ten people in Alaska owns a small plane."

I had heard this before. Finally we get to the lake. Van circles between the mountains and drops down. I cannot see over the top of the mountains. Just a rocky mountainside, trees, and the snowy lake. The engine's rpms drop off as the plane feels for the lake surface. In a cloud of snow and the 'whummmm' of the engine, the plane hits the snow, and the plane drops speed from a hundred miles an hour down to fifty miles an hour and then twenty miles an hour pretty fast. Van swings the plane in a big loop to come back to the cabin. He explains: "Had to land with the wind, so now have to turn around and run back the other way to the cabin." I see a wind sock stretched out that he had been watching when he circled, so he would know what direction to land.

The sled dogs bark like crazy as they always seem to be doing when I see any. I get introduced. The feeding routine is explained. Van tells me there is a ham radio, but I am not licensed to use it, but if there is an emergency I can call for help. He shows me how. Other than that, I will be out of touch and very isolated. No one else lives on the lake or anywhere near here. I will not see any planes, tracks, or human sign, other than Van's. He goes on: "Miles this is the darkest, coldest time of the year, and one of the worse areas in the state this time of year for storms. If storms come along, it might be a week or longer before I could get back."

I nod, "No problem, Van, have a good time. I'll be fine. Looks like there is plenty of food and I have my art to work on." After Van leaves, I am alone with the wind, the mountains, and the dogs. The mountains are so tall I have to crane my neck looking up to see the tops. The lake is big enough I can't see across it. This time of year, this far north, Van only has two hours of daylight to fly.

I am dubious about having much to do with sled dogs. My family has had pets, and I do not like the idea of a dog's life being on a chain, mixed in with many other dogs to where none get enough attention. I saw the life of a sled dog when visiting John in Galena last winter. That one trip we took on his trapline is memorable, but I saw all the work involved, with dogs living on a pile of straw, that being their entire world when not working. I didn't like all the constant noise. Barking non-stop. I enjoy peace and quiet. I saw with Joe, here in Manley, how much a team of dogs can eat. Joe had visited me once, and asked if I had anything to snack his dogs on. I came up with all the moose hide scrapings, five gallons, and we had melted five gallons of snow, yet all this was only a 'snack' for a dog team. A few hours later I understood Joe would have to do all this again for their real meal (the full meal deal). How is there time for anything else at all???? Goodness!

Van has seven sled dogs. I am amazed they calm down and seem to be so quiet. Conscience, *'Maybe every time we have seen sled dogs they are in an uproar because a stranger has showed up and they are excited to see us, but most of the time they are quieter.'* This is only speculation, but it sure is nice. I step out in the dark with a flashlight to start the dog food cooker and see tracks in the snow. I bend down and see they are marten tracks! Right through the dog yard! I had thought sled dogs would scare game away, and anyone who had dogs would never see game out the window. Marten are among the shyest of all animals. So if a marten will walk through a dog yard, any animal will, and the dogs hadn't seen, heard, or didn't care, and didn't go nuts barking. I'm flabbergasted. This is mind boggling to me.

After a few days I and the dogs settle into the routine. The dogs accept me, and do not bark or growl or cower, but come up and greet me. They seem happy. I'm surprised. There is light in their eyes. Someone is home between those ears. There is intelligence. One dog isn't eating tonight. Conscience, *'He's looking over at his neighbor's dish. It looks like he thinks his buddy got more in his bowl and he wants the same amount.'* I stop and look at the no eat dog. He looks at me, looks at the others bowl, wags his tail and whines.

"All right, all right, I'll go get more for you, stupid dog." I put another half a ladle in his bowl and he eats now. A few others see this and ask for more. "Ok! That is it, all gone, no more, settle down now!" They do not believe me so one by one I have to show them the empty pot. Each in turn has to have a look. They all one by one, in turn, sigh and go curl up in their bed of straw.

The dog cooking routine is not that big a deal, once it is part of the daily schedule. I bet it isn't taking me more than an hour a day total to take care of them. It looks like Van has been catching fish with a net on the lake, and has a few thousand fish hanging to feed the sled dogs all winter. Each dog gets one fish a day. The fish gets cooked with rice or cornmeal. Corn is better when it gets cold, more energy. Rice is cheaper and ok when the temperature is above zero. Sometimes commercial 'bought feed' is used, but this is not very often. Commercial feed might have a few vitamins that are missing in rice and fish, and may also have some trace elements. Van has told me there are vitamin supplements to add to fish and rice if one wanted to get away from commercial food totally.

No, the dogs have no breed name anyone outside Alaska would recognize. Broadly called, 'Husky,' but in reality a mixture of all kinds, yet with many things in common. Most are what we call 'village' dogs. Sometimes a specific village can be named. Anyone who knows sled dogs can look and say, "Huslia dog," name the bloodline as, 'Atla,' the name of a racer or family that has breed dogs so many generations the dog has a 'look' to it that is identifiable. Van identifies his dogs as, "Mostly Eskimo." This distinguishes them from interior dogs, and means they have long fur, shorter legs , a different disposition, tend to be stronger, but slower, and easy going in a different way than interior breeds. I do not understand all that yet, but apparently some people do.

I could have tried the dogs out, hooked them up to a sled and gone someplace. It might be an interesting golden opportunity. But I was not even tempted. Part of having a high 'Jesus Factor' is not being stupid or foolish, not taking unnecessary chances. Many people feel folks like Maul, the Adventist 'Flying Peddler,' and I are accidents waiting to happen, taking chances as we do. I have never hooked up sled dogs. I do not have a 'reason' to take chances. Usually when I take chances it is because I must! I need supplies, need to make a living, am not in a position to just sit tight! This is a far off remote place I am not familiar with. Too many things could go wrong. I could get lost, loose the dogs, not be able to control the dogs, get involved in a dog fight. So I'm just going to stay here, sit tight, do my job, and not be foolish.

At a handmade wooden table, I sit in front of the picture window by kerosene light working on my art. Outside, all is quiet, and the northern lights flicker over the lake bright enough I can see the outline of the mountain tops. I make a sled dog of copper, with his dog house of brass, a silver collar is put on the dog. I set it in a piece of moose antler for a belt buckle. I am numbering my pieces, in case anyone one day will collect my work. I have numbered almost a thousand. All one of a kind, never repeated designs. It takes five grades of sandpaper and steel wool, and finally a polish cloth to shine it. My vice is set on the edge of the table to hold the metal. A hand jeweler saw with a blade the size of a human hair is used to cut the designs I scribe in with a sharp special tool. So ends a typical evening.

The next day during the two hours of daylight, I take a walk along the edge of the lake. Windblown snow crunches under my Eskimo mukluks. The fox tail on my fur hat blows to the side in the breeze. I notice the trees are shorter, scrubbier looking then I am used to in the interior. There will be herds of caribou here. I keep an eye out, see none, but surely this is the area they show up. This is Grizzly bear country, unlike the blacks, they could be out at any time, even now. I see no bear tracks. As I study the snow, a flock of white ptarmigan fly up in front of me. I hadn't seen them, so I'm startled. The flock of thirty hugs the ground in flight, trembling their wings rather than flapping, then settle back down just 100 ft. ahead. As soon as they land, they stop and freeze, blending in with the white snow so they cannot be seen.

I look for Dall Sheep on the mountain ledges, but the ledges are too far away, and too white with snow to see them if sheep are there. Conscience, *'Over here - look. A pack of wolves has gone by here.'* I come over to look. My conscience has been away from my body looking fifty ft. off to the side. I bend down to look closer. One set of tracks is the size of bear and is as large as my hand print. I slowly stand up and look off across the lake. Nothing but white, on white, on white. No, one lone alder bush. Everything else is white.

Possibly the wolves had seen me, or knew I was here, for this night the wolves howl, come closer and howl again. The sled dogs are quiet, but the rattle of chains on dog dishes tells me they are nervous. The weather is warm, maybe ten degrees, so I go sit on the porch. The dogs look over to me and settle down. *The dogs see me as leader of their pack.*

While sitting here listening to the dark, I pass the time thinking. From my limited experience, I'm trying to picture seven dogs named Cuddles, taking me across some dangerous lake. Dogs are pets, right? You feed 'em - they lick you on the face and that's all right. They follow you around looking for more food, wagging their tails. If you spend time with them, and are real lucky, maybe they will roll over and shake your hand.

But here I am only a week with these dogs and something is going on. I seem to know how they think. When there's tension in the air I know it, feel it. All of a sudden on cue all the dogs jump up barking like crazy. I look up to see what is going on. I don't see anything at first. Then I understand. I walk over to one dog, pick up the bone in his yard and smack him over the head saying, "That's not your bone. You shouldn't steal!" I take the bone over to the neighbor. He slowly tentatively opens his mouth. I set the bone in his mouth and give him a pat on the head. He gratefully carries it over to his straw pile. The whole team has been watching. All of them glower at the thief, who hangs his head, goes and hides behind the tree he is tied to. Then they all look over at me, leader of the pack who resolves disputes. My opinion of dog teams is changing fast. It's a lot of work, but so is any relationship. Two weeks is spent doing my art work with my hand tools, and enjoying the view till Van returns.

BACK IN MANLEY I'm asking more about dogs.

People in the Alaska bush are divided into two groups. You're a machine man or you're a dog man. The groups do not overlap. Baker Creek Carol and her Indian boyfriend 'Two Rivers,' are part of the conversation. Two Rivers adds, "That doesn't mean we wouldn't appreciate it if you took your machine out the slough and around to Baker Creek and broke trail for us though!" We all laugh. Mostly the dog people complain that snow machines mess up the trails for dogs, put speed bumps in the trail. This comment seems funny. I can cover in half an hour on my machine what will take 'Two Rivers' all day, maybe ten hours with his dogs.

I turn my head to Baker Creek Carol. "Carol – won't any trail I make just blow in after I make it, being no use to you?"

She explains, "The dogs can find it under the snow." *Even so, ten hours compared to half an hour? Hmmm.* There is a snow storm raging outside and Two Rivers is nervous about getting back to Baker Creek, fifteen miles away. They do not have any dog food here in town.

"Sure, I'll break trail for you then." They will spend the night with friends and we will get an early start before daylight (meaning any time before noon! Ha!). They will follow behind and I will not wait for them, as I will be going so much faster than them.

Early in the morning I set out up the slough. We decided on this alternate route, up the slough and onto the overland trail. On my explorations, I have run this route before, so know the way. There is no problem getting started. Eight inches of new snow has fallen. Not a lot, but it has drifted, and in places there are four ft. deep fluffy drifts. I have learned from practice that if I keep the speed up I can float on top to a certain extent. Even so, the drifts come up over the headlight, even over the windshield. Sometimes the snow machine falls to its side, and I have to stop and dig it out. I am sure that with practice I could learn to not allow this to happen. I am concerned about working this newly overhauled engine so hard, but I am impressed when it hangs in there. The engine screams. The snow comes inside, and packs all around the engine. Snow gets sucked into the carburetor. Conscience, *'Do you think the snow going in the engine will shut it down?'* I think not, but I am unsure. One thing for sure is, if the machine shuts down, then what? I walk home through the drifts, which is an all-day back breaking job while the machine gets buried in the newly drifted snow. I fix it how? I get it to a shop how? I get back to the machine how? I bring what with me? But if I get in trouble, imagine how the dogs behind me are doing! The new snow is over their heads!

In only twenty minutes I have run the slough, and come to the easy part out of the wind. Probably Two Rivers can make it on his own from here. I just need to break the trail up the river bank. With the engine full throttle and a good run at it, I head for the bank. The engine unwinds rpm's and finally stops. I haven't made it over the top. We both say, *'Shit!'* "Shit!" at the same time. All I needed was three ft.

more. But three ft. may as well have been eternity. The Citation is buried in the snow over its windshield. I have a little dinky folding shovel with me. Conscience, *'May as well get started - come on give me a hand.'* In a half an hour of shoveling I can't even see the seat yet. I am exhausted and sweating. In two more hours I have the seat and less than half the machine showing, but my energy is winding down. I need a break. Five hours after I get stuck I am still stuck, but I think I will eventually be free. In another couple of hours.

From around the bend I see the dog team coming. Quietly, with only the sound of heavy breathing, the team comes up to me. Carol is in the sled, 'Two Rivers' on the runners. Neither is tired or cold. Without a word 'Two Rivers' unhooks the dogs from the sled and tells them to get in front of the snow machine. The sled dogs climb the river bank. They line up in front of my machine. Two Rivers hooks a carabineer from his line to the machine bumper. He tells the dogs, "Easy; easy, take up the slack," and the dogs walk forward till there is tension on the line and they stop. Two Rivers says, "Over the line, Toe!" But Toe looks back at us and just wags his tail. He's on the wrong side of the line. Two Rivers says, "Bum - move over - give Toe some room!" Bum just wags his tail too. Two Rivers slowly moves his arm and waves his hand. The two dogs follow with their eyes, watch his hand wave. Bum thinks there might be something in his hand and moves over, following, as if 'Two Rivers' might be about to toss something to eat that direction. As soon as Bum moves over, Toe jumps the line. Two Rivers says, "Good Dog!" followed by, 'Ready!' and all the dogs come to their feet with tension on the line. "Hike!" All the dogs leap forward as one. The snow machine pops out of the snow like it was a cork in a bottle, and lands on top of the bank. Without a word to me he calls the dogs back to his sled, hooks up, and as he goes by on his way home salutes me - winks and says, 'Later' and is gone.

Back in Manley I have to stop and knock on the door of my friend taking over the store. She has concern on her face when she opens the door. I have been sweating out in the wind and my teeth are chattering. I might be able to make it another six miles home, but she gives me some hot tea, and keeps me talking. I'm suddenly very tired and can't hardly keep my eyes open. She lets me take a short nap in her rocking chair.

In January of this year, 1979, I get a calendar and keep notes in the little squares. This is not really a 'dairy' as such, but a one sentence record of events. Calendar:

Jan 3 - Nuther marten bites the snow.

Jan 5 - Lynx got in fight with Art's sled dogs - dogs all tore up.

Jan 9 - Check mail.

Jan 11 - Pottery day.

Jan 12 - Joe shot his dog team.

Joe was always a sort of odd one. I am undecided how much I like him. At first we got along well enough. But after a while I noticed that every time he left my place he left with something I gave him. He never brought anything, paid for anything, or did any favors. Not that I keep track, but when you first meet someone, and a couple months goes by and you recollect things, then realize you have given him fifty things, and he has given nothing… you go "hmmm." It was little things. A pint of kerosene for the lantern. He forgot to pick some up, some moose meat, a trapping stretcher. I didn't notice till he asked for some food. I offered frozen potatoes, and he was insulted, saying,

"You expect me to eat this shit Miles, come on, that's an insult, what else ya got!" I replied, "Joe this is all I have. This is what I am eating. I can't offer better than what I got." I don't mind sharing, but when what I have, my best, is insulted, then he can beg food from someone else. I got over it, but I was more cool to him after that. There was also a tone in his attitude over the food that came across as a threat. "Give me better, or else!"

Word around the village, when his name came up, was that he is crazy. Few trust him, or wanted him around. He makes threats, lives on intimidation. He talks, saying he is a Vietnam vet, and had some serious war experiences. Probably so. I heard that a lot of vets moved away from society, want to be alone. So now this news, he shot all his sled dogs. I wasn't there, but was told he simply got mad at them in front of the post office and shot them all right there. *I guess he got them to shut up all right.* I'm imagining the event. Bullets flying, kids and others around, blood all over in the snow, dogs screaming, some wounded, then cleaning up after. It's hard to believe the community just shrugs its shoulders and considers this normal. I take my cue from everyone else and nod, *'yup this is cool, normal, life in the pucker brush, yup'.*

Calendar:

Jan 15 - Get $250 in mail from Alaska House. Alaska House sold some consignment items at Christmas. There is a nice letter with the check. They want more art.

Jan 16 - Finish my art piece; 'Circle of Life.' This is my first major art piece done on the 'full curl' Dall Sheep horn. I was partly inspired by my visit to Selby Lake, the mountain, looking for sheep on the mountain. This is a story piece. I had started it in Squaw Crossing but changed plans. On one side of the horn is the story of the male ram. The other side has the story of the female. Each story is out of sight from the other till they meet in the middle. Each story tells of their life. An eagle swoops down and scares the ram. The parents are killed in an avalanche and he is on his own. There is a grizzly encounter that he survives. The female's story is similar. Across a mountain top they see each other. They pair up and have young. In the last scene, their young look out from the tip, back at the beginning, and you know it starts over. Life is a circle. This is the best piece I have ever done, and has taken all winter to complete. Thousands of hand cut - perfectly fitting metals. As far as I know, no one else anywhere has ever done anything even remotely like this. It is even possible no one else is capable of it. No one has seen it but me yet.

Jan 17 - Visit Two Rivers - trade his furs for some of my art.

Jan 18 - Tan some furs for Betty.

Jan 22 - $200 mitten trade with Betty - beautiful! Betty is a local Native beader. Her daughter was in my art class. I wanted Betty to make me a pair of warm mittens from an otter I caught. She makes me mittens with beadwork and wolverine ruff. The mittens are a museum piece. In return I tanned some furs of mine and traded to her so she would have material to work with to fill orders she has.

Jan 23 - Make half a dozen fox sets near the mouth of the slough.

Jan 25 - 10°

Jan 26 - Visit Two Rivers and Baker Creek Carol again - take river trail home.

Jan 27 - Pottery - made a tea pot.

Jan 28 - -40°.

Jan 4 - Kids dog races still -50°.

Jan 5-6-7-8 - Still -50°.

Jan 9 - Movie night still -50°.

Jan 14 – Still -50°. Moose goes to sleep leaning against houseboat.

Jan 17 - Still -50°. Go visit Joe - chase fox on slough; able to run down.

Feb 2 - movie night.

Feb 3 - Still cold, -50°. Movie night was interesting. I had to smile. It was -50°. Every half an hour the movie was stopped so we could all go out and check on our snow machines. I had a lantern under my hood burning with a blanket over the top of the hood - so it would stay warm enough to start. Conscience, *'Wouldn't this make a great scene in a film? Movie stops - fur clad trappers and miners dash out into the -50°. pink ice fog and cranking on snow machines. All waiting till the machines warm up before going back inside to watch more of the movie. Is this another planet or what!'*

I chase a fox 'hither, thither and yon,' till he runs up a cliff. I am close enough to shoot him with a 22. Is this life in the fast lane? I bring Joe to town. He needs supplies. He now has no transportation. He says to me about shooting his dogs,

"Well, Miles, I needed to get out of dogs anyhow. I was running too low on feed and didn't want them to suffer. It was a planned thing."

"Well then, why didn't you pull your traps first. How come you did this right in town in front of the post office?"

He is asking me to take him on his trapline, or let him borrow my machine so he can go pull his traps. He had left traps out. I do not like to see traps out not being checked, maybe with fur in them being wasted, not picked up, but on the other hand here is someone with a low 'Jesus factor.' A problem person asking me to get involved and sucked in. I am not sure if I lent him my machine if he would even return it. I doubt very much if he would even put gas in it, bet he'd get mad at me for not lending it with a full tank. I'll give him a ride to town, which is more than anyone else is doing for him, give him a ride back. But at some point, he has to get his own shit together.

"Joe, I'm being honest with you here. Nothing about this whole thing sounds reasonable to me. I wasn't there, but I have an imagination. I'm picturing a bunch of screaming ass dogs going ballistic, bullets flying all over the place. Blood everywhere. Bunch of dead dogs tangled up in bloody harnesses; all done in front of half the community, on Federal property, the post office, where it is illegal to have a firearm to begin with. This sounds like insanity Joe. You need to get a grip. I'll help you Joe, the town will help, but damn, Joe, it's up to you if you make it or not! You and I talked before about hard times maybe coming. You told me dogs would be the thing to have. So what's going on now?" Joe and I had talked about politics, about changes going on, about hard times, maybe. We agreed on a lot of basic ideas. It suddenly dawns on me that for all the talks we have had, it is me stock piling, but he has nothing — *hmmm*, so I ask now. "Joe what's with you? We agree hard times might arrive, and agree there are some basics a person might need to get by, yet you don't seem to have set anything by for hard times. It's not just the money, there are a lot of cheap things to be had for almost nothing, even things you can make."

Joe smiles and replies, "If things get tough and I need to survive, I'll just take it from people like you Miles." I knew then that Joe is not my friend, and I don't want much to do with him. I'm bothered though. There are not many like 'us,' who are living out remote, away from the village. There is that bond of so much in common.

I laugh, "Well Joe, thanks for telling me. Now if anything is missing, I'll know who to come see. Hate to see a time I'd have to kill ya, Joe." Once again I wonder why violence seems to be what people understand and live by, the way things get done. I know this though. I'm not going to work my ass off buying stuff so the likes of Joe can come and help himself, leaving me to live without.

Calendar:

Feb 23 - Been -20° to -30° all week.

Feb 25 - Warms to 20 above. Weather is warm and windy for two weeks. Pottery night still happens and movie night.

March 8 - Make bullets. I'm getting more into reloading ammunition now that there is daylight and some warmth. I am out many days shooting.

March 9 - Town meeting – 2nd class city or not. Town people get together to discuss the pros and cons of becoming a 2nd class city - decide against it.

March 13 - Will wins the boat in the raffle!

It came down like this. Talking on the phone with Will.

"Will, what do you mean you won? How'd it happen?"

"Miles, I told you I'd win. Why are you surprised? You gotta believe, Miles. Yes, I was there at the drawing and I told 'em to hook it up right here, and we hooked it up to the hitch I got with the money you lent me."

We talked a while and I say, "So, wow! Maybe you'd like to go with me on a long trip again and put this new boat to use? We can go to Lake Minchumina up the Kantishna. You could haul some of the load for me so I draw less water. I'm worried about my three ft. draft, Will." Will agrees it would be a good trip and we go over some details. I will let him know when the ice goes out, and he will drive to Manley pulling his boat on the trailer he got with it. A $70,000 package he wins, wow I can't believe it. Will sends me some starter parts he thinks I will need for my boat engine that I asked him to look for. He uses the money he owes me. So it is getting to be that time of year, to start thinking about boating season again!

If I go up the Kantishna I will not want the snow machine. I knew before, but know for sure now; I cannot keep a snow machine without tools, parts, and knowledge, not this far out. I will need a dog team.

Calendar:

March 14th - spend day digging up my summer supplies out of the snow.

March 15 - sorting summer supplies.

March 18 - talk of the town homestead land opens at Dugan hills - looking over maps.

March 20 - tried to snow machine to Dugan but wet snow and storm turns me back.

I am interested in this homestead land, but do not know much about it. It is not near the river, so I am only a little interested. Snow mixed with rain and forty degree weather holds over the next week. Even the mail plane cannot get in. I'm a little bummed out. I haven't heard from Maggie all winter. It is not like her to go so long without writing. I'm not sure I have her right address. She was thinking of moving maybe? Last I heard? I'm not sure. She wrote something about meeting her half way in Seattle. I'm not sure if she moved, so have been waiting to hear from her to have an address. No letters got returned as undelivered… Conscience, *'Yes but, the Manley postmaster sent all my mail back when I couldn't pick it up! I bet Maggie's new address was lost.'* I had not been able to get my mail for over fifteen days during a minus fifty below cold spell. The postmaster sent all my mail back as undelivered. There are people who think they lost touch with me and I may not ever hear from again. Maggie is the main one I care about, as I do not have her correct address now.

April 9th - left for Fairbanks—accept dog Kenai from Art.

Art has a dog – my first sled dog. Art says this dog might work for me but he is having problems with the dog, head problems, so will give him to me for free. Art will keep the dog in Manley for a while till I am ready for it.

April 10th - Will and I talk over Kantishna trip.

April 11th - Four dogs from Bill Henry.

As it turns out these are the dogs I saw on the Yukon River when I first got to Alaska. Some are old, but they all have been sled dogs and should know what to do. I sell my snow machine, and what I get for the machine is about what the dogs, harnesses and an old sled cost, so, basically traded straight across, a snow machine for dogs. All the 'machine people' think I am deserting their side, and give me a hard time. I just want what works, and suits the need at hand. I'm not taking sides. Will tells me he will bring the new sled dogs with him from Fairbanks when he comes to meet me at the mouth of the Kantishna River.

Calendar:

April 13th - Back from Fairbanks.

April 14th - Put black powder shotgun together.

April 16th - See Joe across the river about a dog sled.

April 17th - Put lower unit on houseboat engine - go look at dog sled of Joe Reddington.

April 18th - Pick up Kenai. Trade $400 worth of art for dog sled.

Kenai is a trip all right. First thing he does is dashes into my supplies. I yell, "No!" He swerves and dives into my food I yell, "No!" He swerves and dives in the houseboat. I yell, "No!" He dives out of the houseboat and sits in front of me waiting for my command. That is the first ten seconds of us getting to know each other. I have him on a chain but think we are far enough out of the village I can let him off the chain for a few minutes. It seems odd to take a problem dog and first thing give him freedom. Yet, Kenai understood the privilege, appreciated it, and oddly I never really had any trouble with him since. We understood each other and bonded about that fast. I knew what he wanted and he knew what I wanted. At first simply an agreement.

It is time to get serious about packing and leaving, and decide to leave some things behind for Joe to look over. Some items should be good things I just do not have room for, like a stove.

When I saw Joe, it went like this, I say," So Joe I think I'll be leaving some things behind as it looks like I accumulated more than I can carry. I don't know for sure what I'll have room for, but probably I will leave the used stove you asked about. I'll leave some good stuff for you if you get rid of the junk I leave behind and if you kind of clean up. Ok?" I don't like that Joe has been a taker and done nothing for what he got from me, so this agreement at least will help us both, otherwise I am not inclined to help him out anymore. Joe says,

"Sure, sounds good to me, Miles! I appreciate the things you leave!"

Calendar:

April 20th - First rain - God but the woods smell good! Yes every year when the first rain arrives the woods smell so wonderful. The branches open up to accept nutrients and buds try hard to grow. The dirt has a special smell from that first rain.

April 22 - Hear first geese. This date gets a star. A very important day. Geese mean there is open water and means 'probably' there will be no more serious cold weather. Geese are traveling a long way and have passed over a lot of country, and know how the weather pattern is.

April 26 - pack all day - rain.

April 28 - Get big goose with black powder shotgun.

A very special time, getting the spring goose. They taste so darn good! The shotgun was mentioned earlier—a double barrel black powder twelve gauge. It is like "Holy Shit," having a hammer and cap. I have to put the powder down and set a wad over it, then measure a charge of shot, put an over wad on that. This is such a slow ignition I have to 'lead' flying critters by twice what would be needed with modern weaponry. I am also stuck with modified choke, since everything has to get rammed down the front. This means I have a pretty wide pattern. I make up for it by being able to put over two ounces of shot in it.

April 29 - Can't travel anymore. Water and wet snow everywhere.

April 30 - Controls hooked up. Go over engine carb. More packing. House afloat in overflow water - move gear away from water edge.

Small boat still froze in.

In the fall I had pulled the small boat ashore, but not far enough. Some overflow during the winter came up on the ice and froze the stern in solid. My notes based on the diary written maybe two years later say…

Diary: The river must be breaking. I can't rightly tell since I'm stuck up this dead end slough. The river rose maybe ten ft. overnight from an ice jam. Up in the woods I stuck an ax in a tree stump. Only the tip of the ax handle is above the water. My froze-in sixteen ft. boat has only the very top of its bow showing, and even that goes under water. The water is over a lot of my goods stashed on shore. Nothing valuable, but I lost a lot of books, and lots of things need drying. I will be leaving more behind for Joe to deal with than expected, but there are canning jars, a stove, and some things he should be able to use.

Calendar:
    May 2 - Water rises seven ft. in four hours. Much gear wet - some loss.
    May 3 - Water drops a foot - things out to dry.
    May 4 - Tanana breaks up - small boat afloat - walk to town. There is not much snow so I am able to walk the river bank - sort of. I need to let Will know what is going on.
    May 5 - Small boat to town.
    May 6 - Will trucks' to Nenana. He has my dogs and is going to boat from Nenana to Manley Hot Springs to meet me. The roads are too muddy to travel to Manley.
    May 7 - Surprise Birthday Party!

The 7th is my birthday, and Manley put on a party for me, with food and gifts. Almost everyone showed up, showing I am accepted by the community.

Will shows up on the 8th by boat and tells me that at the mouth of the Kantishna he ran up on black ice and almost flipped the boat over. Another concern he tells me about. "Miles, this seventy horse twin jet sucks up fuel like there is no tomorrow." He isn't sure how bad it is but a 'guess' is as bad as eighteen gallons an hour. I have a plan then.

    May 9 - Gas hauled and loaded on houseboat.
    May 10 -Lower unit on houseboat engine falls off.

I lost the lower unit. It fell off the engine. Will almost quits and goes home. I made him stay. He tells me, "To fix it we need to get the boat out of the water and weld it, Miles." Now, where are we going to get a welder, with power to run it? Does Will know what it would take to get us out of the water? It would be a week just unloading the boat! We'd have to build a tripod and winch system to lift it and pull it.

I look around for a while and say to Will, "Give me a hand here can ya? I think these spare eyebolts in my toolbox might fit." The eyebolts are run through the hull, and the lower unit hanger pins are run through the eyebolts. We are back running in two hours. Will comes up with my bear grease to replace the bearing lube. We haven't even started yet.

Calendar:
    May 11th -Take off for Kantishna! Make fifteen miles - fix lower unit bearing.

It takes ten hours to go fifteen miles. At fifteen miles is Baker Creek, where Baker Creek Carol and Two Rivers live. Will and I spend the night. Baker Creek is an abandoned lumber mill camp. Some of the 1920's equipment is still here. I find a complete model T-Ford with wood track replacing the wheels, making it a track rig snow machine. On the river bank is the hull of a sternwheeler, with trees growing up through it. Off in the woods it looks like the boiler to the stern wheel power system was removed, and hooked up to a lumber mill. I took a photograph of the name plate on the steam engine - made in Cleveland in 1908. There are no trails, no roads, no signs, just an ancient story written in rusty steel.

I have mail for Carol and Two Rivers. They have not been able to get to Manley for a month and are glad I remembered them. The mail man holds mail for them, but not mine. Two Rivers has fish nets out, and is getting so many fish he tells me to help myself so I can feed my sled dogs. I trade him a necklace to give Carol, and some other stuff I made - for some dry fish to last many weeks on the trip.

Someone at my birthday party gave me a sled dog to add to my team. I knew they had put a notice up around town saying they wanted $150 for it, so this is a nice gift. Two Rivers just stares at me as I ramble on about sled dogs. "I read all about them and this is what is reliable in the wilderness, same as you figured out! That silent travel, and a close working team you can trust and depend on!" Two Rivers might have used that term, "Educated idiot," but I didn't hear him. My smile is so big it plugged my ears.

This new dog is a female. Not that I had made note of it. *A dogs a dog right? Female, male - no discrimination here! I'll take 'em all!* Will and I had left the team tied up in the sixteen ft. boat. Before we ate, we figured out where to tie them out on shore.

The dogs had been well behaved the whole day. Apparently the female was coming into heat. The male dogs were smart enough not to let me know. The first chance they got when no human is around, they get loose, beat up on each other, and take turns with the female. We didn't hear much. Maybe she cooperated. Hard to know. She slipped her collar. When I got to the boat, the males were all wore out and cut up from fighting with each other, but all had happy grins. Just like a bunch of guys in a bar fighting over a floozy, after being let loose from work.

"Where is she?" I ask? They all laugh and look at each other. No dog knows or cares.

"She's worth $150, you shits!" They all smile and look at each other. I throw my hands up. They all wag their tails. When I went to Two River saying, "Can you believe..." he only stares at me. I have no idea where she is, or how to get her back. "Well, when she turns up and you catch her..." *but I'd be gone and if he finds her - then what?* "Want to buy a sled dog – cheap Two Rivers?"

He just stares at me. *Hmm.* Finally, he says, "If I see her I'll shoot her. I don't need any loose females in heat around here."

I'm not sure what to say. He's right, she is my responsibility, not his. But dang. She was a gift. In the morning she isn't around when it is time to take off. "Well, no more female problems!" Is all I can cheerfully say, not really expressing how I feel, but there are other things to think about. I do not need to begin getting myself or anyone else depressed or mad. Will had lost a dog on the way here from his place. It had run off. He couldn't catch it. Two dogs from my team gone already both females (smile). *Hmmm.*

It's still cold in the morning in early May, below freezing and windy.

"Will, you want to check out this depth sounder I got?" He had never heard of one, and wanted to see how it worked. "Sonar, Will. Pretty slick!"

He asks questions about it. It wasn't perfect, and picked up debris near the bottom, and there is a time delay when traveling, to where we would know where we had been, but not where we are. This helps though, he agrees. We know we have been running in four ft. of water. If we see indication of a change, we can decide if we lost the channel, and need to find it again. We may understand or predict a change. I practice guessing how deep the water is, and looking to confirm. No one told me it was impossible to guess the exact depth of this murky water, but I practiced anyway, just for fun, just in case it could be done, even if it is impossible.

"Miles, the sonar is ok, but it is not much like being a Mountain Man of the old days, it's modern stuff." Will has a point. We talk about this often. Others as well, ask me why I use or do something, since it is not of the right era.

Once again I let Will know. "Will, I'm just not trying to be in the 1800's. That is not my goal. There is a lot about that Mountain Man image I appreciate, and like, and want to learn, know about, use and do. But if some modern tool helps me, I can afford it, and it works, then I consider using it." I go on expressing what I have decided is the truth. "Will, we have both read a lot of the old Mountain Man books and biographies. Here in Alaska someone was a sourdough after one year. People of the gold rush days and trapping years we think of, died at an average age of forty. Few of our heroes lived as we dream and read for more than five years. Most were worn out or dead in less time than that. Only a few lived and trapped long. Jim Bridger survived a while by opening a trading post. The 'hayday' of the free trapper was only ten years. I think the 1850's. Few were really 'free trappers.' Most had to work for a company like Hudson Bay, and did not own their horse, traps, or gear, and earned slave wages. There was trapping before then all right! But it would have been without steel traps. Thus totally different than the story we dream of. Deadfalls, pits, and other various contraptions built on the spot, not portable. Making a living at it was not done. Even the Indians trapped, some for their own use, but it was the white man who brought steel traps and encouraged the Natives to leave the warmth of the teepee and go out and trap to sell to the white man. Before that, the Native spent a lot of winter sitting by a fire telling stories. Just cutting firewood with a stone ax to keep warm was a full time job, how could they be out trapping? Not in these parts anyhow!"

Will and I agree on this. We remind ourselves, so we can adjust our own reality. The romantic idea of the Mountain Man, that first started in the dime novel to sell back east, was mostly made up by eastern reporters, who took the train west and ventured a few more miles past the end of the tracks and got scared, tired, thirsty, and hung out at the fringes, making stuff up or listening to the folks in the taverns, and hearing - seeing what they wanted and what would sell. The western cowboy as pictured in the movies was part of this as well, and not reality. Anyhow starting fires with flint and using buffalo robes to sleep on is 'interesting.'

"But Will, you know what one of the hides weighs? When it got wet it might take two men to lift! Ha!"

"Miles, I think this is Dugan Creek here."

I'm not very interested, but Will has talked about homestead land opening here someplace, and wants to take notice. He thinks he might like to get some of this land. This is too close to civilization to interest me, and I'm not ready yet to settle down.

"Will I want to look around some more. That's why I built the houseboat, to check out more country before calling anyplace home." Un-conscience: *'Canada and all that.'* Not really ready to be associated with any town yet, till I figure out more what went wrong, trying to settle in Beardmore, ended in me getting set up and losing everything. I don't want that to ever happen again. But I'm not going to go into all that with Will. We stop, hang around a little so Will can check it out.

"Miles, I could get mail and supplies in Manley on the road. It's only a few miles here from Manley, and there is the winter trail to get in and out during snow time."

Calendar:
> **May 12th** - Engine spark coil goes out - fixed. Make Kantishna River!
> **May 13th** - 30 miles, bend prop.
> **May 14th** - good run past the Toklat River. Shoot a goose - eat good.
> **May 15th** - Water exhaust problems - engine overheating?

"Will, we'll tie your boat to the houseboat and tow the whole deal. At least some of the load will be distributed between the boats. When I get in some bad places you can unhook and help out with power, or help me through some narrow places." Six sled dogs are in Will's boat along with some gear. I don't even know the dog's names yet. Will's boat of barking dogs and gear is tied on the side of my houseboat.

The sixteen ft. run about is loaded with supplies. Mostly gas, as in 300 gallons, and is tied on the other side of the houseboat.

Calendar:

May 16th - Lost lower unit oil - nothing on hand but bear grease – Will repacks bearings in bear grease.

May 17th - Shallow water by Bearpaw. Rough time.

May 18th - Make 20 miles all day - lost prop, then engine quits. We don't know where we are.

May 19th - Rapids near McKinley River. We are worn out. Gaining less than a mile an hour, early stop.

May 20th - Make the Muddy River. Map shows travel should improve.

May 21st - Held up by ice jam. Have to hole up till it goes out or melts.

Traveling the Kantishna is rough, but there is so much excitement we don't care.

"Have you noticed, Will, there are no other boats? Have you noticed that?"

"Ya, my kind of country, Miles. This is all right." We see no cabins, no road, no planes, no beer cans, no footprints, and not even a blaze on a tree to show someone has been here in the past fifty years. Here we are, spending days and days and a hundred hours of time, and this is nothing but God's country.

"God and us wild animals huh, Will?" It seems worth waiting for. "I've been waiting to be here now for a few years. I heard about this river in Galena from an old timer, and been trying to get here ever since."

"Miles, the way this engine doesn't run we're lucky to be here at all!"

"Ya, I know, but Will, you either got money and no time, or time and no money. Where would I get the kind of money it takes to get a good engine capable of moving this much weight? You know yourself it would cost two to three years of our gross pay combined to do that! And you know how life works, Will, if we had the kind of job that paid the kind of money we need for a set up that would be reliable and safe, the boss would never let us have a month off to do this, right?" Will and I have talked about this dilemma before. Damn if we do and damn if we don't. A catch twenty-two. "As for me, Will, I'd rather be out here doing what we are doing. If our equipment fails us, we drift back to Manley, not that big a deal."

"Sounds good, Miles but you know we could break down and get stuck. Breakdown and drift into sweepers and roll this puppy upside down..."

"Sure, but we could slip in the bathtub and hit our head. Life has risk, Will."

"Yes Miles but most people would not call 'this risk,' the same as the chances of slipping in the bathtub. Some might say we have maybe a 50/50 chance of living."

"Sounds like good odds to me, Will, what do you think?" He doesn't answer so I go on. "And you know, if it wasn't for the hardships, the cost, the cold, the mosquitoes, why Alaska out here would be New York City! Everyone wants to see the Northern lights, hear a wolf howl , catch a fish. If horses was wishes Will--- ya, know what I mean? If it wasn't hard, why, we wouldn't be alone out here enjoying it! This is limited to a handful of privileged people, like us!" After a pause, we both start laughing.

"Miles, you are so full of shit – you could sell snow to Eskimos! You could convince those in hell they were in heaven!" But hey, at least we are laughing. What else did we have to do, ten hours a day of sitting up here on the roof going slower than walking. Sometimes we'd spend an hour going around one river bend. Some would call it boring. We talk a lot.

"Miles, I was thinking. You ever wonder about the good days of the fur trade? When Lewis and Clark went by Yellowstone. Can you imagine what that would be like to see the Grand Canyon, the geysers at Jackson Hole? The days of the buffalo, before the fences? Them must have been the days, Miles!"

"The way I figure it, nothing at all wrong with 'right now.' That's who we are, Will, Lewis and Clark. Think about it! I have no doubt one day you'll be telling grandkids about these days, and their mouth will fall open. 'Yup, the days you could meet a twenty year old moose on the river who'd spent his whole life on the river and never seen a boat, didn't know what people are!' Yellowstone? Why some day, Will, all this will be a park too. And you and I will say, 'I remember when!' Maybe even in our lifetime Will."[1] He looks dubious so I go on, "There's some that say I'm full of crap, Will. Sure this is no Grand Canyon, but it is special in its own way. The kind of place someone could get lost and walk the rest of their life for thirty years, and never find a village." It's a thousand miles to Nome, with no roads in between. Look at the map, Will. No one knows what's down here. The bottom of our maps reads, 'Aerial surveyed in 1952.' There might be gold, oil, or most anything here. A land of opportunity, and you and I are on the cutting edge, no different than them mountain men who went out west. You read about what life was like for them? Just like we are doing, Will! No easier! They were called crazy too! You bet! Building rafts to go down the Ohio. When they got there, dying right and left. Didn't have a clue about life in the pucker brush. But they had balls, Will! And they founded our country as we know it. The Indians messed with them, they lost their food, they sank their boats on snags, they almost turned back a hundred times! And when they got back to civilization? Those few who did, why no one believed the stories they told, Will! Someday some tour boat will putt along here with a glass roof, feeding tourists lunch, while someone talks on a loud speaker. Anyplace along here they might say: "And this here is where mountain men Will and Miles, sank their boat, right over there." And tourists will make the sign of the cross, bow their heads, gawk. Why, we be famous, Will!"

"Sheeee-it. We bite the big one here, Miles, who is gonna know? Just God be our witness. Be years before anyone comes a - looking for us. We'd be long time bear feed, and just another couple of fools." Well it may or may not be true, but discussing it passes the time.

"Think about it Will! The mountain men, who were they in those days to society? They were 'Low Life's', Will! They had no rights once they got to town. No one wanted them around. People crossed the street when they came along to get away from them. The ones with Indian wives, dressed funny, and stinking. They had uncivilized ways and lived in the slums; the bad side of town. The sheriff was asked to keep an eye on 'em. That's how it was, Will, for the people who founded our country. I finally figured that out. Our heroes were nobody, in the eyes of society that reaped the rewards of the work they done taming the wilds."

"But, Miles, the ones that get talked about who founded our country like Jefferson and Washington and all of them, what about them?"

"And who came before them, Will, huh? Who was on the Mayflower for example? Rich people? People with class? No, Will, they were poor people. Some were unwelcome where they came from, looking for a better way. Persecuted people. The ones who dropped like flies, got sick, starved, even abandoned and left by the mother country. Who gave a hoot about them, Will. Look at Roanoke. To this day no one knows what happened to them. Do we know any of their names? The ones who go down in history, who take the credit, came later. The followers, the leaders, the wealthy, the well read, the land grabbers, the ones society respected. William Penn was given the entire state of Pennsylvania, Will! Who went out west? The criminals, the persecuted, the poor. Even Lewis and Clark who got a lot of credit, were not the first. It was the tales of trappers that got Lewis and Clark appointed to go check it out officially. They had trapper guides, whose names are no longer important. There were, of course, Indians there first. We seem to forget. That Sacagawea gal – who was she? At the time, she was just another Indian. It was her association with a white man trapper Clark needed, that got her the job of tagging along. Don't you suppose there were plenty of other Indians who lived there and knew the way? Plenty of other trappers who had been there and done that, who heard about Lewis and Clark and said; 'Sheeeeee-it – who the hell are you two?' Wouldn't you guess it was a joke among the trappers who had been covering that country for years already, to have it suddenly 'discovered' by a couple of surveyors?"

Will and I think about that, and those days, trying to figure what was going on back then, and how it relates to what is going on now, and how we are treated. "Many famous people and American heroes were pirates, and would have been hung by the government of that time, the British! Only considered descent folk because the Americans won a revolution! Enemies of the government at the time, Will!" I read a lot of diaries, accounts, history books, about exploring in general, and famous people.

"Oh, dang, there goes the engine again, Miles!" The prop falls off. The engine quits, and we are alone in the silence, as the bow slowly swings downstream . Once again we hope Sable doesn't snag on anything or roll over. The hiss of the water on the hull is all that can be heard. We hold our breath. We each know what to do and grab a paddle. Will on the left, me on the right in back. Using the big paddle as an oar, we have some control, enough to get us going downstream. Good enough we can drift to a safe place out of the current. This isn't the thrill of a lifetime, or even thrill of the month. In fact it is not even the thrill of the day. It's merely the thrill of this hour. To cheer Will up, I pretend to be a tour guide. "And look to your left folks. This is the view Will and Miles had when they lost their propeller back in the 70's, when men were men! Did they give up?!" I hope Will can picture all the ooh and ahhs, picture taking, "and there is us Will, on the postcard handed out!" *Even if it is not so, God can see! If there is a St Peter, and I meet him at some pearly gate? I'm gonna be there standing at attention as he tries to find my name. When he goes 'Oh yeah here you are' He's going to frown. The scroll will fall off the table and roll across the floor and there will be the list of deeds, rolling across the floor, five feet in small print. 'This is you?' And I'm going to say 'Yes Sir!' St Peter may even swear.*

Diary: We never passed a human sign. No cabins being used. Only a few old ones— with caved in roofs. I'd get to looking for human sign.

Once we passed a bronze cross stuck in the ground up on the bank. It was not a place I could stop so we only wondered. Later Will writes me a letter and tells me what it said. I forget the name - had no meaning to me. Some trapper who died here long ago during the depression. No one I asked had ever heard of him. No cabin, no trails, no other sign – just a bronze cross against a tree - most curious.

"Will, is that a beer can?"

"No only a tube of floating birch bark."

"Will, is that a sawed off tree on the bank over there?"

"No, Miles, just natural broken off."

"Is that a footprint?" No sign of a camp fire or fish camp, nothing.

The river in some places is only twenty ft. across, but in other places half a mile. The land is glacier silt that the wind blew in over thousands of years, like powdered chalk or mica, but the color of burlap. There is little to hold it together. A quarter of an inch a year over thousands of years makes rolling hills of silt. Mammoth herds marched across these hills in the blowing dust under the arctic sun. The river cuts here, there, around, and changes by the day, even by the hour. The grass and trees growing on the edge help contain the rivers bank, but the frozen permafrost is only two to three ft. down. That is all the deeper the root systems go. Silt is suspended in the water, and drops wherever the current slows. Sandbars are really 'silt bars' that shift and come near the surface. Some are above the water, for now. A few have short willows where the river floods only once a year at break up. Some sandbars look much like dunes, and extend far enough to look like the Sahara desert. Sometimes the wind or even a breeze picks up the light silt and creates clouds, dust devils, mist, like sheets of wispy tan air.

"Will? Doesn't this remind you of photos of the moon?"

I look over at Will watching the trees, spruce and poplars here, maybe forty ft. tall, really tall for interior Alaska. *Good cabin logs.* These trees extend for 100 ft. back from the river. Behind that is moss, swamp, and tundra forever and ever. Siberia looks like this. The Indian says stickman lives here. 'Uclainy' (bad medicine). I smile, for anything that keeps people away is all right by me, even spirits. It is not so much 'beautiful,' as 'vast' and there is something 'beautiful' about 'vast.'

I realize I'm tired. I'm wet from jumping in the water to grab the bow of the boat when it swung and got stuck last time. A 'pry pole' had to be used to get the bow off a sandbar, and it had taken several hours. Not that time matters. I yawn.

"Hey, Will, that is a pond we can pull into off the river, look good to you for spending a night?" He's tired, too. Without a word he yawns, climbs off the roof to the bow, with the bow rope in hand, as I turn the boat to the pond. The sun is setting. Half the sky is red and purple. Dinner of fish is already cooking on the stove inside. A little firewood is gathered from the drift on the sandbar nearby to keep the stove going into the night, and keep the night chill at bay. Here and there, snow is piled up that has not melted yet. Bluebell and fireweed shoots are starting to come up, so I pick some to go with the fish. These plants are only good eating when they first come up. While cooking dinner I work on a letter to Maggie.

Dearest Maggie,

You would probably love the view from the houseboat as we travel. The Kantishna River is about 100 ft. across, and the channel is averaging six ft. The color of the water is silty with foam on it, so not as pretty as some rivers, but very twisty, with nice trees hanging over the water ....You'd find the dogs cute. They love people and compete for attention. They all weigh from forty-five to fifty-five pounds, and look like the huskies they are – though different colors and some have longer hair then others.

...Letter interrupted

"Miles, how can you drink that river water without letting the silt settle out!" I had never given it much thought.

" I guess I used to let it settle out, but over time I gave it less and less time. Now, it isn't important, it's only silt." Will just shakes his head and laughs. The feed for the dogs is already cooked. We are giving them some last year's dry fish from Two Rivers with rice added.

"Miles I don't know how this dog thing will go. It sounded nice when you talked about it, but look at all the work! These dogs don't mind us, just like the ones that ran off on us…." He trails off. I have thought about that too. I was used to pets who followed me around, wouldn't dream of running away. The pets seemed never to be much bother, but maybe someone was always at home, and the family didn't have concerns about traveling with them, or dealing with more than six at once. *Or someone else in the family besides me was responsible for them.* These dogs are getting to know us, and wag their tails, with very few growls anymore. They all seem to understand the routine, maybe. Anyhow I'm not going to give up on the idea. I just shrug my shoulders in reply. It's not going to be his problem after this trip anyhow, so what's it to him? I'm feeling miffed over his comment and disgust over drinking muddy water. *He is not understanding the difference between clean dirt and dirty dirt. This mud is better than the chemicals in city water, that's for sure! Just because we can't see it.*

"Miles, why don't you just get a book about dogs?" I sigh back a reply that I have repeated many times on many subjects.

"Because I'm not good at listening? Because when you live at the cutting edge, there are no books. Would books have helped Lewis and Clark? I notice when you work on engines you never have a book in front of you - how come?"

"I guess it's the same, Miles, half the time I've used miss-matched parts never suggested in the book. A lot has to do with feel and sound. Half the time I can't afford those fancy tools suggested, or they are not with me, and there is no way to get them with me because I am out remote like with you."

"Will, it is like that, but also I hear that term, 'educated idiot,' and realize some things come from books and some things not. Fairbanks has not got the biggest library in the world anyhow. Books on dogs are about pets, pet care, or at best, hunting dogs. There will be no books on pack dogs, on sled dogs, on sleds, or harness work, or minus fifty degrees, or traveling by boat with a pack of dogs, or what to do when you're poor and or remote." I can tell though, that Will would do it all different. Everyone has their own great plan. Their own idea on which road gets to Rome. We all tend to think our way is the best. So, knowing this, I listen to Will, smile and nod. So many times someone giving me advice knows less than I do, certainly no more. Even books get written it seems, by people out for a buck, who may or may not be qualified to write about the subject. Will asks me what I'm chuckling about.

"Will, you remember that book called "Free for the Taking" we found at the library? Yes, well, anyhow I showed it to you, and the point is, the book is full of crap. People would go out in the woods and die reading and believing that stuff. Same as learning through Walt Disney. Anyone who knows anything at all could tell you just from the title, the book is nonsense. Nothing is 'free.' There was that part in there on how to carve a lens from ice you could shine light through to build a survival fire with, saying how one should never again be without fire in the woods. Will, I tried starting a fire with a real magnifying glass and that's an art in itself. Could you imagine trying to carve a lens with freezing fingers, and get one carved in time to save your life? Now I read some place how it is possible to get a fire going by taking the projectile out of a bullet, and fire the gun into your kindling. That might work, useful to remember. But it is the only idea in the entire book that was worth filing away in my mind. I'd guess Will, the right books are out there someplace, but how would we find them? Most wouldn't be much fun to read anyhow."

Will gets out his bedroll and sets it up on the floor. He's a big guy and can't fit crossways in the width of the boat, the way the bed is set up. Me being short and having designed the boat for me, I have no trouble with the bed that converts the day table by adding a section in it, to the bed at night. While lying in bed I can push the front door open. This is good in an emergency. I can get out fast.

We sit up reading by kerosene light before drifting off to sleep. This is part of our daily routine. The boat gently rocks as the current, through the pond, 'burgles '— Creeks gurgle, but brooks burgle-related to burping.' Ducks make nervous 'going to bed noises,' across the pond. I know by the sounds, they wonder if it is safe to go to sleep with us on their pond. I smile, wondering if they will still be there in the morning light to be our breakfast.

"You hear that, Will?"

"Uh huh." "I like breakfast to be cute, fuzzy, and cuddly don't you?" *"And help-less – don't forget that."*

The dogs hear the ducks too. I open the door to ask them to be quiet, or our breakfast might take off. They look at me. They look at the ducks. One sighs and lies down. The rest look at Kenai and lay down as well, and be quiet. They are all chained to their own tree in the woods, glad to have more room; out of the boat!

In the morning I'm able to shoot three ducks before the rest get away. I retrieve two, but one must have been wounded and got off in the grass by the ponds edge, and is hiding or died there. The dogs are going nuts. Kenai seems to be most alert and focusing on a specific spot like he might know where the duck is, and he's not barking.

"Will, turn Kenai loose!" I holler from across the pond where the duck might be. Will has been inside getting things ready for a duck breakfast. He turns Kenai loose, and the other dogs go even more nuts, but Kenai acts like he knows what he's doing, so I don't say anything. Most important to Kenai is I trust him and leave him alone to do his job. Sure enough, Kenai dives in the icy water and heads to the weeds where I had shot the last duck.

"Go get it, Kenai!" He swims harder and looks around sniffing the air. Sure enough, he finds the duck and grabs it. But Kenai has had no training, so does not know what to do now. He looks to me for instruction.

"Over here, Kenai! Bring it here!" I tap my leg in the usual communication to dogs meaning 'Here where I am, bring what you have and drop it here,' that most dogs seem to understand. No problem. Kenai gets my meaning and swims to me with the duck in his mouth - just like I see in the movies. He climbs out of the water and comes to me, but doesn't want to drop the duck. He figures it is rightfully his, and doesn't want to share it. I don't get mad I just have to think what to do. I talk to him nice. Kenai only gets stubborn if you yell and get mad.

"Kenai, over here," and I point for him to sit in front of me. He reluctantly sits in front of me, but turns his head so I can't get the duck. I talk to him. "You know, Kenai, I shot the duck and if I hadn't shot it you wouldn't have the duck to fetch. You couldn't have killed it all by yourself. I'll give you part of it, but it has to be cooked first or you might get worms." I put my hand out for Kenai to give it to me. Reluctantly he drops it in my hand. "Good boy, Kenai - you did real good!" But Kenai is not dumb, and does not want a pat on the head and praises. He wants the duck!

As Will and I eat duck for breakfast. Five gallons of water is heated on the stove for the dog's morning broth. The duck guts and feathers are added. There had been a frost last night, but the houseboat is nice and warm. In fact we have to keep the front door open. We wait for the morning fog to lift so we can see to travel. As usual we have to fiddle with the engine to get it to start. Will has taken to draining the oil at night and warming it on the wood stove to about body temperature. The heated oil is poured into the engine to warm it. *Now where would you ever read about stuff like this in a how to book? Where is such a book when you need it? Except for my buddy Will, - who would know about stuff like this? When it comes to engines I listen to Will – that's for sure.* Because he proved he knows more than I do about them. Will does something else I don't see, and the engine starts. He'd sprayed something in the carb mouth after taking the filter off.

"Will, come on out, need you to check this out."

Will was in the house putting wood in the stove. He sticks his head out the front door saying. "Lots of ice, Miles, what's it mean?" We have not seen much ice floating in the river, but now, here is an ice pack coming at us.

"Maybe Lake Minchumina is just breaking up! This is ice from the lake, or some jam just broke up ahead!" I pull the boat into an eddy in a bend out of the main flow of ice while we discuss what to do. The ice thins out after we eat lunch, so we think we can go forward again. After taking off, there is more ice around the corner.

"Miles, I think Lake Minchumina is around the next bend. I've been studying the map while you have been running the boat, and think I recognized this bend." After looking at the map with him I agree, but it looks like we will have to wait till the ice clears to go around the corner and into the lake. Civilization is supposed to be here, rumor has it; but no one I asked knew for sure. There should be a village of maybe twenty people. Van had told me he was in touch by ham radio with someone from here, but not much information of use to me. One ham radio contact could be a lone trapper with a portable radio in a tent.

Diary: May 18th - engine quits twice - almost lost her. **19th -** Fast water rough time - **20th -** Made the Muddy. The Muddy is 200 miles up - and once on the Muddy, the trip gets easier. All the time we worked on that engine it seemed. The time that she quits, would be in the fastest current, or at the sharpest corner. Often as not there would be sweepers – some are six inches in diameter - and thirty feet long; out across the water five feet above the surface. The current bounces them off the surface so they slapped the water and then up fifteen ft. in the air, moving like a live snake. I surely didn't want to go under or into one sideways. Sometimes when Sable quit, we'd jump ashore with ropes and snub her off before she got away. Sometimes we'd throw an anchor over the side and hope it held. I got mad at Will a few times, and he got mad at me a few times. It was my boat and I was the one who had something to lose; but anyhow. Some places I had to dig a channel with my prop. There was no place with 3.5 feet of water. Sometimes Will had to cut in his 70 horse jet to help, but he could barely hold us against the current. I can't say when, or where, or how many times this happened; every bit of the way really. I'd jump off and throw a line over my shoulder sometimes, and pull in the freezing water filled with ice chunks. The fastest we went was about four to five miles an hour. Sometimes we went half a mile an hour against the fast current. I'd sit there on the roof with the engine going as full throttle as I dared, just barely holding the nose into the current - fighting to stop the nose from swinging around downstream - and it was ever so slow. But at no point had I ever considered giving up.

Fish caught for the sled dogs while traveling

CHAPTER NINE

LONG HOUSEBOAT TRIP TO LAKE MINCHUMINA, DOG TEAM, NET FISHING FOR DOGS, SUE

W ill and I tie out the sled dogs, and hole up for a while. We have opinions now about the dogs, since we have been with them a while. Will tells me: "Miles, this one dog, Scorpion from Bill Henry, I think you will have trouble with!"

I agree, but do not know what to do. "We already lost two dogs out of the bunch. I'd guess Two Rivers shot Wiseman." Now I think the dogs would not run off, know us, and would come to us when we called, but it takes time and is not easy.

Scorpion is a 100 pound wolf hound—big, strong, stupid and likes to fight. I hope he comes around and mellows out. The other dogs listen to him somewhat because he is the strongest, biggest, and most aggressive. But Kenai—the first I got from Van, is smarter than Scorpion. Kenai is sixty-five pounds, and has a lot of bird dog in his blood. I'm amazed again, how different all the dogs are. As different as people are from each other.

Kenai watches me while all the rest watch Scorpion. Kenai looks at the other dogs and wants them to behave. Scorpion looks at the other dogs and wants a rebellion. Scorpion is angry because Kenai is smaller, yet gets the better of him because Kenai is smarter. Kenai knows how to steal a bone from Scorpion without getting bit. By the time Scorpion is saying, "Hey you got my bone, that's not fair!" Kenai already has the bone and is out of reach of Scorpion.

Kenai laughs. "Sure you can whup me, but first you gotta catch me. Meanwhile I have your dinner you dummy!" As leader of the pack, it is up to me to decide how to handle various situations.

"Miles, that was pretty cool with Kenai, huh? Getting that duck like that! Didn't you tell me you got him from a guy who had trouble with him?"

"Yeah, Will, but I think dogs are like people, and some will work for one person and not someone else sometimes. I only know I understand Kenai, and how he thinks. He understands me and how I think."

"I don't know, Miles, dogs are just dogs, ya know? You can't put too much into what they think and all."

I know what Will means. "Yeah maybe you are right. I don't know. Whatever works for me right? I mean the bottom line is if I'm happy about it."

"Miles, trouble ahead!" Will is running the boat. I'm down below cooking. I look out the window. A sweeper is across the entire main channel. I take over the controls. "Will, I'll nose up to the tree while you get the saw and cut it down, ok?" He understands what I have in mind, but we both know it will be very tricky. I will have to nose the boat under the tree so he can reach it. When the tree falls I have to back off so the tree does not land on us. If we run over the cut tree, I may have to kill the engine or put it in neutral as it sweeps under the boat. If the tree is strong enough it could tip the boat or get hung underneath somehow and we would be out of control. I ease up under the tree, as Will cuts on it. I have trouble holding the boat in this exact spot fighting the current and holding us even.

"Miles, the tree is about to go!" I hear it cracking and back off the throttle. With a loud 'crash!' the tree hits the water inches in front of the boat. The current grabs the tree, and flips it end for end up in the air as it goes by the boat, scraping the side all the way. With the engine in reverse, the boat backs away from the tree, which is now spinning, wanting to go under us. The current takes over control of the boat, which drifts sideways, but the tree spins just out of reach. The engine is put in forward. I gain control again. We continue on.

WILL and I get all the dogs into the boat. Each dog has a favorite spot. We can turn them all loose, and they decide among themselves, somewhat, who will get what spot. We chain them to the spot they choose. Kenai waits till last. He knows if he gets in the boat with Scorpion loose Scorpion will kill him. Understanding this, and helping Kenai save face, I take all this into account and act like it is my command it be so, "Kenai, last." Kenai seems to understand and appreciate this. Scorpion is too dumb to know what is going on.

Lake Minchumina is only a hundred feet around the corner, just as Will figured. This is exciting for us, as this is our destination! We need gas, and want to touch bases with human beings.

"Check out this lake, Will! Isn't it amazing!" The sun is out. The lake is eight miles across, calm as glass, with ice cakes floating like ice cream in a float. Most of the ice has snow piled on it. Off to our left we see Mt McKinley and Mt Foraker.

They look close enough to touch. So tall we have to look up to see the top. White cones in the blue sky, pretty enough to eat. The thugga, thugga of the engine echoes and bounces off the spruce covered hills around the lake. Even the dogs sit up, look around, and sniff the air. They must smell civilization and other dogs. We do not know where the village is located.

"Will, the dogs seem to be sniffing and looking off to the right up ahead there. Maybe it's the village, so let's go that way." The dogs have told us where to go. The dogs are right.

As we get close to a collection of cabins, we see a fire. When we pull in, we see a bucket brigade, and are handed buckets. Will and I look at each other in astonishment, and do what we are told, fill the bucket and head up the hill. This is a gentle slope, starting with diamond willow and alder, then into poplar trees as the ground gets drier. There is a lot of dry grass and leaves along with rose bushes and shrubs that would support a fire. Someone has been burning brush in their yard and the fire got away. We throw the water on the dry grass as instructed. A log cabin up a path ahead looks safe. The cabin looks new, with well-oiled logs, a nice picture window and smoke coming out a chimney. An outhouse indicates no running water, and there are no power poles, electric lines or other cabins nearby.

Calendar:
> **May 22, 1979** - Ice clears. Houseboat onto the lake. Beautiful day.
> First boat on the lake. Fire.

"Miles, looks like they think we are BLM firefighters." I hadn't thought of that, but some new people are coming up the hill with yellow BLM jackets on. After the fire is out, we introduce ourselves, and find out we are the first with a boat on the lake, which seems to matter to me. No one has even put a canoe in the water this season, and here Will and I have put in 300 miles to get here in a houseboat. I fluff my feathers and strut around. No one notices but me—but I'm mighty proud. Will only laughs and doesn't see why that is important. *If I was to be asked – after a lifetime —what the top ten things are that matter? This would be in the top five. When I die, let that be my epitaph! "The first one in—the last one out."*

I laugh along with him, "Ha! It's a rough life, requiring some motivation, some illogical emotional aspect, something hormonal or stupid, to engage in something so unreasonable and risky."

Calendar:
> **May 23** - 14 fish.
> **May 24** - 13 fish.
> **May 24** - 23 fish

May 25 - 28 fish, leave for Fairbanks.

The most important thing was to catch fish for the dogs. Will and I set the fish net, and catch a few using a pole, so we have fresh fish for the dogs. We are low on food for them. Mostly we catch pike and whitefish. Salmon will not be running yet till later in the summer. There is no mention of meeting anyone. I have to go to town to get 'stuff.' Will is staying here to fish and feed the dogs while I am gone. Will records each day, how many fish caught and what kind. Will writes on my calendar.

June 2 - Heard from Miles I send a letter along with 2 new fish nets.
The catch increases. 37 Fish-34-38-59-47–62
June 9 - Got back from art show. Total fish caught 667.

Will was to tend to things while I am gone. He wanted a taste of life by himself, as I had lived in years past. Like me, he had the Alaska dream. He is more family oriented than I am. There was always wood to cut for the family. He says to me, how his dad is coming home from the North Slope job, and he has to be there when his dad comes in. Always something, some reason he can't get away. Life with his family has its rewards, as my life has its rewards. So this is Will's time to check out my side of life.

Flying the 200 miles to Fairbanks cost $28.

Will adds, "Don't forget my snuff!" Will has a list of things he wants. On the flight to town I drift into a . . .

Past Flash:

Will and I live in his truck and stash our grubstake of goods in the woods here and there, back when we first met, maybe '73. It's hell when you don't have a place, and no one to trust.

We found a hole once; a deep hole in the woods to hide our latest purchases in out behind Alaskaland. We put a lot in there, and covered the hole with plywood and dirt so no one would see it. I remember a nice fishing pole I got at a garage sale I looked forward to using – and some furs I hadn't sold yet. Some locals must know about the hole, and our things were gone. All we saw were tire tracks in and out. Who could we complain to? We'd be asked,

"Did you own the land?"

"No."

"Do you have a receipt to prove you owned anything?"

"No." We'd be lucky if it was not us charged with trespassing! So finding a place to keep stuff we acquired long enough to get it together, and get it out in the wilderness is always a chore. Half of all we acquired we figured, got stolen.

Flash Past ends

WILL GAVE me the phone number of his sister in Fairbanks who has a place and is working. I call, and she comes to the airport and picks me up. I stay at her place a few days. Alaska House needs a few days to advertise I'm back in town. We set a show date for me to sell my art. Karen and Charley are glad to see me, and excited about stories of houseboat life that I can tell the tourists at my show.

As usual, my art is packed in empty tin cans with moss from the woods. Once again I explain, "Where am I going to get boxes, chains, tags, brochures, and displays? I only come to town a few times a year for a few days, and I stay at the Salvation Army or impose on a friend. I need to get in and out. I don't have the kind of money it takes for a motel; anyplace I might sort things, box things." The Parr's understand and can supply 'all that.'

"Miles, you just bring us your art and stories. We can handle all the rest! All that packaging stuff can be bought and supplied a dime a dozen. It is you and your work that is special!" I do not know if it is the truth, or they are just flattering me. Since the tourist season is just barely getting started, the Parr's have time on their hands, so we talk. Charley is not, 'just anyone' but a state senator, so I value his opinion and tell it like I see it.

"Well Charley, one day I hope my work will be better. I recognize a need in myself for attention. The best attention is positive attention. But negative attention is still better than none, or better than being one of the sheep. I think my work depends a lot on flash and dash, without enough on ability. My ideas are great, but I'd like to handle my material better." His wife Karen seems to have more to say than he does. He's pretty quiet usually.

Karen replies, "You don't give yourself enough credit, Miles! Most art is flash and dash. That is what gets the name! You'll get better with the technical part, but the part that can never be learned is the part that is 'you,' that shines through your work. Through the roughness is something bold, creative, and filled with expression. Your work shows the humor in life! This latest work is better than good, Miles."

We are looking over my latest work. I pause at one piece. "See this? This is a duck hiding in the grass at the edge of a pond, thinking it can't be seen and it's safe, a little fat body with head tucked in."

"How precious, Miles! I know we can sell this!" She holds this piece up and looks at it close saying, "I see you are polishing the back now as well as the front!"

I give her a roll of the eyes saying. "Yes, but why does anyone look at the back!" and she laughs as I continue, "I'm doing everything by hand with five grades of sand paper. Doing the back adds another half hour to the time. It's also boring as heck."

Karen replies: "But Miles, people want that added touch and refinement that shows you care!" Well that's why I do it of course.

Karen takes me over to the News Miner. I show up with my leather clothes, my hat made out of thirteen squirrel skins. There is the owl feather in the hat, and ever present blade of grass hanging from my mouth. The reporter eats it up, wants a picture and a story. There will be a good picture and story about me doing a show. I learned a while back it is better and cheaper to have a story done than to pay for an ad, "Latest Adventures of Wild Miles" stuff like that. Headlines like 'Master Craftsman Comes Out of the Bush!' are saved in my pile of memories. I know what the news media wants, and I give it to them. In return they help me out. What the heck, Karen and I smile about it.

Before show time I unveil the latest piece I've been working on over a year 'Winter Trapline.' This is seven ft. of whale baleen with a trapline story in metal. There are trees, snow with footprints, a shack, a pair of snowshoes, some sled dogs, harnesses, traps in a tree, and other details, all in mixed metal fit together in my puzzle work style. Everyone is silent and mouths hang open as I tell the story going with the 'circle of life' on sheep horn. Two sheep meeting, without words, told in metal. "How much?" Everyone thinks it's a steal at $3,500.

"If no one buys it, at least it will draw attention and people can look at the other things." Almost everyone wishes they had the money for it.

At the appointed hour I am dressed in my 'Wild Miles' costume. I wink and say to Karen, "It's show time!"

The crowd is enthralled. One customer says, "Gosh how I envy you! I'd do anything to be able to do that, live in the wilds!" I don't think I have done anything special, except done it, instead of talking about it.

I reply, "So do it—what's stopping you?" There's the usual stops on seeing that through. Got a family, obligations, no money, no knowledge, no time. He buys a belt buckle of Dall sheep horn with copper bear playing in the flowers on it. Conscience: 'Next!' A lady knows what she wants with no story. She doesn't seem to want to think I, *this grubby looking guy dressed like a freak,* made this beautiful piece. *Not a problem my hand is out for your money—next!*

"Enjoy your new art piece..." I'm saying as I'm already looking to the next in line. Everyone here wants a good bear story, so I tell the one about me kicking the bear. I make another $800 in sales off that one.

"Where do you get your ideas?" One of the basic three questions I have a pat answer for. *New unit of time—never heard the question before in my life, what a great and unique question. I reply,* "I use the material I find on the land in my everyday life, and use the metals to tell a story about it. Simple stories like the way a duck comes in to land on the pond, or how the mountain looks on the trapline at minus fifty below…" She's looking at the piece she wants. I tell the story "This is a swan flying over my houseboat in the spring. It's tired and had a long flight. The wing beats are slow and measured, as it fights the wind. See how the grass below is blowing in the wind? Yet the Swan prevails and does not give up. In the end she gets to the nesting grounds, which is filled with everything she ever dreamed of."

"What a lovely story. You are so sweet! So sensitive…" Conscience: *'Ya, ya, ya, fine—so hurry up lady where's your money. Next! Tell her about drinking the silt water— watch her drop the piece like a hot rock."* Naturally I'm not going to tell her anything she doesn't want to know. What good would that do? I smile politely. I'm honestly sad I have an attitude, that these people do not want the truth, but only the dream. I feel like a con artist. Is there another way?

Melissa is one of the clerks at Alaska House has listened in. "You are very kind to these people Miles."

I feel guilty for my thoughts but--sigh—maybe if I 'act nice,' one day I will think nice too. I reply, "I'd like to reach these people but don't know how. I'd like to convey something more meaningful and real. Make a difference in people's lives."

"Miles you can't single handedly change the world. You do your part. You give them beauty in an ugly world. That is enough. You are too hard on yourself." She wants to take me home with her, feed me, give me a good meal 'and all that.' We'll see.

"Next!"

A little girl. "Ooo parts off a dead animal! Look mommy!"

I politely smile, as the family comes over to look, and I'm guessing, to give me a hard time about the evils of killing living things. Ready to yank my chain, bait me. I'm not going to ask them if they ever go to McDonalds or wear leather shoes. As the little girl scowls and brings her family to gawk, I say to her as I show her a polished slice of moose antler with a bull moose on it . . ."Once I was very hungry and alone. There was no store nearby. I was eating moldy food. I might have died. Before I died, a moose came along. I was able to kill it and this meat saved my life. Since I had already killed the moose for food I didn't want to waste any of it! So I made art of the hoofs, bones, and antler. I like to be reminded how the moose saved my life, and to tell that story for all to know in my metal art work, using a piece of that animal."

The little girl softens and says, "Wow, look at this mommy, moose antler with a moose on it that saved this man's life!" Mommy frowns at me as she gets the money out to please her little precious girl as I smile.

I try real hard not to smile a smile that lets her know I'm good, and she's been coned. *Who could do it smoother? Maybe my buddy Crafty? "Next!"* I tell one story after another, depending on what they want to hear. The money rolls in. A few shyly ask for autographs. The famous 'Wild Miles' who kicked a bear, and lives in a houseboat.

Everyone of course stares at the baleen, 'Trapper' major work in awe. Why should I be serious? My art speaks for itself. Get out of it the meaning you wish. "Behold—I stand before you all revealed." The best there is at what I do. But if you envy me, if you wish to be in my shoes, if you wish you could do as I do, if you want the truth, well, be careful of what you wish for!

"Excuse me, Miles, will this chain hold up? I like the piece but am unsure of the chain."

"Well truthfully, I am selling the pendant and throwing in a chain for free. This should be put on a better chain, but there are so many choices in chains, and good ones cost so much. I live in the wilderness, where chains tarnish and get tangled, so I don't offer good chains."

"Yes, ok—thank you for being honest. I do have a good chain to put this on. Here, you can keep the chain then."

A guy asks me about the shotgun on display. This is the black powder shotgun I'd built, and inlayed with a duck scene of silver, copper and brass. I do not really care if I sell it or not, since I use it to hunt, but of course everything is for sale when you're broke. I had put an outrageous $400 price tag on it thinking no one would buy it. It is only worth half that. *The guy wants it!* I whisper: "It's loaded. I shot a goose with it just a few days ago. All you need to do is put a cap on it and it's ready to go!" The only way to unload black powder is to fire it, or run a worm rod down the front, and try to yank the load out from the top. I have such a worm end for the ramrod, but no use letting the world know it is loaded. I assumed I'd be headed home with it, and just use the load. It's harmless enough without a cap. Anyhow the guy thought that was a great story to tell about his new art piece. He will hang it on the wall and tell that story a hundred times.

"This shotgun belonged to Wild Miles, and was loaded when I got it at a show. He'd killed a goose with it just last week!" I smile.

There is some talk about how some of my pieces are not holding up over time. Alaska House has some repairs that have come in. Since every single piece is an experiment, there are some combinations of the glue and material that does not hold up. I am experimenting, trying to solve the problem, but meanwhile back at the ranch...

"This one came apart just sitting on the shelf, Miles." Karen brings me pieces to fix. I will fix for free, but even so, I need to solve the problem. Also I notice over time, people know they need to polish this metal since it is not gold, but when it tarnishes people seem to put it in a drawer and not wear it again. I can experiment with finishes. The whole process just seems, 'slow.' Meanwhile I knowingly sell stuff for high dollars I suspect will not last more than a year. I try to keep the price down and tell people, but that goes over like a lead balloon, and it is hard to do when people smile and want to pay top dollar. Even so, I have much work to do. When I'm alone I have a migraine headache.

"Miles, you need to write your book. Are you still thinking about that? Like your Alaska Magazine story?"

I reply to Karen, "Yes I am working on it, but can't seem to sit still long enough. I am keeping a good diary though." Conscience: *'A book, you mean like my art, that falls apart in a year?'* I think of a reply, "What sort of book would it be? I want to write a Mountain Man book, but all I do is make mistakes. Well, whatever, perhaps all will reveal itself in good time. I can write when I am old and sitting in a rocking chair—but I'll need good notes."[1]

Karen just says, "Well don't forget, Charley and I want to read it when you are done."

We count up the money. There is enough to live on for the next year, maybe. Especially if this winter I trap and make a few dollars. Since I do not keep records, it is hard to know what I am making in a year. I made about $2,000 my first year and lived on that, barely, but think I am making about $7,000 this year, about half what I would make on welfare, but I feel so rich, so do not understand how I am poor. Nor do I understand how anyone on twice my income should complain and cry about it, or why anyone should feel sorry for them. Life is surely puzzling.

At Alaskaland, I visit with my friends at the Diamond Willow shop, Bill and Nora. They are glad to see me! I give each a gift of art. They had put me up when I was rescued and fed me—gave me a place to stay when I couldn't pay. I want them to know I am grateful. A girl running the Alaskaland post office looks sad when I go in, so I go get an extra ice-cream.

"You want an ice cream?" She brightens up, tells me I am thoughtful. Heck it is a small thing to do, no big deal. The TV is on.

"Hey isn't that you?" I look up to see my interview. I shrug my shoulders. She wants to hear all about my life. She wants to take me home and feed me (here we go again!) *"What is it with these women?"* What the heck though. I have no place to sleep tonight. Her name is Sue. *Not really!*

SUE HAS TAKEN ME HOME, fed me, and we have talked. I wonder where I'm gonna sleep. She lets it be known the plan is for me to sleep with her. Well, I'm not a prude. This might be ok. I mean I'm sort of looking for something long term and meaningful but is that likely? How does one meet a long term relationship? By turning everyone down? So I ask, "Well um—what sort of prevention is there—are you on the pill or…?" I'd as soon be responsible here. She replies. "No! I want to have a child. I'm getting to the age over thirty where I may not be able to, and that's why I am so sad!" Conscience: *'Oh no!'* How do I explain to her that just because I gave her an ice cream does not mean I want to be the father of her child? How do I explain that it is one thing to have a one night fling between two alone responsible adults. If it goes further, well we shall see, but certainly not an obligation to! How do I explain that this is not how I want to be saddled and harnessed? I would expect first, openness and honesty. Any woman I'd be serious about would have been up front from the start, and not lead me on, or waited till we were about to climb in bed before explaining. She takes my pause as time to explain. She says further, "I know I should find a good man and settle down first, but what do I do when I am sure that is not going to happen? At least I will have a child to love!" Sounds sort of reasonable, especially with my pants half off.

I do say however. "You think this way now, but it is a great responsibility, hard for a single woman, and a child needs a father. This is not fair to a child!"

She says, "Well if it's not you, it will be someone else! I want to get pregnant!"

This I believe. If she is bound and determined! I might as well have the fun. I ask, "Well I don't want you to go back on your word and say to me later some other story! I don't want any responsibility, no obligation!"

"Oh don't worry! I would be grateful! Really. All I want is a child! I don't want anything else from you!"

"I try to imagine what it would like to be a woman in her shoes wanting a child, no guy, with time passing. The biological clock ticking. That strong instinct to have children. Who am to say I would be strong? Surely she is very sad all right! I should not judge anyone else and their decision in life! She is right, she will go see some other guy! If I were sober I might say, "So go see some other sucker!" But. What the heck, long as she doesn't come to me later with some sob story! I want her to be happy. Even so, I might be an accident waiting to happen. One cannot keep all that desire inside forever and ever, without going nuts.

June 9th - I fly back to Lake Minchumina, greeted by Will.

"So Miles how come you got that grin on your face—get laid or something?"

I didn't really want to explain, so say, "Just town, Will, you know, the usual stuff. Glad to get back!" We are both excited by the fish catch. Before I left, we had started building a fish drying rack in the sun on the pebble beach. I had showed Will how to cut and hang fish so they can dry and be preserved. We have about three months' worth of dog food dried. Not enough for winter, but in fall there is supposed to be a big salmon run. I should get lots, plenty for winter.

On the twelfth, we get 200 fish in one day, but then a storm hits, and for three days it rages with the nets washed ashore not working. *Almost as if the fish knew there was a storm coming and were moving to another area.* For a week, the usual number of fish are getting caught. It is about time for Will to leave to get back home. He wants to run his boat back, so buys some gas locally. I buy his gas for helping me out. We part without much fanfare or goodbye's.

"Have a safe trip, Will, and write when you get back!"

"Watch your top knot, Miles—stay below the horizon!"

Will likes to use the old Mountain Man talk. I mimic him when he begins to talk like a Mountain Man, and speak incorrect uneducated Mountain Man jargon. "Check how your stick floats, Will!" and I wave goodbye.

Photo Section

Launching boat in spring after trapping off it all winter

My best lead dog full of porcupine quills. He does not survive

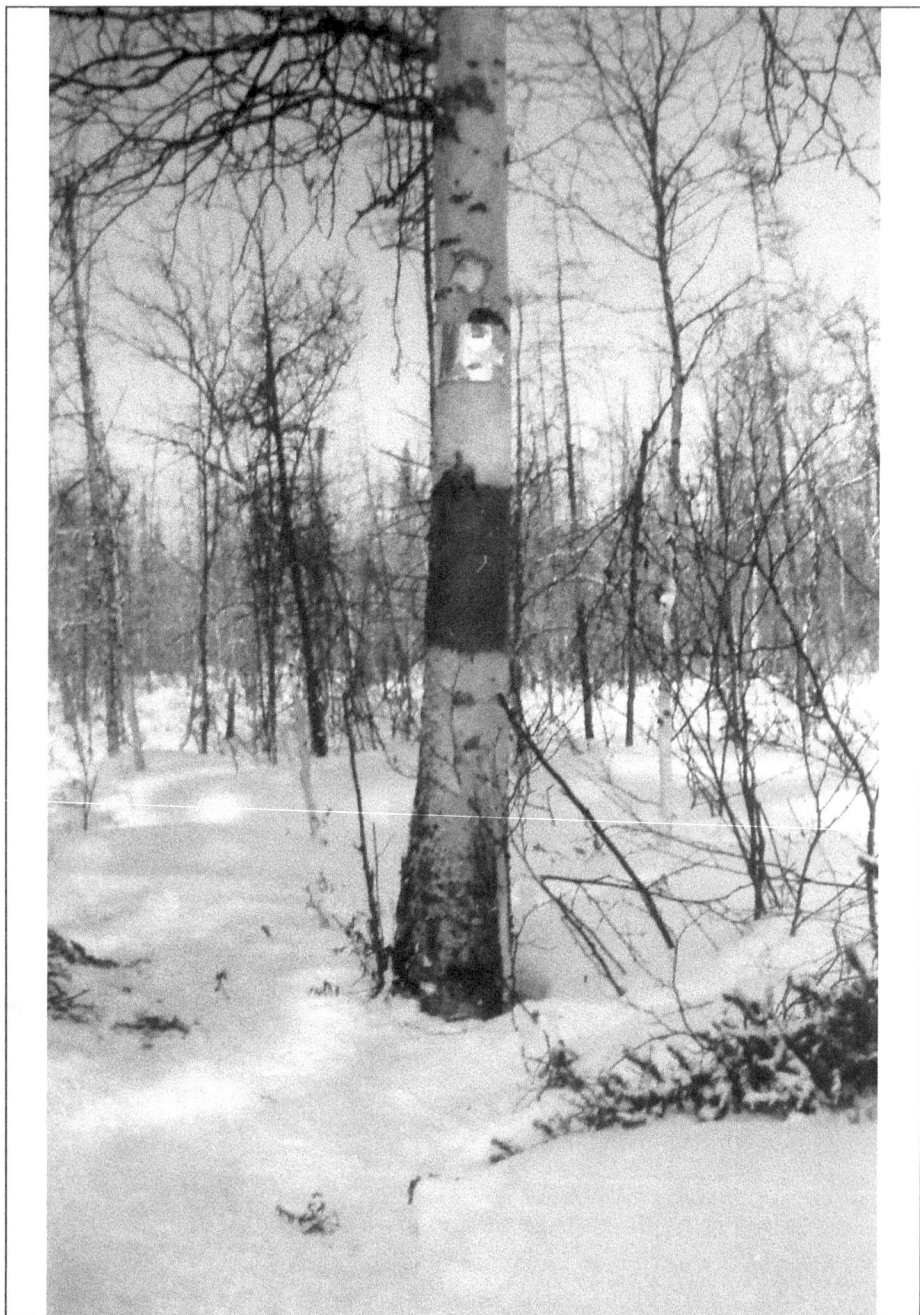

Corner post marking homestead 1st corner post

Unloading houseboat, use smaller boat as runabout

Building trapline cabin in winter, takes five days

Spring goose at the homestead

Emergency steering cable repairs

Built and setting up a fish trap

Tremendous loads I hauled to the homestead with an inch of freeboard

Insulation and tin against logs on the outside of Kantishna cabin for warmth

Grizzly track along the river

Dog sled I built myself with hand cut wood. Set up for long distance.

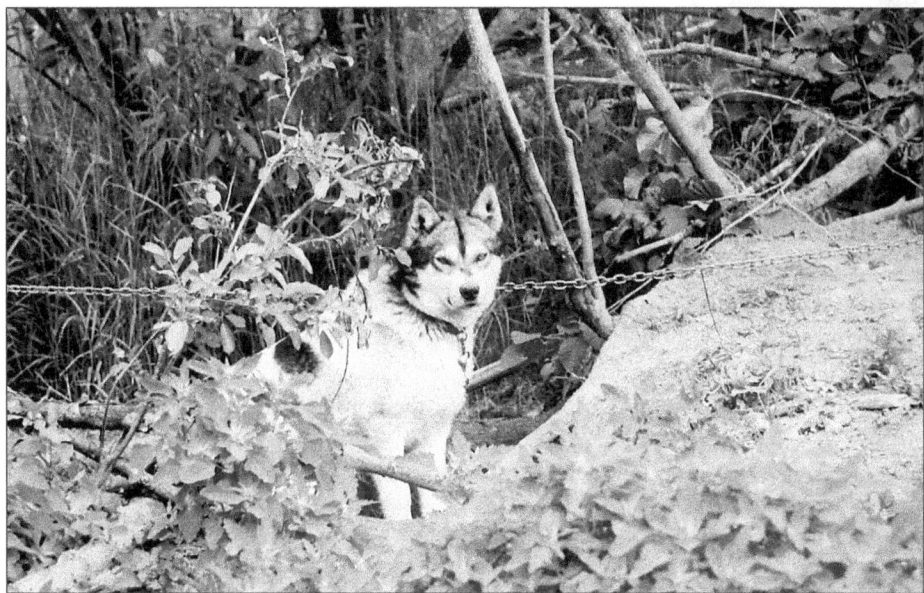

My sled dog 'Map,' whose markings look like my trapline map.

CHAPTER TEN

MINCHUMINA TRAPPERS, MUDDY RIVER, HANSEN LAKE, LOST AND OUT OF GAS

I'd been slow to introduce myself around the village of Minchumina. I don't like these situations, that seem filled with dread. The guy whose place could have burned is grateful Will and I stopped to haul water with the rest of the community. I visit with him. His name is Lenard. Harvey in Galena had asked me to say hi to someone he thought might still be living here. The old timer Kenny is still here so I say hi from Harvey in Galena, and Kenny invites me in. I visit with him often. I learn who is trapping, and where the traplines are, sort of. I look over maps and ponder.

I let it be known I'd like a trapping area. No one is pleased, and say it is all took up. The usual talk. No one wants to let on where any place might be. Everyone who traps is vague about where they themselves are. I don't get it. The area looks like lots of room to me. I'm resentful about the attitude. *People trying to claim the whole darn country with all this room around! How much sign had Will and I seen, the 300 miles coming up here! Too many trappers indeed! Ha!* But I'll be patient and hang out, mind my own business, be honest, hardworking, just see what develops. *But that's what I did in Canada…*I have a while yet to work it out. I think though, I'd like to backtrack down the Kantishna. The boat trip with Will looked like nice country. I may not try to settle in the village. I've had enough of village life for a while. Galena, Delta, Manley were 'ok,' but my chosen path is the wilderness, not village life. Anyone can live in a village, only a chosen few can handle the deep wilderness. *Sour grapes? I'm not being accepted around here and I don't want that life anyhow!*

June sixteenth, my Manley forwarded mail arrives. Still nothing from Maggie. I keep hoping somehow she finds me, or I find her. Kenny is old, but claims a trapline. He seems interested in parting with it. His area is across the lake. It sounds like, from others, he has not been on it in ten years or more. Locals respect his area, but he has no right to sell or transfer it, which would not be accepted by locals. A young kid is friends with Kenny, and seems to want the trapline too, and I think he would have priority since he is local. My take on it though is, Kenny is not willing to give up the idea he is a trapper. He also likes the attention of two guys coming by to woo him over it.

Tom Flood traps by snowshoes, has been here a while, and is a respected trapper. His area seems sort of north of the lake. There are the Collins Twins; two girls who trap, and whose father has been around for ages, running the airport or some such job. Something to do with the FAA (Federal Aviation Administration.) Lake Minchumina has a surprisingly good airport. I hear the reason is because it is needed for firefighting planes to land, to deal with any fires in the area. They can refuel and pick up more fire retardant when there is a forest fire or other village fire. There is no 'community' here as most would know it. Just a collection of log cabins around the lake. There are no roads, just snow machine and four wheeler trails. There are few jobs of course. A handful have work related to the airport. There is snow plowing and grader work. Someone gets some money to sort mail, and deals with the mail in general. It is just part time.

There is no store, but the Holmes family across the lake sort of sells things out of their home if you need something. They keep extra things for that, if you can catch them at home. They sell gas, sort of, when it is around, but often it cannot be counted on. Everyone has their own gas supply. There is a little airplane work, if anyone stops and needs plane repairs. Or at least one guy says he is a repair man. There are a lot of retired people here who get money from 'outside.' A few people trap full time, seriously it sounds like. One guy is sort of a writer. Unpublished yet. He writes and is hopeful. He has to leave the community to go to work for the summer. Maybe others leave as well to find work. I would think at least, they must! I myself am unsure how the future will go for me in terms of needing to leave to get funds. I have not met any natives so this is a white community.

I have enough money now to do ok till sometime in winter. Depending on my needs, and if anything breaks and needs repair or whatever. Can I continue to depend on art sales? I left art on consignment, so when I do get to town again there should be money waiting! I hope to be trapping this coming winter, and who knows what kind of money I can expect from trapping, especially my first year here! I have no doubt I will be trapping someplace. Conscience: *'We can do this the hard way or the easy way...'* Well I do not want any problems for sure. I have heard enough about trap line wars, killings, bad feeling, all that. Trappers are serious about their livelihood. Not having any legal rights doesn't help. It means we all have to work it out among ourselves. I want to be accommodating, but this is ridiculous. *No room! Yeah right!!* What kind of talk is that? If I'm a hundred miles from anyone, how could that possibly affect anyone? Good grief! How much do I want to be played for a sucker, and how much muscle do I want to show. I'll watch all the players in the field. Bide my time, see who is honest, who I want to ally with. Every small community has its clicks.

Ray Jr. is younger than me, but interested in sled dogs, fishing, and has the plans as I do. He's the one who thinks he might get Kenny's trap line. I like him and his dad. His mother is the postmaster. They seem to be a respected family. Ray wants to have a plane and fly. He has some promising pups and is building a dog sled. We talk about such things. While looking at maps, I keep going back to the Bear Paw area. Someone from Nenana is right at Bear Paw, but between it and this lake there is a lot of room. I just keep looking over the map. The Starr's have a lake named after them at the mouth of the Muddy. This is a big family Indian name out of the Tanana area. I didn't see any sign at the Muddy though, looked like no one had been there in a while. Ray tells me what he knows about trapping activities. Since he is young and has not established himself yet, he is more willing to talk than the professional trappers.

"Ray, if you are interested in working something out with Kenny, I will leave that area alone and not try to deal with Kenny in competition with you."

"I'd appreciate that, Miles. I think one day Kenny will let go of it, and I'm the logical one to get it."

The Collins Twins across the lake are visited. They were the ones Van in Manley talked to on the ham radio sometimes, and told me about. "No, Miles, we fly a lot. We do not see much winter trails around that area between the Muddy and Bear Paw."

I tell them I might head over that way. I hear no objection. The Blackburn family is on the lake. An old timer in the family, Val, is a great story teller. He talks about Hansen Lake. I find it on the map. *Sort of in the area I had been eyeing*. He used to trap from that lake, and there may be small cabin—if it is still up—that he sold to someone who is never there anymore. The name didn't mean anything to me, someone who was the first master guide in Alaska, Hal Waugh, used to be well known, died. His wife lives in Eagle now and is school teacher there. No, they never trapped there. If anyone had any rights to the area for trapping, Val has as much right as anyone.

"Val, can I buy it from you for a couple hundred bucks?" I could have just taken it and no one would say anything probably, but I think it would be better all-around if I said "Yea, I bought it." Val hadn't cut any trails, never expected to go back there and has nothing there. He and some old timers, all long dead, used to go there. Val was glad to get the money. Now I just have to find the area!

I ask Kenny, "What do you think? Is it too far? Wondering how I will get mail!"

He gives me a look of disgust. "Do you want to trap — or get mail!?" Well, put like that, yes, of course, the decision is simple. Going back a hundred miles from here to settle might be tough. That's a ways to come in for anything. Trapping is more important than mail.

Calendar

June 17 - Pull nets.

June 18 - Packing to go downriver.

June 19 - Leave camp on the Muddy.

I have all my dry fish and everything I need for a winter, the sled dogs and I are sitting in the water with, I think, two inches of freeboard, and drawing three and a half feet below the water.

June 20 - Made sixty miles - almost swamp the boat.

June 21 - Lost steering - lost power - lost lower unit twice. Heck of a day.

On the Muddy River I lose steering in a critical corner. I have to shut the power down. The current makes a whirlpool here. The pool spins the boat around sharply. My steering chair falls off the roof. The boat takes on a steep lean, and almost takes on water. In the lean, things on the shelves inside fall off, which adds weight to the low side, compounding the problem. In a flash I'm in deep trouble. The boat, however, rights itself before it swamps. I have to spend a long time cleaning up.

I stop to camp, and take the small run about boat ahead to scout out where I am going. I don't want the cumbersome houseboat with me while exploring. If by chance I go past Hansen Lake, I am unsure if I can come back upstream with my big load. With the small boat, I discover I am only ten miles from Hansen Lake. I had guessed it should be coming up soon.

June 22 - Boat into Hansen Lake and lose lower unit again. Hang fish to dry.

The fish I have is not completely dry and needs to be aired as it is spoiling. If it gets too bad - flies will lay eggs, so it is important to keep it drying. I am happy with Hansen Lake.

June 23 - Set fish nets - move houseboat to deeper water - pulled with the small boat.

Hey Will!

I got to Hansen ok but the engine is giving trouble! Without you around, I think I cannot keep it going much longer. I am unsure when you will get this, but I will have a pile of letters going out when I make a trip to Minchumina. I like Hansen Lake and this was a good choice for me. The lake has two parts, sort of like an hourglass with a narrow creek connecting the two halves. There are several islands and some deep spots mixed with nice grassy shallows for ducks and fish. The water is clear, but looks black where you can't see bottom. A creek at the upper end is clear, and has grayling in it. I am pretty sure there will be fish around for the sled dogs. Bear Paw Mountain comes right down to the lake on one side, and Roosevelt is on the other side. I can see Mt. McKinley well, so there is a good view. I guess it is sort of in the flats though, as there is swamp country all around me so good for trapping and getting around in winter I think. I ramble a bit.

Sunshine, Miles

The houseboat engine is on its last legs. I cannot nurse it along as well as my mechanic friend, Will, could. Everything is simply worn out. I am now burning three to four quarts of oil a day. I'm where I think I am going to stay, so the engine has served its purpose. I certainly got my $200 worth that I paid for! Who knows what I will do with it now? One day, maybe next year, I might use the small boat and haul in a new engine for it. Maybe go back to the original idea of steam! I might try a tunnel in it, which would allow me to suck a twelve inch propeller up into the hull so I do not need twelve inches of water below the hull, but only six inches–what the hull draws. All choices have a good point or two, and some bad points. With a tunnel all water pulled by the prop into the tunnel above the waterline is considered payload, as if it were in the boat. It might be fifty gallons. Steam and paddle is only about 20% use of its horsepower, romantic but amazingly inefficient. Anyhow, too many other things to deal with for now. I am now concerned with needing a boat to live on and setting up camp. Somewhere on this river will be home, and this will all be my stomping grounds. I need look no further.

June 24 - Move dogs to new location.

    June 25 - Rain - fix moccasins - make a knife handle.

    June 26 – Set two more nets - move everything off houseboat roof - set up tent on shore. Make a fish cache.

    I need a fish cache against the rain – something I can keep smoke under now and then to keep flies away.

    June 27 – twenty-eight Fish.

    I start getting fish out of the lake. Not as many as lake Minchumina, but at least there are fish here.

    June 29 - Left in small boat for Lake Minchumina.

    June 30 - Make wrong turn up McKinley River and get lost.

I know I have only been here a week, but I sort of want to know how long it will take, and how much gas I can expect to burn going into Minchumina. I want to know before I get in a bind. This is not really a waste of time. Once I get settled in more, with more fish hanging, it will be harder to leave (so I reason) and I have mail to pick up and a few more supplies to get, and leave word maybe, that I found the lake and am ok. Not that there is anyone to inform. Will might like to know. Anyhow—and anyhow.

I leave the dogs behind, thinking I will go fast and light, and be back by tomorrow night. If I break down, the dogs are downstream. I'm told to expect to use ten to fifteen gallons of gas. I have the twenty-five horse engine on the sixteen ft. boat, one of the twin engines the houseboat originally came with. I bring twenty-five gallons of gas. Reading the water going upstream is different than it was coming down. I had been up this way a month ago, but the water level is different now. I had covered so much ground I had no idea where this was, in relation to the trip on the houseboat. I had been doing three miles an hour then, now doing twenty miles an hour, quite a bit different!

Diary entry: I'd see a landmark and expect the next one in an hour, but I'd shoot by it in a matter of minutes. This got me all confused. There had been no possibility of a wrong turn when in the houseboat because I had to stay in the main channel. No side stream would be deep enough. A wrong turn never entered my head, but I did in fact make a wrong turn in the small boat, and went up the McKinley River. The snow in the mountains was melting and making much more water on this river than I had seen a month ago. I kept going. Going up, looking for a familiar landmark. The river got faster, and faster and more narrow the further I went. I run the motor full throttle and should have been doing thirty miles an hour, but looking at the river bank I am barley making progress. I am in three ft. rollers and can go no further. If this is what I have to go through to get my mail then this is very discouraging.

I bend a prop and loose the motor cover trying to put a new prop on. Darkness is near. I make a camp on a sandbar. The sunset on the mountain is so beautiful it is worth the sacrifices made. The mountain goes through royal blue to majestic purples and on into pink, all reflected off the snowcapped peak of Denali—The Great One.

Saturday I backtrack, and see where I had made my wrong turn. I head on toward Minchumina. When the Muddy comes up I stop to think. I only have ten gallons of gas left out of the twenty-eight I had started with! I'd have to turn back. I can't leave the dogs, and if I do not get to the lake and have to drift for several days that would not be a good situation.

"We don't have enough gas back at the houseboat to make another trip to the village." My conscience has nothing to add. No one knows where we are for sure, and no one is expecting us, or will come looking for us. After a pause, my conscience replies, 'We might be here till November— then we can run the sled dogs into the village. Do we have enough supplies to last five months?' That is the beauty of the concept of the houseboat, everything we need for a year goes with us. We will settle into the routine of being the only ones on the planet. I still have no watch, or clock, or radio, to know what time it is, what day it is, or know what is going on in the rest of the world. The dogs are glad to see me return. The routine of fishing for the sled dogs is got into. I do have a few civilization concerns… "That shipment of fossil walrus ivory we ordered will arrive COD and if we do not pick it up, then what?" I sigh briefly till I think of something else.

'Sue will think we don't want to see her again.' I decided none of it is worth worrying about since there is little I can do about it. How in the heck can I ever expect to have anyone in my life if I disappear for months at a time right after meeting them? I'm five gallons of gas short of what I need to get to Minchumina.

I spend my time building a shelter up on shore in a nice part of the lake, up a creek a little way that runs into the lake on the other side from the river. A fish cache and a smokehouse are built. I unload the boat into the shelter so I have room in the boat to live.

The weather turns nasty and there is rain for four days. The river rises two ft. overnight, and my camp goes under water. All my fish, dog food, rice gets wet. I dry 100 pounds of rice in a frying pan on the woodstove in the houseboat and save it all. It, of course, will never be the same again—with leaves, spruce needles, pieces of paper bag and such in it. I'll eat it anyway and be happy to have food.

July twelfth a plane flies over low and circles. I hold up an empty gas can. I think I hear the pilot yell, "Back in a week!" before heading to the lake. It looked like the Collins plane, but I am not sure. The very next day a float plane lands on the lake. The sun has come out. I paddle a canoe out to the plane, now anchored out in the lily pads. A startled pilot opens the door and asks, "Is this Mucha Lake? I think I missed it, and am looking at the maps here." I poke my head in through the door to look at the map on his knees, point to Mucha Lake, and tell him this is Hansen he is on. He is glad to have it confirmed and know where he is. Putting his hand out he says, "Name's Dave - Dave Hafley."

I understand the polite thing to do is tell him who I am. "Miles Martin—Wild Miles."

He nods - he's heard of me. "Miles, any fish here?" He's got his wife with him. They are out for a weekend of fishing out of Fairbanks, just an hour or so away in his private plane.

I tell him how I am doing with the nets. I leave him be, to try his hand at fishing. "Dave, I have some letters if you'd take them out. Got any extra gas by chance?" I wasn't going to say it was an emergency, for in fact it is not.

"Nope, sorry, no way to get it out of the plane tank anyhow." I canoe back to the houseboat to get my letters together.

Dearest Maggie...

I have written hundreds of pages to you and it has been well over a year, and I have not heard from you, so think we have lost touch. I write you but it is like writing my wood stove. You have become my conscience. There is no one else I trust enough to write so much to... Who else would read it all? Ha! 100 page letters! (smile.) You wouldn't believe how beautiful it is here. The lake has two parts sort of like an hourglass. One part is windy and choppy a lot. The other part is in the lee, is shallow, and has more trees around it and the fish seem to have a route they follow along one bank, cross over to the grass, enter the shade of an overhanging willow and on up the creek. There is one place I put a net that is under an eagle's nest. They have young. So when I check my net I see the young being fed and I think it is just so different from what you are doing and seeing every day, but certainly I hope you smile at my word pictures. I imagine you sighing and asking questions. I image what you would be telling me. Married and having kids by now? I mention that a lot? Yes because each of our lives is changing from when we knew each other. Would we recognize each other if we saw each other? I counted sixteen swans on the lake and think there are eight nesting pairs. I saw some other signets that were smaller and gray looking. They fly over the houseboat and the dog yard twice a day, going to and from their feeding, then nesting grounds. They are my alarm clock. Could you imagine waking up each morning to the sound of trumpeting swans flying over? Well, gotta go—some fisherman is here who will take my letters out with him. My letters to you are not being returned so I do not know where they are going. But hope you get this! I chuckle. Huh? Well I just thought–100 years ago not so far from here was the furthest North Hudson Bay company fur trading outpost. I read once where it took three years for a letter to go round trip to England. Imagine writing your loved ones - and knowing it will be three years before you get a reply. This is life... and so I smile.
Sunshine, Miles

"Nope, no fish Miles, but we need to get going. The wind is picking up, looks like I'll be fighting a headwind going home." I hand Dave my few letters going out, and he promises to send them, adding, "Looks like a nice lake here, Miles, prettier than the one I was headed for, so I might be back. Hope to see you again then!" I canoe away so I will not be in the prop wash and watch him taxi, turn around, rev her up, and leave the water. Myself and I stare after the plane for a while. *'He'll be in Fairbanks in an hour, did you hear him say?'* "Uh huh. Pretty wife, did you notice? Pretty flower print dress on, wearing sandals." My conscience chuckles, *'So would you trade places with him?'* "Not really. Anyhow we have to work at being more humble, ya know. It is really hard being so blessed and chosen by God and all... " I trail off... *'Ya I know.'*

Maggie had been told about the lake, but there was one place not mentioned.

There is an old fox farm left from the 20s. During the depression, many wilderness Alaskans had fur farms to make a living. Hansen, who the lake is named after, had a fox farm. Two brothers, Emil and Einer from Denmark settled in here. The fox pens still have names of the fox on the cages. Val had told me the Hansen brothers had a still and sold hooch to other trappers. No one knew where the still was. Val had been drinking with his group of buddies one night, when Emil decided to go feed the fox across the creek while he was still drunk. The handmade canoe is still here that was used to cross over. Emil fell out of the canoe and drowned in three ft. of water. Einer had his home a ways up the river. Apparently they argued a lot, and divided up the goods and split. Emil had not told his brother where the still was.

"And I looked for the still a lot of years, Miles, and never found it. Rumor was that it is in a cave nearby." Val had told me as much as he knew. If it is in a cave, then it has to be in Bear Paw Mountain next to us, and would not likely be a long way off, if Emil was selling out of the cabin. Little details found seem interesting. There is a fox poop scoop made of willow wood, baling wire, and an old square gas can. Some cages were hand woven mesh, leading me to believe these were the first ones made before there was any money. He had a lot of time on his hands. An old grocery list found in a fox pen consisted of lots of corn and sugar, supposedly for the fox farm. Other items on the list looked like fox stuff. But also a cool way to sneak in hooch supplies during prohibition. This looks like a list for a barge order. Old horse harnesses and cart by an old gold rush cabin shows how heavy loads were moved. Val told me the Hansen's hauled ore for miners in the area to the barge for part time work. There is lots of grass around the lake to support a horse. All this together gives an image of life here in the 20s.

"Maybe we can find that still! Might be interesting history for a museum or sell as antiques. There might be copper coils and old jugs and such." I'm also thinking of trapping season. "So let's go explore the country for a trapping area, we are caught up on chores." My conscience agrees! We take off walking with a packed lunch. There are marten tracks, good country for all kinds of fur. It is a hard to get around until everything freezes, but there are a lot of marshes, ponds, lakes that will be easy to cover with sled dogs. There is no sign anyone else has been here in fifty years. The next day a boat stops by. I hear it coming from a long way and wonder who it might be. The Collins twins from Lake Minchumina. That had been their father the week before flying over. They had gas for me. They had planned to boat out this way anyhow. I only needed another five gallons.

"Yeah, I made a wrong turn and went up the McKinley."

"Yes, the McKinley is still running pretty high. It is amazing you made it so far up there! You saw the canyon?"

"Yes, I didn't seem very far from the base of the mountain. I think I hurt my engine in that rocky, shallow water though."

"No wonder! Goodness! No one I know has ever boated that far up!" I thanked them for the gas. I didn't want the Minchumina people thinking I needed rescuing or needed taking care of. Respect in this way of life is doing for your self—being competent etc.

As they take off I say, "I'll be headed into Minchumina soon, so see ya there!"

I'll need motor parts, I think. Something is wrong, but I am unsure what. *'We could use a spare motor if we can afford one… and we have a list of things that would just be nice to have.'* I'm unsure what to do about the dogs, but think if I leave them all a pile of food and water they will be ok for like three days. Unsure what other choice I have.

The twenty-five horse runs rough, and goes through a lot of gas on the trip in. All my props are bent so I'm sure this is a big part of the problem, but there is more wrong… yet I can't haul the entire engine into town. I have to figure it out on my own. But what parts do I need? I arrive in Minchumina on one of the days the mail plane comes in. I can fly out tomorrow. Kenny is glad to see me. I stay overnight with him. "We thought a bear got you, Miles!" I heard all over the village. When people disappear in the woods it is very often because a bear ate them. I chat with Ray about trapping, then Val about the lake. Everyone has plenty of time to talk.

In Fairbanks I first check on Alaska House to see what sold, to see how much money I have to spend. Karen is glad to see me and tells me everything sold. She needs more - so I give her more. I get the impression that if I was willing to live in town I could make a lot of money, but it is hard showing up sporadically, and no one knows when. But I have enough money for a spare four horse engine, just enough to get my sixteen ft. boat someplace if my main engine goes down.

"Hey, Wild Miles, what's the good word?" This time Will spots me on the street before I spot him. "Miles! You still got your top knot huh? What you doing in town?"

We laugh, "Will, once again you simply show up when I need you! Wow, huh!"

"Almost spooky Miles. I stopped what I was doing and decided to come to town for no reason, as if you somehow told me to!" I just smile and wink. We chat and get caught up on the news we each have. "Miles, I'm headed for Delta to meet with my dad. He's got a day off from the pipeline working on the pipe structure crossing the river, and wants to have dinner with me. Want to come along?" This is how I had found the boat builder and worked out the deal to build a houseboat—on trips with Will seeing his dad. Will's dad is a really nice guy who buys our meal, knowing Will and I are broke. He makes no big deal about it. We always know we will eat good. This trip may occupy a good part of a day, since it is a two hour drive to get there. I am pressed for time, since I have dogs waiting back home, but on the other hand, aside from being fun and great to see Will, he is my source of transportation, and is willing to drive me around for a few hours to buy the things I need, then give me a ride to the airport. Plus the boat dealer is on the way to the visit with Will's dad…

"Sounds great Will–lets' go!"

We pick up a spare motor and a few parts for the twenty-five. Will suggests, "The usual would not hurt, a spare water pump, some gaskets, plugs, a few wrenches, lower unit oil…" I buy everything Will suggests. It's not totally Greek to me anymore, but still, Will has forgotten more than I will ever know about engines. We eat at the Tamarack. We all order the usual bacon cheeseburger they are famous for.

I laugh, "Ya, this is sure better than the moldy rice and fish I been eating*!" My life is not about eating good*. Will helps me shop at the hardware store. We work down my list.

"Is that you, Wild Miles? Good to see ya, man - how'z it been!? You got any new art?" I still have some art in a box and get it out. This guy, whoever he is, who says he knows me spends $250.

Will is impressed. "Geez, Miles that's all right - I should get into something like this!" I hold back a smart remark about practicing for twenty years first. This would be like me trying to sell car parts, which Will would be great at, and I might in twenty years. We talk a lot about how to earn a living.

"Will, you still selling rebuilt wrecked cars? Is that working out?"

"Well yes and no. It is not all it's cracked up to be. Not much money in it really. I got a used dozer and am fixing it up. Maybe I can do dozer work on the side. But yes, I buy wrecked cars on Tradio still, and make 'em run, resell them, but the laws are starting to crack down. Need insurance, can't register the cars anymore with mismatched parts, can't get title. People who want a rock bottom deal on used cars are the type who don't have any money' Miles. It's a real bitch." He still gets work on the pipeline for short periods of time. He's in the labor union.

I call Sue and she is glad to hear from me and wants to get together.

"Sounds good, Sue, but my sled dogs are out there. I need to get back pretty quick. My time is filled with getting supplies and dashing back out."

"I could come out to the houseboat and visit couldn't I?" There is a long pause. I am unsure if this is nothing but a mess to try to get out of or what. Do I want someone with me in the boat with broke down engine, maybe floating without food… the usual stuff, with some woman I hardly know? Freak out time and all that. But, what the heck. She wants to come, let her see the reality and get it over with, then she'll quit asking. And if it works out, well that might be nice too. I know I can't always be so fatalistic…

The pause. "Well, Sue, it's a long way. A different life. I have to think if it is irresponsible of me to say 'yes' to someone who doesn't know what they are getting in to, but sure, I think it could be worked out. I know a pilot who wants to trade for art. He could bring us both out in the same trade deal." Unsure how to get her back to town again. Maybe I could boat her in, and Skip could bring her back out? We will talk about that later...

"So ,Sue, want to go to Alaskaland?" I need some things I see for sale there, and can drop off art, see Bill and Nora, leave more art with 'Crafty' at his new craft store. Sue runs me around to these places. We make it to the Howling Dog to dance when our day is done.

"Ya, Sue, I like people, and town well enough on a visit. The biggest problem comes from extended periods of time, involving answers to questions having to do with making a living, where to stay, how to get around. This is where and when it all falls apart. People are glad to see me a few times a year and run me around to shop. I can find a place to sleep for one or two nights, no problem. It is fun to shop and get supplies and then go dancing. But once you have a job to pay for it all you are too tired. There is no time to have fun, to use the stuff you buy, like boats. The costs multiply like crazy when you need to buy food, pay rent, pay electric, trans-portation, and pretty soon it is just the rat race."

"I feel the same, Miles, but am unsure if the answer is how you live. Most people would enjoy the good outdoor times, as you might enjoy the good times in town. The problem comes when people must fish even if it is raining." We fall asleep in each other's arms. I have to keep it all in perspective—after all, 90% of her relation-ship with me is that she wants a child; so I am unsure how much is her bullshit, saying stuff so she gets her goal. Where I'm in favor of getting to know each other first, to see if we get along, before we can be parents... and I'm asleep.

"SKIP, for that art piece I need you to do some flying. If you haul fifty gallons of gas to the lake, and take Sue back home, that'd work out great for me. I'll bring Sue in by boat to the lake."

Sue and I fly to Minchumina on the mail plane with supplies and engine parts. We stay with Kenny. It's July twenty-fourth. I work on the twenty-five horse down on the beach, and get it to where I think it will run ok. Sue and I load the lake boat up and take off for Hansen lake, 100 miles downstream. I at least have a spare motor. As bad luck would have it, a storm comes up and we are traveling in the rain. There is no way to get out of it. This is an open boat. Many of the new supplies get wet. We have ankle deep water in the boat. The twenty-five horse engine is still not working right, but I do not know what is wrong. We mostly lack power, and burn a lot of gas. It could be carburetor problems, but might be weak spark, a fuel line problem, or resistance in a bearing someplace.

"Miles, aren't you cold?" Sue sounds cold.

I take my jacket off and wrap her in it as I reply, "A little maybe—but guess I am used to it."

"Miles, why didn't you bring the houseboat into Minchumina? I thought that was your plan, to travel with the house."

She sounds like she is just curious, but I think behind the question is the thought 'I would do it different and better if it were up to me! This is crazy!' so I try to explain what I have discovered."It was a good plan to start out with. Reality just steps in. Gas is expensive and hard to get here. The houseboat is slow, draws a lot of water. Right now I have a worn out unreliable engine in it, and a new one would cost me a year of my gross wages."

"But Miles, this boat has an unreliable engine as well, so what's the difference?"

"I have been stuck with the houseboat, and it is hard and dangerous. It takes power equipment to get it off a sandbar, or a day of backbreaking work. Drifting in the houseboat is not safe compared to this small boat that is easy to paddle and easy to push off if it gets stuck. But mostly this trip is costing $25 in gas, but would be $100 in gas in the houseboat. Yes, if I had a good engine I'd probably use the house-boat, bring the dogs and have everything with me. That would be the goal." Sue is not complaining a lot. I admire this about her. I don't really mind the rain that much. It is not great, getting supplies wet, but I like how things smell. There is something beautiful and majestic about storms. I just didn't want one this moment, when I am trying to show a woman a good time.

"Miles! How do you know where to go on the water? How can you even see! You are amazing!"

I chuckle, "Just practice, maybe. As you know, I've never driven a car, so this is my world! Where I'm amazed anyone can drive a car, and not get in a wreck."

THE DOGS ARE glad to see us. They are all ok. Most still have water and food in their yard. Judging from tracks circling the dog lot, it looks like a bear has been trying to move in on the dogs to eat one, or all of them. I'll have to keep an eye out.

"Not much room and not much for windows. I had to design it so it would stay warm in winter. A lot of glass is not safe on the river in storms."

"Miles, why don't we use the empty cabin by the creek mouth?" This is the cabin Val told me about. It is unlocked, has a wood stove, but no supplies. Local people stop here on their way downriver for the night. Val had told me it is owned by the Waugh's who are no longer around. I wrote a letter to Julie Waugh but have got no reply yet. I ask if I can use or rent it. Bush etiquette as I understand it, dictates that such an unlocked cabin can be used in an emergency or to stop for a night, maybe a weekend on the way someplace else. It would not be proper to move in, especially being a trapper or hunter, who will use the land and compete with whoever owns the place. I'm sensitive to this, after my experience on the Yukon my first few years. I had things stored in just such a cabin as this, and had everything stolen and had almost been killed. I don't want problems here. But, this might be an appropriate acceptable use, to get in out of the rain for a couple of days, a woman with me. I explain all this to Sue. We decide next day to use the cabin. I get the wood stove going to where we can spread out our stuff to dry.

"Miles did you see this note on the table, under the coffee cup? What is this?" I quote the note to let her know I saw and read it.

"Stopped by to visit. Sorry I missed you—1951.

"Ha! "I was born the year this was written, and it sits here as if it were written and left yesterday. Time standing still, huh?"

Now I am separated from the dogs, from the houseboat, and all my supplies across the lake. I'm not happy about that. That's my life I depend on over there, but neither do I want to move it all over here onto someone else's property. Well — it's only for a few days.

On the twenty-eighth of June, Dave flies into the lake again with his float plane. He has ten gallons of gas for me, if I take him fishing.

"Great, thanks for remembering, let's go!" The new four horse seems to work well out on the lake putting around in the light wind and fighting a current from the creek that runs through the lake. I show Dave the eagle nest and young. We get places he can't taxi into with his plane. He only catches a few fish, and is disappointed, but he likes the view and says he will be back again.

Sue and I are back on the boat living. She is organizing things. I do not know where things are now. "Sue? Where are my socks, I thought they were in here with the tea bags...."

All I hear is "Men!"

"Huh? And the honey jar, it's not behind the books anymore..." But I get used to where everything is, and it is nice to have it clean and organized. A person could get spoiled and dependent pretty easy... "Thanks Sue — for sorting this all out."

We pick berries together in early August. Sue wants to make jam. I get the impression though, that she wants to be a mother and is just practicing on me, like playing house. There are many issues we are avoiding. Many views we each have that are not compatible. So I feel more like, I am going along with the program to keep peace, rather than sharing, experiencing, acceptance, respect, and love.

"Sue, are you carrying the 357? There's bears around, trying to move in on the dogs." She doesn't seem to believe me, and is only indulging me, my paranoid guy macho gun thing, trying to scare her, be her protector. I explain to her, "Sue, I wouldn't step five ft. out the door without my pistol stuck down my pants." She only smiles. Changes the subject. Thinks I'm overly scared.

"Miles, I came across this duffle bag. It looks like dirty clothes, but they look pretty old. Do you even want to keep them?" I had forgotten. I had meant to get to that bag one day. But that was a year ago. Dirty clothes yup.

"Well," I hesitantly start, "Ya, see. I go to the Salvation Army thrift store, and I'm an easy size to find being small. I can get a whole bag of clean cloths cheaper than I can wash these in a machine... so... um... I guess I just sorta keep going to the salvation army rather than doing the laundry..." I trail off. I also guess when you actually move in with someone you learn all kinds of unromantic things about them. I mean on the one hand I hate waste, so I want to save and wash, but reality is, it is a full day's work washing this much stuff by hand, and it can all be replaced for a dollar at the salvation army. So in the balance of things, a dollar, or a day's work, it seems easier to come up with a dollar than a day of free time... Anyhow and whatever. Makes sense to me, perfect sense. "Nope-no dishes. I eat out of the cast iron frying pan, and then put the pan in the wood stove. The fire burns anything off. I retrieve the pan and it is clean, ready to use again; but ya, ya, sure not an issue because over here I have, ta da — two matching handmade ceramic dishes I traded for, knowing that someday I'd have a guest, and eating out of the frying pan would not be polite!"

I laughingly tell her a friend of mine in Galena's answer to doing laundry in the bush. "I ask him what he did today and he tells me he was doing laundry all day. I tell him not all day, because he was out on the river running up and down the Yukon. I saw him. "Ya", he tells me, "I put my laundry in a burlap bag with rocks and soap, tie it behind the boat and run up and down the river. This bounces, slaps, twists it around, and makes stuff pretty clean." He tells me he has to run in a clear creek to do a final rinse to get the Yukon silt out.

"Very funny Miles, sounds like an excuse to go out and have fun on the river to me though. I'll be right back, have to go use the outhouse!" In general Sue's attitude about me and my life is disbelief and distrust. Maybe this is all just so different from the planet she lives on. I catch her studying pictures and notes up on the wall that I pin up. She looks puzzled and asks, "Miles what are these quotes all about, like this one here."

I look at what she is pointing to, and lean in to read it out loud. "There is one thing and one thing only. To turn from the dark night and greet the white dawn." It seems self-explanatory to me. What's to explain?

"Explain, Miles, why it is here!"

"To remind me, I get discouraged sometimes. I need a reason to get up in the morning—to get out of bed when I am depressed. This reminds me of the story it is from—'The White Dawn,' and is supposed to be an Eskimo quote from before the days of white man, passed down many generations." A quote about primitive survival that is universal. Perhaps I feel less alone, knowing others understood hundreds of years ago. "It is so short and so eloquently put. All survival summed up in one rule."

I notice once again Sue has gone to the outhouse without her gun, so I sigh to myself, and decide to follow her a bit to make sure everything is ok, rather than reprimand her about it, *not be to bossy ya know*. I silently follow. As she leaves the edge of the trees, I see up ahead of her, a bear coming from behind the outhouse. Sue has not seen it yet as she is busy contemplating the sky. The bear sees Sue, and comes towards her instead of running away. Not aggressively, but I find this unacceptable. Also I wondered if the bear had figured out our routine over time, knows we go to the outhouse, and has been waiting there as a place to ambush us. I'm not going to take any chances. The meat could be used anyhow.

I get the 357 out and calmly say to Sue, "Could you drop down please so I can shoot the bear?" She looks ahead to see what I'm talking about, sees the bear coming toward her and steps out of the way. The bear sees her leave the path, and leaves the path as well to intercept her. Not aggressively or fast, maybe just curious. I take a shot between the trees.

"Blam!" An eye blink later, the 'splat,' the sound of a 357 copper jacketed 158 grain loc core mushrooming in flesh. The bear is gone from my site. Silence rings in my ears. Sue and I walk slowly to the area, after waiting a spell, to look for the bear. I see blood on the ground, so know I did hit it, but the bear is not around. We have no trail to follow.

"Sue, killing things is just not as easy as it's made out to be. Things have a tendency to want to live. I made a distant shot at a moving target in the thick trees. The bear was coming to you which was not good, so I had to make a judgment call, and made the shot fast. It's not like I wanted to wound it." But of course she understood if she had been armed she was closer and might have hit it better, assuming she knows how to use a gun. If I had not been there following her, it might have been a wounded Sue being followed by the bear. Still, it is strange to me she is mad at me for not killing the bear, and now it might be suffering.

"Miles, it all happened so fast! I barely saw it!"

"Now we have to be more careful as the bear might survive and come back angry. Probably he will go off and die, become food for wolves and other creatures of the forest."

Meanwhile, I decide to work on the outboard engine again, for the hundredth time. I take the engine head off to see if the rings broke, or there is telltale aluminum in there to indicate something wrong. A compression gauge gets put on my 'town wish list.' The head gasket gets torn, so I spend time making a head gasket from my art materials. A copper sheet. I have it almost finished. Sue is talking to me as I work. The boat is on the creek. I'm in the back of the small boat. Sue is sitting in the bow facing me. Tools are spread all over the boat seats. The sled dogs are behind us, lazily sprawled out sleeping. Fall colors dazzle us as shimmering leaves. I look up, and a bear has come through the dog yard, and not awakened one dog. The bear is sitting, just watching us in plain view. No place is safe, not even in the dog yard with all the dogs around.

"Sue, do you have your pistol with you?"

"God, Miles, are you crazy, we are in the front yard with all the dogs around us!"

"Well, have you got your camera with you then?"

"Why?"

"Turn around and smile." She turns and sees the bear sitting there lazily watching us from only thirty feet away, out in the open. It's a black bear again, not huge, but over 300 pounds. Sue is not afraid because the bear is looking so content and lazy.

"Miles, how did it get past all the dogs without waking them? Why don't the dogs smell it?"

"I don't know. Maybe the bear has been hanging around, and the dogs are used to the smell. The bear is used to the dogs, so not afraid of them." I'm reluctant to shoot it, after the fiasco yesterday. So I just holler at it, but say, "Sue, mark my word that bear will be back making trouble. How can he resist the fish in the cache?"

The twenty-five horse runs, but not much different than it had before, after three days of working on it. I still do not know what is wrong with it. This is pretty frustrating, to maybe end up getting a whole new engine. Maybe this one only needs a $3 part to be perfect. "Maybe." We try the small boat with the four horse engine, just to test it out on the main river against the current. There is Sue, the twenty-five horse, maybe thirty gallons of gas. The four horse goes against the current, but only three to four miles an hour.

"Beats walking though, Sue!" I'm not highly impressed, but optimistic that if I was in an emergency, and I emptied my load and went as light as I could, I might expect to go faster. Even with a load though, I'd get to Minchumina eventually, like in five days.

That night we awaken to a loud crash and dogs going crazy. I know right away what is going on. A bear has got into the fish. It is September first today, midnight, dark. I get the pistol instead of the rifle because up close I can maneuver the pistol faster and better. I grab a flashlight. Sue's eyes register astonishment, half asleep. I tell her I'm headed out to deal with the bear. I can't allow the bear to eat or ruin all my winters worth of dog feed. I'm also 'pretty sure' the bear will be content, and involved with feeding, and not very alert to my presence. *Or perhaps ignorance is bliss.*

I can't see the front site on the pistol as I shine the light around to find the bear. I seem to do better without the light, so shut it off, and aim by pointing at the sound twenty feet in front of me. 'Blam!" Followed by the satisfying familiar sound of a copper jacketed bullet slowing down from 2,000 ft a second to zero, in a tenth of a second, increasing its diameter by four times, as it pushes through bone and flesh. In the darkness, a thud. A moan follows. Then quiet stillness. I assume this is a solid hit, but will leave, and wait till morning to go see.

We do not sleep much, but talk till daylight comes. Sue has been telling me how she has to get back by a certain date for her welfare check. She had been filling in for someone else at the Alaskaland post office when I met her. Welfare will of course take care of her, and her new child when she has one. She has it all figured out. I wouldn't want to be a taxpayer, but what can I say? In most eyes I'm just one small step away from her. I have no job, live on nothing, on a shoe string, and even the slightest emergency means I need to apply for assistance of some kind.

I've never got food stamps, welfare, anything like that, but this is the image of homesteaders--free land, right in there with free medical, free food, free, anything else—land just tossed in there on top of the freebies. Sue puts me in the same category. She makes more money on welfare than I do working, so has no interest in finding a real job.

"Why? What kind of job could I expect to get that pays more than welfare?" It's an easy life choice. One to get hooked on. She could actually take care of me, better than I could take care of her. What am I to say? It is not what I want, but I have no real practical argument, and no serious opinion. I'm just hearing the story, digesting the information, going "huh," in amazement. Stuff we never learn in school. She's trying to convince me to move to town, let her take care of me. "Who needs this kind of life Miles? Every time you turn around, you're facing being eaten by a bear. What if you get hurt out here?"

I reply with a happy grin, "I'm dead!" That old timer when I had asked years ago told me, 'When we get sick, we die,' with the same happy grin. He'd never been sick and was in his 80's.

Just before dawn, Sue is cooking fish on the morning fire in the wood stove. I'm cleaning my Ruger 357 Black Hawk. She stares at me as I load, and put gun oil on. I spin the cylinder so the clicks are so close they go 'sssss.' I breathe deeply, loving the smell of gun oil. I wink at her."Miles - you're sick!'

I only go 'hmmm' in agreement. Conscience: *'Ya, well, where would we both be without an equalizer, huh? At the mercy of all the bears, listening to a bear eat the food up we need to survive the winter. I value my gun. I like it, and it is my friend. Without it, right now we'd be holding each other, crying in fear."* We eat and it is time to go deal with a dead or wounded bear.

"Let's do it!" The words from a movie, some cheap spaghetti western no doubt.

The sort of thing my hero Clint Eastwood would say. My words and gesture convey; "This is life - and I love it."

"Over here, Miles!"

"Yup," and I come over. Dead bear. Already getting stiff. Flies are calling to each other. A neck shot that hit the spine, a perfect instant kill. "Find a five gallon bucket, Sue. I'll fetch the knife and sharpening stone." All the insides we want go in the bucket—heart, liver, stuff like that. We get out the pressure cooker and canning jars, get an outdoor fire going. We will put the meat in jars called canning! "I think, Sue, this is the same bear as the first one I wounded, because I found a flesh wound when I skinned it out. Just goes to show you can't always scare these guys away." She wants to learn, and be part of the process. I add, "Nice to have that wounded one accounted for now anyhow; not have to think it is suffering, or wounded and mad someplace, or wasted meat rotting in the woods. I feel better knowing." I do not tell her about the visit from my other female friend in Manley, and how we had killed a bear, sort of similar, girl in bed, I jump up, kill bear, both of us out there cutting it into pieces together…deja vu. "Da vu, in da jar, can ya dig it?"

"Miles, what are you doing now?"

"Looking for the bullet." My finger is following the bullet hole in the carcass. With a satisfied grunt, I can't find it, meaning it went in further than my elbow. After cutting, I see the bullet imbedded in the bone. I roll it around in my fingers thoughtfully. "The 158 grain I used in the past was better, I think. Slower, but made a bigger hole. The 110 grain was pretty useless for sure. Maybe this compromise of 145 grains is best, combine low trajectory, high speed of the 110, with the knock down power, but poor range of the heavier 158…" My mind works it over, wondering if I want to settle on hollow points, which will make a bigger hole but stop at bone, or solid, that breaks bone, or try something else, that breaks what it hits, yet goes in deep. It all pretty much works. All in all, there are differences to note. *When killing is my life, I make it an art form.*

Next day, while we are still pressure cooking bear meat, all the dogs jump up at once and start going nuts, looking over across the creek. My rifle is nearby, so I grab it up. I see nothing, but then a bear shows itself peering out of the bushes. It sees me, turns to run, as I get a quick shot through the brush, with a follow up shot at where it should be in the thicker brush as it runs. Silence. The dogs are quiet. Sue and I take the boat to the other side, but I see little sign. The dogs know what went on.

"Sue, I'm going to bring Kenai over here and see if he knows how to track, for surely he knows what just happened and it wouldn't hurt to try." My only real concern would be that Kenai either gets killed by a wounded bear, or takes off after it and we never see him again as he chases it 100 miles.

The situation is not starting well. Kenai is so glad to be free he is tearing all around ecstatic, as the rest of the dogs jealously scream. I put a chain on him and he is so strong he just pulls me around, tangling us in the trees. "Go get it, Kenai!" I say as I point his nose to the blood spots I see, and he must be able to smell. Maybe he can even hear the bear up ahead someplace, and by watching where Kenai looks, and turns his nose, I might get a hint. I am unsure what will happen, what to expect. Finally he settles down a little. But Kenai does not want to come down the trail I am sure the bear went down. Kenai stops, wants to go another way.

I suspect that after all, the bear did not go down the main trail I am so sure of.

"Sue, do you think Kenai wants us to follow where he is going?"

"I don't know, Miles, he seems pretty ready to just bolt to me." But I give it a try, and walk toward Kenai, letting him go where he will. Kenai walks a little way and stops till we catch up, then walks further, and lets us catch up, and now it looks for sure like he is leading us someplace on purpose. I do not see him stop to sniff anything or look around, but maybe he doesn't need to. For sure he stops me from going down one fork, and has an opinion on where to go.

Kenai stops in his tracks and 'points,' just like I see in pictures and movies. One front leg up, tail out, nose straight ahead, frozen in position. He has been a sled dog all his life, and there is no way he could have learned that, adding strength to my belief, some things are bred in and simply 'are.' As I walk up, he gives me a terrified look that says "He's in there, you go get him!" Yes, Kenai had done his job. Sure enough, I hear the bear still breathing in the bushes. I shoot it in the head. Upon checking, my first bullet had gone through the liver and a lung, just missing the heart by inches. I'm amazed the bear got this far, and lived as long as he did. Something new to learn in the never ending art of killing.

Sue and I 'can' more meat till we run out of jars. We need to make some jerky.

"Jerky is not for us, Sue, has to be for the dogs." She asks why. "Bear is one of the few unsafe meats in Alaska, that might have trichinosis. Some kind of small worm that lodges in the muscle, that can kill you, and there is no cure. The worm is killed with hard cooking, but not by drying." This jerky will be good for dog feed later on in winter when they need more than fish. I was told by a native, and I believe, that the trichinosis is killed by more than five days at thirty below 0.° I'm not convinced enough to eat it myself without cooking. We fill forty-six quart jars with bear meat for people food. "I hope this is the last bear I have to deal with for a while!!"

There is rain for almost a week straight, so we have to stay indoors. I do a lot of art work. We hear a plane, and think it might be Skip looking for us. A plane circles the cabin, then sees the houseboat and we think it lands, but over on the other side. I leave Sue behind while I go out with the boat in the rain to check what is going on.

"Hey, Skip!"

"How's it going Miles? Got your gas, mail, and some fresh vegetables for you!" We go let Sue know it is Skip. She has already been getting her packed things organized to go. Skip takes off with Sue. I am left with the empty silence. It is hard to get used to being alone. Who knows what the future holds for Sue and I. I notice she frowns a lot at the way I am, things I do. I do not know if I can adapt enough, or if she can. I suspect she has no intention of moving into the wilderness, and certainly I have no intention of moving to town. So right there, how can it work? I sigh. *She thinks the lure of good sex will make us give up the path we are on and cause us to see the light, the error of our ways, and we will never look back, but forward, into the light of her eyes and duties of fatherhood.*

Sled Dogs on the trapline

With wolf hide at homestead

CHAPTER ELEVEN

FISH SEASON ENDS, WINTER BEGINS, DOG MUSHING STARTS, MINCHUMINA DOG TRIP

Dearest Maggie:

August is coming to an end, and with it summer. For the first time I have missed the Tanana State Fair. I did not grow a garden, but have picked a lot of wild things and put them up for winter. I have learned what mushrooms to pick, where to look, when to look. I have cranberries, blueberries, and raspberries. I have almost enough fish for the sled dogs. In general I should be ready for winter.

Geese are showing up, and I eat them, or ducks. Almost every day they show up by the thousands here at the lake. If I wanted, I could get enough to can for the winter, but all my jars are filled with bear. I'm always looking for canning jars at garage sales, etc. All my empty jars of all kinds get filled. Empty peanut butter jars get filled with cranberry jam. Even plastic bags get filled with jam! I run out of plastic bags and fill my wash basin with hot jam. I use cardboard boxes for the dry rose hips.

My only female dog Tulip got loose. I got her from Kenny at Lake Minchumina. She was the nervous type. When I dove for her chain she thought I was trying to beat her, so she took off and would not let me catch her. I thought she was one of my more stupid dogs till I saw how uncanny she was about avoiding me and learning my habits. A week has gone by and she is raiding the food at night. She knows what traps are, and how they work so I can't get her in a trap. Oh well.

The water drops and the logs underneath the houseboat are uneven so the boat is a few bubbles out of plumb. I spend a day using a jack and gas cans to shore it up level. I explore trapping country, and get a lot of grouse for fresh food. There is the daily routine of checking fish nets, which will be done right up till the ice runs.

Scorpion is a wolf hound, and as big as a small horse, so I make a pack for him from a part of the bear hide I tan. He can carry my saw and lunch while out hiking. Scorpion is another dog that seems not so bright. Right now he is a big puppy. He is the one that I have to hammer on his head to get it down enough to chain him short in the boat when we travel. It takes a two x four to get his attention. He responds to discipline faster than love. Each dog requires something different. Scorpion likes to fight and he and Kenai have had it out a few times, as I mentioned before. I'd use a pack on Kenai—but I have all the other dogs too and Scorpion is tall and can keep the pack off the ground better.

A larger wood stove meant for winter goes in the boat, and I put the small stove away, along with my summer clothes. four miles of trapline trail is cut for a shortcut to a creek. As the daylight gets less each evening, I spend more time making art by kerosene light. I know I am rambling and this will probably never reach you. It's possible I am only writing to myself and no one will ever read this. I miss you and hope you are well.

Sunshine, Miles

I toss the letter in the stove when done. *It is enough I wrote it.* Many letters are now addressed 'Dear Stove" *I am after all, recording the ending times.* A red letter day for the art is recorded.

Calendar: August 28th - Able to take the art saw cutting to the nearest thousandth-freehand!"

I tell my conscience: "Check it out! This copper duck is a quarter inch long, and has a dozen pieces cut freehand, and if you look through this magnifier, the fit of the metals are perfect!" *'You lost one of the pieces of the puzzle—maybe under my finger nail —it was that small!'* I had to recreate it, or give up on the entire piece. I eyeball the missing hole, and saw the brass sheet freehand with the jewelers saw. I set the pinhead size finished piece over the work, and drop it in place. It is a perfect fit. *'That's impossible. No one can freehand and see to the nearest thousandth, and make a complicated shape!'* I gesture to the piece—to myself with a, 'look and behold—all doubters!' *'Yeah? Well you couldn't do that again in a million tries!'* "No doubt! It is amazing enough it happened once!" My work improves. I have very steady hands. My eyes cannot see something this small, *but my mind can.* Sawing the buffalo out of a nickel would be boring child's play.

Now that there is time to slow down more, since I am about ready for winter, I get to thoughts of my letters. Nothing from Maggie. Not much else matters quite as much. There is a note from my father. His letter does not say much beyond blue sky and clear weather. Who knows what he is really thinking or doing? There is no reference to anything I am doing. No sense that we can discuss any issues, exchange advice or opinions. Yet he has a degree in sociology, is a behavioral scientist. Studies economics. I think one of his PHD's might be in that. I write him, but more from the standpoint of 'what things could and should be' rather than from 'how it is.' I try to be uplifting and positive (as I suppose he tries to do with me…)

Dear Dad,

Nice to hear from you! Yes I am well and happy. The houseboat is set up for winter now, and I have all my supplies. There have been a lot of berries this season, so lots of jam and jelly! Along with lots of berries, there were lots of bears. No—there were no close encounters of the third kind. The lake here is beautiful. Trumpeter swans, eagles, ducks and geese make a constant background noise. My art is going well. At least everything I bring to town sells, and my shows sell out. Of course it is pipeline days so everyone has money. We are a rich state at the moment. (!) Oh—Have you heard from Eileen? Just wondering how she is. Are you still with Kate and still getting along? I assume so. Aaron must be growing up. I don't really remember him well, but he seems a nice kid. One you will be proud of. I think you are doing a good job with him! Is he about the age, and ready to go to college yet? Getting good grades I bet? Well when I think of you I can picture that lake you live on and the dock and the sailboat. I hope you are finding time to get out in it! I'd like a picture of the boat if you have one! Talk to ya later then! **Sunshine, Miles**

Dear Eileen,

Your big brother here-so what's new with you? Last I heard you were getting a new apartment and maybe had work. I hope the job and move worked out for you! Is your friend Peter still with you? If you moved, I just wonder if Peter came with you. Sounded though like you did not move far, as you are still in Portland, Maine--right? So you think you'd like to move to Alaska, huh? Be closer to me? Ya, I know, but it costs a lot to travel from there to here, and I don't really have a home as such. You might have a better chance for a job though. And—did you know all Alaskans get oil dividend money from the state, from the oil money the state gets from the big oil companies? It is about a thousand dollars every year. Pretty cool, huh! Well let me know if you are ok! Sunshine, Miles P.S., I enclose a picture of my houseboat pulled up and ready for winter, with me next to it.

Dear Mom,

Hey, Mom! Are you and Grandma still thinking of moving to Arizona? I know you told me Grandpa needs to move there for the hot dry air and you are all thinking of going there. Wow—be quite a change from Maine, huh! Well I know you are in Oregon now with your new husband and his kids. I forget their names—but they sound nice. You said they were poor and needed a mother, a woman around. So you feel needed and are having a positive effect on their lives? Sounds better for them than for you? Sounds like you enjoy your house and garden a lot, strawberries and lots of flowers! Has it been a good season for them? Oh—no, don't worry, I never told Eileen where you moved to. (Life being as it is—sigh). I did hear Joe is in jail now—maybe Eileen wrote me—and just wondered if you knew. It is good to be away from all those memories? Yes I understand… that it is therapeutic in a way—to spend time around Nature—God's beauty. Certainly not much can get screwed up in the garden—beyond worries of slug infestation! Ha! Yup, I'm fine. Hope you are too! **Sunshine, Miles**

My Step Mom who raised me…

Dear Mom,

Hi, Mom! Yes, been a long time. I am ok, ready for winter, doing my art. Do you still do pottery with that group of artists? I always liked your pottery. Are the fall colors out in Michigan yet? I can picture you out on the porch in the nice country place you and Bob got. A nuclear scientist huh? I do often wonder what studying an atom spinning in a cyclotron would be like. I think of him when I read my Isaac Asimov books! Ha! Well, yes, sometimes I think of Michigan—but suppose every life has choices, rewards, a price—things to balance—what you gain—what it cost—stuff like that. No—I wouldn't trade in what I have. You'd love the beauty here… anyhow hope all is well with you!
Sunshine, Miles

There are letters to different women who are writing me, who seem to come and go. There is the gal from the library, Melissa from the Alaska House Gallery, several ongoing, never met in person but met from an ad. Nothing so far that looks great. I sort of think about Sue and wonder, and surely that was a big thing for her to come here and stay with me. I write a letter to her, since I do not know if I can ever call from Minchumina. All my letters get the usual watercolor envelope, even impersonal letters. Bills get a watercolor, and when ordering from catalogs. All painted upside down, as usual of course.

Dave flies out Sept tenth to hunt duck, moose and fish. My motors are not working. I'm fed up with them. All the money spent, and so little in return. The new four horse is down for the count. Dave and I paddle around the lake. A good Grayling fishing spot is discovered, or at least for this time of year, and we catch a lot of grayling. Moose season is a time of year to expect a lot of traffic in the wilderness. Luckily it is only a brief two weeks. Dave asks: "Miles have you got your moose yet?"

I explain. "Legal moose season is set up with sport hunters in mind. If I got a moose, even the last day of the season, it would spoil before winter comes. The setting of the season assumes we have access to freezers." Dave doesn't want to talk about it. I think he really doesn't understand my lifestyle. He has never gone hungry, has a good job, education, insurance. My guess is he spends time with me because he knows what a guide would cost. He comes here, and for nothing, basically, gets a guided hunt. If he wasn't getting something out of it, he wouldn't give me the time of day. He's friendly enough and I like him. He's interesting, smart, and a nice change in my routine, and brings me stuff.

His only reply is, "If people didn't follow the rules, Miles, there would be chaos, and no moose around. I work hard, pay a lot of taxes, and one of the rewards for working hard is to reap certain rewards. One of those rewards is moose hunting. One individual does not have the right to make up the rules to suit what they want."

He's right, he shouldn't be denied that. So what can I say? I'm pretty sure he sees me as irresponsible, lazy, and a welfare case. He's doing his part, being nice to me to show how big his heart is. I think he might turn me in if I hinted I might wait till after the legal season to get a moose, or gave him specifics or evidence he could provide, so reply: "Yeah, sure, I'll get my legal moose. I just get discouraged sometimes."

The very next day after Dave is gone, hunters get dropped off on the lake by a guide. The pilot asks me my name.

"Miles"

"Ok, I'm bringing some friends of yours out here, didn't they write?" He thought I was expecting them. I hadn't checked my mail in a while, so the letter is probably in Minchumina, possibly two or three months old.

"My friends, the Underhill's from Alaskaland are coming out? Great! Be good to see them." They had talked about wanting to, but didn't know how serious they were. This is going to cost several hundred dollars, so I'm surprised. There are two hunters with the pilot. They heard my name. One puts his head around the float plane seat to talk to me.

"Hey—aren't you that guy who was in Alaska Magazine a few years ago, got rescued and all that, then another article about… " I nodded. "Wow I'm honored to meet you!" hand comes out for a shake. "I always wanted to meet that guy. I live in Michigan and read Alaska Magazine. You're famous where I come from!" Meeting me makes his whole trip, he tells me. He and his friend want me to take them all around the lake. So, what the heck. I take a day off and take them fishing, tell them stories, and entertain them. The plane comes back to pick them up.

"We'll be writing, Miles. You're a very rare and special person!"[1] I nod in thanks. They are off. Next day Bill and Nora show up.

"Wow, Miles, it sure is beautiful here! You are so lucky being able to live here!" They have a tent as they know my houseboat is small, but I show them the small cabin and they stay there. I am very pleased to be able to offer my hospitality to them, since they had taken me in during my time of need.

Bill asks, "Where are all the moose? Have you got one tied up someplace for me?"

I laugh and explain my take on it: "I saw a cow hanging out here all summer. I think it is just too early in the season—weather-wise, for the bulls to be going in rut yet. They are still holed up in the high country. With all these hunters around and noise and what not, it would surprise me if any showed themselves anywhere."

Bill replies, "Well, just wondering. We'll have a good time anyhow, nice to get away from work!"

We sit up talking after dark in the cabin. I ask about their Diamond Willow wood business at Alaskaland: "How did the season go?"

"It is ok. We love it, but the real money is from the oil pipeline work. The company I work for sent me to school and in return I work for them. They pay well and treat me good. We save the money, so will be able to retire. We are getting a new home in Salcha, further out of town, a nice big place on the river. Mostly we like meeting all the people, and talking to the tourists in summer at the shop. We want to help others appreciate Alaska as we Alaskans do! "

"Are the Can Can cuties still putting on the summer skits, and is it the same group?" We all laugh because I hang out with them as they practice, and a lot of the girls took a liking to me, confided in me, and are friends. and flirt around with me.

"Rita still asks about you and wonders how you are. She misses you there."

Yes ,we seemed to be special friends. I miss her as well. Not that she could live with us, but even so it's good to have such a gorgeous woman proud to be seen next to us, willing to be our friend and views us as more valuable in her life than even her boyfriend is. She said to us something about how it's not hard to be sleeping with someone, much more rare to actually trust and share your heart with someone.

My ART DOESN'T FIT in with the kind of things Bill and Nora sell at their shop, so we never discussed them carrying my work, but they like it, and want to know how business is going for me. They mention some people I should show it to, who might be able to promote it.

Nora likes to fish as much as Bill does! We all have fun catching the grayling I had discovered. A fish every cast is very exciting.

"Miles, this is the life! I tell ya! Doesn't get any better than this!" I show them the eagle nest with the young ones about ready to head south. Bill acknowledges Indian blood in him, and how sacred the eagle is, and how honored he is to see them so close. We are like-minded, so pause in sacred silence under the overhanging tree the nest is on. Seeing eagles in the wild, not in a zoo is unique, but especially so out here with Denali, all snow covered in the distance. The fall colors dazzling the eyes. All of it reflected in duplicate on the water's surface, doubling our pleasure. The smell of ripe berries is in the air. Each of us perhaps, focuses on different sensations we treasure most.

"Miles—isn't that a bear swimming the lake over there?" I look where Bill is pointing, and sure enough, it is a big bear. "I don't think I can make the shot this far. Can we get any closer?" Bill is an accomplished rifle shot from his time in the military. He never talked about it much, but enough. I know he was in Special Forces, and knows a great deal about 'guns.' Bill wants the bear and has a bear tag to hunt one. We slowly work our way over in the canoe, as the bear shakes himself, and starts eating something on the shore, probably a fish. Bill rests the magnum rifle in the fork of a tree, after quietly getting out of the canoe. He does not get buck fever, and makes a good instant death shot.

"Miles, Nora and I are going to have a bear rug made in memory of this trip! As long as I live, I will remember this day! We make good money and have been on cruises and other vacations costing a fortune, but this is the best experience we have ever had together."

Bill gives me the meat for winter dog food. The skull is blown to mush, but I knock the teeth out and will use them in jewelry. *No use wasting anything.* For both of us, this is almost a spiritual belief, waste nothing, showing respect for the animal killed. Even though Bill is engaged in a trophy hunt—I would have shot the bear myself for the meat, and this way, both the meat and hide will get put to good use. After all, I have all the bear hides I can use in a lifetime. If I had killed the bear, the hide has little value to me.

"Hey Miles, you know that dog, Tulip, you said is still loose and you have not seen around? I saw some wolves today when I was out alone on the edge of the lake. I think I saw a dog running with them!" I'm not sure I can believe this. I think Bill means well, but is not very bush wise, and more of a romantic. First I doubt a wolf pack would accept a dog, even if she was in heat, they might breed her, but then kill her, or—well, I doubt a dog could even keep up with a wolf pack. If this is so, then she might teach the wolves my habits and all about avoiding traps, etc. So I hope Bill is wrong! Bill and Nora stay for five days, and then once again, I am alone with my thoughts.

Dearest Stove,

My friends, the Underhills, came to visit the other day. I think they had a good time. I look up to them for inspiration. Have I told you their story? Probably—but it is on my mind, so I will repeat it just in case. Bill was in Vietnam. He was in special forces—and highly decorated. He killed a lot of people, but seems too mild mannered and kind.

He was married, and was sending money home faithfully. He came home from overseas to find his wife had left him and moved in with a Mr. Studly black guy. She had sold their house, moved in with him, and was spending all the money on the boyfriend and living in style. All the money Bill thought was being set aside for their dreams together, everything that gave him a reason to be defending his country, went out the window.

Nora was a very beautiful model in Canada. One of the top best paid models. She was in a car accident that left scars. Not serious bad, but enough her occupation as a model was over. Because she couldn't bring home the bacon anymore, her husband divorced her. Apparently in Canada, there is an assumption that if there is money in the family, it came from the man, and the law reflects this. All the money Nora made, went to her ex, and she was left penniless. No job, no future, no husband.

Bill and Nora met, and are the love of each other's life. About as romantic a story as you could ever find. The stuff movies are made of. I think of them. The happiest, sanest people I know. It has me wonder if, somehow, something terribly awful happens in your life—it doesn't have to mean Karma—that you deserved it. That it is possible for things to turn around and be better. Neither Bill nor Nora seems resentful, spiteful, or damaged. They didn't dwell in a world of 'mean, angry and hateful'. Isn't that amazing?

I think about this, and the fact that most of my other friends (or more 'people I know') are very quick to have an excuse to have a bad mood or anger, fuel that fire, as if they want to be mean and angry. The Underhills, by contrast, show me a better way, by example, not by lecturing. They do not cry in their beer about what they could have been or done 'only if.' They dwell on how lucky they are to be alive.

On this note I end my letter to you Dearest Maggie (now my stove).

Have a good day! **Sunshine, Miles**

"Where is the fall run of fish?" *'Should be here—don't know—very strange huh?'* I discuss with myself the problem of the fish run. On the Yukon River, certainly there was a run. I was told the other rivers have runs the same way. At Lake Minchumina the locals talked about the fish run and also in Manley. In summer we are supposed to catch a few local fish—enough to get by. Later fish move around. The local fish head for the big rivers for winter, or move from the river to the big lakes. I'd waited for this big movement to take place, even counted on it. I knew I could not expect many salmon here in Hansen Lake, but some reach as far as Minchumina. I found a place on the river where people long ago put out nets, because up on shore was a good top line with hand carved net floats, right where I thought a good place to set a net would be. There are all varieties of fish here. I get whitefish, burbot, suckers, pike, graying, salmon and a few shee fish. Anyhow... getting too late for a major fish run. I am concerned for the future if I cannot depend on a lot of fish in fall.

Diary Oct tenth

Over fifty Trumpeter Swans gather on the lake to go south. I heard them trumpeting and beating wings on the water, so went down to see what all the commotion was. There cannot be very many people who have ever seen this. Creek freezing up fast—cold spell arrives.

Oct thirteenth - A bull moose responds to my tree banging and comes charging through the brush. I do not see him. The dogs hear him coming and start barking. The bull stops and will not come closer. I never see him. I will have to rely on the bear meat this winter I think. **Diary ends**

I get a moose the very next day. The small boat is being used with a paddle to quietly go around the lake through the weeds. I am concentrating more on getting ducks and geese that are congregating to go south in great numbers. The black powder shotgun, a new one I built, is with me. 00 buck is loaded to see if this helps get geese from a long way.

A moose is feeding in the grass. The big bull makes a move toward the thick willows when he sees me. All I have is the goose load in the gun. I am close enough I think the .00 buck will do the job, so, from fifty feet away, fire on him. Vroom! The usual six ft. of flame, and rotten egg smelling smoke cloud. He drops like a rock in the middle of a stride. *Amazing!* Yes, I am amazed. As usual I want to see where he was hit, and what the projectiles did when they connected with bone, or meat, or thick hide, so I will know better what works and why.

Oddly I cannot find a mark on this big bull moose, so assume the lead hit on the other side, but that would be odd, as I know which way he was facing me. Later, when skinning, I spend more time looking for a hit. Inside the ear is checked. Around the eyes, and even a clip hit on the antlers are looked for. I see no hole in the hide, and no indication he was ever hit. No Mark. That seems impossible. It must be impossible. It might be that the loud sound startled him, and he stumbled and fell and broke his neck. Or he had a heart attack. I have no explanation, only that here is my moose, and I see no evidence anywhere of a hit.

A great many things in this life seem to defy explanation, however. Like seeing three suns that all look the same, or finding unfrozen water at minus fifty degrees. Way back when I walked out to civilization that one year, there was the truck floating in the tree tops. It all must have an explanation, if one only knew what that explanation was. This moose is late enough in the season I do not have to can it, but only have to hang it away from the birds, keep the wolves away, and of course the black bears are hibernating now, or will be very soon, so not a problem. Grizzlies are rare, but could be a concern.

I finally catch Tulip. Only because she wanted to be caught. She had been gone off someplace, and is very thin, weak and discouraged. She is surprised I do not beat her. I just hook her up to the tree and feed her. It is possible she has been with the wolves, and could not keep up, but I do not know. For sure I am excited about winter, looking forward to running these dogs. I have been feeding them all this time, and fishing for the dogs all summer, so getting to know them! Kenai of course is known and understood the best. Scorpion I do not like much, but at least understand. Thunder is a fifteen year old lead dog I was told should be run out front and maybe as a 'leader trainer' to one of my other dogs side-by-side. No, I do not know much about running sled dogs. Like everything else, I am confident I can figure it out.

Van, who gave me Kenai, had told me when I asked about putting a harness on them. "It's easy, just grab all the X's and put it over their head!" Yes, that sounds simple enough. So I think I am going to try to hook up a dog to the sled, just to see how it goes. Maybe get some firewood along that four mile trail I cut.

Right off I learn something. The dogs go nuttso seeing the harness, knowing what it is, and they all want to go, all at once. It's very intimidating. I wanted to do this quiet and calmly, on my own terms. I'm flustered now. I think Thunder is the one to hook up, the oldest, wisest, and the one who knows how the harness goes on, and what to do the most.

With confidence, I grab all the X's of the harness, and start walking towards Thunder. I do not understand what to do next. He puts his head out, and I slip all the X's over his head. Nothing happens. The harness is all bunched up on his neck. I step back to study how the harness sets, so I can figure out where his legs go through. Thunder snorts and steps back, looking at me like I'm an idiot. So now I can't think. I get the harness off, and go in the houseboat, and look at him out the window with the harness in my hand, imagining how the harness might go on.

The dogs have no idea what I'm up to, or why. Are we running, or not, or what? My conscience is with me studying the harness and the dogs. We talk it out together… '*Ok—obviously the padded area is where the pulling takes place. In order for the pulling to take place what has to happen?*' "Right—ok—this hole here, the head has to go here, and therefore the legs have to go there, because here is where the snap is that gets hooked to the Gangline, so we know this is in the back beyond the tail."

We think we have it figured out. I try to sneak up on Thunder again. but he is convinced I'm nuts, and wants nothing to do with me. His behavior tells me 'I can't believe this—I've had a lot of masters in my life, but this takes the cake! You have to be kidding me! I'm not working for this bozo-piece of shit greenhorn!' I have to say in reply, "Come on now, Thunder. I know this looks bad, but I'm a fast learner. We'll be covering a lot of miles together, I promise, because we must. Now, we can do this the easy way, us working together, or the hard way. The hardest way of all is getting a bullet in the head and maybe you hearing as your last words, 'next!' So what's it going to be?"

He is not stupid, and has seen it all, and therefore knows I have him between a rock and a hard place. He grumbles and cusses, but finally sits there with his head out for me to try again, glowering at me. He closes his eyes when I get close. "Ok, Thunder ok, I'm sorry, ok, I'm not going to stick it in your eye I'm not a klutz—I just need to learn here, so bear with me, ok? Don't embarrass me, ok? You make life easier for me, and I'll make life easier for you, ok? "

As soon as I start to put the harness over his head, he wiggles his head, as one might do getting a T-shirt on, but it undoes all the X's I have in my hand. Now I have lost track of where I think all the straps go. I have to take it off again, and go back inside and study some more. Harness in hand, dogs looking with incredible expressions through the window.

Scorpion - "I can't believe this! We got to work for him? Screw him I say!" Kenai is the only one rooting for me.

Yes, eventually I figure it all out. But it starts here, not even knowing the simplest of the simple things. I'm three years old. Alone in the wilderness. To survive, I have to travel 100 miles where there are no trails. All I have is the confidence of youth, stupidity, and an ego that thinks I'm one of the few, chosen by God. My life is a comet across the sky, blazing in glory. Fine then. We start at square one. I hold my head up. I take the first step. A baby crawls, and one day will run the Olympics, but first I must crawl. Fine! *'But some babies learn to walk, and that is all they ever do all their life is walk, and will not, and could never, run the marathon…'* "Yeah? And your point is? You have no point, you know why? Because we are not ordinary. The laws of the universe do not apply to us! Wherever we go, a tear in the universe follows." No other attitude at this time will keep me alive. This is not a time to be humble, or face reality.

I step out the door and address the dog team…. "Fine, you know more than I do! So you will teach me what you know! Fine, I am ignorant, but I am not stupid. I will learn. One thing I guar-an-f+&^ing tee…. We will all go to hell together before I give up. Giving up is not an option!" I'm screaming at the top of my voice now. All the dogs are silent in rapt attention. Not a chain clinks. Not a head twitches. *'Is there anyone here who is not going with us? I will give you early retirement! Scorpion?'* All heads turn to Scorpion. His eyes are big and round. He gets the picture. "This is not a game Scorpion. You mess with me and I'll kill you." Of course they do not know my words, but they do know insanity when they see it, and know what impending death is if they think this is funny.

It dawns on me this is the exact routine of boot camp in the military. Push ups, pull ups, being called maggots, worms, pieces of crap and do it again, be it out of fear or anger. Someday our lives will depend on each other. I stand here, arms folded, daring anyone to do as much as blink without permission. In a calmer voice I say, "I have spoken." A longer pause, and more sane. "Ok, then who wants to step forward and show me how a harness goes on." I hold the harness up. All is silence. Kenai steps forward. His love for me is blind.

Future flash

Thousands of miles together and years later I would learn more about love, kindness, as a way to work a dog team... but like a drill sergeant with new recruits, or a new team coach, sometimes at first there is hate, fear, anger. Slowly respect/understanding. But it is a long hard road, not arrived at quickly or easily, and must be earned, not demanded. Yet in the beginning the first step has to be taken, and the first step is a command. For at first, every new leader is 'stupid and incompetent!'

An important thing to learn is to select good dogs to start with. Ones that I understand, relate to, and have the traits I appreciate. It is hard to make a dog anything, or turn a dog into something it is not. Why waste time trying? I also did not have much knowledge on dog care, nutrition, worms, bedding, but it all starts here, my first dogs, and the long hard road to knowledge. 999 people out of 1,000 quit about now. *'Good, because this is what will separate us from the lemming. The winners from the losers. We will be a Mountain Man, or die trying.'*

Gives new meaning to the line, 'Till death do us part' huh? My story is not about how smart I am, or how lucky I am, or better, or how successful I am. It is about a way to look at life. It may or may not be workable, much less the best way. It is just my story, for whatever that is worth. Even that changes in time, for survival is about being adaptable. The list is very long, of those who went to the wilds with my attitude, and died. Over the years I have known dozens. Dying is easy. It's life that hurts. On the one hand, I have encouraged others to follow their dreams! Yet I am puzzled that so many hold back for a good reason, and if they chase a dream, fail. Apparently being stubborn and having a dream is not enough. Is there a formula?

People who know me best, friends, those, who lived with me a while, worked with me on jobs, think my story is pretty much bullshit. I never did what I say I did, and if so, it is highly exaggerated to the point of being a lie. I have no answer. For sure I am not the same person among people. I do not drive, cannot use the phone, need looking after and such. Perhaps no one is with me when I am at my best. If anyone is, I cannot deal with the responsibility. It's difficult to see me as competent. Later in life I stopped worrying and wondering, and pressed on. For if the story is fantasy and made up, then it is an interesting story about a life revolving around dreams and bullshit. **Future flash ends**

"Hike!" All the dogs leap forward as one. The ice is very marginal for thickness.

Here and there are open holes. If we go fast we can travel on ice less than an inch thick. How much less than an inch we are still figuring out. Ice I couldn't walk on. If we stop, we fall through. If we fall, either the dogs fall in—or the sled falls through, but rarely both. If the dogs fall through it may be one or two dogs, and the others can pull them out, or I can usually walk up and help. If the sled goes through, usually the dogs can yank it out if I step off the sled. If I fall through the ice when I step off the sled, usually getting the weight off the sled helps the dogs get it free, and I can lay down as the sled leaps forward, and get pulled out of the water, even without getting wet. For at the instant I leave the runner, the sled is already moving, and as my body lays down, it is partly on chunks of ice and slush, offering ever so brief floatation, which is all that is needed, a split second. Usually. It is still not fun, or easy, and is dangerous. People die doing this. Sane people do not do this.

"Gee!" Thunder goes another direction, or wait, *is Gee right or left? Dang. I forget.* I'm trying to use the language of mushers. *I think I learned it backwards.* Thunder is grumbling as I punish him for going the right way, and it is me who has it wrong. Thunder comes to a stop without a command. I'm about to yell at him to get a move on. He is looking ahead, sniffing, looking right and left, using his feet on the ice, testing here, testing there.

"You think he can feel the ice better then we can see, and because he is out in front of us, has a better idea what is going on, and so we should give him his head?" "Risk letting the dogs lead us into open water to drown?" "Maybe—but he is an old leader. Maybe picked up a few things along the way. At some point we have to trust the dogs."

I don't say anything, and let my foot off the brake, so Thunder knows it is up to him. He slowly works his way this way, that-a-way, testing, backing up, going forward, and leads us across a section of the creek I could not have done without him. *'Why are we using code to talk to the dog, this gee-haw crap, let's use English!'* Good point. I never use code again, I tell 'em like it is, and say 'right!' and 'left!' Once in a while Thunder looks back at me. I think about what he wants to know, and how to tell him. I say softly, in a whisper, "easy—easy—careful—try the left" thinking he will pick up on my feelings or tone 'danger go another direction.' He does not respond.

I lift my left hand up to get his visual attention. I slowly move my arm left, and point, till he looks where I point. "Yes" He knows what 'yes' means. Visual some-times works better than voice. We learn how to communicate with each other. It is somewhat like learning how to fly a plane by going up in one, and while in the air, exploring what all the knobs do. After a few loop the loops and near stalls and spins, landing without so much as a scratch. Is that blind luck? God at work? Suici-dal? Stupidity? Talent? I myself am puzzled, and do not know, believing different things at different times. I only know I am not going to worry about it.

Dearest Maggie,

I have had experience before with sled dogs, that trip with my Galena friend, John Stam. I have seen dog teams around, so know something about them. It is still too early in the season to begin actually enjoying the silence and cruising along. So far everything is tense because of thin ice and bumpy trails. The dogs got away from me once already. I had to walk a long ways to catch up to them and get them back home...

(fifty pages later after reviewing all going on and my opinion on everything and how I feel about it all...)

Anyhow, yes, this letter is going into the stove like the last one. I now know you will never read any of this. I could write to Sue, who is real? (You ask) Maybe. She does not understand my life. Doesn't want to hear it. No one does, or how do I say, people are used to page long letters with three to four (I assume) with five being a bit much. Fifty pages totally overwhelming and unacceptable. Ten pages is just a note to me. I'm not even warmed up yet. I have never met anyone who can handle it. Most think they have to keep up, and get left in the dust trying, and give up, or tell me flat out to write less. Few want all my thoughts or feelings. I don't want to bother people. So this works. I write to my stove. But rather than facing that, I pretend I am writing you! What is reality anyhow, but what we believe it is. So I can get this mental image of you, sitting there looking as I remember. Reading my letters... sitting on the bed with the cheerleader pom—poms on the wall, school books tossed next to you. Paying attention to how I feel. It helps me organize my thoughts. (bla bla bla)

Letter ends and goes in the stove.

Diary Mid Oct.

Unsure of the date. Losing track of time once again. Today I was excited! Lobo, the only dog that had never been in harness before, took right to it! A few days later, all the dogs lose enthusiasm. I think because we run the same hard five miles every day. No place else to go. Everywhere we go there is open water stopping us. The weather didn't stay cold, so the dog running got frustrating. Lobo quit pulling, so I had to move him back in the team to the wheel position, in front of the sled, and keep an eye on him. Then took him out alone to teach him how to work and pull. I finally get to run the dogs ten miles, and got a better idea of what to expect. I see who pulls, who wants to give up, and the whole dog running is exciting. It is nice to have a personal relationship with your means of transportation! **Diary ends**

My feelings go up and down about the dogs. Sometimes I am frustrated or angry because they will not turn where I want. I may know exactly where to go and how to get there, but cannot convey it to the dogs! I see animal tracks, yet cannot make a set to catch them because this is the downhill trail. I cannot stop or keep the dogs here. I can only stop on flat or uphill ground. That seems nuts to me. Yet the quiet travel is nice. I also like the feeling of being part of a pack. I like yelling "Hike!" Then feel of six dogs hitting the end of the line and snapping the sled forward as one.

I like to see heads come up and ears turn at sign of game. Each dog is so different. Some can be talked to and reasoned with. Others have to be yelled at. Some only get mad or hurt feelings if I hit them, yet it is what others need. I always know what to expect from Kenai. He never has to be disciplined. Tulip is too dainty to be any good, but I like her anyway. If I yell at Tulip she momentarily looks guilty, leaps forward, but very soon slacks off again, with a 'gee, boss, I'm doing my best!' Yet she is not tired like the rest at the end of the day. I think she's scamming me.

Thunder, the old leader with experience, has to be yelled at sometimes, not much. I thought, due to his age, he'd be the first to drop in a pinch. But he is the one who knows how to pace himself. He also knows the strength of each individual and sets the team pace, knows as each kicks in and takes a break, and comes back on again. I learn a lot watching him. Scorpion is biding his time. He works, but it is because he knows he has to, doesn't like it, and is waiting to stab me in the back. The dogs are not totally smart, nor do they deserve to have free choice. Much of what I am learning I need to digest and figure out what to do about.

Thunder leads us into a hole in the ice, and doesn't seem to care. He gets to rest as I sort the dogs and sled out. He feels no specific obligation to me, or the other dogs. He's smart enough to not actually laugh and find it funny, but thinks I'm stupid, and have not figured him out. Time reveals all. An opportunity will arise when I can ask Thunder if he sees the wisdom in working together as a team and caring.

We are all together twenty-four hours a day, at least within sight of each other. We eat almost the same food at the same time, sleep at the same time, and our lives are totally intertwined. We will know each other, spend more time together, than most families, than most husbands and wives. Many people understand what it is like to have an animal, a pet, a dog, be totally dependent on you for its very survival. How many ever have their lives depend on the dog? Those with Seeing Eye dogs, maybe. Few would put another human being in that position, that we totally depend on them to live. Who would allow this relationship with dogs?

Some traps are out, but I caught a mink that was not prime yet and not worth much, so no point in getting serious about trapping. Prime, in human terms, means good to sell. The animal's fur is different from summer to winter—like pet dogs that shed, like rabbits turn white in winter. More than this though, the skin changes, and winter hair is set stronger in the hide. An unprimed fur shows the hair roots on the back, making the skin look black, because the skin is thin. This skin equals thin leather, not as durable. Each animal primes up at a slightly different time and under different conditions. Water animals prime according to water temperature. Some prime more according to daylight.

On November tenth it rains, which is very discouraging. The lake and creek are slush. Some areas of the creek are opening back up. For a while I have to stay in and do art work. I haul a little firewood with the dogs, but get frustrated by the chainsaw again. I depend more on the handbow saw. We resort to an overland trail I worked on to avoid the water. The trail I cut is too crooked to be of any use. Fixing it is more work than starting over from scratch. This represents at least a week's hard work wasted. I'd had maps out, with lines all over, showing where I want to go. My 100 mile long dream trails that turn into, "Geez, I'll be lucky to cut twenty miles this winter!" Even so, each morning I wake up and greet the new day with enthusiasm.

'Hey—snow—it snowed last night—and got cold!' I take a look too. "Yes indeed! Ha —winter always gets here, that much we can count on in Alaska! Winter is long enough, I guess, but somehow I always look forward to it. A new world opens up, traveling overland, trapping." 'And no bugs!' "Yup—no bugs." It is one of those wonderful days, with snow—soft and new, quiet. Spruce trees bent over, all white, with us stepping out the door. The only spot of color in the world, is us. I spend an hour shoveling snow against the boat hull to help keep it warm. I smile at how cozy it looks, wood smoke drifting skyward. I breath in the crisp cold air. There is a touch of birch wood smoke from the stove. The dogs get up and stretch, shake snow off themselves, wag tails, step forward to greet me. Each gets a kind word, pat, and scratch behind the ears. This is our morning ritual. This also gives me a chance to see if anyone is sick, in good spirit, looking thin, slept ok, or is cold. Now and then there is a cut foot to tend, or I brush ice out of one's fur or whatever.

The dogs and I go out to get some wood, mostly just see how the world is. 'All frozen, as we hoped, and now we can get serious!' Several loads are hauled. I can carry about 500 pounds, maybe a week's worth of wood per load. It is easier to haul eight foot logs, and buck them up at home. The dogs learn the routine and when we get to the wood yard and stop, they all lay down till I am loaded and ready to go. I usually do not have to tie them out. If one gets up and starts to pull I look at them sternly, or growl. Sometimes it is easier to talk to them in their language than mine. Stamping a foot, slowly extending an arm and pointing at them, seems to communicate more than yelling. Or even words. I sometimes say, "What are you doing?!"

The dogs get us out more than ten miles for the first time. We see animal tracks. Most important—marten—the bread and butter of the Alaska trapper. Before I put traps out, I think it might be good to make a trip to Minchumina for mail and see what is going on, rather than set out traps, and then have to pull them all up when I leave. It's been well over two months since I got my mail. I'm expecting a few things I ordered by mail, and information on art sales, some art supplies, and wondering how Sue is. (Hopefully she wrote). I also just want to know the trip is possible. I want to find out while there is still daylight, and the weather is somewhat mild and snow not overly deep. If we can't get to Minchumina, then we are here till when? Boating season next spring? If so, I need to know now, so I can ration some of the supplies! The temperature has gone to minus twenty degrees below zero, which is what is required to freeze up the main river. Later the temperature could go as low as minus seventy below zero. I expect to see minus fifty below zero. The daylight travel hours now are about nine hours. In a month, however, the travel hours will be half that. A loss of seven minutes a day.

The dogs are in good spirits. Kenai has been getting bullheaded lately. He thinks he is the boss and watches with concern, how I load the sled. He does not know where we are going, and as boss, feels he should know. There are times he has wanted to go check traps when I need to go get firewood. He will not go on the trail to get wood without an argument. So all is not perfect, even with my best lead dog. Even so, I feel confident... *'Yes, now that we are accomplished mushers, let us have an adventure. The hundred mile trip will be exciting and new!'* "Well, we may not be 'accomplished' yet, but hey, we will be, and we have to start somewhere!" I'm trying to sound humble, but really, I have no doubt in my mind we are 'Smarter than the average bear.' (To quote Yogi- my childhood cartoon hero). The dogs are watching so I turn to them saying "Hey, Hey, Hey!"—still quoting Yogi. *'We should name one of our dogs Boo Boo!'* "After Yogi's side kick? I don't think so! That's a stupid name." My conscience explains why, *'Microphone in the face reporter interview--we step out into the light—after a winter in the woods looking like Charles Manson—"Ok, Wild Miles, could you tell us the name of your lead dog here?"* "Boo Boo?" As I load the sled…. "Yea, if we have pups I want to run double lead, and name them Distance and Time." "Oh? *Yes, good idea—you mean after our other hero, Einstein? What about double leads named 'Mass' and 'Squared'?"* I pause in the loading to consider that. But get back to the job at hand.

'Put the heavy things in the back—the front has to float.' Our sleeping bag will go in the front, but mail and feed will go in the back. I decide there is no room for a tent. *'How much food do we pack—and for how many days?'* "Oh I'd guess a day there, a day b²back, spend a day in Minchumina maybe two days. I'd think five days' worth is more than enough." This way if it takes two days there and two days back, we are still covered. But dang, five days of food for me and six dogs is a sled load all in itself. Dang! Well, we'll make it work. I don't have much going in. Just a few letters. *'And we need a change of clothes in case we get wet and a way to build a fire and cook…'* I don't reply because of course we do! There's a bow saw to cut wood, and the pistol in case of grizzlies or mad moose, Or maybe to get a rabbit dinner. *'Hares—we don't have rabbits in Alaska—they are hares!'* "Ya, ya, what-ever. But nobody goes hare hunting. No one would know what you were talking about. We all go 'rabbit' hunting!" Hmm do you think the tarp will go over everything? We can make a shelter from

the tarp if we have to, ya know. Since we cannot bring absolutely everything we might possibly need, we have to figure out what is serious, and what is only nice. *'Maybe a small sewing kit. Doesn't weigh much, put it in with the first aid stuff, in case like, we have to fix a dog harness or tear our snow suit.'* Yes this seems a good idea, especially when it looks like at least a couple of the dogs chew their harness.

"Thunder?! If you chew that dish up that's it, you'll be eating off the ground!" He only stops while I talk, goes back to chewing his dish. *'Will we need the dog dishes?'* I'm unsure. But think one would work if I had to, otherwise they will eat off the ground. I can water them one at a time as I make and break camp.

The sun rises on a minus twenty below zero, pink, calm, clear morning. "It's pretty amazing really, if you think about it. That in all recorded history, God has never forgotten to load the sun in the chariot and haul it across the sky on time." I feed the dogs a hot heavy meal with lots of bear fat in it. While they are eating, I check to make sure I have the map with me. I have Stars place marked. They should be my nearest neighbors, fifty miles away. I saw the cabin when boating, but no one was there. Minchumina people told me some of the Starrs live in Nenana, are a Native family, and the old man has a lake named after him in the muddy flats. Anyhow, I might be able to visit, spend a night, depending on how the trip goes.

BELCHING DOGS ARE HOOKED UP. I take off for Minchumina. The sled has about 150 pounds in it. There is a breeze and enough light to see. Some of the ground we cover I have run before; we have a tail wind, so there should be no surprises for a while. After about two hours of running, I notice the dogs pick up pace. I look close to see what the reason is. *Maybe it is a moose or a wolf.* Through the dark I see my own trail. The dogs have gone around an island and came back on themselves to head home. I turn them around and make up the distance. We wasted half an hour of time and energy.

There are open leads in the river to avoid. Usually I can find a slough or way around. Now and then we have to stop and go back around another way. The ice is solid enough where we go, but the strong current keeps the river open in some places in the main channel. I try to stay on the back sloughs that are dried up, where I know the water is shallow with no current. In some places there is glare ice where we go ten to fifteen miles an hour. Other places, the snow has drifted and is soft. The dogs slow down to four miles an hour. I have snowshoes to help break trail, but hope the dogs can do the work. At five p.m. the sun gets low, so I decide to make an early camp while I have enough light to see well. I am not used to staying out in the snow, so want to be sure of the routine. I am warm, comfortable, and the dogs do not seem overly tired. My guess is we are within ten miles of Stars. But if it is two hours away it might be getting dark. If the Star's are not there, or there is a reason I cannot stay there, I will be setting up camp in the pitch dark.

There is a fairly long routine when camping with dogs. Five gallons of water has to be made to boil, from twenty gallons of snow. I have to build a makeshift tripod to hang the cook bucket from, and gather enough fire wood. I have to totally unpack the 150 pounds from the sled to find everything I need, first laying the tarp out so nothing gets lost in the snow. The sled basket is six ft. I think I will just sleep in the sled. I cook fish and rice for the dogs. The sled is pulled by the fire so there is some warmth as I sit on its edge, eating my own rice dinner. The northern lights are not out, but the sky is clear. I can make out the constellations above. By the light of the stars I gather dry grass on the island I'm camped on for the dogs to sleep on. The dogs grumble and are slow to settle down for the night. This is new for them too, though I think some of the older dogs have camped out before. Thunder had been in the team when I had seen Bill Henry out on the Yukon so long ago. He had talked about camping out.

I spend the night in the down sleeping bag my father had given me after I had been rescued. This is a bag I could not have afforded to buy, and is very warm. The thermometer I have with me tells me it is only ten below zero. I have to open the bag to cool off. After staring at the stars in the silent void of my soul, I fall asleep, and sleep well. All is at peace in my world.

In the morning, I get the fire going. I have learned in the past how to lay out fire making things to make it easy in the morning in case my fingers are numb. I have a coffee can with a lid on it full of birch bark, a bottle of waste engine oil, mixed and some saw gas. The saw gas ignites instantly, igniting the oil, which gets the birch bark going. This burning bark is hot, and lasts long enough to get fairly large, damp, or imperfect kindling going. Past experience has shown me, it is not always easy to get just birch bark burning with a match. Snow can fall on the match, or there is frost on the bark, or the bark is too thick or too old or, it is just easier to be 100% certain. Nothing beats gasoline for instant ignition.

The snow in the dog bucket I hoped would still be water, is a block of ice hanging over the cold gray fire ashes. I am able to get a hot fire going while staying in the sleeping bag. When I crawl out of the bag to get dressed, it is next to a roaring fire.

The dogs only get fed one big meal a day, but they get broth in the morning to get them to drink so they do not eat snow. I am not sure about all this, but have been told that it is not good for the working dogs to eat snow, and watering them is an answer. To get them to drink, it is usually necessary to put food in it. I cook pancakes with dry apples for myself. Everything hauled is dry to save weight. We are happy, warm, and take off on our second day as if we had just left the cabin.

I do notice the dogs are somewhat slower, more tired, then they first seemed.

They have a tendency to run on the least amount of snow depth, which would be the last ice to form, and thus the thinnest. Thunder is not too bad at testing, but often the sled is on glare ice, not controllable, so slides sideways in sharp turns. I have no command for telling the dogs not to take the turn so sharp. Nor do I have a good way to convey the concept of going slow and easy. I practice and hope to teach them what 'easy' means, but we are not there yet. A few times the sled swings over open water as the dogs hurriedly skirt the shelf ice. We move very fast, and only the back of the runners swings over the open river so we are not about to go in the water, but even so, it seems spooky to swing over open water. Sometimes I think we should not go here. I have to stop and drag the dogs into the snow. They do not know why they are working so hard in the snow when it is so easy to run three feet over on this shelf ice.

A few times we break through shelf ice in a back slough, with no water under it. There is a big crash and that pucker factor. Apparently the river froze, then the water dropped, leaving a hollow. I had seen this before when trapping the Yukon. It is the sled that falls through, not the dogs, so they are happy because they get a break. Now they will go out of their way to cause this. I have to figure out how to let them know that it is not their problem but mine, yet if something happens to me, it becomes their problem too.

I get tired as the day progresses, so as we go slowly in long easy stretches I daydream. Some issues with the sled dogs remind me of boss/worker problems I have been involved in. Sometimes my mind drifts off in such thoughts as we travel the easy areas. Grouse fly up from the edge of the river, but usually before I can think of shooting them, or there's no good place to stop and tie up the dogs if I see the grouse land in a tree.

As we approach the McKinley River, the river ice is worse. I think this water must be warmer or moving faster. *'Maybe it has some mineral in it of some kind that stops it from freezing as fast!'* At any rate we are getting into overflow and shallow water behind the islands that we had not seen till now.

The Star's cabin is only another mile. I get there, but it looks like no one is home, or at least not up. There is no smoke coming out of the chimney. *'It's late. If they are home it might not be good to wake them up.'* "Yes, and we don't know them, so it is not like we are friends. Someone told us they are Natives, and may not be friendly to whites. We don't want any problems. It is not like we are avoiding them. If they were up, or it were earlier in the day we would stop and introduce ourselves."

So we look up briefly at the inviting cabin, but press on. Right in front of the cabin the river has one of the worse fast water open places we have seen. Right in the bend in the river at the bluff marking the edge of the Minchumina flats and the Muddy River. "But if we can cross this spot and get around the bend, we will be on the slower Muddy, and travel should be much better after that, and safer!" *'What about an overland trail? The Muddy is so twisty it is seventy miles on the creek and only twelve miles in a straight line!'* "Yes but the shortest distance between two points in the wilderness is the known route. It is not faster or easier if we get lost, or there is no trail! If there is no trail there must be a reason!" This makes sense, so we plan to follow the Muddy unless we see a definite overland trail.

The ice just froze in front of Stars. No one has crossed yet. We are the first ones across, even with the Star's living right here. We jump across an open lead and hit two inch ice. I can see bubbles moving under the ice as we cross. The ice cracks, but we are moving fast, so the ice holds us. Around the bend however, the snow has drifted in the lee side of the hill. When the main river had frozen, the water backed up the smaller slower Muddy, and made water on top of the ice which melted the snow, then refroze. So there is frozen slush to travel on. This is rough on the dogs feet.

The overflow on the ice has just frozen the day before. It is hard to judge the thickness or strength of ice with the snow mixed in with it. Here and there we break through the crust, dropping into the few inches of water on top of the old ice. Even though this is only a few inches deep, I sometimes have to run behind the dogs, help push the sled, and in general get splashed with water, which instantly freezes on my clothes and on the sled. This is not an immediate problem in terms of getting me wet, just the weight and being hard on the sled runners. Ice on the sled adds another fifty pounds I bet, and ice on the bottom stops the runners from sliding well.

'Looks like a nice spot to camp, out of any wind that could come up—and dead wood for firewood is handy." Even though we are only a couple of miles from Stars, it was getting late. We should make camp, rest up the dogs, get a good start in the morning. Last night went well enough, so this should just be routine tonight. If the trail is good, like if the ice is like this all the way, we might make Minchumina in a long day tomorrow. Seventy miles is not unheard of for a day's travel. Emit Peters who won the Iditarod dog race traveled 1,000 miles and told me 100 miles a day is common. Camp is made in half the time as last night. I have the dog food done before I am even tired. *'Life is good, huh! Out here under the stars, sled dogs all asleep, a hot meal in our belly.'* The warm sleeping bag in the dog sled looks inviting. With a yawn, we drop off to sleep.

Morning is only a little tricky. I get the fire going while still in my sleeping bag. *'At least, no matter what else we have to deal with, it will be in front of a warm fire!'* I had put felt mitten and boot liners on sticks propped up by the dying fire when I went to sleep. They had not dried. My snowsuit is a little damp as well. It is underneath me as padding in the sled. The snowsuit is frozen before I get it completely on. *'Dang this is a pickle . . . should we get back in the sleeping bag and leave the snow suit by the fire till it dries?'* "Well maybe, but it would take a couple of hours I bet. We do not have wood here to last that long. We have to at least go get more wood, which requires the snowsuit being on." So we have to get the snowsuit on and figure we can stand around the fire between doing chores, hopefully get warm and dried out ok. The biggest problem is the metal zippers on the legs of the snowsuit. They freeze first before the cloth does, and will not zip. One side breaks. *'Hey no problem right? We remembered safety pins in our first aid kit!'* In with the sewing goods are enough safety pins to pin the leg shut.

The dogs get up and look happy and healthy, if a bit stiffer and slower than yesterday. At least all are eager to eat, and all look alert. I give them hot broth and have a hot meal myself. I'm warm and feel good. *'The harness are still frozen!'* I hadn't checked them right off, so I have to wait to thaw and dry harnesses a little before they go on the dogs. *'We need to remember this—to keep the harnesses by the fire along with our boot liners!'* Yes, all the details to keep track of when we are winter camping. I turn to the dogs: "So what do you think of this winter camping stuff Guys?" They wag tails and 'oooooh.' Each gets a pat on the head and a good word. "Ya did good yesterday, Scorpion, no fights. I'm proud of you!" He closes his eyes as I scratch behind his ears. "Kenai, you didn't finish your broth! Dive in—it will be a long day!" I have to point and show him and add "Come on now finish up!" He puts his head into the bottom and licks the last of the soup. "Tulip, are you glad to be back with us after a summer running with wolves?" She wants her belly rubbed so rolls over on her back. I scratch her where it itches. *'No one has to do this with a car each morning before going to work. Our life is so different than our friends and relatives.'* "Yes but this suits us. It is what we choose to be doing. Don't you feel sorry for the rest of the world? People out there this fine morning stuck in a traffic jam, with ulcers, plugged into a rat race they can't get out of?"

I relax a little. "Sure glad to get out of that fast water main river. Kind of scary there for a while. Should go smooth from here on in. Even if it takes another day. The hardest part should be over now." We get an early start at daylight, and are moving right along on the frozen slush we had encountered earlier. As we got further from the main river that had backed up when it froze, we get to the old ice, which has deeper snow on it. At first it is drifts here and there on the ice, then glare spots around the next bend. The drift is hard on the dogs, being chest deep sometimes, so I get off and push.

Tulip starts to wobble and falls down. I'm unsure what is wrong with her. Is she is tired, or being lazy, or what. *'Maybe she's pregnant from the wolves?'* She is not showing but hmmmm. *'She might still be worn out from this summer.'* We put her in the sled since she isn't working. The other dogs are not happy with an extra forty pounds in the sled, and one less dog working, but they take off ok. We move along, and get into the travel rhythm again.

"Tighten up, Whitie!" He's slacking off. The team stops now and then. I see it is just to check out rabbit trails in the snow. I'm unsure how much to get on them about this. *'Maybe they need breaks now and then. If we leave them be they will pace themselves and pick up the slack later on, but if we yell at them it will discourage them, and we will keep going, but much slower.'* Someone who worked with animals, horses, or was from a farm might understand better. I'm used to cars. They do not need a rest, and how fast they go simply depends on the model you bought, but they all 'go.' The dogs stop more often as the day progresses. *This is ridiculous- we will never get there at this rate and the dogs do not understand we only have so much food and so much time.* There are clouds forming. The wind is picking up a little. We are in the flats where wind is not fun to deal with, so I hope this is not a storm, and is a reminder we need to get to where we are going without playing around much!

Now Scorpion stops and calls a sit down strike. He is such a big strong dog that when he stops, all the rest stop.

"Ok Scorpion let's get a move on!" He has had his break, and it is time to get with the program. He doesn't even look at me but lays down as if he's going to call it a day, right here in the middle of the creek. "Scorpion, we tried it the nice way. That's not working, so let's move along to Plan B." I break off a stick from a dead tree. All the dogs just watch. I smack Scorpion alongside the head. He gets up, decides to change his mind, and would like to pull now. "Good choice, Scorpion!"

I walk back to the sled. He lays back down and glowers at me. All the other dogs look at him, then look at me, and decide they will lie down too, if that is what Scorpion is going to do. Kenai is the only one trying to get the dogs motivated. I turn to thump Scorpion again. He gets up and growls, saying, "Yeah? Well, you aren't shit without that stick!" All the other dogs are watching, and that never occurred to them till Scorpion mentions it.

Yeah, come to think of it… I'm the leader of the pack, and my authority is being questioned, my ability to keep and maintain order. "It's one thing to play around, put out some half ass effort in for a day, in return for food and a lodging. As long as it is fun and not hard. Humor me. But this is work and a bit much!" Scorpion says. "Yea! What if we just don't feel like it huh? Who are you anyhow? Pulling you around all day long. I say it's time to call it a day. Play time is over! What are you going to do about it!!" Well of course if we simply stop here and stay, we will eventually all die.

I slowly set the stick down in the snow. Scorpion growls, bristles, and says, "All right! Let's get it on then!" *He thinks I'm nothing without the stick.* I walk up toward Scorpion, as all the rest form a circle around us, or as best they can while still in harness hooked to the sled. I let Scorpion out of his harness, and he lunges for me, going for my throat. He weighs almost as much as I do, and is almost as big. He is capable of knocking me down. But as he comes forward, I step back. While he is in midair I reach out and grab his throat.

In the strength born of fear, anger and survival instinct, my fingers lock in a death grip he cannot break. Scorpion tries to get loose, tries to bite me in the face. I grab his nose in my teeth and am able to control his head now. My teeth draw blood. My fingers cut off air. Scorpion will not call uncle, or give up. This is a fight to the death over leadership. If I lose, and survive, I will never get the dogs to move. They will play, look for rabbits, and each night expect food, and when the food runs out, angrily demand I feed them. *I have to kill Scorpion, without a stick.* I'm fighting for my life. I taste hot blood in my mouth, smell wet fur and sweat.

Scorpion gets weaker, but I do not let go. He goes limp, and I do not let go. When he is dead, I roar, and lift him as if he were a rag doll, all 100 pounds, and toss him 10 ft. into the snow bank.

"Does anyone else think they are the leader here?" I smack Whitie just to see if he has anything to say about it. "You going to pull now?" I turn to Tulip in the sled. "I think you are giving me some shit, Tulip. You get over here and be part of the team." She comes forward and accepts her harness.

The dogs leap forward. There is no more trouble about what we are going to do. We will do whatever I say. Conscience *'So much for Old Yeller, Rin Tin Tin, Lassie— love, peace and free love… Man at one with God's creatures"* I only sigh in reply.

Rabbit hanging on the boat steering. "Hasenpfeffer for dinner!"

CHAPTER TWELVE

COLLINS TWINS, MONEY, SUPPLIES, BACK TO THE TRAPLINE

The good news is that the dogs mind, and don't fool around while we are supposed to be working. We get along better after the discussion we all had on the meaning of life, and why Scorpion isn't with us anymore. There is some bad news however. *'More discouraging than anything.'* Yes, mostly discouraging. It looks like yet another day is going by. I am not at Lake Minchumina yet. The snow is drifted into the creek bed in the flats where it is more windy. The creek is a low spot, so the snow blows in the depression from the surrounding area. The top of the bank has much less snow, but is so darn brushy we can't bust through it without expending as much energy as we do in the deep snow. About the time I want to give up and cut overland, we come to a clear spot on the ice, and I can get back on the sled, and make good time following the creek.

I daydream as we travel a slow four miles an hour, with nothing louder than the hiss of runners in the snow, and dogs breathing hard, hour after long hour. *'Have you noticed all the game around?'* "Indeed I have! I bet we have seen 100 spruce hens!" *'Maybe we should have got one of those eight we saw sitting on one branch of birch.'* "Maybe, but we already got a rabbit for dinner and I don't want to stop much." The dogs had jumped a rabbit along the bank. As it jumped, all the dogs tried to grab it. Each dog looked at the other asking, "Did you get it? No? Who did? I still smell it, someone has it!" I reply to the dogs as I hold it up for them to see while they trot along, heads turning to see… "I got it guys!" Whitie had grabbed and wounded it, and I reached down and plucked it up as we went by.

'What's that up ahead the dogs see?' "Looks like a fox!" The dogs go faster trying to catch up to it. *'I think the fox is playing with us!'* I wait before I comment, but it does

look like the fox can go faster, and seems to slow down, lets us catch up a little, then never leaves the creek to get out of our way. The dogs are going nuts thinking they can catch this fox, and we are going through the deep snow at fifteen miles an hour. The fox finally gets tired of playing with us and leaves the creek. Not long after this a muskrat is seen on top of the ice. The dogs see it, but I think they cannot get it while pulling the sled. I stop the team and let Kenai loose. "Go get it, Kenai!" He runs it down and catches it. *'Yeah big deal, he tore it all to hell, we can't eat it now!'* "Well, whatever. At least he got it, and it can get cooked in the dog pot to flavor up the fish.

There are tracks of all kinds overlapping each other up and down the river. There are mink, marten, wolf, wolverine, moose, lynx, rabbit, and about everything else that can be found around here. *'It sure feels good to know there is lots of game around huh! Makes me feel rich and happy, to know this part of the world is healthy and thriving. It makes being cold and tired worth it somehow.'* "Yes, for sure the world would be a sad place without tracks and evidence of lots of animals and good health."

"Should we camp here? It is dark. We have been traveling for fifteen hours with hardly a pee break. Minchumina is ten more miles. No use getting there in the dark trying to find a place to stay and dealing with the dogs in the dark in someone's yard." I am unsure what the procedure is when visiting with a dog team. I do not know if about everyone has some sort of dog food cooker, or if there are trees or a tie out of some kind at everyone's house. I'd rather see, or ask in the daylight when I am not tired.

The rope lashings on the sled got splashed by overflow water, now the ropes are too frozen to untie. This seems like a small detail, but understand what a pickle I am in if I cannot easily get at my gear under the tarp. Even my matches are under the tarp. The temperature might be colder now, as I notice my fingers cannot be exposed long enough to mess with the frozen rope. I'd have trouble even holding a knife in the mitts to cut the rope. *'Next time make an easy knot or use bungee cords and keep matches and fire things in the pocket, not the sled'* I learn that the fire is important, as once the hands are warm and belongings thawed out, all good things can follow from that. The pliers on my Leatherman tool in my pocket gets the frozen rope untied. *'Ta da! Another commercial for the Leatherman tool that saves the day once again!'* No comment.

The sled tarp gets hung up on some high drift wood logs to act as a backdrop for the campfire heat. This also reflects light so I can see better. Once again, as the dogs get fed, I set out the morning fire needs. We all fall asleep warm and full. The snowsuit zipper is frozen again, but by standing near the fire I get it thawed enough to open, and get my snow suit off. The safety pins on the other side are easy enough. *'Don't forget to hang the harnesses near the fire!'* Yes, I have to look out for the dogs. Spruce branches get cut from nearby trees and set down for each dog to sleep on so they do not have to lay in the snow. They are used to sleeping in the snow, but it takes more BTU's from them to melt snow under them, and I assume they appreciate more warmth. It is hard to tell, because often as not the dogs dig up the bedding, and happily go to sleep in the exposed snow. I yawn, staring up at the stars, and fall asleep, not waking up till morning's pre-dawn pink sky.

We are warm, alert, ready to go at it another day. A few hours after taking off we come to the lake. *'There are sorta kinda two versions to that'* "You mean the unedited version, that we didn't put in the diary?" Yeah, well, um. *'We got on glare ice and the dogs didn't know where to go.'* The village is eight miles across the lake. The dogs hear other dogs barking off to the left. That would be the Collins twin's dogs. The twins live across the lake from the village, and we had no need to go there, but on the glare ice I cannot control the dogs. Slip sliding sideways and yelling, "Whoa! Damn it Whoa!" we make our grand entry into the twins yard.

They very politely want to know who I am. "A knight in armor here to rescue you from your distressed life? Perchance Don Quixote?"

I had to say, "Ummm," and sigh "I guess I'm here to visit, because my dogs are here to see your dogs" Long, lame pause.

Reply, "I see." from either Miki or Julie (no one can tell them apart, not even the parents.) I am politely invited in to warm up. I look cold and tired. They may have felt sorry for me. *'I hate that.'* Maybe not, because they gave me a lecture about how my dogs look. I'm puzzled.

"Miles, they are thin, way too thin. They look like hell, Miles. We know how it is out in the wilderness, but some will not understand, and you can be arrested for keeping dogs in this shape." Talk about a pin in the balloon, and looking stupid and ignorant. I'm not going to get a date with either one of these bush cadets, I can see that!

"Miles? How can you travel with the dogs hooked up like this?" I'd never seen how people hooked up sled dogs, and just figured it out on my own. *I figured it out all by myself, aren't I smart! And Brave! Do you notice my high Jesus factor Dear twins?* I walk over to the sled with one of the twins. "Miles, you hooked the tug line to the first stanchions! Our dogs would rip the sled apart if we tied up like that!"

What am I supposed to say? How am I supposed to know what everyone does? The right way is to loop the rope to all the stanchions, or tie to the back ones, not the front ones, and keep it tied low. I do not have any logical reason that would give insight into this new scientific method I discovered on my own. I have to say, *'Well I guess I have a lot to learn yet huh? This is my first dog trip. I've had exactly ten days experience alone running sled dogs.'* The twins never heard me, as that was my conscience speaking only to me in the background. I'm sure it showed. The twins could guess that, but it is also true, some people have run dogs for years and show no more evidence of common sense than I do. *'Yes, well, that is all fine and well—but there goes a grand entry into the village looking good.'* My diary told it different.

> **Diary:** We were off, and got to the lake soon enough. The mouth of the lake was still open water. No one had tried to get here from the lake yet. Once again I am the first one out. I have to hand lead the dogs from ice patch to ice patch, crossing and recrossing the river at the mouth. This part of the Muddy seems shallow and slow—not like the Kantishna River. We have eight miles to go across the lake to the community. The dogs do not know where to go out in the open. I am forever telling the dogs "Right!" Then "left!" "No too much-- !" They tend to go at almost right angles when I give a command.

I finally give up and let the dogs go someplace—anyplace. We travel twenty miles to get eight miles across the lake, very frustrating and time consuming. I stop at Old Man Kenny's, who seems impressed with my mushing abilities.

Kenny tells me that from his place to Stars,' on the Muddy by the route I took is seventy miles. I covered that in about a day, well maybe a day and a half. *'You just told Kenny a day!'* "Yeah well rounded off to the nearest day…" The long trip made the dogs and I closer. We arrive someplace, so the dogs know the meaning of the trip. The dogs are not my pets, nor my slaves, nor merely my transportation. We are a pack, a team, equals almost, with me being the leader, not only out of necessity, but having been voted in, sort of. A forty mile an hour wind rips across the lake and flats as Kenny and I visit into the night.

"Miles, what's your plan? If ya wanna go someplace I can watch these dogs. I used ta have sled dogs back in the 40s. I was the mail carrier for a w—wa—while." Kenny coughs an old man cough, bent over, white hair, eyes that don't see much anymore, shuffling feet in old man slippers, as he goes on, "I'd enjoy the memories, looking after dogs for a while again."

"I don't know, Kenny. I appreciate the offer, but I'm anxious to trap. I think I'll just get my mail and turn around and go back, but need to make some phone calls first."

"Only phone is around the lake at Holmes's place and it doesn't always work. You can get food there too, but only maybe."

"Thanks, Kenny! I'll go see them. What do you like to eat? I'll grab some extra food." I figure if I buy the food maybe Kenny will fix us both a good meal.

"Hello, Maul? How's everyone in Manley? How's the family! We got a bad connection, can't hear you well."

"Good to hear from you, Miles! Everyone in Manley has been wondering where you went, how far you got, and how you are! We thought you might be dead!" I tell Maul how my dog trip was, but am mindful of the long distance call and the bad connection. Maul interrupts. "Hey, Miles, before we get disconnected, I got your food co-op order here. We divided it up and I have split peas and flour and some other stuff here. What you want me to do with it!? I can fly it to Minchumina or to your camp." I'd wondered about the food order. I had thought it would be in by the time I left Manley, but I couldn't hang around. While I'm thinking of who might buy the order from me and keep it there in Manley, Maul comes up with this, 'flying it to me' plan. "I can get it out in about three days. I'm booked till then and this weather is supposed to break soon."

Maul is right, no use trying to travel in this storm. May as well hole up, and maybe get some things done here. Maul has a free dog for me to replace Scorpion. He can also bring commercial dog food. This straight fish with only a little bit added is not the right thing for the working dogs. *Just ask the Collins twins!* Most everyone mixes it with commercial feed. What the heck the old timers did before the days of commercial factory food, God only knows! (So much for the old ways!) Maul needs to go to Fairbanks, so can bring me there and back in the same deal. Usually a trip to Fairbanks from here on the regular mail plane is pretty spendy. If I get a trip in to town as part of the freight haul charter, I should maybe not turn that down. Maul kind of 'owes me,' in my mind anyhow, as I feel he was responsible with that loose string deal for my snow machine engine failure when he borrowed my machine and tied the carb on with string and didn't tell me. This would be a good pay back. I can use that replacement sled dog as well.

Kenny is only too happy to watch the dogs. He looks forward to it. He gives me a list of a few things he would like in the big city. I could pay him for watching the dogs by shopping for him. He gave me some money to get his goods. While I wait the three days for Maul, I have time to go visit Ray, and fill in Val on how Hansen Lake is these days. In the evening I write, while Kenny naps after being wore out talking. He's rocking in his chair snoring by the wood stove. Propane lights flicker over the hand hewn wooden table I sit at. I'm sitting on a five gallon bucket for a chair.

Later I ask Kenny in puzzlement, about how trappers in his day took care of sled dogs without civilization goods. Kenny summed it up like this. "There isn't a big history of sled dogs in Alaska before white man came. Before white man, dogs in villages often ran loose all summer, fending for themselves off scraps they scrounged, like guts left on the beach after cleaning fish. In fall, they were rounded up to work by whoever needed them. They were never wormed, given shots, vitamins or had any care. The ones that were alive and healthy got worked, the rest died. It created a strong bloodline of sled dogs over a period of time." He goes on about the actual trapping. "Trappers didn't go great distances in a day. Traplines were short. There was lots of fur, and good prices, so no need to travel much. Prices were higher in the 20s than now. If a fox was worth $100 that is the equivalent of $1,000 today. Some people could make a year's wages on their own property. Ten miles of trapline made a living often times. Running sled dogs ten miles is different than 100 miles." I nod my head, that this makes sense. "Also dogs could be fed moose, caribou, all sorts of wild game that was often plentiful, and if game was not, then sled dogs died. No great value was put on a village dog, except maybe a single leader who might get taken care of."

I hear that sled dogs were not a big form of transportation with the white man when he first arrived in the north. Horses were used more. There were regular routes kept open by all travelers, so there was almost daily traffic to keep the trails open, so easy to go on for trappers. Trappers used these regular routes between trapline and village to get mail and supplies. Once at their cabins, traplines were short, and line cabins were set up every ten miles or so to stay at. It was not so hard to keep the dogs in ok shape. They were not overworked. Even the Iditarod was based on a serum run to Nome—which was a relay. No one team went 1,000 miles. This can only be done today because of high tech stuff. It takes $30,000 a year to keep an Iditarod sled dog team and race. Winners have a vet, a handler to help, space age plastic runners, aluminum frames, special harness and balanced special high cost diets. The story is not really about one man alone in the wilds with only his sled dogs. Racers get a lot of help and back up. The run itself may be alone, but a year was spent getting ready. Taking off on 100 mile trips through the unknown with no broke trail was not done. We tend to forget all that when nostalgia for the good old days is brought up.

Dearest Maggie

How you been? I miss you. Me? Oh I been busy. (smile) Yes—you know me—up to all kinds of things… Ya, Maul is going to fly me to town. I know, 'town' and here I want to be alone in the wilderness. (?) But, well, a few things are going on. I need dog food. I have a co-op order in I need picked up. There is a storm raging and my dogs I'm told are not in good shape, so it would be good to feed them good and let them rest. That should help for the trip back—to have the dogs well rested. Also, it is early to trap. The swamps are not frozen good yet and there is not much snow in the flats. And Sue? I should see her maybe? How can I ever meet women if I'm never around? Like that you mean?

Thinking of Maul again. I taught his kids art in Manley. Good kids. Nice family. Some people, well even most, say how he never finishes a project and leaves junk all over, piles of lumber he never gets back to—and always preaching to people about the Lord. It's annoying. But, no one is perfect. I think his heart is good. He means well and does good things. He's a man of action that speaks as much as his words do. He flies food to the villages and barely charges gas money to make sure people can eat good. I heard once he landed and the villagers threw his oranges back at him and called him names. He had to leave in a hurry. They wanted to know where the booze was. But he never seems angry or bitter, but instead is cheerful and full of energy. He thinks the end of the world is at hand and it is time to get prepared for ending times like tomorrow.

I have to smile—but I agree to a point. How can the world last as it is going? It might take a year or ten, or 100, but society can't keep crapping in it's own nest and not run out of room someday. We appear to be lemmings headed for the cliff in some mad rush to our destiny. I don't like to dwell on it—but it doesn't hurt to be self-sufficient and have that get away place off in the wilderness. Maul's family had me over for Thanksgiving once and served tofu turkey. They must be vegetarians. That's spooky. One wonders what they really think of trapping and hunting. One wonders what they keep to themselves and talk about after people like me leave. I am perhaps some sinner they hope to bring to the feet of the Lord—so that I may be in a state of grace as they are. They just try so hard, are so very dedicated to what they do. I admire that. But of course there is much I could never tell them. When it is time to pray, I keep my mouth shut, bow my head, close my eyes.

So, my Dear Maggie, who can I really be honest with and write my feelings to besides you? I love Nora and Bill who came to visit me, but they believe the eagles, wolves, and bears are sacred totem animals who can do no wrong and are held in reverence, as all God's creatures should be (except man.) What do you suppose they'd say if I told em I strangled my buddy Scorpion? My guess is they'd disown me. I'd be lucky if they didn't turn me in to some agency and have me arrested.

Who wants the truth Maggie? Everyone wants the dream—a good story. The good times. I can be funny! We can all have a good laugh! Who, Maggie, takes me seriously? Who, Maggie, besides you, would listen? You'd think somewhere would be a friend, relative—I could talk to and be honest with. Oh, well? Life goes on, huh? Yes, I know, I see it too, I tend to get depressed right after a rush—an adventure. Been there before, be there again. So, no, I am not that all excited about town, and sure I'll visit and have a good time, but it's 90% a sham. Well the % of sham depends on my mood that day, huh? Ha!

I go on as usual for my typical 100-200 pages…
Letter ends
I toss the letter in the wood stove as usual. Once again I wish the postmaster in Manley had given me my mail so I would still be in touch with Maggie.

Maul brings gas, dog food, and my food co-op order. Part of the food is left with the dogs and Kenny. We drop most off at Hansen Lake on the way to Fairbanks.

Maul loves to fly, or maybe he flies to love, but it's infectious, that enthusiasm and energy I admire in him.

"Yes, Miles, I put a 185 engine in this 180 frame. I never have to worry about overloading. If it fits in, I can haul it!" He specializes in loads and trips no one else will do. He hauls five gallon cans of unsealed gas. Propane, odd sizes and shapes, like full sheets of plywood, and sled dog teams. He flies at -50° to -60° in weather that grounds commercial planes. He has a high Jesus factor. Never had an accident. He knows his plane and talks nonstop about it. It is wonderful to see someone so in love with what they do.

I ask him: "Got your cabin done and sold and moved into another one yet, as planned?"

"Not quite. There is a place around McGrath we are looking at. People successfully growing potatoes there and it interests us. We have a job offer, with a chance to serve the Lord there. We are blessed with the opportunity to work with some young kids and start a farm. I'm not sure if I'll have time to get the Manley place done, but will probably come back on my own to finish it up and sell it while the family is setting up the farm."

"Well, Maul, sounds like an adventure and opportunity God put into your hands. It would be exciting to be able to grow potatoes in this climate and make it pay. The chance to offer local potatoes at a lower price would be a big help to people, sounds like!" Maul nods. "Won't you miss your friends when you leave?"

"A little, Miles, but remember our time on earth is short, and the most important thing is to serve God."

"Yes, God made us all for a reason and has a purpose for us all. Hey—how is everyone in Manley! fill me in!"

Maul hesitates and goes on. "Most people are saying you left a mess behind, and want you to come back and clean it up. I don't know what that's all about." Maul is embarrassed. Doesn't want to get involved. Hasn't got any facts. I know what happened. Joe had taken what he wanted, and instead of cleaning the rest up as agreed upon, he left it and blamed me.

I begin to explain to Maul, but sound defensive and complaining. Maul doesn't say anything after my outburst, but maybe his mind is not even here on earth, but contemplating eternity in heaven where all is forgiven. We are both lost in our own thoughts. "So! The very same people who send me off with a birthday party are the same ones badmouthing me now." Maul might not be saying much, as folks say the same things about him! "Leaves a mess everywhere he goes."

In Fairbanks Sue picks me up at the airport. I tell Maul: "I'll give a call when I need to get back. Hope you get the things done on your list!" I turn to Sue and give her a big hug. "Thanks for picking me up, it sure is nice to have someone greet me!"

Sue takes me to her place. "I have not found a boyfriend all fall and it is winter now!" Filling me in on the news. I assume from this that I am not her boyfriend. "You're not here, Miles. What good is a boyfriend who is not around, geez, Miles, smarten up!" Yes I need to be smarter. She had picked me up in a broke down air cooled VW bug. I had suggested way back in summer it might not be the car for Alaska winters. Now would be a good time to think about the right kind of transportation before the real cold hits and she's stranded. I'd help her get something suitable. "No, Miles, I like my bug! I'm going to keep it. I don't want anything else!"

I recall how she had told me she had been into sky diving. Had made a bad jump, landed wrong and was told not to jump, but had defiantly made another jump and permanently injured herself. Being stubborn and defiant is all right, but it requires having a high Jesus factor, or so I think. Naturally I am not about to expound on my rabbit cycle theory of civilization. But I think Sue is one of the lemming going off the cliff. I can't save her. Indeed she doesn't want to be saved. Saved from what? She feels it is me who needs saving…

"Huh?"

"Miles, you are always off daydreaming! Pay attention! Geez, I wonder how you survive sometimes!"

I sheepishly ask if I can use the phone for long distance. "I don't like phones much, and can deal with local calls sometimes, but long distance is a problem for me. Can you make sure I get the numbers right and get the call done ok?" One of my girlfriends so long ago understood, and never said anything, just dialed for me and when the party was on, handed me the phone. It wasn't something I wanted to talk about. Something from my childhood.

"Good grief, Miles, just make the call. I'll be in the other room!"

I want to call my father just to see how he is and let him know I'm ok. I have the instructions written out on how to make the call. I carefully dial '1' first then the area code, then the local number, but the call will not go through direct. I must go through the operator to get outside the state. This requires I give the operator the number. "Hello, this is Bob, how may I help you?"

I'm flustered. No one but the operator is supposed to answer, and it is always a woman and she always says, "This is the operator speaking—what number are you calling"

I reply, "Sorry I must have dialed the wrong number, I wanted the operator."

"This is the operator. We have a new policy and are trying to be more friendly. How may I help you?"

I hang up. I have to think about this. The phone didn't say what it was supposed to, so now I don't trust it.

Sue asks, "So how's your father Miles?"

"Oh, great, ya he's great! Guess I'll call Nora and Bill and let them know I'm in town…" I have no idea how dad is. I can write him. I call Nora and Bill who are ecstatic to hear from me and invite me over for dinner. I call my buddy, Will. His sister answers the phone and sets up a time tomorrow to see Will. I call the fur buyer just to chat—get a feel for winter prices. *'Always pays to be friends with the guy you sell to.'*

"Hey, Sue! Let's go have pizza, I'm buying!" This is one of the big thrills for me coming to town, got to go have a pizza with everything on it!

Sue rolls her eyes up. "Miles, you are such a fool and idiot. This Mountain Man thing, so independent, can't even use the phone, what a joke you are!"

That's still on her mind. My conscience, *'She seems to forget I did not come to her looking for anything. I only wanted to give her an ice-cream cone. I did not want to know her name, share private lives, expect anything at all beyond a thank you. If she picked someone she feels is a stupid fool, what does this say about Sue?'*

"Well, Miles. Are you going to answer me?"

"You made a statement. You didn't ask a question. Give me the question."

"The question, Miles, is what I'm supposed to do with you?"

"Sue, I never asked you to do anything with me. You do not need to do anything either for or with me." But of course we both know this is not true, as she wants to get pregnant, and this is not going to happen unless she can keep a guy long enough. But certainly, I do not see someone here who would love me, or who I would enjoy spending lots of time with. But I do not say much, no need to, may as well get along while I'm here, but certainly I need to gracefully disappear in the big picture.

We go to the Howling Dog, which is the next thing on the list after pizza worth doing. Sue can't keep up dancing, so I have to grab up a stranger and she can't keep up, so I grab another stranger. Sue is ready again after a rest, so we dance more till she's tired again. We both fall into our chairs, both laughing. "Damn I love to dance!" I repeat the words to my favorite song to her, "I know it's only rock and roll, but I like it!"

Someone in the room hollers "Boogie Time! Wow!" Everyone hollers and gets up to dance. I drag Sue back up, even though I can't see straight from all the sweat in my eyes. I dance till I drop, as usual. Sue doesn't understand, but is in a good mood. What can I say? Some people are born this way. It isn't something you learn or understand. This is something that simply 'is.' I laugh a reply, "Sue, in the old days the mountain men, cowboys, miners, would come in off the creeks for a night on the town to whoop it up and dance and jump up and down. It was a grand and special time. A break from the normal routine of hard, dangerous work."

"Miles, you are such a dreamer. You belong in another time 100 years ago!"

A record is turned on as the band takes a break. "Knights in white satin/ never reaching the end/Letters are written/ never meaning to send/ beauty had always been/ with these eyes before/ Just what the truth is/ I can't say anymore…"

"Miles! What are you thinking? You seem awfully quiet and distant all of a sudden!"

"Nothing, Sue, got something in my eye, must be the smoke or something."

"Should we leave, Miles?" Sue does not know I would almost sell my soul for love. But how does one get from 'here,' where I am now, to 'there,'—that state of grace called being loved, understood, accepted? The "Letters are written, never meaning to send" part is the letters to my stove.

The Underhills need to go grocery shopping, so I go with them to get groceries. I go to see Crafty at his new shop, and stop at Alaska House, where I find out I am owed more money from items sold. I have more than enough money for my trip to town and groceries. Maul had wanted Christmas gifts from me for his family and friends, so we had traded my art for his flying. He sells food in the villages. Sue and I get all the fixings I need to print my Christmas cards this year.

"Ya, Sue, every year I print my own cards with a linoleum block I cut. Last year was a swan against the mountains. The year before was a woodpecker on a tree. I did an owl another year. I send out maybe 100 cards every year, something I enjoy." She wishes she knew how, and was as ambitious as I am. But there really is not time to show her how, so I change the subject. "Alaska House said one of my consignment pieces got stolen. Real bummer, huh? One of my most expensive pieces too. The mammoth tooth I found. I put an eagle story on it in my sawed metals. It had a $2,000 price on it."

"Wow, Miles, that is awful!"

"Yes—and I'm told insurance doesn't cover that, so I hate to ask them to pay the full value! That's a lot of money. So I told them I'd split the loss with them." I put some money in the bank. The bank is making automatic deposits for me to my land escrow account. *That Quartz lake land I got off Steamer, while the houseboat was being built. Will I ever see that part of Alaska again?*

"I wish I had extra money to invest like that. I can barely come up with rent money!"

She lives from hand to mouth. Well, so do I, or at least it looks like it, to where there is no use saying I think I don't. I'm reminded many people see me as no different from any other poor welfare type. My thinking I'm different is justification and rationalization, not facing the truth. The Alaska permanent dividend check is in the mail, adding another grand to my winter funds. I probably have three grand I didn't have before I got to town.

After the wind dies, the temperature drops to forty below. Maul is not answering the phone. I call Skip, my other pilot friend, but he is out of town. Dave is just learning how to fly with skis, so doesn't want to take passengers yet. I finally get hold of Maul. "Hey Maul, is the cold weather keeping you grounded?"

"No, Miles, this is weather I thrive on. No one else will fly, so I get all the work. I just never shut the plane off so it doesn't get cold!" Maul has no bottom cold cut off, below which he will not fly. "I can be there in an hour. I have another trip for later in the evening, or you can wait three days." He's been flying around the clock, catching naps in the plane.

So I decide to leave in an hour. Sue is upset by that. She had planned some romantic dinner together. She sees where my priorities are, how much I miss my dogs, the trapline. She can't get the car started. When it does run, the windows will not defrost, so she drives freezing ass cold trying to look out windows she can't see through. We travel in silence. Sue has just told me I had given her crabs.

"From that dirty environment you live in, Miles!"

My conscience replies silently in my head, *'You know what the joke is? Crabs come from her dirty environment, not mine. There are no crabs in the wilderness. That means she's been sleeping with someone else.'* Not that I mind. It's just that it's an indicator we are not meant for each other, and she has not been up front and honest with me.

We stop at the post office so I can mail my Christmas cards and letters. I had remembered to send a nice card to the nun in Galena whose wild roses I had thoughtlessly trampled.

Maul greets me. "Miles! I have this load of things I couldn't sell on my last stop. I have to get rid of it to make room for you and your load." I look over what he has left; an empty new trash can, some bread and some dog food.

"I'll take the whole load if you give me a deal on it and we drop it all off at Hansen before we go to Minchumina." We take off at 11:00 am on December fourteenth. I am glad to see at Hansen Lake, that the last load we dropped off has been untouched by animals. There is more snow now, and wonder how the dogs will do in deeper snow on the return trip.

In Minchumina, Kenny greets me, and has had no problem with the sled dogs. The dogs are very glad to see me and look like they have more weight on. I've been gone a week.

"Miles, mail day is tomorrow, plane should be in between one and two!" I'm so anxious to get home I don't feel like waiting for mail. I'm not expecting anything.

* * *

DAWN BREAKS COLD, crisp, clear, and minus twenty. This is warmer than it has been, so I am happy. I take off in the predawn, about the time God is yawning, and just getting the sun loaded in the chariot to haul across the sky. While I am crossing the lake, the sun creeps up from the surface of the ice. If I listen hard, I can make out the sounds of the chariot wheels, the whip and snort of the horses. Denali is outlined in red. *'Most people only get to see this on a postcard or Nova special!'* "Yes this is not just a picture, and not even a movie, this is real life!" There are other sensations besides vision; there is the feel of the cold, smell of the spruce and dogs, and sounds of dog feet on ice.

I stop briefly at the Collins twin's and give them some fresh food from town in thanks for hauling me gas this past summer. We talk about dogs a little. I ask, "So how do you get them to mind you?"

In a quiet feminine voice Miki says, "I pull their head down in the snow and stand on it, or I bite their ear."

"Oh! I see. Hmmm. Very interesting." They have some good advice all right, but I can see already I do not want it to be for me as it is for them. They have all 100 pound and up freight dogs, that travel at four miles an hour top speed. "But we can pull anything!" I think, *Probably, but if I can't go any faster than that, I may as well walk.*

I want to get a good days run in, so keep my visit short. Leonard, who had the yard fire, told me he has a trap cabin on the Muddy I can stop at. I need to keep an eye out for Seven Mile Hill, to know where his turn off is. He has a trail if I can find it, that will save me distance on the winding Muddy River. I want to be sure to have daylight when I get to this area. I don't expect a fast trip home. I know I wore the dogs out on the trip in, so will spend more time going home, and let them rest more. I'm guessing four to five days.

Leonard's trail is found. We get to the seven mile spot. This trail is through willows and has twists turns, bumps, and bad spots. I'm fooled by the few good stretches till I am up against walls of diamond willow again. The day is turning to dark, so decide it is better to stop for the night thea to get lost. The routine is gone through, that I started to learn on the trip in. I tie up the dogs, get the harnesses by a fire and get the sled empty for me to sleep in. Snow is being melted while I sort things and work. Melted snow will make the water for the dogs and myself for our dinner. The routine does not take as long now.

I have trouble sleeping when the wind comes up. "Must be warming though, usually what a wind means this time of year." The sled is comfortable, as I stare at the stars for a while. A comet flashes as I nod off.

In the morning after a fitful night, I note that there are no serious things I forgot to take care of. The dog harnesses are drying, we all got fed, dogs are ready to go, sled is loaded, balanced, and it's just another day on the trail ahead of us. The wind had moved snow around and created new drifts. These new drifts are soft. The dogs have a problem busting through. I have to put snowshoes on and snowshoe in front of them.

Snowshoeing in front of the dogs is not as simple a matter as it looked in the movies. The sled dogs are used to me being behind, so try to pass me. If I forced them behind me, the leader wants to walk on my snowshoes. Whitie and Thunder are tied in a double lead, then I tried a single lead, then single lead with Kenai. I cannot get too mad at them as they are in chest deep snow working really hard.

When we get to Leonard's cabin, it looks inviting. He had said I might find trapped animal carcasses out back.

"Cook them up Miles, be good for the dogs, and we need to get rid of them by spring thaw!" The carcasses will just get thrown out if I do not use them, since he uses a snow machine. The dogs can use the boost of fresh meat, and it buys us time to wait out this storm. Weather is very nasty, with the wind and deep snow. This does mean however, we have only covered about twenty miles in two days. One beaver carcass, four marten, two muskrat, and a half eaten fox, are added to the cook pot, guts and all.

'Trapline Chatter. We heard of this!' Leonard's radio is on. There is an evening spot devoted to getting messages out to wilderness people. I recognize some of the names messages are going out to. In general I am not interested in news or city music or even a message. *'If we want that, we can go live in town!'* I reply to my conscience "Yes, when in the woods we do not want to be reminded of town, it just doesn't seem very relevant. The sound of the wind and water and wolves howling is our music." *'And what do we care that the Arabs are messing with oil prices. It's just depressing stuff we can't do anything about and does not affect us as much as most people.'*

The next day the wind is laying low. We may as well take off and have an advantage of the wrath and end of the storm for now. The cabin is on the Muddy River where the wind has not reached, so there is less snow drift. More frozen overflow ice makes for good travel conditions. Our trail into Minchumina is no longer visible though. I have to jump off the sled in a few places where there is a single drift to get through, but we are making good time now. I get to Star's trapline cabin in early afternoon at the mouth of the Muddy. Old man Star is just coming in on snowshoes. He's in his 80s. Al Star is his name.

"Thought you were with the park service! I saw your tracks when you came through last time! The river had just froze that night and we had not even crossed yet. You are either very brave, and will live a long time, or very foolish and will not last long. I have not decided which." Al's son Paul comes in and is introduced.

"This is the person who crossed the river? Why is he still alive?" He says to his dad not addressing or acknowledging me. They are Athabascan Indians. I'm white, the minority race here, and a greenhorn. My status is lower than that of my sled dogs. The old man seems to have accepted me, so Paul acknowledges me with, "What do you think of the President's Park?"

I know he refers to the extension of Denali Park by President Carter recently. The new boundary includes some of this area and traplines, and subsistence people in this area. It's pretty much not good news to locals, as they wonder who will ever come here, since there is no way in. The only answer I can give is, "It's a bunch of crap!" Which was the right answer. So now I'm invited to sit down. We spend the evening taking about various subjects trappers talk about; the price of furs, land issues, and the new Native Land Claims Act. The Star's planned to claim this cabin and trapline as their 160 acres, but the park expansion might stop that. They might get run out. Al was born here and the lake here is named after him. They blame the white man, but I'm ok, not all white people want to turn Alaska into a park. "Al, who traps down by Hansen?"

"Someone is across the river, but never crosses to the Hansen side. I think more the Bearpaw country." Bearpaw River is across and downstream from me. "They come in from Nenana." I look puzzled as it seems like Manley would be closer. "The old mail trail," he adds for explanation. That would be what is called the Iditarod trail maybe, and used to be the route for the mail when it was hauled by sled dogs not so long ago, maybe the mid 60s. Al remembers those days well. "I remember before airplanes and even before white man was here, first the Russians arrived." Many Russian names still linger, creeks and lakes and such.

I yawn. "Do you have any carcasses I might cook up for the dogs? Maybe marten?" I get a scowl and find out it is 'uclanny' to feed marten meat to dogs. I am able to cook rice and fish on the wood stove and am asked to spend the night. In the morning the temperature has dropped to minus thirty. The weather report is for the weather to get colder yet by tomorrow. I feel good about the weather though, as it is calm, and snow in good condition for travel. I get an early start on the river.

"Miles, the snow rarely drifts around the hill ahead, so you should have good travel conditions!"

Around the hill from the Star's, the snow is drifted. I hope this is temporary and around the next bend will be wind swept, but the snow was just deep everywhere. The sled dogs have a hard time. Snowshoeing in front of the dogs goes easier this time compared to the trip in. Open water on the river concerns me. *'How can there be water at minus thirty?'* I never would have believed it if someone had told me. I have to see it for myself. I have no explanation. I did understand falling in would be death. The dogs want to go near the open water because the snow is not as deep on the very edge where water has just froze, maybe the width of the sled and two inches thick. It seems impossible to explain to the dogs why we need to go in the deep snow and stay off this ice road that is so easy to run on. If they fell in, just before they died, as their eyes were big and round, I could say, "That's why." But short of this, there seems to be no way to explain. I'm too tired, and it wastes energy to stop and drag the dogs into the deep snow every three minutes. Hopefully one of the dogs will fall through, get wet and survive. Hopefully all the rest will have comprehension why thier fearless leader wishes to avoid the water. Hopefully it will not be me going through, or all of us. The sled runners often come within inches of open water, but the sled seems controllable, much like a car running within inches of the guard rail now and then, not a big deal unless you think about it.

Tulip falls through. The other dogs scramble to pull her out. She lives about ten seconds. Time enough to make one gasping sucking sound of death the other dogs understand. As predicted, they now wish to avoid the open water. Within a few minutes her tongue is frozen solid, and I cut a frozen harness off her, and unceremoniously leave her along the ice. In an hour she'll be frozen solid. The living must press on. There is no time or room for the dead.

We get to some better ice once we pass Roosevelt Creek. There is an island in the river with good firewood for a camp fire. *'This is one of the best places we have seen to camp in a while, let's stop here for the night.'* I agree with my conscience, so we stop; I want to get a fire going. I have trouble holding the matches, and realize I'm numb with cold. If I can't hold the matches well enough to light a fire, this could be a serious problem, so I concentrate on accomplishing this task. First I jump up and down to get my blood going, then slap my hands against my sides. Can I feel fingers long enough to get the fire going and start the snow melt process while I set up camp? The temperature seems to be dropping as I notice nothing will dry by the fire. This fact messes with my routine. I now have to stop everything else to work on how to dry things.

Everything seems to take twice as long to accomplish when it is cold. *"Developing a routine that works is also important, don't forget that!"* No, I'm not about to forget that. *"So what's the routine for drying dog harnesses when a fire won't work?"* The biggest issue on my mind is, how am I going to put frozen harnesses on the dogs in the morning? I might try sleeping with them, but know the harnesses might stay thawed out, but never dry. I might put them in the hot water I start before adding the feed, and they'd be thawed, but would freeze again before I got them on the dogs. In the past I learned that struggling to keep items close enough to the fire to dry, meant getting one side burned and the other side staying frozen. At bed time, I realize I can't get my snow suit zippers undone as they are frozen shut. My fingers are too numb to mess around a lot, so decide I will get in my big sleeping bag with everything on and the dog harnesses and keep everything thawed and if lucky maybe even dry out.

In the middle of the night I wake up cold. There's no way to know what time it is, and I could get a fire going, but I have kindling only for a morning fire. It is too dark to hunt around for more kindling, even though I have plenty of logs handy. If I sleep, and the fire goes out, it would be hard to get another one going. I hope I will simply fall back asleep…*'It's the dampness from all the wet stuff we brought in the sleeping bag with us. We are using our own body heat to dry this stuff.'* I had already consciously figured that out.

In the first morning pink light, I lean out of the dog sled I'm sleeping in and get the new fire going. My bunny boots are frozen, so I pour hot water in them to thaw and warm them. I had learned that in past years. Bunny boots are warm wet or dry. Putting cold feet in warm boots gets the day started right. The dog harnesses kept in the sleeping bag are taken out one at a time and put on each dog. *'Let the dog's BTU's keep the harnesses thawed now.'* This is fine. I just have to make sure the dogs get lots of fuel. I have to keep moving to stay warm, and think the damp snowsuit is not helping me. The moisture migrates out to the surface and becomes frost. I start feeling warm enough to where I think I am going to survive. For a while I wondered if I would.

I hook the two slow wheel dogs up front, They cannot keep up with me snow-shoeing so they do not step on the back of the snowshoes and trip me. The rest of the dogs bunch up behind the leaders. Snowshoeing keeps me warm. A rope goes to the lead dog's collar. The other end is held behind me so I don't have to turn around to see if they are following behind, or getting too close. As they get tired I can pull on the rope to encourage them not to get separated from me. As the cold day progresses, pulling the dogs along gets more frequent to the point I was doing a lot of the pulling. I'm as tired as the sled dogs, but saw few workable options for us. There is little use in stopping to rest if I cannot dry things, or sleep well. As we eat up our traveling food, the load gets lighter, but we do not want to run out! My conscience reviews the choices: *'We could leave some of the load behind and come back for it sometime, maybe even by boat in spring. We could travel faster if we were lighter.'* "Yes, but I look at the load and everything is critical and needed. I can see maybe ten pounds that can come off, but this is not going to make enough difference in our weight." *'The dogs are holding us up, and most of this load has to do with them. We could snowshoe home and wait for the dogs to catch up, or not, they can decide if they want to go home or not.'* "Well, that seems like an act of desperation. We are not that bad off yet."

Really the only thing we can do is what we are doing, press on and hang tough. When I get to the base of Bearpaw Mountain, I know I am within ten miles of home. "I'm not sure the dogs can go ten more miles, and it will be dark soon. We'd be committed once it got dark. It might be better to stop for one more night." If I can't sleep I'm not sure how my strength will be in the morning. *'Here's a river cut bank overhang. It's hollow underneath. We read in a Mountain Man book about making a shelter out of a situation like this. Drape a tarp over the front and have a fire for heat and focus the heat, contain it like a cave.'*

While I'm stopped looking at this possible make shift shelter, pondering if the tarp will fit, how to tie it, if the wind might blow into it and such, the dogs have decided we are stopped for the night, and to them it's a done deal. The team is all curled up, ready to go to sleep. I once again envy the sled dogs that making camp is so easy for them—drop and go to sleep. It will be hours before I will be ready. I know I cannot expect to get the dogs going again now, so we are making camp. I am not used to my transportation telling me what we are doing.

Eventually I get the sled tarp rigged as a door, with a fire going, dog food cooked, and camp ready for a night. Once again I cannot work the zipper of the snowsuit, due to the frost on the zipper and my cold fingers. The heat starts to build up in the shelter I constructed, however, so I can manage the zipper. The view from a distance as I get more driftwood brings a smile. The orange glow of a fire shines through canvas. The irregular shape of the canvas against the black mud, and dark toothed scrub spruce looks like the entrance to a magical cave in a child's book of hobbits. I'm too tired to dwell on that fleeting thought as I drag wood to my lair. The dogs are all asleep and do not wake up as I drag the wood past them. I'm warm, comfortable, and well fed now, only needing some sleep to call it the end of a great day, except for missing Tulip.

Several hours after falling asleep I become aware of mud dripping in my face. The frozen mud cave I chose for a shelter is thawing. The sleeping bag is pulled over my face. The mud can fall all around me without bothering me. I'm too tired to think of what the sleeping bag will look like in the morning. *'Muddy cloth ball, just like I told you.'* "Uh huh, yes, but the sleeping bag can be cleaned. We slept well, and will be home by tonight." Dying fire embers are rekindled to a blaze, bunny boots are warmed, and bucket of snow set on the logs for dog water. My own meal of rice and dry vegetables is started. All is done from the sleeping bag so I can drift off to sleep again for half an hour while all the chores take care of themselves. *'Oops! Check harnesses first!'* Harnesses are turned on the stick. I have them hanging to make sure they are dry by the time dogs get hooked up.

The dogs get up when I get out of the sleeping bag. They all have the runs. *'From the beaver meat and beaver guts. They are not used to straight meat.'* I had been told this is something to watch out for. It should not hurt them much, but my Iditarod Athabascan friend, Emit, had told me, when racing long distance, changing feed and having the dogs get the runs weakens them, and is to be avoided. But at the same time we do what we have to do. As I give each dog a gallon of broth I say, "Just ten more miles, guys!" In a happy cheerful voice. I see the dogs respond to being talked to. They all smile and wag tails and 'oooooh' back. Each dog gets a personal greeting, pat on the head, scratch behind the ear, *'Civilized people do not have to do this with their transportation.'*

This reminds me of primitive times long ago, and it pleases me. Something that worked for 10,000 years, while modern mankind thought he could improve on this. Maybe yes, maybe no, but surely 10,000 years of doing something did not just 'poof,' disappear from our make-up. This feels familiar, the way life ought to be, was meant to be. Not everyone feels it though, just some.

In a good mood and feeling stronger, we charge off into the dusky dusk of dawn's early light. God is still hooking his chariot up, preparing to haul the sun across the sky. My feet are still a trifle too warm from the boiling water I had poured into the bunny boots, but at minus fifty, I am glad enough to be too warm. I do know, if I start the day off feeling cold, it is hard to ever get warm again at these temperatures!

Diary: Dec 21st 1979

The hell with this adventure stuff. The snow got deep again. For a while there I was not sure if I would really make it.

I'm snowshoeing in deep snow again. Each mile seems forever. Even when I think I am only three miles away, that last bit seems forever. One foot forward, then the other, counting each step. The three islands. The last three islands. The dogs swing in behind the last of the three islands, and onto the creek. The cabin seems forever. "Let's stay at the cabin. Fish are stored as well as people food we left. Go the last two miles to the houseboat tomorrow." Yes that last two miles to the boat would take hours maybe. The cabin will be fine.

Diary

Dec 22 - Good to be back home. Warms to minus forty. Took seven days to get here. Do chores.

Dec 23 - Caught marten by fish rack. Nose and hands blistered from the cold.

Dec 24 - Another marten. Cut wood

Dec 25 - A warm zero

Dec 26 - Bring goods from cabin to houseboat, minus ten

Dec 27 - Read all day mostly. Marten paid for all the traps I bought!

Dec 28 - Snowshoe a few miles exploring country to trap.

Dec 29 - Two marten

Diary for the year ends

Trapping is going well, and should pay for a lot of my supplies. This is especially exciting, since making a living trapping, being a real trapper, Mountain Man, outdoor person, is my goal in life.

Dearest Maggie

... I lost two dogs on one trip in to check mail. Geez, it is not like I thought it would be. I suspect however, this is not entirely my incompetence. Maybe we get what we pay for and 'free sled dogs' should be held in suspect. There is a reason they are free. People do not generally give away good dogs. (or good anything!)

Scorpion and Tulip may have been shooters from the get go. Sometimes I think people do not want to admit they have a shooter or do not want to face the responsibility, so pass it on to someone else, or think maybe someone else can do something with the dog. Kenai was one good example. I think he would be no good for anyone else, and he simply bonded to me.

Enough about dogs! Yes everything else is going fine. Getting lots of furs and making a profit. It's about fifty cents an hour for my time, but what else is there to do for a living out here? Maybe my art, but I need to work physically and be active outdoors! **Sunshine, Miles**

I go on for a while writing.
Letter ends and is tossed in the stove.

Building a trap cabin in the winter. Most of my early sled dog pictures got ruined when my houseboat sinks in the future.

CHAPTER THIRTEEN

MAJOR ART STARTED, CUT TRAPLINE, SPRING ARRIVES, BOAT TO HOT SPRINGS WITH SLED DOGS, FAIRBANKS, SELL FURS, MY BIG ART SHOW ON TV

'There are three suns out, come look!' My conscience has alerted me, while I am fixing breakfast. I reply "yeah right. Who ever heard of three suns in the sky—dream on. You are hallucinating. God would never forget how many suns to put in the chariot!" 'Yeah? And only a nutcase thinks God hooks up horses each morning and loads the sun on it and hauls it across the sky! So there!' "Ok, well I know the difference between reality and a fantasy. We can't prove anything spiritual, so it simply suits me to imagine God with a face and body and horses and a chariot. It's only symbolic anyhow. That is different than asking me to take seriously, three suns in the sky! Anyhow the Romans were true believers who lasted longer than our civilization will last! "

Yet there are indeed three suns in the sky this fine morning. 'Didn't we read about 'sun dogs' someplace once?' Yes, this must be it. I cannot tell one sun from another. Ice crystals in the air must be refracting light. There is sort of a rainbow around each one. So amazing that even if science can explain it, it's still a miracle! This is just another day however, and I have started a major piece of art. An eight foot piece of whale baleen is polished, and will be the background for my metal story. This one is the story of the new Iditarod race. Two teams will be racing down the Yukon River. There are twenty-eight dogs planned. Lots of details will be included. One team has broken camp fast, and debris is left behind in the snow. There are sticks of firewood, footprints, empty cans, and a flock of white ptarmigan flying up. There are thousands of little intricate pieces of puzzles of metal to cut out and fit. This is perfect when having time on my hands. I feel glad to have this to work on when it is too cold to do much outdoors. No, I do not need to design this art project, nor draw it all out first. I simply start at one end, and work across the baleen. I have it all in my head. It's too complicated to ever draw.

When the weather warms to minus twenty, I eagerly head out on the trapline and cut new trail with an ax, day after day, after day. An overland route to Minchumina is the plan, that I can trap on the way to the lake. This trail I cut is way north of where anyone else says they are going. One day I cut myself with the ax. I just tear the hem of my shirt, and tie it around the wound, and keep on going. The cut is into the bone. February fourteenth, Valentine Day, I record that I am ten miles out on the new trail and think of building a line cabin. This will be a shelter to stay in so I do not have to come all the way home. I can outfit it with emergency supplies, skin furs here, and hole up during storms. In very bad weather ten miles is as far as I might go in a day. On a good trail of course, it might only be an hour away! It's nice too, in case I have an emergency, or am wet, or have a broken sled, injured dog, etc.

At one point I think I am averaging two to three miles of cutting a day. This does not last though, as the weather is warming and I am now dodging open water and bad spots in the swamps. The trail is cut as far as Star's now.

Diary: Get to Star's in less than a day with twenty-three marten for the fur buyer. I stop at Leonard's 'washtub' cabin, named because he keeps a nice copper washtub hanging on the logs. I'm in Minchumina the next day.
Diary ends.

I am not interested in going in to Fairbanks this trip, too much to do. Don, the fur dealer, quotes me good prices for furs. I have more than enough to buy a new outboard. "Don, if I send these furs in, can you buy me an outboard motor. I'll pay extra, and you send it to Lake Minchumina?"

"Miles, usually I do not like to get involved in trappers and their supplies. I have not seen the furs so do not know for sure the exact amount I can pay. But guess I can do that, to save you a trip in." The Collins twins said they'd fly the outboard out to Hansen Lake when it arrives in Minchumina. I get my mail and head home. I'm home in two easy days with nothing to record. The dogs are in better shape, trail is better, weather warmer, and it all sure makes a big difference.

Spring arrives before I know it, time to think about garden seeds, fish nets, and a change of season. *'Still too early yet! It is only March; we have at least a month to go yet, probably more!'* I know, but the warmth and melting snow speaks of a new era.

While out finishing up trapping on the lake, I fall through the ice. Luckily I always carry a long pole under my arm. Up to my arm pits, and the pole stops me from falling further, I would not be taking the chance, but assumed the water was not over my head, since it was shallow when it froze. Yet the water is deeper than it had been in the fall here. This is a surprise. *A current under the ice must eat away some of the mud. Dang. So much to learn yet! Does it ever stop?*

As usual, as it is every year in the wilds for me, there are more ducks and geese then I know what to do with. Every day there are new ones landing, and every couple of days I get fresh meat. There is only a couple of weeks of dry fish left for the sled dogs, so I am more and more anxious for the ice to go out, nets to go in the water. I will not feed my dogs geese or moose except for guts and parts I do not eat. *'In the old days, sled dogs got fed everything I'd think.'* Probably so, but in this more modern day and age, there is just not enough geese and moose to feed to dogs. The law, as well, says not to do this, but the bigger concern to me is what it does to the environment. For the sake of feeding the dogs, I think a lot about open water. No, there seem to be no fish under the ice in the lake, too shallow. Fish must be some-place. Unsure where. John in Galena, had showed me how to fish under the ice in the main river in the middle of winter. I was not impressed with the procedure though. Possibly there would be fish in the main river, but am unsure how to find them. It is a lot of work to drill fifty holes to try and find out. The river is not close by anyhow, as I am a ways up the creek and across the lake. We'll manage as it is.

My main twenty-five horse engine has been acting up. I thought I would either fix it over the long winter and during break up, or the new replacement would be here to use to get to Minchumina. All my outboard needs, I think now, is a new water pump. I have fixed everything else, but without cooling water I cannot use it. This part is only three dollars, but here where I am now might as well be $3,000!

The new boat engine from Don has not arrived. There is a wonder on what is going on with this. It is getting too late to land with a ski plane to deliver it. All I have is the four horse, so plans have to be changed. Instead of an upstream trip to Minchumina with power, I think I will have to go downstream, only steering with the four horse all the way to Manley. This alters my entire summer plans. Break up in spring is a critical time. If I do not catch the early spring fish run, and I do not get the garden planted, the summer becomes different. Now dog food has to be bought, and more food, so more money, more work. Floating to Manley will take up to two weeks. No use worrying about it.

The four horse has problems. A new head gasket is made from cardboard and jewelry copper. This works fine, but occupies two days of time. The ice on the lake did not wash out when the river rose and fell. It is a few more days before I can get to the river through the lake's floating ice pans. While working on the engine, the rewind rope got caught in my life jacket vest. When I let go of the cord it almost pulled me over the back into the river. The life jacket seems to be in the way when trying to work or maneuver in the boat, especially in emergencies. I stop wearing the life vest, just keeping it handy nearby. The rewind rope had pulled the gold nugget I wore around my neck, and tossed it in the river. This was that nice nugget I had found on the Yukon years earlier.

Diary

    May thirteenth - I put all the dogs in the small boat with enough feed for two weeks, and with my mail and other supplies. I head downstream for Manley Hot Springs.

    May sixteenth - Get to Baker Creek, but Baker Creek Carol is not staying there. She must have moved in with her boyfriend, Two Rivers. I stay in the cabin and rest up the dogs.

    Diary ends.

The next day I am in Manley. I run into a local hunting guide. "Miles, are you interested in being a guide? I need an assistant guide! You seem to know your way around in the woods." This is an interesting proposal. It might fit in with my life-style and allow me to make money in the environment I love. Several thoughts against it though. One is that I prefer not to work for anyone else. Next, I am not keen on trophy hunting. I accept it without comment, but do not kill anything myself just to show it off, and what others do is up to them, but I would prefer not to be part of it. Also I am unsure of this guy. I had heard good things, but then, not so good things around Manley. He might be hard to work for.

"Thanks for the offer! That's nice you'd think I'd be qualified. I've got some other things going on for the summer though." Just one more job opportunity I closed the door on. The guide has his own plane and major guide business in the interior of Alaska.

Van, who gave me Kenai, says he will look after my dogs while I go to Fairbanks for a while. He will trade for some of my jewelry work. Since he has sled dogs himself, he has plenty of feed around. I fly to Fairbanks and call Sue. We go out for the usual pizza that is my traditional 'welcome to town.'

"Don, what's going on with my fur and engine. I had to float to Manley and use up a week's time."

"I wasn't sure what to do Miles. Soon after you called the price of fur dropped. Instead of being worth two grand, the furs were only $1,200 and the new engine is $1,500. Then there was shipping and such."

I felt bad, as I thought he would know I was good for the money, and really needed the motor! It is of course easiest to blame someone else for my problems though. *It could not possibly be my fault!* The fur price dropping just at a bad time for me after convincing me to send all my fur, sounds a little like a line run on ignorant trappers. Hopefully, Don would not do this to me. Well maybe I had not handled the furs perfect, so not worth as much as quoted. There is a need to deal with how it is anyhow, not dwell on what got done and not done. I accept the cash Don hands me.

"Thanks, always nice to get cash in the hand with no receipt!" (we both grin) 😊 :)

This is the main point after all, wads of cash. If it is a grand, or two grand, that is only a minor detail. Either way, I'll make do. If I have to sell some more art, what is the big deal really. Money will come to those who work, one way or the other. I buy a ten horse motor. Smaller than what I had hoped for, but good enough to go upstream in the smaller boat. Travel with the houseboat will have to wait a while. *Perhaps I can fix the engine in it.*

"Hey, Karen, Charley, good to see you, any of my art sell at Alaska House?"

"Yes, Miles, we expected you any time now, and have been advertising a show soon. Any day you want we can do that!" I get paid enough from what sold while I was gone, to take care of my time in town. Alaska House plans on a show 'tomorrow.' "Miles, why not do a spot on the radio for the show. We have a spot open to advertise." They apparently pay some discount amount for so many hours of air time per year.

While doing the add, the radio guy is interested, asking, "Can we record a few bear stories to air later, on one of our shows?" I tell a couple of bear stories on the spot.

The TV studio is upstairs. They hear me and are interested. "Miles, you have a good media presence. You can speak the allotted time to the second, you have a clear voice, tell a good story and we think will have a good TV audience."

I go upstairs. Without preamble go live on TV. I'm on The Town Crier, where we talk about changes around town, and the life for those coming in from the bush. As I leave the studio building, a car of girls comes around the corner and I hear screams: "There he is!" Ooo, Ahhh, Eee. It would have been nicer however, if they stopped. *'So we could discuss the various aspects of a life all alone in the vast wilderness. Like coming in for pizza. While eating pizza one might speculate on—well all sorts of topics.'*

Sue and I saw a new movie called "All That Jazz" that the folks at Alaska House had raved about, so I give the line at my Alaska House show.

"It's show time!" with a wink as I adjust my 'costume.' We all laugh. Give the folks a show. There is a story for every art piece.

"That marmot on the moose antler? Once I saw a marmot and did not know what it was. It was asleep on the banks of the mighty Yukon—sound asleep in the sun, with daisies all around blowing in the wind..." *'I don't remember the daises—I think you made that part up.'* The lady gets all starry eyed and buys it for twice what it's worth.

"Next!"

"No the moose didn't suffer. Yes, I got the antler from a moose I ate as part of my recycling beliefs." *'Did the cow have a good life that went into your burger? Is the question relevant to your life?'* "Did the lynx claw come off a dead lynx you found in the woods?" "Did you carefully select shoes not made by overseas slave labor? Do you know it first hand for a fact? Did the wood in your house get carefully selected from already dead trees? You seem quite concerned with the morals of my life, have you examined yours?" Yes, indeed, Ma'am, I found the dead lynx in the forest and salvaged its claws!" You looked! But wait, it was, in fact, in a trap found dead in the forest! We just leave out the 'naturally dead' part.

"It is not common to find anything dead in the woods. Usually dead things get eaten by creatures very fast. The claws I get come from lynx I trap, or other subsistence trappers. The fur buyer prefers the claws be removed because the sharp claws cut the fur in the tanning process. There is usually no market for the claws. Since the animal is already dead for the fur, I do not want to be wasteful, and am creating a market for this byproduct. "Oh yes I remember this lynx now. I had run the sled dogs to the ten mile cabin, and the northern lights were out. This one got skinned at the remote camp 100 miles from civilization, while I was waiting for the salmon to cook for the sled dogs…bla bla bla."

"Don't you get lonely out there?" I consider this an impolite rude question but do not let it show. How would you like to be asked, "Aren't you lonely? How is your relationship with your bimbo?" Do I have any more reason than the average person to be lonely? Why should you think I do? I politely reply for the hundredth time, "No. I am lonelier in town then in the woods. In town I get to see what I am missing. In the woods it is out of sight and out of mind. I enjoy the life and keep busy, productive, and find my life fulfilling, rewarding, and challenging. In town I am only another grain of sand on a vast beach, no one and nothing. In the woods I have myself, God, nature, and my dreams." This memorized answer seems to satisfy customers. "Next!" *In truth, in town there is a desire for me to feel guilty, low, stupid, crazy. Society puts that energy out, through how I am treated. It is desired I be nothing, no one, garbage, with no rights. Worth a story all right, but marry your daughter? Work at your side as an equal? Be your boss on a job? Sit next to you on the bus? No. My place is eyes to the ground, go to the back of the bus, bow and say "yes, Masta!" Much as a black musician is welcome in the night club, many may want an autograph. Compliment the jazz. But ask such a musician what his rights are? 'really?'*

"I thought it was illegal to sell white walrus ivory" "Next!" We never heard that question. Nor should I reply beyond, "Then I suggest you don't buy it." Because all the laws, loopholes, exceptions, exemptions, under fifty various conditions, would lose the sale, take a day to review, and experience has shown, not convince anyone they have misunderstood the laws. Yet I sigh because it would be nice to enlighten folks. I try. The gist of which is:

It's legal, but a gray area not worth discussing in a short answer. The book of laws and court cases is mind boggling, involving the definition of 'Subsistence,' 'Native,' art, traditional use, discrimination, income, place of residence, intent, exact date to the day of when harvested, by who, for what purpose, and could possibly take a week in court to decide. There are state laws, Federal laws, and international laws, many are in conflict. Far beyond what a tourist will digest. As we speak there are international meetings taking place resulting in a Cites Treaty (Convention on International Trade in Endangered Species…), with more specific rules, and a list of endangered animals, with various layers of restrictions and exceptions. The subject is still in flux, and being discussed. For now, Alaska is not paying attention. The Feds are a long ways away. I'm hearing about the issues from native friends, other artists, and the galleries. Charley is a state senator. Another person of interest is a Lt. Governor I meet, that helped write, and signed, the Alaska constitution. Others are or have been on, the board of Game, helping to set the laws. I'm not 100% confident on my beliefs. I'm not confident that even the government is following its own laws.

As usual, I sell everything I made over the winter in this one day show. There is still pipeline money around. The Alaska economy is sound. Karen reminds me again, "Miles, everyone just loves your wilderness stories! You really need to work on a book! It is everyday things to you, but to the rest of the world, it is fascinating!" There had been that success with the first article I wrote for Alaska Magazine; 'Survive' that had paid well, so this is at least on my mind.

"Yes, one day when I slow down. I'm keeping good notes!" I do seem to reach a lot of people with my stories. I hear back from people who remember! I have had a profound effect on them. I do not know why, but do not dwell on it. I make my money, and have other things on my mind then why. *'More interested in living my life than talking about it!'*

"Sue, do you want to go to Manley Hot Springs? I'll pay for the gas."

She had told me earlier or hinted, it might be nice to go there and see the dogs and such. She still has her VW bug, and it still does not run well. "The fuel pump is acting up. I think that is it. I do not have the money for a new one."

The pump is easy to find, and easy to take off, and easy to take apart and see the basics of its internal workings. Even if I have never worked on one before, I am confident I can look at the parts, see what they need to be doing, and if there is anything obviously wrong or broke. "It is as I thought, it just needs a new diaphragm, this is wore out on the edges. I think I can get it to seal with some kind of gas resistant silicone,"

"That is all well and good, Miles—your opinion! But it is my car! If it fails I'm the one in trouble! Did you even read the glue instructions?"

Christ, there will be no place in the instructions saying it is good for car fuel pumps. I realize this instructions word is a button for me, guaranteed to illicit a string of profanities. I try hard to not let it show. "Well, if it does not work, you are no worse off than you were before. You need a new fuel pump or diaphragm."

"Miles, it might ruin my car!"

But I convince her to trust me. I fix it for free, and it works fine now. There is no 'thank you' for that, though. She is still convinced somehow it cannot possibly work. *Because Miles fixed it and I'm incompetent? Because a man fixed it?* I sigh once again because we do not seem to be getting anyplace with our relationship. She acts like she just wants to get out of this alive, and never wanted me to fix the pump, but allowed it because to decline might start an argument, and better to ruin a car then get in a fight. Sue is good for a ride to Manley with my supplies. That's about all I feel about her now.

THE NEW TEN horse boat engine is checked out, and seems to work well on the sixteen foot boat. I am sure it will go upstream at least. The four horse can be kept as the spare. It's now May twenty-seventh. Van tells me I am on the cover of 'Homespun North' with a two page story about me on the inside. I vaguely recall doing an interview, and having my picture taken. I saved the article from the News Miner with my show ad, and big picture spread out there to the public. There is concern on my part of all the publicity. It's hype and glitter without total substance. I'll participate if it is in front of me, but how much do I want to seek it out? I'm a ham all right, and sure the attention is great, but in the big picture 'how it really is' matters the most, not what people think.

One aspect of that is not being totally satisfied with my art. There is a glue stability problem. It's a new glue on the market related to the new crazy glue. What I use is an industrial grade that works pretty darn good, yet sometimes is unpredictable and unstable. For reasons I have not figured out yet, it can let go unexpectedly after a few months. It's not cool to tell someone what is presented is quality art and then have it fail in a few months. I do not have a handle on the percent of failure. So far it appears to be maybe 5%, maybe within acceptable limits. Still I am not pleased.

A letter from the manufacturer explains some issues and how to resolve this. "Keep track of the expiration date, and keep it cool." Sometimes I buy a brand that does not even have a date, with no way to know if it has been temperature controlled or not. A company has been found in Fairbanks that sells this product as a direct distributor with a date and out of a refrigerator for commercial use. "This might solve that problem. Surely there is an answer!" Still, it seems forever! It is all an on-going experiment. *I'm selling experiments, but that is the difference between 'art' and 'science'!* There is a reluctance to speak of such matters, share my thoughts with anyone, except maybe my Dearest Maggie, through letters she will never see. Obviously Sue already thinks I am a buffoon and idiot. No use giving her the rope to hang me.

Likewise I am accomplishing things in the woods I am pleased about, but in terms of the public, I am not as successful as told by the press (told to the press by me of course). The public is not very forgiving. One false move or mistake and the pack is ready to tear an individual apart. I am not under the delusion the public loves me. The public loves what they feel I stand for. Life in town is about staying sober and alert, entering a room and keeping track of the way out, sitting with my back to the wall in a corner. God help any of us who trips and falls. You will die where you lay. The masses will step on you in the mad rush to wherever it is everyone is headed. Off the cliff with the lemming no doubt. It's all pretty sobering, all in all. It does no harm to play the clown, and jester as a survival technique.

"Hey, Miles, your socks don't match!"

"Yeah, huh, and I have another pair just like this pair in the drawer!"

One step at a time in the very long road of life. *'Hey! I think we are crashing after the big heady high of our town visit. What do you think?'* After a pause without comment, my conscience goes on, *'Yeah, we been there before, we'll be there again. You know what? It's ok if we are the jester and the clown. You know why? Because what you and I have done kills most people dead. I wouldn't give someone like Sue more than two days in our life, and it would be freak out time, dead in a week. So we have a few battle scars. But let's walk with our head up. Be proud.'* I smile. My conscience is so full of bull. A chip off the ole block.

Various things kept me in Manley Hot Springs for a while. The glue issue, getting things ordered in the mail I need. My buddy, Will, drives out to Manley on June nineteenth.

"Hey, Will, good to see you. You bring all this rain with you?"

"Ya, good to see you too! Sure is some weather, huh? I see the river is high with lots of drift!"

"Yup, one reason I have not left yet. Fast current, only ten horses and a 1,500 pound load. Hey, check the dogs out!" Will has not seen them since last year. He remembers most of their names, but sees some new ones, and some that are not here. I tell him all the sled dog adventures. He seems envious, but at the same time he has rewards in his life I do not, so 'whatever.' Sure be nice to have a relationship with a father like Will has for example. What's that worth?

"Miles, whatever happened to that woman you talked about last year?" I sheep-ishly think of Sue, and don't want to talk about it, but play dumb.

"You mean Sue?"

"I think her name was Theresa something or other."

"Oh, her, yeah we were writing and it looked good for a while. She was about to come to Alaska, and at the last minute decided to buy a nice car instead. But then the car had a flat and she could not afford another tire. Weird. Tire was wire rimed magnesium something or other worth more than my years income. Anyhow I figured after that she was not serious. Yeah, a year ago. A year is a long time when it comes to love, Will." We both laugh. He has not had much luck in life with love either.

"But, Miles, you sure seem to meet a lot of them!" It is time to part because Will has to get back to town. "Watch your top knot, Miles, and keep below the horizon!"

I give the usual Mountain Man reply, "Yup and you watch which way your stick floats!"

Diary June Twentieth

Head for home. The poor ten horse is pushing 1,500 pounds. They sure don't make horses like they used to. **Diary ends**

Sixteen-hour days are put in facing into the wind and rain, slamming the waves and the clock. When I get to the Toklat River I pull over. "Anyone got to pee?" All the dogs wag tails. We all dive to the woods and find a tree of our choice to pee on. I proudly say. "Hey guys—I can pee the highest check it out!" But Kenai proves he can pee the furthest. I scream "Hey! What are you doing? Who's top dog around here anyhow? You can't do that!" He quits peeing the furthest. "That's better. Don't be dissing me. Dang, guys! How'd we all get in this boat anyhow?" It's a struggle to pack all in the boat with the load.

We never see anyone on the river. The surprise would be if we did. Once we leave civilization, we leave some strange planet and arrive at 'earth,' the planet we live on that no one else does.

Future Flash

It is late summer of 2006. I have been boating past this area of the river off and on, between the Kantishna mouth and Manley Hot Springs. My job is wilderness land survey work, a job I acquire along my path in life. There is a camp near the mouth of the Zits River and I recall various fish camps here. Over the years locals set up a tent and fish for sled dogs for a few weeks. There is a curiosity who this is, and interest in stopping to chat, as is polite in this part of the world. The fellow camped here has a dog or two, a canoe, tent, and fish rack, the usual look of someone 'from around here.'

I wave and plan to pull in, but the fellow hides and acts odd—will not wave back. The message I get is this guy does not want to be visited, so I go on by. This happens three times in a week.

In Manley Hot Springs I mentioned this at the Roadhouse. "Hey, who is at the mouth of the Zits anyhow? Sure is acting odd whoever it is!"

Someone answers, "Actually the community is thinking of calling in a report. Several people have been threatened—it is Glen, from up the Zits, you know him— homesteaded there in the early 80s, I think. Anyhow he's been making trouble, and it's about time someone did something before someone gets hurt."

I was glad I had not stopped in. Word is spread to stay away from there. A week or so later I am in Nenana at home and see the newspaper. A policeman was in a struggle with Glen. Glen was killed. The paper said something about this Glen guy threatening a boater who wished to go up the Zits River. Glen told the boater that this is off limits, his river, his area, and no one can go here. It was the boater who called in the troopers, feeling he has a right to go up this big river to go fishing.

Glen's brother later wrote an editorial saying, "My brother, Glen, only wanted a piece of Alaska for himself, the Alaska dream, what's wrong with that?" This gave me pause. I realize this might be a common wilderness mind set; to think it's 'all mine,' when you are the only one around for months and years on end. Others become invaders of your planet. Keeping a small piece of the earth for you can work, but not when it is an entire 500-mile river drainage. This does remind me of my early years and the sense I owned the earth (and everyone else lived someplace else).

Future Flash ends

My day dreaming ends. At the end of the day we all sleep and eat in the rain. There is no room for a tent, sleeping bag and camp gear. I lay on the boat seat in the rain and sleep. A blue tarp is pulled over me like a blanket, to keep the rain off. I am fine, waking up well rested. On this day the miles go by slowly. The dogs are used to the routine and sleep soundly. Some are dreaming with twitching feet and ears. One young one is sort of awake, and sees something in the water. There is a startled "Woof!" Letting us all know something exciting is in the water! We all need to immediately look. All the other dogs wake up, jump to see over the boat gunnels to get a look. Old Man Thunder is 17, and slow to wake up with creeky joints. He falls off his comfortable spot, and has trouble focusing blurry eyes on the spot in the water everyone is barking wildly at.

The 'spot' on the water is only a stick. Thunder looks disgusted, looks at all the others one by one and snorts, goes and lays back down again. This was so hilarious and human-like I wrote about it later. The most exciting incident of the day. The dogs too, were probably just bored, and needed to create some excitement.

In six days I get home to Hansen Lake. The situation with my supplies left at the lake is drastically different than I left them. A cache had been built to store perishables and keep them away from bears. It was not quite rickety, but to ensure I have no problems, I set a bear snare under the cache to snag any bear insolent enough to eyeball my goods. Across the dog yard from the cache is the creek and my houseboat. The engine is no more use to me. A tripod built over the back of the boat is now in the water. A winch on the tripod was used to hoist the engine straight up. The plan is to move the boat out from under the tripod. Another boat can be put under the engine, and engine lowered in the boat to be brought to town. Will says he is interested in it. A new engine can go on the boat, but do not know yet what to get. Go for the original steam engine plan? Try an outboard hooked on the transom? Try a tunnel hull? Another inboard-outboard? A diesel? Direct drive? Flex shaft? I'm investigating all those options, studied books at the library. The cache is now on the ground! It looks like a bear got in the snare, hooked himself on the cache pole, pulled the cache down, headed for the river, then got tangled in the engine tripod and pulled the tripod and engine into the river.

"Dang!" *'We'd ah been better off just letting the bear help himself to the cache!'* Maybe, but nothing from the cache is missing, damaged, or wet. Everything had been in waterproof containers collected at the Salvation Army. I can do without that no good engine, better than I can supplies of food.

"Hey, the seeds we left to sprout on their own have sprouted!" I take a look, and indeed, the cans have plants growing in them. Some plants from a greenhouse in town are with me and set out in a garden spot. *"Poof, instant garden!"* We both smile, quite pleased with ourselves.

The next day a new net has caught 15 fish overnight. *'We still need to get to Minchumina for our mail order things!'* Yes. I have not got mail in many months. I have ordered more new fish nets, a canoe kit, and various other things.

A week later I am off to Minchumina. Dogs are left behind so I can make a fast trip in and out. The boat does well empty. I get to Minchumina in fourteen hours. The day I arrive, there is a funeral happening. Val is being buried. His coffin is set in a boat, and hauled across the river, so he can be buried on his property. He had been an old time trapper around her—the one who had told me about Hansen Lake. He was the one who knew about the Hansen's and the last word on where the still might be. He had sold the Hansen cabin to a guide named Hal Waugh, the first master guide in the state. But Val had not owned the cabin to have legally sold it. He had merely said 'sure!" and accepted $100 in return for a piece of paper saying he sold it. That piece of paper was used to make it official. Somehow Waugh got legal title, with the ability to keep everyone else out. Originally this was a cabin used by many trappers and travelers as a nice place to camp along the long journey to civilization. Various trappers had used it for a season or two over the many years since it was built in the 20's. The subject and history becomes relevant, as I am inquiring who has rights to it, and how I can contact these people, and ask if I can use it, (or maybe buy it myself). It originally sold for $100. Waughs have not used it in twenty years. A letter has arrived from Julie Waugh, school teacher in Eagle, Alaska.

Hello Miles,

Thanks for your letter informing me of the condition of the Hansen cabin. I am not interested in selling it, as I have hopes my son will have a use for it later in his life. He is a pilot now in Anchorage, but may have an interest in a hunting cabin later on. Since we are not using it and keeping a fire going in it and informing us of what is going on with it is good, we do not mind if you use it as a trap cabin. Have a good trapping season! **Julie Waugh**

So it looks like I can use the cabin at least. Surely I need more room than the houseboat offers. There is at least a possibility in the future this son will have no interest, and be willing to sell. The sale and use of trap cabins and trails is legally interesting. Officially there is no such thing as a legal sale of a trapline or accompanying cabin. I discuss this with Ray at the lake. He is young, and like me, interested in acquiring a trapline. So we go over what we know of the situation.

Officially traplines are considered public land. Trappers have a right to put in trails, use them, but they are public trails anyone can use. They cannot be bought or sold. Unofficially, however, traplines are bought and sold. The trapper puts in a lot of time and work, sometimes a lifetime. Locals recognize this. Trappers have an unwritten code of honor; an unspoken agreement amongst themselves. This can vary with each community, and between each group of trappers. Some claim an area, some claim an actual trail. If what is claimed seems 'reasonable' to locals, it is accepted. No one messes with the trapper. Each trapper has his spot others stay away from. Traplines can be in flux, shift, and border disputes arise. In most cases there is some minor grumbling, but someone backs off, moves over a little, and expands someplace else. Sometimes areas are traded or sold, or favors exchanged— like "I'll turn over my birch creek cabin for beaver trapping, if I can move into Bear Lake for lynx season in your area." Ninety percent of the time there is a peaceful resolution. It works. If a trapline is sold, whatever rights the seller has locally, is transferred. Whatever respect the seller had is passed on to the buyer till he proves his own worth.

Closer to civilization, there are actual rules to follow. You can trap within a mile of someone else. You can't leave you trapline for more than three years without losing it. No cabin within five miles of someone else. In more remote areas the rules are much more loose. Some old timers like Kenny here, have had areas for a zillion years and may not have got out in a decade or more, yet the area is respected anyway. This can represent twenty years of work. Closer to civilization it is more common for the trails to have already existed or cut over the years by more than one land-user. Moose hunters, skiers, clubs of different kinds put in and share trails they all shared in cutting with trappers. "Mostly, Miles, there is just more room to move over here in the wilds. It's why we live here, right?!"

There is, in fact, official recognition between the lines of some laws. Traplines are recognized as being passed on in wills for example, legally binding. Likewise if someone wishes to cross the wilderness with a road or bulldozer, among the permits needed is contacting the trappers in the area and getting permission. It is not legal to mess up a trapline. If an area opens to homesteading, any trapline trail is marked, considered an easement, and cannot be blocked by a parcel boundary. Also traplines with a history can be recorded as a historical trail with legal rights, still a public trail, but recognized as 'untouchable' by timber or oil interests, etc. This can be important, but at the same time having a trapline listed on a public map is to invite all land users to come on down the trapline! All sorts of idiots with a map can show up.

Trapline cabins can be registered with the state for a $100 a year fee. This is more important in an area that gets lots of public use. No one I or Ray knows, has registered with the state. At the same time, it is common knowledge there are hundreds of trapline cabins all over the forest and state. Federal officials must know about it, but it serves no purpose to discuss the legality. Trappers need cabins, trapping provides income, and is useful to society, so the trails and cabins, are simply an understanding of the reality of life in the toolies. Trapping is a good industry in the state. We became a state primarily over trapping interests. An interesting legal position. Ray and I puzzle over it. Now and then of course, some trapper quotes the actual laws. "You have no rights!" And acts accordingly. Now and then such people have been known to disappear. There are good reasons to get along. It is therefore important to understand the unwritten code.

Another letter is opened, also having to do with a cabin and trapping

Hello Miles

I am not thrilled to hear you are in the area and want to cut a trapline and come through my lake. No, I do not get out there much. I got the trade and manufacture site from the Feds many years ago. I was once a school teacher, now retired, and thought someday I might spend more time at the lake, and maybe put a few traps out, nothing serious. I'm in Washington state now. I run a square rigger sailing school and live on the boat sometimes here in Olympia. I'm glad to hear you run sled dogs. I think the thought of a snow machine zooming by would not be as good. I guess you can trap around there, for now anyhow. If you use the cabin be sure to leave firewood and leave it in good condition. Keep me posted on what is going on. I have fond memories of the lake and proving up on the site. It was rough times back then but exciting. I flew my plane in and out of that lake. Later then. **Sandy Sinclair**

I replied I'd be sure to let him know. If he showed up to trap, I'd make room for him. I have no intention on ruining that dream for him.

My canoe kit arrives. It is a canoe in two pieces that needs fiber-glassing together, seats and gunnels put in. It cost me $150. "Cool!" I pretty much rush back home. The dogs need feeding, and I have things to do!

The new net gets twenty-five fish a day on the average. The houseboat gets moved over to where the cabin is, so I can have one spot to work out of. A new dog yard is set up. The canoe is put together, and works great for checking fish nets, and getting around the lake without a motor. Paddling the lake boat was so inefficient! A fish cutting table is built, along with fish drying racks. I'm getting thirty fish a day then fifty fish a day. I'm guessing I need about 2,000 put up for winter.

There are enough ducks on the lake to support my eating habits. I do not seek females or young. Usually a lone male off by himself is spotted. This is not hunting as most people perceive it. There is no specific day set aside to go out for food or fun. There is no date to plan for, in which I pack all my camping gear and head out on vacation time or weekend with the guys and bring beer, to harvest enough to last a season on that one hunt designated by a 'season' with a rulebook to follow. This is not a sport, game, or recreational. I simply have a gun with me at all times. Usually at some point while out doing my chores, I come across some critter of some kind that is edible, crossing paths with me. It might be a duck, a muskrat, a beaver, or any sort of four legged or flying critter. If it is easy to get and I am hungry I take it. Rarely it is more than one a day, and often only once a week. This seems to have no effect on the population whatever, no different than how it is with a wolf, or bear on the lake.

I have no special technique nor do I develop any special skills as a great stalker of game. Perhaps learning how to be a good shot is handy, being ready as an opportunist is a developed skill. The game comes to me. I do not go to the game. This way of life does not fit within the parameters of the laws of civilization, but seems not to be relevant, as I am not in civilization. Not that I give it a whole lot of thought (yawn). At the same time civilization is trying to understand, acknowledge, and accommodate subsistence needs. Yet doing so without asking subsistence people. Much like men discussing discrimination against women, without having women at the discussion table, or allowed any input.

The cabin gets set up to use. Shelving is built from poles. The bed is fixed. Bear proofing is important. The new tin stove is installed. The new glass for the one broken window is installed. Some holes in the roof are patched so the roof no longer leaks. Log oil is applied. Anti-rot painted on the bottom logs. Ant poison is set out to stop the ants from eating the logs. There are few days with nothing to do.

There is a break in the long rain spell. I find an old trapline trail of the Hansen's in the woods. One old style trap is found. The trail is followed as far as I can, till it disappears in a swamp. *'When if freezes we can explore this further!'* The trail is marked with red flagging so I can find it again with the sled dogs. This is exciting, for this trail might go a long way, and save me a lot of cutting! It is also interesting to be following in the footsteps of someone who lived as I do a long time ago. *'Trapping is not weird; people did this for hundreds of years as a way of life.'* I feel a sense of history here. The Hansens would smile and nod. All is well in the world. Seeing where they put the next blaze on a tree, teaches me how they think, what they had in mind. I can see where they were tired, where they got excited, where they were in a hurry, where they were looking for a way out, or in, maybe sixty years ago or more.

A sled runner is found leaning against a tree. A broken runner. Nearby a cut tree. "Someone slammed into a big tree, broke a sled runner, stopped and camped here. They cut this tree down, and made a new runner on this spot and pressed on." A single leather dog collar hanging on a branch tells me where the dogs were tied up, and left in a hurry. The firewood stumps are counted. I can guess about three days was spent here. A story fifty years old, measured by an injured tree's growth rings. Footprints in the land. Someone in furs hunkered down by a fire, arms wrapped around his knees saying, 'Rats!' Telling the dogs to shut up. How can I not smile? How can I not feel at one, and at peace with the world around me? "I know this man more than I know my own family."

Everything in its season. Fish are put up. Berries picked and dried, rose hips for winter tea harvested and dried, mushrooms picked and sorted, as it has been for 10,000 years.

'The bear is back again!' Yup! He has not learned his lesson. We have tried tin cans making noise, tried hanging the fish higher. The bear is bound and determined to have the fish. He sees no reason he is not king of the forest. He helps himself to whatever he wishes. Over a week period I am missing about 100 fish. The fish is needed for the dogs this winter, so something has to be done. The dogs will die without this fish, thus so will I. The bear has learned I cannot see in the dark. He has learned the dogs are tied up. The more he learns, the more dangerous he is to me. Ultimately he could get bold enough to off me (as a way to have all the fish whenever he wants).

I devise a gun set. A string is put on the trigger, around the trigger guard, and up along the barrel. A piece of fish is tied right on the end of the barrel at the end of the string. The gun is hung from the string on the fish rack. The weight of the gun pulls on the trigger, so only a tiny bit more pull will set the gun off. The angle is such, the bear will put his mouth around the fish and pull. It's a little touchy backing away, not knowing if it will go off on its own.

In the middle of the first night the gun goes off! "Bloom!" I wake up, and only smile slowly. I know exactly what happened. There is complete silence for ten seconds as the dogs are in shock. Then the dogs all go nuttso at once. I get up, and slowly get dressed, get the lantern light and take my time getting on out there.

Yup. Dead bear under the fish rack. *'Hey look, his mouth is still wrapped around the end of the barrel with the back of his head blowed off!'* Yes, I see. Glad he died fast and easy. Never felt a thing I'm sure. Death doesn't come any easier. *'Now we have bear meat!'* We are both drooling. We look forward to fresh red meat. Ducks are ok, but it's not all it's cracked up to be to tell the truth, sometimes they taste like mud. Not all ducks at all times of the year are tasty. I'm not complaining or anything. *It's all a gift!* Just that fresh red meat has a special place in our hearts and belly. The fat will be wonderful as well, to add to the beans in winter, and render down for boot grease, and other projects. Liver is the first thing to eat on any big game as it is good the very first day, but after only a day it changes, and is not as tasty. Yum!

FALL ARRIVES. The two young eagles in the nest over the fish net are grown and ready to leave. A grouse is in the woods, and clucks as I am checking the nets. This sounds like my dinner calling to me. The gun is grabbed, and it's off in the woods I go. The grouse is easy to spot. I shoot it and head back to the boat. A few fish are in the boat from the net checking. One of the eagles has decided to steal a fish. As I approach, he is in the boat frantically trying to leave with the fish before I arrive. I charge down on the boat yelling. The young eagle panics, and jumps over the side of the boat with the fish in its talons. He cannot let go of the fish, the way an eagles talons are designed, until he puts his weight down on the ground. Lifting only make the talons grab tighter. The eagle is now in the water with wings flat on the water unable to break free of the surface tension with the fish in his claws.

I get in the boat, and am able to lean over the boat and touch the eagle. A paddle is used to lift the eagle off the water, swing over, and set him on dry land. He is able to let go of my fish, and hobble indignantly off in the brush. A camera would have been handy here. As it is, this becomes only a memory.

I count 1,500 fish by the time I discount what the bear and birds got. Probably enough if I supplement guts and other foods throughout the winter. Roosevelt creek is along my trapline route, so I decide it might be good to boat there and drop off some fish for feeding dogs on the trapline later. There is still a cache standing in the old gold rush village that is bear proof (hopefully). Time is spent fixing the cache up and making a waterproof cover. A ladder has to be built and left behind to get up in the cache. A few other trapping supplies are added as well.

Thoughts of the trapline are on my mind with the ending of summer. Once again the wore out maps are studied. The big lake north of Hansen is where Sandy has his cabin with he said is ok to use. Much of the country is flats, so maybe not so hard to cut to, even though it looks like a long distance. Where to go from there is contemplated. Wien Lake is the next logical place, as it is a bigger lake. However, there are a few people there, and at least one traps, I think. Hansen Creek runs up pretty close, so maybe I can run up the creek and loop over to Sinclair Lake. Few of the lakes have a name, so I just call this one 'Sinclair' since his homestead is there. He calls it Square Lake.

THE FIRST FREEZE on the lake! Snow finally arrives, and the sled is pulled over to the dog yard. Kenai is so eager to go he chokes on his tongue. The rest were barking like crazy as well. *'Except for Thunder. He doesn't look excited, you notice?'* Thunder is the leader and the oldest at seventeen years. He had been slowing down, maybe not feeling so young anymore all summer. He seemed stiff after the rains and not happy.

When I take off with the dogs, the youngsters go full out like crazy, and poor Thunder does not even try to keep up. Thunder falls down, and gets drug a ways before I stop and unhook him. *'Maybe he needs more time to get in shape than the rest, we could work with him a little separately?'* Yes this might work. The older dogs and Thunder are hooked up. But Thunder is in no mood. I'm not sure if he is just being ornery and lazy or what—or just too old!

I try once again to hook him in the main team. All the others are looking down the trail barking wildly to go. Thunder looks down the trail with a frown, looks at me with a frown, and looks at his dog house with a frown. All the other dogs are saying 'Rah, rah, rah, lets go get it! Yes, yes, let's run like crazy in the snow!" Thunder says, 'You idiots. I know what is at the end of the trail when we work hard all day! Nothing! Just another bowl of slop, just the same as if we stay right here all day!' I almost laugh and want to say "Hush, Thunder, don't tell the rest!" He obviously does not want to go. Not today, not tomorrow, not ever. I sigh. He also does not need a pep talk. Nor does he need the facts of life explained. He knows exactly what retirement as a sled dog means. He's seen it all. He's not afraid, and he's made up his mind.

I unhook all the dogs, let Thunder loose, and get my snowshoes and gun. Thunder slowly walks out to the lake. I follow. He sees an old piece of driftwood out and walks over to it, sits down, and waits for me to snowshoe up to him. I, too, look around and say, "Yup—looks to be about as good a spot as any." I scratch him behind the ears and tell him what a good dog he has been. The bullet goes in behind the back of his head as he stares out the trail across the lake that he can never run again.

I don't dwell on it much. I am too full of life and eager to be a comet across the sky. The old and the dead are already the past. If a time in my life ever comes that I can't pull my fair share, take me out back and shoot me. That's perfectly acceptable. That's the rules we all live by out here. When I hook all the rest up again I ask, "Anyone else want early retirement?" No one else in the team wants early retirement. It's all 'Rah, rah, let's see what's at the end of the trail after a long hard day."

There are no easy days. Every single day takes us to the limit. I feel like Tarzan. I feel like one of those guys in a Jack London story. I feel like Muhammad Ali, undefeated heavyweight of the world, never been knocked down for the count. The dogs and I own the world, for as far as we can see in every direction.

"HEY, what's the hold up there, Kenai?" We are going slower. Every dog has been slowing down to pee on a tree along the trail. I scowl. Then I decide *yeah, it's a pretty good tree all right.* "Whoa!" and I pee on it too. On second thought I get my hatchet out and reach up as high as I can and cut the tree bark. The dogs begin scratching up the ground all around the tree. In spring some bear will come by here, and he'll look up at this tree and know what it means. "Wild Miles was here."

"String em out, Kenai! Let's get a move on, tighten up!" Kenai leaps forward, looks behind to see they all have tight lines, and as one, with bent heads, yank the sled forward into the great beyond. The colder it gets, the deeper the snow is, the more we like it. Most days my beard, scarf, and snowsuit all freeze over my mouth so I can't talk. I often give silent signals to the dogs. A tap on the right runner means to turn that way at the next intersection or around the next tree. Pulling back on the handlebar means to slow down. Stomping my foot next to the runner means I saw that, and you better straighten out.

The dogs remember where all the traps are. Usually I do not have to give a signal. They just stop at each set. There is always something to do at a set. If the set did not catch anything I have to at least brush the snow off the trap and stomp around so it can be seen, then leave new bait, add lure, or make a change of some kind. Around here we do not try to hide traps except from wolves. Animals have not seen man before, and know nothing about traps, so have no fear of the trap. There might be hesitation of something new, but stomping around gets them curious and overcoming nervousness, usually. They want to know what we were doing here stomping. Usually activity is related to 'food,' and they want some of it.

Another animal doing this would have buried something. Once the animal's attention is had, it is not so hard to get them to see or smell where we hid the food. Ninety percent of my sets are for marten. Pretty easy, pretty standard.

When there is fur in the trap, the dogs wait for me to take it out, put it in the sled and reset the trap. They seem to know when the last thing is done, and it is time to go, no matter how many times I come back to the sled and open the sled bag. The pole set is preferred. A pole is set in the crotch of a cut down tree, with a notch put on it to accept the trap. The marten gets caught going up the pole trying to reach the fish nailed on the butt end of the pole. He feels the trap grab him and leaps. He is now hanging from his foot on a chain, and cannot get back up on the pole. He freezes off the snow away from mice that might pull fur off to make nests. It usually takes a few hours to freeze, maybe even a day. I honestly think it is not very painful. We get asked that a lot, *'Does the animal suffer, is it humane?'* A loaded question. The purpose is to kill the animal, somewhat like asking about the death of the cow the burger is made of. When it town I joke, 'I hope this chicken didn't suffer!' Freezing is not that bad a way to go. Getting sleepy and not waking up. The trap itself does not hurt much. It is made to hold, not to maim. You could stick your finger in most traps and it would smart, but not hurt or break the finger. Even a wolf trap should not break your finger, or hurt, just grab and hold. It just doesn't sound very pleasant.

One marten is worth more than a day's wages for an average worker in town. I should be able to average a marten a day over the winter. Or is that just a dream? Traps get checked from three to seven days after the last check. If traps are checked more often than every three days, it seems to have a negative effect on catching. *'Because the animals think you are too close, and do not want to come around and take a chance you are nearby. In their minds I cannot hurt them unless I am here.'* Usually if more than a week goes by, something about the set needs changing. More bait, snow brushed off, or some other change. Often a jay bird or squirrel is in the trap that I have to take out in disgust, and use it for bait. However, nothing seems interested in squirrels and jays, so into the dog pot they go.

I have five sled dogs now with Thunder gone. Six to seven is better, but five will do for a trapline team. A tent camp is set up ten miles out. On Jan. third, I am thirty miles out on the trail and setting up 'Camp two' near Hansen Creek, the goal I set for this winter. Sandy's cabin is used a couple of times not far from here, but it is a big cabin and hard to get warm. There is not a lot of firewood around it, as it is built in stunted tundra trees, all there is around the lake. Camp two is better. It is in a birch grove with lots of firewood around, and more protected from the wind. This is better for the sled dogs.

My attention now goes in the other direction. The old trail I saw of Hansen's, headed for Roosevelt and Minchumina. The very next day, Jan. fourth, I cover about eight miles of trail I had seen before. The trail comes close to the Kantishna again near Roosevelt, then disappears. It is assumed the trail goes into the old village. The river is followed from here. I get to my cache left by boat. Everything is fine, and I set up another camp here. A wolverine had tried to get in the cache. I make a set to catch him. Since this is on the way to Minchumina, a mail trip and fur selling is planned.

Diary Jan. Seventh

I went back home and got ready for a Minchumina run. I left on Jan. seventh. Took four hours to Roosevelt, four more to Star's and spend a night with them. I got to Minchumina the next day, picked up my mail and headed home. I had a hard time finding the trail in the muddy flats. The wind had blown in our trail. The trapline trails are about thirty miles, while the Muddy River is seventy. We had to head over to the river and follow it. Because of this it takes two days to get to Star's. **Diary ends**

There, Kenai gets loose at night, and gets into the beaver gut pile out back. In the morning he is round, fat, and grinning. This is Star's garbage pile, so they do not care, but the concern is that Kenai might get worms from the uncooked guts. "Beaver meat is one of the most worm free meats around, Miles, so probably your dog is ok. Lots of trapper feed raw beaver meat to dogs." I am lucky it is not lynx or some other kind of meat then. Roosevelt is reached in an easy day. Home an easy next day. The following day I am back out checking traps and cutting more trails. In the evening at Camp two, I read over one letter I just got from this last mail run. It's from one of the guys I know that I used to work with firefighting. He has a job at the state land office now.

Hi Miles!

I heard you are on the Kantishna now. I thought you might want to know the State plans to open homesteading on the Kantishna this summer. So far the area to be selected is about forty miles up from the mouth to about thirty down from the Toklat. You should stop in the office and talk to me when you come in this summer.

Later. Pete

This would be the first time land on the Kantishna was ever opened up. "Probably we will never see homesteading any closer to here than this, at least on the same river we are on!" The thought of my own land on this river is appealing. This seems like an area I am finally happy with, and feel I could live here the rest of my life. Already I am investing a lot of time and effort into cutting trails to trap from. I'm not about to just walk away from this. Till now, there were few opportunities to settle down on this river and own anything. The probability of Julie selling me the cabin any time soon seems remote. Homesteading would allow me to have land by proving up on it rather than paying for it. More like paying for it, but with time and work, rather than money.

The map is studied. The area being proposed in relation to where I am now is examined. *'Looks like about 100 miles of cutting trail if we get land there and connect to here.'* This is more trail than I really want to deal with, and more trapline area then I want, but... *'We cut maybe fifty miles of trail this year, so in two years we could be here. It's ambitious, but possible. No one traps that whole country. It would be an empire all right. The size of the state of Rhode Island.'* I'd be happier just to stay here, but for sure, owning some land has a lot of advantages. Homesteading was thought to be over, having closed for good in 1972. This might be the opportunity of a lifetime. If I choose to pass this up, I wonder if I'd regret not doing this later in life.[1]

My trail cutting slows down since I do not know for sure what the future plans are. If this homesteading thing works out I would head that way, instead of cutting trail the opposite direction, toward Lake Minchumina. I could well be getting mail out of Manley Hot Springs instead of Minchumina if I get a homestead on the lower river. I'd have no use for this trail I'm working on. There has been more talk at Minchumina about problems of some kind at Wien Lake. A trapline war. Maybe a crazy person. Someone disappeared, probably killed in a trapline war. I do not need to step into that. My trail now is only five miles away from Wien Lake. No one should care, or be able to say anything according to accepted trapping ethics if I cut no closer. If I turn here, do I go west to Minchumina, or east toward Manley Hot Springs? I drag my feet.

My father sends me a radio for Christmas. I'm not sure I like the idea of the other planet, called civilization, invading the planet I live on. But I hooked up an antenna, and listened to 'Trapline Chatter.' I found out about this radio message system when I visited the Star's. *'This is the way bush folks get messages from the radio station KJNP out of North Pole'* I remind myself. A note had been sent off to Pete concerning the homestead land, saying I'd listen to messages every Monday. Pete put my name in for the land opening. It is lottery draw. Those selected pay $10 for a map, part of a staking packet showing where the land is.

On Jan. twenty-forth, Pete sends me a message saying my name is one of those selected. The opening date is in March. I have a year to get my staking packet and select my land. A minus sixty below cold spell has me temporarily cabin bound. When it warms to minus forty-five, I head out to my trapline.

Not far from Camp two, I slam into a tree coming down a hill and break a runner. This reminds me of the old runner I saw on the Hansen trail, and how something similar must have happened. The dogs get me to Camp two, where we can hole up and fix the sled. There is plenty of food and everything I need to live a week or more. We enjoy our time as I carve a sled runner with my trapping hatchet and hunting knife. Some baling wire is used to lash it in place. An old rusty nail is heated and used to burn a hole through the edge to do the lashing.

'Aren't you glad we do not depend on machines! If we had to, we could build an entire sled here! With machines, 'no part, no go.' A sled is all wood! The stuff growing all around us! Not a problem!' Yes, I agree, this is pretty cool. Aren't you glad we broke down!

After we get home the temperature drops again to minus sixty. We'd been traveling at minus fifty-five probably. The last cold spell was spent mostly fixing things, sewing holes in clothes, fixing zippers, the sled bag, snowshoe harnesses, dog harnesses and other chores. This time I have more time to dwell on letters I got in the mail.

Crafty from the Craft shop, who I know from the fair, sent some ivory and horn to do art with as part of a trade we are working out. Sue is complaining. She tells me once again how much she dislikes Crafty. *'She dislikes him for the same reasons we think highly of him!'* He's a garage sale and flea market lover. He knows how to sell things. *'Yeah he could sell warts to a toad or snow to Eskimos!'* His dress is scruffy and his shop more like a dingy rat hole, but he has cool stuff. I'm starting to learn a little about business. Crafty wants to be my agent. We have discussed the percent we each get, and the percent the shop gets. I know what 'keystone' means. That is when I want half the retail value. I have to think about who supplies boxes and chains, who sets the final retail price, the advantages and disadvantages of wholesale, consignment, and retail. If Crafty supplies raw material, will it be trading me his retail value, while I am expected to trade my part at a wholesale value giving him my art? He makes twice as much money off me this way. These are important issues I never considered as just an artist making nice items.

It takes a while to grasp it all. In the chess game of doing business I have to know what moves to make. If I bring in ten grand in art, and Crafty gives me four grand cash, no mess, no fuss, no boxes, no chains, no advertising, no hanging around, there might be an advantage in that. To get the full ten grand retail value I'd have to stay in town, accumulating three grand in costs and miss summer in the woods. How do I value my time? How long does it actually take me to finish an average item? Anyone who goes into business for themselves producing any product faces these same issues. It seems easy, but there are many hidden costs and many pieces of time forgotten about, that need to be accounted for. One hidden cost for example is theft and damage. How much gets lifted at the shows? How much does it cost to fix and repair older unsold pieces before they can be put back out again? Samples are given away as gifts, or for promotion. How does one factor that in? Increased costs from year to year for materials and production need to be taken into account. "Maybe we can high grade it first before showing Crafty? I can do a show at Alaska House, sell the best off, and what doesn't sell, wholesale to Crafty." I doubt I can out-craft Crafty though. Yet what is considered honest, and the way it's done? A note in a box of material makes me smile.

> "If you do your usual work with this, this material can produce $200,000 in finished art."

Yes, I like to play with numbers and dream. I like to think big. Crafty knows how to move a pawn and keep me in the game. I can't help admiring him and appreciating how his mind works. I'm just learning what Crafty already knows. Another smile comes to me as I recall Crafty's line… "For you, a special deal." His friends joke he needs that printed on a T-shirt.

I'm not exactly like Crafty in personality, but yes, something about him is admirable despite the points Sue makes. To quote her, "Crafty buys as cheap as he can and sells as high as he can, with total disregard for what that does to others!" Like buying ivory from drunken Eskimos at ten cents on the dollar, then marking it up by ten times when he sells it.

This sort of thinking is more common than not, like 'If you can't take care of yourself step aside! Make room for someone who can!" There is no room in this world for kindness. I've already seen where that got me in life. 'Yeah, Canada!' "Yeah, Canada." I repeat to myself. I'm still after all this time, reeling from that one. I lost my home and everything I owned. At least I ended up in Alaska and in short order was down to twenty-five cents to my name, a month or so after owning my own home, with river frontage, having a complete photo lab, a boat, and enough money to live a year without working, and only twenty years old. All that pride disappeared mighty fast.

Nora and Bill at Alaskaland are on my mind during my time of spring thinking. . . I sigh. They will never make any money to speak of selling diamond willow sticks. However making a lot of money is not the stated goal, so that has to be taken into account. They seem happy, well adjusted, and well liked, even though they make no real impact on the world. Crafty has money, prestige, respect, and is known by a lot of people. Who knows Nora and Bill? But Nora and Bill seem happier maybe? It is hard to know. Hard to know what or who to emulate, what behavior to choose as a set of laws to live by.

All of this seems important to think about. I, and any of us, can go in any number of directions in our life. We have choices to make. What works? In terms of how to deal with people, and situations. What kind of job will I have, and how will I conduct my business? This question is not on many people's mind maybe. This is on my mind because I feel I was sent out in the world with a toolbox filled with tools that do not work. Finding that out, what tools do I toss out, and what new ones do I look for and put in my toolbox? Who has tools I think are working? How can I acquire those tools? For now it has to do with heroes, and those I look up to—the Mountain Men of the past who made our country, the brave ones who went out into the wilds and were at the forefront of civilization. The ones who were at one with nature, living with the land and God, who worked hard and laughed and enjoyed life, having adventures and being healthy. How can one possibly go wrong following in the footsteps of the likes of Daniel Boone? Other such heroes were explorers like Lewis and Clark. I'm reading about early Alaska explorers and gold rush heroes.

So now is a thought of being a homesteader. It would mean a change in thinking. The true mountain men snorted at homesteaders. The true Mountain Man roamed the land free and wild, following only the rivers and furs. Being a homesteader is only one step up from being a farmer and building fences, a whole different concept from being a 'hunter-gatherer.' The only adventure a farmer has is deciding whether to plant beans or corn. What is the life of a homesteader like? It's certainly about putting roots down and being committed to one spot. Can I accept this?

Dad wants to know how I am, and if I got the radio. Mountain Men of course never had radios. What is the big deal about the news anyhow? Minutemen waited till spring. Getting news from a society going off the cliff and how we need to be afraid, be depressed victims, seems low priority on my list of wishes. I sigh. I'm torn. *To be, or not to be, that is the question.* I am being reminded by my conscience that this has been an ongoing question for as long as man has been civilized. Do I follow my own heart, or do I toe the line and please others. Do I involve myself in a society I am afraid of and do not trust? Does society know what it is doing? Does society have the right to think for me, make decisions for me, or even care about me? If society is as the lemming and going off the cliff, am I obligated to follow along and go off the cliff too? Is there any good news to listen to out there in society?

There is something new on the radio as I listen in the evening. 'Watergate' Scandal.

I'm aware that even in Christ's time, there were those who yelled about the end of the world being around the corner, and the sky falling any time now. Is this just thoughts of people who worry too much, have no reason to, and need to get on with life? This might just be cabin fever and mid-end winter depression. A smile crosses my face. Been there, done that. Normal. We'll tough it out.

A cache at a new homestead called 'bearpaw'

CHAPTER FOURTEEN

ON THE COVER OF RURALITE MAGAZINE, LAND
LOTTERY WINNER, FIRST BOOK EDIT ATTEMPT

I'm in Fairbanks as part of my annual yearly routine, getting supplies and setting up a show at Alaska House. There is more business with Crafty this season than in the past. "Hey, Miles, it looks like you got the art supplies I sent to Lake Minchumina. I wondered how you'd get in to get mail. Did you run the sled dogs? Nice work here. Sure, I can sell this art for you, but we need to talk prices."

"Yes, I ran the sled dogs to the lake and the materials were nice to get; kept me busy the rest of the winter. Since my work is unique, and one of a kind, it is hard to price. There is nothing to compare it to, beyond the prices I get at the shows at Alaska House. They take a third of the retail—like consignment. So if you sell it for me how does that work?"

"Usually, Miles, I buy outright and get goods for a low price so I can make money reselling. Sometimes it's ten cents on the dollar. I admit I buy from vendors at shows who are discouraged and want out of the business. I buy their whole inventory. I'm honest with them though. They agree to sell all they have and get out of the business. They get their few thousand they want to begin a new life. Or I buy outdated items or damaged goods and have it reworked by my employees."

"Well in a case like ours, how would you work it, Crafty?"

"Well the shops I sell to need to double their money. I want a third, so you'd get a quarter of your retail. Just set your retail higher to cover my cut." I'm not excited by the deal. *The artist, creator of the goods, without who the goods do not exist, gets the smallest cut? Is this normal?* Crafty trades me supplies, and used items I need that he collects at garage sales, having an idea the sorts of things I need. I can even give him a list of what to look for. Crafty gives me a place to stay at his shop. There are various perks that do not involve money, but sweeten the pot for me. The beauty is, Crafty will move volume for me. No one else is talking art pieces by the hundred. Most shops will take a few items to try out. I have to admit, the total dollars, no matter how it gets decided, sounds nice. I get over a thousand dollars. Like others who tend to sell to Crafty, 'Who needs the hassle, it's only money, let Crafty deal with everything. Sure, he gets more money than me, but he deals with all the stuff we do not want to even know about. We live cheap. We live in the woods. We deal with bears, and as long as we have a roof over our head and can eat, what does it matter how much each of us makes?'

I'm now creating more art than I can sell at the short shows I do at Alaska House. The pipeline is over. The big money is not as big, not as free flowing as the past. This translates into more effort in selling my art to make money. For now Crafty is an easy answer, so I can get on with what matters to me. He's an ok guy all around. He gives me rides places, lets me stay at his place and sits and chats like we are friends. I rarely get a lot of money out of him, mostly favors, trades, and goods. It could be a bummer to fully comprehend I have $10,000 worth of goods I am getting $1,000 in trade for. Sadly, it is the best deal the average artist can expect. We have no union, and are at the mercy of the shop owners.

"Miles, you seen yourself on the cover of the magazine yet?" One of the cute employees at Alaska House. I forget the name. She's showing me the "Ruralite Magazine," August of 1979. This magazine is put out by the electric company. Ruralite carries various articles, ads, and such, distributed all over the northwest. I'm curious to see what was done. Margaret Van Cleve wrote it, and had interviewed me. "Here, Miles, on page sixteen and seventeen."

I want to look at the cover again—me, wearing my squirrel skin hat with feather in it, staring.[1] I have my hand art tools. I'm working on an art piece in a vice at Alaska House. A pretty romanticized version of the reality of my life, but see why it sells, and understand this is what folks want to hear about and see in a picture. I repeat what I tell people a lot. "Yup, that hat took thirteen squirrels. See all the eyes and faces across the front? See all the whiskers of the thirteen squirrels? The white stripes all line up in concentric rings around the hat, see that?"

My cute female fan smiles and nods and thinks I'm pretty slick. "Made it yourself, tanned it and all that? Where did you learn that, Miles?"

"Oh I just read about it, tried it, and practiced. These skins were brain tanned, but I tried a dozen ways of tanning. Anyhow let's see the story!"

She opens to page sixteen, and there is my picture again, and pictures of my art work. The title of the article is "Wild Miles" The first part goes over my rescue in the wilds, much like the 'Alaska Magazine' article 'Survive' written at the time. The article goes on.

"Miles is also an artist, specializing in metal-inlay work. He cuts out intricate Alaskan flora and fauna from sheets of brass, copper, silver, mounting them on backgrounds of ivory, jade, horn or even claws" Then later "Working without electricity, he works by the light of a kerosene lamp."

I skim further. I am quoted directly.

"I try to express my love of the outdoors through my artwork, instead of carrying a sign and saying "save the animals," maybe someone who buys my jewelry will look at the Dall sheep or whatever on it and be inspired to go out and see the country."

The article ends with a reference to political issues in the news.

"Miles lives a dream few can. In the D-2 legislative controversy, one of the key issues is the right to choose or continue a particular lifestyle—be it traditional native subsistence, or Miles's trapping existence. Some fear that it may outlaw a free life in remote areas."[2]

After a quick scan/read, I say, "Yes, nice enough article don't you think?" Trying to feel out this lady's take on it.

"Sure. A little too much on the conservation slant, but you need to say stuff like that to please the public right?"

"Ya, right, for sure! Ha! Most of my art goes to the ladies you know. I can't go around talking about blood and guts, and expect to sell anything! I have to do a certain amount of hocuspocus and give 'em what they want!"

My fan slaps me on the back with a grin like we understand each other. We are both cool. She tells me about herself. "Miles, I lived a while in the wilderness with a husband. I liked the life ok but we were not so far out as you. Anyhow it ended. We fought a lot. I ended up having to pull a gun on him. I knew I had to leave. I feel so bad to have ever had to pull a gun on anyone. We had various issues. It might be nice to reaffirm my desirability. Maybe you can come over and visit?"

I could guess what is on her mind. She is very pretty, not much like girlfriends I had in the past in that she is very modern, with short Betty Boop hair style, dyed blonde, city dress, high heels, fancy car, just 'different' then I have known, more like the tourists I talk to. She knows my artistic side, and understands fine art. She sees in me a sensitive passionate artist. I see no harm in being this person for her. Maybe I can learn something about women. She is not married nor has a boyfriend.

I've rarely spent more than two to three days at a time with a woman in my life. I feel like I do not really know very much about women, in terms of being close, living together, sharing a house, a life, or bodies. Like her, I feel a certain desperation, or concern, or insecurity about myself and relationships. If I can please a woman even. I have not had much luck, and assumed eventually I would find the right one, and things would have a way of just working out, and it was all natural, and there is nothing to know. But I'm getting in my thirties, and everyone I know is married by now, knows about love and relationships.

I HAVE TO CHUCKLE. We were not alone ten seconds and she is tearing our clothes off. I quietly hold her. My breathing adjusted to hers. My heartbeat in tune with hers, as each valve opens and closes, as one might keep up with a partner dancing to music. Our body temperature's notice each other, and silently tweaks temperatures by tenths of a degree so we would be the same temperature, as one.

This is like, as a skeleton key matches a door latch. Tumblers seek notches and high spots before anything moves. It may require jiggling, pulling, turning and pushing again, till the time is right to click and open. Springs move, greased bearings turn, arms and rods pivot and cycle through. With a 'click' the latch releases, the door opens, revealing all that is hidden behind the locked door. A room filled with light and wonder.

I think we stay awake two days straight. We may have got up to get a drink of water. I think we did not eat. Maybe we slept, but only in cat naps tied together in a knot.

"I can't do this again, really" I say with a laugh. I thought five to six times was enough, and impossible.

She smiles back. "We'll see!"

"Dang!" We are giggling again under the sheets.

More details are probably not necessary. "No probably there is no more to say about it." *'Yes children and sensitive types can turn red and quickly skip that part.'* A time in life to ponder about over the years. I did not have to feel so bad about being short, and all that. She too, seemed a new revitalized person. God does not seem inclined to punish us.

Even though it is not likely this lady and I could live together, the thought of having love and companionship is a strong pull. Many times I live alone because I feel I must and have no choice. Other times I see I have a choice, and could choose to have companionship. It is hard for any woman to live as I do now, on a houseboat, on wages that are half of the legal requirement to be called poor. I cannot ask a woman to live like this. Some women tell me they do not care about this, money does not matter and such, but wait till they have to do without. Wait till they have to make their own clothes, or get used ones at the thrift store and garage sales. Wait till their meals are frozen potatoes that turned black, and eat meat with dried maggots because we can't afford to throw it away. Wait till it is time to live like an animal. Then see how romantic it all looks.

So my interest in getting a real piece of land I own, and a cabin on dry ground where I might keep things, and have a garden and such. This dream has at least something to do with the willingness to compromise, and have something to offer a woman. Maybe someday far off I could have such a woman as I have just met. She seems fine, meaning smart, honest, kind, sane, good looking, all the things one might want in a life partner. Getting together like animals over a weekend is not really what I want, it's just the best I can have for now.

"Hey, Pete! Thanks for putting my name in the hat for the land lottery. Explain it to me and where's the paperwork."

"Sure Miles let me go to your file." While Pete is looking he explains. "It's all in the packet I'll give you. Just follow the directions and you owe me $10 for the packet. Basically you go out to the Kantishna River with this packet. You pick out any five acre parcel you like. You measure it off, put posts in the ground at your corners. There are instructions telling you what you have to write on each of the tags that get nailed to the posts. A picture is taken for proof and reference. Bring all the information and pictures back here and file it. That cost $100. In this program you have to get your own surveyor to survey the parcel you got. When the survey is filed and you prove you have lived on the land for five years, the land is yours." This is pretty interesting, but I have a question or two.

"What is this survey going to run me? I'm looking for the punch line here. What is my total cost going to run?"

"Miles, you can work out any deal you want on the survey. Usually it will run a couple grand. So for maybe a total cost of $2,500 you own five acres of river frontage. It's hard to lose, Miles."

"And what does 'prove up' mean. Do I have to make a lot of improvements and clear land and all that?"

"No. You have to build, and you have to stay at least six months out of the year, I think it is. You'll have to look it up."

"Pete, do you think I could use my houseboat as my prove up cabin?"

"Probably not, Miles, but you do not have to have the cabin up the first year or any specified time, except within the five year limit, so if you are proving up in the houseboat for those five years and have a cabin up at the end of that time I think that would qualify. The intent is that you are actually there and working the area in some way. Basically, this is really your home, you care, and are not just land speculating. Since you trap and will really be out there, this is fulfilling the intent. I doubt you'll have a problem, Miles."

If I go here and stake as it looks like I am doing, I will need to move my entire Hansen camp downriver 100 miles. This may require a good engine for the houseboat. All the money I got from Crafty for a year's worth of art is used to buy a new fifty horse mercury outboard. This engine will go on the long wood riverboat I traded John for in Galena. If this boat is tied alongside the houseboat, I can make headway and steer downriver. The twenty-four foot wood boat will then be used alone with the fifty horse for freight hauling. The houseboat can be left behind as my dwelling wherever I settle in.

The staking packet is opened and examined. Most of it is easy to understand. The introduction lets the potential homesteader know what to expect by saying "This land is remote, it is expected you will need to live a subsistence lifestyle depending on the land." *Exactly like me! This is my dream! Perfect!* One big concern is to stop land speculators from hiring people to go get title to remote land, so it can be sold for a profit down the road. It is important that the staker be serious about living and staying remote.

There are instructions for using a compass, with a reminder to use true north, not magnetic and the declination here is twenty-six degrees, which must be set in the compass. Being an outdoor person, I already know most of this. Maps are easy to read from my experience cutting trails. I use the scale of 'inch to the mile' terrain map. This is a map I already have, and am somewhat familiar with. "It is to our advantage that we already know this map, and what the swamps and symbols mean. Let's study the map and see if there is a place we can spot to check out."

There are two places I see that I think look interesting. Both spots are on water, yet require going up a creek a ways, and maybe even doing a small portage. Such a situation would offer privacy from main river traffic. Both places have numerous lakes nearby, and access to all I might want. The map indicates lots of trees nearby for firewood, hills nearby to protect from wind, water for drinking, and good trapping country in an area no one else I know of traps. There would be a route to follow to head over toward the Hansen country I have already cut trail in. The Hansen cabin could be a trap cabin at that end. Ideally I could boat some supplies there and have them waiting at that end of the trapline when I get there by winter trail.

The more I study the maps, the more convinced I am this can work and be an answer for me. This then, would be my choice as a place in Alaska to settle, call home and invest in.

At Alaska Tent and Tarp I buy a canvas trapline type tent. This requires poles to be set up, is very stout, and can be used in winter to trap from, but also as a place to stay or store things while cabin building. A list of hand tools needed for cabin building is bought, mostly at Sampson's Hardware, still the main hardware store in Fairbanks. This list includes a draw knife for peeling logs, two door hinges, spikes, string, and for the first time in ages, a chainsaw. At a secondhand store I get a hand auger for drilling holes through logs to pin them with wood pegs. There are wolf traps at the store I make a deal on as well.

The sled dogs are tied up in the woods along the Chena River near Alaskaland. There is enough dead wood around to have a fire to cook rice and fish for the dogs. A net is set in the Chena River for fish. The dogs are adaptable, and learn the routine. They keep quiet in the daytime, enjoying the summer sun. I buy a bicycle for $10 for my transportation. This can come back to the homestead with me in the boat. *'But wait! I bet Crafty at the Craft store would let us keep the bike at his place, just chain it up there.'*

Some nights I stay at the Craft store in the basement, and have use of the shower. This is part of the art trade deal we made, since Crafty does not want to part with cash. Crafty tells me the art he got from me is selling, so we have an established relationship. He will want more art later for sure. As with many summers, at least some amount of time is spent in Fairbanks doing odd jobs to make ends meet, even though I am not happy about this, and live in hopes of one day not having to spend so much of the nice summer in the city.

At Alaskaland, I am at home. The girls that do the show know me, vendors know me, and I am still a tourist attraction, an asset to the park. A few still find me to be a seedy character, and do not want me around, but over time the grumbling seems to not be so loud. *'I think these grumblers see me as a nut case–but harmless enough.'* With squirrel hat and blade of grass in my mouth, I visit the leather man, willow shop, ice cream shop, and the tavern where the girls hang out. Sometimes I can sell some art, or offer a boat ride to a tourist for extra money. A few Alaskaland shops buy art from me wholesale now.

"Hi, Nora. Hey Bill, having a good day in the shop?" They seem happy today, dressed up in the old 1800's clothes, sitting on stools in front of the quaint shop on the boardwalk. Such a handsome couple, as one might see on the cover of a magazine. The Alaskaland train whistle toots in the background. The train goes right behind their shop on its small rails, and disappears around the back side of the paddle boat Nenana, an original steam powered boat that once hauled freight on this river system. We all look at the disappearing train and boat in silence for a moment.

"Yes, things went well today Miles, good season I guess. Did Roy get those bolo ties of yours that you hoped he'd want? Sounds like you did good yesterday at the other shops!"

"While I was on the way back I had a chance to tell the story of the sled dog breeding with wolves, maybe anyhow, remember when you saw my dog with the wolves?" I am not sure, but Bill seemed sure, so I tell the story for the tourists.

"So was it good for a free meal, Miles?" Nora has a smile on her face knowing how I trade stories for meals.

I sheepishly reply, "Yup."

One of the places I sort of hang out is the library. As with about everywhere, it is not long before everyone knows me. That's how it is when you are a character. I'm a little standoffish at the library though, remembering my Canada experience. In my mind, it was wanting to keep a library open that got me in trouble and deported.

"Wild Miles, have you been working on the book you spoke of last year? It needs to get done while it is fresh on your mind. It might help support the lifestyle you want as well. I have a degree in English and would be happy to edit it for you. I think you have something important to say, so I would be honored to be part of it. I know you do not have much money, so I might trade for art!"

For the first time I get serious about the book I have talked about so many years. I've been sort of stumped for many years. Two issues; one is that the only character when alone in the wild is me. It is difficult to say, "I saw, I did, I went" all the time. There are no other characters! The second issue is that, I originally started out with the idea I was going to be a Mountain Man, and the book would be about my success. I am willing to tell a story, but I cannot out right lie and fabricate things. I have done nothing yet worth writing about. Any local could tell it better, and has accomplished more. So far the story would be more like a Don Quixote story. Me going after the windmill believing I'm a knight, slaying dragons.

I do have lots and lots of poetry written, and after reading Hiawatha, and being so influenced, I wonder if I could write a whole book as poetry? Not a collection of stories, but one long book size poem? This might be impressive? Writing it all in poetry would force me to slow down and think, weigh my words carefully. One problem I have in general with my writing is I write too much. Writing 100 pages a day is easy. But will I ramble and drag it on? Poetry will stop that. I hand what I have to the librarian gal who takes an interest in me.

"It is hand written, and remember, it is done in poetry so keep the lines intact."

She eagerly takes the work and is ready to give it her best. She is one of the gals who is at least a little interested in me, and talks about what it might be like to join me. Tentatively we might work on books together. A few days later I stop in again. She has one chapter sort of done.

"Wow, let me see! That was fast! Has it been hard to edit?" I glance at the work and see it is not done by lines as poetry. She has ignored the poetry and written it, corrected my words, and changed the lines. She has made more complete sentences, and totally rewritten the words and meaning. She does not recognize it as poetry. There is the knowledge that poetry just does not sell. No matter how good it is, it's poetry. Yuck.

"Wild Miles, I had trouble reading your handwriting..." She trails off. She obviously spent a lot of time on this. She thinks I am not a good writer. I realize I'm going to have to start all over, buy a typewriter, and type it all out. I will have to learn to type first. I can make notes and changes in the margins, but at some point it has to be completely retyped again. At some point someone else may have to type it to a correct format for submission to a publisher or printer. This is just so much more work than I ever imagined. Quite different then writing magazine articles in an hour, or even 700 page letters to girlfriends! I trade this gal some art for her effort, and basically have to toss her work out. I vaguely promised I'd look her up again when the manuscript is all typed so it could be read more easily.

There are already hundreds of hours put in to this. Back to square one. This is the first time anyone else in all these years has seen what I have been working on, and it is not positive or optimistic. It will take a lot of energy not to give up on it. After years and hundreds of hours, I see I must throw it all out and start again from scratch, and spend many more hundred hours on it. I'm not sure myself if it is worth it, or what purpose it serves.

Yet I get a feel for a set of questions and a certain curiosity folks have. As time passes, more and more I have the chance to talk to groups, spin yarns, and see a pattern of what it is people are curious about. This latest letter I get is an example of why I need to write a book. This is only one in maybe 100 communications of the same question. "Why?"

Am curious...after listening to your tape. How many personal ads have you placed?

And one more thing... I'm not sure why you wanted to live the life you did. It seems you almost abused yourself...why with freezing and being hungry and all... I can understand wanting to get away from the city and people and live in the wild and remote but to jeopardize your life?.... when it was not necessary... difficult to understand... talk some more to me about the
WHY.

I reply with a letter

Hello Bobbie!

So you ask 'Why?' You didn't read my poem "Twelve answers to What For?" On what level do you want an answer? When I left one life to enter another I was desperate in some ways. But I was ready to die seeing if I could live my dream. I was not happy in the life I was in. I wasn't getting good grades and would never amount to anything. I was an artist but "So what! What are you going to do for a living?" was the attitude. I didn't like the military. I wasn't qualified for anything, was not good at anything that 'mattered.' Where was I going to go? Do what? My sister and I tried to commit suicide together when we were young. As far as I was concerned I was living on borrowed time. I'd be dead by now (at age twenty-five) if I stayed in civilization... so why not go for what I wanted? My dream? I'd be no worse off than if I was in civilization (dead). So it is hard in the wilderness... but I found something I was good at. I found someplace I belong. I found strength, courage, something to live for. I found pride. I found something other people respect and admire me for. But yes, some feel sorry for me, even my relatives, but no one in Alaska. People here understand. On another level I found masculinity. I proved myself. I am short. I never fit in, and was made fun of for being small, and the family moving once a year never helped. I was picked on, bullied, the brunt of jokes. I was 'sensitive' and an artist. You add that up and it spells 'pussy'... 'faggot.' I was soft. Had no physical skills. Because it wasn't part of my upbringing.

In the wilds it felt good to become 'physical'... feel my body get strong. I once flexed my muscles and ripped my shirt. I felt like a lion when it roars. People didn't make fun of me for being small and sensitive. I was the guy that killed bears with my hands. That bought me the right to do 'sensitive art.' I didn't seek out trouble or pain or a rough life. I didn't enjoy the troubles I had. It was a bitch. But I saw it as the price to pay. You want to dance, you pay the fiddler. If it was free or easy everyone would do it. What I did was exclusive because it was so hard. It weeds out lesser people. It makes me special. I like being special. But I didn't care so much what others thought, as I didn't come to town to get anyone's opinion. It was how I felt about myself inside. I was good at something. I was strong, tough. I felt it. Nothing great is accomplished easily. Anything worth achieving will ask a price. God made a certain personality for a reason. Why does the chicken cross the road? Why do people climb mountains? Why is there now and then a sheep that leaves the security of the pasture to find out what is on the other side of the fence-out there where there are wolves and the shepherd can't protect you?

Why? If I have a problem usually it was because I made a mistake. I could figure out the solution and do something about it. Sometimes it is 'hard' but it is simple. I need food. I need fire. I need a lantern. I need needle and thread. Sometimes I wait a year to have it. But I do know what I need, and that is very clear in my mind. I can deal with that. I'm capable of working hard to achieve that which is achievable. In civilization problems are complex, and have no solution I am in control of. High taxes. What can I really do about it? I get angry and high blood pressure. I do not recall ever getting angry or frustrated in the wilderness. A bear might break in, but I am not pissed off, I simply kill it. Nature is harsh—but understandable. Nature makes sense to me. In the wilderness I laugh a lot. In the wilderness I am a King. I own all I can see, all the way to the mountains and beyond, because who is around to say different? In civilization nothing is mine, not even my property. I am a slave to the system. If I do something those in charge don't like (and they are people I do not respect) they have it in their power to do me great harm, and I can do nothing in return but kiss ass and play games and hide, and hope like hell no one sees me. Is that any way to live? So what sort of question is 'Why?

People want to hear the most about the hard exciting times, and that is what makes the 'story.' When things are hunky dory no one wants to hear about it. Or no, some want the opposite, the romantic view through rose glasses. The best of times and the worst of times. The reality and truth is a blend, and suspect this will take a book to explain.

I live my dream. One line in a Donovan song, 'First there is a mountain, then there is no mountain, then there is.' First we have a dream and we see the mountain in the dream as a perfect picture. We think we understand the mountain; and know it. We move to the mountains and it's not all it's cracked up to be. Well, it's Ok, but a lot is so different from the picture we had. It can be pretty, but then the wind comes up and the storm and the heat and the dryness and the climb up and it's a lot to deal with. We want to give up on the dream. We no longer see the mountain, for we cannot see unless we are far off. We don't understand it as we once thought we did! Reality has been a pin in our balloon. We ask 'Why?' But in time we experience the mountain differently than in the dream. It isn't perfect in the same way it was. We survived it's storms, it's harsh changes, the climb and the muddy roads and flash floods; but we have seen awesome beauty beyond any picture. We smelled smells, done things, been places, and our heart is filled. Once again we see the mountain... and it is perfect. It has all come full circle. Being on the mountain, too close to see it, we are part of the mountain. It has come back to us in a new and better way.

I feel sorry for the rest of the world that wakes up to an alarm clock, gets time off only on weekends, and only two weeks a year vacation. Every life has a price and a reward. We weigh what we get against what it cost. Almost everyone enjoys the wilderness on a sunny day—a good day swimming and good walk, a good fishing hole in perfect weather. But the question becomes, "How much do you like it and what will you pay?" Do we like it enough to be out in the rain fishing? Will we fish when we are cold? Will we accept being poor? Almost everyone likes the city when there is money and a museum or a play or concert. We all love a nice place to eat. Who wouldn't like that? But when it's time to pay for all this, and it requires a job, with bills, and credit, and debt—how much fun is it then? The bottom line? If you really enjoy the rewards—concerts, the library, the meals, picture windows, lack of dirt—then the bills seem worth it. And if you love the sun in the leaves and the sound of a trumpeter swan then you seek it out and pay the price... **because it's worth it**.

After I write, I keep thinking of this common question. I realize I ramble in my letter beyond what this woman wants or needs to hear. I realize this question is a sore spot, now a button. Why? To me it is like asking, why eat food? Why not just take the nutrients in directly, with pills or intravenously? And we say, 'Well, chewing is so fun, it taste so good, is such a pleasure in life. It is hard to imagine what life would be like without eating!" *It's absurd to take nutrients through a needle!*

Most people would think. It is the horror story of all horror stories.... it seems odd anyone would even ask why! If anyone would reply: 'Well by eating food direct, you risk taking in germs. Through food comes dirt; disease. Is it fun to get botulism, worms, even the flu? You can die by eating food! You avoid all that 'risk' by taking it in purified pill form!' We might well open our mouth to reply—but say—what? Obviously such a person is never going to understand. So 'Yes', when you go out on the river ice, you risk falling through. When you go out in the wilderness, you risk being eaten by a bear. When you go explore anything, you risk getting lost, etc. etc. But those who do it, find more reward in it than hardship. I could have gone out with an experienced person? Why would an experienced person want me along? I have no money, no skills. I was in the beginning, not strong. I was a soft city kid. I had nothing to offer. I couldn't do the grunt work. I couldn't offer money and I couldn't offer advice. I would have been little to no help--just a burden. Then, how would I recognize a skilled person? It was three to four years before I met another trapper. I didn't know where to find them. I didn't know how to find them. Any more than a tourist could find a real trapper. Wilderness people don't hang out where tourists go. I met a person or two at the Salvation Army who suggested we partner up together. Alcoholic old timer losers who basically wanted to sponge off me and had nothing in return to offer. I recognized this at least. There had been a couple of offers.

"Miles, you buy the traps and food and cut the firewood. Come with me to my trapline! Catch the fur and skin it. I'll help you sell it, and we split the profits 50/50! What do you say?" Burp. Blurry eyed, weaving on feet silence, waiting for my answer. Most real trappers thought I was a fool. No serious outdoor person would have anything to do with me. I was a starry eyed sensitive artist who would have said, 'Gosh, golly are you a for real trapper?' A real trapper would have said, 'Go away—you're bothering me, kid! Ha, ha!' It did not help that I have a limitless ego. Selective memory. I would have implied we are equals. *I'm so sure I know as much as you do!* In truth when I myself meet such personalities I only smile and reply 'Have at it, enjoy your life!' The best thing for such people is to go for it! Figure it out on your own. Is this a fault in someone. If so, who enjoys having faults pointed out? Especially coming from the opposite sex when contemplating romance! There is a chi on my shoulder I am only vaguely aware of, that my Conscience understands better than I do. My own parents ask why. My own parents think I am retarded, and do not support me. *If you cannot trust your parents, who can you ever trust in life?*

My first real advice by descent folks was, 'Why don't you stop talking about it— and go out and just do it, kid?' I was hanging around street people. I had no money; was dressed in rags. I was around people doing drug, saying 'Far out man-- lets go escape in the toolies!' I was saying to them, "But I mean it—I'm really going to do it!" and they all said 'Right on! Me too!' Not one of them ever did... and of the few of the gang I hung with who did, most died—or came close, and quit. One couple froze their feet trying to walk into a village. None of them had any more of a clue where real trappers and mountain men were than I did. Most wouldn't admit they were that stupid or naive. I admit it because I wasn't the only one who couldn't figure it out. How could I even get to a real Indian village? I didn't have the skill or the money! There are no roads going to them. Flying in cost as much as flying to the lower 48 states, (a week's wages) and the villages have no hotel or place for visitors. You have to know someone—be invited, or have lots of money. You don't just show up in a village and say, "Hi I'm looking for a place to stay and eat..." The response is 'And who the F.. are you?' If you look stupid and dressed in rags, you may end up either turned in to the law, or ripped off by the locals (and that's pretty much how it went at first).

Why? You ask. I wish to experience life—all it has to offer. The reason I stay is not the reason I went out in the first place. I was seeking one thing, and found something else. Like in the Wizard of Oz. Getting sent out on these impossible missions by some yahoo God figure - myths I read about, people defined as Mountain Men. The Lion finds courage, the Scarecrow finds a brain, Dorothy finds home, the Tin Man finds a heart. They had it all along, inside them, but it took an ordeal to have it show, to see it and believe it. It had to be tested. And even the Wizard felt he was just a humbug from Kansas. But he inspired the rest, and he built Oz from the wreckage of his air balloon crash.

The pilot who rescued me flying the jet looked me up, wants to meet me, shake my hand. He thought it was a miracle, and I was blessed. I should have died. Far from thinking I was careless and had a low Jesus factor. He thought God watched over me. The people who took my supplies assumed I would die. I should have. No one would have thought some city slicker tourist outsider could find his way out of this one alive. They thought I would give up and cry. Scream, and run till I froze to death. Curl up in my cabin till I ran out of food and was found frozen in the spring, another idiot hippy freak bites the snow. But I showed them all what I was made of.

"Behold! And remember my name! For you shall hear from me again!" Aside from my words. What do I want out of life? I carved my way here with a knife. I built cabins with nothing but a $100 worth of used hand tools. I didn't read about it from a book. I lived it. It did not have to be this way? I do not know how else it could have been. It if were easy, there would be no more wilderness, everyone would be there. It was not life threatening forever. It was like a movie or a book, only instead of just my eyes I smelled it; heard it. I felt it in my heart. It is the difference between seeing a picture of a good meal, and actually eating a good meal.

To ask "why" is pretty scary Bobbie.
Sunshine, Wild Miles

"There seems little use explaining at such length the 'why' of our life to anyone. Maybe it is more to get a better grasp on ourself. Sort of like if anyone asks why anyone would find interest in swinging a stick at a ball, they will never give their life to baseball."

This year, I am lucky, and have to spend only a couple of weeks in Fairbanks. The wood boat is loaded, and ready to head out. Gas can be pumped in the boat at Pikes Landing. The new merc fifty is nice! I load 150 gallons of gas on board along with sled dogs and supplies.

The boat will not get on step, but think after I burn off twenty gallons or so she will climb up. The dogs are excited to be on the river again. The water changes color where the Chena River dumps into the more silty Tanana. We turn downstream sharply here. There are a few scattered houses and boat landings, but within a few miles the river looks like wilderness. Nenana will be the next village, and next road we see seventy miles downriver. I am not sure if I will stop there or not, but might need gas.

"Kenai!" I call sharp to my lead dog. He looks up at me. I point to Whitie, who is not the sharpest tack in the box. Whitie is leaning too far over the side and causing the boat to lean. He might fall in the river. Kenai looks and growls at Whitie, who pulls his head back in, along with his front paws. More and more I depend on Kenai to be my second in command. I tell Kenai there is a problem, and he straightens it out. Somehow he chose the roll himself and likes it. Now and then Kenai looks at me if he thinks there is some issue to deal with. I usually shake my head no and he leaves it alone. Kenai responds best to hand signals and facial expressions; visual more than hearing. I find that interesting.

This is the month of June. The weather is nice and warm. Eventually the boat climbs on step as fuel is burned off. We double our speed. Nenana is reached in a few hours. No gas is needed, but I stop to take a break. The Nenana River looks inviting, because there is more of an out of the way boat landings here than on the main Tanana River, maybe used more by the locals. The dogs are unleashed and tied out so they can get a brief break from the boat and do their business.

"Hey, where you from?" a voice out of the woods addresses me. The face looks friendly enough. A native man built like me somewhat, short, but more wiry. I explain my trip. He tells me who he is. "I'm Josh, I keep my sled dogs here and just wondered who was around, want to make sure my dogs are safe. These are valuable race dogs you know!" I wouldn't have a clue, and had to take his word for it. Josh rambles along. "Yeah, this reminds me of the Hansen brothers. One brother, Einer used to boat here and tie up his sled dogs, right here where you are tying yours. I used to watch the dogs for him while he went to Fairbanks for supplies."

This talk brings home the old life even more. The connection to the past and the Hansen brothers is here. Josh was just a young lad back then. Josh shows me his sled dogs tied up not far away. He gets water for them from the river and cooks right here in a big cooker. A fish rack on the island across the river has a few early salmon drying—though they might be last years fish still there.

Josh looks at my sled dogs, "This one, Kenai, is loyal maybe, but not built right for long distance. See how his pastures break line? See how his wrists are not round? See the height in the hind end? You want front end strength, deep chest, no sag across the back like here. Look at this dog. See the difference? This is how a sled dog should look!"

I do not see the difference; do not have a clue what this guy is talking about. He seems to enjoy talking about sled dogs. Maybe I can see what he is talking about if I study on it. Josh and I chat a while, till it is time for me to be on my way again. The dogs have had their break.

We are off and headed out on the main river again. I tell the dogs, "Next stop Minto!" this is the old village with no road going to it. There are local natives here who fish and live in the old ways. There may be only five to six people there now. Thirty miles to Minto.

A heavy elder Athabascan greets me, at a fish camp not far from Nenana. "Edmond Lord!" Hand out. He's got a loud voice, and speaks of many disassociated things. He ends the greeting with, "And let me give you some advice. If you ever have to kill anyone, be sure you slit their belly before dumping them in the river!"

What an odd bit of advice. But the man seems sincere, and ready to embrace a stranger, so I reply, "I'll remember that, thanks!" I do not take him seriously and find out later Edmond calls himself, "The Lord," loves to tell tales, shock and impress people with behavior and goofy stuff. Underneath all that he is a fantastic hunter and outdoorsman, and a hard worker who is well respected in the area. Rumor was to watch yourself on any business dealings though, and he's not quite legal and by the book, but very likeable. I meet him off and on over the next twenty-five years.

In about two hours I'm at Minto. There is no stopping here. No one is seen out and about. All looks deserted, with no boats tied up. "Next stop, Tolovana Road House!" This is an abandoned roadhouse from the mail hauling days. The roof has fallen in, and the floor has been flooded by the river over the years. Yet it is a building and landmark. In an emergency someone could sleep in here out of the weather, if one could find a part of the roof still intact. There will be no more roads the rest of the trip, Nenana was the end of the road system.

Camp is made at the mouth of the Kantishna River in the dark. We have traveled about eighty miles today. We have about 120 more river miles to go to get home.

"Hey, guys! You notice we did not pass one boat the whole trip? Is this awesome country or what!" The dogs wag their tails. Actually we are not headed all the way home. The area open for homesteading, that I have a staking packet for, begins about twenty miles upriver, and goes for about ten miles. My interest is on the furthest upstream end closest to my Hansen area. "This is not really homestead land as such. The packet calls this remote homesite land." I am aware of this, but it all seems under that simple heading easy to understand called 'homestead.'

'This looks like the first spot we want to check out. See, this island has changed shape, but is the one to go behind to find the creek.' I agree this looks like the place on the map, even though it has changed shape. When the boat gets up a little ways behind the island, and just out of site of the main river, a pond becomes visible with a short boat-wide creek going into it. The creek is only sixty feet long. The pond seems deep, clear, and about an acre. Sedge grass is at the edge, and it looks like fish hang out here. At the opposite side from the creek is a beaver damn about 100 ft long and six ft tall. The dam has a flat dry top. The map does not show any of this. It is easy to see looking at the map, that the actual terrain that was once a mud depression got washed out and became a pond. Beaver altered the lay of the land by blocking the creek and turning it into a long lake instead. The rest of the area should be the same as on the map.

This is the situation I had hoped for, though I had ideas maybe I could get the houseboat into this creek-lake and on further. The dogs are tied up. A tent camp set up on top of the beaver dam. A hike is made along the shore of this long lake to check out what is ahead around the bend. This looks like a safe place against storms and floods. All my expectations are met. Probably somewhere on this long lake I will stake my land.

The spot where I turn behind the island is marked so I know where to turn off coming down from Hansen. The canoe will come in handy here to check out this lake. I can easily drag it over this beaver dam.

After a long day of nice river travel without incident, the dogs and I arrive 100 miles further upstream at our Hansen camp. Everything is as we left it. Dogs and I are glad to be home. Except now our home is changing again. There are issues to consider when contemplating the move, and when to make it. I consider the likelihood of being able to get the fish I need for the sled dogs at this new location. The main river would have to be fished, and I have never done this. When would the fish run? There is probably no one to ask, as no one fishes this river. Is there a trail to Nenana or Manley from this place? How many others might stake land and be here. Will any homesteaders be trappers and will this area get crowded? Pete had told me the Division of Lands has offered 144 staking packets. It is hard to know how many of these will result in people staying. Even half this many would be a drastic impact, and big change on the country. Am I better off further upstream on my own, with lots of room, outfitting from Minchumina? Surely a lot of questions, and some with no answers till time passes, and we see.

It is decided though, that this is an ok time to make the move and settle in with the houseboat on the pond off the river, and get ready for winter, expecting to live on the boat. It is too early to harvest any berries. There has been no garden this year. There are fish getting caught to feed sled dogs, but only a week's worth is dried. "We better start catching fish in the main river when we get there! I don't think that long lake has fish, as it is blocked off, and we saw no sign of fish."

Looking at the map, the lakes out back look like shallow swamp lakes we see on the trapline, unable to support fish. "At least we have fish to get there, even stay a little while. If we cannot get fish, we cannot afford a trip to town for commercial feed." I dare not contemplate the results of this. There is no communication here. No radio, nor CB, no one who knows where I am, or who will check or deliver a message. No one goes up and down this river I have seen. We are totally dependent on what the river can provide. This requires a level of trust, or belief, or strength from within. With a big grin I head down the river toward a new adventure.

EVERYTHING I OWN IS with me. Only a few supplies are left at Hansen for when I get here with the trapline cut from the lower end, the new homestead area. This might take a few years. There are four boats with me, all tied together. The houseboat, the twenty-four ft. wood river boat, the sixteen ft. run about, and the canoe. *This is a regular flotilla!* All powered by the new fifty horse merc outboard set up on the twenty-four ft. riverboat. The sled dogs are in the sixteen ft. boat tied on one side, so I can keep an eye on them and reach them if one does something stupid. Sled dogs can be much like children.

I kill two Canada geese with one shot. The sand bar backdrop is the color of coffee with cream. Driftwood roots reach to the sky like hostage arms in robbery. Instead of 'Your money or your life!' I arrive through the star gate of time blasting the shotgun. Peace and quiet is turned to chaos in a flip of a page in time. Whump! Goes the shotgun, arf, arf, arf and woof go all seven sled dogs! Honk, honk, honk go all the geese that get away. Two geese go flap, flap and splash, into the gurgling river ahead of us. But one has a broken wing and makes it to shore with a mad dash to the woods. The sled dogs go nuts. My trusted Kenai is turned loose. He dives in the river, swims to the sandbar, and tracks down the goose in the thicket. With cheers from all of us. Kenai does not know if he should jump back in the river and try to swim to us with the goose, or wait there. He has killed the goose and holds it gently.

'Wait there, Kenai—stay." He knows what that means, and sees me slow, reverse, and gently swing all four boats to the sandbar. Kenai will not wait till I am completely ashore. He jumps in the water, swimming to the side of the house. I have to grab him by the scruff of the neck and drag a soaking wet smelly sled dog over the sky blue gunnels. No use reprimanding him.

"Good boy, Kenai, now drop the goose, and please, shake your fur someplace else!" But no. I am soaking wet. Two geese to cook up, though. We stop long enough to clean them. They get put in the wood stove oven on the houseboat. While they cook, I continue on down the river, wood smoke gently floating in the breeze with the smell of poplar wood, and forever sound of fifty horses turning a propeller at 4,000 revolutions a minute. It takes two days to get to the homestead area I selected. I do miss my inboard 'cat' engine and that low rpm 'thugga, thugga' sound. The love of my life and I are now divorced. "Forever is not forever," as my very first girl-friend told me when I was fourteen. *"However in this case, 'till death do us part,' was the reason my cat engine and I are no longer together!"*

The canvas tent is set up at the site where I want to build. I chose this spot because the morning light came in like a spotlight exactly here, lighting up a lovely raspberry patch. Nearby is a dry flat grass spot. Surrounding me is a birch tree grove. This seems a correct distance from the main river. Far enough to not hear boats, close enough to easily canoe. There is a wide spot in the creek, with a good view over water to spot game on.

The canoe is used to ferry supplies over the beaver damn from the houseboat to the land along the long pond I have marked. The tent will only keep the rain off the goods, but not protect anything from bears or mice. There is a flat spot in a grass opening I think will work well for the log cabin. I had noted on the previous trip, there are lots of cabin size trees up and down the creek that can be floated to the site using the canoe. Looking up, the birch leaves are as musical notes, with the bright sun, the space between the lines on the music sheet. Looking down, red ripe rasp-berries in a fertile soil of tall dry grass.

The area on the ground is cleared of brush. It looks to me like there might be permafrost here, but am unsure. It's marginal. I hit ice when I dig down, but it could just be seasonal frost. There are no poplar trees that indicate lack of permafrost (they need a long taproot). The tall grass indicates no permafrost, yet the moss and scrub spruce within twenty ft. are indicators of permafrost. The assumption is there is permafrost. With this decision made, I will build right on the ice, leaving the natural moss as insulation, and maybe adding more moss to it.

I write my thoughts to Palace, a woman I have been writing off and on for a whole year now from my Mother Earth ad. I've been depressed about the Sue rela-tionship, and guess she and I will not be seeing each other anymore.

Dear Palace,

You would like this spot I picked since you enjoy the pictures I send, and I have heard descriptions of what you like. There are raspberries off to the side. Swans nest nearby, and seem to fly over at the same time twice a day, trumpeting. The morning sun flits in through birch and spruce trees into a sunny clearing where tall dry grass grows. There is a beaver house on the property, with beaver all over. They created this mile long creek, twisting with no current through the forest. At one end is a pond to keep the houseboat out of the weather. Fish jump in the pond being fed by the main Kantishna River. At the other end of the creek is a huge lake in the shape of a horseshoe with another huge lake connected to it by a mile long slough. The only access to these lakes is up this creek I'm on, protected from human traffic by a beaver damn that has to be portaged over. Few travelers will have a canoe with them. I am sure no other homesteaders will come into this area.

These lakes have shorelines that could not be run in a day, and are filled with every kind of game. I see beaver, mink, otter, wolf, lynx, ducks, birds of all kinds, as well as moose. I do not know yet if there are fish.I think not, as there is no good connection to the river, and the lakes are shallow, but at least there are plenty of fish on the main river. There is field of mint, so there is mint to dry for tea.

Today I started the cabin. I decided to build right on the ground. Cabins were built like this for many years in the old days. Now modern man suggests setting pilings and building up off the ground. This may work, but I think setting pilings on or in the ice is not as stable as setting the cabin right on the ground and try to insulate so the ground can remain frozen. I do not know the size of the cabin. I cut the first tree, then cut it to the length I can lift. I used a string to mark its length so I can cut the other logs the same unknown length. Looks to be about eighteen feet.

I have a chainsaw and draw knife to peel the bark off the logs. There was a hand auger at a garage sale, made to cut a 2 inch hole through two logs. This was designed to pin logs together with pegs made locally. I have one window, a piece of plywood to make a door, and some hinges. This is all I have for tools. I think my total expenses were about $100 – including the used chainsaw. It is a good feeling to contemplate my own piece of land and cabin, built myself, with such little cost.

I have sled dogs to feed each day. This means checking fish nets, but I am getting enough fish to feed them at least, and everything is going well with the dogs. I'll add on to this letter later. I know it might be a month of more before I get to the post office again.

Sunshine, Miles

As I end my letter for the day I think about Palace. She had not seemed interesting at first. I had been trying to work things out with Sue. Palace is only eighteen, and does not seem very 'stable' in terms of knowing much about life, or what she wants. Even so, she is pretty, and somewhat in awe of my life, fascinated by the lifestyle. It is hard to know if she'd adjust and settle in or not. I could more realistically consider a long term relationship if I had land and a home. Palace hints she might be interested in coming up to join me, to see if we can work out a relationship. She's from Georgia so does not know very much about the cold. We have been writing off and on as friends; pen pals.

Many letters and wilderness thoughts I hear expressed in letters seem to be based on the writings of Thoreau, 'Walden Pond.' Many Thoreau fans do not realize the man lived only a few miles from his mother, near a railroad. His mother brought him muffins, knit his socks, while he was writing. Though it is romantic, and good writing, it is hard to feel such writings are influenced by an experience called, 'the wilderness.' Believing life with me would be like a life with Thoreau is not a good comparison. I'm told Waldon Pond is most popular among spoiled romantic teens, who dream of life away from home, yet not grasping that reality, or pretending not to be dependent, while living off the parents.

Cutting trees, trimming them, peeling them, as well as doing all the chores has me wore out, or maybe not wore out, but totally fulfilled. There is little time to think about much. The bugs are out, but this is simply a normal part of life. It is good to have the houseboat to live in as I build a cabin. I can cook, rest, get out of the bugs, keep warm, sleep well, have things protected from bears, and weather, and have a sense of a home as I work. I have built cabins in the past with no place to live, as I build in the bugs and rain, cooking in the open, sleeping in the rain. It might sound romantic, but it is nice to have the houseboat. I also think I will not get this cabin done in time to move in for winter. This would normally mean being unable to use this winter to 'prove up,' on the homestead. It is a legal requirement to get the land, this 'proving up' thing. There has to be proof you are on the land for a specific length of time. In this case, three years, maybe five years, depending on how much work you do, for there is also a stipulation to make improvements on the land. This can be a bridge across a creek, clearing land for a garden, a farm, like that. There might be a time discount for being a veteran.

Because I have the houseboat, I can stay here through the winter as part of my prove up time. This is also good because I do not have to move to civilization for a job, can trap, and live the subsistence lifestyle I love. There is less pressure to get the cabin done. I can take my time to do it right without time worries. It would not be the end of the world if it took even two years to build.

Moss is gathered in plastic fifty gallon bags, to use to stuff between the logs. This is a break from the log peeling and tree cutting. On a good perfect day I can get a round of logs up, but have only done this one time. I tend to pretend I can average this in the great optimism of youth. Actually I am lucky to average just one log a day. It takes time to lay out the stringer logs to support a floor. Poles are cut to lay across the stringers as a flooring, even though I know one day I will replace it with plywood. I can't afford the plywood just yet.

A trip is made for mail to Manley Hot Springs with the riverboat and fifty horse. I have not been to town in two months. The trip only takes four hours. I have dinner at the roadhouse as I read my mail. The roadhouse has not changed in twenty years. There is the usual wood stove, couch, books to read, and locals hanging out. It is a common scene for people like myself to come in out of the woods to do laundry, hang out at the Roadhouse with mail piled around, and new bought items being organized and packed as I eat and relax. One of my letters is from Palace. Joe has come in and sits by me visiting, asking how my life is going. We had been closer friends at one time when I lived on my houseboat here on the Manley slough, but that seemed a long time ago to me. I really wanted to be alone to read my mail. I need to return soon, since I left the sled dogs at the homestead alone. The sled dogs eat once a day, and feeding them one day then returning the next day to feed them is not hard on them. But still, this does not leave me a lot of time. Van and Dem have already invited me to spend the night at their place, just a block for the roadhouse. I have fond memories of Dem, the school teacher, and her husband, Van, who has an airplane and flew me to the Brooks Mountain Range to watch his sled dogs, and gave me Kenai, my best sled dog.

"Ya, Joe, this is a gal I have been writing for a while as a friend. Suddenly it looks like this might get serious. We met through that Mother Earth Magazine ad where I was looking for companionship in a life on the houseboat. I told you before, I got hundreds of letters. Not much really came of it in the big picture, but Palace is one I've kept in touch with."

"You know what your problem is, Miles? You are such a bullshitter and people figure you out and loose interest. You can run a good con on people that gets them interested though, got to hand that to you. But I bet you do not have a clue what this girl needs, and are not that good at handling women. You get her here, and I'll show her what she needs."

This is somewhat funny, and normally I might crack a joke about his own history with women, as if he knew any more than I do. But in truth, I am a bit irritated today—or more, I just do not care for Joe and his outlook on life. Van just told me how Joe scared Dem, hinted she might get rapped while Van is gone. Joe scared her so much Van had to come home for a while. Joe jokes around and talks like a simple subsistence person with a straight forward honest outlook (even if a bit harsh). I see it as more of a sociopath hidden behind the jokes. I do not dislike him enough to actually run him off, however. I recall another subject to ask Joe about. I want to change the subject away from Palace anyhow. "Hey, Joe. I almost forgot. What's this I hear about you badmouthing me for leaving junk behind when I left Manley? I thought we had an agreement you would clean up what you did not want, in return for the good stuff I left for you!"

"That got exaggerated, Miles, you know how people are. I made one statement to Daisy. You know how she can be!"

Daisy was the one who had threatened to shoot me if I ran my new snow machine past her cabin on the slough. So yes, I know what Joe means. "Anyhow, Miles, you told me there would be lots of good stuff, but most of it was junk, wet and ruined. There was a lot more garbage than you told me there would be!" I sigh. He is partly right. When I had left my winter spot on the slough, there had been unexpected flood waters at ice break up which had got many of my things wet. There was little dry ground to set anything out in a nice pile. Much of my belongings had still been under water when I left. I therefore did not know what it would look like when the water dropped. I had been excited to get going, and not paying enough attention to how it looked when I left. I did feel however, a real friend would have seen this situation, forgiven it, and cleaned it up, kept the problem between the two of us, maybe asked for a favor or compensation in return. I'd make up for it somehow. I at least like to think this is how I would have handled it. Still, Joe is partly correct, and that is one of the issues with Joe, he has a good point often times, it's just that his point is so often ugly. I have never heard a good positive rewarding 'truth' come from him. I have never heard him give a compliment or thanks.

"Ok, Joe. I did leave more junk behind than I expected to. You are right about that, it's just that by the time Daisy repeated it around town, my name was mud, and there was a lot of hard feeling I think, that was just not necessary."

"Oh, forget it, Miles, no one remembers anymore! It's just yesterday's news and needs to be forgotten." So Joe fills me in on what he has been up to. It sounds familiar as a lifestyle, and to tell the truth, there are just not a lot of people around who understand, know what it means to run out of food, to fall through the ice, to have sled dogs quit on you, and such matters Joe and I have in common. I tell Joe a little of my adventures since I was last in Manley. Joe tells me he has things to do and takes off. I get back to reading my mail. The first is from Palace.

Hello Dear Miles,

I have made up my mind and have saved my money to come try life out with you. You told me if it does not work out you would pay my way back home, which I appreciate, as I do not have enough for a round trip. I will not bring much with me as I know space is cramped and most of what I have will not be of much use in this new life. Give me a call when you come in for your mail and I will come join you.

Love, Palace

I am so busy working on the new cabin I am unsure if this is a good time or way to introduce a woman to the great life I live, 'but.' But it has been six months or so since I heard from Sue, and over a year since we have got along, so companionship has a strong pull. I call Palace. She will be here is two weeks. I am to pick her up in

Fairbanks. *Dang, just when I thought I had life figured out, here comes a major change. Perhaps a good one!*

The sled dogs are fine when I get home. I get ahead a little on the fish numbers. There are enough fish to dry some for the future. This means stopping cabin building long enough to go build a fish drying rack and cutting table on a sandbar out on the river. This attracts the local bears. I know soon enough there will be bear issues. I'm only five rounds up with the cabin, maybe waist high when it is time to go pick up Palace.

Summer is half over. I have concerns with Palace, thinking it might be nice to have the new cabin to move into for winter. If we get along that is. I boat all the way to Nenana. This is an eight hour trip. I have the sled dogs with me. Josh says he can watch the sled dogs a day or two. I met him before and now understand he is a Native who won the Iditarod 1,000 mile race. His passion is taking care of dogs. I get a ride to Fairbanks, and have allowed an extra day of time in case I got held up.

There is time to drop off art at the Alaska House, stop at Alaskaland to visit the Underhills, and see Crafty at his Craft store. Crafty will let me stay at his place with Palace. Saying, "Sure, Miles I have room, and we can work out a trade for art. There is an extra room upstairs. I'll give you a ride to the airport, since it sounds like she is arriving after my shop closes." It would be nice to pick her up by myself so I can check her out and get to know her a little first before introducing her around, but I do not drive. This help from Crafty will work out.

PALACE IS a bit freaked out when she gets off the plane, but it is good to meet each other. I reassure her everything will be fine. Her eyes are big and round in shock though. Crafty brings us to his craft shop. Already Palace thinks this arrangement is a bit unconventional. The room at the Craft shop is stacked with postcards and old furniture.

"Well Palace, this is not where home is, and this is not the world we are living in so much. We will be out in the wilderness soon, in our own element!" She is full of trust, and wants to believe me. Crafty will drive us to Nenana the next day. I trade him a pile of art for the rides and a place to stay.

Palace and I have been writing off and on for three years. She knows more about me then I do about her, as I tend to write more. After chatting most of the night, I know a lot more. She has been living at home and unhappy. She is anxious to get into a new life. She has been a bit rebellious, and got herself into odd situations that upsets her family. One story of her life I did not grasp all the details of, had to do with having a black boyfriend and having neighbors burning a cross on her parents lawn. I'm being open minded and just taking it all in. She is short, long black hair, slim, nice looking. She prefers to wear jeans, and looks like she might handle the physical life we will have.

Crafty drives us to Nenana. We load the sled dogs in the boat.

"Will the dogs behave?" I am unsure what the question means. *Behave in what way?* I do not know if she thinks the dogs are dangerous and might bite, or if they might jump out of the boat and cause a problem, or will they bark and make lots of noise, or fight with each other.

"Palace, I have traveled a lot of miles with these dogs. We get where we are headed without much fuss. I guess that means they are well behaved." She is curious about the boat, the dogs, and the lifestyle. I am busy answering questions as I load supplies. The question about the dogs would be similar to a civilized person getting asked, "Will the car be all right?" Palace is already 'freaked out' just by the huge change seeing Fairbanks. That in itself seems to be a huge adjustment. "Yes, Palace, we might see a moose."

"Miles, I notice you are not using zip lock bags to put everything in. I have been camping a lot, and learned zip lock bags keep things clean and dry. I always have a Coleman stove with me too, so we can cook and eat along the way."

"Yes, Palace, this is good for camping trips all right. Homesteading and a subsistence life is a little different. When one camps, money and time are not big factors, pleasure is. As a lifestyle, we think more about time, money, and dependability. We have a lot of supplies to haul, and always will. It is tough to get enough zip lock bags, afford them, have them hold up. It works to just make a pile of goods and use a tarp over the pile in case it rains. If we need to stop and cook, we can use an open fire, which is dependable. Weight is a major factor in the big picture. It cost about $1 a pound to haul freight home. Perhaps one stove would not in itself be a big deal. Yet at five pounds with fuel that is five dollars a trip. There are other things one might take camping that might make life nicer, like an ice chest with ice, paper plates, a tent, and a blow up mattresses. If we add it all up we could have a boat load before we even think of supplies." I go on to say after a pause, since she is being so silent, "I have a friend on the river, a native guy, who travels long distances. All I see in his boat see is an ax. I assume he has a knife and matches. This is his life out on the river, and he has done it all his, life, is a respected man who does not seem to get himself into trouble much. He utilizes the land, which gives him most of what he needs."

When I write people about my life and answer questions like this, I could get a respectful starry eyed reply of, "Yes, that makes so much sense now that you said it." Yet I see from the expression on this woman's face, doubt creeping in. She is used to being at home in Georgia by the fire, with hot cocoa in hand reading about my adventures. She looks into a dirty boat smelling like fish slime, seeing an inch of river silt in the bottom, seeing bags of precious food being unceremoniously loaded willy-nilly in the bilges. For sure there will be dog hairs in everything. If we stop to eat, it might be a fish we catch on the end of a stick over an open fire. Romantic as perceived from a home in civilization, but in reality smoke in the face, either under cooked or over cooked food, no spices, no fork, no salad to go with it, no place to set it on, and it probably has spruce needles stuck in it, and river silt blown on it for good measure. This woman has enough imagination to picture a glimpse of this.

"Anything wrong?" She sighs and is ready to go along with the program 'sort of' but ready to say, "I told you so!" at the first problem. I'm in hopes she sees the light. Sees the wild moose and not the flies and moose poop. I can compromise. If she really desires a Coleman stove in the boat, I can provide this. Palace is not pleased with the seating arrangements. I can tell. There is a, 'You expect me to sit here next to the dogs?' look about her. She expected a camping chair or something, not this 100 pound bag of rice to sit on. She may not have expected an open boat either, but some sort of canopy to block the wind and river silt blowing in the air. I have got so used to all this I tend to forget what life is like any other way. She does not complain, but neither is there a big happy content smile on her face. I assume she'll see how it is and settle in. Would I be better off looking for a farm girl who has been poor? A local Indian girl? My desire is someone raised a little like me, with similar background, who came to the same conclusions I did. Only a woman.

We get out on the river and she seems to enjoy the scenery. At first anyway. "Miles, where is all the game?"

"Well, it is a bit windy today, not the best day for game to be out. Moose and bears get hunted so they smarten up, and tend not to show themselves. Those that do, get shot. They are around, just not showing themselves right now." She seems dubious. I interrupt shortly with a glad, "Look, Palace, a pair of swans flying right over us trumpeting!" This would make most homesteaders smile with love of life, richness of appreciation. These majestic birds are rare worldwide. Few humans are privileged enough to ever see and hear a trumpeter swan.

I suspected I was in trouble, when Palace is not impressed, and does not smile. She replies, "I spent time in Florida. Everywhere you look there is wild life, the sound of birds, and in every direction at any given time something to see, deer, egrets, herons, alligators and game of all sorts."

Put in that perspective, what can I say? I never thought of it quite like that before. There is however no free land in Florida, and no river 300 miles long with no one living on it but us. I personally do not care what Florida has to offer. I'm home, and this is what I have. A pair of Trumpeter swans. I'm silent and in hopes this woman will cheer up. *She may have jet lag still, or is feeling a little homesick at first, with all the new changes.* I'm not going to start an argument, that's for sure.

After four hours of boat running Palace asks, "Where is everyone? How come there are no roads. Are they up in the woods there?" She speaks nervously with big round scared eyes of distrust. She seems to not comprehend what she has been told in the letters.

I happily say, "There are no roads, not in the woods not anywhere. No telephone poles, no footprints, no cabins, no beer cans, just nature all around us!" Again, such words make the women starry eyed when read in a letter in the comforts of home. It does not seem to work in reality however.

Rather than being put at peace, she seems to be even more nervous. The extent of her nervousness shows in her question. "Do you think we should turn back?" I wonder *whatever for*. Forward is home, and all we wrote about. *Back to what?* She is nervous about something. I do not understand what. I've seen it before, however. A fear of the aloneness, loss of strength in numbers, the bond of civilization. She may need human sign around her. She feels safer among people. She is afraid of bears, drowning, and the cold. The more relaxed and at home I got, the more nervous she seems to get. As if I am insane. She says, "What if something happens?"

It would not help to tell the story of how I pulled my own tooth on the trapline. If I feel sick, the first place I want to be is home in the wilderness. At my wilderness home I can sit and wait and have my things around me - food, shelter, herbs, and books on medicine. I feel safe. All I think of in town is that if I get sick, seeing a doctor in a hospital costs about a year's wages per hour. In a single day I'd be broke for the rest of my life paying off the visit. I'd rather be dead. In truth I get better at home, always have.

But she meant something else. "Miles, what if you get mad or for some reason you do not bring me back to civilization. Who would even know?"

I'm just not that kind of person. It's something to decide before going out with someone. I can only guess she has had some past experiences of some kind. I am able to talk her into continuing on. But later in the evening after we stop, I come back to the boat after cutting firewood and see the window is broke. I ask what happened, and she does not have a clue. It turned out she had the window open facing in. The hot lantern was too close to the glass. Its heat broke the cold glass. She was too scared to tell me, because I might get upset. She can't afford to get me upset apparently. I hoped the relationship would improve and there would be trust, given time. I was kind about the window, an accident, not a problem. I now suspect she has been with abusive volatile men.

"Miles I don't think you are going to make it in life. You are too nice, people will take advantage of you."

She is worried I might get mad, then disrespectful. I am too nice? We got along sometimes, and have some fun with the canoe and the different chores working on the cabin, and teaching her about various wilderness skills she is excited to learn about. We identified edible mushrooms, medicinal herbs growing wild, and such. I think about what Palace said. About me not being a survivor. I get the impression her idea of a Mountain Man, is someone who is harsh and intimidating, aggressive and such.

One day, a week or so after arriving, we are cutting salmon, and a bear comes along the path towards us. I explain, "Now you know why I insist we carry the rifle everywhere we go." She thought I was just making it up, exaggerating, trying to make her afraid and dependent or whatever. She has refused to carry a gun, or learn about guns. She believes in peace. Explain that to the bear. Sue went through this same exact conversation with me. The bear wants the fish, and acts like we are in the way. The bear is irritated, and wants us to leave. Explain that to the sled dogs. Tell them they do not get to eat because I let a bear eat all the food.

"I'm going to defend the fish, Palace. The safest place for you right now is in the boat. Find the skinning knife and a plastic bag. We'll need it for the liver and heart." Palace is frozen in horror. She is certain I am crazy. She thinks the bear is boss, and if he wants the fish, let him have it! I only say, "Uh huh" as I step forward with the rifle; off safety, talking to the bear in a pleasant voice. I think the bear can under-stand moods and intent, so my mood will come across as I talk. "This is my fish and I plan on keeping it. If you leave, I will not kill you, and we can share the river in peace. There are other fish, other things to eat. It's your choice. If you try to take it from me, I'll be eating you as well." The bear hesitates and studies me. I am not acting aggressive, but talking in a fairly kind voice without fear or hate. Simply stating a fact as I saw it. The bear rears up from thirty feet away. Perhaps to get a better smell and view of the desired fish, or perhaps to intimidate me. I suspected this is the bear who has come around before, and will come around again, looking to get this fish. He is not leaving. Standing up, he offers a perfect heart shot. The 270 rifle is now a rifle I am familiar with. This is an easy shot. I fire and he drops like a rock.

"Palace, did you find the plastic bags?" I hear no reply from the boat, so walk the path and find her crying in the boat. I do not understand women well, and do not know what to do that might comfort her besides give her a hug and tell her we have fresh meat. I suspect she thinks this is a harsh life for her to live. I think town is the harsh life to live. So we are at odds. It all worked out while we had been writing, but somehow reality is not the same as the dream.

"Miles take me back to town. I need to get back to town."

I explain, "I'm not trying to keep you here if you do not want to be here, but this is not a good time to leave. There is a bear to deal with, and it will take a few days to get him canned and taken care of. Also, I am concerned with the weather. It has been raining, especially upriver. The river is rising fast. I think it could flood. Flood time is not a good time to be traveling. It's unsafe. There are logs in the river we might not see and there will be a stronger current with bad undertows. I know you are not used to your life being dependent on the weather, but that is how it is in this lifestyle. The weather can tell us sometimes what to do, where to go, and when." I do not mention the economics. In this lifestyle we do not have lots of money, we are rich in adventures. Trips to civilization cost a month's wages, so need to be planned. Unplanned trips are possible but perhaps one a year, or you become too broke to survive. Or, 'feast and famine.' There are times of the year I have money, and other times to hunker down. This is a hunker down time, with important tasks to get done that affect the whole rest of the year. We do not walk away from all this meat and let it rot for, example.

"Then it is not a life of freedom as you promised. I want to go, and you tell me I am not free to go! If you keep me here you can be arrested you know!" I'm sorry she is thinking this way. I'm not going to say 'arrested by who?' Nor point out there is no one around but us, and never will be. She is still living by civilized rules she understands. *She is pr-chance expecting to dial 911?* If she feels this strongly, then I will take her back, but do not feel good about it; this is a bad time. I am reluctant to waste all that bear meat. If nothing is done with it within hours, it will be full of maggots and no good. I need to at least skin it, gut it and hang it. It's pouring rain.

We head for Manley Hot springs after the rain stops. The river is rising fast. I am concerned about leaving the houseboat in the pond. I have no choice though; we have to take the river boat and cannot take the houseboat. I get Palace to Manley through the flood waters, logs, and strong current. When I get her there with all her belongings, she is unsure what it is she wants to do now. She does not want to return with me, at least not right now. I'm frustrated because I have a life to live. This includes dogs that depend on me, and a home to finish building. I cannot afford idle time off to hang around civilization till Palace is in a better mood. I do tell her she can stay here maybe with friends, and I can come back in a week or so and see what she wants to do then. She acts like this is not the right answer.

I tell her, "I am responsible for you. I said I'd get you back home if things did not work out. I'll give you enough money to get back home and you decide what to do." I assume she will find her way back to civilization on the mail plane, head back where she came from, and I will never see her again. I go check my mail, and take care of a few things while she hangs out in the roadhouse. Maybe if we are apart a short time she can think, regroup, and be able to tell me better what she wishes to do and how I can help. If she stays, but does not want to be with me, I might be able to help her find a place to live, or get her some basic supplies to get started.

The situation between Palace and I is becoming the talk of the small community. The typical comment is a laugh. "Dang, Miles, what were you thinking? The grass is greener on the other side of the fence? You can't bring a greenhorn kid from Georgia and drop her into a situation of subsistence lifestyle and expect it to work! Ha!"

I have little to say. I came up to Alaska at a young age, and went into the wilds cold turkey without even advice or help. Why would I assume everyone is going to freak out? Surely if a personality like mine is created, why couldn't it happen twice? Why wouldn't there be a like-minded female out there someplace? That sounds like a reasonable expectation to me. Not a big deal, anyhow. Someone thinks they will be like me and wants to give it a try and it doesn't work. Ok. No great loss. There are lots of fish is the sea. I just say "next!" Right? It's not that easy of course. The situation is more complicated than this. I also believe in this new concept, of equal rights. *Why should women be treated as a weaker sex? Needing protecting? Why can't women be as tough as men? I say they can! And are!* She may expect me to make her my number one priority. Forget the bear, dogs, fish, and houseboat. Are all women like this? 'Yes, Dear, whatever you wish!' No food, transportation, or home, all neglected as I wait to hear what she wants. *How is that going to work?*

I meet Palace at the roadhouse later in the day. She is in a better mood. She is sitting next to Joe. "Joe has told me he can give me a place to stay, and will help me out. I think I'm going to stay here in Manley." Joe winks at me. I'm thinking that if Palace is attracted to someone like Joe, I can see why she and I would not get along. Joe, who got mad at his sled dogs and shot all seven of them in front of the post office? I had warned Palace about him, even saying he said he wanted to take her away from me. Perhaps I came across as just badmouthing a rival. Maybe I should have just kept it to myself.

Joe says, "You know what your problem is, Miles? You are just such a talker and bullshitter. People can see through that. The great need for attention and being better than everyone else. People feel sorry for you and your insecurity. You get people into trouble with your wild romantic stories. Women do not need that, they want the truth." So Joe is going to give Palace the truth? She seems to trust him.

I'm somewhat bummed that three years of writing is worth about a week, and turns into this situation. I reply, "You might be right, Joe! As long as Palace is being taken care of and is happy, that's the main thing. Guess I'll see you two around then. I've got to get back to the homestead to feed the dogs and get working on the cabin."

They both laugh at me as I leave the roadhouse. I've had a good meal, loaded the boat with gas, a few supplies, and am ready to head back to the Kantishna.

One of the women I meet learning to butcher a bear

CHAPTER FIFTEEN

MAIL ORDER WOMAN COMES AND GOES, HOUSEBOAT SINKS, ALASKALAND, FAIR TIME AND FIRST TIME WITH A BOOTH, ART STORIES, CABIN WALLS UP, MEET KAREN AND TAKE A SLED DOG TRIP

W hen I left the Kantishna River homestead with Palace I had been concerned about the weather. Flood time is not a good time to be gone. This is time to stay around and look after my belongings. There are not a lot of specifics to worry about. One issue can be, like odd weather events and having various repercussions not thought if. Water rising fast, then dropping fast, can wash land into the river, trees to fall, and might affect the pond or the beaver damn in some way, maybe even the houseboat. Palace would not hear of it, and thought this was my usual long winded excuses used to always get my way and be controlling. Like Joe told her about me.

"Miles, you always have an excuse for everything you do. You act like you know everything and have to have your way all the time!"

I think about this as I travel. The trip from Manley Hot Springs to the homestead, about eighty miles, is slower than usual because of the fast current, waves, and logs to dodge. I had lost an engine in weather like this in Galena. The engine had hooked on a log that pulled the engine off the back of the boat. There had been a friend nearby to rescue me. Now there would be no help if I had problems. If my engine quit for any reason I'd be in a bad way as this boat would not float well in the rough water. If this boat got sideways it would roll over. I'm not especially afraid and have been out in conditions like this before, but I'm more alert and going slow.

355

I end up having to spend a night in the woods. *No, I do not have zip lock bags, or a Coleman stove, or a cooler full of ice and goodies.* I build a camp fire to stay warm and cook. I shoot two grouse for dinner. I do have some survival food with me—rice, spices, tea, a candle, matches and a single pot. I cook the rice to go with the grouse using pepper and some wild sage I pick from the rocks. There is one lone wild mushroom spotted, slightly overripe, but will do in a stew. Some cranberries are my salad sauce.

There is no tent, but my sleeping bag is with me. I cut spruce bows for a padding to sleep on. I have bug dope for my face as I sleep. Curled up next to the fire, I am comfortable, happy, at peace. There is enough left over grouse and rice for breakfast in the morning. Tea is made from Labrador leaves growing all around me rather than using the single tea bag I have with me.

I EASE into the pond behind the island where the houseboat is parked. My heart is heavy. The houseboat has sunk. Part of the nose is all that is showing above water. All my supplies in the boat are under water or have floated away. I can see what happened. There had been a crest of high water that washed the nose of the boat up on the cut-bank shore. When the water dropped two feet, the bow did not slide back in the water, but stayed up on that high bank. As the water dropped, the back dropped, but the front did not. The angle was sufficient for water to come into the stern. Somewhat of a freak accident, but preventable. *I had known it was not a good time to leave. Leaving had been to please Palace. I had gone against my better judgment.* Not that I can blame her, as she does not have a clue what happened, or that it would be preventable, and does not understand how in this lifestyle one pays attention to and respects, Mother Nature. If I had refused to take Palace to town 'right now,' she would have wigged out, tried to have me arrested for kidnapping, rape, who knows what-all. Anyhow, no use thinking of that.

I feed the sled dogs, then move into the tent I had set up to keep supplies in. Getting the houseboat off the bottom requires a plan. *'Let's build a tripod over the back.'* Yes this seems the most logical method. I can use a come along winch to lift on the boat. *'But how do we get a purchase on the stern to get a good lift on it?'* My Conscience and I both know we have to get a rope under the boat, and this means swimming under the boat.

The weather is cold and drizzly; not ideal conditions for diving in the pond. In my underwear I stand in the water up to my neck and feel branches and snags under me in the water. I cannot see more than an inch underwater due to the mix of mud, silt, and water.

'Hold your breath, one, two, three!' We dive down and feel along the side of the

boat to determine where it touches the bottom and how to get under it. It takes several attempts to determine where I can get under safely. With rope in my teeth, I dive for the last time, swimming under the houseboat. With relief, I come up on the other side. I know now the hard part is done. The rest will be hard enough, but at least known, and doable. In three days of work I get the gunnels of the boat above the surface of the water. The rope broke once, the winch slipped another time, and the tripod needs bracing more. Once the gunnels are out of the water I can use a bucket and start bailing.

When I can get inside the house, there is the expected mess. Rice floats everywhere, mixed with swollen beans. Books and paper are water soaked. There is not much room on shore that is dry and sunny; the land still flood wet and drizzling rain keeps it damp. The sun eventually comes out. The water drops. The land dries up. Dry grass is laid down and paperwork is laid out. Books get grass between the pages so they will not dry stuck together. Some rice and beans can be re-dried, but mostly it is a loss that needs replacing. More than the direct loss, is the fact that goods cost a dollar a pound to transport here. I am unsure where to get the money to replace the loss. The trip to Manley had been unplanned and unnecessary in terms of needs. Usually each trip is planned and accounted for in the budget. The money given Palace is a loss. Though I realize she spent the money to get here and took a chance as well. *'It's just that 'dang' women sure do cost a lot, sigh.'* Maybe we can't afford one.

😄 :)

The bear meat is being fed to the dogs, so is not a total loss. The dogs do not mind rotten meat full of maggots. *Sinking the bear carcass underwater helps keep the maggots at bay.* The water is much colder than the air, and seems to keep the meat longer. For sure there is less smell! A lot of sighing takes place. I'm way behind now on the cabin work, quality of life in general, and I now need to rethink the whole year.

Eventually the boat dries out and appears to be undamaged. The wood stove on board helps dry it faster. I'm moved back in. All that can be saved has been saved. It is going to be state fair time soon. *'Let's make as much art as we can and get to town for the fair. We can sell the art and replace the supplies we lost.'* I'm not sure what to do about the sled dogs when at the fair, but this is a detail that can be worked out.

Instead of working on the cabin to be ready for winter, I concentrate on doing art work to sell. I'm not terribly unhappy. I'm still in the wilderness, still doing what I love. There are no real setbacks. *'It is the journey, not the attainment that is the secret to happiness!'* My Conscience reminds me. *'Like Jack London. It is not so much the gold, as the looking for it.'* Since much of my art material is lost, I look around at what I can use. Old antler found in the woods is sliced up and used for belt buckles and necklaces. Bones from the bear are cut and used in carved objects. Teeth and claws of all sorts are salvaged from the dog yard as parts they cannot chew. These are strung with beads I also make. Here and there, I use real sinew I salvage from animals to sew and decorate. There are feathers to use, with various things from the land that have a story.

My customers like the hand crafted aspect, done without electricity out in the wilderness, and used to support a simple lifestyle. I'm told there is a sense of peace and harmony in the finished art.

'Peace and harmony! What about that letter we got from the bible thumper filled with judgment about us and our violent lifestyle.' I have to smile and look over my long reply. Often I write thoughts out as much for myself as I do for the one asking the questions.

Dear Stove,

I used to feel guilty about what I'm not good at and let it depress me. I've always been terrible about remembering people's names, keeping appointments, remembering a time line of events, meeting deadlines, returning calls. Such things drive me crazy. Likewise, I seem to require excitement, a challenge, and insurmountable obstacles. Rather than go crazy, it seems better to me to concentrate on what it is I'm good at. Nobody is going to be good at everything, and I figure I'm good at enough things I shouldn't have to feel bad about what I'm not good at!

The Sword—When I was younger I heard the line, 'Those who live by the sword, die by the sword,' and think it's quoted as some bible passage. Certainly the phrase is supposed to help us behave, toe the line, be nice, passive, and content being sheep.

I thought about this line, because a time came that I did 'pick up the sword,' so to speak, when I realized I needed to know more about guns. I faced a life with a lot of violence in it. I wondered then, what is so bad about dying by the sword? There are few pleasant ways to die. Do sheep mostly die in their sleep? Ignorance is bliss. My guess would be, that their life is tolerable, right up until slaughter day. I decided life is special, and when it goes, I think I'd prefer knowing about it, fighting for it. I decided it was the sheep who wrote such a line, not leaders, survivors, warriors, defenders, protectors of the world.

The meek shall inherit the earth comes to mind. I think this is a line spoken to sheep by conquerors. Being strong doesn't have to mean picking up the sword, diplomacy works sometimes, and kindness, forgiveness, understanding, seem to be a good place to start, but given by those who have something to give, spoken from a position of strength, a position respected for what it took to get there.

To 'give' first one must 'have.' To give, first one must be in control of what is up for grabs. To give, first one must 'be', and to be, requires surviving in the first place, and it is not the meek who have the highest survival rate. It is not the meek who have anything to give, and it is not the meek we turn to when we need help. It is not the meek who will ever change anything. The meek are the mat of bodies lying in the mud the conquerors walk on, so they do not get their feet muddy. Such a life in the mud seems a rather pointless waste of life. If meek is the best a person can be, so be it, but me, I have more to give than this. I hope to be cause over events in my life. Sometimes that means living by the sword. The secret to me is to be able to know when it is time to put the sword down, and when to pick it up.

I have heard words about being more humble. We must strive to be as humble as we can. Hmm. This is another word that seems to fit in with being meek and inheriting a dead earth, knowing nothing about swords; spoken to sheep, by those who run things, as a nice way to keep everyone subdued. Something Hitler might have said to the Jews, making it easier to march them passively to gas chambers.

I would guess there is a time to be humble. There is a time for everything, even being nailed to a cross. A time to sow, a time to reap, a time to live, and a time to die, and somewhere in there I assume, 'A time to stand up for what you believe.' I feel that somewhere along the line, someone has been teaching all of us a bunch of crap. It doesn't make sense to me, that the time to be humble would be when you are weak. The time to be humble is when you are in charge, or at least reached some level of maximum efficiency, based on your ability, strength, and intelligence.

There was a time I thought all the bullshit came from stupid or misinformed parents. Then I thought it might well be some 'master plan' concocted by a foreign country, as a way to take us over. Other times I considered it takes place 'within,' information put out to the masses, by those 'who have,' spoken to 'the have nots.' I mean it makes sense. If I was in charge, and had more than the average, and could only keep what I had by keeping the masses at bay, I could only gain more by convincing the masses to serve my purposes. I would teach the masses exactly what I was taught, what our society is being taught.

There is nobility in being humble. To be meek, passive, turn the other cheek. Swords are implements of violence, and violence is a terrible thing, always. I might encourage the masses to eat unhealthy junk food that will keep them alive, but not strong; allow the masses to work, but not revolt. I might encourage drugs, to keep the masses content with their simple lot in life, unaware of the reality of the real world, keep them laughingly happy with a rat race, and collect a tax, a profit off keeping them passive, under control, disorganized, unaware. I might then cure a few as a way to increase profits. I might convince the masses that guns, knives, dangerous chemicals etc. are 'the cause' of all sorts of problems. People who are terrified of guns, who have no knowledge of them, are fairly easy to keep in line.

Behold. I have a sword, and am not ashamed.

My letter ends one of those kinds of moods.
I have a long list of wants that are in civilization. The wooden twenty-four ft.

riverboat along with the houseboat are loaded with sled dogs. I head for Nenana and Fairbanks, several days journey away. It is August. The river level drops a little, as normal for this time of year. *Due to the first freezing in the mountains*. The weather gets clear with blue sky, as is usual and expected this time of year. Early fall smells are special. The sedge grass seems to be among my favorite outdoor smells. Sometimes there are enough rose bushes along the river, that the smell of roses drifts down the river. Other times the smell is of the sappy poplar tree.

We camp along the way. Fish are caught each night for the sled dogs and myself. There is a stop in Nenana, but Josh is busy, and would not be able to watch the dogs. I decide to just bring the dogs on to Fairbanks with me. In Fairbanks, I park at my usual spot, the dock at Alaskaland. There are the familiar woods across the river to tie the sled dogs in. I can live on the boat while in town. It might even be possible to sell my art off the boat, if I wanted to stay a long time. I'd have to promote where I am to get customers. But no, it is better to just go to the fair, see Alaska House, and Crafty. There are also some individual collectors of my art I can look up, with a few more shops to check on. Arctic Travelers and The Paint Pot, as well as Santa Clause House in North Pole Alaska are new places I sell to.

"Hey. Miles, what are you doing in town, must be fair time again?"

"Hello, Bill and Nora, good to see you. Yes, it's fair time. I have my usual art to sell. How has the season gone for you here at the Willow House?" Bill and Nora have been here selling all summer at Alaskaland. They are their usual cheerful selves, filled with optimism and good feeling. We get caught up on the latest in each of our lives. Shifting my ever present blade of grass from one side to the other in my mouth, I decide to take it out and examine it thoughtfully. "Well I better get my show on the road here, things to do and places to go. See you later. I expect to be around a couple of weeks maybe, staying here on the houseboat, so I should be able to see you two again."

"Hey, Crafty! How's the Craft store going for you? Had a good season so far?"

"Yeah, making money. Can't complain. The season is slowing up though. I had a good July, saw some thousand dollar days." Crafty and I chat about people we know, art, the price of supplies, and the ivory market. Crafty wants to see all my latest art, but I hedge, and tell him it's not with me, but on the boat. *It is better to sell my best at higher prices to the galleries before showing it all to Crafty.* Alaska House will pay better, and I can get full retail at the fair. Crafty will be good for unloading volume at discount prices. He might be offended to be told that though. My problem with this whole issue is, Crafty is so good at what he does, that if I even show him all my art he will talk me out of all of it at some bargain price, leaving me thinking I got a good deal, till I go home and count my money and think about it. It can be a good deal in that Crafty will buy a large amount, so I do not have to go look around to sell. Crafty is more an agent, a middle man, a representative. He will take my art to the shops up and down the road and resell most of it. Those shops then resell it to the tourists. He can only make money if he gets it cheap. He only retails some if it in his shop, while the rest is wholesaled .

The atmosphere at the Craft shop is unique. Crafty lives at his shop. His two employees live at the shop. There is a kitchen with only a partial door separating it from the selling area. Crafty's employees and regular customers come on in, step into the kitchen, make a snack, sit at the table and eat, use the phone, talk, and discuss business. Like one big family. Customers get phone messages here. Some customers go in the basement to use the tools or help Crafty with repairs or projects.

Crafty likes to trade, and gets customers to work for him in exchange for materials they need. He'll say something like, "Here help me load the truck, I'm getting ready for the fair. I'll give you some jade bears." Or "Hey, can you watch the shop a minute I have to go to see Tusk about some carvings."

"Miles, can you watch the shop a minute, I need to go see Tusk about some ivory." *I knew it! Rats!* "I guess, Crafty, but I have a list of things to do today, I'm kind of busy."

"It will only be a minute, thanks!" Crafty is out the door. I make some sales for him. I have to figure out where the change is, and where to write it down. Crafty is gone two hours.

'Thanks, Miles, Tusk just got in some new stuff from Savoonga." Crafty is carrying a big box of Eskimo artifacts. There are 2,000 year old harpoon heads, broken dog sled runners made of walrus ivory, and all kinds of related items. Some will go in the Craft Museum room, and the rest will get sold for big profits. It is interesting to learn, and soak up the knowledge here at the shop. I learn what the artifacts are, what they were used for, who made them, and the value of each item. I give Crafty credit for this knowledge and passing it on to me.

"Miles, check out what I found at a garage sale yesterday, see if you need any of this. I was thinking of you when I got it, it's in the basement." We go into the basement and Crafty has a box of nails, a carpenter level, a lantern, and the sorts of odds and ends as what would be found on a homestead.

"Sure, Crafty, I can use all of it, what kind of a deal are we talking?"

"For you, Miles, a special deal."

"Un huh, so how much." We both laugh. I know Crafty is going to make money on it, but that's business. It's still cheaper than if I had to go find all this stuff. It is a bit interesting to see a guy running a $200,000 a year business going to garage sales and buying used oil, buckets of dry paint and worn out drill bits. Crafty agrees to bring the load to my houseboat at Alaskaland. He has business to deal with over there anyhow. In the deal is a better bicycle and some of those ivory artifacts. In the end, Crafty gets my art he wants, and gives me no cash, as often happens.

"Sure, Crafty, I can use the bike. I can use it in town to shop. Maybe I can just keep it on the houseboat."

"When you leave, just lock it up alongside the building here, where your older one is, so it's here when you get back again." *This ensures I keep coming back to do business, so is good for him, good for me.* I'm also more inclined to give him a better deal on the artwork he expects me to bring by. "No use you trying to bring your art around to all the shops. I know everyone. I see them anyway and make appointments. I can rep you like I do other artists. I can give you a deal, buy it all, and you can get back out in the woods. You'll sell some by riding around on a bike and a little box of goods, but it's not displayed, not in enough volume to interest the big shops, and you didn't make an appointment." I see his point, but also see for this 'favor' he is doing me, he wants to trade me garage sale junk.

"Hi Karen! Where's Charley? Is he still politicking?" Karen from the Alaska House is glad to see me, and is interested in my latest work. "No I don't think I will do a show this trip. I have to go to the Fair and that is ten days long. Hopefully I can sell most of what I have there. But I wanted to show you gallery items that I think would be best suited for display here with you." I want to sell outright this time, since I need some 'around town' money and need to get supplies. I lose 60% selling outright, but that is still $1,500 cash in my pocket, half a year's wages, for maybe $100 investment on my part (and my time).

"Miles, stop in again when you have more time to chat. I know Charley is always glad to see you, he'll be sorry he missed you. Oh wait here he comes. Charlie! Wild Miles is here."

Charlie comes in looking like he can use a break. Tall, thin, handsomely gray, and dressed well. He smiles with his hand out to me. Reminding me of Abe Lincoln. "Hi, Miles, good to see you." He is always formal and polite, speaking in a quiet, strong voice. The first impression one gets when meeting him is a sense of extreme intelligence. He has time to sit and take a break, so we have coffee, chat, and discuss the problems of the world. Today we discuss the pros and cons of various forms of government. Something in the headlines of the newspaper Charlie holds in his hand that he has been reading prompts our discussion. Since he is a state senator he knows a thing or two.

It is over my head, but he reviews with me how our own government is set up. How it is supposed to work, and it's shortcomings we need to resolve. This ends up a rare glimpse of behind the scenes, behind the headlines, of how problems really began and will get resolved. This is view few ordinary citizens ever get. I'm truly honored to be in his presence. Not because of the position he holds, but the dynamics of the man himself. I cannot help but think those who say all politicians are no good scoundrels, have never sat down with one, having an open mind, and truly listened. Once again I notice we do not agree on everything, but we treat each other's views with the respect they deserve.

"Miles, what's this art piece about here that you are leaving with us? Looks interesting."

I have it in my hand, so hold it out. It is a letter opener—dagger knife in a stand. Interesting in that it is not for men. It is for a woman, and not done as an instrument of destruction. I show Charlie the name tag and hand written out story that goes with the piece. He knows from the past that I like to do what I call, 'story pieces,' where I explain the material, why it was chosen for this piece, and what the piece symbolizes to me.

Story Knife

This Knife was designed to be a woman's decorative protection knife—to be displayed on a nightstand or someplace in the home. The knife is made of 440 stainless steel with brass inlayed heart. The handle is Alaskan mammoth ivory found by the artist on the Yukon River. The sheath is from the same tusk and has brass-silver-copper, hand cut soldered and pinned unicorn. The stand base is the same ivory with local caribou antler. The stand has silver-copper-brass and Mexican opal flower centers.

Story- On one side is the tranquil unicorn in a beautiful setting, symbol of love, peace, magic and non-violence. Yet we know the unicorn is a mythical animal! Is the scene also mythical?? Is there ever love, peace perfect and forever beauty? Turn the sheath over. The back shows the unicorn rearing in anger. You never really know—or can predict the future of every situation. Perhaps it is wise to have the ability to defend yourself close at hand—just in case. Thus, the functional dagger as part of a beautiful art piece—something that does not have to be hidden away where you can't get at it if you ever need it. The heart in the blade? A symbol of love. This is not for attack or for crazy people. This is for someone who loves life, peace, honesty, and simply understands these qualities need to be defended sometimes. If you have anything, be it beauty or material goods, there is always someone out there who wants to take it from you. Life should not be lived in fear.

Charlie gives me cash for items I leave at the gallery.

My friend Will helps me shop around. "Once again, Miles, I decide to come to town, stop what I am doing. What happens? I run into you within five minutes. How many times now has this happened? Over a dozen? What are the odds!" Once again he expresses shock. We have had this conversation so many times, there is no reason to answer. We go to garage sales. Lost supplies are slowly replaced. Will tells me the guy who stole the leather jackets years ago at the fair, who got me in trouble, is still around. Some of the others from those days are still around, but some are dead now. Mostly drugs killed them, while others are in jail. None who said they were headed for the wilderness ever got there. Of the group of those I met my first few years, I'm the only one, 'doing it.' Or 'struggling to' or, 'getting by,' *but not yet proficient and good at it like I want to be.* This is good to be reminded of since I am so bummed out about Palace, Joe, and their words which reflect words from my family.

"You still got the black powder bug, Miles?" We laugh. I got out of black powder years ago, and here Will is, still excited about it. It is good to see Will again. He had a good trip home after our adventure at Lake Minchumina. His life is pretty much the same. Looking for work, doing mechanic stuff, wishing he could do something else. He gets by at least, and seems happy enough. *Not really.* "Problem is, even though I won that boat motor and trailer in the drawing. I couldn't afford to keep it! Had to sell it. Burns more gas than I can afford to pay for. A jet lower unit is no way to go when you want to go long distance, Miles!"

I had already figured that out. It's still a shame not to be able to keep something worth seventy grand. Sold it for ten grand. All he could get.

"Will, looks like I have a booth space at the fair this season. Coming up in the world maybe. Ha! No sneaking in pretending I'm a delivery guy. I'm not sure how to do it yet. I think Crafty has tables and displays. I can work a deal in trade for more art with him. For sure he knows all there is to know about fairs, and what one needs to set up to sell. He'll have the display cloths, tags, cash box, everything. *Crafty gets my $30,000 in art, and parts with zero cash.*

My space at the fair is alongside the big craft tent in the 'hand craft' area. Not much has changed over the years I have been coming here. There is a big open field. A few dirt paths crisscross the grass. Along the paths are wood stakes in the ground marking each person's ten x twenty foot space. A huge tent is set up for those who wish to rent a table under the communal roof. If I do not get a table in the tent, I have to provide my own tent and table in the grass clearing provided. There are not a lot of rules. I set up whatever and however I wish. As in years past, some natives from the villages bring only a blanket and tree stump to sit on, and this is their booth.

I have some visqueen and Crafty's old table, a chair and some well used cloth to cover the table. I have about a hundred finished pieces of art, mostly pendants in the $30 range but a few for $75 or more and a few art pieces for $500 or more. There is only my wallet to make change. There is no sign saying who I am or my business name. Even so, people know me and come and buy from me.

"Hey, Miles, I see you at least had business cards made! Making copies of your magazine articles is a good idea as well. That 'Survive' one in Alaska Magazine was a good one! I'd like a copy of that myself!" Crafty is checking things over for me. He suggests in the future, I have a brochure made as well as the business card. A few local galleries even have representatives come by who ask for wholesale inventory for shops they work for.

There is a wood sign maker at the fair. We trade my art for a plague with my business name. 'Sunshine Jewelry.' (I change this to 'Miles of Alaska,' later.)

This is now familiar to me. I have had good experiences here. Because of this, the sounds, smells, all forms of 'input,' are recorded as 'fun,' and good, bringing happy familiar memories. This is a significant change slowly taking place, as this is one of the very few social situations where I feel at ease, happy, safe, and look forward to. For I do not in general consider society a safe place to be. *I see more dangers in society than I do in the wilderness.*

"Miles, what's up with you? Thought you were the hermit for life. The recluse. The Mountain Man who vows to live and die alone in the wild!" I laugh good naturedly.

😄 :)

This is a customer I should know, but forget the name of. Just a face I recognize in the crowd."Yes times are changing all right! Maybe I'm getting smarter? I still love and want the wild, but it takes money to get the rice, beans, and gas for the boat! This is a good opportunity for me to make some fast money at doing something I'm good at. It's hard to look to regular jobs. I can at least work for myself, and create art in the wilderness. If I have to come to town for ten days to sell it to get supplies, this is better than having to spend all summer to grub stake myself. I see what you mean though, big changes for me and my image! Ha!" The guy buys a belt buckle and turns to move on. "Hey, wait a second; I forgot to show you something!" I show off a black powder rifle I built and want to share, all inlaid metal art scenes on it. Lots of my customers are village people, and most here at the fair at least go out to hunt for moose or caribou. A crowd starts to gather as I start to tell the story and make my sales pitch. Ten guys stand in front of my booth admiring the art piece.

Beauty and the Beast

While out for a walk in the wilderness you come across a scene of beauty. This is on one side of the rifle. A grizzly is feeding, geese fly overhead. They know you are there and leave, but the bear pays no attention, he fears nothing. Late flowers are in bloom, the sun is out, and it's a hot, clear, calm day.

For reasons only the bear understands, he suddenly rears up. Did he get wind of you? Is it a female, and there is a cub somewhere you do not see? All you know is, the world is now dangerous, ugly, loud, and full of chaos. All hell has broken loose. The geese are squawking and the flowers are torn up. This is the scene on the other side of the rifle. These were the days when you only had one shot and you pray your powder is dry.

Your black powder rife comes to level and as you pull the hammer back, you automatically check to see that the cap is on the nipple. You hear the double click as the hammer engages the sear; and in the same instant you pull the trigger. A microsecond before ignition, you can make out the cap snapping. There's a "Wooomph," the familiar smell of rotten eggs, the pull into the shoulder. Through the cloud of blue smoke you see the wounded bear, charging like a runaway train.

Is it a scene from the past? The present? A distant future? Is it timeless? All in all, neither life, death, or power plays have changed a great deal. Is this something familiar in all our genes if we care to see it? Most of us never met the bear? But isn't it so, that so often things are going along so smooth and beautiful, then all of a sudden things turn ugly? I know a great deal more about grizzlies and rifles, but I would guess that Big Brother, the landlord, a takeover company, can be 'facing the beast.' There is often one single moment to act, or be crushed. There is no time to explain, to call 911, ask the police to take care of us, this is a time to act, or be acted upon; 'survival.' At such times the only thing between us and total destruction can be one tool. It might be a credit card, a phone, a pen, gunpowder. They can all do the same thing; protect us, help us, defend us, lift us from the Stone Age, or be our worst nightmare.

Black powder says it all so eloquently. Gut feelings, instinct, preparation, one chance-one shot at the big one, having the right stuff, it's all said right there in a black powder rifle. This symbolizes what separates the sheep from the wolves, the eater from the eatee. A fearful life from a confident one; but mostly, the living.... from the dead.

And as for what's beautiful, and what is beastly? I pause and sigh.

In some ways the day gunpowder was invented, was an amazingly sad time in the history of the world. Those were the days? I smile. The real days were the days of teeth and claws. I smile slyly. But who of us would really appreciate such days? (Think about it).

So by all means, let's raise a glass, cheers, "to civilization!" Go ahead! Pick up the rifle. Be at one with your history. Balance it, look at the grizzly. As you do, ask yourself this, "Do I feel lucky today?" And when you look at each side? Do try to remember, how very quickly things can change. I wink. "Never let your powder get wet." I laugh and add, "Or your ink run out, your contract expire, or your phone go dead. Try to find the beauty in things, but when the bear rears its grizzly head, don't freeze up."

The changes I have seen and am going through are on my mind. One reason is the books I'm working on. Why am I writing them, who is my market, what is it I'm trying to say or accomplish? Partly, I am still upset over losing Palace, and how, to who, and why.[1]

More money is being made than when I was just walking around in past years selling out of a shoe box. *'Display really makes a difference!'* There is not as much time to enjoy the fair though. This year I miss watching the kids' 4-H entries and reading the short stories they write. *'This is getting too close to having to work for a living!'* I smile, as we know there is no such thing as getting out of work. Still, one can enjoy what must be done.

"Hey, Miles glad to see you finally got a booth of your own!" One of the vendors that used to reprimand me for selling on the street now has something good to say, and we chat.

"Yes, Ozzie, I think this works out better. I have more inventory these days. The shows are not as short and swift as they once were during the pipeline days. Want anything I have? I'll trade for some meals at your booth!"

"Sure. Miles, I think Annie was eyeing the one hummingbird on the shell over here. We can trade for $60 worth of food. Come on by, we'll write up a tab. You'll be number twelve, just mention the number and the workers know where the book is to enter it. Might as well please Annie, she works pretty hard. You'll learn yourself one day, Miles, how to keep a good woman!" He and I had talked about my various experiences with mail order women. We both laugh.

Ten days is a long time to hit it hard selling ones soul through art. I'll certainly feel like replenishing the well when this is over. I have known since I first started coming here that this suites my personality. This is like the feast and famine of the wilderness life. There is lots of hard intense work, with huge rewards, lots of risk, followed by more slow times when one can take a break. I explain to a village friend who is also a customer I am chatting with,

"I do not enjoy regular work with regular hours. There is the loss of security of a regular paycheck, knowing my income, but there is something good about feast and famine. It seems good for dreamers. It's like life with the wild creatures. The wolf runs and runs till his heart about bursts to get the moose. He risks life and limb. But once he has eaten, he sits around with a fat belly for a week belching." The villager and I laugh as we both know about this kind of life.

AFTER THE FAIR, a boatload of supplies is loaded up and tied aboard so it will not fall overboard. Every space on the houseboat is packed with boxes of necessities for winter. One customer I sort of know, trades me his driving time around town, taking me shopping, in trade for a wolf claw necklace he likes.

Will and I also run around together, looking for things for winter we both need. Fall colors are showing, and the first freeze has arrived. The water level will drop fast, and not come back up. With a farewell to Will I nervously take off. There are a lot of river miles to cover before I am settled in at home. The sled dogs seem as eager as I am to get back to the river life. They enjoyed the woods behind the park as a change, but I know they miss 'home.'

I am in Nenana the next day visiting Josh. Going downstream is faster. This is good, since I have such a big load! "Miles, you may as well spend the night, the sleeping bag you left is still here behind the couch, go ahead and set it out by the stove whenever you are ready to go to bed."

"Thanks, Josh. Yes, pretty tired, but need to go to Manley for my mail before heading up the Kantishna."

My mail is in Manley Hot Springs. To get there I have to pass the mouth of the Kantishna River, and keep going down the Tanana River and on to Manley another forty miles beyond my turn off. Nets are set out to catch Chum salmon for the sled dogs while camping at Baker Creek. It has been a while since I was in Manley and had dropped Palace off. I am surprised in a tense way, to hear she is still in Manley. It implies it was not Alaska she could not handle, but me. Someone I sort of know, but forget the name of in the roadhouse tells me.

"Yes, Miles she moved in with Joe. I think they are getting along well enough. I hear some negative talk about you around the Roadhouse though. Something about being a know it all and having an ego problem, not admitting when you are wrong, everything having to be your way—stuff like that."

There had been the complaint in the past when Joe had told the community I left a mess behind when I moved. We are both smiling, sharing what sort we think Joe is. I reply to that smile, "Uh, Huh." I am curious about Palace and Joe. I'm hurt, but what the heck. Life goes on. Palace gets word I am in Manley but chooses not to see me to say 'Hi.' She and Joe stay at the cabin across the river he has permission to stay in. I'm unsure what he does for a living, but think he gets some sort of disability as a Vietnam War vet. Life might be pretty easy over there at his cabin. Sigh. *Life is easier when you don't have to work for a living, do not go anywhere, have no goals.*

Before leaving civilization for a long time, I am in a mood to hang out a bit longer, have a cheeseburger, fries, and a coke, just soak up village life a moment. As I eat, this guy I sort of know joins me. I'm trying to untangle the web of my woman issues. The subject partly comes up because there is mail from some mail order women in my pile this guy spots on the table. I try to explain what type of woman I seek. "There is one bottom line about the woman who is my soul mate. She will have power over me and know it. But she will not abuse it. She will use the power she has over me to help me. This is the woman I will worship, put on a pedestal, who will have my soul in her hands."

"Ha! Dream on, Miles! There is no such woman!"

'Then I will live alone forever looking for her, and go to hell crying for her. Maybe she will be there, or in the hereafter in the next life. Or the life after that."

He adds, "You are a dreamer all right! Ha. Meanwhile she can have something of mine in her hands, but it won't be my soul!"

"Now you're talking sense." I play along, there is no point in arguing. *And if I cannot find her, then she must find me. Step out of the dark and tell me she is her, my other half. Till then we do the best we can as half a person, both her and I. When she finds me, the first year will be spent crying, rocking back and forth in each other's arms. Both of us. But then we will never need to cry again.* I speak out loud, "I got a letter from this one gal I have not met yet. Here's her picture. Seems nice enough. Hard to know though. I can't share the letter, you know, too personal for your innocent mind. She is in competition with no one. I have bought her a treadle sewing machine and it waits for her. I have never slow danced. She will be the only one I ever slow dance with. The only one my eyes focus on. Everyone else is just a blur. She need not be concerned with anyone else I may have been with. For when I meet her, I will be born again, and there will be no past, only now and forever."

The picture is stared at in awe. "Dang, Miles look at these—" I do not let him finish…

"Uh, huh. A wolf could have fun running this one down, ham stringing her and having a feast."

"You got that right, Miles, you wolf, you! You gonna share any?"

"She's not even here yet and…?" I grin good naturedly.

"Well, who are you to know what women want. I been hearing you can't keep em around. Maybe you need advice from a real man!"

"That'll be the day! When a man can give another man advice about women! I think if I want any advice I'll get it from a woman!"

"You got that right. I like you. Miles, you tell it like it is. Problem is when a woman talks, you can't understand em, they talk Greek or something. But I can keep em at least. Yah don't have to understand em to keep em. Like a dog. Yah feed em, and when they do something nice you give em a treat, and when they mess up you spank em."

"Are you sure it's not you that's the sucker and the dog on the leash?" Said with a good natured smile. "Life is a circle. What goes around comes around. The hunter ends up the hunted. The cat can become the mouse, the mouse can become the cheese, and the cheese can kill the cat. The con artist is the first to be the sucker in a scam… the pike with biggest teeth, the first fish to die in the net… "

"Hey, did you hear me Miles? You are one space case, Dude! You been in the bush too long? You better get that woman here quick and latch onto what's real!" He grins and winks, pointing at those big 'items' in the picture, in case I do not catch his meaning. "Gotta run Miles—dang woman of mine ran away again, gotta drag her back. Shouldn't waste my time. She always comes back begging forgiveness when she realizes who pays her bills." I cue in on how his mind works.

"You got that right! Spank her good now, teach her a lesson. Give her a nice treat too." I wink.

"Sure thing, Miles! See ya around my friend."

'Friend? I think not, you piece of dog dung!' I smile and wave good bye. I close my eyes briefly and go into a Zen thing. To make it all go away because… because? Yes, because the proof is in the pudding right? Mr. Dung is right. I am alone and he is not. What else matters? For everything else is just words. He has reality, and I have only me, myself and I. If he is dung, what am I? Poof! It is done, forgotten, a magnet swipes over the memory tapes. A new memory is created in its place. What is real? *That which we remember, that which we want to be real, that which will keep us alive and sane, that which cannot be proven false. That which your Conscience decides to tell you about, distorted by the curve of the time space continuum that is a universe that ultimately comes back on itself. That which blends with everyone else's agreed upon reality enough to not be over the edge.* I open my eyes with a big smile, blade of grass shifting to the other side in my mouth. Life is good.

I gather up my mail, gruffly speak to the dogs, and we are off for the homestead. As we travel to the purr of the engine, I think about being ready for winter.

A food co-op formed in Manley. I missed my food pick up once again, as the community order has not arrived yet. Money is saved by lots of us ordering in bulk, then dividing the order up when it arrives. Mine was paid in advance, since I am unsure when to get it. One of the co-op members will keep my food.

As I travel the river I think about the homestead, and how I can get to work on the cabin more seriously, now that making lots of art and making money are out of the way. No more money is needed till I sell furs in winter.

When I get home, salmon are caught in nets and hung to dry. Mushrooms are picked and dried. Field mint is picked at my secret spot. Cranberries are picked, and jam is made. This is all healthy reality. The cabin walls are up, but not all chinked with moss yet. *'We should be able to get a roof on before winter.'* "But probably not get moved in for winter." I reply to myself. Luckily, once again, we have the houseboat to live in.

It is September, time for one last trip to Manley for mail, and my food co-op order. There is some art to send off to fill a few custom orders I got at the fair. There is enough business to make it worth a trip into Manley. This will be fast, so the dogs will not come with me, nor the houseboat. The wood boat with fifty horse will get me in quick enough, maybe five hours.

The fall colors are still out, but fading. Weather is still great. In Manley, I pick up my food order from Van and Dem. Van still traps in the Brooks Range, but is moving more towards a guiding business in the area. He reminds me how I watched his sled dogs for him in the Brooks Range, and now I have my own sled dogs! Dem is still one of only two school teachers. Dem asks, "Miles, how come you ordered so many split peas? Eighty pounds, gosh!"

I never really thought about it, and thought this is a rude question. I see she is only curious. I have no answer beyond, "Well, it was cheap, and I didn't think much about it, and they keep forever." But yes now that you mention it, this is enough to last one person several lifetimes. But at a sale price of $20 who cares? We all laugh.

😄 :)

I spend a night in their small guest cabin that was the main cabin when we met, but now they moved into a newer bigger place!

"We don't mind, Miles. We lived like you for a while, and had to find places to stay and others helped us out. It is our turn to pay this back to others. What goes around comes around. One day it will be your turn to help others." My friends the Underhills feel the same way. I'm too busy to think about it. I have a place to stay, that is off my mind. Next issue.

I get an early start after a breakfast at the roadhouse. There is no inquiry about Palace and Joe. If they are happy, fine, but I do not need to hear the details of why life with him is so much better than life with me. Humph! In a miffed mood, I take off into the early morning mist.

Soon the ducks flying up, the morning warmth of the sun, and hum of the nicely tuned outboard get me into a good mood. *'Yeah who needs a woman when a man can have a boat he can depend on!'* So we purr along, me and the love of my life, the water, and a future.

I get to Baker Creek, and think I might stop, maybe spend the night. I had left three days of feed with the sled dogs. They are used to being left this long. The Baker Creek cabin is a nice place, pretty, a good place to fish and relax, and has good memories associated with it. Baker Creek Carol and Two Rivers were here a while back, and I had visited them. Now it is an empty cabin, good to stay in for a night. However the cabin has guests. As I approach there are two woman and some children in the yard. I recognize Baker Creek Carol.

"Hi, Miles. This is Karen who lives outside of Manley, and her two children. We are teamed up fishing for our sled dogs."

I notice they have only a kayak, and are using this to check fish nets with. I acknowledge Karen. Without being Conscience of it, I admire the children who are hard at work helping the two adults hang fish and do chores, even though they are only three and nine years old. There is disappointment that I probably cannot stay here the night as I had planned, so will move on and camp in the woods someplace along the way. I reply to the women, "How is the kayak for checking nets? Seems like it would be hard. I can help with my boat before I go if you want." The two women acknowledge they are getting fish, but not easily, and would welcome the help. One of the children is struggling with firewood on the path to the house. I comment. "Geez, looks like you women could use a guy around her to cut wood and bring fish!" I'm flirting, and at the same time offering help. The women respond. We happily go check nets together.

Karen dominates my time and wants to talk to me, ask questions of me. "I distributed the food for the Manley co-op, and wondered who the heck ordered eighty pounds of split peas! I had never heard of you, so was curious. Someone said you almost starved once, so maybe food is a big thing with you?"

I never saw it like that before, but maybe this is possible. But this initial inquiry about me brought out a lot of information, and Karen was all the more curious. She is trying to live the same lifestyle, and is still learning, as I am.

As we do chores, Karen and I talk a lot. She is a little older than I am, but not enough to matter. Very fine looking, blonde, fit, my height, German. "Miles, I want to get into the sled dog transportation lifestyle. I have dogs, but have never been on an overnight dog trip before. I am a little afraid to do it alone!"

"Well, Karen, it is not so hard, once you know how to run the dogs, as it sounds like you know. I have been on long trips with my sled dogs, and know something about it. I guess we could go on a trip together if you wanted company."

This begins sort of a 'relationship.' We are interested in each other. She tells me about herself. "Why not spend the night here. It is late. You helped us out a lot and we can feed you. There is room to set out your sleeping bag by the stove. If you cut some wood for us with your chain saw in the morning before leaving it would really help."

They are cutting wood with a bow saw and struggling to keep up, doing ok, but using up a lot of time. I can cut in half an hour what would take them days to cut by hand. I'm more interested in getting close to Karen than being a Good Samaritan though.

"I'll be glad to help out, thanks for the invitation. I was sort of counting on staying here and did not know it was occupied." Here at least is an available woman, who already loves Alaska and the wilderness life. She is right here living it. Way into the night we agree to take a trip together, and tentatively see if we can get along and have a relationship. Neither of us really wants to be alone. We can be alone if we must, but there is an attraction here. As for me, maybe I was ready for a relationship when I met Palace, and this idea got set on the back burner when things did not work out, but the seed was planted and here is reseeded. A little water and sunshine revives the dry plant.

The trip back to the homestead from Baker Creek is made much lighter, and done in good spirit. The winter dog trip is thought about as I run the river home. One plan is for me to mush to Manley and pick Karen up. We could mush to Nenana together. This should be about a two day trip, three for me including the day trip of sixty miles to Manley. When I get to the homestead, the sled dogs are glad to see me; there have been no problems while gone.

Fish nets are put back out in earnest. I catch more than ever, as the water level drops and late fall turns to winter. To be ready, one big project is to get the houseboat secure for the cold and ice. Logs are jammed under the boat between the pond bottom and house bottom, till my house is resting on logs. Rose hips get picked for tea. Late mushrooms get dried over the wood stove. Many things from the land end up preserved in jars I save. This is a necessity, not just fun, cute, romantic, and healthy. I run the smaller boat to check nets as the ice is running. The very next day, I cross the river with sled dogs!

"Kenai! What do we do about the boat getting frozen in the river? Can all of us pull it out onto high ground?" There are no trees nearby to run rope to use the winch. Just soft river silt for a quarter mile. The gang line is unhooked from the dog sled, and hooked to the river boat rope. All seven dogs are hooked up. "Tighten up!" all the dogs walk forward to take up the slack and wait my command to pull. Without my command, they begin to lean into the harness and put strain on the rope. "Easy" They back off a little so I can walk to the back and check the boat out and help rock it. "Tighten up!" They all pull hard together as a team. On their own, they figure out how to pull, slack off, pull, slack off, to work the boat loose from the ice. The rope gets taught enough to ring the water out of it. This takes about 1,500 pounds of pull. With creak and groan, like beaching a whale, the boat comes free of its element. The bow drops to the silt, slides, and is free of the ice till next spring, seven months from now. Before the engine freezes I take the oil drain plug out to make sure any water in it drains out. Forgetting this little detail can cause water in here to freeze, breaking the gear case, causing thousands of dollars in damage. Poles are cut for tarp extension in back of the houseboat from its roof to create the usual extra storage area outside my living space. This is just normal routine now. Pole shelving is lashed to hold boxes organized and away from mice and snow.

It is time to think of trapping and winter activities. This year the weather warms a little and the ice gets bad, so for a week or so I cannot travel with the dogs, and am held up at the houseboat. Traps are cleaned, new drag chains put on, bait made ready, and lure created. *'While we are at it, let's repair the dog sled!'* So, we fool with the sled. Nothing major is wrong, but lashings are retied that seem loose, and the bottom of the runners smoothed for slicker sliding. Extra firewood is cut for later use. This is not an idle time, and means a lot of work, but the sort of work that keeps a person happy and healthy. My winter moose is shot without incident. I hang the quarters near the new cabin, and set a tarp up to help keep it from view of the ravens and other birds. The meat can keep two weeks or more at temperatures below 50° before it freezes. *'As long as fly season is over!'* Good point, yes, as long as there are no flies out! Dog harnesses are mended, and the sled bag repaired on the treadle sewing machine.

I do not expect to get mail till I mush to Manley to see Karen. I'm not sure when, as it depends on weather. My guess is November, two months away. There might be a trip to Nenana first. In late fall a new plan develops. There are two new homesteaders about six miles downriver from me who said they might try to get to Nenana when the weather freezes. There is an old mail trail from Manley Hot Springs to Nenana, but no one has put in a trail from this area.

There has been talk of oil exploration involving seismic work being done between the Kantishna River and Nenana. It is only rumor to homesteaders, who would not be part of the direct knowledge of those protecting their interests. Supposedly though, there may be a new bulldozed winter trail to find. Till then, there is a winter route locally called 'The Commission Road.' It is a railroad right of way that was bulldozed many years ago in anticipation of a train getting to the Yukon River one day. There is no talk of that set of train tracks getting built, but the land was set aside, and now used as a winter road by travelers with sled dogs or snow machine in winter.

There would be about twenty-five miles of wilderness to negotiate to get to this trail. If several of us work on it in pieces, we can make it happen. I had thought Manley Hot Springs would be the place to go for mail and supplies. Maybe I'd follow the Kantishna River to the Tanana River, and pick up the mail trail there. Rumor has it, a Manley trapper gets to the mouth of the Kantishna and comes up a little ways. This would be thirty miles before hitting his trapline if I follow the river.

I look at the maps, and mark where I think trappers and old trails might be. Nothing would show up on a public map anyone could buy. This is an aspect of a lifestyle many do not grasp. The idea that outsiders do not have access to the same information, and information is simply not available to everyone. Information is hard to get, and even knowing where to get it requires being local.

My original plan was to cut almost straight west across country with a trapline to tie into my old stomping grounds at Hansen Lake 100 miles away. But it sounds like there is someone who has trapping rights not so far off, in between me and my old area. Dan Bettes in Nenana tells me he just acquired an old native trapline. He himself is Native. I can cut a trail around him by cutting an extra thirty miles. I tell him I'll do this. Two native families trap in this valley, the Ketslers and the Duyckes.

Both spend most of their energy on the other side of the Kantishna from where I plan to go, so this should not be a problem if I do not cross the river. Though the youngsters in each family feel I should not be any place in the entire valley because I am a white outsider.

I need to balance standing up for my rights against bowing to traditional custom. The rules are not the same as in the city. Hopefully there will be no serious hard feelings. This sounds like a lot of activity, but encompasses an area the size of the state of Rhode Island. There are five people to work the trapping rights out with, each with over 300 miles of trapline, as I hope to have myself one day.

My neighbors, Tom Forest and his wife, downstream have no interest in trapping. The Forests are dog mushers, and do freight hauling and dog racing. Their interest is fishing for dogs, and training on trails for races. The single guy near them seems to just want to kick back. I'm unsure if he intends to even stay. He may use this as his vacation home. The land was promoted by the state as traditionally subsistence. The land is still open for homesteading, so it is hard to know for sure who and what types will show up.

There is talk that there is a pilot based out of the Wien Lake area who traps any empty spot he finds out this way. This lake is quite a ways away from me, but at Hansen, I had cut trail to within five miles. He would be landing on skis on any marsh or lake with his plane. The trapping situation is reviewed, again, looking over maps, and making my own marks with notes. The lakes out back have been seen in summer, now it will be interesting to see them frozen. The country beyond the lakes can be accessed by the sled dogs once frozen. I'm anxious to see what the trail work will be like headed towards Hansen Lake and Bearpaw Mountain. In the evening I write to dad.

Dear Dad

I will not be able to get this letter sent for a while, but thought I'd write and keep you filled in on what is going on. I'm sure it is quite different than what is going on in your world. Things did not work out with Palace, I think I told you. Oh Well? There might be someone new, but hate to talk all excited since I do not know yet if this is just another misunderstanding.

All else is going well. I am ready for winter. Sled dogs are fat and healthy, with lots of fish set aside for winter feeding that I caught myself. I built my own dog sled and it is fixed up and in good repair. This seems like a good spot I picked to homestead. The morning sun comes in and warms the spot up fast, and the evening sun sets on the backside. There is a nice calm creek out front where I keep the canoe. There seems to be lots of game, like moose and bear around. My winter moose was easy to get. Wolves howl off in the hills some nights. So far no one else has shown interest in staking land on the same creek. The soil is fertile, and will make a good garden when I have time for that. I look forward to a good trapping season. It will be a hard season with lots of trail cutting to do, but I am excited to open new country. My nearest neighbors are downstream about six miles and we are working on a short trail between us so we can visit over the winter. We could just take the river, but this is more dangerous and is ten miles. I think we will work on a trail to Nenana overland. Otherwise, I hope to make it to Manley Hot Springs instead. I do not know which will be my place to get mail! I have spent more time in Manley and am inclined to go there, but Nenana gives better access to the hub, Fairbanks to sell my art and get supplies. My art is selling well. For the first time I had a spot at the state fair, which is a big change for me. I'm acting civilized! I still do not drive. I know you keep asking, as if this was really important, but it is not so important in my world. I'd rather have a boat and sled dogs.

How is life with you? What new classes will be taught this season? Is being Dean stressful? I know it is not something I could handle, and marvel that you can do so well at it! I know when I visit it is fun to watch you operate. Well, better go feed my seven sled dogs.

Sunshine Miles

I write another letter to Maggie who I have lost touch with but still write.

Dearest Maggie

Once again I think of you and the changes I have gone through since we knew each other and shared the same lifestyle. I wonder if you would recognize me, recognize my personality, and understand or approve. I think of this with a smile and humor, not sadness. I often imagine you seeing what I see and wondering about your reaction. The beauty and also the hardships. It would be nice to have your advice. Right now, I am having trapping rights land issues and struggle with what is the right thing to do. Am I selfish and greedy to have the dream of carving a trapping empire out of this wilderness? Should I bow down to the native rights and local concerns? Where is the balance, for one either goes for it or not. I have an empire or I do not.

My thoughts go back to Canada and being deported, losing my home and all I owned. My story at the time was that all I was trying to do was keep a library open for $2 an hour, a job the town asked me to do. I did not need the money, and knew I could not work, but was told this was an exception and believed what I was told. Never did I dream it could end as it did. What other factors were at play I am not facing?? What part am I responsible for?? For I believe we are all cause over our life.

I begin to see this. As an individual, we do not have the right to do what we want. You and I were raised during the 60s, in the flower child era. Over the hill was thirty, and there was no life beyond that worth considering. It was the age to be free. Personal freedom was everything. The rule that sounded ok to me was 'You can do anything you want as long as it does not interfere with anyone else.' What you do to your own body is your business. What you do in the privacy of your own home is your own business. If you want to wear a seat belt, who is anyone else to say one way or the other. If you want to smoke, it's your business. If you want to do drugs, just don't force them on anyone else. The arguments seemed sound to me and made sense. If someone else does not like it, they have a problem, not me. At the bottom of many of my problems is a flaw in this basic premise, that freedom is a right, when it is not, it is a privilege...

I wonder if we are social beings and the group matters ultimately more than the individual. For if the group fails we all perish, but if an individual fails, there is still survival for the rest. There is very little an individual does that does not affect others. There are new seat belt laws when driving. The argument goes 'If you die in a crash because you were not wearing a belt, my insurance goes up.' I thought that was a farfetched absurd connection.

Responsibility used to be on individuals, and now is more social. If I shot someone it was once my fault. The fault shifted to our parents. Now it is the company who made the gun who is at fault. If I drank and that created a problem it used to me, my problem. Now it is the problem of the one who sold the liquor, the one who made the liquor and responsibility is on the farmer that grew the grain that made the liquor. The change is quite interesting to see. It means perhaps we are all responsible for each other.

Along these lines I do not have the right to be free. I do not have the right to make others nervous, scared, or apprehensive. Individuals cannot go around causing the herd to stampede, even cause the herd to bleat nervously. Biologically, survival of the group is in testing any changes, being harsh on change, for it might be good, but it might not be. Being different must come with a price. It cannot be happy and carefree. I cared about others to the extent I wanted a library kept open. Yet I dressed how I chose, expressed radical ideas with no concern for how it affected others. I did not care what anyone thought, as long as my conscience was clear. I did not drink. I did not commit any crimes. I paid my bills. I did not fight. I considered myself an asset to the community, someone who gave and did not take. What else matters? I thought the rest is no one else's business. But now I wonder as I ponder the facts of life.

Anyhow! I'm on the edge of carving out an empire. I am in the prime of life, blazing across a dark night as a comet, burning with energy and dreams. I laugh. I wink. I'm stepping out the door into the vast and dangerous unknown, like in the song by the Who, "Can you hear us Major Tom?" and the last words "I'm stepping out the door."

Sunshine Miles

The letter gets tossed in the stove because I have no address for Maggie. I fix dinner. Freedom is not free. Those who dare to step into the unknown, lay your cards down and play the game, be amazed, and look into the void. To do so and laugh, and wink, that is courage.

Early in October the creek and swamps have the first serious ice form. The first snow arrives. The dogs and I have to wait for the ice to get a little thicker. Warm weather follows. We are aggravated by watching the snow melt. The time is spent working on art projects and getting ready to trap. Cabin work is put off till next spring. Finally, at the end of October, the ice in the swamps is thick enough to go out on. There is very little snow, so I could ice skate around if I had skates with me. The dogs and I slip slide around the creek. The first time out I cannot expect much from them. They are so excited to get out we just go and have fun. There will be plenty of hard work in the months ahead. They may as well start off pulling with a good attitude! That first day we go about three miles.

The next day we do about five miles. The lake is beautiful, and all I expected. The lake looks shallow, so there will not be any fish in winter here. This is a disappointment, but good to know. Several large beaver houses indicate a healthy beaver population. Otter slides in the mud banks show where they enter the water and travel between lakes. Wolf tracks circle the lake.

"Kenai, what's up?" All the dogs are going fast and looking at the ice. The sled catches up to where the dogs are looking. A beaver swimming under the ice only a foot away from us! I squat down on the runners to be closer and observe. The view is like through a glass bottom boat in the tropics. All is crystal clear. There are lily pads, cattails, logs and the beaver who cannot get away from us blowing bubbles as he swims.

There is open water here and there, but enough ice on the edge to get around it. I smile because the books say one needs four inches of ice, and here I am traveling on less than half an inch. (But sticking to the shore edge) The map indicates a narrow spot where I can work my way to another similar size lake. I find this spot and see a creek that might connect the two. The creek drains a swamp, but does not connect the lakes, as it did when the map was made, but does get me closer. It takes two days to cut willows and alder trees between the two lakes. Thick alders and willows are just head heigh, but like spaghetti on a plate, all crisscrossed. When cut, nowhere to put the cut trees.

The sled dogs do not like to sit still for long while I cut. The quiet travel when we are on the move is nice, but the quarreling among the dogs while I am trying to work is not fun. There is plenty of animal sign around, especially marten, the critter I most depend on for fur money. Life is good.

A trail is worked on to the neighbors, the other direction. There is some rough ground through tundra to negotiate, which is hard before there is a lot of snow. The Kantishna is not frozen everywhere, so travel is overland.

"HEY, Tom, how is life in your part of the world?"

"Hi, Miles, Lana and I figured that was you headed this way when our dogs were barking a few days ago. How's the trail? We need a new direction to go. Our dogs are tired of running the slough. Can we try out your trail? "

"It's rough through tundra towards my place. Are you working on the trail to Nenana?"

We talk about dogs and trails. Tom gets the map out and shows what he has in mind. I see from the map I could work on a trail straight across the river from me, that hits his trail, and saves me five miles of travel on the Nenana trip. But for now I might come this way and go out to help cut. Bob is down the slough, but I do not see him this trip. He too is working on the trail. [2]

I do not come by often, as I am busy trapping and the Forests also have their life filled with things to do. The plan though, is to cut and hit the North Commission Winter Trail marked on the map. This goes straight to Nenana, and has been used for years between Manley Hot Springs and Nenana by trappers and winter travelers. The route we plan will be about fifty miles. Another aspect of my trapping trail work is cutting around the neighbor trapper Bettes, who has not showed up, and may never show up. I agreed to honor his request to not cross his trapline. This is hard to honor, as I see how far I must cut to get to my old stomping grounds at Hansen. I see at least a year's hold up cutting around a trapper who has not showed up, starting the opposite direction! Yet I wish to be respected as an honorable man, good to my word, and fair. Like my heroes, the early mountain men I read about. For now I will cut around an old man's trapline so he does not feel some young whipper snapper is running him off. But dang I want so bad to begin my serious trapping and be that comet across the sky.

"KENAI, get off my snowshoes. How many times do I have to tell you?" I do not turn around as I talk. The lead dog likes to get close enough to me to walk on my snowshoes so he does not sink in the deep snow. I get to where I finished cutting last time and stop, tie the lead dog off to a tree, and the sled off to another, and begin to sort my supplies and begin cutting for the day. A sip of hot tea is taken from the thermos. The handmade canvas tarp has Velcro flaps that need to be redone. The trees here are short, and all bent over by snow. We are in the forever tundra that all looks the same. The dogs watch, but mostly are curled up in the snow taking a nap. Kenai, being second in command, stays alert, sitting up in case I have any last minute orders.

"Just cutting trail, Kenai, as usual, see the machete. Looks like a pond ahead though. I might move us all up when it is time to cross the pond." The machete is sharpened on a wet stone as I sit on the rail of the dog sled. There are dry fish for a few days of feeding for the dogs that I can smell in the sled. There is a separate bag of traps, bait and lure for trapping. My sleeping bag sets furthest up front to keep the front of the sled light and easy to steer. We'll spend a night out so I can make faster progress. After a night out, two days of hard work, I think I'm ready with the trail to head to Nenana, believing this one creek will connect me to Tom's trail work.

Dear Karen

I do not know when you will get this, but I am working on the trail to Nenana and expect to get in any time now. The sled dogs are in good shape. Trapping is going well. I run the dogs about thirty miles a day with one day a week off. Cutting trail and trapping occupies 90% of my waking day it seems. There is no other life. I spend more days on the trail sleeping in the dog sled than I do staying on the houseboat. Have you come up with enough sled dogs for our trip?

Sunshine Miles

I write a long letter about this and that.

The letter is put into one of my hand painted envelopes as I always do with letters, even business letters and bills! I smile. Even bill collectors need to know they deal with humans and need to smile. The letter is deliberately addressed upside down as well.

The sled is loaded with camping gear and mail for Nenana. The dogs are excited. They can tell by how I load the sled we are headed for town. The day is clear and a warm zero degrees—warm enough to use gloves instead of mittens, and a wool hat, not a fur hat. Seven dogs are hooked up with Kenai out front.

"Hike!" Kenai leaps forward, and all the dogs are pulling their hardest till we settle into that all day pace. The Forest cut off is reached in a half an hour. The swamps are crossed in another half an hour. We reach the hills, and get to the harder part of the rolling hills. I had helped cut here only two times. I note someone is ahead of me. The trail turns west after another hour, and I know this is to connect to the North Commission Trail. We have not been here before, so this is all new to us. The trail is narrow and twisty, but we manage because of the experience on our own trapline trail, which this is a lot like. Anything on the trail smaller than a couch we climb over. Logs are jumped without a change of pace. The sled got redesigned to run this kind of trail.

'Yeah that was good advice from old time Athabascan Josh!' He runs the big races, won the Iditarod, so knows a thing or two! He suggested three inch wide runners on the dog sled, "no wood cross members below the bed, a short tapered handle-

bar, a nicely toed-in front brush bow." All these features have a reason. Three inch wide runners stop my foot from being swept off the runner by sticks in the trail, mostly cut off small trees that still stick up we call 'pobbles.' The wide runners also allow a trail for the sled dogs to be able to run in next trip. Tapered brush bow steers through the brush and allows going closer to big trees without hitting them, and offers a glancing blow when I do hit. This sled can hit and go over stumps in the trail eight inches across and over a foot high. Few sleds can do this. Most sleds are built for racing, not wilderness use. Also that idea about old style dog collars instead of the usual race harness designed by George Atla that is the big rage, is great for pulling more weight. The old style is more like a horse harness, and allows the dog to pull from a lower center of gravity, and has a spreader or single tree in the back so the hips do not get rubbed. All this makes sense as I run this trail.

By night fall I am still on the trail, but have reached the North Commission Road, so know I have a clear shot to Nenana now. Camp is made. We are very used to this, just routine. Spruce bows are cut and set down for the sled dogs. The dog food is started even before I eat. The five gallon gas can with top cut out and hanging bail on it works well to melt snow. Spruce bows are laid in the sled for me to sleep in later, done now so I am not hunting in the dark when I'm tired. There are things I already know I want to get done before dark. Extra wood is cut, harnesses hung near the fire and the sleeping bag set out. Now I can eat. I eat the same rice the dogs eat, only cooked in my pot with grouse, and spices are added. My own clothes are checked to see if any need to hang out to dry, but nothing is damp. The clothes are set on top of the spruce bows in my sled for bedding, and to keep them dry and warm. A shirt and sweater are used as my pillow. Morning wood fire starter is set out. I can start the fire without leaving the sleeping bag, so will have a roaring fire to stand by as I get dressed. This area has my favorite birch bark, but often I can find dry spruce branches under big trees.

Sled dogs are all around me, and once again I feel like part of a team. Not the master, but one of us, the dogs, part of the wild. We speak to each other with looks and grunts. With eyes closed in the sleeping bag, I say "Kobuk, leave Kenai alone and go to sleep." Without opening my eyes I know what the problem is and who started it. Everyone is satisfied I have resolved a dispute. We are all at peace. "Long day today guys, you all did a good job. See you in the morning bright and early." No, they do not know the words. But they know my tone. Know I am pleased. Know I am addressing them. That's all they need to know. I've met married couples who know less about each other than this, after lengthy complicated conversation.

Stars overhead swim in my head out of focus as I drift off to sleep in the dog sled. In the morning, the jet between Anchorage and Fairbanks flies over at the usual time, and lets me know it is between 6-6:30 am. This is the same jet that flew over at Hansen and on the same flight path. It's only half an hour different in time going over.

Dogs get fed first. The five gallon bucket of snow had been set over dying coals in the late evening so there is some water with skim ice. Even if the water is frozen solid, the ice is easier to turn to water over the fire than filling the bucket with snow ten times.

"Another five hours or so and we should be in Nenana."

The trail I get to is well used by snow machines. The sled dogs are not tired. The trip is without incident. Since I know Josh, the dogs are tied out near his dog yard on the river bank. Josh invites me to the house. I eat with the family, and spend a night on the floor in my sleeping bag.

Letters are sent. Letters are picked up. Groceries are bought in Fairbanks. Those friends I know are visited. My furs are sold to Don as usual. I have money for supplies, with some left over for hard times.

"Miles, I saw your article in Alaska Magazine! Good story!"

"I haven't seen it yet myself. I think the January issue of 81?"

"Yup, She be named, Have Cabin Will Travel." There had been a wonder if the title or story would get changed. I'm reassured when it is quoted to me with a subtitle added "Nomadic House Boater," with some cool appropriate pictures I'm told. It is hard to understand this guy's accent so I am not quite sure. I'm able to buy a few copies at the store. Others stop me and let me know they read it.

"I saw the article, Miles, but what's it about?"

"Well, you know about the houseboat I built; this is the story of places I've been, things I've done with the home on water. The story might help sell my art. People might like to think of the art being made on the river by hand with no electricity out on the Yukon River. I also got paid for the article so it's like getting paid to advertise. "

"Cool concept, Miles, I like how you think, always looking for an angle. Ha, Ha!"

Dear Miles

So when are you coming to get me? I look forward to our trip.

Karen writes more …

"Saw your article in Alaska Magazine. Didn't you exaggerate a bit?" **Love Karen**

Old lost loves are forgotten. Maybe this will be the time things work out. This is already a wilderness woman, and so there should be no lifestyle issues. From our talk at Baker Creek, I know she is a New Englander, like me. Educated in a similar way, and has a teaching degree in English. She got married to someone who wished to homestead in Alaska. He did not like homesteading as much as she did, so when they parted, she kept the lifestyle!

I give her a date I will try to be in Manley - a month from now. I head back to the homestead. The return trip is done in one long day because the dogs know the way, and the trail is broken all the way. After a day's rest at home, it is time to go check traps and cut trail. *'A wolverine. We finally got him!'* We had been trying to get this guy all season, and finally he gets caught in a wolf trap. There is a local market for wolverine for ruffs on parkas, so I know this will fetch top dollar. There is one wolf in a trap, two lynx, and over a dozen marten. *'Not bad for fifty miles of trail!'* The fifty miles is usually a two day trip out and two days back. I spend time cutting so it takes a while. *'Should we build a cabin someplace out here for a line camp?'* I thought about it, but believe one day I will cut straight across this land, and not use the detour around the old man's part. This depends if he ever shows up and how serious he is about trapping. I'll give him a few years to show up, then talk to him again, ask if I can cross through. If so, I need a cabin further along the trail as all I have done this year would be abandoned.

A tent is set up as a temporary shelter. "We need to know what tent life is like anyhow, and this seems to work ok." Tent and Tarp sells canvas wall tents that require long poles to be cut and used for supports on location. This has been common practice since at least the 20s. *'Yeah, but the biggest issue—two actually—is that it takes a huge stove and lots of wood to keep it warm and when the fire goes out at night the temperature drops like a rock. Then two, there is little room to hang anything except from the external structure poles supporting the tent. Thus a whole shelving system has to be built to hold clothes to dry, food and such.'* With a log structure we only have to put lots of nails in the wall to hang things and nail boards to the wall, or use brackets to have instant shelves and tables. But for sure, the tent is nicer than out in the open in terms of drying, storing, and having a place to stop! It is downright comfortable when the stove is roaring. Neither wind nor snow gets in—it is much like being in a cabin!"

Sometimes furs get skinned in the tent so I can travel home with a lighter load of only furs and no carcass. This also saves time at home as I can spend an evening at camp skinning, though it cuts into what used to be my reading time. The tent camp can be taken down and moved in the future when I know better where I need to have a camp.

It is time to head for Manley to meet with Karen for our trek to Nenana together. *'Problem is... tell us the problem again?'* The problem is, it is freezing cold out, with no sign of warmth in the future, but we gave a date we'd be there, so by God we better be there if we know what's good for us!

So we take off on the sixty mile trip with no trail at forty-five below zero. The temperature drops to minus sixty on the trail. I know this because I get as far as Burke's camp at the mouth of the Kantishna. "Hey, Weedz! You staying warm?"

He is surprised to see me. "Miles, the pilgrim! What are you doing out in this weather?" He tells me he is thinking of heading in to Manley with a snow machine, maybe tomorrow.

"Going in for the same reason you are Weedz. A woman!" We both laugh. He is interested in Liller, who is in Manley right now. They are sort of an item. "So, you can break trail for me and the dogs tomorrow with the snow machine, huh?"

But no, he had more in mind, I break trail for him! I'm not thrilled with this idea, as the machine can do so much better, and do it so much faster than the dogs can. But whatever he is going to do, I'll deal with it. He has a simple log cabin that used to be his mothers, now a native claim. Weedz has the saw mill and this is his trapping cabin. I see him in summer when I'm boating by here. I have mushed the river down all the way. We have a good talk, but I'm tired. "Weedz, do you have some carcasses from trapping by any chance, that I could cook up for the dogs?" He is glad to get rid of the carcasses. He has some lynx which are cooked on his wood stove as we talk. The sled dogs are used to this, and eat the same thing at home when I get furs. The dry salmon I carry, is saved for later use by the dogs, like if I need dog feed in Manley.

Weedz comments on my sled. "Where did you get this? It looks like an antique!"

This is a sled I got from Josh that was used to haul the mail in the 50s. It is twelve ft long—most new sleds are long at six ft. This has steel on the runners, great in wet snow, but not as good as the new plastic sold now. "I think this twelve footer hauls a load much better than the short sleds, just like a long boat does. The front can float and steer better. He is impressed this is pulled by six dogs, and I have 400 pounds in the sled, breaking trail sixty miles.

In the morning, I leave ahead of him, as he plans to take his time and go in much later. *'Well maybe he will pass us later in the day and we will have a trail to follow.'* We leave in the dark with no light. The sled dogs are trusted to know how to get downriver and avoid all the various problems, like drift and open water, sand bars. The leader can figure out the shortest way across the bends. I cannot see the sled dogs, much less the river or trail.

We do not get far before we suddenly drop off a ledge about five feet. "Dang, guys! What are you doing up there! Who decided this?" Someone up front thinks it's funny and chuckles. No one is hurt. We press on. There are some good, smooth places that are windblown, so we make ok time in the cold. One method to stay warm is to keep a tiny stove ready in the sled. This is no bigger than a shoe box, sold as a small tent stove. It is kept filled with kindling and fast burning wood. The stove pipe is in sections—two inches in diameter and five ft. long when put together. When I get cold, I just toss a match in the stove and wrap myself around the pipe. My hands warm up fast. Much of the hot pipe is inside my snow suit, trapping its heat. My face is next to it, to catch heat. The stove is between my knees as I crouch down by it. The stove only takes a minute to get warm. When the fire is out, I find new kindling to load for the next time and press on.

Weedz snow machine is heard, so I know he will pass us and give us a trail to follow. The high pitch scream of a two stroke engine comes around the bend. The black dot in the distance quickly turns into Weedz. He is not following in our trail. Very odd. When he stops he speaks to me. "Miles, you and your stupid dogs almost got me in serious trouble! The trail lead over a five foot drop!"

I had to laugh. He is the one who wanted to follow me, this is what he gets. Dogs can go places snow machines cannot. He forgot that. I had forgotten all about what that drop might do for him, till he mentioned it. I have the snow machine trail to follow now, so make good time. I get to Karen's about dinner time. I'm expected any day now. The older seven year old daughter answers the door of the one room sod house they live in. The place is warm, clean, and comfortable. There is much excitement about the trip. The two girls will be with their father for two weeks while their mother and I go on our dog trip. [3]

"Karen, did you come up with more sled dogs?" She tells me we need to stop at Baker Creek to see Baker Creek Carol for a couple of extra dogs she will lend us. She mentions "That Joe guy told me I'd die traveling on that cold river with sled dogs!" She doesn't believe that, but Joe is for sure not helping me get along with the woman I'm trying to share a good time with.

The dog trip goes well. We have two teams, and make good time on the river. Sharing a one man sleeping bag is challenging. Plans are made for her and the two children to join me on the Kantishna in spring.

A second floor is planned for the cabin before I put the roof on. Karen and the children expect to spend time chinking the logs with moss. I finish the log work on the cabin and it is two stories so the two children have their own rooms.

Houseboat hauling cabin insulation

CHAPTER SIXTEEN

LIFE WITH KAREN AND KIDS, ANOTHER HOMESTEAD ACQUIRED, FISH AND GAME PROBLEMS, LIFE AS A FAMILY, FAMILY BOATS TO MANLEY, 10 PEOPLE JUST MURDERED, ALMOST US

M y diary gets confusing. Someone else (a woman!) writes diary entries on the calendar.

Future flash:

Karen is reluctant to have me talk about her and our relationship over the past four years. Like some others, she does not want her life put in print for all to read. I respect and care for her a lot, and wish to honor her feelings. Much happens. Both our lives are changed forever. We learn about gardening and dog mushing together. We raised her two girls in the wilds. I think of them as my own children. We home school them.

Other things happen that were just about myself. My trapline got cut to Hansen Lake. The family moved into the cabin I started, that ends up being built two stories so the girls can have their own rooms. We fish for our sled dogs that are our only winter transportation. We live off the garden, fish, and wild game. Off the grid, off the map. The garbage we accumulated in a year fits in one garbage bag. We are proud of this, not being big consumers. Karen took over writing diary notes on the calendar. Many notations are hers.

Future flash ends

I look back over the diary entries

May twenty-seventh 1982 - Miles got black bear. We canned up and saved hide. Dogs enjoyed the rest.

Mostly the entries are about daily life. Times we set the fish nets and pulled them, and how many fish we caught.

July fourteenth - Houseboat to Manley. Made it all the way up the slough. Fifteen gallons of gas and ten hours.
    August second - Steamed sled runners.

I remember this. I build a new dog sled. I have to first make a wood steamer from old stove pipe to get the runners to bend. I hand cut some birch wood. Josh told me how, "For sled runners use either tamarack or birch. The straight grain birch is often found with poplar trees on top of a hillside. Take an ax and make a cut. Pull on the cut and see if it pulls long or runs off." This advice helped me get strong, straight grain wood, hand split for runners.

August twenty-eighth - First frost. First real meal in cabin. Miles works on roof.
    This is an important day! We have al worked hard over the summer to get the cabin ready for winter. There would not be room for all of us in the houseboat! I cut and haul logs, the girls mostly do the chinking between the logs. The two stories are done but some roof insulation still needs work.
    August thirty-first - Canned ten pints of fried chicken mushrooms
    Sept twentieth - Refrigerator hole ready to use.

We dig a hole under the floor into the permafrost, then make a trap door to keep food cool in summer. This is our only refrigeration. We also discover if we use a lot of vinegar, food items keep longer.

Sept twenty-fifth - Dug up carrots. Miles varnishes dog sled. Sixty-one salmon.
    Sept thirty - Wet snow fell. Fifty-five fish.
    Oct fourteenth – minus ten - Miles out on trapline.
    Oct twenty-first - Miles went out overnight on trapline.
    Oct thirtieth - Miles back. Six marten - total nine marten.

The diary for the month of November is filled with days I left and came back, how much fur I got and the temperatures.

Dec twentieth minus five. Went on trail. Miles has made a trail towards the drop.

THE DROP IS a place we named on the trail to Nenana. We run the Kantishna flats to the hills about fifteen miles by our trail, and reach a cliff we have to get up. There is a narrow cut that seems like a drop straight down when coming back. We name the area 'Chicago' because it is always windy. I went to Navy boot camp in Great Lakes by Chicago, and remember a constant cold wind. So we drop off the bluff into Chicago. There was a big wind and snow on the way in with supplies, and it takes me two days. The dogs are beat. Some of the important supplies had to be left on the side of the trail to lighten the load. Karen comes with me with a separate sled and team to help get the load we need back home. There are now thirteen dogs in the dog yard. We sure appreciated the supplies when they were finally at the homestead.

Feb 1983 Miles and May head for Nenana. Pick up new dogs Poncho and Scrappy.

A big deal for May! She is just twelve years old and going out with her own team on a 120 mile round trip! She runs dogs she owns and takes care of herself. She stays with her father for a while, so I return alone.

March fifteenth - Miles home with supplies. Took twelve hours. Had to leave some supplies.

It was stormy and the trail blew in. I had to abandon fifty pounds of supplies. I go back later and get them out of a snow bank. May, the elder daughter, now thirteen, comes with me with her own dog team.

April third - Miles sets beaver snares in Swan Lake.
   April tenth - Planted garden in jiffy pots on window sill.

If we expect a garden in interior Alaska, it is important to start seeds early indoors or there will not be enough time in the growing season to have a harvest. Many seeds are started two months in advance, like tomatoes squash and cucumber. We compost all our garbage in a big cage I built. Even the dog poop is composted! We end up with wonderful produce that would win prizes at the fair.

April twentieth - All of us walked to see the swans and geese on the lake.
   We just must go to the lake because we hear the birds, and it sounds like thousands! What a sight to see!
   Miles gets seven beaver.

April twenty-third - Miles fixes canoe and paddles to the houseboat.

April twenty-sixth - Miles builds a greenhouse. Plants out in day. Sixty degrees.

April twenty-ninth - The ice in Nenana went out. We hear this on the radio. We all sleep on the houseboat this night. There is flooding so we are uncertain of the water level. We also need to make sure the boat stays safe during ice break up.

May first - We make a gallon of birch syrup from trees we are tapping.

May seventh Is my birthday! The two girls have a birthday about the same time, so we celebrate all on the same day! We haul water, get clean, dress up, have a special meal, exchange homemade gifts. It's a very special time. This is what families do. "Wow, this is awesome!" I had been so worried I could not adjust to being around people, three females, children, in a small cabin, no peace, obligations, so scary, so different, so unlike what I have known in my life. I feel like I took to it like a fish in water. No problems with needing more space, or any issues I worried about. The children needed a father figure and took to me. I enjoyed being 'Mr. fix it,' as they called me. I made them toys and when they broke I fixed them. One girl liked the outdoors and the sled dogs most, the other liked the indoors and art the most. Momma liked having a man around. I liked being wanted. We all agree on a lifestyle that we love and share.

May ninth - Left at 8:30 – Burkes by noon, 4:30 in Manley, walk in to town.

I have to park on the main river because the six mile slough is too shallow. There is a five mile dirt road into the village and I get mail and come right back to the homestead.

May twentieth - Two big pike, Miles works on motor reverse.

May twenty-fifth - Plant potatoes

May twenty-ninth - Black bear troubles for Karen and the girls.

This bear problem shows me it would be a good idea if the girls learned how to use a gun better. I will not always be around. They do not want to, so we hope for the best, that there will be no serious consequences. Already the bear got some of our supplies and the girls could do nothing about it.

When we make birch syrup, it takes two weeks of cooking to get one gallon of syrup. June and July are filled with records of the temperature and daily routine of picking berries, tending the garden, feeding sled dogs, and fishing for the dogs.

In August, I head for Fairbanks for the Tanana Fair and get supplies for the family. At the end of the calendar is a note in Karen's hand, "Please keep your own record of events." I start a new calendar diary. One of those 'getting used to someone else in the house' issues.

After the fair, Karen and I decide to go to Hansen Lake for the winter, while her girls are with their father for a year. I apply for a Federal home site north of Hansen Lake. This would be on the trapline between Hansen Lake and the lower river homestead. Time is spent hauling supplies with the houseboat up to Hansen Lake with the family. This is partly meant as a smart business decision.

"Karen, I am concerned about our legal rights to the trails I have spent so many years cutting. There may be a time in the not so distant future when civilization will encroach. Maybe for the timber, the fish, to expand, or maybe oil. Surely this big chunk of wilderness will not stay un-noticed forever." I explain the legal status of access to my legal property. I might call the trapline my only winter access to legal property, and thus have it called an easement road. Much better legal status than "My trapline." So having legal land along the trail may help me keep my lifestyle longer. Likewise the line cabins I build wherever I want is accepted now. But for how many years?

I'd feel a lot more comfortable to own something along the way. Also, I am concerned about our far off one day retirement! We are not paying into social security. "What have we got when we get old?" I have met old time trappers in the streets of Fairbanks, at the salvation army, with nothing to show in their ending years.

My idea is to use our youth and wilderness skills to acquire land that we can use, and when we get old, and can no longer use it, fifty years from now, sell it for some retirement money. The value of the land should increase faster than interest in the bank or any standard retirement investment program. We do not have cash to invest anyhow. Karen is more for just settling down in one place, spare the details and 'what if' ideas. I think too much. She goes along with the plan, but is not happy.

Sept fifth Indian summer continues. Water drops a little. Talk to Weedz on CB radio. This is our first CB contact with anyone.

Sept seventh - AP comes by with rest of my load, and then Weedz comes by with 130 fish. Karen goes to Manley with Weedz.

Sept ninth - Radio message from Bill. To meet him at Joe's slough and meet the land surveyor. Expect to pick Karen up too.

Sept tenth - Spend night at Weedz.

Sept eleventh - Fetch gas from three people paid $1.20 a gallon for gas, prices going up.

Sept seventeenth - See Steve and Sarah at Toklat River fishing. Spend night below Coy's. Burning lots of gas pulling three boats. Trying to get to the Bearpaw and Hansen.

These are people I meet that are new homesteaders. They are not part of my life, but we meet, I know them, we get along.

Sept eighteenth - Stop at Bearpaw River. Burned eight gallons of gas. Percy at his cabin and sells me thirty gallons of gas.

Sept nineteenth - engine lower unit quits. Make it to Hansen Lake limping. Burned 100 gallons of gas going eighty miles.

While the engine does well downstream or upstream without a load, when overloaded any two stoke engine is hard on fuel. I did not realize how bad it could get until now, less than on mile per gallon.

Sept twentieth - Catch seven fish on the lake. See fifty trumpeter swans.

Sept twenty-first - twenty fish in two nets, whitefish and suckers. Set up propane light on houseboat. Getting dark by 8:00 pm.

Sept twenty-second -Look for moose. Snow. Ice forms. 11 fish.

Sept twenty-fifth - Creek freezes pretty solid. Thirty-two fish.

Sept twenty-seventh - Walk on lake.

Sept twenty-eight - Warms up. Work on dog harnesses. Rain all day.

Oct seventh - Pull nets. No more boat travel.

Oct eighth - Fetch moose. Karen had heard a bull moose bellow during moose season. She came back to the cabin to get me. I shot the moose from across the lake. We had time to gut it but darkness came.

Ice forms on the lake the next day, so it was decided we'd walk around the lake, hang the moose and cover it, then come back for it later when we could use the sled dogs to haul it. So On Oct eighth we can cross the lake to get the meat home. We found a frozen swan in the ice that had not been able to fly south. The sled falls through the ice and we have to save everything. We were glad to get back home.

Oct eleventh - Houseboat afloat from its winter foundation as water comes up due to warm spell. three days of solid rain.

Oct fourteenth - Move houseboat to new location by new fish racks.

Oct seventeenth - Message on radio, Bettes dies, the Native who hoped to come out here to trap, whose area I am cutting around.

Oct twentieth - Run sled dogs for the first time of the season. Minus three degrees. Glare ice hinders dog mushing.

Oct twenty-second - Walk towards Federal place with Kenai, who carries a pack. Camp eight miles out.

FEDERAL HOME SITE land opens in this area. I selected some land north of Hansen. I got flown in to stake the land, and now must prove up, build, and stay in this land for five months. I get time discounted for being a war veteran. Five acres are staked on a knoll overlooking a creek with a view of Denali. This land would only be reachable by the winter dog trail. No access in summer unless I walk in ten miles. I tell

Karen, "Just in case hard times arrive and we need to live someplace away from people that no one can get to." She looks dubious. "Social unrest, revolution, invasion, or widespread disease. You never know. Otherwise, just a trapline place along my long trail that I can own."

Oct twenty-seventh seven mink caught.

Oct twenty-eighth Take six sled dogs and camp out six miles. Cut one mile of trail.

Oct twenty-ninth Cut one mile of trail.

Nov ninth A red letter day, arrive at Federal home site. Set up a tent. Select a cabin site.

Nov sixteenth Head back to Hansen. Takes three hours.

Nov nineteenth I leave for Federal Land with plywood and heavy load. Takes nine hours. Have to drop half the load for later.

Nov twentieth return for load left behind.

The building of a cabin begins in winter and slowly I get the logs cut and up, plywood floor done as I live in the tent.

Dec fourth Move into cabin.

Dec fifth Karen comes out with three sled dogs and black sled. We spend night in cabin. I make door and secure window. We work on a trail to Lake Minchumina. Even though I had been living in the cabin since November, it was rough living till this red letter day we could call 'comforts of home.'

Dec seventh My new sled dog Swizzle bites me and will not let go. He has hold of my wrist. I have to kill him with a chunk of firewood.

Dec ninth Plan to leave for Lake Minchumina for supplies and to sell fur.

Dec eleventh Fly to Fairbanks with Dell. Get a dog from the Cosgrove's.

This is a significant event because it is the first time I pay money for a good sled dog. This family is known in the racing group. Up till now I have rejects, free dogs, and some of these work out, but a proven bloodline does make a difference. I pay $300 for a female I can get pups from. She is Rita (lovely Rita the meter maid, from the Beatles song). Paying money comes with some guarantees and warranties that I will be satisfied. "You got Scorpion from Henry? Ha! We had him first and were going to shoot him! What a worthless dog!" What could I reply?

Dec fourteenth minus thirty-five I take a load of insulation to the cabin from Hansen Lake.

Every day is filled with something I feel is worth writing down. There is fur to catch, loads of firewood to haul, dog trips, bitter cold, snow storms, and surely never a dull moment.

Jan eleventh 1984 Rita has pups in the cabin. Minus sixty-three.

Jan twenty-third minus fifty, Tree house. I stay a night in a tree house I built as a trapline cabin, with the idea being to keep bears and other critters out in summer when I'm gone. Also it will not get buried in the snow. No digging out.

SPRING COMES. Summer arrives. I have proven up on my Federal land. Karen and I get the girls back. We settle in for a while at the lower Kantishna two story cabin homestead. Fall arrives, winter arrives, and life has been a routine with not much to talk about that is different.[1]

One winter day Fish and Game shows up in a helicopter.

"We have a search warrant." The family is very puzzled. We wonder what we might have done, even what we possibly could have done wrong, as we live alone out here and see no one. *Who even knows what we do out here?*

"Looking for evidence you got a moose out of season!" Legal sport season is a two week period in September. In truth it is almost an impossible time to get a moose if you do not have reliable electricity and own a freezer. The meat will not keep as the weather is too warm. It turns green and or gets maggots. (I repeat this over and over to whoever will listen!). Canning is possible, but this is a lot of jars for 1,000 pounds of meat, as well as a lot of time and heat for the boiling, cooking, and processing. Sometimes we could not even afford to buy the lids! The quality of meat is not as good as fresh or frozen. The jars cannot be frozen in the winter. It is almost impossible not to freeze things when we are gone from home and the wood stove goes out. This two week moose season is already an extremely busy time of year getting ready for winter. Jerky is possible to make, but anyone who has lived on jerky understands it is a very inferior product compared to fresh steaks. Maybe for snacks, but not meals.

Up until now there has been an understanding, an agreement, not in legal writing however. That those who live remote get a moose when they need to, as part of a subsistence lifestyle, as long as the meat stays in the woods and does not end up in town, and as long as there is no waste of meat. We have not heard of anyone living as we do who gets a moose in the September season. We all wait till October. At this time the moose will easily keep seven months, till about the end of next May. Whatever might be left over in May can, at our leisure, be dried or canned for the rest of the summer's needs. Getting ready for summer is much easier than getting ready for winter, and spring is a time of year with more time available for caning.

Also there is often old firewood left over to get rid of, rotten wood that can more easily be used for cooking fires outdoors then the wood stove indoors. There are no flies and few germs in spring, so jerky is easier to make, and there is no rush to keep meat away from flies.

One advantage of taking a moose in October is that we can take one far off on the trapline, in swampy areas no one has access to during sport hunting season. We thus harvest moose where they are more plentiful. Let the sport hunters harvest the moose along the river, which becomes a highway during the two week sport season. This seems to make better biological sense, in terms of being best on the moose population.

The family is in shock. A helicopter cost $800 an hour to run, and here these government people are investigating our lives at such a cost, like a serious crime. Some thoughts have been shifting. More and more often, subsistence is becoming a native only rights issue, not a lifestyle issue. 'Only Indians can live this life,' is the way the new thinking goes. This of course is racial discrimination. Maybe this is best, or necessary, but why not then say, "We believe in discrimination," and explain why. Why should a definition of a lifestyle include 'must be poor'? More to the point, this is all new to us, and the first time we are informed of the changes, and informed in such a hostile manner.

Karen and I wonder why the state invitation to homesteaders encouraged 'subsistence' and did not mention needing to be an Indian? If, in fact, there was a good reason to believe in discrimination, shouldn't the state have said "While subsistence is native only, we wish you good luck!" So we would know not to count on it!

The house is getting torn apart in a search for evidence. "Do you have any firearms in the house?" Now the assumption is that I might be armed and dangerous?

"Yes, sir, of course. This is a part of our lifestyle." The fire arms are gathered up and put under the control of one of the two agents.

I'm told, "Standard procedure. We do not want any problems."

Which is understandable, except the officers are well armed, and I'm expected to trust them. There are stories of hostile folks being investigated, but also stories of crooked cops beating up people for no reason, interrogating, planting evidence and such. This very situation does not look great so far. *'No problems for whom?'* I wonder. I certainly am not feeling very safe.

Books are pulled off shelves and thrown on the floor. If the investigators are looking for illegal moose, what do our reading books have to do with it? One investigator is looking at my art and art records. "I heard of your art, Wild Miles, interesting. How much money do you make?" He's looking over my records, tossing them on the floor, scattering my supplies. "Where's Karen's diary?"

Karen screams, and wants to know why she has to turn over her diary. It is personal, and even I have never seen it, and respect her right to keep a private journal no one can read but her. We vaguely wonder where these guys would ever hear about a diary?

They read it, take their time, and have fun laughing and reading her personal stuff. Karen is mortified. I can understand their right to look for evidence of what they consider a crime, To be resolved later in court, *but till then innocent, unless proven guilty. I think I'd win in court, judged by a jury of my peers. I am thus, not a criminal with no rights.* What right do they have to ask me about my art and income, and focus on, laugh about, personal diary entries unrelated to the warrant?

It gets a little comical though. The older girl May, sneaks out of the house and moves the cache ladder so it cannot be found, thus stopping the officers from gaining access to the evidence of an illegal moose kill. *The hide is up in the cache.* Interestingly we had a moose roast in the wood stove oven, and the investigators never look in the oven. Old bones out back are found and confiscated as proof and held for evidence. A ticket is written up. I'm charged with poaching. This seems odd because, how can one tell on what day bones were taken from a moose? Also just who is being charged, as three of us in the family are capable of harvesting a moose?

In truth, these bones are gathered over the years and stored. I use them in my art work. All these bones have dried marrow and maggots in them—proof the animals were harvested before winter. Some were as old as five years. I was not asked to explain, nor given time to point this out. It would have to come out in court. This raid did not seem to us like anyone trying to understand what is going on, or even about gathering evidence against an illegal moose kill. It was about hurting and scaring us.[2]

My guns were going to be confiscated. I have to argue they are needed here in this lifestyle. We cannot have a woman and children out here with no way to protect them from bears. The attitude of the officer in charge is mean. There is nothing friendly about him. We are treated as hardened criminals. I get the impression if I lost it and got angry, he'd kill me. Maybe be glad to. Karen is German, and tells me she has heard stories like this back in Germany direct from her grandparents. This is exactly Gestapo behavior, and she thought we were safe in this country. She is in tears. I can do nothing. She tells me she will never keep a diary again, it is not safe. As her protector, I am helpless. What can I say?

The court date set to face the charge is a time it is not possible to get out of the woods, in late April. The officers know this. If I do not show up, there will be a warrant issued. The law will come and drag me out as a criminal in handcuffs. There is no money for a lawyer. No money to fly out, or back in, and no money to stay in town as the trial goes on. If I manage to trial and win, but have no money to get back home, the family will be left here without a man during break up. Karen does not know much about the boat. *A situation like this is why I had encouraged Karen to learn how to survive without me! What if something happens to me!? Karen is content to depend on me. She is not interested in how the boat runs.* Spring is guaranteed bear raid time. Bears are hungry and will find the cabin. No one but me is a marksman, skilled with firearms. There are not enough supplies to last till after break up. I have no way to get back after the ice goes out if my boat is at the homestead, and I am in town.

Scared does not even describe how we feel. We are terrified. All of us. My big terror is how helpless I am in this situation. How can I fight this? These men can do whatever they wish. So can society. We are nothing. Who would believe us if we managed to tell our story? It's such an incredible story, so far-fetched. It would not surprise me if they raped Karen, or killed us all, saying we tried to escape.

BY A FLUKE of luck the children's correspondence school teacher flies out one last time. I am able to hitch a ride with the pilot in time to go to court. He can bring me back again. He will fly for free, but I find out he flies free only because there is no use asking for money. We do not have enough, and he is not happy about that. He's disgusted, and feels we should not be out here if we cannot take care of ourselves. He sees us as welfare people living off the system.

"Why do you think you deserve to get a moose whenever you want? What makes you so privileged? You contribute nothing, only take, all you people out here. I pay taxes, those I know work hard, and they have to obey the laws, and do not get moose all the time. They deserve to hunt more than you do. Just because you need one! Well, la dee da! Your whole life is an emergency. So what! You chose it, so face it, and live with the consequences. I have no sympathy for your situation. You want my opinion, you belong in jail." He tells me most homesteaders are like this, and he should know, he says he flies for us, and flies the teachers in to home school families all over the state.

"Everywhere you people are, there are broken-down snow machines in the woods, empty drums and five gallon cans, blue tarps blown off roofs, piles of dog crap, junk piles of wood, metal and garbage. Other people have a right to use the wilderness, and you folks ruin it for the rest of us." He comes back to me about not being able to pay for what I need, like this flight.

I tell him, "First I do not want to come out, it is not my choice. Next. I usually can trade for what I need, often times I trade with pilots. I'd be happy to trade for this flying."

"Sure, Miles, but some of those you trade with do not need or want what you offer. It is only that they know the deal is to take what you offer, or get nothing! Or feel sorry for you, and offer it as charity, making you feel better by taking some token or other of appreciation. I have no use for your trinkets. Others like you offer me furs, dry fish, and other things I have no use for. You say you do not want to come out, but you are forced to? Why is that any concern of mine or any tax payer? Why does that become my problem? Wake up and smell the crap, Miles. Take off those rose glasses. You will always have to do what you need to, and not what you want to do. There will always be emergencies, unplanned happenings requiring coming out of the woods unexpectedly. At any time you or the family can get sick, hurt, need a doctor, a dentist. There can be bears, storms, fires, loss of supplies and even court cases. It's life Miles, and you can't pay for it!"

There is little I can say in return. I'm vaguely curious why he keeps this job if he hates those he flies for so much. It seems to me, there are other flying jobs he might enjoy much more. He goes on. "If you paid me what this trip cost, like if you called me and chartered a round trip flight with me, it is $500 each way. A total of $1,000. That is with a discount, not the tourist price. If a tourist calls to go fishing or hunting it cost $300 an hour, about $700 one way to get to your homestead from Fairbanks." We are flying over country with no roads and no people, nothing but swamps, lakes, clumps of trees as far as the eye can see. I make out my trail below and we are following it.

"Yeah, I use your trail sometimes as a landmark, it's a straight line to Nenana. Then I jog over to Fairbanks. Nenana makes a good emergency landing with its good runway, so it's a good idea to be in the area as a routine."

I think *So see! I cut that trail, and it helps you. I contributed something that helps you.* From the air I see it would not be possible to get through with sled dogs. As I suspected, the swamp is opening up. The one lake I wondered about is open already.

I find out later in town, it was this pilot who turned us in. He flies to all the homesteads with the teacher, working under cover for the law. Asking questions, taking pictures, gathering evidence and turning homesteaders in. I recall a situation he had commented on while we were flying, and I had brushed it off. While the teacher was giving tests to our kids in the small cabin early in the winter, the pilot and I had gone outside. We talked as I did my daily chores. One chore for that day had been to sort my stash of moose leg bones. I organized them by size and condition, noted how many I had, so I could plan projects for them. The pilot thought they were all fresh. I may have gone to the dog pot after or before, and this pilot assumed I was feeding moose to my dogs, and even killing many moose to feed dogs. But he had said nothing, and made assumptions that were false.

If he would have said 'Wow, this is a lot of dead moose Miles, why do you need so many?' I'd have chuckled, "Oh this is ten years' worth of leg bones I save!" Shown him the dried maggots in the ends to prove, not fresh. Maybe some of the broken bones I cannot use for art get tossed to the dogs, but absolutely nothing a human could eat. In court, I never face or know who my accuser is, so that I may defend myself. Nor did charges reflect what the pilot saw, that the law believed, and what he said was happening.

In court, the investigating officer takes me aside saying, "We do not mind if you get a moose for the family now and then out of season, but we do not like more than one moose being fed to dogs." I am shocked. None of this was in writing, or part of the charge, or brought up in the open. It explained at least part of the treatment we got. I myself would be disgusted and totally against, and would turn anyone in, who was killing moose to feed dogs. This resource is much too valuable to humans to be feeding it to the dogs. I end up winning my case. Yet I won nothing. The case was dismissed because all cases involving subsistence are being categorically dismissed at this time.

The judge put it, "The state has failed to adequately define subsistence." The Federal government is ordering the state to deal with the subsistence issue, while the state stalls and does not want to. One aspect is to define just what subsistence is, and who qualifies. The prosecuting officer is livid. I got off on a technicality. He feels I'm guilty as hell and I'm getting off. There was no presenting of evidence, no proving the bones were old, no proving dogs are fed this, no proof of anything wasted, etc. As a matter of fact, no one uses more off of a moose than my family. When we are done eating, bones are made into tools and material for art objects. We use the hair to stuff pillows. I use the ears for knife sheaths. There is hardly enough left for a meal for a raven when we are done.

I'm extremely angry to be told I am wasteful. I am angry to have had my family made to tremble and cry, to be in terror, to be hurt. I have a strong instinct to protect my family as the role of the man, head of the family. I did not want to win on a technicality. I want to clear my good name. That chance was not given to me. I told my lawyer so, and want to fight this, and fine, let this be a test case for subsistence, make a stand right here, right now, and clear this up. Force the state to define subsistence. Give me a jury of my peers and let me talk. Let's make history here. If we want discrimination to be legal, let's do that. I do not approve of laws that are not in writing that get a 'wink, wink and this is how it is really done.'

I had a lawyer appointed by the court because I am considered poor. It was obvious to me everyone here knew everyone else. It is me who is the outsider in the room. I am the trouble maker. My lawyer jokes with, and goes out to lunch with, the prosecution. Maybe the next case he will be the prosecutor. I'm guessing his loyalty is going to be with his peers, friends, the judge, those he sees every day. Not me. Nor to a set of ethics he wants to stand by. He wants to know what my problem is, I won! He says. "Geez, let it be! Anyhow you can't sue the state and go around proving the government is wrong! Good grief get a grip. Who the heck do you think you are? I cannot believe the audacity of you people. Give 'em a free lawyer,' who gets them off, and they complain! Now you want to fight the state on society's dime! Ha!" Another lawyer tells me it will take about $30,000 just to get started, am I interested? *I am referred to as 'one of them' none of this 'one of us,' a citizen.*

"Ha, Ha Miles! Since when did you think we live in a democracy! You are funny!"

Future Flash:

"**Lawmakers Hesitate on Subsistence**" April 1, 1985 Northland News. By Don Joling.

Gov. Bill Sheffield unveiled a proposed bill in early March, an attempt to match state law with regulations…that violate the state's 1978 subsistence law."

One line in here catches my eye… "Senate Majority Leader Rick Halford questioned why Alaska hunters should give up a newly acquired right for priority in shooting game they consume in favor of trophy hunters and out of state hunters,"

…and further on someone named Fisher says… "As I read it, it would put us in total compliance with federal law" "but Senate President Don Bennett said he does not think the legislature will act on the matter this year."

My future flash keeps on zooming ahead in time.

I saved this as an interesting article at the time, without really understanding its meaning or implication, or how it might affect me. At the time I am not even sure what a legislature is, or what they do. It's… you know… big government… it's 'them.' Let the politicians figure it all out. Just leave me alone. I want a simple life in the woods. I'm not interested in going to court, writing letters, doing public comments, or writing proposals. I'm out here in the wilds trying to stay alive on fish and moose in an area few hunters get to, and civilization with all its mess, and politics is far away! That's how I want it. The same as 'they' see me no doubt. *'You know, another one of those long hairs, they all look alike, act alike, and are all worthless, poor unethical immoral criminals.'* That's fine. *So you go your way and I go mine and our paths never have to cross. I leave you alone and mind my own business, do not interfere with your corruption. Live and let live.*

I attend a fisheries meeting, and recall one of the board members reading the laws on subsistence gill netting. His comment to the state that I recorded was:

"I'm on the board and I do not understand this. I'm trying to put myself in the place of an ordinary fisherman out there on the river, and it's incomprehensible." Here we are, simple river people, subsistence folks wanting to live with the land in peace. We are responsible for understanding and knowing the laws… laws the board members who wrote them cannot even understand. Laws the state and feds cannot agree on, argue over, and do not understand. How are the officers in the field to know the law? How are those in the office responsible for enforcing and setting policy to understand?"

So I am not the only one who has trouble figuring out what is right and legal.

The train between Fairbanks and Anchorage (passing through Nenana, our area) kills an average of 800 moose a winter. No one seems to care, or even knows about it. That fact goes unreported. Fish and Game declared the surplus of moose in the Nenana area a major problem. (not a blessing!) To solve this problem cow moose season is opened seven years in a row to help thin the population. Moose are not endangered in the area and never were. In 2013, there is serious gas and oil exploration going forward, with a bridge across the river, a road going right down my old trapline trail. I notice everyone who once lived in this area 'subsistence,' and called this area 'home' is now gone.

In truth I get hot headed. In truth I am frustrated and do not understand. I am human and sometimes I cannot separate the facts from the myths, and what is the real danger. I only imagine and get paranoid about what I believe. I hear radicals speak 'Those socialist government people have cameras in the sky, listening devices in the woods spying on us!' Quite a few refer to being Jews and the government head as Hitler. I shrug it off, try not to listen. My own experiences seem amazing and impossible from an honest government, living up to what it says it stands for. It makes it difficult to defend myself, or come across as being in the right, or even sane. I cannot keep my facts straight, my times and dates right. This makes it harder to defend myself within the system. It does not however mean I am wrong. My thought was to fight any issues I have in court, within the system, in what is supposed to be the appropriate civilized manner. I attend meetings, write comments to proposals I ask to get copies of. I try to get informed. More to defend myself, not to attack.

Future Flash ends

Hey Will!

I have not heard from you in a while. How are things with you? Trapping is good this year. I got a wolverine the other day. I got an idea to build a trap cabin as a tree house so bears and critters do not get in and get at my supplies. This seems to be working out ok. I do not have to build it as solid as on the ground, so I'm using 2x2's. This trapline camp will double as a cache the rest of the year. Almost always bears get in my shelters on the ground. Maybe this will solve that. I have tin on the support trees so the bears can't climb. Right now it is wrapped in visqueen with only a little insulation. It was pretty cold at minus fifty° I have a tent camp in the area, but the canvas tent is frozen down. I am unsure how to get the tent up at the end of the season because everything will still be frozen. I got the usual set up from Tent and Tarp, like the one we looked at. They sure want a lot of money. I'm unsure how long these tents can be expected to last.

Oh! I'm a lifetime member of the Alaska Trappers Association now. I was able to trade the usual $800 lifetime membership fee for a major art piece. They auctioned it off and got over $2,000. So that worked out good. I cannot make it to any meetings, but maybe I can write for the magazine. I have my trapline registered with the association. Not that it does much good. As you know there is no legality to traplines on public land. The Association is not in favor of wanting legality. As it is explained to me, that means keeping accurate records, paying taxes, being regulated, watched, restricted, limits set, length of trails set and such. Registering with the association might help the honest people who want to know where they can trap, and where others are. There is a rumor of problems ahead for me at Wien Lake. Another trapper is concerned with where I'm going with my trails, but as far as I know, no one else is where I'm going. The trappers association helps me understand what might be expected and acceptable, and how to deal with various trapping disputes and issues that come up. Anyhow that's all the news from here.

Later, Miles

WINTER COMES TO AN END. In March a pen is built for the growing puppies. The puppies already know about being sled dogs. They had traveled in the sled with the mother, nursing as I tend the trapline. They see the dogs clean their feet, hear the commands I give, and have seen fur in the traps. They all appear to be good sled dogs. In April, I'm able to hook the pups up to the sled, and we make our first journey together. I see how the pups perform and am optimistic.

This is how our life goes month by month as a routine, as the seasons come and go. This is a routine I look forward to. The year always begins with break up when the ice goes out and boating season begins. There is always the first trip to town for supplies. The garden gets planted the first of June. Fish get caught as soon as the ice goes out, but the serious fish runs, like salmon, begin about the fourth of July. Berries get picked in July, with late berries in August. The state fair is in August; I always go and meet with friends and customers. Food is put up in August and Sept. A moose is got in late Sept or Oct. Trapping season begins, working with sled dogs. The children and Karen do home schooling about four hours a day, then the kids have to work on their own a while. A teacher flies out to give tests and check on this once a month. The teacher surprises us by telling us this costs less than having a child in public school! We find this amazing. Sometimes the plane bringing the teacher also hauls propane, mail, and takes outgoing mail for us.

"Karen do you think you understand which is the heavy load and which is the light load for the 357 pistol?" I ask her once again to show me the difference, so I am sure she knows. I am taking the boat to get supplies and she and the girls will be at the homestead alone. We are pretty sure a bear will come around. We have a trash can filled with commercial dog food outside we suspect any bear in the area will come to. There is no easy way to protect the feed beyond shooting, and then eating the bears.

Karen goes to the boxes of ammo and picks up one and says "This is the light one!"

"No this is not one of the light ones." I reply.

"But the light ones are brass, and the hot ones are silver right?"

In most cases she is correct, but this is not a good thing to memorize. Brass or the silver is only a type of metal, and both light and hot loads can be in either, though I had mostly brass light loads. I come upon a solution. "Ok, look at the end of the bullet, Karen. The heavy loads will say 357, and the light load will say 38!" She gets that. We go over what she needs to do if a bear comes. Though not good with a gun, she accepts they are needed, even carries one sometimes, but it is just not her focus of interest. Point and shoot is all she wants to know about it.

"Ok, Honey, I'm off, and hope to be back in four to five days if all goes well. I'll send a trapline chatter message over KJNP." This North Pole radio station has a time set aside each evening to pass messages over the air to those of us living in the wilderness. It is used by pilots to tell folks their supplies will be arriving, and to meet them on a lake or sandbar someplace, or the school teacher is arriving. Often one family member heads in to civilization as I am, and sends messages saying they arrived safe. Relatives say happy birthday and such. One message we just heard was, "I'm pregnant, what are you going to do about it!" But it was sent as a joke by a wife to a husband, but the whole listening world laughed. At any rate I'm going to send a message.

It's a normal trip in and part of my routine not worth mentioning. Almost like, 'Went to the store, got milk, came home. 'It is not an adventure anymore. The adventure was when I got back home.

"Miles! I am glad you are back! I shot a bear and he got away!"

I groan. I am glad everyone is fine, but now we probably have a mess on our hands. A wounded bear running around to keep an eye out for. I ask what happened.

"Well, I woke up and looked out the window when I heard the trash can get banged. It was a bear. I got the pistol and made sure I had the heavy loads in it as you told me. I go out the door and the bear will not leave the trash can. I walk up close, like fifteen feet, and the bear goes 'woof!' He slams his paw on the lid saying "Mine!" But I was determined to keep our dog food! We need it! I will not let the bear have it! So I shot him in the head! Gee the gun is loud!"

I'm puzzled and surprised. Shot in the head from fifteen feet should have knocked him on his butt. I ask Karen to show me exactly what load she used in the gun. She grabs one that says '357' on the back. It is a load I forgot about, a 357 all right, but the projectile is blue plastic, and filled with tiny shot pellets. It might kill a squirrel from twenty ft.—maybe. It is frustrating to me because I can tell the difference between a thirty-eight and a 357 practically across the room. To me it is not complicated. But, yes, I guess when I think about it, there are quite a few combinations to learn and memorize. There is lead, there is copper, there are wad cutters, there are hollow points, there are silver ones, brass ones, shot shells, and light fast ones, then heavy slow ones. Probably more than that. What they all do and are used for is obvious'to me. I explain to her what happened.

"Oh. Well, he did look awfully surprised, shook his head and ran off." I'm worried he has been blinded. But something very interesting happens as a result. The bear comes around, but never touches anything belonging to us! Not in six years. About twice a year he walks through the property to check it out, but keeps on going. The really cool part is, he keeps all the others bears off his territory, and so off our property. We see bear sign along the river nearby, and in the woods out back, and see bears off and on, but they never bothered us. I assume there had been an encounter between Karen and the bear that the bear understood. The bear knew this was our supplies and wanted them, and there had been a standoff. The bear had been bested and accepted that without anger. This turned out to be a good and workable relationship. As a result I will try in the future to leave bears alone as much as I can, and consider teaching them a lesson first to see if it works.

A few days later one of the girls comes in the cabin. "There is a squirrel in the garden, come shoot it!" We do not like squirrels around, as they run off with cabin insulation and damage the crops in the garden, so the children know to tell me if a squirrel shows up. Out comes the 357 with the light loads, and out comes the whole family on the doorstep.

Karen says, "I see it! Going up that big spruce tree by the garden. See it Miles?"

Yes, I see it, but it is such a long shot from here. Maybe three times as far as anyone would want to shoot something this small with a pistol. A hard shot even with a rifle. But I'm going to go for it, what the heck, test my marksmanship. If I miss I can go get the rifle. I think I cannot get much closer, or I cannot see the top of the tree where the critter is chattering at us like he owns the world. He is so far we can hardly even see him.

"Here watch this!" The whole family goes silent and watches me draw, and look down the sites with the hammer back. 'Blam!' and I could not believe it, the squirrel falls from the tree dead, into the creek. I am just so proud of that shot, *with witnesses no less. A call shot no less.* "Am I good or what!" Ooo wee! I fluff up my feathers and strut around. "Did ya see that? Huh? Was that a good shot or what!" No one paid any mind, or knew enough about guns to know a good shot when they saw one. I was just so crest fallen. "Ok, now you look, and you remember, because when I repeat this story, I want you to remember how far it was!"

"Oh, Miles, it was just a squirrel, geez!" Everyone walks away. A shot that belongs in the book of world records and they walk away. Women!

I had found a slide for the kids at a garage sale to set up in the sand by the creek. The girls can slide into the water, where we bathe and play. Stuff for the CB radio was on the town list, and now we have a booster, antenna and other stuff. We have been reading about how to use our CB. It is time to test out these long distance additives. The cabin has the home base with antenna on the roof.

"Karen, you man the home base! The girls and I will go over by the slide with the portable and see how it works!"

The girls and I get in the canoe, and go down the creek to the slide. We fiddle with the squelch and other knobs. All we hear is hiss. We are disappointed. With heavy hearts, we canoe back towards the house. As we approach we hear Karen in a loud voice, "Hello, Hello, can you hear me?"

We were silent in the canoe, and the girls look at me. I hold my finger over my lips for them to be quiet, as we sneak up to the house. The girls can hardly stop giggling. We tie up the canoe, as quiet as we can, and sneak up closer to the house. *Like Wile Coyote sneaking up on the road runner"* I whisper, and the girls nod. Fingers over lips, we all tip, tip, tippy toe. I get hide and the girls get hidden behind trees, I say: "Hello, Hello! Can you hear me, Karen?"

Karen screams in the radio, "Yes, yes, it works!"

Me'n the girls jump out from behind the trees, no radio in our hands, as she is still holding her radio talking in it. Just homestead family fun. The radio sort of works for when I am out on the trapline, but I never liked it. I'm fine. If I'm not, it's too late for a radio. There is a lot of time spent fixing and dealing with the radio, and trying to find a good signal. It was only needed for me to say 'Hi, I'm ok.'

Once the family was in a panic because I never checked in. Another day a storm came up, and I was so worried the family would wonder about me that I traveled in the storm and had a rough time of it.

"I just couldn't get a signal, batteries too cold or something. I wanted to just hole up at one of the trapline cabins for a few days, but knew you'd worry about me so I pressed on." Karen is glad I'm ok, and has things for me to fix. The family calls me, 'Mr. Fix It,' especially the youngest. I'd get home, sometimes gone a week on the trapline, and there'd be a pile of 'stuff' on my work bench needing to be fixed. Maybe mom would have a knife to sharpen, girls have toys needing wheels put back on, or a part made. Everyone would be hopeful I could take care of it.

"That dang meat grinder lost its handle again? Have to try antler this time maybe." I built an airplane for the little one, Joy, that slides down a hill. She can reach her hand out and spin the propeller. She has her own trapline. She is five, and the trapline goes around the cabin logs. It takes her half a day to cover it. Send her out with supplies, just like when I go. A little back pack with a snack, water, sewing kit, extra mittens, headlamp. *Teaching her what she needs to know if she expects to go out in the Arctic winter dark.* Twenty feet, down one wall, twenty feet around the corner, then twenty feet twice again, back to the start. Fall, crawl, get back up, and fall. Looking for rabbits. We'd look out the windows now and then to see how she was doing.

"Is THIS DONE YET?" Little Joy would ask, holding up a slice of ivory she'd been trying to polish for a week. She sits next to me, watching me do my art in awe. She was fascinated with all the tools, ideas, and art stuff. It takes her a week to polish her piece of ivory. She is proud when it is finally done, and shiny! She watches me skin furs, and sits right there asking questions.

"Is that the liver? Where is the kidney, is it out yet?" One day she stared at the intestine coming out of the marten. I squeeze the last foot into a bottle to make lure mixed with secret ingredients.

She has seen this before, but today she stares, and never says a word. Unlike her. Till I'm all done! Then she says with conviction, "When I grow up, I'm not doing that part!" I smile. I know for a fact it is true. Sometimes, someone says something, and you know it's the truth. It never occurred to me anyone would ask her, or expect her to do the fur skinning. She is with mom all day, so when I come in off the trapline for a few days the kids hang around me.

The older girl, May, likes to be alone a lot, working on her cabin, being with her sled dogs. Very different personalities. I love them both for different reasons, for who they are I guess. I did not want to make them into anything, but wanted to help them be whoever they are.

In the spring of '84 Karen, I, and the two children boat into Manley Hot springs running the houseboat from the Kantishna homestead. We have not seen anyone for over a month.

"Miles, wasn't the last time we saw anyone about a month ago when the school teacher flew out and gave tests to the children?"

"You must be right; flying is the only practical way to visit us. No one could find and decipher all the dog sled trails to find the way. Sure will be fun to see what has gone on in the world while we have been spending break up in the wilds. Sometimes I feel like society is a rat race going off the cliff, and we are among the lucky who decided we do not want to go off the cliff with the rest of the lemmings!"

"Yes, Miles, at peace with God, living life as was intended, without war and greed." I kept quiet as I feel this is a bit over stated and not quite true. I do not see how there can be life without war. Even plants fight each other for light. Those people that are living without necessities will always be willing to fight for what they need to survive, as is their right. Likewise it is not realistic to expect those who have the goods to give them up voluntarily. They may have earned it, worked hard for it, and anyhow it is hard for people to take a step backwards. Motion is always forward. Those who speak the loudest for peace are the ones who already have control of the majority of the goods. Peace means being able to keep it. But I understand how Karen feels in general.

"Yes, we sure live a good life. I almost feel sorry for the rest of the world that does not know the life we have. Honey, do you think Weedz will be at his homestead?"

"Who knows. We were at his place last fall when he told us he'd wait for us to come downriver so we could go in together. I'm not sure I believed him. Ha! When he is ready to go, he will go in! He may even want to be the first one in as you do! It must be a guy thing. Who cares who is first anyway! If women were running the world…"

"Yeah, yeah." I smile and we laugh. We have gone here before; we are just talking, passing the hours on the river as we run by the halfway point. "Look, Karen, the log cabin that is our halfway marker is falling in the river. We will just have to remember where this bend in the river is."

"I think I can remember because this is the spot you have to cross over to the other side, and where the swans hang out so often. There must be a big lake nearby. Also this is where so many Tamarack trees are in the left bend."

"Yes, but I have to cross over many places and we see swans all over, and there are Tamarack up and down the river. I think I will remember as well, but because of this tiny island, and here is where, after I cross the river I run behind this island that is so narrow and looks like it should not have enough water. Should we stop at the small creek around the next bend to see if we can catch any fish? I'd rather not myself, as I want to get to the mouth before Weedz heads in."

"It looks like the creek is still blocked with ice so we have no choice but to go on. Do you think the ice pack seems thicker to where we should pull over and wait?"

"Maybe. I'll sure keep an eye out ahead. Why don't you get the fire in the stove stoked up and start lunch. Don't we have some left over goose and rice we can heat up? Will it serve us all?" The two girls are hungry and want to help with the cooking. I'm steering from up on the roof as the women go below to cook. Alder wood smoke smells good coming out the chimney going by me as it snakes down the river behind us. The sounds of dishes clanging below and kids arguing over who will have to do the dishes afterwards are good sounds. It's a scene out of Tom Sawyer, the gold rush days, or the Mountain Man era. Days when families would float the river with everything they owned. Geese are overhead as in a painting. Snowcapped mountains loom far off. Spruce forests go on for a thousand miles up north of us. Not a soul is on the river. Not a footprint or a sign, or a beer can. Even that cabin falling in the river was an ancient shack from a past era. If the engine broke down it might be months before another boat would come by. We could float out, but getting stuck would not be good.

"Ice ahead, I'm pulling over, someone get out front with the rope, please." I stomp on the roof to get the women's attention.

May jumps on the front deck with the rope, as I pull in a slough. We wait while tied up, eat our meal letting the ice pass.

May asks, "Do you think it is an ice jam up ahead. The water looks like it is rising fast." She is only fourteen, but getting very bush savvy. She loves this life. I know in my heart, this is her home forever. She had gone off on her own trapline, and spent an overnight, and built her own log cabin by herself already.

"Yes, I think a jam is ahead and maybe just letting go. We might make it through ok if we press on, but it is better to wait and make sure. An hour or two is not going to make a big difference on our trip. Hey, May, see that whitefish along the bank near the shore? Grab the fish spear and see if we can spear him!" She is excited, and Joy comes out and wants to watch. With hollers and screams of encouragement May spears the fish after four tries.

"A whitefish, something to cook up for dinner tonight!"

"You can have whitefish, girls; I plan to have a burger at the Roadhouse!" They forgot we are expecting to be in town! Ha!

Karen comments. "We eat so much fish and moose and garden things we really look forward to some junk food, and so many Elders would about die to eat that whitefish dinner we want to give up! Looks like the ice has thinned out, want to get going again?"

The day is calm, spring is sunny. Not a cloud can be seen against the robin egg blue sky. The sound of ice hitting the shore is heard along with the geese honking in the distance. The 'thuga, thuga' of the low rpm engine is a constant sound that is not an intrusion, but a natural sound in this environment. It is forty miles to the mouth of the Kantishna where we hope to meet up with Weedz. Three people live in that forty mile stretch, and only five on the 300 miles long Kantishna.

We arrive at the mouth of the Kantishna and expect Weedz to come out to greet us from the cabin. It seems odd no one is here, not even Liller. The door is wide open. No boat, and the pet dog is running around.

"Hey, Weedz! You home?" I call out, but think if he is home he surely heard the boat engine.

"Weedz must have left ahead of us again! Dang! He sure must have been in a hurry!" No one comments. We have thirty more miles to go to the Manley boat landing.

The Tanana River is bigger, and a different color than the Kantishna River. The Kantishna is more gray from glacier silt, while the Tanana has more brown from local rain run-off and dirt. The current is usually a mile an hour stronger on the Tanana River. This does not sound like much, but the difference between five miles an hour and six miles an hour is noticeable in a five hour run.

"Miles, look at all the drift! Lots of whole trees headed down, with sweepers all along the cut banks!" Karen is concerned, but trusts my judgment on river running.

"We will go slow. Weedz must be ahead of us, and he made it. If he got through, then I can." But in all honesty Weedz is twice the river man I'll ever be. He's been on the river since he was a child. He's a local legend, along with his entire Athabascan family. Yes. This sure looks formidable with the acre size chunks of ice and huge trees going end for end down the river. I've done this before though and know what the boat can handle. The biggest problem would be to have the engine quit at the wrong time. Baker Creek is passed, where Karen and I met. We exchange a smile. The Zitziana River is passed. Finally we approach Manley Hot Springs.

"Miles, how will we get from the landing to town?" It is a few miles of dirt road. We may have to walk. But there is no way the slough that goes through town will be free of ice yet, so no use trying to get up that way. And the entrance is six more miles downstream. We see the main landing on the Tanana River way up ahead.

"Hey, looks like a party or some gathering at the landing, maybe an ice break up celebration. It means we probably have a ride in!" We are thrilled. There is a bad cutbank right at the road's end, so we cannot safely park there. The houseboat gets parked up a nearby creek mouth I think called Hagen slough. It takes half an hour to get the boat secure, put the fire in the stove out, cleaned up, and ready for the village. We walk through the tangles of alder and willows along the path to the landing mud parking lot. When we get there, we are greeted by stern faces. This seems surprising.

"Who are you? What are you doing here?" Only then do I realize it is a policeman. It seems odd that a policeman would come to Manley for a party. Manley has no police and no form of government. No taxes and no services.

"Miles, from the Kantishna and Karen from here in Manley. We just boated in from the homestead, looking for a ride to town."

The cop wants us to talk to another cop, saying "Here are some folks off the Kantishna!"

Talk to us about what? This is all very odd. A stern: "Did you see any other boats up there?"

"No. We were in pack ice, and had to be the first on the river except for Weedz. No one can boat upstream yet."

Another cop comes up,"Any more bodies?"

The cop who had spoken to us replies, "We do not have to go look for these folks. They just came in from the Kantishna."

Only then do I look around and see blood here and there around the cutbank of the river. From the expressions, this is not a picnic or party. There is no cook fire. No food out, no tables, nor happy faces celebrating the ice break up. *'Bodies? Did I hear him say bodies? See the blood. See all the cops, and see all the expressions on the faces?'*

I ask a local standing by, "What is going here? We just got in off the river. We spent break up at the homestead. Have you seen Weedz around? He was supposed to meet us."

"Weedz is dead along with we do not know how many others. At least five, but still counting and looking. Some guy shot them all ,we think, but do not know for sure, only that there are dead bodies in the river with bullet holes in them."

Someone else nearby adds, "Yeah Joe is dead, and it looks like problems may have started with him. Some crazy guy was camped here at the boat landing waiting for the ice to go out. He wanted to homestead at the new land opening somewhere near Lake Minchumina. All he had was a canoe to go up the Zits river. Most of us had met him; he seemed like a nut, but harmless enough. Apparently yesterday Joe and him got into a nasty encounter. We think Joe told this guy what a fool he is and he'd never make it. You know Joe… likes to push buttons. He may have pushed the wrong guy around. This guy was insulted; killed Joe, as well as those coming to see the river condition. They got shot as witnesses and this Silka guy killed Weedz, as Weedz pulled up in the boat. Silka took Weedz boat and has not been found yet. At least all this is what fits the facts we have."

Karen and the kids start crying as they hear the names of those missing or dead. Karen and her children knew every one of them. One death was a pregnant woman, husband and a three year old. The Klein's were well liked in Manley. Silka apparently had issues of some sort in Fairbanks before he arrived in Manley Hot Springs and may have killed someone there. There was not enough evidence to prosecute. He ran away and ended up here… another end-of-the-roader. It is hard to say if Silka would have gone on his way if not provoked by Joe.

I get my cue on how to respond by those around me. I do not seem to feel the same as anyone around me, and I'm puzzled. I am not surprised at what has happened. I'm not shocked. *Welcome to life in the pucker brush.* Those who live by the sword shall die by it. I do not like it and am not happy, but I am not the one who made the rules. Honestly, what do we, the people expect? The one who would be in charge, the mayor of the community and the one who owns the biggest business and controls the town pretty much is the one who wanted to toss me out a window. Made fun of me, tried to bait me. With ten others who shared the same view. One wrong word or move and there would have been a pile of bodies.

Another upstanding pillar of the community said she would shoot me if I went where she did not want me to go. Guns and violence are a way of life tolerated by all. Joe is the one who shot all his dogs in front of the post office in front of witnesses. No one suggested this is an aberration. Someone had held a bunch of people hostage in the roadhouse once, and how many brag about the bullet holes in the wall, and find pride in that? No one is concerned at what I observe. I did not spend a lot of time here, but assumed people dropped like flies from the feuds and crazy people. What happened seemed to me inevitable. Yet I see shock, how it was something unexpected, totally out of character and out of the blue. I do not want to hurt anyone's feelings, so take my cue.

In a daze, we make our way into the village, plans totally changed. The next day I come back to the boat landing to check on the houseboat. The police are still around with search teams. Reporters have shown up from the big cities. A helicopter lands as I am there. A city woman gets out in high heels, and a city dress on. She scowls at the mud she has to walk in, and looks confused. She appears to have never seen any sort of life like this. Just a cement flat sidewalk. She is scared of bears, furtively looking around, trying not to get mud on those high heels. She wants a story and looks determined. In her world, she is ruthless. She's from Chicago. A camera man follows her, as she looks for interviews from the locals. No one really wants to talk to a reporter though.

"They got Silka! He was shot in the boat on the river. A police helicopter found him. Silka was able to get off a shot and kill one of the policemen in the chopper. That raises the count to ten dead so far." One of the locals is filling me in on what has transpired.

"Silka's car over there got burned by the locals. Everyone is going around armed or scared, not trusting strangers. I think things will not be the same around here for a very long time."

I add, "For sure we are not used to this sort of thing going on. This is more like what we expect from the crazy big city. This is the place people leave their doors unlocked and strangers are welcome."

We all hang our heads in sorrow. The crazy woman, who said she'd shoot me if I went on the slough, comes up crying in hysteria, throwing her arms around me sobbing, "Thank God you are all ok, I was so worried!"

Human beings are amazingly strange to me. Here I was having dreams of her being found dead, stuffed head first down an outhouse hole. She had made my life miserable, as every time I went up the slough that one winter I cringed and wondered if I'd feel the bullet that hit me, that she told me she'd fire at me, adding what a good shot she is. Is the problem me? Everyone else smiles and nods, till someone really does what they say they are going to do, and then is shocked? *Get off me you crazy woman! It might as well... could have been... you who did all this! You two faced witch!* But no. I smile, go along with what everyone else is doing.

"Yes, we are ok. Thanks for your concern." Give a hug back. Reassuring pat on the back as she cries.

Houseboat in winter. Wood smoke drifts from the warm home. In summer I ride the bike along the beach.

CHAPTER SEVENTEEN

1984-85, FAMILY LIFE IS OVER, FREEDOM RINGS, STAKE LAND, FISH AND GAME, OUTFIT FOR WINTER, BACK IN THE WILDS.

"I'm going to miss my girls, Miles."

"I know, Honey, but they will be with their father. That will be a good experience for them. We have to look at the bright side. He loves them, and will treat them well I'm sure. I'll miss them too! There is nothing we can do about it. We tried. Our lives were investigated by social services, you went to court, all that can be done has been done. I'll be with you through this. I know what your children mean to you. Having them taken away is hell."

We are boating upriver, headed for Hansen Lake in the houseboat.

"Karen, what do you think of the plan to hole up at the Hansen cabin, and stay with the houseboat, then when winter comes, spend time on the Federal land. This will be the most remote land, with no roads, no river, and no one can get to us. A helicopter cannot even land there. We might be safe there."

"I suppose, Miles, but it's your land, your dream, not mine. It seems such a crazy way to live to avoid problems. There must be another way. We can't keep moving and running. I cannot raise the girls like this. Like you, I want to stay in the wilds and never come out! But I'm wanting to stay in one place!"

We still live the same subsistence life, and this land is just owning a trapline cabin which gives us some legal rights. *I have explained all this before, but we keep reviewing it.* The trail we use will be access to the home site. A trapline has no legal rights associated with it. I'm trying to find ways to keep our rights to use the land for our lifestyle where we fish, pick berries, hunt, trap, cut logs, get firewood. *Our lifestyle takes mobility and lots of space. But I see an age old argument between being a mobile subsistence gather hunter, or a farmer.*

"Karen, we know President Carter expanded Denali Park, and this new park boundary affected trappers we know, as well as us. It borders on our area, and we dip in and out of this new expanded park area. Suddenly park rules apply to land that did not have these restrictions when we arrived. So far, no one cares, and it is so remote it is hard to believe anyone will ever check or do anything about these new rules. The Federal government is very far away. Someday it may not be! Some day, we both know, someone will enforce the rules, like with the subsistence moose issue. A lifetime of trail cutting, a way to make a living, will mean nothing, and can get taken away. This idea I have is part of our insurance, like an ace in the hole, preparing for a future problem."

The Native Rights issues are coming along, but few white rights are mentioned, or being fought for. All subsistence issues revolve around Indian rights, not white homesteaders. Partly, I think, the natives are organized, and have funding to lobby and fight. Indians are selecting land all over the place, and kicking everyone else off. The trend of the bunny huggers wanting to stop the killing of animals is getting stronger, more radical, and even looking to me like terrorism. In the news recently was the Greenpeace sinking of a whaling ship. A whaling ship engaged in legal activity. The news media played it like a victory. As a member of the trappers association, I received ashes in the mail with a note saying this is what will happen to me if I keep trapping. There is oil exploration, huge timber tracts being offered by the state, some proposed in our area. We can close our eyes and pretend it is not so, and lose all we worked for, or we can look at the chess game of life, and move a pawn or two in place to protect our dream.

"It's an investment in time, something that can be sold when we get old. It will get things off our mind and accomplish something positive. Keep us busy in a healthy way." She sort of agrees, but maybe is not excited to be a trapper's woman, or living the life of the woman of a Mountain Man. She has a teaching degree. I feel she is an environmentalist, bordering on preservationist.

She thinks in terms of taking long dog trips for fun, not as a way to earn a better living. She has called my art superfluous. "Selling people items they do not need, and forcing people into poverty." She feels I have too many dreams of a future she does not envision. "You like to move too much, Miles, and I want one home, keep it simple, not all these homesteads far apart and huge traplines, being in the limelight, the focus and symbol of political issues and all this. Can't we be more low profile?"

I feel frustrated. If she is against a trapping life and feels art is an unworthy occupation, what are the solutions for our basic needs that cost money? In my mind, *if the government gets in my face, and illegally takes away my rights, who is going to change that? I'm not attacking, I'm defending.* Various problems and issues between couples

415

are not always logical, nor does it always make sense, but this is a part of the concerns between us, symbolic of a division in our thinking. Neither of us can change who we are. We are both stubborn, hard headed. There is tentative talk of us parting while the girls are away. Maybe in the spring. She joins me, but her heart it seems, is not really in this, like this is more my plans, not our plans. In truth, I did not ask her what she wanted to do. I never suggested a Plan B.

TRAPPING IS EXCITING. Running the sled dogs is rewarding, challenging, and fun, as usual. We are both healthy and enjoy various aspects of our life. Fish and Game officers fly out with a helicopter again, and follow my trapline, finding me 150 miles in the wilderness, landing in the trail in front of me.

"Whoa, Kenai." The dogs stop. I tie off the sled as the chopper blades wind down, snow flies, as the scream of the engine fades. An officer climbs out and makes his way in the deep snow my direction. He has never known the silence that he just interrupted.

"Kenai, be good, settle down guys, let him by!" My dogs are scared, inquisitive, want to sniff at the officer who is trying to get past the dogs to talk to me. I greet the officer. "Hey, how are you, what's up?"

I'm scared and not happy, but think this might be... oh... wanting information of some kind about something going on in the area, on his way someplace else, sees me, and stopping to say hi. Maybe part of a game population study or something.

One of the dogs leaps forward and grabs the officer's pant leg, and will not let go, aggressively growls, scaring the officer. *This is such out of character behavior! My sled dogs are very well behaved, friendly, and not mean type dogs. I got rid of that mean sort long ago.* I holler, "Spike let go! Stop that!" Another sled dog wants to act aggressive, so I show up with a stick and get the dogs calmed down, apologizing to the officer, but in the back of my mind, *'Good boys, ya did good! I'm proud of ya'* and am amazed— and assume—somehow, the dogs pick up on my dislike of this situation, and are not hearing my words, but reading my mind. In truth, right now, I feel like a Jew, and this is Hitler.

"You're out here trapping? Got your license on you?" I'm flabbergasted. 150 miles in the wilds, and I'm supposed to have my wallet on me? Of all the things I need out here to survive, I need to have a wallet on me? The officer does at least believe me when I tell him the situation. I do have it all at the cabin. This is a green to Alaska twenty year old, perhaps fresh out of school who is quoting me what he was taught in civilization, what the rules are. Even the rules concerning how to deal with people you run into who are not following the rules.

"I noticed you have a trap within a few feet of a beaver house. It has to be at least

50 ft away, you know." Actually no. I never read those rules. Or did and forgot. *In truth, I make the rules, not read them. Probably this is not a good thing to say though. Nor would it be wise to inform this guy there are only two laws out here, God's and mine. If I got in a pissing match with this guy, he'd win. I'm not stupid, he carries a gun. So do I. But if I kill him, my life is over. I may as well kill myself too. If he kills me he's covered, he's an officer, and only has to come up with a story that fits - how I resisted arrest, drew my gun first or something. But this guy is not being aggressive or mean, he's just doing his job. He does not really understand where he is. He's only half an hour from McDonalds. I'm a hard week away. He just talked to someone else 10 minutes ago.*

I have not talked to anyone but Karen in four months. He does not understand how intimidating a helicopter with all its noise and blowing snow is out here in the quiet peace. He thinks there is nothing cooler than a helicopter. He sees no reason to apologize for being an intruder. I would not love a free ride to town in his cool machine. He does not arrive thinking being my friend has any advantage or might be useful or called for. How hard would it be to offer me a sip of hot coffee from his thermos, ask me how everything is. Introduce himself, as is custom in my culture.

He does not, I think, because he does not have to; has no time. He is the law, carries a gun, his position is so far above mine, there is no reason to be nice. I have no choice but to obey, so let's dispense with the niceties. *The issue is, I think that is very stupid and dangerous on his part. All it takes is meeting up with someone not as nice as I am that responds to rudeness, intimidation, and threats with violence as in 'make my day!' or 'You call that a knife!?' Because I feel this way I have little respect.*

He does not comprehend the sheer terror the wild things have for his chopper and so called civilization. I have to forgive his ignorance. So I'm polite. But I am polite also because I must be. There is no choice, other than death. Because if I burst out laughing. If I tell him, 'No thanks, that is not what I am going to do, but thanks for the suggestion.' I know what the outcome will be.

I finally answer. "I will move the trap when I go by again. Sorry. Sometimes I just forget. The beaver house is not active, no beaver there, the trap is for lynx." We part on friendly terms. But still. A helicopter 150 miles in the wilderness, wanting to see my permit. Expecting me to have a tape measure with me and such. I'm concerned. This young officer is friendly enough, probably a good kid. All it would take would be some more aggressive hot shot officer in this same situation for all hell to break loose. Another blurb on the back page of the paper, another one bites the dust. *'Officer Gunned Down in Cold Blood in the Wilds by Mad Trapper.'* Followed by how we need more laws, more protection, how unsafe it is for our protectors of citizens' rights. My entire lifestyle and reason for being here hinges around my freedom and rights. There would be no headline reading 'Respected citizen defends himself from Gestapo.' If I have it wrong, or how I feel does not work, or is not right, or will not be allowed, then my whole reason for being here has a hole in it. Life out here is hard enough, and marginal enough, with no rules but God's. As soon as it becomes a game, a sport, recreational, filled with rules, then what? I'm already risking my life at an occupation that pays about fifty cents an hour. My mind has to focus on something else.

One goal is to get to Lake Minchumina for mail and get furs sent out to Don.

Jan first 1985 - minus ten and windy, do not leave for Minchumina as planned.

January second - Leave for Minchumina at plus ten degrees. Camp three miles before Leonard's trap cabin, cover thirty miles with eight dogs. I have 200 marten skins in the sled to sell.

Jan third - Travel fifty miles, but wear dogs out in a twelve hour day. Make camp. Lost the trail in the dark. I thought the lead dog knew where to go, but Kenai did not remember. I think he did not want to leave the better going on the creek to take off overland in deeper snow.

Jan fourth - Make another wrong turn, up Spencer Creek, lose three hours and travel twenty extra miles. Walking in front of sled dogs. Arrive at lake Minchumina about noon, see the Collins Twins.

On Jan fifth, a snow storm keeps the mail plane from getting in. I have to hole up at Kenny's. If I had been caught in that snow storm on the trail, it would have been a rough time as my dogs are already beat. We went about 100 miles breaking trail. I get dog feed from the Collins. Don is contacted, and will pick up the furs at the small airline office when they get in. The fur price is better now than it would be if I bring the furs in by boat in spring. I have learned this the hard way in the past!

I rest up another day visiting with Wildricks and Collins. Sled dogs are ready to go on the eighth. We travel twenty-five miles through six inches of new snow and camp at Leonard's trap cabin. I shoot some ptarmigan birds along the trail, enough for me and the sled dogs. Out of a flock of about seventy, I shot twenty-seven. On the ninth, I camp up a creek at the end of the day, about thirty more miles down the trail. I sleep in the dog sled with the tarp pulled over me by the fire, dogs all around me. It is a scene from 10,000 years ago. Home made snowshoes stick up out of the snow, bird feathers are all over from our left over dinner. The sled dogs are alert, looking for game and danger. The northern lights flicker dull green. Spruce trees bend over the creek from the upper cut-bank, a block against any possible wind. Dog harnesses hang on sticks in the snow near the fire to dry. We are content; at one with the world around us. In the morning the dog harnesses are dry, we are all rested, and it is easy to get a fire going. Broth for us is hot. We both eat the same thing from the same pot; fish, rice and ptarmigan. I'm spitting out a feather, and so is Spike. We both look at each other at the same time, feathers hanging out of our mouths. We both stop. He wags his tail and I wag mine.

We get as far as one of my trapline camps by dark. There are supplies here that have been relayed all the way from Nenana, one camp at a time over the entire winter. "At least we have a good trail now, guys!" I jump up and down on the trail and they do not know my words, but understand why I am happy, for it means even more to them, with easier pulling and knowing where they are. I am home on the thirteenth. It takes almost two weeks to get mail.

All the sled dogs get rabies shots that arrived in the mail. I'm excited to get more trapline trail cut, as this is a critical point. I can cut as far as the edge of Dell's trapline if I head more north. He is a trapper who flies in from Fairbanks to trap on a remote lake. We have been in touch on the phone in town. He knows I am arriving. He's seen my activity by plane. We think we can get along, since we are in communication, and he does not feel threatened that I will take any of his trapline. I will be cutting close to the Wien Lake trails, trappers north of me. I'm basically arriving at the end of what is open for trapping. Dell has offered to pick up a sled dog for me with his plane so I can replace one of the dogs not working out. I can get a good breed of dog I heard about from a dog racing family named Cosgrove. They have a dog named Salty for me.

I take off at minus forty-five on the trapline to cut and reach Dell's trail. There is a lake on my map called Jean Lake. A plane once crashed here. The survivor had to hold up a spell. When he got rescued he named the lake after his wife. I have about a quarter of a mile to cut. Not far, but it takes a long time just to mush to this lake, then there is no cabin nearby to stay. I have to backtrack twenty miles to my trap camp. It takes two days to get there. This is part of my 200 mile dream trapline that I have cut over 100 miles of already. So far, there are four trap camps with simple cabins, as small as six x six ft. The cabin at the Federal land Karen and I proved up on is a blessing, and a major place to stop and regroup. Karen has been gone visiting her parents back east, as our futures drift apart.

When I hit Dell's trail, I have only five miles to follow to his camp. He keeps a snow machine there, with a shed to keep it in, and work on it. He is a recreation trapper who mostly just wants a getaway place. He seems an all right guy; ten years older than I am; honest, happy, smart, hardworking and reasonable. It's nice to chat trapping with another trapper.

The new dog, Salty, is thin, does not have a lot of miles on him, but is good natured enough, so I'm happy. Dell does not have dogs; his fur carcasses are piled up, so is glad to give them to me for dog feed. "Go for it, Miles, these carcasses will only attract bears to my cabin in the spring!"

He likes the idea of my transportation consuming a by product of the fur industry, so there is no waste, and no need to buy gas! He has a heck of a time getting gas out to his camp in the small plane, trying to keep cans sealed so they are not a hazard flying.

I laugh. "Who knows Dell, gas prices might go up and be unaffordable, it is something we are not in control of, but we are in control of the meat we get!"

He thinks gas will be around forever, as after all; it makes the world go round. "Miles, the entire country, every country, needs gas, so how can we not be without it? How can we not afford it? If anyone can afford it, it will be us in the good old US of A."

Probably true, but even so, we both agree getting rid of carcasses by feeding it to your transportation is cool. He wants to know how much time it takes to take care of sled dogs. "I guess I invest two hours a day, Dell. I have to go through a total of ten gallons of hot water between the morning broth and evening meal. That's a lot of snow to melt. It is hard to calculate the total time, as there is time working on the sled, repairing harnesses, gang line, and dealing with the dogs themselves. There are disputes to resolve between dogs, shots to give, poop to scoop, scratches behind the ears, as well as reprimands. It's a way of life, it's like raising kids, and it's a relationship. But I suppose the two hours of time I spend cooking, feeding, and shoveling poop, is time you might work a job in town, and use the earnings to buy the gas for your transportation. So realistically it may not be the savings it's made out to be. One difference is that I get to work at home on my own time, in the wilderness I love, while you have to work for a boss in the city."

Dell is retired, so he has money coming without having to work. We discuss retirement. The possibility social security money not remaining available, and not to be counted on, even though we paid into it. We are among the baby boomers. The government borrowed our retirement, gambled with it, lost it. Oh well. Likewise, working for wages to buy needed supplies is not in our control, and might change if times get hard in the future.

My work at this end of the trapline goes faster with Dell to stop and see. There is the chance to get rested up, so I can make improvements on my remote trap cabins. Dell could maybe fly in supplies for me in trade for stuff. He wants one of my custom knives, so already we are talking flying in return. Dell does not know the Wien Lake trappers any more than I do, but I reach a couple of them on CB radio. They know I'm arriving, and none seem especially happy. None really want a connection to either Nenana or Lake Minchumina. They all fly in. I'm unsure what to do, so not pushing that direction as much as I had planned. Yet I need to get north and around a mountain before cutting south again. This direction allows me to make a loop with the trapline someday if I cut far enough. It would encompass an area about the size of the state of Rhode Island. There would be four to five trappers to deal with who dip in and out, or go near, or claim a lake here and there, who fly in; but in general, it is an ambitious idea to cut that much trail and run that much trapline. Maybe I could make more of a living. Just getting by is not going to work forever in the big picture. A person has to get ahead a little bit, like when you need a lawyer or doctor, or new twenty horse boat engine.

Dell and I are sitting in his shack skinning fur. "Miles, that's a nice Marten, reminds me of Russian Sable."

"Yeah, I think the same thing, and even think it is the same animal, since Russia used to own us, and Alaska is only fifty miles from Russia. So it makes sense the animals are the same. Russian sable is worth $200. The same animal here, called a Marten, is only $50. All we'd need would be a Russian stamp!" Reminds us of the Russian 'Gorky Park,' a book about this very subject; based on a true story of some guys who smuggle a breeding pair of sable into the US. We are both doing ok trapping this winter. It saves me weight when at this end of the trapline I can come here to skin and bring home just the fur, and not the carcass. My houseboat and Hansen is two days travel from here. I sleep in the dog sled more days of the winter then I asleep in my bed!

"Hey, Dell, speaking of distance traveled and lots of camps? On the way here I was tired. I woke up last night and was not sure where I was in the dark. I had to think, and put my hands out to see what side the wall was on. I thought I might be at home. I couldn't remember. I was at my line shack, but could not recall which one."

Dell laughs. "At least you found the line shack comfortable, huh!" I spoke of the days I only had tents to stay in. He has a few trapline tales. Once his load shifted in the plane. He was hauling long timber for the shack here. The plane lost its ability to fly, and was nose heavy. He crash landed in the stunted spruce trees. One of the Wien Lake trappers was out flying and spotted the wreck next day. "I was able to get back later and fix the plane, cut out a strip and fly it out."

On another trip to Dell's, we get out maps and compare old trails, discuss lakes and what we both know about the area. Since Dell flies, he sees a lot during the year. Being on the ground I know more about what lakes have fish. I only visit three times, but it seems like a lot of socializing.

The sled dogs seem to never learn to stay off the back of my snowshoes. I taught them to lay down. I'd get so far ahead, turn around and call them and they jump up and work their way to me. I'd have them lay down again. The new dog Salty learns fast.

I gave up using a chain saw years ago, and rely more on a machete, but more and more the chain saw seems handy after all. Electronic ignition, and making saws lighter in weight helps. Still, 75% of my trail cutting is done with a machete. The chain saw is great for cutting the night logs at camp when it is dark and I have no time to cut it with a hand saw.

I come up with a routine for building trap cabins. I can build one in five days. A tent and enough supplies for five days is brought with me. The trees are cut, but not peeled. They can be drug with the dogs to the cabin location. The chain saw quickly makes the notches in the logs. It helps to bring one sheet of plywood, and a couple of sheets of tin, a door and a window. I can build without any of that, but the time increases by a lot. These items can be old and used, not new, so not a lot of money invested. I go up only two rounds of logs and get a floor in. The plywood has to get cut in two ft. x eight foot ft. sections to fit in the dog sled. If I build a six x eight shelter, four x eight of that will be solid floor to walk on in the middle. So much gets stored against the wall, it does not matter if there is no floor for two feet. A log is run down the middle to nail the two sections of plywood to. Often one log wall is also the floor support log. One more long log has to go down to support the other edge of the floor that is two ft from the wall. The door is cut when the logs get too high up to easily climb over to get in. It is easy to just make a flat roof when the logs get high enough. The tin is supported with lots of cross poles. Moss has to be used in the roof. Sometimes before the tin goes on, I lay down visqueen, and toss a lot of moss on top before setting the tin down. All the fixings can be acquired during the year at garage sales. Fold cots, or beds, old lanterns, a chair, table, wood stove, wash basin can be had at thrift stores. A fifty-five gallon barrel in the cabin is used as an animal—and bear—proof container to store food and sleeping bag in. The lid is cut out with a chisel, and hinged to the barrel with a clasp on the other side. Even if animals get in the cabin, my supplies are safe. The supplies need to have survived when I get here, even if the cabin has been breached. A bear seems to be unable to get the lid off because the lid drops slightly inside the barrel, so there is no edge to get hold of. Such a container is not forever, but is good for ten to fifteen or twenty years.

The first half of February is minus thirty to minus fifty. The dog sled needs repair, so I have it in the Federal cabin to work on. The sled is wood, material from the land, so to fix it, we only have to step out the door, and select a tree to cut, then make a stanchion. We are self-sufficient. Repairs are not a major problem. This is in fact a happy thought, and source of peace and security. When it is minus thirty, I get out on the trapline to check traps. Due to cold and deep snow, I only get twelve marten all month. Time is spent working on 'Going Wild' my first book, and doing art work. I'm able to stop off at various trap cabins between the houseboat, Hansen cabin, and my Federal cabin. Trails between all get cut better; trail cutting never seems to end.

The sled dogs are in good shape, and getting feisty. It is hard to control them as they get faster on better trails. We average ten miles an hour and get bursts of twenty. This sounds slow to civilized people, but think in terms of running as fast as the fastest human can run, through the forest down a narrow, twisty trail, jumping logs, ducking under branches, dropping in and out of creek bottoms.

Dell lands in the swamp by the Federal cabin with supplies for me. I have little time to get out there to help unload, so only hook up Kenai. Almost 500 pounds is loaded in the sled, and Kenai pulls it by himself to the cabin. He weighs about sixty pounds. I have eight dogs, more than needed because of Karen and the girls. All the dogs have to come with me since Karen is gone. 100 mile days are possible on good trails, sometimes in as little as eight hours. *We need to be careful what we say, these are Iditarod speeds capable of winning the race!* But the difference in the race is, this mileage has to be done ten straight days in a row. I can do it once, and then rest the dogs up a day. I easily have 3,000 miles on the sled dogs this winter so far. Finding time to rest them is the problem. Most mushers have problems finding time to run them! We are averaging fifty miles a day when we run.

One aspect of running sled dogs I notice is, the longer you have a dog team and the more miles you put on it, the better the team gets. A snow machine is at its best the day you buy it, and it's all downhill from there; it wears out. Once you buy a dog team it never wears out, you have pups, and the team replicates itself. Even a better version, for the dogs that make the team are the breeders, and the pups that survive the lifestyle are the ones that end up in the team. The team adapts to your specific needs. Not just trapping, but twisted trails, jumping logs, sleeping out on the trail, the type of food I serve, are all factors in which dogs I select.

In March, I get a trail open to Square Lake and the cabin I have permission to use that Sandy built. The cabin is in ok shape; Sandy is still in Seattle. He homesteaded long ago, and acquired this site as 'trade and manufacture' under Federal laws. He used near by birch trees to make crafts, and set up a camp for children, teaching wilderness survival skills. He still comes out now and then on vacation to see the cabin and fish. He owns an airplane he keeps in Nenana. I think he is joint owner, or leases his plane out when he is not using it. The cabin is too large to easily heat in a short time, so I prefer my own shacks. There are lots of lynx tracks around this lake so I am excited that maybe I have hit the mother lode. *I'm going to get rich at last.* Only a few lynx are caught though, wondering where all the lynx went. Teasing me.

Karen returns in March and does some dog mushing with me to work on cabins and trails. Some new young homesteader shows up near Dell, who wants to trap. Dell and I wonder how this will go. Can this new person between Dell and I find room to trap without stepping on us? We go over the latest Wien Lake story. "I never knew Dell. I was talking to this guy I think 'Conner' on the CB a few times. No one else was coming on the air. He invited me to visit. When I get to the lake for the first time, the others on the lake warn me. Conner is far from happy I'm here, even though he invited me to visit. A trapper who was here not many years ago disappeared, and probably Conner killed him. This is how Conner got his trapline. Locals here even know the date and method of the murder, just can't prove it. There was a hole in the ice that looked like Conner cut, the day the trapper disappears. He's a lunatic, and everyone is afraid of him."

Dell too, heard some things while he was flying, and talking to other trappers. "Yeah, Miles, I ran into this Conner guy. He was spooky all right. He waved a gun around and told me how good he is with it. He hinted he has a way of dealing with rival trappers that works."

The point is, we like to know something about the people around us, and what sort they are. If this new guy gives us a hard time we have to have a plan. Mostly trappers get along well enough, at least work things out somehow without serious problems, like Dell and I do. What do any of us do when someone is not reasonable? This gets discussed. We are both going to stay away from Wien Lake though. I show the map to Dell and explain how I need to get within five miles of the lake in order to get around a mountain, and head east to my state land, lower cabin, then over to the trapline at that end. Dell sighs and is not totally happy I am coming around the mountain. "I had future plans there, but I agree, a big dream not likely to ever happen and Oh well!"

I reply, "I cut a trail earlier over here" and I show him on the map. We both lean over the wood table and have to move the kerosene lantern to see. "I can show you were it is and you can have that trail." I show what I offer, then show what I want in return. " I'll back off here, but need this area across the lake, so I have this other more critical area around the mountain." This is not something I have to do, but for the sake of getting along, this is what should be offered - a trade. I take something, I give something.

"I'd feel good about that Miles, thanks." In this way we know we will watch each other's backs, care about what each wants. I must believe this is what works as a life plan. I must believe those like Conner who get a trapline by killing someone, or get anything with threats, intimidation, bullying, power plays, is not workable in the big picture. I want to see evidence of this!

The end of March and early April offer good dog team travel days with long daylight and good snow conditions. I get to Twin Lakes east of me, and towards my lower Kantishna land as I try to connect those trails with trails at this end. Twin Lakes is the border line about halfway for me. I had reached Twin Lakes from the Nenana end, so it is exciting to connect from the Hansen lake end.

"Karen, I can alternate years trapping. One year be at this end and trap 100 miles, then the next year go to the other end, and trap the other 100 miles. Let the last year area recover and build back up! My own game management plan."

April is spent bear proofing my camps. One camp needs a new door, another needs a better roof. There had been hope of one more cabin near Twin Lakes to reach from the other end, but I'm out of plywood, tin, and time.

The first Trumpeter Swans show up April fifteenth, so there must be open water someplace, but we are still dog mushing. Sun glasses must be worn against the glare of the sun on the white snow. Going mushing means getting a tan! We have been based out of the Federal home all winter, and now it is time to think of moving supplies back to Hansen Lake and the houseboat.

By April twenty-sixth we record plus fifty degrees, with lots of geese. Still we are dog mushing. "Karen, you would not believe the trip I just had today!" She looks in the dog sled and sees a fresh goose for dinner and wants to hear how I got it. "The dogs came out on to Hang a Left Lake and there was a beaver house with open water. Swans and geese were all around the ice by the open water, maybe 100 of them. The dogs saw. Wow was that exciting. The sled leaps forward, slip sliding on the ice, me grabbing for the shotgun holding on for dear life. Headed for open water, but no one cared! Geese knocking each other out of the air trying to be first airborne. Blam! Blam! goes the shotgun into the flock! I was able to shoot a goose from the dog sled as the dogs went crazy! What a blast! I could hardly hang on to the sled! The dogs got the goose first and I had to fight them for it. A big tangled mess as we laughed and fought."

"That's why the goose is a little tore up!" Said with a happy grin.

"And how I got the tear in my snowsuit, Spike bit me trying to get to the goose first, and I bit him back, if you notice the cut on his ear." I feel like Hagar the Horrible bringing his prize home to Helga.

But Karen was not listening or paying attention. The high feelings and laugh are held in suspended animation, alone. She likes that we have meat, but the details are bothersome. "Getting meat is supposed to be sad and tragic. And legal Miles!"

By the end of the month we have a first rain, and that pretty much ends the dog mushing season. It is now break up. We cannot move till the ice goes out. It is hard to even leave the cabin, as there is wet snow that snowshoes do not work in, mixed with mud. Nothing works. It is a time for me to get art work done. Now and then the weather is right to go work on the boat. The twenty horse outboard is worked on yet again.

As ice thaws, I am able to get some beaver to feed the sled dogs, very greasy meaty animals. The fur is saved to be tanned for our own use. Tanned beaver fur ends up as seats in chairs. Dogs get fat, and shed their winter under fur. Like me, they like the changes, and summer is time off for them.

We get a trapline chatter message from my Nenana Iditarod winner friend, Josh. A radio message tells us that the Nenana river ice went out May tenth. On the thirteenth, the Kantishna breaks. We are able to reach Liller at the mouth of the Kantishna on the CB radio. She has spent winter there alone without Weedz, and may have had a rough winter. Just one of the tragedies of the Silka killings. I can give her a ride to Nenana as I pass her place. Karen wants to continue from the mouth of the Kantishna on down the Tanana to Manley on her own, to live there where we met in her sod house. She will continue on her way by canoe.

IT TAKES four hours to get to Nenana with Liller from her place at the mouth of the Kantishna. We burn twenty gallons of fuel in the wood boat going to Nenana, without the houseboat. I left the houseboat and dogs at the lower homestead on the way down from Hansen lake. "Miles, look at the hats I made this winter. I hope to sell them in Fairbanks. Do you think your friend Crafty would buy them whole-sale?" I had told her in the past, how I can go to town, sell everything, and come back to live the subsistence life I wish.

"Sure, Liller, but the cut he takes will be steep. I suggest selling at least a couple of them retail on your own, maybe a craft show. Nice hats!"

She trapped the marten herself. Weedz taught her. "Miles, I learned to do the add on value, rather than sell just the furs. Three marten in a hat, $350." I had hoped Karen would be interested, and make clothing from my furs. Liller adds, "Trapping is not all it's cracked up to be. I wanted to be humane, treat the environment well." I'm puzzled. She adds, "I suppose in all industries, everyone wants to be efficient, environmentally friendly, recycle, and humane, not wasteful or hurtful!" I'm still puzzled. "I had a beaver that got caught wrong in the snare, so did not die. It came up on top of the ice, so was still alive when I arrived." Ah yes, now I get it. She sighs. "I had to shove it back in the water, hold it under with a stick till it drowned. It took half an hour Miles."

I just say, "Hmmm." I understand of course. I try to comfort her, "Drowning is a common natural way beaver die. I've even seen Nature dish out worse." I tell her what I saw just this spring. "A lake dried up. The beaver on the lake thought they could survive and stayed, got ready for winter. Water dropped and separated the beaver from their feed pile. I saw six dead beaver on top of the ice with trails going way up into the woods where they tried to live off spruce trees, which they cannot do. It took all winter to die. They were skinny, teeth growing around and up into their skull. Each having to watch the others die, weeks apart. I can tell by the marks in the snow, they tried to revive, comfort each other, in the last days. This is common, Liller." She knows, but not how she pictured when she got into this life-style with Weedz.

ENOUGH MONEY IS MADE TRAPPING to get my basic supplies for the year. It's fishing season, and time to put up 2,000 fish for next year, so the dogs can live. I'm not with Karen any more. In spring I helped her get all her things back to her cabin in Manley Hot Springs. We are not angry with each other. On my part, I feel she will be happier with someone else. Someone who has ideas more like hers. Or she'd be happier alone. I see no point in being with someone who does not like who I am, what I stand for, and such. If I thought there was a way to work out our differences I'd work on it, as I do care, even love her, but see no solution other than parting. So! Here I am, alone again, checking fish nets, trying to forget.

A float plane. Huh. I keep checking the net and loading fish in the boat. The plane circles, comes in low, comes in again, and lands. It's Fish and Game again.

"Just letting you know fishing is being closed today, no more fishing allowed. Emergency closure. By the way, I see your net is not marked. You need to start putting your name and contact number on the net so we know whose net this is. New law, just letting you know." All there is to do is shrug my shoulders and acknowledge I heard, and will comply. Another young hot shot that has not got a clue about life out here. Just doing his job, big smile, happy to be out flying in the wilds of Alaska. Feels good about his job. He has no clue what he is doing or involved in. The problem originates with the folks in the office, and the big picture, behind the scenes. I sigh and write it out to Maggie in a letter. A letter I have to toss in the stove as I have lost touch with her.

Dearest Maggie,

You will never get this letter. I miss you. I believe it is not healthy to write someone and then throw the letter away, writing to a nonexistent person. But life is as it is. I will do what it takes to survive, and sometimes survival requires strange things. I get my mail in Nenana now instead of Manley, and will hang out in Nenana.

Anyhow Fish and Game. Where to begin. There is beginning to be a low salmon population problem being recognized. Legally, subsistence use of fish is to have priority over commercial use. In other words, those who need the fish have priority over those who merely want it...

The loophole Fish and Game uses is, they are allowed to shut down fishing anywhere, any time, under a provision called 'emergency closures.'...

One local commercial fisherman officially reported personally getting 30,000 salmon in one season. Only the eggs were salvaged. This is legal....

I wrote a proposal, that commercial and subsistence fisherman work together. The commercial fishermen I talked to told me they thought this would be great. I, and those like me get the fish, and the commercial people get the eggs. I do not have to figure out what to do with eggs, and they do not have to figure out what to do with fish. Under my plan I would not fish at all. Commercial fisherman are allowed to increase their quota, and keep the eggs, but deliver the fish to me and those like me. This is the chum salmon, not kings, and there is not a big market for human consumption of chum salmon, just the roe for caviar. Fish worth $2, roe worth $10. I am ready to take delivery and salvage the fish for my needs. No waste. I do not have to buy nets, wear out my boat and engine, or spend time fishing. The extra profits off the eggs, more than makes up for having to make a 150 mile run to deliver me fish.

The department was not interested. Furthermore, a new law is in the works to make fishing with nets illegal. I must use a fish wheel. I assume the reason is wheels are easy to see from the air, and it is easy to see if they are catching fish or not. Nets are easy to hide.

Wheels cost a lot to build and are efficient; get more fish then I need! I could end up with 800 fish in a single day; more than I can easily cut and hang! A net never gets more than eighty fish but usually twenty to thirty fish, which is a number I can manage on a daily basis. A net can be easily replaced. A wheel, if it gets taken out by a log cannot be replaced till next year. A wheel needs stuff from town and is somewhat complicated and hard to build. It takes skill. It's pretty much a commercial tool. I tried to build one with my small boat, a hand saw, some wire, etc. It was very rickety. It took two weeks to build. It caught no fish, after the first day it was ruined by a log in the river. I have no more material for another try. I am wondering how I can move and push a wheel around with my twenty horse engine. I think it is not possible. There is more, much more, an entire book worth. The subject is just fishing and related issues. How concerned are you as a citizen far off, about fish! It has zero effect on you and your life. At some point it's boring. At some point all you know is I am upset and you care, but the exact 'why' is confusing.

Well, I'm probably spouting more feelings then facts. It's one of my problems. I get so emotional and wrapped up I cannot separate facts from rumors, so no one listens. I'm seen as a radical. Also, I realize there are only a hundred people in the world affected by these laws. Bid deal, how selfish to feel indignant. Who cares about the intricacies concerning salmon fishing in Alaska. It's like the guy in Forest Gump going on and on about all the ways there are to fix shrimp, as if anyone cared. It was humorous, not serious. Only you will listen, and now, you are the stove.

Sunshine, Miles

This is not one of the best times in my life. A tenth of the population of Manley, where I get my mail and have friends are killed involving people I know. My woman and I have parted. Fish and game is being a monkey wrench in my gears.

I get home, and wonder how Liller is doing as I pass by the homestead with no one there. I have a routine boat trip and get home to some footprints on the sandbar. It looks like a bear and a wolf got in a fight. I do not know how common this is, but want to study the tracks to see if I can understand what the issue with each other is. They appear to have had a fight over my goods, hanging fish and dried commercial feed to supplement being unable to fish anymore this season. I am reminded I cannot legally fish to replace any loss. The wolf is dead and torn up. It appears the bear is wounded enough to leave to take care of his wounds. I am pretty sure this bear knows me and will not come around with me home. In fact, this looks like the bear that Karen wounded, that hangs around, yet has not been bothering us. No food is missing.

If there is in fact a poor fish run, it could be affecting the local wildlife as well as me. Wolves and bears are going hungry. Subsistence fisherman are being blamed in the news to the public for the fish loss. We feel like the scapegoats. Global warming, pollution in the ocean, over fishing in the ocean, very far away from me, are all important factors doing more damage than subsistence fishing. *Who knows this, and who cares!* I have to joke with people because I cannot be serious as no one believes me, when I say, "It is not bears, the dark-cold, that is the hardest to deal with in a wilderness lifestyle, it is Man, civilization."

I LOAD up the sled dogs in the houseboat in preparation for another trip to the big city. The sled dogs go nuts fighting for the best positions in the boat. I let them work it out and pick their spot. Except, "Map next to Kenai? I don't think so! Dream on! You two will be in a fight before I get the engines started. Map, go pick a female to be next to!" He does not know what I'm talking about beyond, "No, I am not letting you fight with Kenai." I show him a good spot next to a female and he wags his tail. All the dogs have to be short chained in, but at least they picked the spot. There are eight dogs. The trip to Nenana is uneventful. I drop the sled dogs off with Josh, and spend a night. I have extra dry fish left over from winter to give Josh for his dogs as well as mine, for payment to watch my dogs. My mind is more on the things I need to do in town.

Back in Fairbanks I run into Will, as usual. "Miles, this time I did not argue. I got the usual feeling you would arrive and I stopped what I was doing and came in and just drove around, knowing you'd be here and I'd see you."

I only smile. "Will, is Fish and Game being the monkey wrench in the gears, or me? Because this is not the first time I have had issues with the government and the law. There was my Canada experience. There seemed to be the difference between my sense of what is moral, and society's sense of what is technically written." I did not mention this is also not the first or last time I have had women problems.

"Well, Miles, you pretty much have to follow the law, that's for sure."

"Ya, but Will, I do not want to. That takes the fun out of life. Doing what I want, when I want, how I want, is so much nicer." We both laugh. "The secret, Will, is not to get caught!" More and more the planet I live on that is separate from the planet civilization and everyone else lives on, are coming together. My planet is being invaded. My planet is Earth. Civilization is a zoo of some kind. But now Earth, my world, is becoming a zoo as well. My planet, Earth is not having any problems till civilization shows up. Then civilization blames me for the problems.

Will has told me his family story before. From Czechoslovakia. His family told him the story. How the country was taken by the communists. Registered guns was the law. So the communists came to the villages and demanded the registered gun list at the police station, then went door to door with the list.

"Give us your gun or die." It did not take long to control the country. A couple of days, only a few shots were fired. Poof, suddenly communist.

There were other such stories, like Karen's from Germany, that closely match what we see today in our country. I think of Berlin in the late 1930s. There were parties, money, and good times for those not in the gun sites. Many did not believe there were concentration camps! Ha! Those were good times, for the superior race, drinking good wine, listening to concerts. They all treated each other nicely, I think! We forget now; money was good, production was up, unemployment down. There were many US companies investing in Hitler's plans and getting rich; few admit it today. It was all about money. Even if there is a little crap going on here and there, *probably the Jews deserved it, anyhow, none of my business, why look a gift horse in the mouth?* Who wants to investigate, get to the bottom of anything, and ask too many questions? *It's their fault for being Jews. Thank God I'm not one.* Meanwhile the good life goes on. How lucky for the civilized.

"Or Will! Maybe the lemming herd, which is civilization, is getting closer to the cliff, and my world is between civilization and the cliff, being swept along with everything else, headed for hell."

Will nods this might well be so. "Miles, you are pretty lucky all in all. I have been stuck here all along, and I have had no choice. I'm plugged in with no escape. I have to have licenses and permits and rule books for everything I do. Remember how I used to make money buying junk cars and working on them and reselling them? Well, now every little part needs a record and registration number, and I cannot legalize something I build from five different wrecks. I need a license to sell. I need insurance. I have to keep records. I need to be certified. I'm shut down. I'm out of business. No more small-time, home-run, hobby stuff, or mom and pop outfits. It's all about the big boys. Steam rollers across the business world."

"I wouldn't know much about that. Sorry to hear it though, as I know how much you liked and depended on that business. Anyhow, to change the subject, Will, I proved up on that Federal land homesite. I could maybe acquire a Federal trade and manufacture site in the same area. I'm looking into that. I think twenty acres."

"What would the trade or manufacture be, Miles?"

"Could be any number of things. You have to utilize the land for the trade though. I could build dog sleds using birch off the land. I could utilize something from the land for my art work, like antler, wood, gold, other stuff found maybe. I like the idea of medicinal herbs to dry and sell. I'd have to see what the exact requirements are and what they have to say about my ideas."

"What do you need more land for anyhow?"

"Oh, I don't know, Will. Land is money; retirement. Or, more like money is just paper, you can't eat it, and its only use is as trading material for stuff that you can use. By itself it is useless, only worth what the bank and government says it is. Nothing backs it up. We went off the gold and silver standard. We just print more money when we need it. But land, Will, is forever. It will always have a value. Having land all over is to be adaptable, so I can move with the fur, change as I need. But I think really, I just feel more safe. No one knows where I am. No one can reach me. I can't be found. It's a good feeling. No one is as likely to drag me out of my home in handcuffs screaming in the middle of the night. No one is going to hand me a ticket, or ask for my paperwork, or inform me of some restriction or negative news of some kind. I move here. I move there. I drift around, get my mail in one place. Then another. What I'm up to, where I am, is only a rumor. Wild and free like a myth. Or a mist. I cannot be touched. I have no truth. I give no facts. Nothing is evidence. It's just stories and bullshit. Sleight of hand. Now you see it, now you do not, a trick. Magic. What is the truth? What is fiction? Rob Roy. Clint Eastwood. Indiana Jones. Grizzly Adams. Billy the Kid. The Mad Trapper of Rat River. Like that." We both laugh again as we drive around in Will's old beat up truck belching smoke, and backfiring with turn signals that do not work, looking out for cops.

"Samson's! More stove pipe." Will whips into the left lane after crossing the bridge over the Chena River.

"I need a do-hickey I heard about, that transfers propane from a big bottle to a smaller bottle."

There is a small pause and the clerk who knows me says, "That's not legal! It's not safe!" Another slight pause as I look annoyed.

"I didn't ask if it was legal or safe!"

The clerk chuckles. "Ok, then, right here, this is what you need."

I wink at Will. Get out my list and "Oh, yeah, Down under Guns, right around the corner. I got a bullet load I'm working on for the 180 grain Barns Bullet in the 270 caliber. No data on it. Can't buy that weight, got to load it yourself. Only one guy I know who might have some advice on what powder will be right to start with. I got an older low twist rifle. I assume the 4831 military surplus powder will work, but Peabody might have some ideas. The 150 grain spitzer or partitioned is ok, but not perfect for the thick brush on bears." Will and I talk ballistics for a while. He likes his 375 H & H. Way too big for me, but Will can handle 'big.' A foot taller than me, and a hundred pounds heavier.

"Yeah, Miles, but you are always maxing out your small stuff. So why not just go bigger?"

"Because it's part of my little dick syndrome, Will, don't worry about it!" We both laugh again because he has heard about my various women in the past, met some, talked to them, and has asked me what I got that he doesn't have! He met Palace who was a knock out. There was the library gal, a couple from the Can Can Cuties at Alaskaland, the Alaska House gal, Nancy, Karen, and others. He sees me as a ladies man.

"Seriously though, Will, it's not what I want or look for. I'd about sell my soul for love, peace, and something lasting. I'm faithful to the ones I'm with, and try real hard to work things out. My heart is truly heavy to not have anything last." I'm not sure Will believes me, Miles, the bullshitter with the smooth words. The one who could convince you white was black, or sell snow to an Eskimo. The truth with me is elusive. I can argue about any side of any point and win depending on the situation and what point is required, regardless of how I really feel. *It's a gift!*

"Miles, don't we need to stop at Alaska Feed as you usually do? Let's see the list. That's pretty cool how you buy animal feed much cheaper and eat the not for human consumption and it's better quality!"

"Yup, better quality all right, but do not forget, more bugs in it, and rat shit. But that's natural stuff, Will. Alaska Feed!" My list is on an index card. We have been scratching items off. He's right about the animal feed. It has no preservatives. It's just natural food. There is a higher level of weed seeds in the corn meal and flax and stuff like that. Big deal. It's less than half the price of human food. There may, or may not be, a higher percent of rat shit. As long as I do not see it, it's not there. Reality is anything I want it to be.

"Miles, looks like 100 pounds of wheat flour, 100 pounds of whole grain rice, 25 pounds of rolled oats, 25 pounds of pinto beans, 25 pounds of noodles, a five gallon bucket of honey, a five gallon bucket of peanut butter, five pounds of split peas. That's it for here. Looks like you wrote 'Fred Meyers' for the yeast, baking powder, ketchup, pepper, garlic powder, powder milk, dry fruit, corn oil. What do you do for something to drink? I see no coffee here!"

"I'm not a coffee drinker, Will. I can pick Labrador tea or rose hips to dry for tea. If I have extra money, I might get this new crystallite since it is light in weight. I add that to tea sometimes. I could even do without honey if I am poor and make birch syrup, but it takes so much time and firewood it's just better to buy sweets." I explain how I get a few cake mixes if I can afford it. I also try to be adaptable and buy what is on sale in the way of dented cans of vegetables or fruit, and if there is damaged food or case lots of something in season that I can dry or can then I grab that. Like that time we got a case of mushrooms for $3, and the case of peaches for $10! That stuff is just nice, but not necessary.

"No sugar, Miles?"

"I figure honey is enough. I learned a while back that sugar is not so great on the body. I provide all my meat from the land, and pick some berries to go on the pancakes. I make a lot of bread, as that goes with about any main meal; all kinds of things can be put on bread, and it's cheap. Noodles, rice, beans are the staples as well. They are cheap, compact, keep easily, and can be adapted for all kinds of meals with things I can add from the land. Noodles and rice get wild mushrooms added, moose meat or fish, leaves of different kinds, Eskimo potato, wild rhubarb, stuff like that."

"Why so much peanut butter, Miles!"

"In the eastern countries nuts go with meat, usually cashews. Peanut butter tastes good with meat as well and any kind of nut has high nutritional value. A bean, a nut, and rice is balanced protein, and oil in nuts is good energy in cold country. There's the B complex vitamins. The main vitamin I need that I buy separate is Vitamin C, because it is unstable and does not keep. Vitamin C is in the rose hips I dry for tea, but am unsure if I can count on it. Old timers on the ocean used to carry limes for that. Without vitamin C you can get scurvy, and C is needed when there is lack of light. My diet lacks fresh things, leafy vegetables, but hey, my diet is probably as good or better than most people's."

"Miles, what do you do on the trail for quick fast traveling food. I always wondered that. I'd get cup of noodles and ramen myself."

"Sometimes I get that. But in the 70s that was not around as much. Local natives relied on pilot bread, just a hard cracker. I learned how to grind my own dry items into something I can add hot water to for instant food. I use peas, noodles, dry mushrooms, spices, dry meat. It's healthy, and does not cost much. I just put it in a mess kit and add boiling water. Oh, one thing I add that is unusual is, I dry carrot tops from the garden, if I have a garden. It is like parsley. It's a great spice. Also dry turnip and beet leaves. I add this to rice dishes as well. Not much gets wasted! Ha!" We talk about a few other things on the list like spare bow saw blades, matches.

"Miles! No toilet paper! What do you wipe with!"

"If I can afford it, I get it, but it sure takes up a lot of space, Will. If you are dying to know, I re-use rags and wash em out. I do what I gotta do, Will, it's not all romantic and pretty!" We both have a good laugh. He thought I might use corn cobs like real mountain men do. Eskimos used to use rabbit furs. In summer I use moss. "For a while, I saved bags of moss in the cabin for winter use, but it takes up too much room and is not fun when it dries out." We are driving around, and looks like I have most things on the list now. "You got your education for the day Will! Thanks for running me around. I know you got things to do, but it is always great to get together and get caught up on what's been going on. Might as well drop me off here at the Craft shop. I'll stay with Crafty here and do some trading."

"That you, Miles? Hey, good to see you, wondered if you made it through another year out there." Crafty wants to get filled in on the latest adventure.

"Well I got a wolverine this past winter I couldn't kill—I shot it, I hit it over the head with an ax. I finally gave up and tied him in the sled alive by four legs. Had to, he jumped out of the sled and almost caught up to the wheel dog! Dogs go faster and I grab the wolverine by the scruff of the neck as I go by, and toss him back in the sled, tie him down with traps. I get home and Karen has a fit, asking me why I don't kill the poor thing! Told her I had been trying all day!"

"Dang, Miles, they are one tough critter, huh? How'd you finally kill it?"

"I didn't. I left him hanging in the snare in a tree. I think it took two days. I could have used dynamite or something, but wanted the hide. Enough to give a guy religion, Crafty. Spooky. I admire the wolverine almost as much as dandelions."

"Dandelions, Miles? What are you talking about? What have wolverines and dandelions got in common!"

"Dandelions, Crafty, cannot be killed. The more you stomp on them, the faster they grow. They push up sidewalks, and grow through asphalt. If there is a nuclear war and the earth is flattened, the first thing to recover will be dandelions. We can all learn from that, Crafty. If there is any animal I respect and want to be like, it is the wolverine." We move on to getting money and trade goods for my art work. We eat at the Chinese place down the street, and go see a movie at the theatre. I tell Crafty that Karen and I parted.

"Yes, I figured. I saw it coming. You're both too stubborn to be under the same roof! Ha! Where's the sled dogs? "

"I left 'em with Josh in Nenana, safer than here in town. I look after his dogs in return, so it works out. I'm parking the houseboat at Alaskaland. I sold some things to shops there." We are interrupted with customers in the shop. Interestingly, the customers are looking at art work Crafty has bought from me in past years and has out to sell.

I smile as I overhear, "Wow, look at this fine work. I never saw anything like it!" There are four guys looking at my art all dressed alike. The others agree they think this is some of the finest art they have ever seen... ever... anyplace.

Crafty wants to make a good sale so tells them, "The guy who does this work is right here, Miles. He lives in the wilds and just happens to be here today."

I step forward and tell them about the art they are looking at. They all want something similar. That is when I wonder who they are, all dressed alike and pretty flashy, sort of like 60s rock stars. They seem to have money, are well traveled, so think they are not drugged out hippies. I ask who they are and one says,

"Steppenwolf, here to do a concert." This seems a real honor to me. I had admired them as a band in my youth. Now they are admiring my work! They want my autograph and I want theirs! Ha! Each one leaves with a wolf claw necklace, custom metal art wrapped around it. After they leave, Crafty gets back to our business at hand. I had told him I went to Alaskaland before seeing him, and I saw this on his mind.

"Hey, Miles! You didn't high grade on me did ya?!"

"Well, yeah, probably. Start paying the best price and I'll see what I can do for ya, maybe then you'd be my first stop and not my last!"

He laughs, "I taught you well."

"I learned from the best! Hey, by the way, where do you get that glue I use?"

We both laugh again. He is not falling for that one. "Protect your sources, Miles!"

I look hurt. "But Crafty, what's a few sources shared between friends?" He knows I'm baiting him, so we both laugh again. I have a role I play with Crafty. I see what he wants, expects, and I give it to him. I'm not the same person as I am with Will or the Parr's.

Crafty is not interested in any Fish cop problems I might have. "Miles, you bring it on yourself. You want it all your way, and expect no price to pay for that!"

"Maybe, Crafty, but are you any different? You got problems with the IRS, problems at the fair. Wasn't that you carted off the grounds for selling knives to kids after being told not to?"

"That's different, Miles! Those fair people are not honest and lied to me; set me up; had personal issues with me and were underhanded about it! I have my side of the story! The dang tax people, too. Wanting taxes on inventory I have stored for years is nuts. I'd go broke following that! And that thing about almost losing my business over city taxes! Ha! I told Tom to pay it while I was gone and assumed it got done. There was no notice, no questions, no nothing but ready to shut me down!"

I only smile and go "hmm" He does not see any similarity between his situation and mine. *My poop stinks but his does not.* So I smile. When someone is your friend you forgive them.

"Miles, scientology is being attacked! Can you believe it? We still have meetings here though. Did you read that book I gave you? The Science of Survival?"

As a matter of fact I can believe, even understand the attacks, but why tell Crafty? What good would it do? "Yes, sure did. Good book. I like how survival is defined as maximum survival which involves being ahead a little. I also like the concept of right and wrong, where 'right' is defined as 'the most good for the most number of people,' and being wary of those who tell the truth, when the truth they tell is always negative, destructive, and does no good to anyone but is only rude. Where 'bad' might be illegal, but can still do the most good for the most number of people. It helps me a lot to figure out what to listen to or not, and how to behave myself. But this whole thing about a tone scale, and those below a certain level not worth saving, and wondering who decides where anyone is on this scale is scary."

I understand my friend well enough. When we met he could not read or write well enough to make out a receipt to do business. He was pushed through school. No one cared. It was Scientology who forced him to face stuff, taught him how to read and write. Someone cared. He will never forget and will be forever loyal. Scientology invested in a good soldier. If he's a little radical on the subject, who among us is perfect? I understand the basic principles of Scientology and get along with Crafty fine.

When we met, Crafty was a garbage man selling on the street out of a suitcase. Now he owns the biggest craft shop in the city, and is one of the biggest distributors of local hand done art of anyone in the entire state. He had a vision. A craft market. A distribution point for craft, and for artists to gather. A vision of a place to bring us all under one roof in a shop that represents the craft people. Like a flea market. Crafty made it happen. He has artists working for him sort of like employees. Some actually work in his basement filling orders he takes from galleries. Crafty takes an order and subcontracts it out among his fleet of loyal workers. A beautiful concept. He made the vision reality. From an illiterate street person, he took his dream and is the best there is, maybe in the state, at what he does. Not much else matters to him. It's his life – that and Scientology.

"I got some more literature, one on the role of the artist in the world, and this other about the founder L. Ron Hubbard." I politely thank him and take the books. Only the art one interests me and it does have some good ideas.

"Art is peaceful revolution. By postulating possible future realities, the artist changes the future…" The two concepts Crafty introduces me to, affect me deeply. Defining right and wrong in terms of the most good for the most number of people and seeing my role as an artist as the chance to bring about revolution and change peacefully. Oddly, this is what I get out of Scientology that Crafty does not, and he seeks and finds something else. But maybe all spiritual beliefs are like this. We gravitate to what suits who we are, and what comes natural to us.

"Miles, your mind is wandering again! Did you hear me? If I was a bear you'd be dead now!"

"Ya, ok, what are you saying?"

"I got three piles. One is your last years and damaged I have to move in bulk, fast and cheap, so I need a deal on it! This number two pile I can offer to galleries and higher end places maybe. It's popular at the moment, and I got asked already for more of this, so can offer trade value. Keep in mind the big picture, Miles. What the tourist seeks and why. Watch trends. This last pile I want to retail here in the shop. I need to trade because I have to sit on it longer and it may not sell for a year or more so cannot offer cash."

"Ok, Crafty, but spare me all the details for now. I have a number in my head I came up with, so add it all up and tell me what your number is and we'll go from there." He wants to know ahead of time what my number is. But I know if I tell him, he will no way offer more than that! I only tell him my number if he is much lower than me with his offer. He hedges, hems and haws. He's sizing me up, wants to know how bad I need money, how desperate am I, what can he reasonably offer that I might accept? How low can I go? I yawn. Sit back. Life is good. I'm not broke, not between a rock and a hard place. If I do not like his offer, I can go someplace else. I want him to know that. It's all part of the chess game of life in the business world of Crafty.

He sighs. "Four grand with two grand in trade."

It's in the ballpark of my own estimate. But I gotta play my hand; it's what Crafty expects. I look a little hurt. I sigh. I get out my calculator and punch in some numbers, looking at the pile and frown. With exaggerated elaborate gestures I look thoughtful. I sigh again. I punch in some more numbers and divide by two. I had watched Don, my fur buyer in action doing the same thing. He'd be proud of me.

"Cash within two days, no checks, and I'll cut ya some slack on the trades, but trade has to be my wholesale to your wholesale not my wholesale to your retail." There are a lot of people who think my buddy Crafty is a bit cutthroat and ruthless. But he's also the biggest game in town. Who else has four grand cash? My buddy knows how to move goods and money. That alone makes me watch him with interest. I'd do it different? Well I am not stupid. The proof is in the results. What's my business look like, what's his look like? How is everyone else in the game looking? It's a cruel world. It's quick and it's dirty. God helps those who slip and stumble, not your fellow man. I wish it wasn't like that, but I didn't make the rules. I do, in fact, think I want to do it different from Crafty, but I have no position of strength to speak from, so keep it to myself for now.

"A week, and your wholesale to my 10% discount."

"Ten percent off your retail is nothing, and you know it. You pay ten cents on the dollar. I'll go 30%" It's all about the trade part, which is two grand compared to the four grand cash. I can find a way to make up for the shady trade agreement one small trade at a time. It's chess. I'll let him think I left a checkmate move open. That pleases him. It appears money is Crafty's God. But I know all the reasons why.

Crafty gets ten grand worth of art for four grand cash and some trade goods for what he gets at garage sales and discount stores. He deals with suckers who can't cut the business world who want to bail out, so sell to Crafty, the shark. But four grand is cool. I can live on that. I get my bush life with no mess, no fuss ,no hassle and that's what Crafty offers, take it or leave it. He has the stuff I could not sell fast. He's a hustler and can move it. In some ways, he has a big heart. In some ways, he only thinks he has to be ruthless. I've seen him get talked into lending money, then not getting it back, lots of money, like thousands of dollars. If I was down and out I know he'd give me a job in an instant. If I was in a bind I think Crafty would front me a few grand or more to save me. Pay him back with no interest. Would my bank? Ha! Anyone else? Ha! Not everyone sees that side of Mr. Crafty.

Behind Crafty, is the picture proudly hung of himself next to Grizzly Adams from the TV show. They look like twins. Crafty is never dressed like most successful business people. He dresses and looks like he lives in the wilderness. Some would see him as an unsophisticated slob. His shop is a disorganized mess filled with moose antler dust drifting up from downstairs, and looks like my home in the wilds. He can only get half the price of the shops that have things nicely displayed under glass and lights. Fine, but take a look at his sales and profits. Money talks. There are many aspects of Crafty I see in myself. It is easier to see stuff in others than seeing it in yourself.

"Hey, Crafty, you ever hear much from the old crowd from the 70s? I often wonder how they did, and who ever got out to the woods and what they are doing these days."

"Nope, not really. That one guy who stole the jackets at the fair came by here. I told you a long time ago, and think siphoned fuel from my fuel tank and I told him not to come around anymore."

"I heard from others he's dead now. He went back east and got stabbed in some drug deal or some such. But there were some others, Jim and Jamie and their girl-friends, folks from the Howling Dog that used to give me rides, and we'd show up here or see you at the fair. I was thinking about it, and a lot of them are dead! Before they were forty! Seems strange." Crafty is not interested. He's going over catalogs comparing prices. I tell him good-bye till next time. He absent mindedly dismisses me as he gets into his money plans.

So four grand and I already have most of my supplies for winter. Life is good. *Ya, money talks and bullshit walks.* I still look at how much I have then figure out what I can afford. I do not dream about things I have no money for and then try to come up with the money. I say good bye to the Underhills at Alaskaland where the houseboat is parked. After leaving them, my mind is on my sled dogs, missing them, wondering how they are, and looking forward to being with them again.

"Hey, Miles, hold up a second!" My blade of grass shifts to the side of my mouth as I turn to see who calls. I recognize the guy, but forget the name. *Think he owns the saloon where the Can Can girls I hang with dance. One of the people who tried to get me kicked out of Alaskaland.* "Miles, I saw a copy of the book manuscript you have been talking about writing." We sit on a bench along the path that has been made to look like a village path between log cabins in the gold rush days. My hunting knife clanks on the bench as I throw my leather coat open and lean back to catch the sun. The guy talking is in a clean suit, and sits properly as he has been taught, a little annoyed at my uncouth exaggerated posture. Yeah, some first copies of the manuscript are out among folks at Alaskaland as a preview. I'm curious about the response. So far everyone likes the story, but it needs more editing and my style needs help, I'm told. I still need practice learning to type. I'm using a manual ribbon typewriter. It's pretty rough looking yet. I do not notice that as much as I should, as this is my child I'm proud of, and you better not say anything bad about it.

"It's ok, but it is just not that believable. I was ok with the exaggerations till I read about you kicking that bear. It made everything else bullshit, Miles. It's ok as a fiction, like Tarzan or something, for a fast read, like a comic book, but I expected more like a biography. You get some of the incidents mixed up here at Alaskaland and the fair. Some of your dates are off. It's still pretty rough and needs a lot more research!" I inwardly sigh. Somehow I feel like this reader has missed the point and purpose of the book. Yet this is a common line of thought I hear. Especially from those who know a few of the facts, locals, and those who know Alaska and the wilderness life somewhat. Tourists who do not know any better, love it. Also many seem to be expecting the book to fit into a category of some kind and duplicate the style of that category like biography which usually reads too dry in my opinion. A lot of thought has gone into what these comments mean. And what I might do about it. I'm not going to appeal to every reader. I cannot please everyone. So who am I writing for? Who do I want to please? Who is my market?

I speak seriously with this reader. "I see two extremes of people in the world. Those who think of, and record events as a series of numbers, and those who record events as a series of feelings." To explain this idea, I use as an example. "We ask two types of people the same question. 'Describe a time you bought strawberries.' A scientific mind might reply, 'On August first, I got in my 98' Ford and drove two miles to Safeway and parked in lot number one. I saw strawberries on sale for $1.50 a pint marked down from $2.40 so I bought two pints.' We call this personality a bean counter. An engineer, draftsman, scientific mind, that looks for order in things. Someone who looks first for straight lines, correct spelling, rules and regulations, law and order, and is a whole way of thinking, doing, and viewing life. If we were to ask "What did they taste like?" We might get a puzzled look, a blank stare and this reply: 'Good. I guess, like strawberries. What else would they taste like? What a dumb question! Why, was something wrong with them?' Such a person would laugh if told, "How can you say you got strawberries and not be able to describe how they taste, maybe you never ate one."

The other type is an artistic mind. The dreamer who sees events in color, with sound, smell, and feelings. There, answer to the question is: 'Strawberries? Sure. I went to Safeway, I think, maybe in August, I forget. I remember the strawberries! Big, red, juicy and ripe. I could smell them across the whole store. Before I left the store I had to try one. I ran my tongue over one before I bit it. It goes to my nose and I sniff, close my eyes, and hold my breath to treasure the aroma of spring. Memories of mom's pie and strawberries and ice cream. Strawberries on cereal makes me drool. It smells like happiness, tastes like love, feels cool, refreshing.' If we ask, "What did you pay for them?" We might get a puzzled look, a blank stare and, 'I assume the going price being asked. Who cares. What a silly question. Why, does someone think I stole them?' Such a person might laugh if told, "How can you buy strawberries and not know what you paid, maybe you never had any."

I glance at my reader to see if he is catching my drift here.

"Sure ,Miles, sounds good all right, but there you go again, trying to convince me red is blue, and that shit is really valuable. It's an ego thing with you, Miles, face it. Look at you. Haven't had a bath in over a week, dressed in leather, wearing that blade. The sun does not circle around you, Miles. The universe does not part wherever you go."

I very carefully take the blade of grass out of my mouth and set it down, look at the fresh growing grass by the bench and select a nice tall juicy blade. I inspect it carefully before inserting it contentedly into my mouth. My reader friend is extremely irritated by all this. I pretend I do not know it. I smile, like I am the only one in the world. He assumes I will feel guilty. He assumes he has properly insulted me. Put me in my place. *Someplace beneath him.* I reply, "Yes. The sun revolves around me. Yes, the universe indeed parts wherever I go and, closes behind me, forever changed. There is one thing you fail to see. The sun revolves around you too. The universe parts wherever you go as well. You are unique in the world. No one else is quite like you. Like snowflakes, no two are exactly alike. You are the best in the world at what you are, which is being you. No one else can be you. You can choose to focus on this and notice, or not."

My reader friend is not pleased. He looks nervous. Some people want to focus on how snowflakes are all just snowflakes and blend in as the storm. Such people do not want to stand out, be noticed. Their strength is in numbers as part of that storm. Others, like me, focus on how each snowflake is different. It's only perspective. Each view is the truth. What truths do we focus on?

"Many of the readers I write for have maybe been camping once." I go on to explain my point. The analogy is like explaining Wall Street to an Aborigine who says he understands because he figured out what money is for and is the village hero because he was able to buy a burger and fries once. Yet some villagers ask, 'How can anyone be a success, when they can not even knap a spear head from flint? How can anyone say they went any place at all who never went on a Vision Quest?' How does one respond to this line of thinking? That Aborigine who learns a thing or two eventually about Wall Street even makes a living and goes back to live in his village. He tells of what he learned. Will he be respected and understood in his village? Chances are, he will be seen as a storyteller, jester, and a bit touched and crazy, but harmless enough. For in his village he can barely get by making good spears, tanning leopard hides for his loin cloth. He does not deserve a woman and is tolerated, not admired. He says, 'There are lights that direct traffic. They go from green to red automatically, using something called electricity.' I could picture a hush in the aborigine tribe.

"What an imagination! Ha! What a great story teller! Where does he get these ideas? Lights, people living in huts far above the ground! A material you can look through, but cannot walk through, what did he call it, glass?" Obviously the tribe sees him as doing the lecture circuit so to speak. A teller of tales. OZ. So he smiles and accepts the role. He gets fed, he has a place. It is easier that way. There is nothing to prove. There is no reason to get indignant or make a point of any kind. Few seriously want the truth. But the truth can be hidden someplace for those who seek it. There will be those in the tribe saying, "I heard of this place called civilization, Oh, Wise One. I saw it once on a screen in what they call a documentary or movie. Show me, take me there. I wish to live there too. I wish like you, to make this stuff called money on Wall Street! Yes, I think this would be a good way to live. I wish to be like this one, what they call it, the President."

And here is this guy in a loin cloth who once wore pants when he went to the city, but does not own a pair. His life skills are making spears and tanning skins. Maybe if he is lucky he might get paid in the city to do demonstrations on spear making. Only maybe. Would he accept this? No, he will not accept this. He wants to be President, have respect, money, status, success. He wants OZ to take him there and teach him how, give him directions. This Aborigine does not comprehend. You cannot get there from here on the dirt road to the village—the biggest place this Aborigine can imagine. He has to be willing to go back to square one and be three years old knowing nothing. He must get on a plane and fly, forgetting all about the taboo against flight. He will be lucky not to get laughed at for carrying his spear, lucky not to end up in jail for carrying his spear. It would be a very long hard journey that might take twenty years with no promise of success. I met a native once who was headed to the city to find work and his father gave him something to help. A rabbit snare. So he could eat while there. You tell me how useful a rabbit snare will be anywhere in civilization.

It is the same going the other direction, when the city dweller expresses a wish to be a Mountain Man, live like an Indian chief. My reader cannot get from here to here, to live like an Indian chief. It is not much like camping. The very first step is to be able to dream. For anything to become reality, first you have to be able to see it in a dream. If you cannot imagine it, then it can never be real.

I sigh. If you go out in the wilderness with the tools you have in civilization, you can be a visitor and camp. But it will never be home, and you will never treat it as the safe place to be, and if you go out and plan on not coming back? You will surely die unless your mind is open enough to accept a land of OZ. For there will indeed be munchkins, witches with ruby slippers, people made of straw, rusty tin men, women lost looking for a home, flying monkeys, strange things to eat, odd places to sleep, and if you do not see it? Well, you may run out of supplies and panic and keep running. Happens all the time. Your mind must be a blank, open to accept all the wonders you will see. One must say 'Huh a mastodon, I'll be darned,' and keep washing your face in the creek. Coming unglued is not going to work. Numbers do not work here. Neither do degrees, permits, or 'How to' manuals. None of this would help you be President of the United States, and none of this would help you be an Indian chief (or a Mountain Man, or hero type, living the good life). An Aborigine would be very lucky just to exist in civilization as a dumpster diver on the street in the welfare line, without becoming a drug addict and a statistic. Very little of what the aborigine came to civilization with will he still have as survival tools. A civilized person choosing the wilds as a lifestyle is lucky to be in the wilds and live, eating rotten meat, crawling in a muddy cut-bank at night for shelter. Very little he brings with him will be of use in his new life.

Oh, the Aborigine might find a use for the rabbit snare he brought with him. Maybe to jury rig a broken carburetor cable in the junk car he stole. But this will never be in the manual he was given by his tribe when he took off for civilization. Just so the civilized person's car keys might come in handy when it is time to make arrow heads, but is that going to be in any manual he carries? That manual got rained on and fell apart and lost in the first month.

In a way, I am trying to get the reader to think outside the box. The only truth is that which is in your head. Reality is on a slide ruler. The past, present, and future come together in a parabolic curve of the universe. The same Big Bang that started it all, is the same Big Bang that ends it all. Staring at the future is not a lot different than staring at the past.

If you do not have it in you to eat rotten meat with maggots in it, your days in the wild are numbered. No amount of supplies, no amount of matches, no amount of how to books, will save you. The story of survival is not told in lists, direction, maps, numbers, weights, permits and rules. I'm trying to explain this in the best way I can. I feel like the Aborigine trying to explain glass to those who have never seen it. A material you can see through but not walk through.

I am explaining in my book in the most basic, simplest terms I possibly can, and still have lost this reader on the bench. His chances of survival in the wilds could be measured in hours, not days. But no use making him wrong. I tell him, "Do not pay attention to that man behind the curtain! I am Oz, the great and powerful!" I shift the grass in my mouth, stand up with much ceremony, and wink at him, as I follow the yellow brick road to my boat. He is shaking his head, believing I'm on drugs. I am sad, even a little afraid. This man is in the majority and represents the power of civilization, the vote of the common people. The laws of civilization revolve around numbers, dates, times, names, statistics, not feelings. Warranties, permits, rebates, grants, loans, credit, unemployment, retirement funds, insurance, all revolve around keeping track of, records of, numbers. How we feel is an opinion, not a fact. But numbers too are an opinion. Or, numbers are about as easy to fake as feelings, if one is deceptive. But never mind.

The check list is gone over of all my new supplies. I have almost 300 wilderness river miles to travel to get to where I'm going. I wish I had room for more gas because the price is better in Fairbanks then Nenana, the last village with a road. I'll need a total of 200 gallons of gas for the round trip. I'm in good spirits, and look forward to time alone in the wilds. There will be bears, moose, and geese. Fish to catch, a new cabin to build, trails to cut, and God to talk to. I feel lucky. I know what I want. I know how to get there! The tarp is put over the back of the houseboat to cover the goods not under the roof. The boat is drawing over two feet of water, with only six inches of freeboard. I'll be going about ten miles an hour with the current to save on gas, because I have more time than money. I laugh to myself as I head downstream, "So what's worth more? Time or money?"

In Nenana, I stop to spend a night and go over my accumulated mail. Josh and I feed all the dogs. Of course they are glad to see me! Usually we spend twenty-four hours within sight of each other, so this is strange for them, to have me be gone, to see me, and to leave them alone again. I feel bad that they do not understand. I want to visit with Josh, need to go over my mail in case there is a bill, or important information needing a fast reply before I leave for months. Josh and I are watching TV at his house while I sort mail. "Miles, what's the matter?"

"Josh, looks like a letter stating I have a court case I must be at in a few weeks over the subsistence moose issue! You know, being charged with taking a moose out of season."

"I thought that was all taken care of! Anyhow what is the big deal, locals, and especially wilderness people try to wait till winter to get a moose so it keeps without having to own a freezer! There are plenty of moose around. It's not like you are being wasteful."

"I know Josh. I do not know what the problem is. But having to come in for court is a monkey wrench in my gears. I cannot afford the 200 gallons of gas it will take to come in from the upper Kantishna. This is where I had plans to go, to work on the upper end of the trapline and fish, look over some new land. I have supplies stashed, and that is home now. I think I can't get up there now, not do that and come back in less than a month. Neither can I afford to hang around here for a month! I think this moose issue is a misunderstanding, and I'll get off once the facts are out. Their evidence is some moose leg bones with dried maggots in them they claim represents moose killed in the winter. All they have to do is look inside the bones and see maggots could not have been there in winter. But meanwhile for them to look inside I have to show up for my hearing, or I'll have a warrant out for my arrest for not showing up. I thought this was all taken care of, but looks like it is not. If I had money for a lawyer, the lawyer could get the time postponed for me till I can get back in. I do not think I can do it on my own Josh, because there was a situation like this before. Karen and I got a notice about court, custody, issues over the children. I tried to call and find out what is going on, and set a time when we'd be in. I was told indignantly no one is going to talk to me, have my lawyer get in touch. No one cared I do not live in the world of lawyers. I do not have a lawyer, nor do I have money for a lawyer and I do not even have a phone to find a lawyer, Josh."

"I do not understand either, Miles. If anyone deserves or qualifies for subsistence it is you! You are more subsistence than most natives!"

"I know, and this is part of what scares me. Subsistence is defined by the color of our skin, not by how we live. That's discrimination, but try to argue that and get anyplace. My fear is, I can be made an example of to get the word out to white people, homesteaders and trappers, who think they are subsistence, and equal to natives. I could be a sacrifice to make a point. Even though Fish and Game has no evidence that will hold up, if they want me bad enough, they can plant evidence. So now what do I do?"

I am able to contact a local lawyer Josh suggests, who handles cases for people without much money and specializes in Fish and Game issues. I'm later getting back on the river, but at least the lawyer gets the case dismissed. It cost me $800 - half a year's wages. I head to the lower Kantishna home to drop off all my supplies, catch a few fish to feed the sled dogs, and plant a garden. The whole summer plans are changed now. I had planned on being at the upper end of the trapline, and working down. The good news is, there should be fur to catch at the lower end since I was not trapping here last winter. I try to look at the bright side. "We are healthy, alive, able to trap, in a bind, but not down and out. We shall recover. We could have lost our case and be in jail now." The thought of jail of course makes us shiver, as we'd lose all our sled dogs probably, lose the boat. For who would take care of all this without money?

One concern is that I tend to get emotional, ramble, rant, rave and carry on, till I sound radical, paranoid. Fact and fiction blend in emotional outbursts. I can forget what is real and what is perceived. Going off the deep end is not going to get me anyplace. Plans have to be adaptable. Many things can change our plans. At any time we can fall and break an arm or get sick, or deal with various losses, a funeral or even a wedding and there we are, changed plans. So now I am back where I was a month ago, ready to head upriver and get lost. Safe, away from civilization where no one can hurt me. Where I do not need to be helpless, and where it does not take money to make the world go round. My spare twenty horse engine has been acting up. I cannot afford a new one right now. For a while, nothing seems to be going right. I miss the family, Karen and the girls more than I want to acknowledge. Being unhappy has a ripple effect.

EVENTUALLY, winter sets in, with me being ready for it. I'm on the homestead, and have enough salmon for the winter dog feed. Fur prices look like they will be good this year and there is no reason to think I will not get a lot of them. Josh expects me at my usual time, about Christmas, three months from now. I have 150 miles of trapline trail cut. I am a full time professional trapper making a living at it. Not many trappers can say that. I have been at this lifestyle long enough I seem to know what I am doing, to where it is routine now. I'm at the peak of my physical health, and the peak of my career as a trapper, mountain man, subsistence person. Once again, life is good.

THE END OF BOOK 2

A personal note—

Reviews help! If you enjoyed this book, please leave a review where you purchased it—it would be greatly appreciated!

Sign up for my newsletter, "Keeping Up With Miles," @ www.milesofalaska.com

Deals, new books, comments, links to YouTube. Stay updated!

The Alaska Off Grid Survival Series Summary

Book 1 - Going Wild

In 1973, I am 22 years old, and a city kid. I enlisted in the Navy and got out after the Vietnam War.

I travel to interior Alaska, a 'Cheechako' (Greenhorn) by Alaskan standards. But I have been raised on Walt Disney and feel qualified to be a mountain man!

I arranged with a pilot to drop me off in the wilds of Alaska. I do not have everything I need and have things I do not need. I learn about guns, trapping, and the loneliness of living in the vast wilderness with no other humans around.

I do not see anyone for many months, then walk out of the wilds to civilization in the spring. After working odd jobs to make supply money, I return to the wilds in the fall and have a hard time my second winter. I almost die, and need to be rescued.

I decide to build a houseboat so I can travel around without having to build another cabin. I have to accept summer work in Fairbanks to pay for the boat materials and work under a builder. The boat takes much longer to build than expected.

I live as a street person much of the time to keep expenses down.

Book 2 - Gone Wild (This Book)

I have many adventures on the houseboat and acquire a dog team. There are issues with the police, a bear on my boat, and a trip to see my family who live a civilized life.

My houseboat sinks. I get lost and learn other hard lessons. I start doing artwork and end up on TV. I win a land lottery and start my first homestead.

There are mail order women, and I live with a woman and her kids. Ten people are murdered in a village we visit, and myself and the family are almost among them. Family life is more difficult than I imagined.

Fish and Game becomes a concern.

I head back into the wilderness, which leads into book 3.

Book 3 - Still Wild

I acquire a couple more homesteads and cut more trapline.

I give up sled dogs and enter the world of snow machine adventures.

I winter in Galena and visit many native villages. There are bear encounters, and many survival situations to learn about.

I become a serious mammoth hunter and find fossils as part of my living. I work with a land surveyor specializing in homesteads and wilderness surveys, getting paid to use my boat.

My art sells well, so I do some big shows. I become more social and understand civilization better. I see the wisdom of being accepted by others. I learn. I grow. I try to change, as the world does.

The economy changes. It is less acceptable to be a trapper. I never become totally civilized as a city person defines it, but maybe I do, relative to the life I had in book one.

Book 4 - Beyond Wild

I am getting past just survival and doing well, even prospering. I own more than the houseboat can easily haul. Gas gets expensive. I need a new houseboat engine.

There is a homestead and trapline that keeps me in one place now. There are more bear stories and adventures into the wilds, including a 300-mile boat trip looking for mammoth tusks, which has disastrous consequences.

I find where I want to live on the Kantishna River. A river 300 miles long with about five people on it. I hang out in the native village of Nenana, spending a lot of time here.

I get my first computer and learn to build a website. People are looking at the pictures and buying my raw materials and art. This is a chance to make a difference.

Life is beautiful. Life is precious. I Dare to live it.

Book 5 - Back To Wild

I acquire a home in Nenana and start a web store. I am forced out of my subsistence lifestyle, partly because of changes in the laws. I do some serious mammoth hunting.

Unstable power causes a lot of computer data loss. I learn by punching keys to see what happens. It takes a long time to get good enough to create a book.

I continue the Mammoth hunts. The Tucson fossil gem show and State fair do well for me.

This period of 'being civilized' that I am trying out, has advantages, but also a price to pay—a big change from the wilderness life and being alone!

I am a suspect in a murder investigation. Another trapper tries to move in on my territory. There are neighbors and infringements on my property.

I fear I cannot change who I am. There is difficulty blending the two lives and ways of thinking. There are mail-order women coming and going, as well as the usual adventures and situations I manage to get myself into.

Book 6 - Surviving Wild

Iris is my partner. Business grows, with money coming in, but causes 'complications.' I understand why I left for the wilds in the first place.

I get better at fossil hunting and have some exciting trips getting mammoth tusks and other ancient treasures. I am viewed as an expert on a few subjects and Discovery TV and reality shows contact me several times.

The new life in town causes legal issues that have been nipping at my heels off and on throughout my time in Alaska. Fish and Wildlife ask, "Why are you alone out here where we cannot keep an eye on you? We know you are up to something. What is it you have to hide? We will find out!" This mentality is that different is bad and of concern. I end up being investigated. A SWAT team shows up at my property with a dozen cars and 20 cops.

My arrest makes headlines. I'm sentenced to Federal Prison for six months as a felon. This is a stark contrast to 'Book 1-Going Wild,' where I have as much freedom as it is possible to have.

How did I get from there to here?

Book 7 - Secretly Wild

I am a convicted felon, describing life in prison from the viewpoint of someone used to freedom and the wilderness life. The same feather in the hat I wore on the cover of Ruralite magazine in 1979, is now worth five years in prison.

What do I need to do to survive here? There are classes to take, books to read, farm work to do, and people to help. There are interesting felon stories.

I observe more crime within the prison system by the system than I am accused of committing. "The prison could not survive if we operated legally," I am told by officials. I do my time. Now what? Am I a better person? I see the error of my ways. I am saved. Society is safer now.

Book 8 - Retiring Wild

I talk about news relevant to living off the grid as an individual in the wilderness that few citizens are aware of. I adapt my business, and still have adventures, depending as much as I can on the subsistence life I love and understand that is now becoming illegal as a white man.

I ponder whether the end of my life is in agreement with the views I held dear from the beginning. I have hope that even in times of control and suppression, I can still focus on the plus side, and continue to find ways to enjoy personal freedoms and individuality.

I continue to explore choices, how to have better control of my destiny, happiness, and success. I refer to this as 'Survival.' I have few regrets, and hope my life's path as written can provide entertainment and insight.

As someone who is interested in being different, not one of the sheep, I look realistically at the rewards that choice offers, but also the price that has to be paid.

Please visit www.alaskadp.com for links to the books.

Visit www.milesofalaska.com to find a bio of Miles, additional photos, stories, how-to videos, handmade artwork, and raw materials for sale.

Magazine and News Stories

Alaska Magazine

Alaska Magazine July 77—Survive by Miles Martin two pages, Photos. By Miles about my rescue, walk out on the Yukon River, five days at 50 below zero.

Nomadic House Boater Have Cabin Will Travel January 81—by Miles. Three pages, four color photos, a map. About life living on a houseboat, trapping and selling art (photo of my art), and all the adventures I have had on the river.

Would You Make A Good Bush Homesteader? June 86—by Miles four pages, six color pictures (One shows my custom knives.) A story I wrote about what it takes to be a homesteader.

Surviving The Big Lonesome— March 98—by Jim Rearden five pages, two color photos, one double page photo of Miles. Photos by world-famous photographer Jean Erick Pasquier. Describes life in the wilderness.

GEO Magazine

GEO in Germany is like "National Geographic" in the US.

Life in The Wilderness Alaska Special—87 by Miles Martin ten pages, sixteen color photos, a map

Photos by Jean Erick, one of the best photographers in the world, I Wrote it myself, winter life in the wilderness.

Alaska Special - 95 Einer gegen den Rest der Welt

Eight pages, seven color photos, three are double page. A follow up story to the first, written by New York Times reporter Ted Morgan, with Brigitte Helbing, photos by New York Times photographer Rex Rystedt. My fight for a lifestyle.

The New York Times

New York Times Magazine an insert to the paper, April 17, 1994, section six, The Vexing Adventures of the Last Alaskan Bushrat.

Six pages, four color photos, one is a double page Written by New York Times writer and bestselling author Ted Morgan. Photos by Rex Rystedt (World-renowned photographer). Facing twenty years in jail and a $10,000 fine for putting artwork on a bear claw and selling it.

Book-- A Shovel Full of Stars 95—Published by Simon and Schuster — New York

By Ted Morgan about ten pages with Miles. About one of the last homesteaders, and the lifestyle I live, of a Subsistence person.

Ruralite Magazine

Put out by Golden Valley 180,000 circulation

Wild Miles August 79, two pages, four black and white photos, Full cover page photo of Miles doing artwork. Story and photos by Margaret Van Cleve — Mostly about my artwork, some about my lifestyle on a houseboat

Newspaper, Daily Newsminer, Fairbanks Alaska

Associated Press, date unreadable, think a Thursday, and think spring of circa 74 **'Trapper rescued by Chopper**; Vows to Return to the Bush' headline, one column, National news, about my rescue after five days walking at 50 below.

Alaska Trapper Magazine

Put out by Alaska Trappers Association, a cover photo of me with Wolf. Five-page story by Miles comparing snowmachine and snowshoe trapping Nov. 99—four pages. Over the years, another six-seven articles on various trapping and related issues. Contact organization for exact issues.

Me in 1975.

OTHER TITLES AVAILABLE FROM ALASKA DREAMS PUBLISHING

Visit www.alaskadp.com to see these titles.

Books by Miles Martin:

- Going Wild
- Gone Wild
- Still Wild
- Beyond Wild
- Back To Wild
- Surviving Wild
- Secretly Wild
- Retiring Wild

Titles by other ADP authors:

- Rookie
- Alaska Freedom Brigade
- Apache Snow
- In Search of Honor
- A Coming Storm
- Arizona Rangers Series – Blake's War
- Legend of Silene
- Inspiring Special Needs Stories
- My Life In The Wilderness
- All Over The Road
- Ghost Cave Mountain
- Inside the Circle
- The Silver Horn of Robin Hood
- Alaskan Troll Eggs
- Through My Eyes
- The Professional Ghost Investigator
- The Adventures of Jason and Bo
- Seeds Of The Pirate Rebels

FOOT NOTES

CHAPTER 4

1. Eating wild foods in general is not like food I buy in the store. City food has a minimum standard that is expected, and met. Food in stores or restaurants is rarely 'horrible' in quality. Meaning meat will never have maggots, fruit rarely has worms or bugs, vegetables seldom are as dried up as rains. Though food will never be horrible, it also is rarely 'grade #1.' Few people have seen in a store or restaurant grade #1. Meaning eating right off the vine, or out of the ground, fresh, when it is ripe, not an hour old. Liver, even two hours old, already taste different. Thus I find town food is maybe middle of the road. Not great, not bad. The variety is what is nicest. I learn that in the wilds there can be extremes. I can sometimes eat the best there is of fresh wild blueberries or fresh game. However, it is also true the worse gets eaten sometimes, for a variety of reasons. No refrigeration, lack of skills in handling it, a sick animal, an infested crop of plant life, lack of other ingredients to add, not much other choice around.
2. I have forgotten about the oil pipeline. 1,000 miles corridor built without an environmental study or purchasing the property. Mostly Natives got displaced, ordered to leave their property to make room. Some claims were settled, but 20 years later.
3. Many years later I understand better. 'White man' often uses this term 'friend,' loosely. In the Athabascan culture 'Friend,' is a big deal, and carries specific obligations and understandings. Early Athabascan survival depended on these relationships their very life depended on. In the same way 'Grandpa,' means I have all the rights, but also obligations of a true grandson. Whiteman has contracts, Indians have handshakes.
4. Not that I ever wanted one, but the time comes when John's $10 permit is worth $80,000. In general there seems to be a predictable progression when it comes to permits. Most citizens resist the change. "Not going to get no darn permit!" The argument goes, that it is easy, cheap, no big deal, for our own good in some way. Registering boats is, "In case your boat gets stolen." Steel shot in shotguns is about saving the endangered ducks. Fishing permit is about keeping track of the fish so we can manage them, as well as being asked to tag furs we catch. Time passes and we are no longer asked, the permit is required. More than required, a crime not to. More than a crime not to, the permit can be denied along with the activity.

CHAPTER 5

1. Thirty years from now more than one barge captain still recalls my antics zig zagging across the river trying to get out of the way and being a hazard. Eventually I would get offered jobs piloting barges, but this is many years from now.
2. Some sections of the various rivers are illegal to gather anything off of. I am on a piece of private land I have permission to be on.

CHAPTER 6

1. 30 years later much has changed. Mike, I , Manley , the world. Mike has done a lot for the community, has a new woman in his life, seems happier, more mellow. We get along well enough. But also in this time, there are a lot of dead bodies.

CHAPTER 7

1. Remember who Joe is. Many years from now he is involved in a shootout where ten people in Manley are killed.
2. One aspect to consider when looking at my profits is the fact this is pipeline economically flush times in Alaska. I assume at the time this is normal. Profits are high enough I do not even need to consider what anything cost to make. What cost me $5 to make is selling for over $50. Also at this time no license, permits, fees are required. Though I am making $3,000 in a few days, it is a winters worth of work, and I am only doing the one show a year. There is a total business called 'Miles' that includes trapping. Trapping is operated at a loss being subsidized by the art part of the business. Considering I have a new snow machine to pay for and new traps, gas costs etc. I'm not making enough to be paying taxes. I'm not wise about this yet, and the enthusiasm of making $3,000 in a few days is how I measure my worth, and what I focus on.

CHAPTER 8

1. Ten years from now President Carter expands McKinley Park. It gets renamed 'Denali.' Some of the places we cover now are indeed park land. My friend Van's property is in 'The Gates of the Arctic' wildlife refuge. He can keep his land, but is not allowed to put up a wind sock for landing his plane, and must pick up all the dog poop along his trails least the wildlife be impacted. Some Kantishna land becomes homesteads - semi settled country, with guides, float trips, and tours offered. Civilization advertises this as a 'wilderness' adventure. In 2014 a bridge is being built across the Nenana river, with a road to the Kantishna River. There is major gas, maybe oil drilling going on. Rumor has it the entire river drainage is an oil basin bigger than the North Slopes ANWAR. There are other changes. Bottom line being, the truth of what I say, we are having a very special experience, that we will remember all our lives, and future generations may well envy, yet not be able to duplicate.

CHAPTER 9

1. And here I am a senior thirty years later, very slowed down with the time needed to write a lot. I've saved all my written material, including original first print low run books done, not by computer.

CHAPTER 11

1. These two write for a lot of years. One sends Christmas cards till 2020. I see him have kids, the kids grow up and have children of their own. He sends me pictures of fish he catches, deer, turkey, he gets. All life's up and downs I hear about. I have a lifelong influence on this fellow from Michigan who read my stories.
2. Travel gear has changed over the years. At this time 'tents' are fifty pounds of canvas. The cheaper nylon dome type tents are not available yet. Likewise 'the dark' is overcome with flashlights that require a big square battery clipped to a belt and a cord going up my back. Halogen and low wattage LED high light output is not available, nor powerful compact batteries. There are no light weight reliable cook stoves for camping out either.

CHAPTER 13

1. I call all 'free land' from the government 'homestead.' Technically there is homesite, trade and manufacture, recreational sites. The end result is the same, you get title to the wilderness by living on it.

FOOT NOTES

CHAPTER 14

1. The feather in this hat is a feather I am arrested for having , worth ten years in prison, among twenty-eight felony wildlife charges against me in 2003.
2. This ending of the article with a political reference to D-2 legislation went right over my head. I focused on the good news, on my art, publicity and recognition. I see validation for my path in life. "Yes, people care! This lifestyle is not a mistake!" I understand reality, survival is to be 'one of us' among the protected. This may not matter alone in the wilds if civilization never finds me. Still, I need supplies, must interact to some extent, must get along enough to be left alone. I am told "What do you contribute! You and your kind leaches off the rest of the hard working people of our country! You and your kind! Humph! You should be more like me! Like a responsible citizen! Toe the line like the rest of us! " I can reply due to such articles, "I bring you dreams, hope, stories, entertainment, lost knowledge from our historical past" So forth and so on. "What do you mean it is all at risk through government legislation! The government is us!

CHAPTER 15

1. In 1998, a manual typewriter is found, and new ribbons bought for it. The hand written manuscript done in poetry, the dairies, calendar notations, that all got wet and dried with grass between the pages, are all put together and typed. Already my writing is not going to work. I have started all over from scratch. A few people are looking it over and giving comments.
   The first hand held calculator was built in 1965, costing $2,600 and required a power supply the size of a car battery. The first computer is barely out and expensive, unreliable, and hard to learn to run, as it is all in DOS. But I hear about these computers, and think I might keep track of the progress, as something useful to have one day for the book work.
2. Bob does not remain part of the story for long. He dies in a private plane crash up north.
3. I'd talk more of 'women' the trips, add pictures and such. But the women do not even want to be mentioned! Geez! Was it so horrible to know me? I respect their wishes as best I can. Name changes, keep it all to a minimum, and all that.

CHAPTER 16

1. Partly, I am respecting that Karen does not want our life made public. I think there are people who would like to know what 'family life' in the wilds is all about! Raising children, especially girls, compared to life as a hermit. I seemed to have little trouble adapting. I was worried I had been too many years alone to adjust to life with others. I found it very rewarding, and helping to raise the children, one of the greatest rewards in my life. But there are other books, well written, on family homesteading.
2. One of these fish cops I later learn, many, many years from now, ends up in prison for molesting his daughter. Women who had encounters with him snorted and told me he came on to them. Implied if they slept with him , he might not give the a ticket. I also later find out oil exploration is about to go on in this area. All subsistence people who have rights over resources, were run out of the area, only recreational people remained.

455

www.ingramcontent.com/pod-product-compliance
Lightning Source LLC
Chambersburg PA
CBHW070326090426

42733CB00012B/2382